FLYII

"The fun of fu-oops- **"THE FUN OF FLYING"**
CAPAIN JACK RESLEY BECK
REALLY**TIRED**
CAPTAIN OF THE CLOUDS
****

40,000 HOURS & 6.96969 MILLION MILES &
THAT DOESN'T INCLUDE THE 1500 HOURS OF P-51 TIME
P-51 TIME=PARKER PEN 51---Phony time
Or the 27 parachute jumps

XVIII AIRBORNE CORPS---KOREAN "CONFLICT"
FLYING TIGER AIRLINES
TWENTIETH CENTURY AIRLINES
AEROVIDAS SUD AMERICANA
PACIFIC SOUTHWEST AIRLINES (PSA)
USAIR

VOLUME 1

Becksflyinghigh@aol.com
Fax 928-754-5319

© 2005 Jack Beck. All Rights Reserved.

No part of this book may be reproduced, stored in a retrieval system, or transmitted by any means without the written permission of the author.

First published by AuthorHouse 11/03/05

ISBN: 1-4208-5875-0 (sc)

Printed in the United States of America
Bloomington, Indiana

This book is printed on acid-free paper.

FLYING "HIGH"

A TRIBUTE TO

CHIEF PILOT

CAPTAIN BILL BUTLER

NORTH AMERICAN AIRLINES
TRANS AMERICAN AIRLINES
TWENTIETH CENTURY AIRLINES
TRANS INTERNATIONAL AIRLINES

Loretta Coppney
My flying days 1960-1967

<u>Becksflyinghigh@aol.com</u>
Fax 928-754-5319

My name is mentioned as part of the crew in chapters on page 172 - 1963
Page 306 June 1, 1963
✱ Page 309 August 1, 1963
Problem with engine on this flight!

EDITED BY
Missis BILLIE LEE HUGHES

INPUTS BY---
RICHARD & BILLIE HUGHES--- OWNERS
J.K.J. ELECTRIC CONTRACTORS
928-768-4657
&
CAPTAIN MARK RESLEY BECK
Yea dad---I'm looking it over now.
CAPTAIN KEVIN SHAUN BECK
You told me you were coming to my house to read it.
MISS SHELBI DAUN BECK
???Huh???---What book ya talking about pops???
CHRIS ROBERTS & SUSIE ROSE
are "EARTHBOUND" –Inventors of the "SingClean" -
The Only Karaoke Mic Sanitizer on the Market Today!
For Karaoke Equipment & More see EARTHBOUND DESIGNS
At----www.singclean.com. Ph#1-877-323-7246
(Located in Arizona right by the beautiful Laughlin, Nevada Casinos!)

Becksflyinghigh@aol.com
Fax 928-754-5319

PREFACE

Before you turn the next zillion pages, I want you to know that travel by airplane is still the safest mode of transportation available, ---so far, ---in this millennium.

There are unannounced drug & alcohol checks for the entire crew, ------------------Crews&Stews--------------------------

These inspections are made prior to going to work---at the airport.

Volume I of Flying High occurred mostly in the last of the fifties and the **"Whoring Sixties"**.

Color Television was playing in the display window of your local department store.

Dick Tracy and buddies had the only "Cell Phones".

"Mary-juanna" started taking money away from the liquor and tobacco industry.

The hippies were moving into the Haight-Ashberry area.

The "pill" had become the Catholics answer to birth control.

That didn't work. ---The world's population has doubled since one-niner-six-zero. ---------&

Jet airplanes were leaving contrails in the sky for the first time.

Aviating, at that point in time, was a litta, no a lotta loosa, than it is now.

I have written in **Co-Pilots and Flight Engineers as Captains---** if later on in the course of **FLYING GIANT AIRLINERS** they achieve the----**SKY GOD STATUS AS CAPTAINS.**

And by the way, ---some of the players names have been changed to protect the guilty.

ALL I CAN TELL YOU IS---

---"IF I HAD MY LIFE TO LIVE OVER AGAIN"---

---"I WOULD DO IT EXACTLY THE SAME WAY"---

What you are about to enter now is the flylight zone.

--- CIRCA ---

APRIL---1957

I left Webbers Falls, Oklahoma in the spring of '57 with my---

---AIRCRAFT AND ENGINE---
A&E
License #1364068
nka
---AIRCRAFT AND POWERPLANT---
A&P
---License #1364068---
In one hand, ---my **Flight Engineer's Written,** ---in the other hand.
My Lovely Bride---Dorothy Mae Beck,
Nee **Dorothy Mae Wright** by my side.

I had just graduated from
---**SPARTAN SCHOOL OF AERONAUTICS**---
In
Tulsa, Oklahoma.

---**Thanx to Uncle Sam's Korean "Conflict" GI Bill**---
Eighteen months of intensified schooling *eight to five* at **SPARTAN SCHOOL OF AERONAUTICS** "larnin' which side" of a hammer to hold.
Working *six to Midnight* at Tulsa's Douglas Aircraft Overhaul Plant---workin' as a "gofer" mechanic on Boeing B-47s.

The **EXIT** sign above the **EXIT** door at---
      SPARTAN SCHOOL OF AERONAUTICS---
      That I espied as I **EXIT**ed for the last time.

SIX MONTHS AGO

I COULDN'T SPELL ENGINEAR

AND

NOW I ARE ONE

I virtually pushed that old broken down '46 Plymouth to California.
    When I arrived---I got lucky---First interview. ---
First job as a civilian with **FLYING TIGERS AIRLINES INC.**
    A cargo carrier that was hangared at---
---**BURBANK "INTERNATIONAL" AIRPORT**---
    "International" because Burbank Airport had gambling junkets to T-Town. --- *(Tijuana, Mexico)*
    Two dollars and ten cents ($2.10) an hour.
  I figured it out mentally. With overtime I could make close to **400 BUCKS** a month.
    "I WAS SQUATTIN' IN TALL COTTON."

To you city folk, that means if you're out chopping cotton in Dixieland & the cotton is tall enough & you gotta give a dump-you can pull down your britches & let it go without anyone seeing you.
Modesty is of the essence to a Dixie chick.

I got the job at Flying Tigers at ten in the morning and at four o'clock that afternoon. ---

I punched the time clock at "Tigers" and started one; ---

        A---HELLUVA
        B-----CAREER
        C-----------LIFE
        D---YEP---ALL THE ABOVE

What do you do with brand new snot-nosed-not-dry-behind-the ears?

???A&E MECHANIC???

You put him in Flying Tigers Overhaul Hangar where he can't wrench/screw anything up.

I walked into the overhaul hangar and walked past a DC-4 up on jacks.

!!!NOW I'M EXCITED!!!

I might be able to replace a cylinder on one of the engines, or shoot---even replace an engine.

I had visions of grandeur. I finally was an---

---AIRCRAFT MECHANIC---
!!!WRONG!!!

I went up to the **LEADMAN'S SHACK** with my brand new coveralls on---checked in.

Mister Lead-man gave me a couple rolls of tape.

Mister Lead-man took me over to the DC-4 up on jacks.

Mister Leadman took me under the DC-4's wing where all the fuel cell access panels had been removed, ---"Crawl up in there and line the fuel cells with the tape that I gave you."

So much for the grandeur bullshit

It took me four swing shifts.

The vapors from the RED 110/130 High Octane Gasoline lingered in the fuel cells and each night I would get a litta---no---a lotta drunkey-wunkey.---Then a litta---no---a lotta nausey-washey.

Then toss up my tacos on the way home.

I would decorate the side of my old windowless '46 Plymouth by hanging my head out the window and throwing up.

My next "A&E" job, after the taping of the DC-4s fuel cells was to paint the inside of the DC-4's baggage compartment.

Mister Lead-man gave me a spray gun and five gallons of Zinc Chromate Primer, "Get the job done in two shifts---this DC-4 is leaving in three days."

I worked over time for two swing shifts and finished the job.

I got eight hours of time-and-half pay that helped a much needed first payday.

Only one problem, the baggage compartment on a DC-4 was/is very confined.

The H2o was H2ZINK.

I sucked in a lotta Green Zinc Chromate fumes.

When I arrived home that night I got in a spat with my wife. She got irate and hit me in the chest with her fist.

!!!BIG MISTAKE!!!

I spewed green vomit "all over her body".

Sorta looked like a scene from the movie ---**"THE EXORCIST"**.

The next evening I noticed a bulletin on Mister Lead-man's Shack asking for bids on the---

---FLYING TIGER MAINTENANCE FLIGHT LINE---

Bid it--Got it. The only thing that I didn't like about it was the hours.

Midnight till Seven Thirty, Ante Meridiem.

---THE GRAVEYARD SHIFT---

Aptly named because your social life & existence become virtually

---DEAD---

I would be mechanizing on ---

THE LOCKHEED SUPER CONSTELLATION MODEL 1049H.

Aka

"CONNIE"

Love ya Connie.

The Mechanics on the Graveyard Shift were very, very, very---

---SENIOR FLYING TIGER FLIGHT LINE MECHANICS---

There was very little work to do on the graveyard shift as all the cargo planes launched before midnight and except for an occasional "C" check, the---

---FLYING TIGERS AIRLINES---
---FLIGHT LINE HANGAR---
was
"UNOCCUPIED"

We played ping-pong, poker and chess to while away the night.

Every so often, there would be a Connie in the hangar for a "C" check. I never knew what the "C" stood for but it must have been "Complete" because we checked everything she wore under her aluminum skirt.

By the time we clocked in at midnight, ---all of the gravy jobs had been done. About the only thing left was replacing the de-icing boots on the leading edge of the Connie's wings and changing **"GROSS"** spark plugs on the Connie's four Curtis Wright 3350 Supercharged Engines.

Not real mind boggling, but to me, it was great to work as a mechanic.

*****

4 Curtis Wright 3350 supercharged engines---18 cylinders per engine---
2 spark plugs per cylinder---144 spark plugs.
=== One **"GROSS"**===

Changing spark plugs on the Connie was not an easy task. Because of the high compression and heat caused by the power recovery turbines (PRT), the spark plugs would weld themselves to the cylinder. At times we would have to use a 3 foot cheater/breaker bar to break them lose and it was not uncommon for 1or 2 spark plugs to break off at the cylinder. Then we would have to break off the ceramic part of the spark plug and drill a hole in its base--- then use an "easy out" to remove the spark plug. This was not an easy task because if one iota of metal filing should enter the cylinder, the cylinder would be scrap pile material on the pistons first stroke.

Ouch, ya know what I mean guys?
*I got a **hernia** from replacing those spark plugs. Still got it.*
---MECHANIC MISTER BOB COMFORT---

A mechanic, as young and inexperienced as Self were always assigned these jobs.

The **SENIORS** would go to the break room, drink coffee, play games and sleep.

Mechanic Bob Comfort and Self would go to the stock room---get a couple of gallons of Acetone---start removing the rubber de-icing boots off the leading edge of the Connie's wings.

*****

The **de-icing boots** on the **LOCKHEED SUPER CONSTELLATION 1049H consisted** of multiple tubes that expanded and contracted with air pressure from the #2 & #3 engine driven pumps, ---after allowing the ice to build up on the leading edge of the wings.

This method of removing ice from the wing's leading edges is---

---DE-ICING---
Very primitive as to what jet airplanes have.

If you screwed up and turned the de-icing on before the ice had built up---there was a possibility that the ice could build up on the inflated cycle and render the de-icing ineffective causing the airflow over the leading edge to become ineffective.

Not conducive to the longevity of flight. Get what I mean???

Jet airplanes have compressed hot air, aka ex-wife mouth, ducted from the compressor section of the jet engines. (Compression causes heat)

This method of removing ice from the wing's leading edges is---

---ANTI-ICING---
And is a whole lot more effective.

*****

Mechanic Bob Comfort and Self needed the acetone to break down the sealant that held the de-icing boots to the leading edge of Connie's wings.

This is a long tedious process.

Put the acetone on a corner of the de-icing boot---let it eat its way in for a few minutes---pull off 6 inches of de-icing boot---more acetone---wait---pull back 6 more inches of de-icing boot---etcetcetc.

The fumes from the acetone would put us on cloud nine. It was a cheap drunk. We became a couple of wild and crazy guys.

Mechanic Bob Comfort and Self would finally get the de-icing boots off and go to work replacing spark plugs and feeling no pain.

Ah, yes, life can be fun---even on the graveyard shift.

We'd be just about done. The acetone was mostly off our brains The **SENIORS** would come out of their playpen to help us clean up. The sun would start to infiltrate the dark night.
MY THOUGHT---*"How nice of the **SENIORS**."*
!!!**WRONG**!!!

The day shift was arriving and the **SENIORS** wanted the appearance of working all night.

Ah, yes, for them another night of fun and games but they didn't get as high as Mechanic Bob Comfort and Self did on acetone.

One night I showed up for work and the Swing-shift Foreman by the name of Funk (real name) was waiting for me.
MY THOUGHT---*"Oh man, what did I do now?"*

I was always late for work. Not real late, but just late enough that when I inserted my time card in the time clock, it would click over to 12.01. ---One friggin' minute late.

I look back on it now and I think that time clock hated me and did it on purpose.

Mister Funk Real Name informed me that our Leadman Andy had called in sick and that I was to be the Lead-man for the Graveyard Shift.

"Why me, I'm junior to all these Mechs."
"You're the only one here with an A&E License."
"HUH?"
"You're the only one on the graveyard shift with an A&E License."
"???HUH???"

"We can't operate the shift without a Lead-man and the Lead-man has to have an A&E and you're it. It's in the Union Contract."

"Are you telling me that none of these mechanics have an A&E?"
"Yep, you're the big Kahuna tonight."
"I DON'T WANNA BE A LEAD-MAN."
"You have no choice." Was Mister Funk Real Name's reply, ---as he strode fastly to his car to go home to Miller time.
Well it paid fifteen cents an hour more.
You put that on top of two dollars and ten cents an hour---
I was in hog heaven.

"Okay by me" I shouted and sauntered over to the hangar with my newly found power.

---I WAS SOMEBODY---
!!!WRONG!!!

I started assigning jobs for the night.

The **SENIORS** looked at me as though I was "nutz"---told me to go piss up a rope---left for the break room for fun and games.

My moment of glory was short lived.

The only mechanic that listened to me was Mechanic Bob Comfort. ---**a**nd he only did it out of friendship.

Mechanic Bob Comfort and I changed the Connie's de-icing boots. Comfort, Self and Connie got a little drunkey-wunkey on acetone.

---HERECOMEDEJUDGE---
**THE PRESIDENT
OF
FLYING TIGER CARGO AIRLINES INC**

El Presidente stopped by at 0400 hours and observed my "Kahunaship." He stayed till dawn and observed the **SENIORS** playing games and Comfort, Self and Connie staggering around and apparently drunk on our ass.

Needless to say---
---**EL PRESIDENTE DE AEROVIDAS SUD LOS GATOS**---
Was not amused.

Later that day I got a telephone call from Mister Funk Real Name.

---**FOREMAN OF THE SWINGSHIFT**---

"Can you come in a little early tonight? We would like to talk to you."

I didn't know who we was, but figured I was going to be the, ---**Leadmanofnochoice** again for the **graveyard shift.**

I was already spending that fifteen-cents-an-hour more that I would be making.

!!!WRONG!!!

I swaggered in thirty minutes before midnight and punched in on the time clock. I believe the time clock ate itself because I was thirty minutes early. ---Made sort of a dying swan gurgling noise.

I walked up to the Mister Funk Real Name's Office.

I swaggered right in---
I didn't even **knock**---
I was **somebody**---
I was a **Grave-Yard-Shift-Leadman.**

There sat Mister Funk Real Name and this fat old man sitting next to him, ---"Mister Beck, I would like to introduce you to the---
 ---**PRESIDENT** of **FLYING TIGER AIRLINES**---
I can't remember his name and could have cared less, ---
"Nice meeting you Mister So&So.
*MY THOUGHT---This **LeadmanoftheGraveYardShift** job must be pretty important to have the head honcho down here at midnight to greet me & he even called me Mister Beck.*
I was feeling like I was really somebody.
!!!WRONG!!!
Mister Funk Real Name, ---"Mister Beck, we're going to have to fire you."
Well---BLOW ME---D
O
W
N
"???WHY???"
"PresidentSo&So here observed your actions this morning as, ---
Leadman-of-the-Grave-Yard-Shift."
It appears that you, Mister Beck and Mister Comfort were drunk on your ass and the rest of your crew slept and played games all night.
I explained to them about the acetone and what it did to our heads. I also told them that I assigned the **SENIORS** jobs and they told me to "go piss up a rope".
I was fighting for my job---no, life.
 EL PRESIDENTE DE LOS GATOS, ---"Did you know that you were getting an extra fifteen-cents-an-hour for being a Leadman?"
"**Yes**," was my quivering response, "I tried to do the job right but no one would listen to me."
Mister Funk Real Name and President So&So Pissoffidism turned to Sympathyism.
Funk Real Name and President So&So knew the SENIORS were on the graveyard shift because they were allergic to work. They also knew damn well that there wasn't anything that they could do about it because of the---**SENIOR-S-ENIORITY.**
Mister Funk Real Name looked up at me, ---"Step outside for a minute Mister Beck."

Me---Mister? ---
Me---obliged. ---
Me---was shakin' like a dog shitin' razor blades.
Me---looked through a window trying to read their lips---quite unsuccessfully.
They were waving their arms and shouting at each other.
---Quote---
$^*(**&%%&())*&^$#$^*)__(&^%$$^*)&$#%&())^^**(%Period
---Unquote---
Mister Funk Real Name motioned for me to come back in, ---"We have reconsidered and we are not going to fire you."
I breathed a sigh of relief. ---Amen.
---FOREMAN FUNK REAL NAME---
Had saved my jo---li---ass---bacon. Nice man and I needed the job.
I started to leave before they changed their heads.
Did you say head?
Mister Funk Real Name, ---"We need you to be a Leadman again tonight."
I turned around, ---"Take the Leadsman's job, ---the extra fifteen cents an hour---
---AND SHOVE THEM UP YOUR ASS."
El Presidente de Los Gatos looked like I hit him with a torque wrench.
Now it was his turn in the barrel.
*****

???HIS TURN IN THR BARREL???
The Hillbillies would drill a hole in a barrel and a Hillbilly would get in the barrel and the others would cornhole him through the hole. ---The Hillbilly that couldn't get his dick through the hole you might ask???---Got to screw the barrel owner's wife.
Cornhole you might ask???---That's buttfuckin'.
*****

*A man quit his job in the United States Patent Office in 1903 because he felt that everything that had been invented ---**had** been invented.*

"HAINT NOBODY KNOWS NUTHIN"

Guess what---the year now is 2003---100 years later and still---

"HAINT NOBODY KNOWS NUTHIN"

I believe his great grandson is the same person that said, ---
"The NASDAQ will be way over 5,000 by the end of the year."

*****

I spent all my money on wine, women and song.
I wasted the rest---on the stock market.

*****

A plane was taking off from Kennedy Airport. After it reached a comfortable cruising altitude, the captain made an announcement over the intercom, "Ladies and gentlemen, this is your captain speaking. Welcome to Flight Number 293, nonstop from New York to Los Angeles. The weather ahead is good and, therefore, we should have a smooth and uneventful flight. Now sit back and relax... OH, MY GOD!" Silence followed, and after a few minutes, the captain came back on the intercom and said, "Ladies and Gentlemen, I am so sorry if I scared you earlier. While I was talking to you, the flight attendant accidentally spilled a cup of hot coffee in my lap. You should see the front of my pants!" A passenger in Coach yelled, "That's nothing. You should see the back of mine!"

*****

--- CIRCA ---

1 MAY 1957

*Hooray hooray---it's the first of May.
Outdoor fucking starts today.*
PER CAPTAIN LELAND

There was no Graveyard shift that night. ---No Leadman.
We all went home and they had to pay us for the Graveyard shift.
I awakened the next morning and said to myself, ---"Self---I donwannabeee a mechanic anymore."
"I WANNABEEEA FLIGHT ENGINEAR---er---ENGINEER."
After all---I had my FLIGHT ENGINEER WRITTEN passed.
I envied the Flight Engineers on the "Connie". They had their own panel---wore **cowboy** boots. ---
Swaggered around like John Wayne.
They virtually ran the "Connie"---thought they were shit hot.

*****

I was lucky enough to go up on a training flight on the Lockheed Super Constellation 1049H one time. The Check Flight Engineer even let me sit in the Flight Engineer's seat for a few minutes in cruise. The thrill of my lifetime**, in an airplane**, at that point in time.

*****

!!!Here is a story of an egomanYical Super Constellation 1049H Flight Engineer!!!
SCENARIO

ACT I
LOCATION---LEADMAN'S SHACK
Leadman Andy, ---"Beck, run over to Slick's Hangar and get our fuel truck and fuel the "Connie" out on the tarmac---it's due out in an hour---hurry---move it---hubba-hubba."
I ran to the Slick hangar. Got in the fuel truck and drove beneath the left wing of the "Connie".

I drug the fueling hose up a ladder and proceeded to fuel up the #1 fuel tank. ---PURPLE 115/130 gasoline and very **VOLATILE.** You can't light a match within a country mile of it.
*****

Numbering starts from left to right, facing forward on airplanes---i.e.
Left wing---#1&#2 fuel tanks---#1&#2 engines
Right wing---#3&#4 fuel tanks---#3&#4 engines
*****

ACT II
There was this one Flight Engineer that would stand underneath the wing and---shout, ---
"HURRYITUP---HURRYITUP---HURRYITUP."
Never could figure that one out---like I should jack off the hose to get it pumping faster.
One night egomanYical Flight Engineer hollered one too many times.

ACT III
I shut off the fuel nozzle---
slid down the ladder---hauled ass for the hangar.
"Where are you going?"
"I have a need to shit, but I'll be back."
I entered the hangar and went into the men's restroom.

ACT IV
There was a **littlecrackinthefrostedwindow** and through it I watched the Loudmouth EgomanYical Flight Engineer pacing back & forth.
I wasn't about to fuel "his" airplane, even if I had to stay in the john all night and read, -----**"If you want a good time, call Rayette at 480-6969"**---till quitting time.

ACT V
EgomanYical Flight Engineer kept checking his Big Ben Watch.
*****

"How dja know it was an Airline Captain that raped you maam?"
"He had a big watch and a little peter."
*****

The Super Constellation 1049H was due out in forty minutes and the other wing hadn't been fueled yet. Mister EgomanYical Flight Engineer was running out of airspeed, altitude and ideas, ---all at the same time.

The Connie needed her tanks topped off (*full tanks*) because she was going to Hawaii.

All of a sudden Mister EgomanYical Flight Engineer started for the hangar.

ACT VI
I got in a toilet stall and locked the dodedodo.
In he came, ---"Aren't you done yet?"
"I've got the runs and my hemmies are hummin."

ACT VII
He left and I could hear him pleading with the **seniors** to put fuel in his "Connie".
I heard a **senior** say to him through a
littlecrackinthefrostedwindow, ---
"I'm a mechanic.
I'm not a fuckin' fueler and you can go fuck yourself."

ACT VIII
Once again I went to the frosted window and looked through the crack-hole. There was Mister Mouth dragging a fueling hose up the ladder. It was/is the Flight Engineer's responsibility to make sure there is adequate fuel on the airplane, no matter who does it.

FINALE
!!!Bye---bye---bye----EgomanYicalmuthafuckinfrightengineer!!!

--- CIRCA ---

1 JUNE 1957

Hooray---hooray it's the first of June.
Outdoor fuckin' started last month.
Per Flight Line Mechanic Jack Resley Beck

There was a "Connie" on the tarmac one night.
*****

The TARMAC is the concrete-asphalt that surrounds the HANGAR that houses the Airplanes & Offices & Carports & Wheels & Their Lug-nuts & Sexrataries & Mechanics & Stockroom & Unisex Shit-house.
*****

The "Connie's" #3 Curtis-Wrights 3350 Engine's PRT (Power Recovery Turbine) needed replaced.
*****

The PRT uses exhaust gasses from the engine to force more air into the Fuel Manager, aka Carburetor, upping the horsepower of the engine. ---Good idea except it was too much oomph for the cylinders. Many a time a "Connie" would come taxiing up with a cylinder that **BURST** *through the cowling and be hanging there by the fuel injection line.*
*****

Replacing the PRT was a tough & dirty job---Some one had to do it---

Three guesses who got the job---

First two don't count---right.

YEP

Lower case Mechs---comfort&beck.

The exhaust gasses cause corrosion on the stainless steel nuts & bolts on the PRT's housing causing them to weld together. Damn near impossible to unscrew them without a cutting torch.

Mechanic Bob Comfort **went** with the **SENIORS** to do fun and games, ---leaving me to replace the PRT by my lonesome. Now, I was wagging my tail like a hound dog on possum heat meat.

When you replace a PRT on a Curtis-Wright 3350 Engine, you have to run up the engine so you know that you have full power for take off. I was the only one there, so that would be me.

I replaced the PRT and quickly "buttoned up" (*closed)* the cowling, hoping that the **SENIORS** wouldn't "accidentally" wander "near" the "Connie".

I pulled the ladder out of the propeller's way and proceeded fastly to the boarding ramp. I have/had never seen so many Mechanics come out of the holes in the walls in my life.

The **SENIORS** loved running up engines---they just didn't like busting their knuckles on them. Reckon they were watching me and the minute, no second that I buttoned up the cowling they came a runnin' to see who would get to run up the engine.

The most **senior SENIOR** mechanic got to do it.

With my seniority---I didn't have a chance---no play Hosay.

The Mechanics started asking each other what their date of hire was.

The hub-bub stopped as fast as it started.

Out of the hangar comes this Old Fart---

Older than dirt, he was---

Methuselah in coveralls---

Turkey neck mutha.

Didn't take long to know who the Top Banana was.

*****

Methuselah lived 969 years---without TV or night baseball. ---
Wonder how many children he begat???

*****

The Old Fart said, ---"I'll run 'er up" and proceeded up the mechanics stand boarding ramp to the cockpit.

The Connie had a cockpit door that was located between the Flight Engineer's panel and the cockpit-cabin bulkhead.

*****

The Flight Engineer's panel, on the Connie was situated behind the Co-Pilots seat and the Flight Engineer sat sideways--- even had his own desk and his own set of throttles.

*****

I pulled the cockpit boarding ramp away and stood under the #4 engine and sulked.

My moment of glory was over---
Short lived---
Acetone-sniffer---
Spark plug-ace---
Hangar-broom man.

I moved forward so the Old Fart could see me out of the cockpit door—so as to give him clearance to start the #3 engine. The move placed me under the propeller of the #4 engine. I held up three fingers on my left hand and waved my right hand in a circular motion as a clearance to start the #3 engine.

---SENIOR MECHANIC HARLEY CHALMERS---
&
---SENIOR MECHANIC PAUL ICARDI---
---BOTH---

Grabbed me and violently pulled me out from under the #4 propeller saying, ---"You never know what switch that Senile Old Asshole is gonna hit."

Just about that time, the #4 Propeller started turning. The Old Fart selected the #4 Engine start switch instead of the #3 Engine start switch.

The propeller would have cut me in half, --- **SHISHKABOBBED**---if Senior Mechanic Paul Icardi and Senior Mechanic Harley Chalmers hadn't pulled me out of #4 propeller's path of rotation.

*****

*Mechanic Paul Icardi called engines---**engYnes** and to this day, every once in a while I say **engYnes,** instead of engines.*

*****

**Later on in life, when I finally obtained my
COMMERCIAL PILOTS LICENSE,
I PROUDLY SHOWED IT TO THE OLD FART.
"Might as well wipe your ass with it, you'll never use it."
---Very disheartening to a 23 year old punk kid---**

YOU NEVER KNOW, PILGRIM--YOU JUST NEVER KNOW

*****
We all live in glass houses---
Some are just a little less shatterproof than others.
*****

It's not whatcha got---its whatcha do with whatcha got.
*****

"Doctor, my husband thinks he's a dog and all he will eat is dog food"

"Lady, you have to get him off the dog food or it will kill him."

Several weeks go by and the lady runs into the doctor at Wal-Mart.

"How's your husband doing maam---did you get him off the dog food?"

"He died."

"Lady, I told you that if you didn't get him off the dog food that it would kill him."

"That isn't what killed him doctor. He was sitting on the couch---Licking his balls---fell off and broke his neck."
*****

--- CIRCA ---

1 JULY 1niner57

**Hooray---hooray---it's the first of July.
Outdoor fuckin' starts today.
"Anonymous"**

One night there was a Curtis-Wright C-46 in the Line Maintenance Hangar---a twin-engine airplane with tail wheel. The fuselage was shaped like an hour-glass and had many, many scab patches over the bullet holes from doing its tour of duty flying for Chenault's Flying Tigers in Burma.
*****

Scab Patch???---You just take a hunk of aluminum and place it over the hole and buck some rivets into it---no streamlining there.
*****

---MY JOB---
Remove the nuts and bolts from the aileron's and flap's push-pull hydraulic actuators.

---I DID---
One of the three inch long, 3/8" diameter flap bolt that I removed was worn so badly that it was *U* shaped where the hydraulic piston was attached to the flap.

The **seniors** of course were there to replace the bolts.

I watched as the **seniors** pulled and tugged the same piston that I had removed the injured bolt from to align up the holes to put the new bolt through the flap mount fitting---no could do---just an RCH from putting the bolt through the hole.

(RCH???---Red Cunt Hair---what does RCH stand for---I know it's something technical, but all I've ever heard was Red Cunt Hair---which means low tolerance---especially in the throat.)

They tugged and pulled---to no avail---the rookie---me---lifted the flap assembly an **RCH** and the **seniors** pushed the bolt into the now aligned holes.

The **seniors** were amazed---flat-fuckin' flabbergasted---looked at the rookie---me---with flat fuckin' amazement.

Didn't matter though---
    I went back to---
        Getting smashed on acetone---
            Changing spark plugs---
                Sweeping hangars---
    ---Which soon became old---

*****

The C-46 was designed for carrying cargo and paratroopers. The designed lifetime for the C-46 was 1,000 hours. The C-46 that we were working on that night had well over 10,000 hours.

*****

As I wrote before, all I had was my Flight Engineer's written passed. That and a dime would buy you a cup of coffee in nineteen hundred and fifty-eight.

I kissed the Chief Flight Engineer's "**ASS**" at Flying Tigers for a Mechanic Flight Engineer's position.

---Many "**MOONS**"---

No dice---No license---No fuckin' way Hosay.

I walked across the tarmac to the Slick Brothers Airways' hangar.

Slick Brothers Airways, a cargo carrier, consisted of four DC-6s, two DC-4s and a bullet riddled Curtis-Wright C-46 that flew "The Hump" with Chenault's Flying Tigers out of Burma.

I got an audience with Slicks **Chieflightengineerw/cowboybootson**.

I proudly showed him my Flight Engineer's Written.

Chieflightengineerw/cowboybootson was not impressed.

Chieflightengineerw/cowboybootson, ---"Can you change a chevron seal on a propeller governor on a Pratt & Whitney twenty eight hundred engine?"

"???HUH???"

Chieflightengineerw/cowboybootson stood up, ---"Come back and see me when you have a Flight Engineer **LICENSE.**"---

Turned around---Rode off into the sunset.

I sent resumes to American Airlines, United Airlines, Northwest Orient Airlines, Continental Airlines, Pan American Airlines and every Non-Sked Airlines in the world.

---NO LUCK---

I was doomed to be an---Acetone sniffing-sparkplug changing-hangar floor sweeping lackey-junior mechanic.

---FOREVER---

*****
If you do your best---
What ever happens will be for the best---
At least 70% of the time---
And that's passing in any grade school in the good old U.S. of A.
The most used-useless words in Webster's Dictionary
A: Someday

B: Probably

C: I think

D: All of the above

The least used-useful words in Webster's Dictionary

A: I'll try

B: I'll try

C: I'll try

D: YEP

--- CIRCA ---

NOVEMBER 1-NINER-57
Hooray---hooray---it's the fir----oh shit---
You must know the words by now---unless you are a real pilot.

About this time in life, ---the Major Airlines were starting to hire Co-Pilot/Flight Engineers instead of Mechanic/Flight Engineers.

Now you needed a Pilot's License and a Flight Engineer's License to hire on as a Flight Engineer w/Cowboy boots---of which -
--I HAD NEITHER.

This was a ploy by **ALPA (Airlines Pilot Association)** that would put a Pilot in the Flight Engineer's seat.

When the layoffs came---which they did every September and October, ---

Junior Captains could bump into the Co-Pilot's seat---

Junior Co-Pilots could bump into the Flight Engineer seat---

Junior Flight Engineers could go to selling shoes at Kinneys and look up women's skirts.

*****

*Who was the butt-hole that invented **SKORTS???**---Probably the descendant of the butt-hole that invented panty hose and the chastity belt.*

*****

This ploy, by **ALPA,** caused a battle with **FEIA**---the Mechanic Flight Engineer's Union.

**ODDS 2 to 1
2 Pilots per cockpit.
1 Flight Engineer per cockpit.
GUESS WHO WON?**
??

There was a fiery battle between the **AIR LINE PILOT'S ASSOCIATION (ALPA)** and the **FLIGHT ENGINEER'S INTERNATIONAL ASSOCIATION (FEIA) in the early '60s at Western Airlines.**

The Western Airlines Flight Engineers went out on a "wildcat" strike. (Non-sanctioned by **FEIA**)---There were a lot of busted noses & windshields during the three week melee.

From then on, all the Major Airlines started hiring Pilot Flight Engineers.

THE MECHANIC FLIGHT ENGINEERS---
---WENT THE WAY OF THE BUFFALO HUNTERS.

Some airlines even allowed the Pilot Flight Engineer's to wear **THREE STRIPES** on their uniform.

*****

I finally realized that my destiny was busted knuckles and dirty fingernails.

About that time, Mechanic Bob Comfort **t**old me that he had started taking Flying Lessons on the GI Bill at San Fernando Airport near the San Gabriel Mountains in Burbank, California.

---GOT ME TO THINKIN'---

MY THOUGHT---"I finally "larned" how to spell e-n-g-i-n-e-e-r and now I have to "larn" how to spell p-y-l-u-t."

*****

A FLIGHT ENGINEER WAS HITCHHIKING---

A car stopped & the driver said, "I see that you are a flight crewmember. What's your position?"---I'm a Flight Engineer."---

The driver drove away---another car---another stop, --- "I see that you are a flight crewmember. ---What's your position?"--- "I'm a Flight Engineer."---Another drive away. ----Etcetcetc---

"Huuuum, next car that stops, I'm gonna tell them I'm a Captain.- A good lookin' blonde stops, ---"I see you're a flight crewmember--what's your position?"---

"I'm a Captain."

"Get in Captain."

As they drove away, the newly anointed Captain noticed that the good lookin' blonde had no clothes on underneath her coat. ---

"Do you like what you see?" the good lookin' blonde asked as she turned off on a rural road. ---

"YES MAAM"---

*They were having at it & all of a sudden the Flight Engineer burst out in laughter. **"What's so funny Captain?"***

"I'V ONLY BEEN A CAPTAIN FOR TEN MINUTES
And
ALREADY I'M SCREWIN' SOMEBODY."

*****

IN 1980 a salesperson offered me a remote with a Quasar TV at the Price club in El Cajon, California for the same price as a manual one.

I declined, saying, "When I get too lazy to get up and change a TV channel, I'll quit watching it."

*Today I learned how to turn on the TV and the VCR manually—
I couldn't find any of my **TEN** remotes.*
*****

Dja hear about the lady that backed into a propeller???

Disaster
Diss-ass-t-her

--- CIRCA ---

WINTER OF 1958

Hooray---HOORAY
I'M STILL WRITING ON THIS CHERE BOOK

I stopped by Grand Central Airport in Glendale, California on the way home from the Graveyard Shift at Flying Tigers.
*****
Grand Central Airport was the airport that Will Rogers and Wily Post took off from on their ill-fated flight to Alaska.
*****
I drove across the 2,000 foot, alley-wide, strip of dirt runway to---
---RYAN AERONAUTICAL FLIGHT SCHOOL---
I went there because they had the biggest sign---ah---actually the only sign.

Mister Ryan was very courteous and very informative.

"The GI Bill will pay for seventy-five percent of your flight training. A "wet" single engine Aeronca Airplane, a tail dragger, will cost you fourteen dollars an hour with an instructor and after you solo, it will cost you ten dollars an hour when you go up by yourself."

"Your out of pocket costs will be two-fifty an hour solo and three-sixty-eight an hour with an instructor."
I SIGNED UP.
*****
Mister Ryan gave me my Private Pilot's check ride. When we got back, he told my instructor. ---"Mister Beck flew a good flight and he has excellent judgment."

I always remembered those kind words and they helped me at times when I was trying to get on as a Flight Engineer and Co-Pilot.
*****
"Wet" means full tanks of gas.
*****
I got a little cocky in the Aeronca. Yep, I ground looped her upon landing at Grand Central Airport. All I can remember is

*watching the right wing---**winging about five (5) inches above the grass as the Aeronca went around one time in a very tight circle.***
(360 degree turn)
Sorta discockyed me
Mister Ryan wasn't bragging about my judgment as he pulled grass out from the wheel's hubcaps of his "Airknocker". (Aeronca)
*****

Every morning on the way home from the Graveyard shift, I'd stop by Ryan's Aeronautical Flight School and take a couple of hours of flight lessons.

Within the next year, I managed to get my Commercial Pilots License and my Instrument Rating.
*****

My Instrument Rating didn't cost me one thin dime, thanx to the State of California's GI bill.
*****

During this time, I was sending out resumes to every Airline that had an address.

Hand carrying resumes to Airlines without an address.

---No bites---Not even a "nipple"---
NADA
Dis-fucin-scouragement
I was 23 years old, an old man without a college education in the airline industry. ---

---And not getting any younger---younger---younger---

At this point in time, if you didn't have a flying job with an Airline by the time you were twenty-eight (28), you might as well go to selling shoes at Kinneys and looking up women's skirts.

*Who was the fuckin' feminist that invented **SKORTS**???*

PREREQUISITES FOR A MAJOR AIRLINE
A---2000 HOURS OF <u>TWIN</u> ENGINE TIME
B---FOUR (4) YEARS OF COLLEGE WITH A BACHELOR OF ARTS DEGREE
C---20/20 VISION---UNCORRECTED
D---GOOD PHYSICAL HEALTH---UNCORRECTED

*****
"Got any naked pictures of your wife, Captain?"---
"NO---*of course not."*
"Dja wanna buy some?"
*****

"Cap'n, I hear you watch porno movies with one hand."

*****

My first dirty joke that I heard when I was a kid---Little Johnny Fuckerfaster was detained after school for slapping the teacher on the butt during class.

When he didn't come home, his mother became concerned and went to the school looking for him---walking up and down the school hall looking for him hollering---"Johnny Fuckerfaster---Johnny Fuckerfaster."

A voice from one of the classrooms---"I'm going as fast as I can, mom."

Remember that one???---Right down dirty filthy talk---at that point in time.

Actually, ---any point in time.
*****

--- CIRCA ---

SPRING ---1-NINER-5-NINER

One night my luck took a change for the better.
While **MECHANIC BOB COMFORT** and self were on our acetone trip,
Mechanic Bob Comfort informed me that
---TWENTIETH CENTURY AIRLINES---
was hiring Mechanics for Flight Engineers.
"Where's Twentieth Century Airlines based, Comfort?"
"Right here at Burbank Airport. It's a "Non-Sked."
*****

*What's a **NON-SKED**? --- You might ask,* ---**which I did.**
*A **NON-SCHEDULED AIRLINES**---at that point in time--- flying mostly Military Service personnel and their families to their assigned bases. They were called **CAM** trips---I don't know what that **<u>acronym</u>** stands for---so if you do---let me know.*

*<u>Acronym</u> (ak'ra nim) n. A word formed from the first (or first few) letters of a series of words, as radar, from **RA**dio **D**etecting **A**nd **R**anging.*
*****

"HOW DO I GET THERE?"

"Just go out of Tiger's parking lot, hang a left and turn left at the first open gate. A Trans American Airlines sign is on the hangar door."

"???TRANS AMERICAN AIRLINES???"

"Yea, they used to be
---NORTH AMERICAN AIRLINES---
Then **TRANS AMERICAN AIRLINES** and now---
---TWENTIETH CENTURY AIRLINES---
Yea, you know their game. The owners go bankrupt, change the name, go bankrupt, and change the name and so on down the line."

"Thank You ---Bob Comfort."

*****

    Ole Swenson was giving a lecture at Split Tail College in Bumfuc, Idaho---an all female college, about the perils of World War II in his hometown. ---"Those fokkers were flying all over the city shooting at our airplanes. ---Those fokkers were strafing the city buildings. ---Those fokkers were shooti ---"

    At this moment--- the Principle of the college stood up and interrupted Ole Swenson, saying, ---"Ladies, ---the Fokker Airplane that Ole is talking about was made by Fokker Aircraft Works in Berlin."

    Ole quickly interrupted saying---
"Oh no Mister Principle, those fokkers were Messerschmitts."

*****

Sign on a country store in Phenix City, Alabama

"YOU CAN WHIP OUR CREAM
BUT
YOU CAN'T BEAT OUR MEAT"

*****

--- CIRCA ---

Same day---early in the morning

I punched out of Tigers at 7:30, did a couple of left turns and parked at a door that read---
"TRANS AMERICAN AIRLINES OPERATIONS."
I knocked on the door hoping that someone would be there that early in the morning---figuring that this would be a waste of time.
"Come in." a pleasant voice said.
I did. ---This was my first encounter with---
CHIEF PILOT
CAPTAIN BILL BUTLER

THE BEST CHIEF PILOT THAT GOD EVER PUT WINGS ON
AS I LOOK UP TO THE SKY

ON THIS RAINY DAY ALONG THE COLORADO RIVER

BILL, I KNOW YOU'RE ON TOP OF THOSE CLOUDS.
---IN THE BIG AIRPORT IN THE SKY---

YOU STILL ARE THE BEST CHIEF PILOT THAT GOD EVER PUT WINGS ON.

I THANK YOU CAPTAIN BILL BUTLER FOR GIVING ME THE OPPORTUNITY TO HAVE THE MOST WONDERFUL CAREER AND LIFE THAT ANY MAN COULD EVER HAVE.
CAPTAIN JACK RESLEY BECK---REallyTIRED

P.S. ---Bill---could you give me a hand to finish writin' this friggin book?

---CHIEF PILOT CAPTAIN BILL BUTLER ---

Invited me to sit down and asked me a few questions about my background.

For a couple of minutes---*or a lifetime---*

---Chief Pilot Captain Bill Butler---

Just sat there and stared at me.

I was glad that I had my coveralls on so Chief Pilot Captain Bill Butler could not see the rivers flowing from my pits to my waist.

Chief Pilot Captain Butler started reading my resume.

All this time---**Chief Pilot Captain Bill Butler** was scratching his head---muttering to Captain Bill Butler, whose attitude was nuthin' but negative.

MY NEGATIVE THOUGHT---"He haint happy with me----might as well leave."

"You don't have a Flight Engineer's License. All you have is the Flight Engineer's written passed."

MY NEGATIVE THOUGHT---"No shit, Sherlock."

Chief Pilot Captain Bill Butler hemmed and hawed for another ten minutes.

All this time scratching---**Chief Pilot Bill Butlers head.**

MY NEGATIVE THOUGHT---"I might as well leave---I'm wasting my time."

Now that I had my Commercial Pilot's License and Instrument Rating, I had found a new hobby. I'd stop by the Blue Moon Saloon in Glendale, California on the way home---have some brewskies.

Yes, folks, the Blue Moon Saloon opened for business at 0600 hours and was packed with---

A---Graveyarders.

B---Blue collar workers.

C---Drunks that were alcoholics but wouldn't admit it because they didn't want to attend the Alcoholic Anonymous meetings.

D---Yep---all of the above.

This guy was cutting into my Miller Time by scratching his---

headandruff&hemming&hawing.

Chief Pilot Captain Bill Butler asked me only one question, ---

"Have you ever worked on a DC6?"

I "liednodded" my head, "Yes"---Couldn't "liedspeak".

Heck, lining fuel cells with tape in a DC-4 baggage compartment was close enough for me.
Another ten minutes of hemming&hawing&scratching went by.
Now I started scratching my head---guess it was contagious.
Chief Pilot Captain Bill Butler picked up the phone and called the CAB (Civil Aeronautics Board) which is now the FAA (Federal something or other).
I heard **Chief Pilot Bill Butler** ask if they had someone who could give a Flight Engineer Check ride tomorrow.
"Okay Jerry, see you at fifteen-thirty tomorrow."
Captain Bill Butler looked at me---asked, ---"Can you be here at three thirty tomorrow afternoon?"
I **head** nodded "**YES**". I was so nervous that I couldn't speak.
"See you then and don't be late."
*MY THOUGHT---"I'll be the person that you'll have to step over to get into your office tomorrow. Did you say **head**?*
My heart was pounding out of my chest and my legs felt like jelly.
I tried to be composed.
---SIR CHIEF PILOT CAPTAIN BILL BUTLER---
Knew that I was one scared hombre, but---he never let me know that he knew.
---I LEFT---
*****
Jack Warner said of Clark Gable after he had interviewed Clark Gable—"Gable will never make it---His ears are too big"---
!!!Ya never know---ya just never know!!!
I dated a girl, while I was in the Army 18th Airborne Corps at Fort Bragg, North Carolina, by the name of Abbey Jean, a share cropper's daughter near Goldsboro, North Carolina. She showed me the one-room shack that Ava Gardner was born and raised in. Ava Gardner---what a beautiful lady---as Ava Gardener grew old---some one suggested that she get a face lift---Ava declined saying that it would not be what god had given her.
*When I was an usher in the Alhambra Movie Theater in Alhambra, California at the age of 17, the movie **"SHOWBOAT"** starring **AVA GARDNER, KATHRYN GRAYSON, HOWARD KEEL** with **JOE E. BROWN, MARGE&GOWER CHAMPION, ROBERT STERLING, AGNES MOOREHEAD, WILLIAM WARFIELD**---from the immortal musical play **"SHOWBOAT"** by*

JEROME KERN & OSCAR HAMMERSTEIN II based on **EDNA FERBER'S NOVEL.**

    I saw it **33** *times---actually I was in love with Kathryn Grayson and didn't give poor Ava a second look.*
    I bought a "Showboat" DVD the other day and have watched it over & over while I'm social finger typing this bullshit--- singing, ---

"OLD MAN RIVER"
"THERE'S AN OLD MAN CALLED THE MISSISSIPPI---
THAT'S THE OLD MAN THAT I WANTS TO BE---
WHAT DOES HE CARE IF THE LAND AM WEARY---
WHAT DOES HE CARE IF THE LAND AM FREE
OLD MAN RIVER---THAT OLD MAN RIVER
HE MUST KNOW SOMETHIN'---BUT DON'T SAY NUTHIN'
HE JUST KEEPS ROLLIN'---
HE KEEPS ON ROLLIN'---ALONG
HE DON'T PLANT TATERS---HE DON'T PLANT COTTON
AND THEM THAT PLANTS THEM ---
AM SOON FORGOTTEN
BUT OLD MAN RIVER---
HE JUST KEEPS ROLLIN'---ALONG
YOU AND ME ---WE SWEAT AND STRAIN
BODIES ALL ACHIN' AND RACKED WITH PAIN
YOU TOTE THAT BARGE---YOU LIFT THAT BALE
YOU GETS A LITTLE DRUNK AND YOU LANDS IN JAIL
I GETS WEARY AND SICK OF TRYING
I'M TIRED OF LIVING AND SCARED OF DYIN'
BUT OLD MAN RIVER ---
HE JUST KEEPS ROLLIN' ALONG
*****

--- CIRCA ---

0100 HOURS   NEXT DAY

My luck was still working for me that night.

There was a Slick Brothers Airline DC-6 in Tiger's overhaul hangar that night.

I spent the entire Graveyard Shift sitting in the DC-6's Flight Engineer seat. Screw the **seniors**. I did all their dirty work for the past two years and now it was their turn to bust their knuckles and get acetone smashed.

I simulated-practiced-pretended-shammed-acted-imagined-played.
**STARTING ENGINES---SHUTTING DOWN ENGINES---
ENGINE FIRES---FEATHERING PROPELLERS---
HYDRAULIC FAILURES---ELECTRICAL FAULTS---
RAPID DECOMPRESSIONS
AND EVERYTHING ELSE THAT I COULD CONJUR UP, ---
INCLUDING---GEAR-UP LANDINGS.**

Thank God the DC-6 was up on jacks. *Just kidding*

I read all the emergency checklists and anything else that might help me get through the check ride of my life---up to that point in time.

Many more check rides to come & not all flying airplanes.

I practiced all night long---

I was so enrapt that---

I had lost track of the time---

I heard someone riveting on the side of the DC-6.

I knew it wasn't the **SENIORS.** It would be beneath their dignity to venture into the overhaul hangar and besides that, someone might put them to work.

I checked the five hundred ($500) dollar **Chronometer** on the Captain's instrument panel.

Crap, it was 0800 hours and the day shift had started.
Captain's Chronometer, --- A high tech---over priced---clock.

I snuck out of the DC-6 and went home.

Tried to sleep---I couldn't---I was "all shook up---uhuhuhu."

Right Elvis?

I got to the Twentieth Century Airlines hangar a litta early and a lotta over anxious.
---CEO BOSSMAN CHIEF TRAINING CHECK PILOT--- ---CAPTAIN BILL BUTLER ---
His brother---Flight Engineer Bob Butler ---
And CAB Inspector---Mister Louis Best, ---
All were in the cockpit of the DC-6 awaiting my arrival.

Bob Butler was the Co-Pilot for the check ride. He was a Flight Engineer and I don't believe he had a pilot's license.

The CAB Inspector was about to retire and appeared to be a litta drunkey-wunkey.

Aviating at that point in time, was a litta—
---no a lotta loosa than it is now.
We took off.
Captain Bill Butler shut down the #1 engine by shutting off the fuel with the mixture control and calmly said, ---**"Engine failure number one."**

I pushed in the #1 propeller feathering button that's located on the forward overhead panel.

Captain Bill Butler, CAB Inspector and Pseudo Flight Engineer Beck all looked out the left side window to make sure the propeller was "feathered".
!!!IT WAS!!!
*****

"Feathering" the propeller rotates the propeller blades with the edges facing forward in a position of minimum drag. ---When Captain Bill Butler shut off the mixture control---the propeller was wind-milling causing a whole shit-pot full of drag and possibly a damaged engine due to low oil pressure. ---Not good---not conducive to get to your destination 'because you're gonna burn a whole shit-pot full of fuel if you don't feather that propeller.

Take a sheet of paper and face it into the wind---feel the drag?---take the same sheet of paper and put the edge into the wind---feel no drag?---you feathered the paper.
*****

We did a few more emergency items. I would just pick up the emergency check-list and read it to Captain Bill Butler.

Captain Bill Butler would just nod and point to the stricken system and I would simulate solving the problem.

Forty-five (45) minutes after we took off, Captain Bill Butler greased the DC-6 on the numbers on Runway 33 at Burbank International Airport.

Now known as --- (Nka)
--HOLLYWOOD BURBANK INTERNATIONAL AIRPORT--

Captain Butler taxied the DC-6 to the hangar---didn't stop---taxied **inside** the hangar.

*!!!And that, old buddy, is a major **NO-NO!!!***

I shut the engines down, read and did the **complete shut down** checklist.

*The shutdown checklist has asterisk (*) items for **shutting down** if the airplane is going back out.*

My shirt looked like someone had turned a **fire** hose on me and was **navy blue** instead of the **sky blue** shirt that I put on that day.

We deplaned and went into the office that read---**TRANS AMERICAN AIRLINES--**on the dodedodoor.

"Co-Pilot" Bob Butler and CAB Inspector Louis Best went to the coffee machine mumbling to each other.

I sat down in my interview chair---

---TRAINING-CHECK PILOT CAPTAIN BILL BUTLER---

Sat at his desk and started---
More hemming---
More hawing---
More muttering---
More head scratching.

*****

MY THOUGHT---"Screw it---I blew it---hey, that rhymes. "I'm a poet and don't know it but my big feet show it, —
They're LONGFELLOWS"---
Do you remember that one---Dearie???
"Do you remember? ---if you remember—Dearie---you're much older than I."

*****

---CHIEF PILOT CAPTAIN BILL BUTLER---

"Mister Beck, ---Why don't you go somewhere and get a cup of coffee? Be back here in an hour---please."

I figured that he was going to get rid of Mister CAB Inspector and be courteous enough to shit-can me gently."

I left

I took off my saturated shirt, hung it on the driver's side rearview mirror of my pastensed '46 Plymouth and circled the Burbank Airport till it dried.

I was heartbroken---in tears.

ONLY thirty minutes went by---very slowly.

I went back to the door that read **TRANS AMERICAN AIRLINES**. Might as well get the hangin' over with and go sip some suds and lick my wounds.

I walked in. Mister CAB Inspector was still there. MY THOUGHT---***"beckballhangingtime"***---*"These guys are gonna hang me up by the nuts."*

---CHIEF CHECK PILOT CAPTAIN BILL BUTLER---

Walked over to me---
Put his arm around my shoulder---
Shook my hand--
"CONGRADULATIONS"

"!!!I MADE IT!!!"---
I shouted for the all the world to hear.

"SIX MONTHS AGO I COULDN'T SPELL ENGINEAR
AND
NOW I ARE ONE"

The C-A-B Inspector was sitting at---**CHIEF PILOT CAPTAIN BILL BUTLERS** desk penning out my temporary license.

I sidled over to the desk with tears of joy in my eyes---praying that I wasn't dreaming.

Yep, sure enough, there was my **FLIGHT ENGINEER'S LICENSE**. Signed, sealed and almost delivered.

MISTER CAB INSPECTOR---Stood up, shook my hand and gave me my license.

---**"CONGRADULATIONS"**---

"I'm a DC-4 Maintenance Inspector and have never seen a Flight Engineer at work before. Captain Butler told me you were inexperienced, but eager and to pass you."
DC-4s don't have Flight Engineers.
    I'll always wonder if Captain Butler finagled to get this DC-4 Inspector, who just happened to be one of his Co-pilots at one time, to give me my Flight Engineer's Check Ride.
I'll never forget
CAPTAIN BILL BUTLER
And what he did for me.
---THANK YOU---THANK YOU---THANK YOU---

*****CAPTAIN BILL BUTLER*****

*****

    THE FLIGHT ENGINEER LICENSE THAT I GOT IN FORTY-FIVE (45) MINUTES---Now takes over two months to graduate.
    Three (3) weeks of ground school---ten (10) to fourteen (14) hours of simulator training---and a whole shitpot full of flying hours with a Check Airman looking over your shoulder.
I did it all in forty-five (45) minutes.
---With an unlicensed Co-Pilot---
And a
---CAB DC-4 Maintenance Inspector---
???Guinness Record Book for the world's fastest Flight Engineer check-out???
    The CAB Inspector and I started to leave.
Captain Bill Butler, --- "Jack, I need to talk to you before you go."
I stayed
MY THOUGIIT---"Oh shit, what now?"
    Captain Bill Butler asked me to sit down and said, after hemming&hawing&scratching, ---"I know that you're a mechanic at Flying Tigers with close to two years of seniority which is going to be hard for you to give up. I talked to Mister Funk on the phone

while you were driving around drying your shirt. He told me that you were a bit of a hothead, but a hard worker."

I said nothing---while washing out my pits again.

"The problem I have with hiring you Jack (*hemhawscratchhemhaetcetcetcetc*) is that Twentieth only has four months of the years Military Contract left."

"DO YOU STILL WANT THE JOB???"

"YES SIR"

---I LEFT---

As I walked out the dodedodo, I heard

---CHIEF PILOT CAPTAIN BILL BUTLER---
SNICKERSAY
"STAY OFF THE ACETONE----BECK."

--- CIRCA ---

Same day --- only two beers later.

I stopped by the Blue Moon Saloon, had a couple of well-earned brews and went back to my apartment.

My intentions were to go to Flying Tigers in the A.M. and give them two weeks notice.
!!!WRONG!!!
"RING---RING---RI--"
It was Captain Butler, ---"Beck, this is Butler, ---we need you for a trip tomorrow."
"What time?"
"Check in at midnight---2400 hours."

"I'LL BE THERE" was my breathless reply. I hung up.
MY THOUGHT---"How am I gonna give Flying Tigers two weeks notice?"
MY SECOND THOUGHT---"I worked hard for this & I haint stoppin' now."

I CALLED IN SICK THAT NIGHT. --Screw it. If you're gonna sin---sin **IN BOLD TYPE.**
I slept in till noon--I was beat--I got out of bed and did the 4-ESSES.
!!!SHIT---SHINED---SHOWERED---SHAVED!!!

I put on my pastensed wide lapel gray flannel suit that I got when I graduated from Alhambra High School in California. If I'm gonna slam dunk Tigers---might as well look nice.

I phoned Captain Butler before I left the apartment, ---"This is **Flight Engineer Jack Beck.** What about a uniform? I was so nervous yesterday that I forgot to ask."

"All you need is a pair of brown slacks and a white shirt. You don't even need a tie. You're the only Flight Engineer that we have tonight. If you don't have them, wear what you have on. You can get a uniform when you get back from the trip."
MY THOUGHT---"Shit, they need me---I'm somebody---but I haint wearin' this gray flannel suit."
"OK---Bye"

The only formal clothes I owned, other than my pastensed gray flannel suit, were a-pair of Levis and a holey Tee Shirt. No white shirt and certainly no brown slacks.
First things---first.
I got my Montgomery Ward's credit card---
I stopped by "Monkeys" on the way to "Tigers"---
I charged a five-dollar pair of brown slacks---
I charged a two-dollar white shirt---

I was walking **tall.**

Never did occur to me that I'd be gone for more than one day and need more than one shirt.

I arrived at Flying Tigers Airlines Inc ---went into the overhaul hangar, for the last time, ---I hoped. I climbed the stairs to the offices that overlooked the hangared overhaul wantabee airplanes.

I espied a door that read---
**VICE PRESIDENT OF MAINTENANCE
FLYING TIGERS AIRLINES INC.
ENTER**
I did

"My name is Jack beck---may I talk to the vice president---please." I asked a pretty brunette lady with the name tag that read---

---**"MISSES IDELLA BROWN"**---

"He's in the hangar---I'll page him for you---please sit down Mister Beck."

MY THOUGHTS---*"Mister---wow---told ya I was somebody."*

I DID

An **"eternity"** passed by and with each year---my confidence rating was going fastly to zero---as a matter of fact---I was getting a litta, no, a lotta noivous.

*****

An **"Eternity"** *is the time---from when you pop your nuts till she up & leaves---*

CAPTAIN LELAND (LEE)

Also from Cap'n Lee---"10 seconds don't seem like too long a time---try hanging by your nuts for ten seconds & it will seem like an **"Eternity"**.

*****

I heard the door that read Flying Tiger Maintenance open.
I looked up from my assumed Sunday School Posture.
Guess who? ---**MISTER FUNK REAL NAME.**
Mister Funk was now Vice President of Maintenance.
Mister Funk, like me, had become somebody.
Mister Funk walked over and shook my hand.
Mister Funk invited me into his office.
I stood in front of his desk with a gold sign that read---

FRANK FUNK JR
VICE PRESIDENT OF MAINTENANCE

---Oh man---
I was not only sweating---
I was shaking---
I was shuckin'&jivin'---
I was about to piss off the man that saved my job.
Mister Frank Funk Junior started---
Scratching his head---
Hemming and hawing---
Muttering to himself.
MY THOUGHT---"These actions must be a common/contagious/communicable disease among head-shed people."
Vice-President Mister Funk finally, ---"Son, I know why you're here. I think your making a big mistake by giving up your seniority here at Flying Tigers for a four month flying job."
MY THOUGHT---"Captain Butler has already talked to him."
"I'm probably screwing up, but I'm going for it. I have to quit today."
"???WHAT???"
"I can't give you two weeks notice. I have a trip tonight."
"Well, Mister Beck, ---now you're really screwing up. When the four months are up---I can't hire you back if you don't give Tigers two weeks notice."
"This is FLYING TIGER AIRLINES COMPANY POLICY."

Vice-President Mister Frank Funk Junior knew by now that there was no changing my mind---got up---walked around his desk to my quivering body and shook my sweaty hand.

"Kid, you got guts---you'll do alright."

On the way to my apartment, I stopped at a hardware store and bought a six-cell flashlight. The flashlight had enough candlepower to light up a **new** moon.

*****

*A **new** moon is dark---*
Hidden from the sun by the earth---
*Then the moon **waxes**---*
*Becomes a **full** moon---*
*Then the moon **wanes** back to a **new** moon.*

*****

One item I have to confess before I leave Los Gatos Airlines.

Leadman Andy, ---"Beck, remove the sparkplug on the number one cylinder *(the top cylinder)* of number four engine on that Connie in the hangar. Get a Boroscope and check the cylinder for metal. The Flight Engineer that flew it in said the ignition analyzer pattern was indicating okay, but every once in a while he could see a small distortion in the pattern. Hurry it up---the airplanes due out in less than an hour. It's quittin' time and I'm outta here. If you find anything wrong---tell the day foremen---it's not a write-up in the logbook."

I wrenched out the spark plug and boroscoped the #1 cylinder. I found no evidence of metal fragments. I put a new spark plug in and closed up the cowling. I left.

Later that night, **LEADMAN ANDY,** ---"Beck, I need to talk to you in my office!!!"

"Yesssssir?'

"They had to abort the take-off on that Connie that you worked on this morning."

"Huh?"

"Apparently you didn't tighten the sparkplug tight enough and the thermocouple under it jiggled on the take off roll and gave an erratic reading of the cylinder head temperature. They had to abort and come back to the hangar. Did you write anything in the log-book?"

"No"

"Well---keep it quiet---if they find out about it---they'll fire your scrawny ass."

"Okay"
I LEFT

MY THOUGHT---"Bye---Bye---Flying Pussy Cats."
*****

One more Flying Tiger Story---then I am outta here.

When Flying Tigers received their first Lockheed Super Constellation---they were doing their training at the Burbank Airport.

A shit-pot full of Chief Pilots & Check Pilots & Chief and Check Flight Engineers & CAB Flight Inspectors were on the Connie.

They were doing **"touch and goes"**--- (taking off---staying in Burbank's traffic pattern---landing and taking off again without stopping).

To do these maneuvers---the throttles are constantly going from flight idle to maximum power and back to flight idle. ---Every time the throttles are retarded to flight idle and the landing gears are not in the down and locked position, the landing gear warning horn sounds---**BEEP-BEEP-BEEP-ETCETCETC**---to warn the Flight Crew that the landing gears are not down and locked.

Now, let's listen in on "what's the hops", ---

"Hey Joe, let's get rid of that ^&(^%&# landing gear warning horn---its driving me nuts."

"OK Ed, I'll pull the landing gear warning horn circuit breaker." ---Famous last words.

---WHAM-BAM-THANK YOU MAAM---

As "Connie" came to a screeching ass halt on her belly and the occupants of the---

---FLAMING---
---LOCKHEED SUPER CONSTELLATION 1049H---

Scurried to save their asses from turning to ashes. ---

Someone was heard to say, ---**"Guess we shouldn't have pulled that circuit breaker---what say Joe?"**

I saw a picture of that Connie and all I can write is that 115/130 purple gasoline sure knows how to blacken shiny aluminum.

I did get to fly jump seat on a Super Constellation 1049H training ride---one time.

They even let me sit in the Flight Engineer seat for a few minutes. Thrill of my life at that point in time.

I heard that landing gear WARNING horn go BEEP-BEEP-BEEP many times.

Not one person reached for the landing gear warning horn circuit breaker.

*****

An old lady picked up a young man hitchhiking on a very cold night-
"My hands are freezing."---
"Put them between my legs young man & that'll warm them up."---
"Thank you Maam, they're warm now."---
"Are your ears cold?"
*****

If you are what you eat---does that make me a pussy?
*****

Red Skelton---"I don't want you dating her---her necks dirty."
"Her do!!!"
*****

--- CIRCA ---

TWO-NINER APRIL--- ONE-NINER-FIVE-NINER

I was all set, a brand new white shirt, a brown pair of store bought britches and a flashlight that any woman would be proud to have on her night stand.

I went to the Blue Moon Saloon. ---Sipped some suds. ---Contemplated my future. ---

---Bleak---but---**EXCITING---**

Just to sit in the Flight Engineers seat for take off one time would make it---

---ALL WORTH WHILE---
No turning back now---too late---
All the bridges behind me were ashes.

I got to the apartment---drank another beer to put me to sleep---tossed and turned---got back up---watched television on my "sleeping" couch---too excited to sleep.

---IT WAS GOING TO BE A VERY LONG---
---BUT EXCITING---NIGHT---

My wife got home from work at five-thirty and I told her of the events that happened the last two days, ---"I'm leaving tonight and have no idea when I'll be back. Maybe a roll in the hay would be nice."

"It's still daylight. What will our neighbors think?"

"Screw the neighbors."

MY THOUGHT---*"At least someone's getting screwed."*

I went back to bed---finally dozed---off and on---got up---suited up---tried tooooo prepare my mind for my first flight.

Unfortunately my wife was still up, ---"You're giving up all your seniority at Tigers for a three month flying job---you're nuts. **What are you going to do at the end of three months**? Collect unemployment? You can't if you quit a job, ya know."

"I don't know---besides that---it's a four month job."
--YA NEVER KNOW, PILGRIM---YA JUST NEVER KNOW--

I arrived at the Burbank International Airport two hours early, partly to get away from the nagging bullshit, but mostly out of excitement of my new adventure.

All I had with me was my overnight case with toothbrush, toothpaste and a double edge Gillette Razor, my trusty six- cell flashlight, a small tool box and my newly acquired---

---**Temporary Flight Engineer License**---

I drove directly to the door that read Trans American Airlines with a gorgeous body in front of it in the form of a Douglas Aircraft DC-6. I "de-carred" and drew a bead on her with my trusty 6 celled mega-powered flashlight.

I was ready for action, ---sort of a Wyatt Earp at the OK Corral. I found the Clampetts in the form of a Mighty DC-6. I drew my trusty 6-cell and shone it on her. She glistened in the beam, but she stood her ground. She knew I loved her and was in awe of her.

She was a beauty and I was going to get in her and ride.

Sound sexual? Not really---just a love of flying that most aviators have.

I walked around her---**twice**.

The landing gear---the wings---the flaps---the engines---the propellers---the tail section and every orifice she had.

Still sound sexual? Guess I was in love.

I found a bird nest in one of the air-conditioning ducts---woven with aluminum filings left by a sloppy Aircraft Mechanic. Picture perfect, as only God with Mother Nature's hand could make.

---**A real work of art**---

I holstered my 6 cell and went through the door that read

---**TRANS INTERNATIONAL AIRLINES**---

Full house---3 Pilots---2 Stewardess and the

---**President/Owner of Twentieth Century Airlines**---

This was the inaugural flight since---

---**TRANS INTERNATIONAL AIRLINES**---

Became

---**TWENTIETH CENTURY AIRLINES**---

The President/Owner espied my prized aluminum bird nest, ---

"Where did you get that? That's beautiful."

"In the DC-6's air-conditioning duct, sir."

"You found it on my airplane. It's mine. Give it to me."

I reluctantly relinquished it to the prick. I didn't want to piss off the head honcho on my first day on the job.

Captain Bill Butler got up from his desk and started introducing me to the Crew.

"Jack---this is Captain Bud Eweing. This is Beck's first flight Bud."

CAPTAIN BUD EWEING shook my hand**,** ---"Nice meeting you Jack"---turned around to the rest of the crew, ---"This is my Crew briefing---I'm tired, it's late---so let's get the airplane in the air."

As we "EXcITED" through the door that read, ---
---TRANS INTERNATIONAL AIRLINES---
I heard **CAPTAIN BILL BUTLER** say, ---
"Have a good flight Jack."

*****

Dja hear about the girl that rode a bike down a cobblestone street---
*Said she would never **come** that way again.*
*****

*****

Part of a flight attendant's arrival announcement: "We'd like to thank you folks for flying with us today. And, the next time you get the insane urge to go blasting through the skies in a pressurized metal tube, we hope you'll think of Bumfuc Airlines."
*****

Heard on a Pacific Southwest Airline flight. "Ladies and gentlemen, if you wish to smoke, the smoking section on this airplane is on the wing and if you can light 'em, you can smoke 'em."

*****

--- CIRCA ---

APRIL 30   0100 HOURS   1niner5niner

As we entered the DC-6, after climbing a mechanics ladder, Captain Bud Eweing introduced me to the rest of the crew.
"This is our Co-Pilot, John Wayne."
"That's your real name---no shit?"
"Yep---that's exactly what they call me, John Wayne Real Name No Shit. Nice meeting you."
"These are our two Stewardesses---Miss Kay Klause and Misses Kay Robey."

I still remember their names. ---After working the graveyard shift for two years, ---they were--------beautiful.

I descended the mechanics ladder and did one more walk around the DC-6. She hadn't changed a rivet and was just as beautiful as the first time I saw her.

I climbed back up the mechanics ladder and entered her---she creaked and groaned.

Yea, she was beautiful, but she was old.

I silently entered the cockpit, unsnapped and let down the 12X16"X¾" Naugahyde covered hunk of plywood Flight Engineer Seat---just aft and between the two pilots.

I put my small toolbox beneath it and quietly sat down so as to not to disturb the Sky Gods.

*****

The Flight Engineer's seat was behind and between the two pilot's seats. It would fold up behind the Captain's seat.

*The seat was sixteen inches butt wide and twelve inches back of ass to knee in depth. A piece of ¾ inch marine plywood with a skimpy Naugahyde cover and hard on the ass after a couple of hours---No **minutes**. Needless to say there were not many---no---not any---**Fat Flight Engineers**.*

*****

Captain Bud Eweing and C0-Pilot John Wayne Real Name No Shit were discussing the route of flight and the weather we were about to encounter.

The instruments were a red glare and I could barely see them.

I was snow blind from the beam of my 6-celled, zillion candlepower flashlight refracting off the silvery body of my newfound love.

We did a before start checklist.

Captain Bud Eweing looked out his side-sliding glass window and got clearance to start the number four (#4) engine from a Mechanic, who had positioned himself so as to see all four engines. The Mechanic was standing in a surrender stance with his right hand waving in a circular motion and his left hand holding up four fingers.

Captain Bud Eweing looked around at me, ---"Start number four engine and don't backfire it."

This is like telling your brand new puppy not to shit on your brand new carpet.

This was a tricky job on the DC-6. There were four toggle **PADDLE** switches on the overhead panel---right above my head.

Three toggle switches in a row and the other toggle switch was centered about two inches across from them---this being the thumb safety switch and when depressed armed the other three switches.

Looking up at them, from left to right---
FUEL PRIMER--STARTER ENGAGE SWITCH--IGNITION

FUEL PRIME--START ENGAGE—IGNITION

O   O   O

O

THUMB SAFETY SWITCH
(Looking up at the overhead panel)

The thumb safety switch was to prevent somebody's head from hitting the starter switch & decapitating some unsuspecting soul standing in a propellers path.
Head---did you say head???

I reached my right hand up and simultaneously depressed the thumb switch and the starter engage switch.

Co-Pilot John Waynerealnamenoshit looked out his side sliding glass window at the #4 engine propeller and counted out loud the blades of the propeller as it turned.

"Onetwothreefourfivesixseveneightnineteninetenelleven"
---**"TWELVE BLADES"**---
*****

The reason for counting twelve blades was to ensure that there weren't any liquids in the bottom cylinders of the radial (round) engine. The twelve-blade count put the engine through its complete intake-compression-combustion-exhaust cycle so that when you put the fuel & ignition on & the engine started---there would be no engine parts lying on the ground beneath the engine.
So much for the ground school bullshit
*****

I **SIMULTANEOUSLY** depressed the **thumb switch**---
The **starter engage switch** with my social finger---
The **ignition switch** with my ring finger---
Toggled the **fuel primer switch** with my index finger---
The #4 engine started.

When the engine's rotation reached 600 R$_s$PM (Revolution$_s$ Per Minute) ---I reached down, between my legs, to the floor with my left hand and raised the #4 engine fuel lever up to the up/rich position.

This has/had to be done with precision or the engine will/would backfire.

---**KAPOW**---
Was #4 Engines response to my ineptness?
BOTH pilots looked at me with a "Who hired you?" look.
It was 0130 hours---I had just given the city of Burbank a piss call.
Three more engine starts ---
---**KAPOW**---**KAPOW**---**K-FUCKIN-POW**---
Three more "Who hired you looks?"

Now I knew that the whole town of Burbank was heading toward the bathroom.

---W---I---D---E---AWAKE---
Screw 'em----if I'm awake---everyone should be awake.

*****

In my defense. ---The DC-6's, that Twentieth Century Airlines owned, were purchased from American Airlines. The DC6's still had American Airlines' orange paint on some of the engine cowling. (Engine cowling===that hunk of aluminum that wraps around the engine.)

Some **Murphy Law** *American Airlines Mechanic had installed the* **smaller** *DC-4 primers in the DC-6 engines and when the engines on the DC-6 were started and would get to 500 R(s)PM (Round(s) Per Minute) the engines couldn't get enough fuel to sustain rotation, they would stagnate, take more air in---KAPOW.*

Normal rotation for bringing in more fuel with the mixture control was 600 RsPM. Bringing in the mixture control before 600 RsPM could cause the backfire to go through the internal workings of the carburetor causing damage to the carburetor.

Murphy's Law*--If there is a way to screw something up---somebody will.*

*****

I read the Before-Taxi Checklist and both pilots actually listened to me and responded loud and clear.
Was I somebody or not???

Co-Pilot John Waynerealnamenoshit picked up his hand held mike, ---"Burbank Ground, this is Twentieth Century 775---Ready to taxi." (*775 was the tail number of this DC6B.*)

"Roger, Twentieth Century 775---taxi to Runway 15---taxi on the runway if you like---How ya doin' John? Stay on this frequency---I'm working tower too. When you get to the end of the runway---taxi into position and you're cleared for take-off."

"Fine Paul---We're starting our taxi. We're gonna have to make a full run up before we go."

Captain Bud Eweing released the brakes---Pushed the throttles forward till the creaky old DC-6 started rolling and then---pulled them back to idle.

"Oh---in that case, John, use the taxiway and run up at the blast fence. They won't let you run up the engines on the runway anymore---a Tiger Super Connie blew a Volkswagen Van across San Fernando Highway---on its side."

"OK, Paul, we will taxi on the taxiway---run up at the blast fence."

Captain Eweing, ---"Taxi Checklist, please, Jack."
Gosh---he called me by my first name.

I read the Taxi Check-List as Captain Bud Eweing taxied down the taxiway that paralleled Runway 15/33.

We got to the blast fence on the side of the taxiway. Captain Eweing positioned the DC-6 so the tail of the aircraft pointed at the blast fence and parked the brakes.

Captain Bud Eweing, ---"Do the run-up, please Jack."
MY THOUGHT---*"God, please don't let me screw this up."*

I ran the engines up to 1,000 R(s)PM (Round(s) Per Minute) ---I checked out the magnetos and the propeller's ability to change pitch. All this time the pilots were hawk-eyeing me---praying that I wouldn't destroy their engines---and their jobs.

*****

---Checking out the magnetos---

Aircraft engines have two (2) spark-plugs per cylinder to give better combustion and to keep the engine running in case one magneto should fail. The left engine driven magneto fires the front set of spark-plugs and the right engine driven magneto fires the back set of spark-plugs.

*You check the **magnetos** with a selector switch labeled---*

L---BOTH---R

*Selecting **L** puts your engine on the left **"mag"**--- disables the right **"mag"** & then you will experience an RsPM drop of 60 to 100 RsPM---indicating that your left **mag** is operating properly. If the engine quits---you quit & go back to the gate.*

*Samo, samo for the right **mag**.*

*You then select to---**BOTH**---& then **mag** check the next engine etcetcetc. This whole procedure for all 4 engines takes less than 30 seconds.*

You also have an ignition analyzer oscilloscope, which is located next to the Flight Engineer's left ear (a convenient pillow at times) that you can check the firing pattern of each & every spark-plug individually.

---Checking out the propeller's ability to change pitch---

When you start the engines---the propeller blades are in a fine pitch-flat mode causing the least amount of drag on the engine. You taxi in fine pitch.

When you advance the throttles forward for Take-Off power---the propeller blades automatically go towards full pitch giving the propeller blades a bigger bite of air.

*To check the propeller's ability to change pitch---there is a lever that manually changes the pitch of the propeller blades. This lever, located on the forward pedestal---conveniently next to the Captain's right hand---is kept in the full forward---**AUTO**---position.*

Pulling back on the lever puts the propeller blades in the full pitch position causing a RsPM drop of 200-300 RsPM.---& that ladies & gentleman---boys & girls & Electrical Contractors, Richard & Billie Lee Hughes is how you make a magneto check & a propeller check on a Pratt Whitney 2800 Reciprocating Engine---if I remember right---me thinks.

*I've had enough of this ground school bullshit so we'll get back to **KAPOW** City.*

*****

Captain Bud Eweing, as he scanned the engine instruments, ---"Everything check out okay Jack?"

I nodded ---lest I say the wrong thing.

"Okay, tell the tower we're ready to go, John," Captain Bud Eweing said as he released the parking brakes and started to taxi from the blast fence to Runway 15.

"Burbank tower---this is Twentieth Century Airlines 775---ready for Take-off."

"Roger, Twentieth Century 775---This is Burbank Tower---wind's calm---Altimeter's two-niner-niner-niner---Runway one-five---cleared for take off---see ya later John."

*****

*Why say **NINER** instead of just plain **NINE**???---*

*"Way back when"---I was taught that you said **NINER** instead of **NINE** because **NINE** might be mistaken for the **Number FIVE**.*

Now I've been informed by my son---Captain Kevin Shaun Beck, who flies for America West (Actually Kevo is not a Captain yet but he probably will be a retired Captain by the time I finish this book) ---that you say **NINER** *to distinguish the English number* **NINE** *from the German* **NEIN**---*which means---no way Hosay---oops----I meant Meinkoff.*

*****

"Roger, Burbank Tower, Twentieth two-zero-five-niner is on the roll. See ya later. Pablo."

CAPTAIN BUD EWEING, ---"JACK, set take-off power please."

---I---me---self---

Slowly pushed the throttles forward very carefully, so as not to get another KAPOW.
I set Take-off power. Shazam---Gomer---I was hot---no---shithot.
This was exciting and I was getting paid for it.
!!!WE LIFTED OFF!!!

Hallelujah---Lord, come through the roof---I'll pay for the shingles. Flight Engineer Jack Resley Beck is in the air. This was fun & I was getting paid for it.

CAPTAIN BUD EWEING, ---"GEAR UP"

Co-Pilot John Waynerealnamenoshit reached down behind the pedestal with his left hand, which was near my left ankle and put the gear lever to the **UP** position.

Captain Bud Eweing waited for the three RED landing gear in-transit LIGHTS to extinguish.

"CLIMB POWER, PLEASE, JACK."

I retarded the throttles to where the manifold pressure gauges indicated that we had climb power, checked the engine instruments to make sure they were in the tolerance for climb power and said, ---

---"CLIMB POWER SET---SIR"---

I was squattin' in tall cotton. I was somebody.

LANDING GEAR INDICATING LIGHTS

LEFT　　　NOSE　　　RIGHT

GEAR DOWN AND LOCKED

GREEN---GREEN---GREEN

GEAR INTRANSIT

RED-------RED--------RED

GEAR UP AND LOCKED

ALL LIGHTS EXTINGUISHED

I scanned each and every instrument so many times that my eyes got blurry from trying to read the dimly lit instrument panel.
Problem? ---**No problem**---I whipped out my trusty 6-cell---turned it on. Shazam---the cockpit lit up like Las Vegas on---
*MONDAY*TUESDAY*WEDNESDAY*THURSDAY*FRIDAY*SATURDAY*SUNDAY*

----DAY or NIGHT----

"Turn that dadblamed flashlight off---PLEASE!!!"
I did
Captain Bud Eweing sounded a litta---no---a lotta--- **IRATE** and up to the time of being blinded---seemed to be a very easy going type of guy.
I shut off the 6-celler---muy pronto.
In the last twenty minutes ---I had managed to wake up the City of Burbank and blind two Pilots.
---Shoot---haint nobody perfect.
The rest of the flight went smooth and we landed at **TRAVIS AIR FORCE BASE.**

This airport is located about halfway between San Francisco and Sacramento, California.

Captain Bud Eweing greased the mighty DC-6 on the runway numbers---reversed the propellers and turned off the runway on a high speed turn off---less than a fourth of the way down the runway---never touched the brakes.

---I was flabbergasted---
*****

I look back on it now---not that big a deal as the runways were over two miles long at Travis.---A safe place for Air Force pilots to land and not run out of runway.---Just kidding guys---go back to shining your shoes.
*****

As we turned off the runway on the high speed---Captain Bud Eweing took the propellers out of reverse by stowing the reverser levers that are attached to the throttles.

!!!#3 DID ENGINE NOT COME OUT OF REVERSE!!!

Captain Bud Eweing, ---"**Shut down number three engine, Jack**---as a matter of fact---shut down the number two engine also---we're empty and no use burning all that gas and loading up the spark plugs for nothing."

I DID---by putting the #2 & #3 fuel enrichment levers to the **FUEL CUTOFF** detent.

Captain Bud Eweing taxied the Mighty DC-6 to the desolate civilian tarmac and parked the brakes, ---"Jack, shut down number one and number four engines, please."

---I DID---

I read the shut down check-list---stood up, ----folded up, ---buttoned up my seat.

I fastened up my seat to the cockpit bulkhead and walked backwards out of the cockpit so Bud and John could get out of the cockpit.

Captain Bud Eweing, ---"Jack, I hate to ask you this. It's zero four hundred hours and there's not a mechanic in sight. I need you to slide down the escape rope and get us a mechanic's boarding ramp stand so we can get off the airplane and do the **MOUNTAIN** of paper work that's required of us. We're due out at zero six hundred hours and it's gonna take almost that long to do the mountain of paper work to get out of this place. We can't wait for a mechanic to show up so we can deplane. There's a whole bunch of ramps on the side of that last hangar that we just passed."

"Would you mind doing that for us, please?"
"Sure"

I went into the cabin to the forward cabin door, opened it and pulled out the emergency escape rope, which was stowed inside the forward cabin door jamb, just below the top main cabin door-closing latch.

I let the loose end fall to the ground and pulled muchly hard on the other end to make sure it was attached to something solid.

---I slid down the rope---

MY THOUGHT---"This must be the Emergency Evacuation Training that someone told me that I would need if I ever got to fly for an airline."

I ran across a couple hundred yards of tarmac---found a useable ramp behind the airplane hangar---pushed said ramp, at a run, back to the forward entrance door of the Mighty DC-6.

I stood back and watched Captain Bud Eweing and Co-Pilot John Waynerealnamenoshit as they came down the ramp and walk away towards the Travis Air Force Base Military Operations Hangar.

As they walked away, Captain Bud Eweing looked over his shoulder, ---"If you can't get the number three engine out of reverse on your own, call Travis Ground on the VHF radio and tell them to call me at Travis Military Flight Operations and I will get you a couple of Air Force Mechanics to help you. Travis Ground frequency is still on number two VHF. You do know how to operate the radio, ---don't you?"

"YES SIR"

"YES SIR---I'll get the engine out of reverse---SIR"

---was my shaky-confident response---

I went back into the cockpit. I found the dust covered logbook jammed under the Co-Pilot's seat.

Now I knew why Co-Pilot John Waynerealnamenoshit couldn't adjust his seat, ---

---FORWARD OR BACKWARD---

The **last** entry in the log book had been made six months prior and that entry read, ---"Test Flight Satisfactory" 11/23/58

---signed---
Rube Goldberg
A&E #6969696969696
American Airlines---LAX

MY THOUGHT---*"Humm---five months of **SALT AIR & METAL** without a gulp of fresh air---*

---***BAD-BAD-BAD-COMBINATION***---

I dusted off the logbook, dirtied my hands on the cockpit floor so it looked like a real mechanic's writing and scribbled in the log book, ---

"Test Flight Satisfactory" 04/30/59 and I signed---
"Jack R. Beck"
A&E No 1364068   FE No. 1439372.
Twentieth Century Airlines

*****

First time I ever got to use my credentials & I used two of them. Was I somebody or not???

First time I ever penciled in a bogus log book item and the last time---and **you can take that to the bank---well, pretty close to the bank---maybe just to the drive-up window.**

*****

SALT AIR + METAL = CORROSION

The DC-6 had toggle-type circuit breakers, much like the wall switch on your bedroom wall that is more off than on.

I found the #3 propeller reverse toggle-type circuit breaker that was located on the aft cockpit bulkhead among the zillion toggle-type circuit breakers, ---labeled, ---

**#3
PROP
REV**

O

I jacked that circuit breaker off until my thumb and index finger got sore---hoping to get the salted corrosion off the circuit breaker contacts.

I started up the # 3 engine *(KAPOW)* and the # 3 propeller immediately went out of reverse into a positive pitch position.

As I was shutting down the #3 engine---the cockpit door flew open. Stewardesses Kay Klaus and Kay Robey ---groggily & excitedly, ---

"WHAT HAPPENED???---ARE WE ON FIRE???"

"We heard an explosion and the whole side of the airplane lit up."

Me---unexcited & ungroggily, ---"Nah---everything's okay---I just back-fired an engine and raw fuel came out of the exhaust stacks in a ball of flames."

"Oh yea---I remember now when you started the engines at Burbank. ---Do you back-fire them to clear the engines? We both just hired on---we're new." inquired the much younger stew by the name of Kay Klause.

"Uh---uh---Yea---This airplane has been idle for a long time so it helps to clear the engines when you backfire them."

"Uh---okay---we're going back to sleep."

"G'night"

I descended the mechanics boarding ramp and did another walk around the DC-6.

I heard a noise and shone my trusty 6-cell at it.

Captain Bud Eweing---a litta---no---a lotta surly, ---"Will you please shut off that dad-blamed flashlight, Jack---You're blinding us."

---I did---

"I know you ran up an engine Jack. ---We heard the backfire clear over at Travis Field Operations. Did you get the prop out of reverse?" ---Captain Ewing inquired as he watched me rub the "grease" off my hands with a greasy grease rag that I had found along with the log-book underneath the Co-Pilot's chair.

"YES SIR---sir"
---Captain Bud Eweing---
---Didn't ask me how. I didn't tell him how---

*****

I flew Flight Engineer on that particular DC-6 many times---
TAIL NUMBER-775.

???Mechanicals???---You might ask---

I'd just wait for the Pilots to leave---jack off the associated toggle type circuit breaker and "repair" the "mechanical" 90% of the time. The other 10% of the time---grease under the fingernails and busted knuckles.
The Pilots thought that I was one helluva Mechanic Flight Engineer.
   As---**CAPTAIN JOHN FRAZIER** ---Used to say---
"Ya gotta do it with mirrors, Beck, Ya gotta do it with mirrors."
      "NEAT---NEAT---NEAT"
    "Yea, Frazier, I know---I know."
      "NEAT---NEAT---NEAT"
*****

  "Good deal---How much fuel do we have?"
  "Plenty, sir, ---we left Burbank with full tanks. I dip-sticked them all. We have twenty-four thousand pounds."

*****

Gasoline is 6.7#s per gallon---how many gallons did we have in our DC-6 wing fuel cell tanks? ---you might ask---you figure it out---I'm a shit hot mechanic flight engineer---not a mathematician---besides that---the **FUEL QUANTITY** *gauges on airplanes are calibrated in* **pounds**---*so, it's not a need to know item.*
*****

    "Let's get the show on the road."
  As we climbed the mechanic's boarding ramp, I could see by the "Daun's" early light, some busses approaching us from the Military Concourse on the other side of the Travis Airport.
  "Here come our passengers," Captain Eweing mumbled as he slid into the left seat, --- "Read the before start checklist, Jack, so we can get off on time. These people have been up all night and we want to get them to their destination as soon as we can. ---Seems like every couple has at least one diapered child who has slept all night and will start squallin' and shittin' as soon as we start the engines and won't quit till we land."
    I read the Before Start Checklist.
  We were on a **CAM** trip. I do not know what that acronym stands for, but we flew Servicemen and their families to their Home Bases throughout the United States and across both **BIG PONDS.** ---That's the Atlantic & Pacific Oceans---Tex.

The Stewardesses, **KAY ROBEY & KAY KLAUSE**---
Refreshed after their abbreviated slumber---
Greeted the people aboard---
Brought up the manifest---
Tit fucked the back of my head and handed the paperwork to---
CAPTAIN BUD EWEING. ---
Who politely said, ---"Start the engines Jack. Please don't backfire them because you'll wake up the squalling babies."

!!!KAPOW---SQUALL---KAPOW!!!
!!!SQUALLSQUALL!!!
!!!KAPOW!!!
!!!SQUALLSQUALLSQUALL!!!
!!!K-fuckin-POW!!!
!!!SQUALLSQUALLSQUA LLSQUALL!!!
!!!S-fuckin-QUALL!!!

And we were on our way to Detroit, Michigan. The flight went without incident, except for the four KAPOWS, which both pilots pretended to ignore.

I even got bored.
*****

Now I had learned that flying as a crew member was---
HOURS & HOURS of TEDIUM---
And later on in life---occasionally interrupted by---
TEN SECONDS of ADRENILIN RUSH.
*****

We landed at Ann Arbor Airport (ARB), Michigan at mid-afternoon, ---taxied to the Cargo Terminal. I shut down the engines and K&K deplaned the Passengers.

Captain Bud Eweing, ---"When the Stews get done cleaning the airplane, do a complete shut down---close all the doors---including the baggage doors and do a thorough post flight check of the airplane. John's going to call the hotel to pick us up and I have to finish the paperwork for Uncle Sam and check in with Captain Butler. See ya at curbside. And, Oh yea, don't forget to dump the biffys. There's a turd-hearse parked behind the airplane."

---I DID---

And found my way to curbside by following Kay Klause & Kay Robey---where there was a Texas sized herd of Non-Skeddar Crews&Stews---and a caravan of hotel busses.

*A Non-Scheduled Airline (Non-Sked) --- lives up to its name. ---No scheduled flights. A Non-Sked operates on contract flying---a lot of the contracts were/are Military Contracts which were normally yearly contracts---SO---when a Non-Sked Airplane took off from a Military Base Airport or a Civilian Airport---a half-dozen or more followed suit and landed within an hour of each other at the same destination. ---SO---the Non-Skeddars had the kind of closeness that comes with being together through---"Thick&Thin---Air&Ground". Their backgrounds were varied---World War II Cargo Plane Vets---Korean Civilian Soldier's of Fortune---& some, like me---just plain civilians. The Non-Skeddars worked closely together (Those that didn't'--- soon weren't) ---**DRANK AND PARTIED TOGETHER** and took care of each other in time of need---mostly with hangover sympathy aspirins.*

---The best of Pilots and Stewardesses---

The Captains paid for the fuel and maintenance cost for the airplane---paid the Crews&Stews their per-diem every day---made sure that there were hotel accommodations---took care of the hotel expenses---fired and hired Crews&Stews and in general was Boss and friend---and was paid 6 cents per mile---Co-Pilot---2 1/2 cents per mile---Flight Engineer and Navigator----2 1/4 cents per mile.

*****

We found our hotel bus and boarded. ---Seating assignments???---Crews sat on seats---Stews sat on Crews. Me???---I was the last one on and I got to stand and chat with the hotel bus driver.

On the way downtown to Downtown Detroit City Hotel, the Crews&Stews that had just came in from flying the Pacific broke out a couple of bottles of Canadian Club and passed it around.

They had stopped at Wake Island where Canadian Club was $1.10 a Fifth---and if you were a real cheapskate, ---you could buy a **QUART** of Beefeaters Gin for 90 cents a Quart.

By the time the bottles got around to me---there was only a sip left---which was more than enough to make me, a two beers on Saturday night kind of guy, ---woozy.

Captain Bud Eweing checked us in and gave us our room keys.
Captain Bud Eweing gave us our Per Diem monies.
The Crew&Stews headed for the bar.
I went to my room---to bed---"Goodnight."
*****

A story told to me by a laughing Captain Bud Eweing, ---

"Twentieth Century was the first Non-Sched Airline to get a DC6. Up till that time we flew DC4s which does not have prop reversing. --We were the last to land and taxied to our parking area."

"There was only one parking space available and we couldn't park there because we would not be able to taxi out. There were a lot of Non-Skeddars sitting around and laughing at us."

"I taxied past the parking space. Now the Non-Skeddars were laughing and scratching their heads wondering what I was going to do. I simply put the propellers in reverse and backed into the parking space. They quit laughing and scratching and ran for cover---too late."

*****

After a real crusher of a landing in Phoenix, the attendant came on with, "Ladies and Gentlemen, please remain in your seats until Capt. Crash and the Crew have brought the aircraft to a screeching halt against the gate. And, once the tire smoke has cleared and the warning bells are silenced, we'll open the door and you can pick your way through the wreckage to the terminal."

--- CIRCA ---

Same day---*Me thinks*

"RING---RING---RIN--"
I was awakened by a blaring telephone.
Hello.
Captain Bud Eweing, ---"Jack---would you please come down to the bar and bring your flashlight with you."
"OKAY"
MY THOUGHT---"*My **flashlight???**---What now---Am I gonna have to go back to the airport and work on the airplane???*"

I got dressed and went down the elevator---found the Detroit City Hotel Bar & Grill and walked in. The place was jammed---with Non-Sked Crews&Stews---still in uniform---having one helluva drunken time.

The Non-Skeddars saw the rookie---pointed at my flashlight and howled. Apparently Captain Bud Eweing told them all about it.

Captain Bud Eweing walked up to me, ---"**LET ME HAVE YOUR FLASHLIGHT.**"

MY THOUGHT---"*He's gonna fire me for blinding him. ----How am I gonna get home???*"

The Crews&Stews became deathly silent.
I nervously handed it to him.

Captain Bud Eweing took the flashlight---walked over to a chair and bent it in half over the back of it.

MY THOUGHT---"*I'm dead meat.*"

Captain Bud Eweing took a flashlight from his hip pocket and handed it to me, ---"Turn it on, please, Jack."
---I DID---
The beam shone **blood red** because of a **red lens** fastened to the front of the flashlight.

The Detroit City Hotel Bar&Grill remained **VERY** silent.

"I'm giving you this **red-lens** flashlight and if I ever see you without it, be it day or night, I'm going to fire you."
"YESSSSSSSIR"
EVERY Non-Skeddar in the Detroit City Hotel Bar was staring at me---

-silently-

THEN---**CAPTAIN BUD EWEING**---Put his arm around my shoulders, ---"Congratulations on your first flight---except for a few **MINOR** things---you did a very good job."---Shook my sweaty hand and put a bottle of Millers in the other sweaty hand.

The Non-Skeddars broke the silent silence with laughter and each and every one came up to me, shook my hand, and patted me on the back---said, ---**"WELCOME ABOARD"**.

Stewardesses' Kay Robey and Kay Klause took my sweaty hands and led me to a table laden with **FULL** bottles of Miller High Life.

I drank a couple---well maybe more than a couple, said thanks and goodnight to everyone and staggered to my room---for some much needed sleep---with my clothes on.

*Non-Skeddars are a different kind of Aviary Breed---Sharp---love to fly----love to party hearty---and by the way---the whole time I was with Twentieth Century Airlines---be it day or night---night or day---I had that **red-lens** flashlight clutched tightly in my hand.*
*****

One gay guy to another gay guy---
"Whose boat is that out there in the bay?"---
"That's the Staten Island Ferry."---
"Oh my, I didn't know we had a Navy."
*****

It haint what cha got---It's what you do with what cha got----
chachacha
*****

This man was at a party and had to go #2 potty---he ascends the stairs to the bathroom---the line to the bathroom is as long as tickets to a Shania Twain Concert. ---

He can't hold it much longer and goes into a room off the hallway---there was a hole in the floor and he shits in it---all done, he goes back down stairs---lo & behold---everyone at the party was covered with shit---no shit! ---The hostess came up to the man, looked him over---"There you stand so spick and span.
Where were you when the shit hit the fan?"
*****

--- CIRCA ---

---The day after---

"RING---RING---RIN--"

"Where am I?"
Oh shit I'm flying airplanes. I answered the phone.
"Jack, this is Captain Eweing. I just got a call from Central. The company needs this airplane in El Paso as soon as we can get it there. Be down in the hotel lobby as soon as you can."
"UH-UH---OKAY."
I was groggy---but still excited. I de-clothed---took a cold shower---re-clothed---elevatored down to the hotel lobby.
I expected to see nothing but pain and suffering among the Non-Skeddars---and at least a couple of comatose bodies.
!!!WRONG!!!
The Non-Skeddars were standing around, coffee clutching, chatting like they had eight hours sleep. Sorta looked like the early morning bullshitting social meeting around the coffee urn at Big Time Office, USA.
Like good athletes---Non-Skeddars kept their livers physically fit. This was a way of life for a Non-Skeddar---party hearty and be ready to take to the sky at a moments notice.
My liver was not in condition---nauseous---throbbing headache---close to upchucking.
We arrived at Ann Arbor Airport, Michigan en-mass and after four more---

---KAPOWS---
---WE WERE WINGING OUR WAY TO THE---
---WEST TEXAS TOWN OF EL PASO---
Ala Marty Robbins
Dja hear about the woman sheriff???—
-She had the biggest posse in El Pusso.
Captain Bud Eweing and John Waynerealnamenoshit never flinched when the engines---

!!!KAPOWWWED!!!

**Other than trying to blow up the engines---I did a helluva job---
The ace of the base.**

I was starting to gain some confidence.

Captain Bud Eweing painted the Mighty DC-6 on the numbers upon landing at El Paso City *(ala Marty Robbins.)* and taxied us to the Cargo Ramp. Captain Bud Eweing "borrowed" a tug with baggage cart attached.

Co-pilot John Waynerealnamenoshit, Stewardesses Kay Robey and Kay Klause& Self got on the baggage cart. ---

CAPTAIN BUD EWEING drove us to the---
---AMERICAN AIRLINES OPERATIONS SHACK---

Captain Bud Eweing made a zillion phone calls and came back to our briefing table with another Captain.

Captain Bud Eweing said, ---"I just called Captain Butler. He needs me for a trip to Tokyo. Captain Hal Boresly here will be your Captain for the rest of the trip."

Captain Hal Boresly *(Real name---**NO SHIT**)* waved his hand without any emotions and rudely turned around and raced back to a "Covey of Stews."

We stood up and bid---

*****CAPTAIN BUD EWEING*****

A fond farewell

I never got to fly with Captain Bud Eweing again. Our "flight" paths crossed many times throughout the next year. Captain Bud Eweing would always shake my right hand and look for his **red-lensed**-flashlight---which I always had in my left hand.

Captain Bud Eweing would look at me---smile and walk away saying, ---**"Jack, try not to backfire the engines today."**

CAPTAIN BUD EWEING

A GENTLEMAN AND A GREAT PILOT

--- CIRCA ---

MAY 1---1niner-5-niner

Hooray---hooray, ---It's the first of May.
Outdoor Fucking starts today.
Per Cap'n Leland

---Herecomedejudge---
Cap'nhal-fromhell
MAYDAY---MAYDAY---MAYDAY
PAN- --PAN---PAN
My first encounter with
---PILOT EGO---BUT NOT MY LAST---
!!!EGOMANYICALJEALOUSY!!!
---THE MOST DEADLY OF ALL THE DEADLY SINS---
A CESSPOLL FOR
CARBUNCLES & POTTYGROWTHS
---WHICH GIVES BIRTH TO BLIVETS---

BLIVET---*5 pounds of shit in a 1 pound bag*
"Define egomanYicaljealousy for me please."
"OK I will."
Beckster's Dictionary;
EgomanYicalJealously---n.v. ---is when a person causes harm to another person, sometimes a best friend, because his **egomanYicaljealousy** cannot stand to be in the shadow of another person.

Think about it. Have you ever deliberately done something to a person because of your egomanYicaljealousy???---**and** that includes **MALICIOUS GOSSIP about your friends and neighbors.**

SCENARIO
AIRPORT OF DEPARTURE---El Paso International Airport
AIRPORT OF DESTINATION---Lake Tahoe Municipal
AIRPLANE---DC-6B
CAPTAIN---Hal-from-hell, ---Part time captain---
part time movie extra---full time asshole.

CO-PILOT---BOB ROBEY
FLIGHT ENGINEER---BECK
STEWARDESS---KAY KLAUSE
STEWARDESS---KAY ROBEY---Bob Robey's wife

Co-Pilot John Waynerealnamenoshit went back to Burbank with Captain Bud Eweing. He had flown with Captain Halfromhell before---just once---and in Co-Pilot John Waynerealnamenoshit's words---and I quote, ---"I flew Co-Pilot for that asshole once---first time---only time---last time that I'll fly with that incompetent egotistical fuckhead."

I WAS SOON TO LEARN WHY.

ACT I

Stewardesses Kay Robey, Kay Klause and Self boarded the one seater "borrowed" tug and I drove us back to the Mighty DC-6 where I met Bob Robey, Kay Robey's husband, for the first time.

Nice person and with pretty Kay along side of him---a nice looking couple that appeared to be very much in love.

Good –looking well-built man with a shit-pot full of old sayings in his mind. A line of bullshit that make/made a lot more sense than most people has/have in their everyday conversations.

ACT II

Stewardesses Kay Robey, Kay Klause and Co-Pilot Bob Robey went into the cabin and started cleaning up the baby shit and puke.

I went into the Cockpit and did an originating pre-flight by my lonesome---which consisted merely of turning on the Airplane's APU. The APU was a gasoline motor driven generator that delivered direct current, in parallel with the battery, to the Aircraft's electrical system. (Auxiliary *electrical* Power Unit)

The APU was not an integral part of the DC-6 and was attached to the front bulkhead of the Aircraft's forward baggage compartment with tie-down straps. Its exhaust was vented through a hole that some "Jury Rigging Mechanic" had drilled through the bottom of the fuselage and attached the exhaust pipe to.

*****

"Jury Rigging Mechanic" is a Mechanic that can make any mechanical thingamabob work by using common sense and any

piece of equipment he can get his greasy paws on—including "chewing gum".

Case in Point ---

I was sitting in the cockpit of the Boeing 737-200 at Fresno Air Terminal (FAT) California.

A Stewardess came in and said, ---"Captain, where gonna have to ground the airplane."

"HUH"

"The restraining strap's snap for the aft door exit-way is broken and **IT IS A NOGO** item."

"HUH"

I reluctantly put down my New York Times Crossword Puzzle and went to the aft cabin to check out "The 'No-Go' Restraining Strap". The **no go restraining strap** was only an inch wide and couldn't "restrain" a piss ant---and I'm supposed to ground a giant airliner 'cause it haint got a good snap button.

No way-Hosay---I found a safety pin---attached the "restraining" strap across the exit way---went back to my New York Times Crossword Puzzle---proud to be a "jury rigging mechanic."

*****

ACT III

I turned on everything electrical and checked all the gauges for proper operation.

All systems checked out fine---lasts a long time. I then turned on all the exterior lights---including the landing lights.

As I exited the Aircraft---I shouted to Co-Pilot Bob Robey in the aft cabin---still trying to get the baby-shitty-pukey smell out of the airplane, ---"Bob, when I thump on the fuselage---turn off the landing lights and retract them---please."

Landing Light limitations on the ground is five (5) minutes---the reason I had Co-Pilot Bob Robey retract them???---You might ask---So I could make sure that they retract because when left in the extended position---they cause a whole lot of **DRAG.**

ACT IV
EL PASO---HOT AND HUMID---SWEATSVILLE

I acrobatted my legs on top of the rails of the mechanics boarding ramp, slid down to the tarmac and started my exterior pre-flight inspection.

I was standing in the nose gear wheel well checking to make sure all the trunion bolts were secure to the nose gear strut assembly, cannon plugs, hydraulic leaks and nose gear landing lights---etcetcetc---when I heard a whole lot of shoutin' and cussin' going on.

I kneeled down to see what kind of calamity was happening. ???Guess who???

Cap'nhal-fromhell---In the face of a very weary-sweaty baggage handler, ---**"I TOLD YOU THAT I WANTED THE FIRST BAGGAGE CART THAT ARRIVED FOR YOU BAGGAGE SMASHERS TO PUT THE BAGS IN THE AFT BAGGAGE PIT."**

"Sir---the weight and balance indicated for me to fill the front pit first and put the remaining bags in the aft pit. All the bags are duffel bags and are full of the fire fighter's equipment and clothes---they all weigh about the same---and they are **HEAVY**. If I had put them in the aft pit first---the airplane would have fallen on its tail."

"I DON'T GIVE A SHIT WHAT THE WEIGHT AND BALANCE SAID---NEXT TIME DO AS I TELL YOU---I'M THE CAPTAIN."

MY THOUGHT---*wow*

"HEY BECK---GET YOUR SCRAWNY ASS OVER HERE."

"Yes sir," as I ducked out of the nose gear wheel well and ran to the forward baggage pit where **cap'nhal-fromhell** stood."

"YOUR NEW, AREN'T CHA?"

"Yes sir, this is my first trip."

"O--Okaaay---I'm gonna follow you around on your exterior preflight. I've already walked around the airplane once. I didn't find anything---but I'm gonna follow you and make sure you do it right."

"Yes sir."

As we neared the left main landing gear---I noticed that the left main tire looked a little flatter than normal. ---"Sir---that left tire looks a little low---I'm gonna get someone to check the pressure."

"Haint necessary---I already had the baggage smasher look at it. ---He's a mechanic too, ya know. The reason the tire looks flat is because of all the fat Apaches and their fire fighting equipment on board."

"The fire fighters are still on the bus, sir---they haven't boarded yet."

"**Where ya goin'?**"

"I'm going to go get a tire pressure gauge, sir."

"**DON'T YOU BELIEVE ME?**"

"Yes sir---This airplane has been idle for six months and I'm gonna check the pressure in all the tires."

"O---kaaay---get it done fast. I want to get the fuck out of this god-forsaken place."

"Yes sir."

I did the rest of the exterior pre-flight check and went to get a pressure gauge from Mechanic/Baggage Handler name tagged---**MECHANIC BOB FLORES,** who along with **cap'nhal-fromhell,** now owned the position of **Passenger Boarding Agent** and was in the process of boarding the fire fighters.

ACT V

I asked Mechanic Bob Flores for his tire pressure gauge.

A weary, but smiling Mechanic Bob Flores pointed toward his Craftsman's roll-a-way toolbox on the other side of the airplane.

"I ducked under the Mighty DC-6 and procured the tire pressure gauge from **Mechanic/Passenger Agent/Baggage Handler Bob Flore's** Craftsman rollaway tool box. I went straight to the left main gear wheel well.

The left main landing gear tire looked even flatter. I also noticed that the left tire was on a bit of macadam build up and the right tire was barely touching the ground.

I checked the pressure of the right main landing gear tire.

ZIP
ZERO
OOOOOOOOOOOOOO

Apparently why the left tire appeared flatter was because the firefighters boarded---causing the left main tire to take all the weight of the now horrendously over grossed airplane.

I found **Passenger Service Agent Bob Flores** sitting on a tug, who now was wearing the hat of Dispatcher Bob Flores, working on the manifest, weight and balance and dispatch release.

I told Dispatcher/Pax Service Agent/Mechanic Bob Flores about the flat tire.

Back to being a Mechanic---Bob Flores, rolled his eyes, threw the Clip-boarded paper work on the ramp and said, "Get on."

I did

We drove to the nearest American Airlines Quonset Hut Hangar and "borrowed" a hydraulic jack and a fully inflated tire.

ACT VI

We drove back to the airplane where **cap'nhal-fromhell was waiting.**

"WHERE THE FUCK YOU GUYS BEEN? ---What's the tire for? ---That fuckin' tire haint flat."

New Hat Mechanic Bob Flores---calmly---but firmly, ---

"Captain---the right tire is flat and we're going to replace it."

"Oh---O---kaaay"

Mechanic Bob Flores said, ---"That jack will never work with all the firefighters on board. We're gonna have to deplane the Firefighters."

Cap'n-Hal-from-hell, ---**"I'LL GO DO THAT."**

Mechanic Bob Flores---looking at me and rolling his eyes---under his breath, ---"Good---just go."

I placed the jack between the wheels, under the landing gear strut---proceeded to jack up the airplane. It didn't take very much as the left tire was bearing the weight of the airplane because of the rise in the asphalt. Actually all I did was jack the left main tire off the ground about an inch and **MECHANIC BOB FLORES h**ad the right wheel off and was motioning to me to help him roll the new wheel off the tire cradle cart and roll it into position.

I did

About the time that Mechanic Bob Flores was putting the torque wrench to the last lug nut---the last firefighter had descended to the ramp and **cap'nhal-fromhell** was acomin' our way---
SHOUTING, ---"WHAT'S TAKING SO FUCKIN' LONG---WHAT'S TAKIN' SO FUCKIN' LONG---ETCETCETC?"

As Cap'n Hal-from-hell approached us still **SHOUTING,** --- Mechanic Robert Flores **a**ppeared to take a more intense hold of the torque wrench that he had just tightened the last lug nut with---stood up and calmly and said, ---"The tire has been replaced sir and the airplane is ready to go. I filled the main fuel tanks and there is one thousand pounds of gasoline in each of the four auxiliary tanks---you can board the fire fighters now---**SIR."**

Cap'nhal-fromhell looked at the multi-veined hand that held the torque wrench that was tapping heavily on the newly appointed tire, **DID AN ABRUPT ABOUT FACE.** ---started **SHOUTING** at the firefighters who were sitting under the airplane smoking cigarettes. ---

**"GET YOUR DEAD ASSES ON BOARD---
GET YOUR DEAD ASSES ON BOARD---
PUT THOSE FUCKIN' CIGARETTES OUT---
ETC ETC ETC."**

I shook---
**MECHANIC/STATION AGENT/DISPATCHER/FUELER-
RAMP AGENT/BAGGAGE HANDLER
MISTER ROBERT FLORES**

Greasy---now untorqued hand, ---"Thanks for fueling the airplane for me, Bob."

"You're welcome---see ya again and good luck with that Captain."

*****

I did see Mechanic Bob Flores again later on in life. He was a Mechanic for Pacific Southwest Airlines **(PSA) in Oakland (OAK)** *and he did change another tire for me---as a matter of fact---it was the left main landing gear right tire---only this time it was on a Boeing 727-200. Look for it in a later* **CIRCA in Volume II.**

*****

I walked around the Mighty DC-6 one more time---making sure the Apaches didn't get rid of their cigarettes by shoving them in one of the airplanes orifices---mainly the Pitot-static tubes, which supply pressurized/static air to the aircraft's airspeed indicators.

---NO AIRSPEED INDICATION---NO TAKE OFF---

This happened to me once---on the Mighty Electra. I'll write about it at the end of this CIRCA.

ACT VII

I did one more walk around and went up the Mechanics Boarding Ramp and entered the cabin through the aft cabin door. I wanted to make a final check of the hand carried oxygen bottles and the hand carried fire extinguishers.

Cap'nhal-fromhell was there to greet me, ---"WHERE THE FUCK YA BEEN? I've checked the emergency equipment---so let's get the fuck out of here."

I followed **Cap'nhal-fromhell** up to the cockpit---stepping over firefighting equipment and sashaying around drunken Apaches leaning out of their seats---some snoring---some upchucking.

DISPATCHER HATTED BOB FLORES---
CO-PILOT BOB ROBEY---
STEWARDESS KAY KLAUSE---
STEWARDESS KAY ROBEY---
Were standing by the cockpit door, looking at the passenger manifest weight and balance---shaking their heads in disbelief.

CO-PILOT BOB ROBEY looked at **Cap'nhal-fromhell** and mumbled one of his many bullshit sayings about how too much weight is gonna break the horses ass and then said, ---"Sir, we are way over grossed----about eight thousand pounds. Sir, that's four tons. **We can't take off at this weight."**

"WHO THE FUCK ARE YOU??? ---I'M THE CAPTAIN---GET YOUR DUMB SHIT ASS BACK IN THE COCKPIT---WE'RE GOING---YOU TWO STEWS---GET BACK TO YOUR FUCKIN' STATIONS---AND YOU, BAGGAGE SMASHER---GET THE FUCK OFF MY AIRPLANE AND BUTTON HER UP."

MISTER BOB FLORES rolled his eyes one more time, turned around---exited---closed the forward cabin door behind him and knocked a couple of times on the door signaling the Stews to check that both main cabin doors were locked and the emergency evacuation slides were snapped into their locks.

*****

On the DC-6---there was a lanyard (rope) to pull to inflate the slides.

On modern day aircraft*---the emergency evacuation slides are automatically inflated if they are armed and the door is opened.*

So if the Stewardesses---nka as Flight Attendants goof and forget to disarm the emergency evacuation slide, except in the emergency that they are intended for---the emergency evacuation slide becomes a big balloon expanding between the jet-way and the modern day aircraft.

Needless to say---it is part of the F.A.-Stewardess job to make sure the emergency evacuation slides are disarmed before opening any cabin doors. Hence the announcement---from the---

----NUMBER ONE FLIGHT ATTENDANT---
"FLIGHT ATTENDANTS"
"PREPARE THE CABIN FOR ARRIVAL"
*****

Murphy's Law *sets in again---Sometimes you bite the bare (pussy) ---sometimes the bear bites you.(and you pay alimony).*

I saw Ole Murphy work on Emergency Evacuation Slides in action only once---in San Francisco. ---

The Flight Attendant forgot to disarm the emergency evacuation slide. ---The emergency evacuation slide became a big bubble between the jet-way and the Boeing 727-100.

The Boeing 727-100 was leaning to the right---the jet-way was holding its ground.

I watched as a **Jury Rigging Mechanic** *surveyed the situation---reached in his right coverall pocket---pull out a pocketknife---stabbed the Emergency Evacuation Slide to death several times and ended the tug of war.*

ACT VIII

I followed **Cap'nhal-fromhell** to the cockpit as Stewardesses K&K made a bee-line to the back of the cabin---muttering and shaking their heads all the way.

Cap'nhal-fromhell was in the left seat, looking out his sliding glass window---

SHOUTING---AT EVERYTHING THAT MOVED.

Co-Pilot Bob Robey was in the right seat, looking out his sliding glass window---silently.

Me---I was scared---shitless---if that's possible.

"Sir---would you like me to read the before start checklist???

"I already did the before start check-list---just sit on your hands and be quiet."

"Yessir"

"Stow your seat up and get out of my way. I'm gonna check out the cabin---can't get good help nowadays"

I did

I came back in the cockpit, unsnapped the ass hating, skimpy naugahyde covered, marine hunk of ply board called a seat, lowered it, turned around and sat down.

Co-Pilot Bob Robey was scanning all the cock-pit instruments---muttering one of his many sayings, ---**"Ninety percent of all captains have hemorrhoids---the other ten percent are perfect assholes."**

*****

I didn't know how to spell hemroids---the micro chip put a red line under it so I looked it up in my Random House Webster's **LARGE PRINT** *Dictionary and being that I went to all that trouble to make all you armchair, sitting on your ass, "drinking the weather channel and watching beer", critics happy. ---I'm gonna write what I read, ---*

Hem'or-rhoid' *(hem'a roid), n. (Usually pl.) painful dilation of blood vessels in anus.*

I believe--- in layman's terms---that means—
---RFPA ---Royal Flaming Pain in the Ass---

*****

Co-Pilot Bob Robey quit scanning and muttering at the same time, looked around at me, ---"Would you mind reading the before start check-list Jack? I know the Captain said he did it---but we need to make sure. I've heard about this Captain---he tries to do everyone's job and forgets about what he's on board for---watch him closely Jack"--- and Co-Pilot Bob Robey started mumbling something about "a jack off of all trades and a masturbator of none."

I read the **BEFORE START CHECK-LIST** to Co-Pilot Robey

ME   **ROBEY**

"**LANDING GEAR LEVER**"----------------"**DOWN & LOCKED**"

"**BATTERY SWITCH**"---"**ON**"

"**APU**"---"**ON**"

"**HYDRAULIC PUMPS**"---"**ON**"

"**PARKING BRAKES**"---------------------------------------"**SET**"

"**ETCETCETC**"-----------------------------------"**ETCETCETC**"

"Before start check-list complete---Bob."
"Thanks, Beck---the Captain did not do a thorough job. We got it all done for sure."

"**GET OUT OF YOUR SEAT BECK---MOVE IT.**"
"Okay" I uttered as I swiftly got up, stowed the Flight Engineer's seat and stood up as cap'nhal-fromhell rudely squeezed by me."
MY THOUGHT---"WOW"
Robey said, ---"Beck and I did the before start check-list---Captain."
"Oh---kay---**I'LL START THE ENGINES BECK---you fuckin' Flight Engineers need to go to school on engine starting---haven't had one yet that didn't backfire the engines.**"
"Okay"

With that thought in his egomanYical brain, **cap'nhal-fromhell** reached up on the overhead panel with his left hand for the engine start switches.

    FUEL PRIMER   STARTER ENGAGE   IGNITION
        0   **0**   **0**

0
THUMB SAFETY SWITCH

    Cap'nhal-fromhell turned his face away from **MECHANIC BOB FLORES** who was doing all kinds of body language trying to tell us not to start an engine.
    I glanced out of the Co-Pilot's side window and saw some baggage carts underneath the propeller of #4 engine---I grabbed **cap'nhal-fromhell's** left hand.
    "WHAT THE FUCK YA DOING-DON'T EVER TOUCH ME."
    "There's a baggage cart under number four engine---sir."
    "OH---YEA---**SHIT---DON'T START ANY ENGINES**," shouted Co-Pilot Bob Robey as he also went for **cap'nhal-fromhell's** hand."
    Cap'nhal-fromhell slammed open his sliding glass window and started shaking his fist at Mechanic Bob Flores, --- "WHAT THE FUCK YA DOIN? ---YA TRYING TO KILL US? ---GET THEM FUCKIN' BAGGAGE CARTS OUT OF THE WAY."
    MECHANIC BOB FLORES just shrugged his shoulders---slowly walked over to the tug that was attached to the baggage cart underneath the #4 prop---got on board---started the tug's engine.
    ---Drove off into the El Paso red sunset---

Cap'nhal-fromhell proceeded to start the #4 engine.
!!!K---FUCKIN---POW!!!
#3 engine
!!!K---FUCKIN---POW!!!
#2 engine
!!!K---FUCKIN---POW!!!
#1 engine
!!!K---FUCKIN---POW!!!

Co-Pilot Bob Robey just sat there---calmly staring out his window---mumbling one of his many sayings.

Me---I couldn't help but laugh---I tried not to---I just broke out in hysterics.

*****

Actually, it wasn't really funny---the backfire is no big deal as long as you're just using prime to start the engines. The backfire just comes back up through the throat of the **carburetor** (first time I spelled that right) and no harm is done.

Once the Mixture Control is brought in to play and the engine backfires---there is a potential of the backfire going through the internal workings of the carburetor and kapowing it to death.

*****

"WHAT'S SO FUCKIN' FUNNY? READ THE BEFORE TAXI CHECKLIST."

I did,

"WHAT ARE YOU MUMBLIN' ABOUT ROBEY? --- CALL THE TOWER FOR TAXI INSTRUCTIONS. I HAVE NO IDEA WHERE THE FUCKIN' RUNWAY IS."

"El Paso Ground Control---this is Twentieth Century Flight seven-eighty-five---need to taxi. We're new here."

"Roger Twentieth---Runway Niner is active. Wind is out of the East at fifteen knots---altimeter---two-niner-eight-five---Cleared to taxi."

"Roger, Twentieth Century seven-eighty-five cleared to taxi---uh---we're new here---can you give us directions."

"Yea---Twentieth Century Airlines seven-eighty-five---there's a **"FOLLOW ME"** truck coming up behind you. He will take you to Runway Niner run-up area."

"Roger---seven-eighty-five sees him now and we're starting our taxi."

Cap'nhal-fromhell released the parking brake, added a little power and we started our taxi. Co-Pilot Bob Robey put the flap handle to the **TAKE-OFF** position and we watched the flap position indicator needle go to **T-O.** *(Take Off position)*

We arrived at the run-up area. **Cap'nhal-fromhell** positioned the Mighty DC-6's tail toward the wooden blast fence---set the parking brakes.

I sat forward on my seat as far as I could to make sure I could get the throttles forward to the take-off power setting and reach the propeller pitch change lever, with my left hand, which was even farther forward. I put my right hand on the Co-Pilot's throttles and looked at **cap'nhal-fromhell** in askance.

"I'LL RUN THEM UP,' as he pushed my hand off of the Co-Pilot's throttles. **"SIT BACK IN YOUR SEAT AND WATCH, MAYBE YOU'LL LEARN SOMETHING---I DOUBT IT--- WHY THEY EVER PUT A THIRD MAN IN THE COCKPIT--- I'LL NEVER FIGURE OUT."**

I sat back in my seat and folded my arms.

Co-Pilot Bob Robey looked around at me---rolled his eyes--- shrugged his shoulders---muttered something about "a one man circus"---turned back around---reclined his seat back as far as it would go---closed his eyes.

Cap'nhal-fromhell pushed the Captain's throttles up less than halfway---pulled them back to idle.

He didn't even attempt to check the magnetos or ensure that the propeller pitch control was working.

Cap'n Hal shouted to a now sleeping Co-Pilot Bob Robey, -- **"WAKE UP ROBEY---TELL THE TOWER WE'RE READY TO GO."**

"El Paso Tower---this is Twentieth Century seven-eighty-five---ready for take off."

"Roger Twentieth Century seven-eighty-five---taxi up to and hold short of Runway Niner---you're number two for take off following the American Airlines DC Seven already in position."

"Roger---Twentieth Century seven-eighty-five---Wilco."
"READ THE BEFORE TAKE OFF CHECK-LIST BECK AND HURRY IT UP---AMERICAN'S ALREADY ON

THE ROLL---I GOT A PRETTY BIG ACTING PART AT PARAMOUNT STUDIOS TOMORROW AND I WANT TO BE THERE AHEAD OF TIME."

I read the check-list.

"ROBEY---TELL THE TOWER WE'RE READY TO GO."

"I already did---sir." And Co-Pilot Bob Robey muttered something about "some people listen but don't hear".

---"BUG 'EM AGAIN---GODAMIT---BUG 'EM AGAIN"---

"El Paso Tower, Twentieth Century seven-eighty-five---ready to go," and Co-Pilot Bob Robey muttered something about "a squeaky wheel getting shit on".

"Roger, Twentieth Century seven-eighty-five---wind is zero-niner-zero at three-zero knots---temperature is---uh—one hundred-ten degrees---altimeter is two-niner-seven-five and falling---**looks like a big storm coming in from New Mexico**---maintain runway heading---cleared to ten thousand feet. ---Cleared for take off runway niner."

*****

Looks like a storm coming in???—Decreasing altimeter setting (falling barometer) and increase in wind-speed and change of wind direction are indications of an impending storm.

'"HIGH TO LOW---LOOK OUT BELOW.
---SAYETH CAPTAIN PATRICK JOSEPH MCGANN---
Aka
---EAGLE BEAK FROM EAGLE CREEK----ALASKA---
*****

"Roger---Twentieth Century Airlines seven eighty five's on the roll. Have a good one."

"I'LL SET THE POWER BECK---JUST SIT BACK IN YOUR SEAT AND FOLD YOUR HANDS---DON'T BOTHER TO PUT THE COWL FLAPS IN THE STREAMLINED POSITION---THOSE ENGINES ARE RUNNING HOT AND I'LL DO IT RIGHT BEFORE LIFT OFF."

I did
*****

Why streamline the cowl flaps???---The cowl flaps, located on the aft part of the engine cowling are regulated manually to keep the cylinder head temperatures at optimum operating temperatures.

On the ground---with very little airflow---the cowl flaps are set at full open.

For take off---the cowl flaps are **streamlined** for minimum drag and minimum disruption of airflow over the leading edge of the wing.

Once airborne---the cowl flaps are regulated manually between the open and closed position to maintain an optimum cylinder head temperature.

Did you say head?

If the engine cowl flaps are left in the open position for take-off---the disruption of airflow over the leading edge of the wing and the induced drag are not conducive to flight.

Just about as horrendous as leaving the landing gear down.
Why write all this bullshit??? Read on Macduff.

STREAMLINE

↑

FULL OPEN | FULL CLOSED

"Take care Twentieth---contact El Paso departure control on one-two-zero-point-niner."

"Roger---one-two-zero-point-niner"---And Co-Pilot Bob Robey muttered something about, "This chere airplane is shakin' like a dog shitting razor blades."

"El Paso Departure Control, this is Twentieth Century Airlines seven-eighty-five climbing to ten thousand feet---heading zero-niner-zero."

SHAKE---RATTLE---ROLL
SHUCKIN' & JIVIN'
The MIGHTY DC-6 did not want to fly and she was telling us so.

With "folded hands"---I scanned every instrument in the cockpit---looking for the reason that she was having internal problems. She acted very sick.

The instrument panels were shaking so violently that I couldn't read the gauges---except for one---
        ---The **RADIO ALTIMETER**---

A scrolled instrument that reads feet Above Ground Level (AGL)

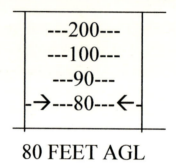

80 FEET AGL

**THE MIGHTY DC-6 HAD CLIMBED TO EIGHTY FEET
AND
SHE WASN'T GOING ANY HIGHER.**

The age-ed American Airlines discard was quakin'&shakin' so bad that I feared that she would start de-aluminizing.

I looked out the forward windscreens and saw the desert floor coming up to greet us. I was too naïve to be scared----thought this happened all the time.
        AHA---EUREKA---I FOUND IT.

Cap'nhal-fromhell did not do my---no, his job. ---The **egomanYical** son-of-a-beach had forgotten to streamline the Engine Cowl Flaps.

The engine cowl flaps were still in the full open position---destroying the lift over the leading edge of the wings.

#1 ENGINE COWL FLAPS

STREAMLINE

FULL OPEN  FULL CLOSED

---SAME SETTING FOR #2--#3--#4 ENGINE COWL FLAPS---

In less than a heartbeat---
**I unfolded my hands and put all four cowl flap switches to the
STREAMLINE POSITION**

∧ ∧ ∧ ∧
1 2 3 4

She quit quakin'&shakin' and started moanin'&groanin'.
But STILL **NOT GAINING ANY ALTITUDE.**
Once again I looked out the forward windscreens. *Windshields*
Now the DC-6 was wooooooing the Cacti and Yucca Trees.
We were un-pretty close to "buying the farm" or should I write, ---
"having desert for dessert".
I glanced at **cap'nhal-fromhell.** He was shaking like a dog shitting razor blades and as white as the towering cumulous clouds up ahead---that also appeared to be touching the desert floor.
I glanced at Co-Pilot Bob Robey---he was muttering something about, ---"If the airplane is in the air---keep it in the air."
I once again scanned all of the instrument panels that I could now read---everything appeared normal---

OH SHIT---they left the gear down.

LEFT MAIN LANDING GEAR---NOSE LANDING GEAR---RIGHT MAIN LANDING GEAR

GREEN------------GREEN------------GREEN

Landing gears down

I didn't ask---I grabbed the landing gear lever located on the aft of the center pedestal between my feet ---
SQUEEZED THE SAFETY HANDLE and

PUT THE LANDING GEAR LEVER TO THE UP POSITION.

LEFT MAIN LANDING GEAR---NOSE LANDING GEAR---RIGHT MAIN LANDING GEAR

RED---------------RED---------------RED

MOMENTARILY

Landing gears in-transit

LEFT MAIN LANDING GEAR---NOSE LANDING GEAR---RIGHT MAIN LANDING GEAR

BLANK-----------BLANK-----------BLANK

LANDING GEARS UP

The ugly duckling became a beautiful swan.

I watched the radio altimeter as it indicated **100---150---200---etcetcetc---very slowly though as we were about 8,000 pounds (4** tons) over Maximum Gross Weight.

Captain Hal very politely, ---"Bob, would you please bring the flaps up?" ---"Thank you."

"Jack, would you please set climb power for me please?" ---"Thank you."

Captain Hal put the Mighty DC-6 in a very shallow bank, picked his way through the now towering cumulus clouds, rolled out on a heading of 270 degrees. *(Westerly heading)* and we were on the wing to Lake Tahoe, California.

*****

Why a shallow bank? ---You might ask---The more the bank---The more decrease in lift---proportionately.

What are cumulous clouds? ---You might ask---They are the beautiful, fluffy white clouds that some times will build up to 50,000 feet.

Pretty on the outside---Mean as hell on the inside. (Sort of like your ex-wife.)

Full of violent vertical wind currents.
SEVERE---FUCIN---TURBULENCE
HAIL STONES, SNOW, RAIN, SLEET AND
THE WRATH OF GOD.

*Or as Texan **CAPTAIN BILL FARIES** would say---"Those mutha-fuckas are* **"NUT BUSTAS".**

These Cumulous clouds paint the color magenta on the radar screen and must be avoided.

FAA LAW---Thou shalt not be dispatched into SEVERE TURBULENCE conditions.

*****

Gotta write you readers this one while I'm thinking about it.

One of PSA's Boeing 727-200s was coming back to San Diego's Lindberg Field from a pilot training mission at Blythe, California. *(PSA had installed landing system instrumentation at the Blythe Airport when they got a contract to train Japan Airline (JAL) crew-members.)*

There was a shitpot full of PSA's Check Airmen and FAA dudes on board.

Blythe Municipal Airport is in the Imperial Valley in Southern California. The Imperial Valley, once a hot yellow desert and now a fertile green farming area irrigated by the Mighty Colorado River, has many Military **RESTRICTED** areas. When they're hot---they're **HOT**---and you better not fly into them 'cause **our US Air Force** fighter jets will blow your ass out of the sky.

SCENARIO
AIRPLANE---BOEING 727-200
CAPTAINS---A Shitpot Full Of Check Airmen And FAA Flight Inspectors
CO-PILOT---ONE SWAMPY ARMPIT TRAINEE
FLIGHT ENGINEER---J. P. LEWIS---THE BEST
LOCATION---10 Nautical Miles from Blythe Municipal Airport Heading West To San Diego at 11,000 Feet
TIME---MARTINI

ACT I

"Hey Ed, get your ass up front here and take a look at this."

"What dya need, Bill?"

"Look at those cumulous clouds up ahead---they're right on the airway."

"Yea man---they're at least thirty thousand feet and still building."

"I'll call Los Angeles Center and see if they can lift the restricted areas for us."---"Los Angeles Center, this is PSA Trainer 123---we're looking at some build-ups ahead and they're painting magenta on the radar screen."

"Roger PSA---they're on the airway---tops have been reported at thirty-six thousand feet by Military Aircraft."

"How's it looking to go around them?"

"**NEGATIVE---negative---all restricted areas are hot."---"Suggest you make a right turn---come in over Palm Springs.**"

"Stand by." ---"What dya think Ed---Palm Springs is a long way out of our way."

"Hell Bill, I can see a lot of clear spots in the clouds---looks like we can weave our way through there. Ya might have to climb a little."

"**PSA---what are your intentions?**"

"Uh---uh---we're gonna continue on---there's some clear spots up ahead---looks like we can get through okay."

"Okay---keep us posted. ---Proceed on course."

"Roger PSA 123---cleared on course---looks like we're gonna need a higher."

"Climb to any altitude you need to miss the clouds---you're the only one on the Airway. ---Report level."

"Roger, PSA 123 is starting our climb---looks like some holes about seventeen thousand feet."---"What do you think Ed?"

"Yea Bill---that's my guess."

"Give me climb power J.P."

Well they didn't find the holes, but they did get the shit kicked out of them.

ACT II

LOCATION---PSA Maintenance Hangar at San Diego's Lindberg Field.

Mechanic Val, ---"What happened? Looks like somebody took a ten pound ball-peen hammer to the wing and tail leading edges."

"Uh---uh---a cloud closed in on us and we hit one helluva hail storm."

"WOW"

EPILOGUE

The Boeing Engineers left their roost in Seattle, Washington---Flew the coop to San Diego---Chirped---
"If the Boeing 727-200 would have been in that hailstorm **TWENTY (20) MORE SECONDS** ---It would have---in a word---

"DISINTEGRATED".

*****

---BACK TO BULLSHIT---

ACT IX

Captain Hal or should I say **Captain Neat** flew around the towering cumulous clouds and Co-Pilot Bob Robey got us clearance, ----→Albuquerque (ABQ) -→Las Vegas (LAS)-→Lake Tahoe, California. ---Muttering something about, ---"Doctor Jekyll and Mister Hyde."

We arrived over Lake Tahoe just as the sun was setting---
Beeeautiful sight.
Captain Neat circled the lake a couple of times---not to sight-see, ---but to **burn off more fuel** as we were still over the---
---MAXIMUM LANDING WEIGHT LIMITATIONS---
We landed, ---deplaned the fire fighters and helped them get their gear on the busses.
I did a walk around preflight all by my lonesome while Captain Neat and Co-Pilot Bob Robey went into the terminal to fill their thermos bottles with coffee.
Captain Neat and Co-Pilot Bob Robey came out of the terminal, brought me a Pepsi and we all three went back into the cockpit chatting as if we were old fuck buddies.
"Read the before-start checklist, **please** Jack. Bob **please** cancel our instrument clearance to San Diego. We'll go VFR---I checked the weather and there's not a cloud in the sky between here and Travis."

*****

VFR---Visual Flight Rules---
Simply means---you're on your own. You pick the altitude you want to fly at---
EAST---ODD ALTITUDES   WEST---EVEN ALTITUDES
And pick the course you want to fly.
*****

"Start the engines Jack---Bob, fly us to Travis."
We stopped at Travis Air Force Base just long enough for Captain Hal and Co-Pilot Bob Robey to make out the

^^OUNTAIN of paperwork and load another load of servicemen and their families---went back to Detroit City---ferried the Mighty DC-6 home---to the Hollywood Burbank Airport.

We said our goodbyes---
Captain Neat went to do his acting part at Paramount Studios.
Co-Pilot Bob Robey and Stewardess Kay Robey, looking just as sharp as pretty as when I first met her---got in ex-Co-Pilot Bob Robey's '47 low rider souped-up Chevy Coupe and proceeded to Mountain City, Nevada.

ME
FLIGHT ENGINEER BECK
I smelled like Billy Goat Hill
-Same shirt---same underwear---same socks.
A rose is a rose is a rose I was not.
I went home.

EPILOGUE

Captain Hal Boresly got killed, when all four engines quit due to fuel contamination, taking off from Burbank on a DC-6 a few months later. Captain Boresly crashed head on into a mausoleum in a graveyard located off the end of Runway 15.

Co-Pilot Bob Robey quit after the flight with Cap'nhal-fromhell-CaptainHal-Captain Neat.

CAPTAIN BOB ROBEY
Went to Mountain City, Nevada.
And I heard him declare---as he drove out of sight, ---
"Sucky baby-titty mouse---crying all around the house."
Whatever the fuck that means???
**In a matter of a few days---
The Rookie learned---
The Ying & Yang---
The Black & White---
The Good & Bad Of---
FLYING WITH A COMPETENT---CONFIDENT---
NICE CAPTAIN LIKE---**
CAPTAIN BUD EWEING.

&

---Flying with an egomanYical asshole like captain halfromhell---

*****

I found out later on in life that Co-Pilot Bob Robey came from Mountain-City, a mining town in Northern Nevada and after this trip with cap'nhal-fromhell---QUIT---went back to Mountain City, Nevada.

Mister Bob Robey became a silver miner, wild horse ranch owner, bronco buster, Judge and---eventually the owner of Mountain City Saloon & Casino.

The reason I know this---I ran into Mister Bob Robey and wife, Kay Robey, nee Klause, a couple of years ago in the WESTERN BALLROOM at the RIVERSIDE CASINO IN LAUGHLIN, NEVADA.

KAY ROBEY nee KAY KLAUSE was just as pretty and sweet as ever---and---Mister Bob Robey???---You might ask---

MISTER BOB ROBEY was still the same---Slim & Trim---easy goin' gentleman---nothing changed---except---MISTER BOB ROBEY'S---**Buckets** of bullshit sayings have grown into a **barrel** of bullshit sayings.

---NICE PEOPLE---

Just a little plug here for---
---SUSIE ROSE and CHRIS ROBERTS---
*****

---CHRIS ROBERTS AND SUSIE ROSE---
Host KARAOKE Sunday, Monday and Tuesday nights at the Riverside Casino Western Ballroom."

They're nice people and everyone just loves them.

"Chris Roberts and Susie Rose are the ones that invented the **Karaoke Microphone Sanitizer**. ---You know---the sleeve that you slip your microphone into after you sing so the next person that uses it doesn't catch your germy diseases.

*****SUSIE ROSE & CHRIS ROBERTS*****
At
*****www.singclean.com*****

From all reports, ---Susie Rose and Chris Roberts are the best Karaoke Emcees in the United States.

Chris Roberts and Susie Rose also perform at the Riverside Casino Western Ballroom---Sunday---2:00 P.M. till 5:00 P.M.

--- CIRCA ---

1-NINER-68

I promised you readers this CIRCA about Pitot static tubes and here it is---

Location---San Diego International Airport---Lindberg Field

We got airborne---I called for the gear up and did a full cockpit scan----Captain's Panel---Center Panel (Engine instruments and assorted airplane system's gauges) ---Co-Pilot's Panel---

!!!HUH---NO AIRSPEED INDICATION!!!

"Hank----what's wrong with your airspeed indicator???"

"Yea---it haint working."

"Shit---call the tower and tell them we have to come back to the airport."

"Lindbergh Tower---this is PSA 723. We need to come back and land."

"Oh---ah-ah---PSA---do a one-eighty and come back and land on Runway zero-niner. Do you need the emergency equipment?"

"Nah---we just got a minor problem that needs fixed. We're not coming back to San Diego for two days and we wanna get it taken care of at our maintenance base."

"OK---PSA 723---cleared to land Runway Niner."

We did.

I taxied to the gate, parked the brakes and said to **Flight Engineer J. P. Lewis,** ---"Shut down Number One & Two Engines---Leave Number Three & Four engines running."

I opened my sliding glass window and shouted to a couple of PSA Mechanics that were hooking up our external power unit that we lost the Co-Pilot's airspeed indicator on take off.

I stuck my head out of the sliding glass window and watched one of the Mechanics named Val check the Pitot - static tube on my side of the airplane.

He did and looked up at me, shook his head no, alternately held up 3 & 4 fingers with his left hand and "cut" his throat with his right hand.

I looked around at **Flight Engineer J. P. Lewis,** ---"Chop #3 & 4 engines." ---He did.

Val disappeared underneath the Electra and I watched the E&E *(Electric & Electronics)* Compartment door RED warning light illuminate.

Flight Engineer J. P. Lewis was already off the Electra and right behind him.

I wrote a squawk in the log book---simply, ---"**Co-Pilot's airspeed indicator failed on take off."**

The E&E *(Electric & Electronic)* compartment door RED warning light extinguished and soon---**FLIGHT ENGINEER J. P. LEWIS and PSA MECHANIC VAL** were standing in the cockpit snickering.

"What's so funny?"

"We're just looking at your write up" snickered Val as he signed off the squawk. "The cannon plug was off---might have fallen off except it was a new cannon plug and still had the red protective cap on it. I don't know who installed it---but apparently he forgot to hook up the cannon plug. Do you want me to find out who installed it?"

"Nah---forget it happened."

Val left.

*****

Pitot-static tube---pronounced pee-toe---measures the difference between air pressure and static air and supplies the mixture of air to the Airspeed Indicators and Altimeters.
Three (3) Pitot-static tubes---which supply measured pressure/static air---

To the Captain's Airspeed Indicator & Captain's Altimeter. That's one. 1

To the Co-Pilot's Airspeed Indicator & Co-Pilot's Altimeter- That's two. 2

To the Standby Airspeed Indicator & Standby Altimeter--- That's three. 3

*****

An Airline Captain was having his six months mandatory 1st Class FAA physical and said, --- "Doctor, my wife and I have been married for thirty-six years. Our love life is as wonderful as ever--- but our sex life is not as ardent as it used to be."

"Any suggestions?"

"Captain---you've let it get that way. ---You have to spice it up. When you go home tonight and walk in the door---no matter where she is---grab her and rip her clothes off and make mad passionate love to her."---

"OK, Doc, I'll give it a go."

A few days later, the Captain happened to see the Doctor at Wal-Mart.

"Well Captain---how did it go---did she enjoy it?"

"Well, she didn't much care for it---but her bridge club got one helluva kick out of it."

*****

--- CIRCA ---

15 MAY 1-NINER-5-NINER

"RING---RING---RI--"
"Hello"

Chief Pilot Captain Bill Butler, --- "Jack, can you be out here in thirty minutes?"

"Do I have to put my uniform on?"

"You have a uniform???"

"My white shirt and brown britches."

"Oh---that. No just come as you are."

"Ripped Levis and greasy tee shirt with holes in it?"

"Doesn't matter what you're wearing---just get here as soon as possible, ---PLEASE."

I took a few seconds---put on a clean holey tee shirt---put a note on the refrigerator door for my wife---got in my trusty '46 Plymouth---boogied to the Burbank Airport.

It usually took me twenty minutes from our apartment in Glendale, California---took me 12 minutes.

When Chief Pilot Captain Bill Butler said---"**ASAP**"---I became **A-SAP**.

When I arrived at Twentieth Century---I drove across the tarmac and parked right behind the Mighty DC-6---figuring that they were in the cockpit waiting for me.

---Not so---

No pilots around the airplane---Just a **PARAMOUNT STUDIOS** industrial sized van and a whole shitpot full of people with movie cameras taking pictures of everything that moved---and didn't---including me. They surrounded the---

---TWENTIETH CENTURY AIRLINES HANGAR---

I warily went into Chief Pilot Bill Butler's 8X8-office shack. Captain Butler took one look at me, ---"You weren't kidding were you?"

"No sir---what do you need me for?" I asked cautiously figuring it was back to changing spark plugs time.

"We're gonna fly around a little bit. Paramount Studios needs to film a DC-6 in flight for a picture that they are making."

!!!WOW!!!

I was somebody---from a lowly graveyard mechanic to a movie star---in less than a month. ---Will success ruin Jack Resley Beck???

Flight Engineer Bob Butler---Captain Bill Butler's brother entered the office, **---"The studio has the airplane ready to go."** *I still don't think he had a pilot's license.*

"Okay---let's get going. ---Jack, do a walk-about pre-flight and get on board and start the checklist."

"Bob, get on board and get us an **IFR clearance** out over the Pacific Ocean. We'll do the air work out there---a lot less aluminum flack."

"I'll call the bosses and tell them what's happening---this airplane is due to go out on a **CAM** in a couple of hours."

IFR clearance??? *---You might ask **Clarence** ---***I**nstrument **F**light **R**ules---*simply means that you are under FAA control from take off to touchdown.*

I got on board and was curious as to what Flight Engineer Bob Butler meant by "ready to go". For some reason, they had put black paper over all the windows in the passenger compartment.

???WHY???---

I don't know why---**CELEBRETIES** don't need to ask questions.

The airplane that they were going to film us with was a World War II A26 owned and operated by Hunts Hall Productions.

*****

*I think Hunts Hall was the name of the Production Company. If I'm wrong---don't bother to tell me---many "**MOONS**", both on the ground and in the sky---have passed by since I was a movie star.*

Speaking of "moons"---Why doesn't some one manufacture toilet paper for men with hairy asses and Italian Women???---

Eureka---I found it---Pampers---Natural Aloe Touch. Goodbye streaky shorts. Put the brown ones in a wastebasket. It haint pretty but your septic tank will love you for it.

And after that's all wiped and done---
*Put some **GOLD BOND on your hummin' hemmies.***

*****

We taxied into position on Runway 07 with the Twin Engine A-26 nestled **CLOSELY** behind our left wing.

"Co-Pilot" Bob Butler asked Burbank Tower for take-off clearance and we departed the Hollywood Burbank International Airport. ---**!!!AS ONE!!!**
---Just like they do in the Air Force---**at times**---
Didn't frighten me---too naïve.
Captain Bill Butler dodged the zillion light airplanes in the Los Angeles Airspace and flew us out over the Pacific Ocean.
"Co-Pilot" Bob Butler cancelled our **IFR** clearance and Captain Bill Butler dead reckoned toward Santa Catalina Island at 500 feet.
Captain Bill Butler put the Mighty DC-6 on Automatic Pilot and all three of us watched the A26---still to the left of us and too close for comfort.
I just happened to glance out the forward windscreen.
In front of us appeared a Beechcraft V-tailed Bonanza.
*****

*V-tailed Bonanza???---You might ask. --- The **V** tailed Beech Bonanza is a combination of rudder and elevator and is controlled by the yoke (Steering wheel)---no rudder pedals---easier to learn to fly so doctors flew them a lot---crashed them a lot---so when one would fly by---*
Some one would always say---
"THERE GOES A DOCTOR LOOKING FOR A PLACE TO DIE."
*****

My voice froze---couldn't talk. ---I grabbed Bill's left shoulder.
That was all that CAPTAIN BILL BUTLER needed.
In a "fast" heartbeat, Captain Bill Butler clicked off the Auto-Pilot and climbed up over the Beech Bonanza---calmly looked around at me---grinned, ---"Let that be a lesson to you Jack---if a mid-air is about to happen---show him your belly."
I did---MORE THAN ONCE.
The A-26 missed the Beechcraft Bonanza because he was flying in tight formation with us.

"ALLS WELL THAT ENDS WELL"
PRFPACPJM
Chief Pilot Captain Bill Butler circled around Santa Catalina Island for a few minutes to allow the A-26 to get all the shots they

needed. This done---Captain Bill Butler "put the pedal to the metal" and headed home.

The A-26 passed us like we were "flying still"---wiggled his wings in a show of thanks---headed back to the Hollywood Burbank International Airport.

We followed.

Captain Bill Butler greased the Mighty DC-6 on the Numbers---taxied to the---

---TRANS-AMERICAN HANGAR---

Captain Bill Butler parked the brakes---I shut down the engines.

We deplaned and went into Chief Pilot Bill Butler's Office.

Standing room only as the crew of the A-26 was already in there---toasting each other with Martinis. A camera was still shooting on a tripod in a corner of the room.

We joined in.

The Captain of the A-26 handed Bill a "Martin"---shook his hand, ---"Good job, Captain Butler---we got some great shots. The only thing that we couldn't figure out was the abrupt climb. We could hardly keep up with you and we were in an assault aircraft."

"Did you get nervous by us being so close?" The Captain of the A-26 grinningly inquired.

Now it was Captain Bill Butler's turn to grin, ---"Just trying to wring the old lady out to see if she still has it." Captain Butler looked at me and winked. ---I said nothing.

CAPTAIN BUTLER HAD ICE WATER IN HIS VEINS.

Nothing riled Bill---not even Attack Aircraft.

The Head of Paramount Studios came into the office with a wad of bucks in his hand---paid us in cash. ---One hundred dollars for Captain Bill Butler---fifty dollars each for "Co-Pilot" Bob Butler and Self.

After they left---Chief Pilot Captain Bill Butler wrote me a check for fifty dollars.

I got one hundred smackaroos for two hours work and half of that was tax-free.

In less than a month---I went from two dollars and ten cents ($2.10) an hour to fifty bucks an hour and became a movie star.

**The name of the movie was---
"THE CROWDED SKY"**
Starring
DANA ANDREWS as the Captain,
And I believe **TROY DONAHUE** was the Co-Pilot.
YES---THE SKY WAS CROWDED THAT DAY.

I went home to my apartment in Glendale, California---proudly showed the monies to my wife, ---"Sure---you made a hundred dollars today. What are you going to do a few months from now when you haven't got a job?"

She left and went shopping with her friends.

I had stopped on the way home and bought a six-pack of **BREW 102**. At ninety-six cents a sixer---you can't go wrong. I consumed the whole seventy-two ounces and went to bed.

I woke up at ten that night---ready for work. The beer was still on my brain and my mind was a little "fizzy".

I started to put on my coveralls when it came to my gourd, ---"I don't do this anymore."

I took off the coveralls and went into the living room---stark naked.

A Santa Ana *("Devil Wind"---aptly named by the Native Americans)* was blowing to the south in Southern California and the sixty-dollar-a-month apartment was without air-conditioning and insulation.

I turned on the idiot tube---stretched out on the couch. I fell back asleep watching the late news.

*****

**HIGH TO LOW
LOOK OUT BELOW**
*High pressure area---becoming a low pressure area. ---
A storm is coming.
The more the drop in pressure. ---The more severe the storm.*
*****

I spent all my money on wine women and song---
*And wasted the rest---**on the stock market***
HAINT NOBODY KNOWS NUTHIN
Ask the man who said---and I quote---
"The NASDAQ will be well over FIVE THOUSAND by the end of the year."
Unquote
*****

Is the glass half full or half empty???
Depends on whether it's beer or water.
If its beer---either way works.
If its water---who gives a shit? ---unless you're a camel.
*****

Talk is cheap---it takes money to buy whiskey.
*****

Dja hear about the girl that was eight before she was seven.

*****

--- CIRCA ---

16 MAY---1-NINER-5-NINER
Actually it was just the next day.

"RIN-"
The phone woke me up and I caught it on the first ring so it wouldn't wake my wife.

It was---**Chief Pilot Captain Bill Butler.**

"Jack, I'm sorry to wake you up at this hour, but I need a Flight Engineer this morning."

"What time?"

"It's zero one hundred hours."

"No. I mean what time is check in?"

"Zero-six hundred hours---Can you make it?"

"Sure thing---I'll be there. Where are we going?"

"Frankfurt, Germany."

"HUH? ---Frankfurt, Germany---Shoot---that's on another planet."

"Yes. Can you do it for me please?"

"Sure---I'll be there."

"I'll see you then---gotta hang up and find us a Co-Pilot."

EVERYONE
That worked for Chief Pilot Captain Bill Butler would go to work on a moment's notice. Chief Pilot Captain Bill Butler was well respected and liked by his Pilots and Flight Engineers.

*****

Zero one hundred hours (0100 hours)Zero six hundred hours (0600)

The twenty-four hour clock is what we should be using by now in the good-old USA. ---0001 hours till 12 noon is just what it says---0100 hours-1: 00 AM---0200 hours-2: 00 AM and same-o---same-o up till noon---then add the number of hours past 12 noon to get the 24 hour clock setting---I.e.---1200 +1hour becomes 1300 hours Aka One PM----1200+2 hours-1400 hours Aka Two PM and so on.

Maybe when Timex runs out of the present day clock---then the powers to be might---and I say might, will put the 24-hour clock into play and work.

--- CIRCA ---

SAME DAY IN MAY---0105 HOURS
5 minutes later than the last CIRCA

Hooray---hooray---it's the first of May.
Outdoor fucking starts today.

I got ready to fly before I went back nite-nite.
One grungy white shirt and a pair of wrinkled shit brindle brown uniform pants.
I took them to the apartment complex's laundry room---washed, dried and ironed them.
I got our one and only suitcase, which looked like it came in on the Mayflower and I'm not talking moving van, and packed it. I wrapped it with duct tape that I had "borrowed" from Flying Tigers to keep it closed.
I set the alarm for five. ---Fell asleep on the couch. ---Over slept.
I got to Twentieth Century Airlines at 0630 hours. Captain Bill Butler was pacing his office, ---"Where the devil have you been? I called your house and woke up your wife. She wasn't very happy about it and said, 'I don't know where he is.' Then she hung up on me. I was just about to drive over toward your apartment to see if I could find you. That beat up old Plymouth that you drive is on its last wheel and I figured that you had stalled out some where."
Like I have written, ---Captain Bill Butler always looked out for his crews---and---he was in need of a Flight Engineer.
I did a fast walk around preflight and we were on our way to Frankfurt, Germany.
VIA
Newark New Jersey---Goose bay, Canada---Keflavik, Iceland---Shannon, Ireland---Frankfurt, Germany.
Iceland is green---Greenland is ice

---MULTIPLE CREW---
---TWO CAPTAINS---
---ONE CO-PILOT---
---ONE FLIGHT ENGINEER---
---ONE HAMMOCK---

---PILOT FLIGHT TIME LIMITATIONS---
DOMESTIC
100 hours per month---1000 hours per year

INTERNATIONAL
120 hours per month---1000 hours per year

---FLIGHT ENGINEER FLIGHT TIME LIMITATIONS---
DOMESTIC
100 hours per month---1000 hours per year

INTERNATIONAL
0
---ZERO---ZIP---NONE---
---FLY TILL YOU DROP---
Which some Flight Engineers did---not from the flying---but the partying.

*****

100 hours a month may not sound like much time. ---IT IS---
It takes just a little over three times that amount of hours that you are gone from home.
In layman's terms---to get 100 hours of flight time---a person has to be gone over 300 hours and if you get a shitty block of flights for the month---it will be close to 400 hours away from home---and if you get an egomanYical flight crew member in the cockpit---it will seem like **1000** *hours before the month is over.*
A normal month of flying is 80-85 hours---and that is plenty.
*****

We ferried the mighty DC-6 to "Newock, New Joisey"---picked up our load of Service Men and Women and their families and flew to---**Goose Bay, Canada.**

The approach into the Goose Bay Airport started out over the iceberg dotted Atlantic Ocean---was executed on an easterly heading---through a canyon of snow about a mile high on both sides and less than a mile wide.

If you had to make a missed approach, ---you had to wrack the airplane around in a sixty **(60)** degree bank and ---go out the same way you flew into the **BOX CANYON.**

Normal MAXIMUM bank is THIRTY (30) degrees.

WE LANDED.

I deplaned---dragged a fuel hose up on top of the wing---gassed her to the max.

I was freezing my ganooches off---never occurred to me to bring a jacket.

We took off for **Keflavik, Iceland.**

We departed the same way we came in, causing us considerable delay due to landing traffic---which took priority.

The approach into Keflavik was identical to the approach at Goose Bay---one way in---one way out---except the approach path between the snow-capped mountains was a lot wider and a lot less scary.

We landed and I topped off the fuel tanks one more time.

Four (4) main fuel tanks---Four- (4) auxiliary fuel tanks.

A Pan American Airlines Eskimo Mechanic looked at me in my white shirt and blue arms---shook his head---gave me a parka.

I was still freezing my ganooches off and if Mother Nature was protecting me---my scrotum sack with the squiggly sperms must have been well up into my stomach.

I gave the **PAN-AM** Eskimo Mechanic back his parka---went up the boarding ramp---closed the forward cabin door---entered the cock-pit---read the before start checklist to Captain Bill Butler and we departed for---**SHANNON, IRELAND.**

Horrendous tailwinds of up to 150 Knots prevailed which gave us enough fuel to overfly Shannon, Ireland and fly directly to Frankfurt, Germany. We had been on the "road" for thirty-four (34) hours.

The Pilots took turns relieving each other and lying on the hammock.

The only relief that I ever got was when I went to the **BIFFY**.
*****

Biffy---airplane crapper (toilet)
Why is it called a crapper???---You might ask---
Man by the name of **CRAPPER** *invented the modern day biffy---er---I mean toilet.*
*****

We landed at Frankfurt, Germany---waited for the rest of the Non-Sked Airplanes that had to stop at Shannon, Ireland because they didn't fill their auxiliary tanks---like Captain Bill Butler had me do. ---*Told you Captain Bill Butler was/is sharp---*

We proceeded en-masse on hotel courtesy busses to the ---

---FRANKFURT ON THE MEIN HOTEL---

The Non-Sked Crews&Stews went directly to the Frankfurt Hotel Bar. ---They had to get their livers back into condition.

I was "comatose on the mind" and went directly to bed---"did not stop at go" but passed out.

I woke up and went down to the bar. The bar is where you went when you want to see a friendly face. It sure as the "devil" wasn't the local church.

There was my crew, ---the Crews&Stews that I had met in Detroit City and a whole barpot full of Non-Skeddin' Crews&Stews that I had never seen before.

One by one, they came up to me and introduced themselves---asked to see my flashlight.

Embarrassed---I showed it to each and every one of them.

Apparently the flashlight that Captain Bud Eweing gave to me was the "Non-Sked topic of the day".

I had a couple of beers and went back to my room---washed my one and only white shirt and sacked out what was left of my emaciated body one more time.

I started a pleasant dreamland of a zillion airplanes and I was the Flight Engineer on each and every one of them.

"ALLS WELL THAT ENDS WELL"

PRFPAPJM

*****
Who invented woman---a Pollack—
-Who else would place a lunch counter next to a shithouse?
By the way—
Pollacks are the most honest hard working people on this planet---
And if that makes them "dumb"---
Then the rest of this world is pretty stupid.
*****

*****
One old maid to another old maid---
"Do you remember the minuet?"---
"No dear, I can't even remember the ones I screwed."
*****

Young bull, "Dad---let's run down to the pasture and screw a cow."
Old bull---"No son---let's walk down and screw them all."
*****

--- CIRCA ---

A GROGGY DAY IN MAY.
Hooray---Hooray---it's the fir---
Forget it---I'm too tired for the "outdoor fuckin" bullshit.

"RING---RING---RI--"
!!!FIRE WARNING---SILENCE THE BELL!!!
Shoot, ---it was the friggin' phone.
MY HAZY THOUGHT--- *"Time to fly and my only white shirt is still wet. ---When I get home I'm agonna buy a dozen white shirts and I'm agonna pay cash for each and every one of them.*
I was getting dish-pan hands."

Captain Bill Butler, ---"Jack, we're going to the Bruckenkellar Hoffbrau to get something to eat. Wanna come along?"

"Sure---thanks---I'll be right down---wait for me please."

Bruckenkellar=Cellar under the bridge---me thinks.
MY THOUGHT---*"Did he say eat? This will be a first."*

Over two dozen of us Non-Sked Crews&Stews **descended---**
*told you it was a **cellar**---*on the Bruckenkellar as one.

I watched as the Non-Skeddars rearranged the furniture to suit their needs.

The Maitre'de watched also, ---with one hand over his heart and the other hand white knuckled on a chair back.

Surprise---surprise---Gomer---these people actually did devour food. ---Of course, they needed gallons of wine to build up their appetite.

The Non-Skeddar, who selected the wine, *which by the way, was delicious*, professed to be a "Cona-sewer---oops---Connoisseur of fine Wines'. When asked later why he had selected that vintage of wine? ---"Shit, I don't know, ---I didn't see anything that I recognized so I just ordered the most expensive thing on the menu."

After we wined&wined&wined---we dined.

The "Wine Connoisseur" suggested that we go to a German Bier Garten that he had been to.

The Non-Skeddars declined as one, ---"We don't want to waste time traveling. ---The Bier Gartens are about to close."

"This Bier Garten stays open all night."

"What are we wasting time for---let's get going," ---the Non-Skeddars said as one.

We hailed a bunch of cabs and taxied to the German Bier Garten, which was less than a block away.

The German Bier Garten was rockin'&rollin'.

The Krauts were drinkin'&singin'&dancin'.

Not wanting to be "Ugly Americans"---the Non-Skeddars joined the melee---with both hands---clinging to bier steins.

I joined in---with both hands---got "beer" drunk. Not to bright on German Bier when you're used to Brew 102. ---*Which has the potency of horse piss and tastes like it---me thinks.*

I decided to purloin one of the German Bier Garten "Steinguts" that I was drinking out of and hid it under my shirt---half full of bier.

This **HUGH** German Bier Garten Waitress Fraulein saw me hide the Bier Stein under my shirt.

This **HUGH** German Bier Garten Waitress caught me by the shirt collar. ---Picked me up---shook me like a cat does a mouse---at chow time.

The bier spilled and ran down into my crotch. No big deal---but even though it looks like a straw---it doesn't work like a straw.

I tried to get away from ---**BIG BERTHA** ---to no avail.

The **Big B** reached inside my one and only white shirt and pulled the coveted Bier Stein out, taking some buttons along with it.

I grabbed the Bier Stein Handle and hung on to it.

!!!HUGE GERMAN FRAULEIN!!!

Took an ashtray from a table and started beating me on the wrist with it.

I hung on.

The Non-Sked Crews&Stews were in hysterics. The Non-Skeddars were having a lot of laughs at my expense.

!!!HUGE GERMAN BOUNCER!!!

Picked my shirt up and threw it out in the street. I went with it. Somehow, during the course of all this manhandling of my body, I had managed to hold on to the---

---GERMAN BIER GARTEN STEIN---

I had no idea where the hotel was---or the name of it.

I sat down on the curb---waited for the Non-Skeddars to come out---hopefully on their own power.

They did---

Saw me sitting on the curb---more hysterical laughing---slapped me on the back. ---Hoisted me on their shoulders---didn't work. We hit the bricks.

I had finally become a real Non-Skeddar.

We all went back to the hotel.

The Non-Skeddars stayed in the lobby drinking out of their flasks.

I went to my room and hit the sack.

*****

"I didn't know whether it was night or day."
"It was dark so I opted for night."
"I just didn't fall off the moon-lit turnip truck."
(Sung to the tune of an old German Bier Garten Stein Folk Song)
I wrote it when I was drunk on my ass.
Sauerkraut

*****

When I get drunk---I get 6 feet tall and I can "lick" any woman in the house.
I don't have a drinking problem—
I get drunk---fall down---throw up---
NO PROBLEM.
I can drink a whole fifth of Ten High and not even stagger---
Hell, I can't even walk.
*****

--- CIRCA ---

A GROGGIER DAY IN MAY

Hooray---ah screw it. I aint got the strength.

"RING---RING---RING--"

"Jack, this is Bill Butler---be down here in thirty minutes---we're going back to the States."

"I'm on the way." ---I was a litta---no---a lotta fuzzy.

I had sat on the curb for some time without a bier, if you don't count the bier in my crotch---so I was somewhat sober.

I knew the Non-Skeddars would be "hertin for certin".

I slid into my damp shirt---went down to the lobby.
!!!WRONG!!!
I couldn't believe it. The Non-Skeddars were standing and sitting around the lobby coffee clutching and chatting as though they had just got out of church and never been near a bottle of bier in their life.

???Me???
---URPITY & NAUSEOUS---
My stomach was regurgitating into my esophagus and my head was throbbing.

I reckon that I was not a real NON-SKEDDAR yet.

We flew back the same route that we came in on, except we had to stop at Shannon, Ireland because those wonderful horrendous tail-winds that airborne the Mighty DC-6 eastbound across the Atlantic Ocean became horrible horrendous headwinds going westbound.

We stopped at Keflavik, Iceland---Goose Bay, Canada and on to Newock, New Joisey, --where we deplaned our passengers, United States Military Service Personnel and their Families---including a zillion squalling/shitting babies.

They had only got out of the airplane once---in Keflavik, Iceland---where the frost was on the pumpkin and breathing was a chore.

Needless to say---as much as the passengers needed to walk around a lot---**They did not.**

Thirty hours of sitting in a modified aluminum engine-driven sardine can that reeked of puke---baby shit---cigar smoke---cigarette smoke---B.O. bodies---without a breath of fresh air.

We ferried the now empty DC-6 back to the
---Burbank International Airport---
We landed at 2100 hours.

*****

What time is 2100 hours???---
You might ask. You figure it out---I wrote you how to do it.
I.e. ---2100 minus1200 =9:00 PM.

*****

XXXXXXX causes Cancer in Canadian Field Mice.
How long did it take them to figure that one out???
Twenty Years???
I just read that XXXXXXX is back on the market. What did they do? --- Kill off all the Canadian Field Mice?

--- CIRCA ---

---SHIT---I DON'T KNOW---
---SOMEWHERE AROUND THE END OF MAY---
Me thinks
Hoora---forget it.

"Thirty six hours on the "road" and I'm gonna get home tonight." I bought a sixer of Brew 102 on the way to the apartment---
---EXHAUSTED---
I drank two---put my Flight Bag down---drank the rest---passed out on my white imitation Naugahyde couch.

My wife woke me at 0700 hours---needed a ride to work. Her car was in the Garage.

"You can't imagine the things that I've been through since you left. One crises after another."

"Huh?"

"Vera and Bob want us to come over for dinner tonight."

"Huh?"

"Are you listening to me?"

"Huh?"

"By the way---how was your trip?"

"Ok"

I dropped her off at the Car Insurance Agency where she was employed as a secretary---got another sixer of Brew 102 on the way home---drank it---re-passed out on my white imitation Naugahyde couch.

I was re-awakened by my wife, ---"How dja get home?"

"Vera dropped me off---I have something important to tell you."

"Huh?"

"I'M PREGNANT."

"???HUH???"

"I'm pregnant."

I got up from my white imitation Naugahyde couch and looked out the window.

"What are you looking for? Didn't you hear me?" ---

---"I'M PREGNANT."---

"The last time this happened, ---there was a Bright Star in the Eastern Sky and three Magi were driving Camels toward it. We could have two Christmases this year."
I was trying to figure out when the "event" occurred. In reality---I was **thrilled.** ---I wanted children.

*****

It was Christmas time and everyone was making Merry.
Merry left and everyone jumped for Joy.

*****

*****

I predict by the end of this century that man will evolve a third thumb with a fingernail shaped like an X-acto knife solely for the purpose of opening plastic containers.

Plastic haint that tough---it's the surface tension that makes us mortals grunt and groan to open what manufactures seal up so much that it takes a machete to open it.

By the way---plastic takes **400 years** *to* **biodegrade**---*re-cycle if you can---and for nature's sake---don't litter it.*
Aluminum---samo-samo, ---400 years.

*****

I would have had a wet dream last night but I fell asleep.

--- CIRCA ---

LAST OF MAY- ---1-NINER-5-NINER

"RING---RING---RING--"

Chief Pilot Captain Bill Butler, ---"Can you do another Frankfurt trip for us?"
"When?"
"Tonight---twenty three hundred check in. I hate asking you---but---you're the only Flight Engineer that I have."
I was exhausted. ---
All of a sudden---all of the glamour of flying---didn't seem so glamorous.
"I'll be there---er---2300---ah---er---that means 11:00 PM---right."
"Heh---heh---yes that's right, Mister Flight Engineer Beck. Eleven o'clock tonight."
"Thank you---sir---I'll be there."
As beat as I was, ---I couldn't refuse Chief Pilot Captain Bill Butler anything---besides that---I was getting paid by the mile and it was a lotta mileage to Frankfurt, Germany and back.
-I WAS IN HOG HEAVEN---SQUATTIN' IN TALL COTTON-
When we arrived in Frankfurt---the Non-Skeddars went to the bar.
I went to my room---washed my white shirt---went to bed.
I slept for 24 hours, ---till departure time.

We landed back at "BUR-BONK" Airport.
I bought a sixer of Brew 102 on the way home.
There was a note on the refrigerator door, ---"Went to Oklahoma to visit my family."
Thank God for small favors.
I had two brewskies---passed out ---slept for another 24 hours.
*****
"BUR-BONK" Airport???---You might ask—
That's what---Captain Bob Berson nicknamed it after my sphincter-puckering landings at Hollywood Burbank International

Airport when Captain Bob Berson was---Co-Pilot Bob Berson and flew with me.
    Thanks Bob---I needed that. Do you remember, Berson? ---Don't laugh old buddy---you bonked a few at Burbonk yourself.
*****

Speaking of Burbank International Airport

**When I first started working at the Burbank Airport---
The East-West Runway was numbered 07-25.
---Take-Offs and Landings to the East on a 070 degree heading--
Take-Offs and Landings to the West on a heading of 250 degrees
At a later point in time---I can't remember the year.
Runway 07 became Runway 08.
Runway 25 became Runway 26.
---Take-Offs and Landings to the East on a 080 degree heading--
---Take-Offs and Landings to the West on a 260 degree heading-
---SAME HUNK OF CONCRETE---**

Was it the San Andréa's Fault's fault or did some Pilot have his magnetic compass too close to his **BIG** watch when he designated the East-West Runway 07-25???

*****

For some reason---these old sayings keep going through my gourd as I write this bullshit, ---

"Never judge a man till you have walked a mile in his shoes"
I think that goes in line with
---*"YE WHO HAVE NOT SINNED---CAST THE FIRST STONE"* ---
--- *"People that live in glass houses should not throw rocks"*---
---*"JUDGE NOT---LEST YE BE JUDGED"*---
"Do unto others as you would have others do unto you"
Seems to me that the
"MICRO CHIP AGE" *has put them in the* **"RE-CYCLE BIN".**

*****

???HOW'S THAT SAYING GO???

"Do not judge a man till you walk a mile in his shoes."

---THAT DOESN'T WORK WORTH A BEDIT---

ANY ONE CAN FAKE IT FOR A MILE.

"DON'T JUDGE A PERSON

UNTIL

YOU HAVE WALKED A LIFETIME IN HIS HEARTBEATS."

ONLY GOD CAN DO THAT.

SO GET OFF YOUR HOLIER THAN THOU PULPIT---

MIND YOUR OWN BUSSINESS.

TAKE CARE OF YOURSELF AND YOUR FAMILY.

---WHEN YOU GET THAT ALL SQUARED AWAY---

---WHICH YOU NEVER WILL

GET BACK UP ON YOUR HIGH HORSE---

RIDE OFF INTO THE SUNSET.

---YOU HAINT GONNA CHANGE ANYTHING ANY WAY---

---AS DEAN MARTIN USED TO CROON---

"IT'S STILL THE SAME OLD WORLD."

"YOU'LL NEVER CHANGE IT."

"AS SURE AS THE STARS SHINE ABOVE."

*****

CAPTAIN JACK RESLEY BECK REAllyTIRED

--- CIRCA ---

6-9---5-9

"HAPPY BIRTHDAY TO ME"

I woke up and started to assess my future---in a little over a month I would be out of a job.
---TWENTY FIVE YEARS OF AGE---I PANICKED---
I went to the library and got the addresses of every Major Airline on the Planet Earth--- made out a zillion resumes for---

PILOT---FLIGHT ENGINEER---A&E MECHANIC
COMMERCIAL PILOT LICENSE #1418059
FLIGHT ENGINEERS LICENSE #1439372
A&E MECHANIC LICENSE #1364048
INSTRUMENT RATING
FIRST CLASS FAA PHYSICAL
20-20 VISION
ALHAMBRA, CA HIGH SCHOOL DIPLOMA
500 HOURS DC-6 FLIGHT ENGINEER TIME

I fudged a litta bit---no---a lotta bit on the 500 hours of DC-6 Flight Engineer time. Seemed like all the Major Airlines needed 500 hours for insurance purposes.
NADA
Not A Damn thing Anyway
I was home for a week---no bites---not even a "nipple".
ALL REJECTED---NO COLLEGE.
I finally remembered that I needed white shirts---went to Montgomery Wards---bought five white shirts---**with cash.**
I actually paid cash for something. I received a $700 dollar paycheck from Twentieth and still had part of the 100 bucks that I received when I was a movie star---that's 800 bucks in less than three weeks. ---That was more than I made a Flying Tigers in two months---with overtime.
I WAS SQUATTIN' IN TALL COTTON.

I left "Monkeys" and went to the Blue Moon Inn---bought the "house" a drink.

Diamond Jack had emerged---had a couple of brewskies---departed---went home---wife was still in Oakie-Land---got bored---drove to the Burbank Airport to see if Captain Bill Butler needed me for anything and when I say anything---I mean changing sparkplugs---washing airplane windows---sweeping hangar floors etcetcetc.

---CHIEF PILOT CAPTAIN BILL BUTLER---
Was doing his usual hemming and hawing.
Scratching and fidgeting---**THINKING**---
"What's wrong?"

"Ernie Tin Man just quit. He enlisted in the Air Force. I don't have anyone to replace him for a trip to Tokyo tonight."
MY THOUGHT---"Am I fired? He can't find anyone??? Here I am standing in front of him, in loving-living-color, and he isn't gonna use me for the trip."

"Can you use me for the trip? I'd like to take it."

---CHIEF PILOT CAPTAIN BILL BUTLER---
Scratching and fidgeting. Hemming and hawing, biding his time---
Always trying to make the right decision---

---**And Doing it**---
Now I started to fidget and scratch.
MY THOUGHT---"Did I do something to make him mad at me?"

You had a week flying the States and two trips to Europe. I was trying to give you at least ten days off."

---CHIEF PILOT CAPTAIN BILL BUTLER---
Would cancel a trip before he over worked his men.
"I'd like the trip---**please**."

"Okay---if you feel up to it---you got it. Check in is at 2300 hours.

"I'll be here at 2300 hundr---er---11 PM---right."

"Yea---Eleven tonight---once you get used to the twenty four hour clock---you'll like it."
Okay you guys---look at your watch and figure out what time it is.

"Who's it with?"---Hoping it would be **Captain Bud Eweing.**
"DIRTY DAN"
???"Who"???
CAPTAIN DIRTY DAN TIBBETTS.
"Why do you call him Dirty Dan?"

"You'll find out in the first ten minutes."
"You're kidding me."
"Nope---you'll see---better go home and get some rest---you've got a long night ahead of you."
"Are you gonna be here tonight?"
"No way---I just landed a couple of hours ago---got in from Honolulu. I'm going home after I make a few phone calls."
"Okay---see ya again."
"Have a good one Jack and oh yea---Happy Birthday."
"Thanks Bill---you just made it happy for me by giving me the trip."
Did I say Bill---WOW—I was on a first name basis with a **CHIEF PILOT**.

I stopped at a Luggage shop near the "BurBonk" Airport. I bought a new Samsonite Suitcase and a Brain Bag aka a Flight Bag---with cash.

Diamond Jack Beck lives.

I tried to sleep---no way-Hosay.

I got up and packed my Samsonite with all the clothes I owned, including my antiquated wide lapelled gray flannel suit.

I put my red-lensed flashlight and tool box in my flight bag and boogied out to the Hollywood Burbank International Airport---a litta---no---a lotta early.

I walked into Chief Pilot Captain Bill Butler's office and for the first time I met---

---CAPTAIN DANIEL TIBBETTS---
---DIRTY DAN---
Bespectacled and slight of build.
---CO-PILOT NELS JENSEN---
Tall good-looking blonde man.
STEWARDESSES
---GINA&TINA---

Gina was Dirty Dan's girlfriend. A real pretty young "thang"---about twenty years younger than Dirty Dan Tibbetts.

*****

Young meat and old meat
Sometimes it works---
Sometimes it doesn't.

*****

---I left---

I went across the tarmac to the Mighty DC-6 to check with the mechanics to see if there were any squawks that we should have signed off before we departed for Japan.

!!!No mechanics!!!

I connected the External Auxiliary Power Unit (APU) to the airplane *kissed it* turned it on---went up into the Cockpit.

I put the battery switch to the **ON** position, then put the external APU switch to the **ON** position---lit up the airplane's cockpit and cabin so the Crews&Stews could do their pre-flights---checked the aircraft's logbook for "no-go" items---got a fuel dipstick---left the cockpit---did an interior inspection of the cabin---straddled the mechanics ramp---slid down to the tarmac---took the mechanic's ramp---pushed it up against the leading edge of the left wing between the #1 & #2 engines---climbed back up the ramp---got on top of the left wing---checked the fuel level in #1 & #2 main fuel tanks with the dipstick, which was a long wooden stick with a glass tube attached, that read in gallons, that you held your thumb over when you pulled it out of the tank---empty---checked the fuel level in #1 & #2 auxiliary fuel tanks---empty---straddled the mechanics ramp---slid back down to the tarmac---went back across the tarmac to---

---CHIEF PILOT CAPTAIN BILL BUTLER'S OFFICE---

I entered, ---"Captain Tibbett---Sir---the number one and number two fuel tanks are empty."

"WHAT?"

"All the fuel tanks on the left wing are empty. I haven't dipped the right wing yet---sir."

Captain Tibbetts said, ---"Those damn on-call mechanics never fuel the airplane like they-re supposed to. I'll call Butler."

"I'll fuel them---sir---if you want me to."

"You don't have to do that, Jack," Captain Tibbetts said as **he handed me the keys to the fuel truck.**

---I left---

All counting ---on airplanes--- are as if you were sitting on the tail—looking forward---from left to right. I.e. 1-2-3-4

Ran back to the Mighty DC-6---took the mechanics boarding ramp from the forward entrance door---ran-pushed the mechanics boarding ramp to the leading edge of the left wing---between #1&#2

engines---ran across the tarmac to the fuel truck---got in---drove the fuel truck up to the Mighty DC-6---parked it in front and as close to the leading edge of the left wing as possible without hitting the propellers of the #1&#2 engines---got out---turned on the fuel truck's fueling pump---took the fueling hose nozzle from the reel---dragged the fueling hose up on top of the left wing---took off the #1&#2 main fuel tank fuel caps---topped off #1&#2 main fuel tanks---secured the #1&#2 main fuel tanks caps---dragged the fueling hose down the mechanics boarding ramp---reeled the fueling hose back into the fuel truck---turned off the fueling trucks fueling pump---got in ---drove the fuel truck around the DC-6 to the right wing---in front of #3&#4 engines---got out---ran back to the left wing---got the mechanics boarding ramp---ran-pushed it around the DC-6---put it against the leading edge of the right wing---between #3&#4 engines---ran to the fuel truck---turned on the fuel trucks fueling pumps---took the fueling hose---dragged the fueling hose up on top of the right wing---took off the #3&#4 main fuel tank caps---ah-oh-the #3&#4 main fuel tanks were full---took off the #3&#4 auxiliary fuel caps---ah-oh-the #3&#4 auxiliary fuel tanks were full---secured the fuel caps back on all four fuel tanks---dragged the fueling hose back down the mechanics boarding ramp---reeled the fueling hose back into the fuel truck---turned off the fueling truck's fueling pump---got in---drove the fuel truck back around to the left wing---positioned it in front of #1&#2 engines---ran back to the right wing---got the mechanic's boarding ramp---ran-pushed it around the Mighty DC-6---positioned it against the leading edge of the left wing between #1&#2 engines---ran to the fuel truck---turned on the fuel trucks fueling pump---took the fueling hose----dragged the fueling hose on top of the left wing---took took off the #1&#2 Main&Auxiliary Fuel Tank caps---topped off the #1&#2 Main&Auxiliary fuel tanks---secured the #1&#2 Main&Auxiliary fuel tank caps---dragged the fueling hose back down the Mechanics boarding ramp---reeled the fueling hose back into the fuel truck---turned off the fuel truck's fuel pump---got in---drove the fuel truck back to the fueling dock---ran back across the tarmac to the Mighty DC-6---positioned the mechanics boarding ramp up to the forward cabin door---ran up the steps to the cockpit---turned on the DC-AC Inverter---checked all eight (8) fuel gauges to make sure they were working properly.

# 1 MAIN	# 2 MAIN	# 3 MAIN	# 4 MAIN
LBS-→ F	LBS-→ F	LBS-→ F	LBS-→ F
# 1 AUX	# 2 AUX	# 3 AUX	# 4 AUX
LBS-→ F	LBS-→ F	LBS→ F	LBS-→

AOK

I sat in the Captains chair---read the before start checklist---checked the fire warning on #4 engine---**RED LIGHT---R-I-I-I-I-N-N-N-N-G-G-G-G**---started #4 engine---**KAPOW.**

I looked out the forward windscreen---
Saw four figures, with coffee cups in hand exiting---
Chief Pilot Captain Bill Butler's 8x8 Chief Pilot Office Shack.
!!!MUY PRONTO!!!

"What happened? ---What's wrong?" asked an excited Captain Dan Tibbetts as he ran into the Cockpit, "Are you okay?"

"Yea---I'm fine---it's the dad-blame primers on this American Airlines Airplane. Captain Eweing told me that an American Airlines mechanic put DC-4 primers on the engines somewhere along the way."

"Oh---yea---I remember now. Captain Eweing told me about you and how you back-fired the engines. I saw Captain Eweing the other day on Wake Island when I took over his airplane. You're not the only one---ya know. Everyone does it---even the mechanics. Ya know---you have to be careful when it's backfiring and you bring in the mixture control. As long as it's backfiring when you're just priming it---it can't hurt anything, but when you bring in the mixture control---it could backfire through the carburetor and blow out all of the carburetor seals---ya know."

"Yessir---I'm aware of that. I started the number four engine so I could get some air conditioning on the airplane for the Stews. The airplane was super cold when I first boarded her. They took our internal APU out of the baggage compartment because of weight problems going to Honolulu. ---I have to go down and disconnect the ground APU and get it out of the way. I also gotta get the mechanics boarding ramp away from the airplane. We will have to make a battery start on #1#2&#3 engines."

"How are you gonna get back on board?"
"I'll use the emergency escape rope on the forward cabin door."
"Huh---have you done that before?"

"Well—uh—I've slid down it---never came up it---yet---probably need some help getting in the door."

"You don't have to do that Jack. I'll go call a mechanic in if you want me to."

"Uh---oh---no. I'll be glad to do it---actually it's a lot of fun."

"As you like---go get it done and let's get the show on the road."

"Okay---will you have the Co-Pilot come up here and monitor the number four engine for me, please? I can't remember his name."

"Jensen---Nels Jensen---**NELS---GET YOUR ASS UP HERE AND LEAVE THE GIRLS ALONE.** ---Beck needs you to watch an engine while he secures the equipment outside."

"COMING---BOSS."

I went back to the forward main cabin door---pulled the emergency strap/rope out of its hiding place in the forward main cabin door jamb---made sure it was securely fastened to the aircraft---threw it out the do-de-do-door.

Once again I put my legs over the rails of the mechanic's boarding stand---slid down to the tarmac---ran to the other side of the Mighty DC-6---shut down the external Auxiliary Power Unit---pulled its umbilical cord from the DC-6's side belly button---pushed that electric generating monster---by hand---out of propeller harm's way---ran to the other side of the Mighty DC-6---un-braked the mechanic's boarding ramp---pushed the mechanic's boarding ramp out of harm's way---re-braked the mechanics boarding ramp---did a "run" around pre-flight exterior inspection---ran back to the forward main cabin door---**tugged one more time on the emergency escape rope strap to make sure it was still secure---hand over hand---climbed up to and entered**---face first---into the cabin of the Mighty DC-6---closed the forward main cabin door---went to the aft cabin---secured the aft main cabin door---checked all the emergency exits for security---checked each and every seat back pocket for burp bags and oxygen masks--- checked the **NO SMOKING & FASTEN SEAT BELT** signs and switches for proper operation.

I went back up into the cockpit. Gina was sitting in "my" Flight Engineer's seat.

With a smile on her face---with Dirty Dan's hand up her skirt.

Co-Pilot Nels Jensen was looking out his side sliding glass window---at nothing.

Captain Dirty Dan looked at me, ---"Do you want a feel of this?"
*****

Well it took longer than 10 minutes, but now I knew why they called him Dirty Dan.

*****

I blushed---blanched---even shivered---went back into the cabin---checked the forward main cabin door for security---went to the aft cabin---and did all the checks all over again trying to hide my embarrassment---waiting for Gina to exit "MY" seat. I didn't want Captain Dirty Dan to know that he had a very shy introverted momma's boy for a Flight Engineer.

We departed **Hollywood Burbank International Airport** for **Travis Air Force Base.**

Shortly after we got airborne---#2 engine started running rough. I switched on the **ignition analyzer**---checked the spark plug ignition patterns on each and every cylinder---with a rotary switch that allowed me to check each and every cylinder.

AHA---#1 CYLINDER ON #2 ENGINE---No ignition pattern.

"Captain Tibbetts---sir---the number one cylinder on number two engine is dead!!!"

"FEATHER THE MOTHER FUCKER."

"YESSIR" as I reached up to the forward overhead panel and pushed the guarded #2 **RED FEATHERING BUTTON** that feathers the propeller---shuts OFF all the fluids to the engine at the engine firewall---closes all the air ducting.

I reached down by my left leg and put the #2 mixture control to the **cutoff** position. ---To back up the firewall fuel shutoff valve at the carburetor.

I checked all the #2 engine instruments to insure that the shutdown of #2 engine was complete and read the---**ENGINE SHUTDOWN CHECKLIST---ALOUD** ---to myself.

*****

Nowadays---no shutdown switch is operated unless all eyeballs in the cockpit are locked onto it like a pair of tits at Hooters.

Then and only then does the person that is doing it, after looking at nods from the locked on eyeballs---initiates the action.

Unless the situation is panicked. ---Then you do what you have to do---!!!NOW!!!---Which happens very seldom---if at all---on jet aircraft.

*****

I went back into the cabin and checked out the #2 propeller to make sure that it was feathered and was not rotating.

"CAPTAIN TIBBETT SIR, ---#2 ENGINE IS SHUTDOWN, ---THE PROPELLER IS FEATHERED. THE NUMBER TWO PROPELLER IS NOT TURNING AT ALL."
"Thanks."

Nels, ---"Captain Tibbetts---dya want me to tell departure that we shut down an engine?"

"NO-NO-NO---NELS---DON'T SAY NUTHIN'---NUTHIN' AT ALL."

"Okay"

MY THOUGHT---*"My first engine shutdown and I did it right. Hallelujah---Lord come through the roof---I'll pay for the shingles."*
MY AFTER THOUGHT---*"We're gonna turn around and go back to the Burbank Airport---*

Being that I was getting paid by the mile---I wasn't gonna get paid. I figured it out in my head—I didn't even have to write it down---Burbank Airport to Burbank Airport---000.00 miles===000.00 bucks."

!!!WRONG!!!

Dirty Dan had a hard on and didn't want to waste it.

Me??? I was bucks up.

"We're gonna continue on to Travis you guys---haint no use to go back to Burbank. ---It'd take us all night to get a mechanic out to the airport. It's just a cylinder---we have a spare cylinder in the spare parts kit. Beck can replace it at Travis. I know a couple of mechs up there that I'll get to help you Jack."

Nels---"Okay"
Beck---"Okay"
---We continued on to Travis---
---Three turnin' & burnin' ---
---ONE NOT---
We landed.

Captain Tibbetts handed me a Motel Card, ---"Call me when you are completely done and have the engine run up and the airplane is ready to go---not a fuckin' minute before.

Dja understand Jack?"

"Yessir"

Captain Tibbetts---Copilot Jensen----Stews Gina&Tina---boogied to a motel.

I stayed to replace the cylinder with the help of the two mechs that showed up as we taxied in.

I figured three hours max.

!!!WRONG!!!

We found metal on the engine oil screen and magnetic plug---as a matter of fact---it looked like all of the internal parts of the engine were on the magnetic plug and oil screen.

*****

A litta---no—a lotta exaggeration makes the story more interesting.

That's what McGag told me when he was always bragging about how big his dick was. Claimed that people with big noses had big dicks and McGag had a honkin' honker.

*****

One of the mechs drove me to Travis Base Operations. I called Captain Dan Tibbetts.

"Captain Tibbetts, ---I can't fix the engine."

"HUH---WHY THE FUCK NOT?"

"It ate itself when the number one cylinder imploded."

I heard noises in the background---sounded like one helluva party going on. I'm busting my knuckles and freezing my ganooches off and these people are partying---haint no justice.

"CAN YOU GET ANOTHER ENGINE?"

"Don't know---I'll try," and hung up.

I asked the Ops agent where I might find an engine.

He looked at me like I might be playing a joke---saw that I was serious, ---"You might try the maintenance office down the hall---second door on the left.

"Thanks."

I walked into an office that read---

---TRAVIS AIRFORCE BASE MAINTENANCE---

I didn't even knock---went right on in---screw'em----I was a civilian. I served my time in the 18th Army Airborne Corps kissin' brass butts.

The gold sign with black letters on the walnut desk read---
COLONOL SHAPIRO.
The schmuck even spelled Colonel wrong on his nameplate.

The Colonel was sitting at attention with phone in hand, "YessirYessirYessir"---obviously annoyed by my intrusion---looked up at me---cupped his hand over the phone and curtly said, ---**"What do you want?"**
MY THOUGHT---*"Back to ass kissing---army style."*

I snapped to attention---stared at the wall---shouted, ---
"FLIGHT ENGINEER JACK R. BECK ---REPORTING SIR"
"RA19451559"

The "Colonol" said good-bye to the person on the other end of the phone line---softened.
Dya see how army training pays off sometimes?"

"At ease---Sergeant---what's your problem?"
"SIR---I NEED AN ENGINE FOR MY DC-6---SIR."
"At ease Sarge. ---Did you say you need an ENGINE?"
"YES SIR"

"Quit shouting Sergeant---I got a hangover. What kind of engine do you need Sergeant?"
"PRATT AND WHITNEY 2800---SIR."

"Sergeant---sit down and please quit shouting---okay---tell me what I need to know."

"Yessir---I'm a Flight Engineer for Twentieth Century Airlines. It's a Non-Sked out of Burbank. Our number two engine ate itself on the way in here."

"Who was the Captain?"
"Captain Tibbetts---Sir."
"Did he declare an emergency?"
If you have been paying attention up to now---you will read---
I lied.

"No Sir---we were on short final---Sir. We didn't have time to declare an emergency before we touched down."
"Did you tell Travis Ground Control that you had lost an engine?"

"No Sir---Captain Tibbetts was to busy looking for a place to park the airplane. I think he figured that Travis Tower could see that we had a prop feathered and didn't feel that it was necessary."

"Air Force regulations state that you must declare an emergency, no matter where you are, if the airplane is not configured for normal flight."

"Yessir---I'll tell the Captain," being careful not to say Tibbetts name again.

"What was the nomenclature of that engine that you need again? You were shouting so loud my ears went deaf."

"PRATT AND WHITNEY 2800---SIR."

"Colonel" Shapiro picked up the phone---dialed it, ---"Briggs, do you have any Pratt and Whitney 2800 engines in stock? ---Okay---good---I'm gonna send a Sergeant Beck over to pick it up. Is it on a cart? ---Okay---good---see ya at the Officers Club tonight. ---Yea, I'm bringing the old lady. ---Yea, I know, ---see ya there."

Colonel Shapiro wrote something on what appeared to be some kind of requisition form---handed it to me, "Take this requisition over to the Overhaul Hangar to Captain Briggs---he has an engine for you. ---Do you need a ride?"

"No sir---one of your mechanics drove me over from the airplane. Thanks anyway."

"You're welcome, ---have a good one."

I stood up---**Came to attention**---watched the "colonel" cover his "hungover" ears.

"THANK YOU SIR"

Saluted sharply---did a brisk about face,
I left.

So much for kissin' butt---I was a good soldier---you do what you have to do to get what you need---ask your ex-spouse.

I walked out of the Travis Operations Building---no mechanic on the tug---must have been quittin' time.

A Military Policeman (MP) was sitting in his jeep---sleeping. I woke him up and asked him where the Overhaul Hangar was. The MP pointed to a massive building---a long-long-wayaway.

The dawn was starting to show her lovely face, silhouetting the hangar.

"Need a ride?"

"Sure---thanks."

I entered the Overhaul Hangar---went up a flight of stairs to the row of offices on one side of the hangar---found a door that read.

---OVERHAUL MAINTENANCE---

I politely knocked. I didn't want to piss anyone else off. I needed an engine bad---was willing to brown nose anyone to get it.

"Come in" a voice said as I heard the auto-lock on the door snap.

I entered and politely introduce myself to Captain Briggs. He was older than dirt---wizened like a prune---gray as a Bald Eagle. *How can an eagle with feathers on its head be called bald?*

I handed Captain Briggs the note.

"I found an engine for you Sarg. How are you going to pay for it?"

"GULP"

Never thought about that! ---"May I use your phone---sir?"

"Sure---use the one on that other desk---I need this one open."

"I found the now greasy hotel card in the pocket of the greasy mechanic's coveralls that one of the mechanics had lent me.

I dialed the number and asked for Captain Tibbett's room.

"No one here by that name."

I then asked if he had the room number of an airline crew that had just checked in a few hours ago.

"I just have one airline person staying here. Would you like me to connect you to his room?"

"Yes please."

"Hello"---a female voice said.

"Is there a Captain Tibbetts there? I have a need to talk to Captain Tibbetts---this is Beck---the Flight Engineer that is working his flight."

"It's for you honey---it's the Flight Engineer."

Whatsh a matter Beck---told you not to call me at the office---ha-ha."

MY THOUGHT---"Oh my"---I knew then that these crazy animals were drunk on their butt and no help would be forthcoming from Captain Dirty Dan Tibbetts."

"They will not give us an engine unless we pay for it."

"HUH?"---A little more coherent.

"THEY WANT C-A-S-H ON THE LINE BEFORE THEY'LL GIVE US AN ENGINE."

"Ya got any bucks---Beck? ---that rhymes---ha-ha."

"No---I'm serious---they want money up front before they'll let me have an engine."

"Now I get cha---pay first---drive later---ha-ha."

"What do you want me to do Captain?"

"Okay-okay-okay---I'm alright now---let me think---okay---try thish number---no that haint it---Gina, whatsh Melvin Ward's number---heeeeres Gina."

"Jack---try 7147684154."

"Whose number is it?"

"MELVIN WARDS---he owns the fuckin' airline." Dirty Dan said as he took the phone from Gina. ---"Call us back when you get the engine replaced and don't be in a hurry about it."

"Good luck---Jack." I heard Gina utter in the background."

"Thanks---bye."

Shoot, now I was on a first name basis with the head honcho of the airline.

I dialed 7147684154---ring ring---ring---ring---ring---etcetcetc. *No answering machines in '59.*

Finally a sleepy voice answered, ---**"This better be important."**

"My name is Jack Beck---I'm the Flight Engineer on Flight 304, ---Number two engine ate itself on the way in here and has to be replaced."

"Who in the hell are you and what the devil do you want?"---*Groggily.*

"I'm the Flight Engineer with Captain Tibbetts. My name is Jack Beck and we have to replace an engine---we're still at Travis."

"Where are you?"

"Sir---we are at Travis Air Force Base and we have to replace the number two engine."

"Well replace it and get going---you were due out hours ago." Caffeine awake now as he slurped his black metabolism upper.

"Replacing the engine is not the problem sir. They will not give us an engine unless we pay for it."

"Where's Captain Tibbetts? ---Mister Melvin Ward inquired with caffeine heartbeats.

"He took the crew to a hotel to get some rest."

"What hotel?"

"I have no idea which one he went to sir." Mister Melvin Ward hearing Dirty Dan schlurrr his words was not a good idea at this time---actually---at any time.

"Let me talk to someone there."

I gave the phone to Captain Briggs.

Captain Briggs wrote many words on his memo pad. Captain Briggs hung up. Captain Briggs made out some kind of requisition form---handed it to me, ---"Take this to Field Operations."

"Where's Field Operations?"

"Down the hall---last door on the left. The Second Lewy in charge is an arrogant asshole---bottom of the food chain. Be careful what you say to him and for your own good---kiss his ass or you are not gonna get your engine."

I saluted Captain Briggs.

I left.

I knocked softly on the door that read **FIELD OPERATIONS.**

"Come in"

I did.

I was confronted immediately by Lieutenant Arrogant Asshole---not much older than me.

"What do ya need Sergeant?---Who sent you?---What do you need?"

"Stand at attention when you're in my presence."

"Sergeant, what's that in your hand? --Is it for me? --Give it to me."

I handed Second Louie Arrogant Asshole the requisition that Captain Briggs had given me with warning---took a step back---saluted briskly.

I could already feel my nose turning brown.

Lieutenant Arrogant Asshole scowled the requisition over---scowled me over, ---"Sergeant, the United States Air Force is not in the business of selling aircraft parts to civilian airlines."

I snapped to attention---stared at the wall.

Second voice---same as the foist.

"YES SIR"

I needed that engine and would kiss anyone's ass to get it.

Who says that army training doesn't pay off?

"Sergeant---where did the engine fail?"

---"SHORT FINAL---SIR"---

Second Louie Arrogant Asshole, ---"I do not want to do this, but if Captain Briggs wants to sell you an engine---it's yours Sergeant."

"THANK YOU LIEUTENANT---SIR."

MY THOUGHT---If this bozo calls me Sergeant one more time---I'm gonna deck his ass---engine or no engine. I found out later on in life that most Flight Engineers in the U.S. Air Force are Sergeants---A few Warrant Officers are---TOO.

Lieutenant Arrogant Asshole signed the requisition that Captain Briggs had given me---handed it to me---stood there waiting for me to salute him, ---"Take this to Master Sergeant Bond's Office across the hall."

I took the requisition with my right hand---saluted him with my left hand---slouched out the do-de-do-do.

The hallway clock chimed 0800 hours. I had been at this bullshit for four hours now---still no engine in sight.

How in the hell did we win any wars?

---Because of men like **MASTER SERGEANT BONDS**---

"Sergeant Bonds---HOLY COW, what the devil are you doing here? I thought you were gonna retire."

"Come on in and sit down Sergeant Beck. Give me that requisition, ---I'll get your engine for you."---As he picked up the telephone---dialed a number---said a few words into the mouth-piece---hung up---leaned back in his wooden swivel chair---clasped his hands behind his head, ---"Your engine is on the way to your aircraft, ---along with two mechanics to help you hang it."

"C'mon, I'll give you a lift over to the airplane. I'll tell you what happened on the way."

"Thanks Sergeant Bonds---sure is good to see you again."
*****

Master Sergeant Bonds was the Section Head of the Chemical-Biological-Radiological Section when I was a Clerk Typist/File Clerk in the 18th Airborne Corps at Fort Bragg, North Carolina during the Korean "Conflict".
*****

Sergeant Bonds said, "Here's what happened," as we climbed into his Jeep.

"Remember Major Gilbey in the Air Force Section down the hall? Well---he got promoted to Bird Colonel and assigned to Travis as Head of Maintenance. He offered me a big bonus and this Jeep if I re-upped in the Air Force for four more years and came along with him---so here I am. ---So what have you been doing since you mustered out?"

"Well---you might remember---I left and went to Spartan School of Aeronautics on the G.I. Bill to become an airplane mechanic. When I was at Spartan, some of my buddies pushed me into attending the Flight Engineer Course---which was only a four month course but cost me an extra twenty bucks a month. I never heard of a Flight Engineer before nor did I know what they did."

"Well---anyway---I attended the Flight Engineer Course, --- which got me the written portion of the Flight Engineer License, and then I got married and virtually pushed that old Plymouth of mine out to California."

"I landed a job as an A&E Mechanic with Flying Tigers at the Burbank Airport. Worked graveyard for a couple of years and got this job as a Flight Engineer with Twentieth Century Airlines. Do you know Chief Pilot Captain Bill Butler?"

"Yes---I do---good man."

"Well---he was good to me. Took me up for a Flight Engineer's check ride---passed me---got my license signed off for me and sent me out on a trip the next day. You're right---he is a good man---he sure helped me out."

"What about you? ---How's married life for you? ---If I remember right---you had just gotten married right before I got discharged."

"Great---she's the greatest---well here we are---there's your engine and the two Mechs I promised."

Sergeant Bond then reached around to the back seat of "his" Jeep---grabbed a pair of mechanics coveralls and handed them to me. "Here---these are GI Issue---you can keep them."

I de-Jeeped and walked around to Master Sergeant Bond's side of the Jeep---put out my hand to him. Sergeant Bond jumped out of his Jeep and gave me a bear hug, ---"Good Luck to you Jack---you'll go a long way---you've got the right stuff."

"Thanks"---I stammered as I got out of his grasp. "Thanks---thanks much and the best of luck to you **Sergeant Bonds.**"

He left.

The mechanics already had the cowling off the #2 engine and were working on the **"GARBAGE"**. I suited up in my new GI issue coveralls and joined in.

It took us twice as long as normal to get the engine off the airplane. Six months of corrosion sitting by the Pacific Ocean's corroding salt air at the Los Angeles International Airport was the cause.

Nowadays the Airlines put their standby and worn out aircraft out on the desert.

*****

"GARBAGE"—-*All the cables, cannon plugs and tubing that connects the engine to the FIREWALL.*

*****

We finished her up---buttoned her up---ran her up.

Works fine---lasts a long time.

It was **NIGHTIME.**

As we deplaned I swiped some miniature bottles of booze and gave it to the mechs and put a couple in the pockets of my new GI coveralls.

The mechs "borrowed" a tug and drove me back to Travis Operations.

When I got off of the tug---the mechs pulled out their mini-bottles---saluted me with them---"uncorked" them---chug-a-lugged---drove off in the California sunrise.

--- CIRCA ---

6-10---1-NINER-5-NINER

HAPPY UNBIRTHDAY TO ME

  I entered Travis Air Force Operations---found a pay-phone. I deposited one thin dime--- called the motel---asked for Captain Tibbett's room, hoping that he would be in his room by now.
 "RING----RING----RING ---RING----RING----RING----RI--"
  "Sir---Captain Tibbetts doesn't seem to be answering---may we take a message?"
  "Yes---would you please go knock on the doors of all the people that checked in with Captain Tibbetts and have them call Beck at Travis Operations as soon as possible? It's very important."
  "Sure thing---bye."
I told the Travis Operations Agent I was expecting a phone call.
  I went over to the make shift boarding lounge room where all the Service Personnel and their families had been housed for the last eighteen hours.
  Most of them had babies---just ashittin'&agittin'. Not a pretty sight ---and they still had over thirty hours to go before they could bathe their bodies and lie down in a bed.
  I went back to the Ops Room---found a vacant corner---laid down on the floor.
  It was 2100 hours. I was vegetated.
  I have been on the job for almost 24 hours and have only made 5 bucks. Remember I was being paid 2 1/4 cents per mile and Burbank to Travis Air Force Base was about 400 miles.
*****

OK you guys---2100 **hours**---*what PM time is it---you forgot how---I knew you would---ok---*
This is the last time I'm gonna tell you how to figure it out.
2100 minus 1200 noon = 9:00 PM
Or
1200 noon +9:00 PM =2100 hours
And I haint gonna tell ya again.
How's that for Army talk?

--- CIRCA ---

10 June 1-niner-5-niner

Same day---just a whole lot later

"RING----RING----RI-"
"IT'S FOR YOU SERGEANT BECK."

It was the motel, ---"Your crew is on the way---They asked me to call you."

"Thanks much."

I attempted to make out the mound of paper work on the clipboard that read---

---TWENTIETH CENTURY AIRLINES ---FLIGHT 304---

That didn't work past the first entry.

I hitched a ride with an MP back to the DC-6.

I did a pre-flight walk around with the mechanics that helped me hang the engine, or should I say a "stagger around". Apparently the Mechs had got some more booze from the airplane or they were a cheap drunk on a couple of mini-bottles of booze.

We put power on the airplane and they sat in the cockpit with me and helped me run the checklists necessary for departure. Their breath was, literally--- "intoxicating".

I checked the---
FUEL QTY

#1 MAIN	#2 MAIN	#3 MAIN	#4 MAIN
--→ F	-→F	-→F	-→ F
#1 AUX	#2 AUX	#3 AUX	#4 AUX
-→ F	-→ F	-→ F	-→ F

Wasn't good enough for me---too much water to cross---
I grabbed the **FUEL MEASURING DIPSTICK.**
I went to the left cabin overwing window **EMERGENCY EXIT.**

I unlatched the **RED HANDLE** and pulled the over-wing **EMERGENCY EXIT** window out. I put it on a passenger seat and **crawled** out on the **dew-wet** wing.

I checked #1 & #2 main fuel tanks---**FULL**---to the brim. I didn't need the dipstick---as a matter of fact, I had to put the fuel caps back on muy pronto because the fuel came spilling out over the wing.

I checked #1 & #2 auxiliary fuel tanks---**FULL**.

I crawled back to the left over-wing emergency exit and back into the airplane's passenger cabin.

I opened the right cabin overwing window **EMERGENCY EXIT.**

I crawled out on the right wing.

I checked the #3 main fuel tank---overflowing.

I checked the #4 main fuel tank.

AH-OH
E ←--MPTY

I couldn't even get the end of the dipstick wet.

Haint nothin' worse than a dry hole where you can't get the end of your dipstick wet.

I crawled back to the right over-wing emergency exit and back into the airplane's cabin---went into the cockpit. I tapped on #4 main fuel tank quantity indicator with the middle knuckle of my social finger of my right hand.

It went from → F to E←.

I called Travis Operations on the VHF radio, ---"Travis Operations---this is the Flight Engineer on Twentieth Century Airlines DC-6---Flight 304."

"Yea---go ahead Twentieth---whatcha need?"

"Yessir---we need a fuel truck."

"Sergeant---that aircraft has already been fueled. Did you look at your fuel gauges?"

"Yessir---they all indicate full. I got on the wing and dipsticked all the fuel tanks. The number four main tank is completely dry."

"Godamit---hang on." as he covered the mouthpiece.

I heard muffled obscene shouting---looked toward Travis Ops---saw a pair of headlights turn on---watched them come my way---post haste. *Whatever that means*

I went down the passenger boarding ramp that a Travis Air Force Base Boarding Agent put there when we parked---met the fueler man as he jumped off the fuel truck running to get the fuel hose.

I followed him up his ladder---to the top of the wing.

I checked the #3 & #4 auxiliary fuel tanks while he fueled the #4 main fuel tank. They were full.

I went over by the fueler man to make sure that he did it right this time. He finished filling the #4 main fuel tank and left. I put the fuel cap back on and went down his ladder.

When I got on the ground---fueler man took his ladder---secured it to his fuel truck---rode off in the darkness. ---Never said good-bye.

*****

After that knuckle rapping session---I made it part of my pre-flight check. I found many of the gauges to be sticking---not as drastic as the one mentioned above, but as high as a 700# error (that's over 100 gallons---6.7#s =1 gallon) No matter though---unless I put the 115/130 purple gasoline in myself---I used the dipstick.

I might have got a little overanxious with my social finger middle knuckle rapping because one time that I knuckled the fuel gauge---I busted the glass on the instrument---

Pissed Captain Doyle Bunch off.

One more item---

Why was the #4 main fuel tank was empty? I can only speculate because I filled it to capacity at Burbank.

The flight from Burbank only took less than two hours and I cross-fed the fuel out of the auxiliary tanks first (the fuel is used out of the auxiliary fuel tanks first for Center of Gravity (CG) limitations as the auxiliary fuel tanks are located aft of the main fuel tanks) so the # 4 main fuel tank should have been almost full.

I believe that the fueler man parked his truck under one wing---filled all four tanks---went under the fuselage---got the cross-feed handle which allows you to cross-feed from wing to wing---opened it and then filled the fuel tanks on the other wing---closed it and then went up on the wing and filled the now empty tanks that he had cross-fed from and missed the #4 tank in the progress. Any-hoo---that's the way I see it.

*If we would have departed with the #4 main fuel tank empty---the possibility of the **OVERGROSSED** Mighty DC-6 gone on its back was eminent---and if it didn't go landing gear tits up---we would have landed short of Honolulu with a very wet airplane and swimming with dorsal fins.*

Maximum fuel differential (out of balance) between wings, for dispatch, is zero for take-off and 1,500 pounds differential for flight and landing.

Any out of balance will cause considerable drag because you will have to put aileron in to maintain straight and level flight.

*****

Just as the fuel truck disappeared into the darkness---the motel bus brought Dirty Dan and Crew up to the Mighty DC-6. I watched them de-vanning---figuring that at least one of them would fall on his or her behind.

!!!WRONG!!!

They stood beside the passenger boarding ramp---personalized coffee cups in hand---chit-chatting like they just left a church social---instead of drinking booze and pounding pee-holes.

They went up the passenger-boarding ramp into the passenger cabin---nary was a drop of caffeine spilt.

A new crew member---with two stripes on his sleeves---remained on the tarmac with me---AND---for the first time, I met—

---NAVIGATOR NORY ELLIS---

Who had a shit-eating grin on his face like the cat that fucked flat the canary.

*****

I have to tell this story about Nory Ellis before I forget it.

After we got back from this trip that we were about to embark on---Nory Ellis asked for a ride home. I gladly took him home because he was such a nice guy.

On the way to his house---Nory slipped a Trojan rubber in my front shirt pocket to avoid taking it home saying, ---"Throw this in the trash somewhere before you get home---don't forget??"---

And as **STEVE MARTIN quips**---*"When they come to take you away---simply say—*

"I FORGOT".

And sure enough---I simply forgot.

When I got home---I reached in my shirt pocket with my right hand for a pack of Camels---pulled the pack of cancer sticks out of my pocket---the Trojan Rubber came out along with it.

In less than a heartbeat---my left hand had grabbed the rubber---in mid air---put it in my hip pocket.

My wife---who was standing right in front of me, never saw it.

*****
NAVIGATOR NORY ELLIS

Shook hands with me, ---"Hi---Beck---I'm Nory Ellis. I'm the Navigator for the trip to Tokyo."

"Nice meeting you Mister Ellis. Where did you join up with Captain Tibbetts?"

"Call me Nory. I had a room at the motel where Captain Tibbetts stayed. I just got in from Tokyo yesterday morning. No use to go home to Van Nuys because I was supposed to deadhead up to Travis with Tibbetts to take this trip last night, so I just got a motel room."

"Every one partied in my room when you guys came in last night."

"Okay Nory, ---I'm gonna do one more walk-around inspection to make sure that everything is buttoned up---see ya on board."

"Okay Beck, ---here come the busses with our passengers. Better hurry up that walk around and get back up in the cockpit---it's gonna be a zoo out here in a few minutes."

I did.

--- CIRCA ---

STILL THE SAME FRIGGIN' DAY-A WHOLE LOT LATER

Captain Tibbetts snored.
Co-Pilot Nels Jensen got us clearance to Honolulu.
I read all the checklists---to myself.
Nory Ellis ate an orange.
Tina & Gina sardined the passengers on board.

The **FWD CABIN DOOR** light extinguished and I went back into the cabin to make sure that all doors and **EMERGENCY EXITS** were secured.

As I walked down the aisle---Gina & Tina passed me as many times as possible---rubbing their tits on my back. They found out early on that I was shy and blushed crimson red when they even got near me.

I checked everything and made tracks to the cockpit, where---Captain Daniel Tibbetts---was now wide awake and briefing the crew.

I got in on the last part of the briefing and all I heard was, --- "Jensen---we are way over-grossed---we have well over one hundred knot headwinds. I had them top off all the fuel tanks."

"**Beck---did you check all the fuel tanks visually?**"
"Yessir" I started to tell him about the erratic #4 main tank fuel gua—.

"**Yea---okay---we're flight planned for eleven hours. We have twelve and one-half hours of fuel on board, which makes us legal. That will give us the required one and one-half hours of fuel at our destination that the International Flight Rules require.**"

"Jensen---make sure you pull the landing gear lever up as soon as you get a positive indication on your rate of climb gauge. If we lose an engine before the landing gears get in the wheel wells---I'm gonna set her down straight ahead into the rice paddies---cause that's all she wrote---she haint gonna climb any at this gross weight with the gear down on three engines. If we lose an engine after the landing gears are up and locked---we'll continue on straight ahead and when---and if we gain any altitude---we'll do a one-eighty and land straight in on the runway we took off on. We'll have a twenty-knot tail wind but we have two miles of runway---so we should have plenty of concrete to stop on."

???"EVERYONE HERE UNDERSTAND"???

We all said **YES** in unison---including Gina & Tina who had completed securing the cabin and had come up to report to "Danny" and were now rubbing their tits all over Nory sitting at his make shift desk behind me.

MY THOUGHT---"Haint nothing like this ever happened on the graveyard shift."

*****

Two drunks sitting at a bar---
"Letsh have another drink and go get laid."
"Not me---I got more than I can handle at home."
"Good---Letsh have another drink and go to your house."

*****

Say you leave San Francisco for Honolulu with a steady 100 knot head wind all the way. Then you fly Honolulu to San Francisco (SFO) with the same 100 knot tail wind.

???QUESTION???

*Is the **fuel burn off** for the entire trip the same as if there had been no wind both ways?*

!!!ANSWER!!!
NO

The fuel burn-off *would be more---because you're in the headwind longer than you are in the tailwind---anyhoo--- that's what*---Captain John Stuckher *told me.*

*****

A little levity note here on---Captain John Stuck-her---
Seems that Stuckher listed his name in the San Diego City Phone Book as----**Captain John Stuckher**---
Seems that---Captain John Powell & Captain Les Deline---
Got a little drunkey-wunky---called the San Diego Telephone Company---

"This is **CAPTAIN JOHN STUCKHER**---*I have just been promoted to*---**VICE ADMIRAL JOHN STUCKHER"**---

"Will you please put my name in the San Diego Telephone book like that?"

"YES SIR ADMIRAL STUCKHER, ---
"The new phone books come out next month and congratulations on your promotion sir."

One month later---Vice Admiral Captain John Stuckher was---to say the most---pissed.

*****

--- CIRCA ---

6-11---1-NINER-5-NINER ---0100 HOURS

We took off,
The landing gear retracted into the wheel well and locked.
Dirty Dan was asnorin' before---
Co-Pilot Jensen retracted the flaps to the **FLAPS UP** position.
Navigator Nory Ellis ate an orange.
???ME??? I checked---
Each and every spark plug on each and every cylinder on each and every engine on the---
---**IGNITION ANALYZER**---
I checked all of the instruments and every switch that could be---or not be moved---**30 ZILLION TIMES.**
We **COASTED OUT** over the Farallon Islands, an extinct volcano a few miles West of San Francisco, and the world ahead of us consisted of a "hole" lot of water---namely the---
---**PACIFIC OCEAN**---
*****

PACIFIC---Derived from the word: **PEACEFUL**---*me thinks*
COASTED OUT & COASTED IN---*International Airline Jargon for leaving the coast and arriving at another coast---that's how I interpret it anyhoo.*
*****

The longest airway in the world---without an alternate airway to land at---IS---
UNITED STATES---→---→---→---→ ---→---→---→HAWAII
1OO+ KNOT HEAD WINDS---FLIGHT TIME 11 HOURS
---OR---
HAWAII---→---→---→---→---→UNITED STATES
100+ KNOT TAILWINDS---FLIGHT TIME 9 HOURS
These times are for propeller driven aircraft.
Five hours to Hawaii---Four hours to the States for Jet Aircraft.
*****

Co-Pilot Nels Jensen hand flew the mighty DC-6 to 10'000 feet---engaged the **AUTO-PILOT** and put the **ALTITUDE HOLD** on.

We were 4000 pounds over our maximum take-off weight.
The Mighty DC-6 could not go any higher.
Our **optimum altitude**, for fuel conservation, was **17,000 feet**.

If we stayed at **10,000** feet, we would land about **100** miles east of Hawaii and have a very wet airplane.

The closer you get to your optimum altitude, with out going above it, ---the less fuel you burn.

We had to step climb to our optimum altitude of 17,000 feet as we burned off 115/130 purple gasoline and got lighter---so we could climb.

Does that make sense? ---Anyhoo---you'll see what I mean as you read what I write as we fly along to Hawaii. ---Does that make sense??? If it does---please explain it to me.

I looked back over my right shoulder at Navigator Nory Ellis.

Nory was standing on his chair taking a fix on the stars through the airplane's Sextant that he had put through a hole in the ceiling of the cockpit that was made for that purpose.

Navigator Nory Ellis pulled the Sextant out of the self-sealing hole---sat down---pulled a chart out of his flight bag---unfolded it. *Self-sealing hole---hummmm*

THE CHART WAS HUMUNGUS.
---TO SAY THE LEASTMOST---
THE CHART FILLED UP THE WHOLE COCKPIT.
THE CHART FILLED UP THE WHOLE COCKPIT.
TWICE

Navigator Nory Ellis took a pair of scissors out of his flight bag--- Cut a two inch strip from

---

SAN FRANCISCO--→--→--→--→--→--→--→**HONOLULU**

2 INCHES

Took the rest of the chart---wadded it up---trashed it.

Navigator Nory Ellis looked at me ---saw my chagrin---teethed his Cheshire Cat grin.

He knew that this was my first trip across---

---THE BIGGEST POND---

"Simple as this, Beck---if we get off this strip of paper------WE'RE SHARK BAIT."---

Navigator Nory Ellis stood up---leaned over my left shoulder---tapped Jensen on his right shoulder, ---"Turn five degrees to the left."

Nory made sure Co-Pilot Nels Jensen complied---then laid down in the fetal position on a gym mat that he had brought with him, ---"Beck, wake me up five minutes before the hour." Ate an orange---snored.

I checked the **HOW GOES IT CHART** where I had recorded the airplanes fuel burn in pounds. This was recorded by the **FUEL FLOW METERS** to keep track of our fuel remaining and the gross weight of the airplane for step climbing to the airplane's optimum altitude. The fuel flow meters were more accurate than the **FUEL QUANTITY INDICATORS.**

Recording the fuel flow meters is/was the most **CRITICAL** job of the Flight Engineer on long over water flights.

The **How Goes It Chart** (Official name PULMART, me thinks) also showed us our---**POINT OF NO RETURN--- (PNR).**

The place where either we continued on to our destination ---

OR

We went back to "whencesoever" we departed.

I tapped Co-Pilot Nels Jensen on the shoulder, ---"We can climb to twelve thousand feet now."

"Oakland Center---this is Twentieth Century Airlines 304. How do you read?"

"Loud and clear, Twentieth Century 304. How me?"

"You're five by five---we need to climb to twelve thousand feet **AS SOON AS POSSIBLE!!!"**

*****

*5X5???---No, it's not a fat man---remember that song---"He's Mister Five by Five---Five Feet Tall and Five Feet Wide etcetcetc."---**5X5** in airplane radio transmissions jargon means, on a scale of one to five and five being the highest---*

MODULATION X CLARITY---*me thinks.*

If you're confused, as I am---Just say **LOUD AND CLEAR** *or say---on the bottom part of the scale "We can't read you" and if that doesn't work---just take your headset off and pretty soon your company will SEL CAL you and gives you another frequency.*

*****

Co-Pilot Nels Jensen had been across the **"BIG POND"** many times and knew the urgency of getting to our optimum altitude. He didn't like to do his swimming with dorsal fins.

Sharks or Lawyers---depends if you are in warm water or in hot water.

Hesitation---Oakland Center had to make sure that there was no conflict traffic **COASTING IN f**rom Hawaii.

Twentieth Century 304---climb to twelve thousand feet---acknowledge."

Roger---Twentieth Century 304---climbing to twelve thousand feet."

"Report level---please"
"Wilco" *Will comply*
"Climb power Beck."

I adjusted the propeller pitch and pushed the throttles forward. I put on just a little less than the charts called for. **We needed to conserve fuel.**

The "ancient" American Airlines DC-6 FINALLY struggled to 12,000 feet. She didn't want to go swimming either.

---**SHAKE---RATTLE---ROLL**---

Once again I checked the---**How Goes It Chart**.

The fuel that we had burned in the climb, from 10,000 feet to 12,000 feet made us light enough to climb to 13,000 feet.

"Nels---we're light enough to climb to 13,000 feet."
Nels, ---"Oakland Center---this is Twentieth Century 304---we'd like a higher altitude."

No response.

We were out of range for our Very High Frequency (VHF) Trans-Ceiver Radios (Transmitter-Receivers). VHF is line of sight and the curvature of the earth was blocking "our line of sight".

*****

Just like your television set is blocked out of watching Bob Barker at 0900 hours by a mountain between the television transmitting station and your television set. Of course that was before Direct TV and Cable. By the way---how does Bob Barker keep his composure after all these years? He's a better man than I am---Gunga Din.

*****

I tuned in one of the two High Frequency (HF) Trans-Ceivers to 10.8, a frequency that was put on the **How Goes It Chart** by Navigator Nory Ellis that he got from Travis Operations when he made out the **FLIGHT PLAN.**

TRAVIS AF BASE -→-→-→-→-→-→-→-→HAWAII

The reason that the Flight Engineer tuned in the High Frequency Radios was because they were temporarily installed on the overhead panel, right above his head, for over-water flight operations.

High Frequency (HF) follows the curvature of the earth---and---if the atmospheric conditions are right---you can talk to Tokyo from Bum Fuc, Idaho on any given day.

*****

Dja hear abut the queer electron that blew a fuse?

*****

I reached up and pulled the HF microphone out of its temporary wire holder and handed it to Co-Pilot Nels Jensen, --- "Oakland Center---this is Twentieth Century 304---How do you read?"

"Twentieth Century 304---This Is Houston Center---**WE** read you loud and clear. How me?"

"How did we get a hold of you?"

"Full moon---all the crazies are out and the High Frequency waves are skipping all over the country."

Nels and I laughed---Dirty Dan and Nory snored.

"Have you got anther frequency for us to try?"

"Yea---try one-zero-point-three."

"Thanks---be careful going home tonight---those Texans screw German Shepherds, not to mention their aunts and sisters and some of their off-springs turn into Werewolves."

"Bow-wow---Bye."

I reached above my head and tuned in.10.3 on the **HF TRANS-CEIVER** radio dial on the **OVERHEAD PANEL.** *Did you say head?*

Once again Co-Pilot Nels Jensen keyed the HF mike, --- "Oakland Center---do you read Twentieth Century 304?"

"Five by five---how Oakland?"

"Uh---you're loud and clear---we're level at twelve thousand feet."

"Are you requesting a higher?"

Co-Pilot Nory Ellis looked around at me in askance?

I checked the **How Goes It Chart---I** shook my head **NO**---said, "It will be at least another thirty to forty minutes."

"Oakland Center---we're too heavy at this time---be another thirty plus minutes."

"That will work---we have conflicting traffic above you. First one is twenty miles---eleven o'clock---your position."

Nels and I strained our eyeballs into the darkness---looking for the two **RED** rotating beacons and the---

---RED & GREEN NAVIGATION LIGHTS---
*****

Green light's on the right---
5 letters in the word **G-R-E-E-N**---*5 letters in the word* **R-I-G-H-T**
Leastways that's the only way I could remember it when I first started out in aviation.
*****

"There he is---Nels."

"Where? I don't see him."

"He's more at our ten o'clock position."

I had 20/10 vision in my left eye and 20/20 in my right eye up until I was 63. Never wore sunglasses.

"Yea---Okay. Oakland Center---Twentieth Century 304---got the traffic in sight. He's at our ten o'clock position."

"Yea---Twentieth---that's him and there are two more behind him. One World Airways Super Connie and the second one is Northwest Orient SevenOSeven on its inaugural flight---twenty miles in trail of each other. We can let you climb up as soon as they get by you---that's if you're light enough to climb."

"Thanks Oakland---you'll be the first to know."

"No doubt in my mind---Twentieth---we need a position report before the hour---go ahead."

"Roger We can do that---we'll talk to you then. Twentieth Century---over and out."

I waited till ten minutes before the hour---woke up Nory Ellis, ---**"Nory, Oakland Center needs a position report within the next ten minutes."**

Navigator Nory Ellis stood on his chair and took a look through the **SEXTANT**---sat down---turned on the **LORAN**.

*****

What's a LORAN---you might ask. Nory explained it to me and if I can remember right---The LORAN (Low Frequency---curvature of the earth reception like High Frequency (HF).

The LORAN takes a fix between three stations and the airplane is located where these three fixes intersect---me thinks.

*****

Within five minutes---from the time I woke him up---**NORY ELLIS** the **NAVIGATOR** ---was handing the **POSITION REPORT** to **CO-PILOT NELS JENSEN,** ---**"Turn left another fifteen degrees, Nels.** That wind is blowing out of the South a lot more than was reported and we're getting too far north of course."

Navigator Nory Ellis looked at me with his Cheshire Cat Grin, ---"Next time---don't wake me up so early."

Navigator Nory Ellis was the best and he knew it. He ate an orange and went back to nite-nite land.

Thirty minutes later, ---

"NELS---OUR FUEL BURN OFF FIGURES ON THE HOW GOES IT CHART SHOWS US LIGHT ENOUGH TO CLIMB TO FIFTEEN THOUSAND FEET."

Co-Pilot Nels Jensen felt the urgency in my voice---depressed the HF Mike button, ---**"Oakland Center---this is Twentieth Century 304---we need to climb to fifteen thousand feet---WE NEED TO CLIMB NOW."**

Oakland Center felt the urgency in Jensen's voice, ---"Twentieth Century 304---we need a position report---**WE NEED IT NOW."**

Our loud voices had awakened Nory and he had already had taken the Sextant and Loran Fixes. Navigator Nory Ellis handed Co-Pilot Nels Jensen the **POSITION REPORT WHICH** Nels passed on to Oakland Center.

Oakland Center read back our **Position Report** then said, --- **"TWENTIETH CENTURY AIRLINES FLIGHT 304, CLIMB IMMEDIATELY TO FIFTEEN THOUSAND FEET---report out of thirteen thousand feet."**

"Roger---**Twentieth Century Flight 304 is cleared to climb to fifteen thousand feet**----we'll give you a call out of thirteen."

"Give me climb power---Beck."

I did.

"Oakland Center, this is Twentieth Century 304 out of thirteen thousand."

"Roger Twentieth Century 304---thanks----no hurry to fifteen thousand---call level at fifteen thousand, please."

"Wilco"

I retarded the throttles, just a little, to conserve our precious gasoline. The rate of climb dropped from 700 feet per minute to 300 feet per minute.

The aged DC-6 creaked and groaned and moaned.

Nels looked at the **RATE OF CLIMB** instrument---looked at the throttles---looked at me---shrugged his shoulders---looked out his side-sliding glass window at the Pacific Ocean in full moon splendor.

We finally reached 17,000 feet. I set cruise power and leaned the mixture controls to the point of engine coughing, and then enrichened the mixture controls just a scoche to stop the engines from sputtering.

Dirty Dan snored---Nels watched the moonlit Pacific Ocean fly by---Nory snored---Me---I watched the chronometer on the Captain's instrument panel and entered the fuel burn on the **How Goes It Chart---every fifteen minutes.**

Unless the headwinds increased significantly, ---we should touch down at the **Honolulu International Airport** with more than enough fuel to meet our over water fuel FAA requirement limitation of **one and a half hours of reserve fuel.**

We had been airborne five hours and only six more to go.

*****

Being that I haven't anything to do for this next hour, except listen to Dirty and Nory snore and look at the Pacific Ocean---I'll write you a scary story that Dirty Dan told me when we were having drinks at the Drifter's Reef Bar on the Atoll of Wake Island.

CAPTAIN DANIEL TIBBETT'S---story---

"We were just about at the POINT OF NO RETURN, on the way to Honolulu from the States, when Gina came into the cockpit and told me that a drunken Indian Paratrooper was raising all kinds of hell in the aft cabin."

"It was my first trip with Gina and I was trying to impress her so I got out of my seat and went back to the aft cabin. Sure enough there was a paratrooper sitting all by his lonesome in the middle seat of a full airplane---**'AN APACHE INDIAN THE SIZE OF ARIZONA".**

"Still hoping to impress Gina into shedding "cotton" at the Honolulu Biltmore Hotel after we arrived, I got in the Apache Paratroopers face and said,"---**"KNOCK OFF THE BULLSHIT OR I'M GONNA KICK YOUR ASS."**

"HE DID"

"Then, in a half-a-heartbeat, the Apache Paratrooper methodically reached up---put his left-arm around my neck---lowered my face into his piss-wet crotch."

"I held my breath and kicked my legs frantically, which I hoped were still attached to my body and in the aisle where someone might see and come to my aid."

"NO ONE CAME"

"**The Apache Paratrooper eventually released me** out of his Half Nelsen. I **ran** back up into the cockpit as fast as I could---jumping over the trash in the aisle. That is the last time that I ever went back into the cabin, except to piss, while in flight."

"Didn't matter to Gina though---she started taking her laundry off before we got to my room at the Honolulu Waikiki Hotel."

"LET THAT BE A LESSON TO YOU BECK."

I DIDN'T
Or as
CAPTAIN JOHN FRAZIER
Used to say
"YOU LIVE AND YOU DON'T LEARN"

I was flying Flight Engineer for Captain John Stuckher on the Lockheed L-188 Electra. We were taxiing out for tak---oops ten minute before the hour---gotta wake Nory---I'll finish this at the end of this **CIRCA.**

*****

"Nory---wake up---it's ten till the hour."

I watched in amazement as Nory went from a sound sleep---did a star fix on the Sextant---did a triangular fix on Loran---penciled it in on the **Position Report,** ---hand the position report to Co-Pilot Nels Jensen and say,---"Turn left twenty degrees---looks like our one hundred knot headwind is becoming a quartering crosswind from the South. We're a lot further north of our course than I like. Hold this course for thirty minutes---then turn back right ten degrees. It looks like we're going to land at least thirty minutes ahead of our scheduled **Flight Plan.**"

Navigator Nory Ellis watched as Co-Pilot Nels Jensen turned the auto-pilot knob to the left and turn it back to center when the desired 20 degree left heading was attained—ate a **"BIG ORANGE"**---lay down and snored. This whole process, from eyes open to eyes closed, took less than five minutes.

NORY ELLIS the NAVIGATOR WAS THE BEST---
And he knew it.

I entered Nory's **Position Report** in the **How Goes It Chart---CHECKED AND RECHECKED the fuel burn that I had recorded off of the fuel flow meters**---tapped Co-Pilot Nels Jensen on the shoulder, ---"Nels---we will be at our **POINT OF NO RETURN** fifty-five minutes past the hour."

"Thanks Beck. I'll tell Oakland Center."

"Oakland Center---this is Twentieth Century Airlines 304, ---How do you read?"

"Five by Five---Twentieth Century 304. How me?"

"Loud and clear, Oakland. Twentieth Century Flight 304 will be at our **POINT OF NO RETURN** at fifty-five past the hour."

"Roger Twentieth Century Airlines 304. Appears the winds have switched around to the South. You're already thirty minutes ahead of your scheduled estimated time of arrival at Honolulu. Contact Honolulu Center on one-zero-point-eight."

"Roger---one zero point eight. Twentieth Century Airlines over and out."

"Roger---Twentieth Century Airlines 304---**OUT.**"

"Honolulu Center, ---This is Twentieth Century Airlines 304 at seventeen thousand feet. How do you read?"

"Five by five---Twentieth Century 304. This is Honolulu Center. How me?"

"You're loud and clear, Honolulu Center. We're just about forty minutes from our **POINT OF NO RETURN.** We'll give you a position report then."

"Uh---that's not going to work. We have a Boeing 707 jet above you that's declared an emergency---pressurization problem and we have to get him down to ten thousand feet as soon as possible. We need a **POSITION REPORT** as soon as possible---**over.**"

"NORY---Honolulu Center needs a position report right away."

"Yea---uh---okay---Beck. What time is it?"

"It's not our hourly position report. They want to descend a disabled 707 through our altitude and they need our location."

"Okay---give me a second------------------------here ya are Nels."

Co-Pilot Nels Jensen gave Honolulu Center the position report, then said, ---"We should be getting Ocean Station November soon."

OCEAN STATION NOVEMBER---a weather station--- was a Coast Guard Cutter anchored mid-way between Hawaii and the United States.

Ocean Station November was also used for **sea rescue.**

It was a welcome sight for airliners giving them reassurance that they were on course **"along the longest airway in the world without a piece of real estate to land on".**

Co-Pilot Nels Jensen keyed the VHF mike, ---"Ocean Station November---do you read Twentieth Century 304?"

"Loud and Clear---Twentieth Century Airlines 304. Good Morning."

Co-Pilot Nels Jensen looked over the position report that he had given to Honolulu Center, ---"Twentieth 304 is in your South-East grid."

"We confirm that---we have you on radar and can see you visually."

The sun was rising behind us.

Nels and I stared out his sliding side window. Nory opened the Cockpit door and shouted for Gina & Tina to come up and join us.

We scanned the early morning Pacific Ocean for the **Coast Guard Cutter November**.

Gina & Tina maneuvered their bodies so they could rub their tits on the back of my head while scanning the Pacific Ocean.

Captain Dirty Dan Tibbetts snored.

I saw Ocean Station November first, ---**"There it is---about our two-thirty position."** *20-20 vision and I never wore sunglasses---on or off the airplane.*

Nels keyed the VHF Mike, ---"We have you in sight---**nice to see a pretty face out here."**

"Ha-Ha---Thanks---I needed that---see you on the way back---have a good one Twentieth."

"Roger---over and out."

Navigator Nory Ellis ate a **BIG ORANGE** and went back beddy-bye---Captain Dan Tibbetts snored---Me???---I was in the twilight zone.

*****

The reason I put **BIG ORANGE** *in* **bold** *capital letters is because I found out later that the best of the Navigators would take oranges and lace them with syringes of Vodka. In other words---they were eating* **SCREW-DRIVERS AND SLEEPING** *across the Ocean---interrupted only by a few minutes each hour of taking fixes on the stars.*

"Not a bad job---if you can get it."
On the flip side of the "kern" as Norton used to say on
---*"THE HONEYMOONERS"*---

The worst of navigators stayed awake---THEY *were always climbing up and down off their chairs to look through the Sextant---making annoying noises and keeping everyone awake.---One of which got us so badly lost going into Tokyo that the Japanese Air Force scrambled up after us. I'll write you about that one later.*

*****

It has been close to forty hours since I have slept. I was seeing animals coming out of the fuel flow gauges that I knew did not exist.

I looked at Co-Pilot Nels Jensen. Nels was bright eyed and **bushy tailed. Another animal that I knew did not exist.**

I checked out each and every spark plug on the---

---IGNITION ANALYZER OSCILLOSCOPE---

Hoping that some distraction from watching the fuel flow gauges would fire up some adrenalin.

Didn't fill the ticket.

I asked "bushy tailed" Nels if he wanted some coffee and that I would go back and get us some.

Nels looked around at me with the eyes of a hoot owl that had red and yellow flames dancing in them, ---"No---no thanks Beck. I don't need caffeine to stay awake and beside that, I got a good five hours sleep at the motel."

"Sure---okay," as I stood up, turned around and folded up my ¾ inch thick, naugahyde covered, ass bustin' Flight Engineer's seat and attached it to the bulkhead along side the---

---IGNITION ANALYZER---

I carefully stepped over a snoring Nory with orange saliva oozing from his mouth, exited the cockpit door, which was on the side of the cockpit, rather than the middle, and went back into the passenger cabin.

I literally had to crawl over a mountain of trash to get into the passenger cabin. Gina and Tina were somewhere in the back of the cabin---serving their second meal.

I poured a tepid cup of coffee from one of the carry-on urns in the forward galley, that I found behind a mountain of trash, that was put on at Travis and chug-a-lugged that puppy.

Poured me two-to-go and juggled my way over trash back up into the cockpit.

I mis-stepped on Nory's gonads on the way back to my station. Didn't faze a Screwdrivered Nory. Nory never missed a snore-beat.

I put one cup of coffee in its designated holder and the other cup on top of the ignition analyzer, which was a no-no, unfolded my ass-bustin seat and sat down.

I offered a cup of, now cold, java to Co-Pilot Nels Jenson who once again looked like the man I first met in Burbank.

Nels said, ---"No thanks---I can go for days without sleep. I don't need caffeine to do it. Besides that---I don't drink airplane coffee---period."

With that in mind---I laid my head against the ignition analyzer.

!!!STARTLED ---I WOKE UP!!!
I KNEW SOMETHING WAS AMISS.
!!!WE WERE ALL ASLEEP!!!

I reached up to the overhead and pulled the HF Mike out of its wire grip---**SHOOK** a "I can go days without sleep" sleeping Co-Pilot Nels Jensen by the shoulder---handed Nels the Mike---hollering, ---"NORY---NORY---WAKE UP"!!!!

"What's happening---where are we---where are my oranges?"

"WE NEED A POSITION REPORT NORY, ---I fell asleep."

Nels, ---**"HONOLULU CENTER---this is TWENTIETH CENTURY 304---DO YOU READ---DO YOU READ---DO YOU READ!?!?!?"**

"Twentieth Century Airlines 304---this is Honolulu Center---I read you five by five. How me?"

"LOUD AND CLEAR---LOUD AND CLEAR."

"No need to shout---Twentieth---I can hear you very well. What's your position?"

"Standby" Co-Pilot Nels Jensen whispered as he picked the **Position Report** up from beneath his rudder pedals where Navigator Nory Ellis had thrown it in his groggy haste.

Co-Pilot Nels Jensen read the **Position Report** to Honolulu Center---turned on the **over head speaker.**

"Where have you guys been? We've been trying to reach you since you first reported in close to two hours ago. **YOU GUYS BEEN SLEEPING???**

!!!"SLEEPING!!!SLEEPING!!!NOBODY'S SLEEPING"!!!

SHOUTED ---Captain Daniel Tibbetts **as** he rose from the dead.

Nels, ---"Oh---no---no way. We've been trying to reach you with our last two hourly **Position Reports** and all we could hook up to was Houston Center. Oh---this is Twentieth Century 304."

"Houston Center???---O—kaaay. Well this is Honolulu Center. We need another **Position Report** on the hour. What's your estimated remaining time in route and your **FUEL ON BOARD?"**

"Stand by Hous---er---Honolulu," Co-Pilot Nels Jensen uttered as he looked around at Nory and I with a wink, ---**"How are we doin'---guys?"**

Beck, ---"Nory has us **FLIGHT PLANNED** for ten hours and five minutes and according to our **How Goes It Chart**---we should land with over two hours of **RESERVE FUEL."**

Nory, ---"Yea---Nels---that one hundred knot head wind has turned into a direct fifty knot crosswind. I'm glad you fell asleep and didn't turn back right ten degrees like I told you because we would have been looking at landing at Anchorage. Just kidding, but we would have been way too far North of our course---probably would have used up all that time we saved when the headwind quit."

"Honolulu Center, this is Twentieth Century Airlines 304."

"Go ahead Twentieth 304."

"Twentieth Century 304 estimating Honolulu in ---
**---TWO HOURS AND TWENTY MINUTES---
---TWO HOURS OF RESERVE FUEL---
---NINETY EIGHT SOULS ON BOARD---"**

"Roger Twentieth Century Airlines---we need one more **POSITION REPORT.** Call it in at fifteen past the hour."

"Roger---Twentieth Century Airlines---WILCO."

*****

*After the sleeping incident of "sleeping on the job" ---for the rest of my flying years---I could not sleep in the **COCK---PIT** and had a hard time, even falling asleep in the passenger cabin no matter how tired I was. ---*
!!!GOT MY ATTENTION!!!
*****
???"COCK---PIT"???
We now have female aviators in the cock-pit and the term is now
---SEE-YOU-NTEE---PIT---
*Just kidding the feminists.
The term is now*
---FLIGHT STATION---
*****

Captain Daniel Tibbetts listened to the fiasco with a bored look on his face.

Apparently sleeping and missing radio calls was part of the job---nothing to get excited about.

Dirty Dan reached up to the overhead panel and pushed the Stewardess Call button.

"**GINA---I want my coffee---I want it now."**

Gina dropped everything but her drawers. Gina was saving that part for later. Gina---in less than a minute--- "squeezed" by Nory---handed Dirty Dan his coffee and was rubbing her tits on the back of my head.

Gina knew that Dirty Dan was a grouch when he woke up and didn't have his caffeine in his gut.

GINA & TINA
In the last 8 hours had served ---
---BREAKFAST---LUNCH---DINNER---
Gina looked a little disheveled, but none the worse for wear.
---Pretty lady---

Dirty Dan--sitting side saddle facing us--- looked at me, --- "Why don't you go in the back for a while---you've done your part---take a break and come back up when we start letting down."
What a neat Captain---he looks out for his crew.
!!!WRONG!!!
I stood up---turned around and folded up my Naugahyde covered, ¾ inch, marine plywood seat.

Gina titted by me and sat in Dirty Dan's lap. Nory backed into the passenger cabin so I could depart the cockpit.

I entered the passenger cabin.
INSTANT URPY---PUKESVILLE
The stench of puke and baby shit permeated the place. I walked up and down the aisle trying to get rid of my nausea.

Didn't work.

I went back up into the cockpit. Gina was sitting on my Naugahyde covered, ¾ inch, marine plywood seat---with Dirty Dan's hand up her skirt---with a smile on her face.

Co-Pilot Nels Jensen, always the gentleman, was watching the Pacific Ocean fly by.

Navigator Nory Ellis was standing behind Gina---doing his Cheshire Cat imitation---with one hand.

I blanched---blushed---went back into the passenger cabin. Haint nuthin' like this ever happened on the Graveyard Shift.

Once again I walked up and down the aisle to keep from up-chuckin'.

The overhead bins, the **EMERGENCY EXITS** and the galleys were crammed with trash left from Gina & Tina serving------
---breakfast---lunch---dinner---.

Every exit was filled to the maximum. If we had to **DITCH** into the Pacific Ocean---there was no chance of "exiting the aircraft in an orderly manner".

How do you prefer your demise?
???SHARK CHUM or DROWNING???

Gina finally came back into the passenger cabin and I went back into the cockpit.

Dirty Dan had a smile on his face.

Co-Pilot Nels Jensen was watching the Pacific Ocean fly by.

Navigator Nory Ellis was Cheshire Cat grinning with one hand.

They knew that they had embarrassed the rookie.

Co-Pilot Nels Jensen made his last call to Honolulu Center.

Just about that time---the #1 & #2 **AUTOMATIC DIRECTION FINDER** needles slewed around a couple of times---then steadied out---right on the nose. Navigator Nory Ellis tapped me on the shoulder---pointed at the gauges---Cheshire Cat grinned, ---"I told you so."

NAVIGATOR NORY ELLIS---was the best.

Nory knew it and everyone that ever flew with him knew it.

WE LANDED

The Crew that was taking over the airplane met us at the bottom of the ramp. Dirty Dan briefed-----**CAPTAIN BUD PLOSSER**---As to the condition of the Mighty DC-6 and the winds aloft.

I briefed **FLIGHT ENGINEER DICK GREENBERG on** the mechanical we had at Travis and other minor squawks that I had encountered---stressing the sticking fuel gauge.

Hawaii was not yet a State and we had to go through customs. The weary passengers deplaned and were herded into a holding area with bleacher seats. They had more than eighteen hours before they touched down in Tokyo.

We crammed into a taxi---Nory and I got to sit in the front seat---naturally.

Captain Dirty Dan uncorked a quart of Canadian Club—passed it around---offered the Cabbie a drink, which he took,---said, ---"Waikiki Biltmore and don't hurry."

The cab driver didn't and took the last swig as he pulled up curbside.

Me? I had two small swigs and was on my butt. I couldn't remember the last time that I had slept. The sun looked about noonish.

Dirty Dan checked us in.

I took my room key, waved goodbye to everyone---went to my room---hit the sack---comatosed.

They were building hotels everywhere in Honolulu.

THE JET AGE had arrived.

A person could "707 JET" to Hawaii in less than half the time it took a Douglas DC-6 or a Lockheed Constellation 1049G airplane.

The tourist trade was ten-fold. ---That's the good news.

The bad news?

Hotel rooms were still one-fold. "No room at the inn."

The good news?

Plenty of warm beaches to camp out on.

In order to build a hotel in Honolulu---they had to sink 6-foot diameter pipes---100 feet into the sand---then fill them with concrete.

It took massive pile drivers to do this.

Massive pile drivers made mucho noiso.

Massive pile drivers piled 24 hours a day---7 days a week.

Haint no-body gonna snooze---except me.

"ALLS WELL THAT ENDS WELL"

PRFPACPJM

--- CIRCA ---

ONE WEEK BEFORE

---A SLICK SLEEPING STORY---

I gotta write just one more story while "sleeping on air" is the topic of this CIRCA. This event occurred a week before our "sleep flying" episode. ---

A Slick Brothers Airlines DC-6A-Cargo Plane was less than 100 miles from Hawaii---inbound from the States---cruising at 2,000 feet.

The flight crew fell asleep. The auto-pilot got a bad signal and clicked off. The DC-6A pan-caked into the Pacific Ocean.

The Co-Pilot and Flight Engineer were killed on impact.

There was one soul on board---a Japanese Cook that was sleeping in the aft cabin.

The Captain grabbed his "Mae West", which is a life jacket, when inflated---so named that you look like Mae West---from the neck to the belly button.

The Captain opened his side sliding-glass window---maneuvered his body out into the Pacific Ocean---pulled the drawstrings to inflate his life jacket---didn't work---he then inflated his Mae West by blowing in the tubes installed for that occasion.

*****

Dja hear about the guy that blew in his blonde-airhead girlfriend's ear???

She said---"Thanks for the refill."

*****

The fuel tanks were nearly empty giving the DC-6A buoyancy like an inflated raft.

The Captain swam back to the left wing and pulled himself up on it. The DC-6A floated for several hours and then began to sink. The Captain somehow managed to pull himself on top of the fuselage.

Soon the airplane started to nose over.

The Captain crawled along the top of the fuselage toward the empennage. *(Tail section)* As he crawled by the aft cargo door---he could hear the Japanese Cook banging on the aft cargo door trying to get out---apparently trapped when the cargo shifted upon impact.

The Mighty DC-6A Cargo plane gave up the ghost and descended to Davy Jones locker.

The Captain jumped off before it sank and swam away, with mucho gusto, ---from the aluminum coffin that would be sure to suck him down to his drowning.

The Japanese cook Sayonara-ed with the air-ship.

The Captain tread water and soon The Rising Sun came up out of the Eastern Ocean.

Now---the Captain could see that he was in a Conestoga wagon surrounded by many Indians---only these Indians had dorsal fins and his Conestoga wagon was salt water.

At first they were far away swimming in a circle around him.

The circle began to tighten.
CHOW-TIME---FEEDING-FRENZY-
!!!MUNCHY-MUNCHY-CRUNCHY-CRUNCHY!!!

A coast guard cutter, that was dispatched to the area when the Mighty DC-6A flew off the Honolulu Center Radar Screen---

---SHOWED UP---

The Coast Guard Cutter Sailors shot at the sharks---killing some and wounding some. The unharmed lawy---oops---I mean sharks turned on their wounded brethren and forgot the Captain. The sailors pulled the Captain---**ALIVE**---out of the Pacific Ocean.

LIFE OR DEATH
IS A MATTER OF TIMING

"ALLS WELL THAT ENDS WELL"

PRFPACPJM
*****

LOVE IS LIKE AN ICECUBE
ONCE IT MELTS
IT'S GONE
*****

"Got any naked pictures of your wife???"
"!!!HELL NO!!!"
"Wanna buy some???"

*****
"Where's the remote??" "Which one???"
"Turn it on at the set."
"I don't know how."
*****

I watched a porno movie with one hand.
*****

If your sweat soldering a copper pipe and that last trickle of water keeps the solder below the melting point---jam a piece of bread sans crust into the copper pipe---samo-samo with PVC.
*****

This is the story that I promised you at the end of this **CIRCA**---the one that Captain Dirty Dan went into the cabin and the Apache Paratrooper almost throttled him.

Remember---Dirty Dan warned me about going into the passenger cabin when some kind of disturbance was happening.   .

I'll take it from the top when **Captain Dirty Dan Tibbetts** looked at me and said---

"LET THAT BE A LESSON TO YOU BECK"
I DIDN'T
Or as---
CAPTAIN JOHN FRAZIER
Used to say---

"YOU LIVE AND YOU DON'T LEARN"

Next page ---please.

--- CIRCA ---

1-NINER-63

SCENARIO

AIRPLANE---LOCKHEED ELECTRA L-188
CAPTAIN---JOHN STUCKHER
CO-PILOT---CAPTAIN JOHN POWELL
FLIGHT ENGINEER---BECK
STEWARDESS---ANN GARAFALO
STEWARDESS---LORETTA COPPNEY
DEPARTURE AIRPORT---SAN DIEGO---SAN
DESTINATION AIRPORT---BURBANK---BUR

ACT I

First&Final Act

Upon taxiing out for take-off---Stewardess Ann Garafalo burst into the cockpit crying, ---"There's a wild man back there raising all kinds of hell. He's standing up in the aisle and won't sit down."

We didn't have to open the cockpit door---it was latched wide open at all times.

Captain John Stuckher set the parking brakes, turned to me, ---"Go back there and set him down Beck."

"Okay"

I stood up---folded up the Flight Engineer's seat---snapped it to the bulkhead---oops---wrong airplane. I got out of my easy chair and followed Stewardess Ann Garafalo into the passenger compartment.

Ann made a left turn and went into the Forward Galley.

Me???---I stood face to belt buckle that read---**P-O-L-A-C-K.**

I looked up at a mountain of a man that was so tall that his head was bowed toward me because his neck was against the overhead.

I pointed my right index finger up at him and meekly said, --- "If you don't sit down, we're going back to the gate and have you taken off the airplane."

"Oh---I'm so sorry sir. I didn't know that I was doing anything wrong. Of course I'll sit down. Please forgive me."

I went back up into the cockpit---sat down. Captain John Stuckher was busy reading his Girlie Magazine with one hand *not a joke* ---completely unaware of what had happened.

Co-Pilot---Captain John Powell, a 6 foot 6 inch goliath himself, had been watching the fiasco through the open cockpit door, ---"Man that is one big mother-fucker Beck. --- What dja do to make him sit down?"

"I don't know---M-m-m-my mind went blank when I ran into his belt buckle. All I know is that he sat down and I'm sitting in m-m-m-m-my seat.

And that---ladies and gentleman---boys and girls is the first, last and only time that I went into the passenger compartment to take care of a problem.

*****

Why the cockpit door was latched open on taxi-out??? You might ask.

PSA COMPANY POLICY
FOR
PUBIC-oops---er-PUBLIC RELATIONS

The cockpit door was latched open on the first flight of the day and remained latched open till the Lockheed Electra was put to bed at night.

We had as many as six or seven passengers in the cockpit at one time. I would slide my seat back as far as it could go so the passengers could get in front of me to look out of the windows.

The women, at times, would sit on the laps of the pilots and I would hold their babies. I even burped a couple of the urpy little ones at times. Puke all over my uniform shirt.

"BABY---HOW THINGS CHANGE"---*Is that a pun?*

*****

    *The newest addition to the AH City Police Force was their first female police officer. She was assigned to Officer Wilam's Squad Car. A tall skinny **blonde**---but fuckable.*

    Officer Wilams---a heavy gambler, ---"Bet you guys 100 bucks I'll be in her pants before midnight." ---as he bought a sandwich out of the machine and left the Police station to go to his Squad Car where she was waiting.

    "We'll take that bet." His fellow Police Officers shouted after him in unison. How are you gonna prove it?"

    "I'll leave the Squad Car's radio on so you guys can listen in."

    Officer Wilams got in his Squad Car---put his sandwich on the dashboard---drove off in the AH City sunset with tall skinny blonde.

    Later that night, ---Officer Wilams parked his Squad Car along a deserted desert road---turned the Squad Cars radio on so his fellow officers could hear them---began his seduction of tall skinny blonde.

    Every thing was going according to Officer Wilams' plan until he knocked his sandwich off the Squad Car dashboard on to the Squad Car floor. He picked it up and started to take a bite.

    "You're not gonna eat that dirty thing---Are you?"
!!!"SAY SANDWICH---SAY SANDWICH"!!!

*****

--- CIRCA ---

12 JUNE---1-NINER-5-NINER

"RING---RING---RI--"

"Uhhh---uh—yea---hello."
"This is Dirty Dan---wanna join us for breaky?"
"Uhhh---uhh---**sure**---what time is it?"
"I dunno---we just watched the sun rise on Waikiki Beach."
*****
"When the sun goes down in Honolulu---I'll go down on you."
"NEAT---NEAT---NEAT"
CAPTAIN JOHN FRAZIER
*****

"I'll be right down," ---as I scrutured out of bed.

I took a long, cold shower trying to get the grutchies out of my gourd and went down to the Coffee Shop.

Nobody there. ---**N-A-D-A**

I asked the waitress where they might have gone.

"Who?"

"My flight crew---a bunch of pilots and stewardesses."

"Haint nobody been in here this morning yet."

MY THOUGHT---"They're funnin' the nonsked rookie."

The waitress handed me a menu and I sat down.

Captain Tibbetts walked in, ---"Where the hell you been? **What the hell ya doin' sittin' in the coffee shop?"**

"You told me that you guys were having breakfast."

"Oh---oh---okay. We're having breaky in the bar. Follow me."

I did.

As we neared the Waikiki Biltmore Hotel bar, I could hear screaming and shouting and laughter from inside.

MY THOUGHT---Nobody could be partying at this hour.

!!!WRONG!!!

The bar was packed, *standing room only*, with Non-Sked Crews&Stews. Some still in uniform---some departing---some arriving---some about to cum---er---come..

The bar was capacitated with martini glasses---everyone was juiced---on their keesters. They were old friends and had been through many crises together---both on and off the airplane and they knew when to party hearty. Which looked to me, a rookie Non-Skeddar, **anytime that they weren't on an airplane.**

I nursed a couple of Japanese Asahi Rice beers and watched the action.

A few Crews&Stews paired off and left.

The uniformed Crews&Stews slowly left for the Honolulu Airport.

The remaining Stews&Crews screamed and shouted and laughed.

???Me???---I was on my butt. I said bye, which nobody heard, and went back to my room beddy-bye.

I didn't even stop for "breaky".

--- CIRCA ---

Same day---only later.
Hooray Hoo---heck, it haint even May.

"RING---RING---RI-"
"Hello."
"This is Dirty Dan, ---We're going to Do Hos for dinner."
"Wanna come along?"
"Yea---sure---thanks."
"We're in the lobby---hurry on down---we'll wait for you."
"Yea---sure---thanks."

I showered one more time---got dressed and elevatored down to the lobby.

---Standing room only---

The Crews&Stews that had departed for their flights were replaced by the incoming Crews&Stews. Everyone was having one helluva good time.

Kissin&huggin'---dancin'&romancin'.

Passing the quarts of Canadian Club and Beefeaters Gin around the room.

We crammed into some taxi cabs and went to Don Ho's.

The Crews&Stews didn't wait to be seated---just pushed the tables and chairs around to suit their own seating arrangement. DeMaitre'd just watched.

DeMaitre'd had seen "the wild bunch" in action before.

DeMaitre'd knew that to intervene would be futile.

DeWaitresse warily approached us.

DeWaitresse, too, had seen the Non-Skeddars in hand-to-mouth Martini combat before.

"MARTINS"
"Martinis for everyone." Shouted Dirty Dan, ---"I'm buying."
"???MARTINIS???"
DeWaitresse said with raised eyebrows.

We were in Hawaii and drinking Martinis. DeWaitresse look was a scowl. We should be drinking Mai Taïs or some other exotic Hawaiian drink.

"I believe I said MARTINIS," was Dirty Dan's curt reply.

She left.
---THE CURTAIN OPENED---
The Wahines shook their hula skirts. ---The Hollies sucked fire balls.
Don Ho sang, ---"The Hawaiian Wedding Song"
"This the moment that we've been waiting for, Aloha."
Alohaalohaalohaalohaalohaalohaalohaalohaalohaalohaalo haalohaalohaaloha&on&on&on&on&on&on&on&on---

I got so friggin' sick and tired of hearing that song over the next year that it reminded me of acetone. I'd get nauseated and want to upchuck.

They played
---"ALOHALOHALOHA"---

In every bar---every restaurant---on the streets and even in the dad-blamed elevators.

Strictly for the tourists from Flat Rock, Kansas---looking for the romance that they once had. They hadn't sniffed each others pee-pees for ten years and this trip to Hawaii for one week was going to make up for all their indifferences toward each other over the years.

I observed them

The Mainland Hollies drank Mai Tais. ---Got wasted. ---Passed out.

The Mainland Wahines ogled the crotches of the fire eating natives. ---Stroked themselves. ---Passed out.

This was Hawaiian foreplay and it only cost them two thousand bucks to get---**LEI-ED.**

Ma and Pa Kettle could have went out in their pasture in Flat Rock, Kansas, watched the goats mount each other and got turned on for the price of a Mason jar of White Lightning and a couple of T-Bone steaks.

Heck, I would have even gone there and sang the Hawaiian Wedding Song for them.

How's that song go???
"ALOHA---ALOHA---ALOHA"

See---I heard it so many times that I remember the words.

We had some more drinks and then ate---after all, we had to check in for our flight to----
---THE ATOLL OF WAKE ISLAND---IN FOUR HOURS---

Atoll---a ring shaped Coral Island nearly or completely surrounding a lagoon

We walked back to the Biltmore Hotel. The Crews&Stews went to "their" respective rooms. I went to bed, solo, with my clothes on---couldn't sleep---got back up and walked the streets of Honolulu trying to relax and sober up at the same time.
Is that possible???

"Aloha-Aloha-Aloha. This is our wedding day." was everywhere that I went. Pukesville---Hawaii was a phony tourist trap.

No matter what you did or where you went, somebody had their hand out for a tip. If you didn't tip, they would actually snarl at you and walk away waving their arms shouting obscenities. If you did tip, and they thought it was too small, they would look at you and shake their head in disgust.

Their **GOD---KAMATACHEEWHOTHEFUC** taught them how to fleece the tourists well.

!!!TIME TO FLY!!!

We met in the Biltmore Hotel Lobby at midnight and taxied to the---
HONOLULU INTERNATIONAL AIRPORT.

The Stews went out to the airplane to help clean up. The Stews worked a litta-no-a-lotta harder in those days.

Yadafitinwell **STEWARDESS MUFFIE BURKE.**

---CREWMEMBERS---
CAPTAIN DANIEL TIBBETS
CO-PILOT NELS JENSEN
NAVIGATOR NORY ELLIS
FLIGHT ENGINEER BECK ---

Went into Honolulu Airport Flight Operations.

"Wind is out of the West at **ONE HUNDRED-FIFTY KNOTS,**" was the first and only thing that the Operations Briefing Officer said.

Got Dirty Dan's attention, ---a seven hour piece of pie flight was going to turn into a nine hour piece of pie crust marathon flight.

"Beck, we're flight planned for twenty three thousand pounds of fuel. Put on twenty six thousand pounds. Two thousand pounds for the headwinds---one thousand pounds for grandma."

*****

Gasoline weighs 6.7 pounds. You figure out how many gallons we had. I'm a half-assed author that's been writing on this friggin book for 15 years, make it 16 years, now make it 17 years, not a mathematician and besides that, all the gauges are calibrated in pounds. So haint nobody cares how many gallons we had---do you?
*****

Grandma fuel---You are an old lady and need the extra fuel as a crutch to help your get-a-long.
*****

Honolulu Operations Briefing Officer**,** ---"Captain Dan Tibbett**, y**our aircraft is at the terminal and needs to be fueled**."**

"Beck, taxi over to the fueling docks and put twenty-six thousand pounds of fuel on her."

As Don Ho would sing, ---**"This is the moment that I've been waiting for."**

I was in hog heaven, squattin' in tall cotton and the thrill of my life was about to happen.

I got to sit in the left seat and taxi a big airliner.

I went on board, closed all the doors and sat in the coveted left seat.

I looked out the right side-window.

I was somebody. ---**Captain Beck**.

I was wallowing like a pig in mud.
*****

His name is mud---

Mudd was the doc that set John Wilkes Booth's broken leg after he assassinated Abe Lincoln.
*****

I looked out the left side window. A Maui Mechanic was swinging his right hand around in a circular motion and pointing at the # 4 engine indicating to me that it was clear to start the #4 Engine.

The # 4 engine started without incident---not even a kapow.

The Maui Mech walked over to the left side of the DC-6 and with a circular motion of his right hand, pointed at the # 1 engine with his left hand and gave me clearance to start it.

I commenced the start cycle on the # 1 engine.

KAPOW

It backfired and spewed burning fuel all over the engine and the tarmac.

It was midnight, but the terminal was aglow like it was "High Noon".

"Do not foreskin me oh my darling."

My **left** hand fingers and thumb were manipulating the starter switches which are located on the overhead panel to my right. I couldn't let go of the starter switch because if I kept the engine turning, it **might** start and suck the burning fuel back into the engine and extinguish the flames, ---like maybe put out the fire.

  I looked under my left armpit and saw many Maui Mechs with fire extinguishers, scurrying around, ---putting out fires.

   The engine finally started. All the fires were extinguished.

    Once more midnight descended on the Mighty DC-6.

"ALL'S WELL THAT ENDS WELL"

PRFPITACPJM

  "Honolulu Ground Control, this is Twentieth Century. Need to taxi to the fueling docks."

  "Aircraft that's on fire and keying the mike---Honolulu Ground haint reading ya old buddy." *Snickering*

    I tried again---a little bit louder, ---
"HONOLULU GROUND CONTROL, --- THIS IS TWENTIETH CENTURY."
"NEED TO TAXI TO THE FUELING DOCKS."

"Twentieth Century Airlines, we can barely read you. Say again."

  I looked at the mike. I was so clanked up over trying to burn up/down the Honolulu International Airport Terminal, that I had it turned around and was speaking into the back side of the mike.

  I finally got clearance to taxi from Honolulu Ground Control and taxied to the fuel depot. I fueled up the DC-6's main gas tanks to the brim. I put on an extra thousand pounds for my grandma and taxied the DC-6 back to the terminal.

Now we were four thousand pounds over maximum gross take-off weight.

    Hell, that's only two tons.

Captain Daniel Tibbetts entered the cockpit---sat in the Co-Pilot seat, ---

"Heard there was an airplane on fire out here. Know anything about it?"

    "Nah never saw it."

  Captain Dirty Dan Tibbetts might not let me taxi his airplane again if he knew I almost put it into aluminum ashes like the "Phoenix."

Nah---Dirty Dan would just grab Gina and go back to the Biltmore Hotel and tell me to call him when I got it fixed.

We loaded our passengers on board and took off for---

---THE ATOLL OF WAKE ISLAND---

*Wake Island is a tiny **coral isle**---halfway between Hawaii and Japan.*

---OVERGROSSED---

Captain Daniel Tibbetts**, —"GEAR UP."**

Co-Pilot Nels Jensen reached down for the landing gear lever, which is located aft of the center pedestal just about where my left foot was, ---tried to put it in the **GEAR UP** position.

No dice---it wouldn't budge.

NADA

The squat switch located on the right main landing gear strut failed and did not activate the solenoid that held the landing gear handle down.

This left the landing gear lever thinking we were still on the ground.

This is a safety feature to keep some "Tinker Bell" from raising the landing gears or lowering the airframe, *depending on how you look at it*, when the airplane is on the ground.

Is the glass half-full or half-empty???---Depends on whether it's whiskey or water.

Now we have the landing gears hanging down which is a whole lot of drag and we were way over grossed---as usual.

We climbed to less than fifty feet and could go no higher.

Captain Dan Tibbetts was now maneuvering us between the new Honolulu high rise hotels and condo buildings, hollering, ---"Get the fucking gear up---**GET THE FUCKIN' GEAR UP."**

Co-Pilot Nels Jensen, a well muscled man, no longer watching the Pacific Ocean fly by, was tugging at the gear handle---"**panickidly**". ---

Nothing gave.

N-A-D-A —*NotADamnthingAnyway*

I looked down at the gear lever/handle—instant **red** out.

In Co-Pilot Nels Jensen's panic, he had turned around the red guarded light that shown on the landing gear handle.

I turned the **red** guarded light guard back around where it showed on the gear lever, --- espied the solenoid's plunger that held the landing gear lever down.

I pushed it aside with my social finger and raised the gear lever/handle.

There was a button beside the landing gear lever that released the plunger of the solenoid that was activated when the landing gears struts extended.
We were ignorant of this button.

The landing gears went into the wheel wells and our landing gear safe/unsafe lights extinguished indicating that the landing gears was up and locked.

One engine fart and we would have been part of Honolulu's landscape.
---FATE IS THE HUNTER   ERNIE GANN---
The mighty DC-6 started climbing.

Captain Daniel Tibbetts stopped shouting.

Navigator Nory Ellis patted me on the back.

Co-Pilot Nels Jensen watched the Pacific Ocean fly by.

I do know one thing though. The city of Honolulu had an early wake up call that morning.

The cockpit door flew open and in came Stews, ---Gina & Tina.

We didn't lock the cockpit door in those days. No need to. Who would want to hi-jack an airplane that reeked of puke and baby shit anyway?

Gina & Tina said as one, ---"That was the most beautiful take off we have ever seen. We could see people out on their lanais waving at us. Next time you're going to do that, tell us and we'll come up here and watch."

Captain Dirty Dan Tibbetts, never the one to miss out on a chance to be a hero, --- "That was nuthin'---I've been through there much lower than that."

Navigator Nory Ellis Cheshire Catted.

Co-Pilot Nels Jensen looked at the Pacific Ocean fly by with a full moon over it.

Fright Engineer Beck suppressed barfing & massaged the scar tissue around his aorta.

We winged on to **The Atoll of Wake Island.**

Captain Dirty Dan Tibbetts went night-night.

Co-Pilot Nels Jensen was already snoring.

Navigator Nory Ellis had a fresh supply of oranges.

Flight Engineer Beck leaned out the engines till they were farting.

We were alive and I was wide awake.

*****

In the ensuing thirty six years of flying, I could never sleep on an airplane, even when commuting or deadheading in the passenger cabin.
    The incident when we all fell asleep on the way to Honolulu lay on my psyche forever.
*****

I awakened Navigator Nory Ellis every hour.
    Nory would take a star shot with the sextant---check the Loran---make out a position report---hand it to me---eat an orange---go back to sleep.
    I'd call Honolulu Center with the position report---set the new heading with the auto-pilot turn knob---listen to the snoring.
    We flew across the International Dateline and lost a day, meaning Sunday now became Monday. I really didn't give a rat's ass because I didn't know what day it was anyway.
*****

---INTERNATIONAL DATE LINE---
---SATURDAY---EAST OF THE DATE LINE---
---SUNDAY---WEST OF THE DATE LINE---
---EAST IS LEAST AND WEST IS BEST---
*****

I met an author by the name of Wally Depew on the Atoll of Wake Island. He gave me an autographed book that he had just completed writing. Never did read it and I can't remember the name of it---I do remember it was about flying. Anyone out there in reader-land know?
*****

We landed at Wake Island just around noon-time.
"High Noon"
"Do not foreskin me oh my darling" ---*I love that song.*
High Noon---Hot & Humid   Low Midnight---Hot & Humid
    The landscape was blinding---white-sandy-white-white.
    Navigator Nory Ellis got two-sixers of Asahi, a Japanese rice beer at the Pan Am PX located in the Wake Island Airport Terminal near the **AIR CONDITIONED,** painted white Quonset Huts with **PAN AM** painted in blue letters on the roof.
This housed the elite crack aviators of---
—PAN AMERICAN AIRWAYS—

We all crammed into a 211.99 degree "renovated" World War II Red Cross Van of 1942 vintage and proceeded to our quarters on the other side of the crescent moon shaped---

---ATOLL OF WAKE ISLAND---
About two miles to domed shanty town. ---Unpainted Quonset Huts.
---Also of World War II vintage---
No air conditioning and thin partitions between the 8X8 rooms.

You could hear a person fart four rooms down the hall. The only heated water was solar. If you waited to shower until after sundown, you showered in cold water, which was apropos, because unless you imported your own "care package", ---you were going to sleep alone.

The Stews had a separate Quonset Hut nicknamed,—
—"THE IRON GIRDLE"—
There was a ten foot chain link fence around it with barbed wire on top for De-Icing **HOT Non- Skeddar-Crews and the ENTIRE Workforce of Filipinos on---**
---THE ATOLL OF WAKE ISLAND---
Kept the Filipinos out but not the wild and crazy Non-Skeddars.

*****

Co-Pilot Nels Jensen spent the day playing cards.

Co-Pilot Nels Jensen wound up in the Wake Island infirmary with second degree burns.

Co-Pilot Nels Jensen had been sitting in the shade.

*****

I drank a couple Asahis---went to bed---couldn't sleep---too hot.

Too hot to sleep. I put on my swimming trunks and went down to the lagoon which was near our *"Hotel De La Quonset"*.

A whole bunch of Crews and Stews were sitting around the lagoon drinking Asahis and raising pandemonium. I joined in.
When in Rome

I looked across the lagoon and recognized another Flight Engineer sitting all by his lonesome---picked up a couple of Asahis---left fifty cents in the cooler *(One beer, one quarter. Two beers, two quarters, etc)* ---swam across the lagoon.

It was---Flight Engineer Muldoon---who was to become my friend for life.

"Hi, ---want a beer?" dumb question.

*****

I found out later that Flight Engineer Muldoon never turned down a drink in his life. As the years went by, I found out that he never turned down a drink ---or food. I think it was, and still is, against his religion.

Muldoon---at the age of 75---is still flying Flight Engineer---started at the age of 22.

That's fifty-three (53) years as a Flight Engineer and still going strong.

That, my friend, has to be an item for the Guinness book of records.

*****

"Sure" Flight Engineer Muldoon said as he wrenched the Asahis out of my hand.

We drank beer ---swam a little to cool off---went to **THE DRIFTER'S REEF BAR.** Like our quarters, the Drifters Reef Bar was an old army Quonset hut left over from World War II, except the Drifters Reef had the luxury of two ceiling fans.

LEFTY was the bartender, a Filipino also left over from **WORLD WAR II.** Drinks were forty cents a pop and Lefty would pour until you said stop. If you meditated in silence, Lefty would fill your **water tumbler** till it overfloweth.

I had a lot of religious silent moments in the Drifter's Reef Bar.

Hallelujah Jehovah lives

Christmas still comes once a year amen---so much for Mass.

Muldoon and I got Asahi drunk---solved the problems of the world.

The bar closed and we went back to the "Beverly Hilton" Quonset hut.

All kinds of fun and games were happening---no fights---fighting would have interfered with the Non-Skeddars drinking and carousing.

Two Stews passed us in the hall "bear" assed naked.

They were casually chatting as if they were walking down an aisle at Nordstrom's.

I turned around and stared. Muldoon continued on to his room.

Two Non-Skeddars passed me like I was standing erect. ---*I was*

Two Non-Skeddars had hard-ons with towels draped over them.

Two Non-Skeddars looked like human towel racks.

Two Non-Skeddars grabbed the prize pussies.

Two Non-Skeddars took them to their rooms.

Muldoon went to his room. Muldoon had a lovely wife at home by the name of **JO ANNE** back in Long Beach, California—who, ---Muldoon was very much in love with and didn't want any out side inn-trusions.

Joanne and Muldoon are still a happily married, as a matter of fact---

*****

Muldoon & JOANNE ---

Recently celebrated their 50TH WEDDING ANNIVERSARY JOANNE IS STILL AS LOVELY AS EVER.

Muldoon haint changed either.

*****

I took a cold-soapy shower---went to bed---fell asleep.

I was awakened by a lot of animal noises in the room next to mine that sounded like a couple of bull elephants at rutting time.

It was Gina and Dirty Dan.

His room was right next to mine. They consummated their act and all was quiet. *I would have had a wet dream but I fell asleep.*

---I comatosed---

Next thing I heard was someone pounding on my door.

It was Muldoon, ---"The mess hall is going to close in thirty minutes. If you don't get your butt out of bed, you're going to miss breakfast."

I was groggy, ---**"Did he say mess hall? Am I back in the friggin' army?"**

I became lucid and put on my bathing suit. I went with Muldoon to the Quonset Hut Mess Hall for breakfast. Now there were two things that I had found out about Muldoon. He never turns down a drink and he "never" misses a meal. ---Still "nevers".

We had "Shit on the Shingle." ---*Gravied chip beef on toast.*

"Not bad. It's better than the dehydrated eggs and Spam they usually serve," said Muldoon.

Muldoon went to the lagoon for a swim and to cool off.

I checked out a fishing pole, got some gristle meat from the cooks at the mess hall and went down to the Standard Oil pier. I ripped off a couple chunks of meat and did some chumming.

To you folk that haint never dropped a worm in the water, ---Chumming means throwing bait in the water to lure the fish to your---fishing hook, line & sinker.

The Parrot Fish, so named because their mouths are shaped like a parrot's beak and just as hard---so they can crush the coral that they mostly feed upon, ---went into a feeding frenzy.

The water was a-boil.

I fished for a while, chummed for a while and fished some more.

Plenty of bites, ---but I just couldn't hook the Parrot Fish because of their hard mouth.

The Filipino cooks were not going to be happy with me. When they gave me the meat, I told them that I would bring them back some Mahi-Mahi.

I was sitting on the pier---half-baked by the sun. I happened to look down in the channel that was dredged out for the Standard Oil Tankers.

There were three sharks, about the size of the Jap two man-submarines which were lying in rust next to the Great Whites, ---lurking down there, ---eyeballing my bod and lickin' their chops.

The pier that I was on is not what you have in your mind's eye. It was actually just a walkway, about a foot above the water, floating on empty oil drums. The Great Whites were lying there treading water and salivating at the mouth trying to figure out how to get to the pier because the water got shallow near the pier.

I departed the pier muy pronto. ---The sharks went back to the deep.

I went back out on the pier---took most of the meat---threaded my hook and line through it---cast it out as far as I could.

The ocean tide was ebbing and took the bait out even further.

It was late in the day---the sun had baked my head---I was daydreaming.

I even missed noon chow at the mess hall.

Muldoon probably ate my share.

The Pacific Ocean "Hiroshimad"---looked like Neptune pinched a giant zit.

I saw a Great White take the bait and go ten feet in the air. My fishing rod bent and it's reel hissed as the shark went to visit Davy Jones Locker. (*Went for the deep*)

I tried to tighten the drag on the reel.

No help---**NADA**

I was running out of line and put both thumbs on the spinning spool trying to stop it. Not very bright. Instant "water" blisters.

The shark ran around some coral and cut the line. Bye, bye, bye big shark.

—THANK YOU NEPTUNE—

I don't know what I would have done with him anyway.

One small guy---

One small pier---

One big shark---

I'll take odds on the shark.

On the way back to the barracks, I stopped by a lagoon.

There were a couple of Japanese two-man tanks lying on the

bottom of the lagoon. Apparently, when the Yanks took over the island during World War Two, the Yanks pushed the tanks into the Pacific Ocean.

I had one hook, very little line and just a little bait left. I cast into the lagoon hoping to catch something to take back to the mess hall.

I DID.
I caught a friggin' Moray Eel.

I was fishing from a bluff about twenty feet above the Pacific Oceans floor. I could see the Moray Eel stalking the bait through the transparent teal-blue waters of the Pacific Ocean. I actually slewed the bait around trying not to catch him.

2 little---2 slow---2 late.

The Moray Eel glommed on to the mess hall gristle meat and hooked himself.

Uh -Oh. ---I was "un-happy".

I tried to dislodge the Moray Eel from the hook by violently whipping the fishing rod from side to side and up and down.

"No-way, Moray," as sung to the tune of "No-way, Jose."

The Moray Eel was "un-happy".

The Moray Eel did not like the "Big Hook."

The Moray Eel violently whipped his body from side to side and up and down.

The Moray Eel's gyrations tied him up in knots.

The Moray Eel looked like a snaky hula-hoop and wound himself all the way up to the tip of my fishing rod.

What do you do with an un-happy Moray Eel? Put him on the coral reef and beat him on the head till dead.

I did.

I threw my pole and the **monster Moray Eel** on the ground---found the barrel of a machine gun from one of the tanks---beat the Moray Eel's head to a pulp. He lived until the sun settled into the Pacific Ocean.

*****

AS ---DIRTY JOHN FRASIER ---USED TO SAY TO THE STEWS "WHEN THE SUN GOES DOWN IN HONOLULU— I'LL GO DOWN ON YOU" REMEMBER CAPTAIN JOHN FRAZIER aka DIRTY JOHN ---THE LEGEND OF THE SKYS---

*****

Sometimes, you can see a phenomenon that looks like a puff of TEAL-GREEN SMOKE---*when the sunsets over the Pacific Ocean.*
*****

I took the Moray Eel to the mess hall---quite embarrassed.
The slimy Moray Eel was all I had to show for my "day in the sun".
The Filipino cooks went wild.
The Moray Eel is a Filipino delicacy.
I was their hero.
Some Filipinos claim a male Moray Eel's brain is below his "waist", right next to his nuts, (*maybe where mans is*) and beating him on the head may have had only blinded him.
The Filipino cooks said, ---"You go fishing tomorrow, catch Moray. We give you meat for bait."
Hell, I almost brought them a shark, ---"Sure"
I left
*****

The legend of **"MAG CHECK CHARLIE"**.
It was rumored that a Great White Shark would go to the Take-off end of the runway and listen to the airplanes run up their engines. If the engines ran rough while the pilots were making the Magneto Check, --- Mag Check Charlie would go to the other end of the runway and wait for the airplane to go into the ocean. ---**CHOW TIME**---
*****

I went to the Drifters Reef Bar. The hot sun had permeated my brain and I was in need of liquids, ---booze type.
I needed some moisture in my bod. ---Some libation---some coolant from the ceiling fan's in the **Drifter's Reef Bar** that cooled the **IAT** down to 99.99 degrees Celsius.
IAT---inside temperature---OAT---outside temperature
All the Non-Skeddar Crews&Stews were there. The Non-Skeddars had been there since an Asahi breakfast, having an **"Asahi Time"**.
I got drunk on Asahis. ---At twenty five cents a pop---you can get wasted with a "fin in your creel".
I found Muldoon and had another beer with him. The sun had settled in the West and my sanity was going "South", ---"Muldoon, you had better get some rest. You're due to fly out at midnight."
Muldoon laughed, ---"They switched trips on us and you're the one that's going out at midnight."

I staggered over to our "Quonset Hut Hotel". There was a chalkboard there that told us what flights we were going out on and the time of departure.

Sure 'nuff, Muldoon was right. I was going to Okinawa at midnight.

I tried to nap---no luck. ---went out for a run.

I ran up and down runway 09/27 trying to get the Asahis out of my brain.

The east/west runway was strategically placed on **The Atoll of Wake Island** because of the **Prevailing Westerlies.** *Or whatever blows your skirt up*

Actually, runway 07/09 was placed that way because it was the only piece of blinding white coral reef real estate that was long enough for a six thousand foot (6,000) GI World War II landing strip.

Didn't work, ---still groggy.

I went back to the "Hilton" Quonset hut and took a cold shower.

It helped a litta but I was still a lotta of woozy.

---PUMPKIN HOUR---

We Boarded the "Renovated" World War II Red Cross Van of 1942 Vintage.

The Crews&Stews were silent and appeared to be stone cold sober.

How did they do this? Training, ---they kept their livers in shape.

We arrived at the Wake Island International Airport---went into Pan Am Operations.

Captain Daniel Tibbetts gave me a fuel load of twenty-six thousand pounds.

"Take the airplane down to the fueling depot and gas her up."
MY THOUGHT---"I shouldn't be driving a car, let alone taxiing an airplane."

I did it and did it well. No backfires---no burning fuel on the tarmac---I even talked into the mike the right way.

I laddered up on the wing and put some of life's blood into my sweetheart in the form of 115/130 octane purple gasoline.

I buttoned her up. She knew that she was well fed and well loved.

I started her up---she purred. I taxied her back to---

—THE ATOLL OF WAKE ISLAND PAN AM TERMINAL—
Gina & Tina boarded the passengers and we took off for Okinawa.

---OVER GROSSED AS USUAL---

The DC/AC inverter crapped out on us before we got to ten thousand feet.

This is the **motor** that takes direct current from the **engine** driven generators and converts it to alternating current which is needed to operate the flight and engine instruments, and most importantly---
---THE AUTO-PILOT---

*****

*The difference between an **engine** and a **motor**???---You might ask---An engine is self contained. ---Your car has an engine.*
A motor needs an external force to power it. ---
Your refrigerator has a motor.
****

I tried my usual jacking off of the inverter toggle-type circuit breaker.
---Didn't help---
I looked at Dirty Dan who was working his butt off trying to keep us straight and level.
"I can't fix it Captain Tibbetts."
Captain Daniel Tibbetts, ---"We're going to have go back to Wake Island and get it fixed. I can't fly all the way to Okinawa on needle ball and airspeed without an auto-pilot."
Poor Dirty Dan. ---It would cut into his siesta time.
Co-Pilot Nels Jensen picked up his VHF Mike, --- **"Wake Island Departure Control---we have a slight problem and have to return to Wake Island."**
MY THOUGHT---"Slight---Bullshit---Dirty Dan hasn't flown on basic instruments for over twenty years."
Wake Island Departure Control, ---"Twentieth Century 304, turn right to a heading of 350 degrees, maintain eight thousand feet. Contact Wake Island Approach Control on 124.3."
"124.3---Roger----Twentieth Century 304---see ya."
"Yea, ---I'll be talking to you on approach control. I'm the only one in the tower."
"Wake Island Approach---this is Twentieth Century 304---heading 250 and maintaining 8,000 feet. We're returning to Wake Island."
"Roger Twentieth Century 304---proceed direct to the airport at any altitude---the sky is yours---the closest airport traffic is over two hours from here. Are you declaring an emergency? What's your problem?"
"Ah---No---no emergency. We just had an inverter go tits up on us. We've got some inoperative instruments and **NO AUTO-PILOT---** Twentieth Century 304."

"NO AUTO PILOT---IS Dirty Dan hand flying that old tub?"
"Yep"

"Well, in that case, Twentieth Century 304, ---**WE'RE declaring an emergency**---we'll have the Emergency Equipment standing by. Just kidding---our emergency team needs to get off their dead butt once in a while. I can't remember the last time they were out of their Quonset hut."

"OK---we're about five miles from touchdown, ---we have the field in sight."

"Roger Twentieth Century Airlines 304---I have you in sight---you are cleared to land on the runway of your choice---wind is calm."

Co-Pilot Nels Jensen looked at Captain Tibbetts as to which runway he wanted.

Captain Tibbetts was one busy Airline Pilot earning his money with muy sweat beads on his forehead---gave no response.

Co-Pilot Nels Jensen shrugged his shoulders, ---"Wake Island Approach---we'd like Runway 27---we'll be closer to your maintenance hut when we roll out to the end of the runway."

"Roger Twentieth Century Airlines 304---cleared to land Runway 27---wind is calm---altimeter is two-niner-seven-niner."

"Roger---Twentieth Century Airlines 304 is cleared to land Runway 27."

I tapped Captain Dan Tibbetts on the shoulder, --- "We're way over our landing weight limitations. We're going to have to dump fuel."

Dirty Dan snapped at me, ---

"DO IT AND DON'T BOTHER ME AGAIN."

Captain Dan Tibbetts had his hands full of something other than "stew-meat".

Captain Dan Tibbetts was doing all he could to keep the DC-6 sunny-side up or straight and level---whichever comes last.

Dirty Dan had his hands full and was assholes and elbows at work.

Dirty Dan was busier than a Cat covering shit On Tennessee William's Hot Tin Roof.

Co-Pilot Nels Jensen heard the fuel dump necessity, ---"Wake Island approach---this is Twentieth Century 304---we're gonna make a go-around. We have to dump fuel and we can't dump fuel with the flaps down."

"Roger Twentieth---fly where ever you want. You're the only aircraft within 200 miles of Wake Island. Dirty Dan needs the practice anyway." *"Chuckle---chuckle"*

I checked the fuel dump charts. I figured that we were going to have to dump fuel for five minutes to get down to our landing weight limitations.

I started to tell Dirty Dan but didn't. Dirty Dan was one muy busy hombre.

"Nels---it's gonna take five minutes to get down to our landing weight."

"Thanks Beck." ---"Wake Island Approach---this is Twentieth again. We're gonna be out here another ten minutes."

"Roger Twentieth---take all the time you need. I don't get off till zero-seven hundred hours. I still have you in sight."

"Roger Wake Island," ---Nels responded.

Co-Pilot Nels Jensen looked at Captain Tibbetts, ---"Do you want me to bring the flaps up? ---Beck's gonna dump fuel."

"DO IT AND DON'T BOTHER ME AGAIN."

Co-Pilot Nels Jensen put the flap lever in the up position detent, watched the flap position indicator go to **UP**---turned to me, ---**"DUMP."**

I noted the time on the "company clock" and pulled the---

---RED FUEL DUMP HANDLES---

The initial tug swung the drains about two feet below the wings.

The second tug opened fuel valves to allow the fuel to exit the fuel tanks.

I went back in the passenger cabin---looked out the windows to ascertain that we were, in fact, dumping 115/130 Octane Purple Gasoline.

WE WERE.

The mighty DC6 was taking a dump.

The fuel was hitting the slipstream and vaporizing as it came out of the dump chutes causing a white smokish effect.

I went back into the cockpit and watched the Captain's Chronometer.

When five minutes were up, ---I pulled the adjacent dump closed handles, which closed the drain valves first and then pulled the drain chutes back up into the wing.

I went back into the cabin to make sure that everything was secured.

I looked out both sides of the airplane. We were no longer dumping fuel.

I was about to go back into the cockpit when one of the serviceman grabbed me by the arm, ---**"Sergeant, your fire is out."**

Poor guy thought we were on fire.

Poor guy thought I was in the Air-Force.

Poor guy thought I was a Sergeant.

At that point in time, we never made any announcements then as to what was happening up in the "front office." Now-a-days, if you fart, you've got tell the passengers which cheek you raised and if you streaked your shorts.

We landed back at Wake Island and taxied up to Pan Am's maintenance Quonset hut.

I deplaned and asked a Pan Am Mechanic if he had any inverters in stock.

"Nah-we don't have any in stock. Our stockroom is limited to one spare engine. There's a fuselage of an old Air Force DC-6 out back with a lot of the parts still intact. Come with me---I'm not doing anything for another couple of hours---I'll give you a hand finding one."

"Thanks"

We walked around the Quonset hut and found the DC-6 fuselage half buried in the coral sand. We went into the no door airplane and up into the cockpit. The only component that had not been scavenged through out the years was---an **inverter**.

"Let's take it in to the maintenance hut and I'll bench test it for you."

I looked at the Mighty DC-6, thought of the people on board sweltering in the hot and humid airplane, ---**"No thanks---I gotta get some air going through that airplane before people start passing out on us."**

"I understand---I'll give you a hand with it."

"Thanks"

We replaced the inverter---"works fine-lasts a long time". The Mech helped me refuel the Mighty DC-6. I thanked him and gave him a buck for some beer.

I started the engines without incident and we taxied out for take-off.

We always taxied with the Captain and Co-Pilots Sliding Glass side windows open to cool our sweaty bodies and closed them before the take-off roll.

Co-Pilot Nels Jensen started to close his sliding glass window.

Captain Tibbetts, ---"Leave your window open Jensen---we gotta get some cool in here. I'll close mine."

"OK" with a Co-Pilot shrug of his shoulders as all Co-Pilots do when they think that the Captain might be just a little bit tetched.

We took off.

IT WAS BREEEEEZY AND NOOOOOOISY
BUT COOOOOLING

Co-Pilot Nels Jensen couldn't take it any longer and closed the Sliding Glass Window at 9,000 feet.

It did the trick though---our soaking wet clothes were like they just came out of the dryer.

---CAPTAIN DAN TIBBETTS FELL ASLEEP---
---CO-PILOT NELS JENSEN FELL ASLEEP---
---NAVIGATOR NORY ELLIS WAS WIDE AWAKE---
!!!HUH!!!

I wrote, Navigator Nory Ellis **was wide awake.**
???You're kidding???

There were no oranges on Wake Island, thus, no fleshy screwdrivers to pass away the tedium to ---OKINAWA.

Navigator Nory Ellis would check our Sextant and Loran positions.
I did the heading changes with the turn knob on the **AUTO-PILOT-**
--about a foot in front of me.
I also made the position reports to Okinawa Center.
We skirted the line of cyclones off to our right as shown by our RADAR.
The Radar, at that point in time was as good, if not better than the ones we have now---just not as pretty. Sorta like a good hard-on. If it works and you want to keep it, don't screw with it.

Nory Ellis and I bullshitted all the way to Okinawa, talking loud enough so we could hear each other over the roar of the engines and the snoring of Co-Pilot Nels Jensen and Captain Dirty Dan Tibbetts.

I came to find out that this was Nory's fourth crossing within the month.
That is approximately over two hundred hours of flight time. ---Not counting time on the ground.

Nory Ellis, with his side-mouthed-shit-eating-grin, said, ---"I'm making two thousand dollars this month, ---and I'm spending it like I'm going to make it every month."

Pay for a Navigator was usually about eight hundred bucks a month.
The other three times---Nory had stayed on the same airplane for the complete round trip with no layovers. There was no time limit as to how many hours a Navigators could fly.

Thank God and Sunkist for oranges.

About two hours out of Okinawa, Dirty Dan uncomatosed.
A good seven hours rest behind him.
You know the routine.
Ding, ding---
"I want my coffee now."

In came Gina. ---
I left and went back into the cabin.
I wasn't about to watch the stink-finger action again.
*****

I like to eat shrimp frozen---gets away from that pussy smell.
*****

While I was waiting for Gina to get her mayonnaise maker massaged, the same soldier grabbed me by the arm and said, ---"Nice job of putting out that fire, Sergeant."

"Thanks."---What else could I say?

Gina left the cockpit with a smile on her face.

I re-entered the Cockpit---looked at Dirty Dan, ---"Do you ever wash your hands?"

Nels Jensen and Nory Ellis cracked up. They couldn't believe that a straight laced rookie would ask a question like that.

We landed at Okinawa and cabbed to the Daichi Hotel. I went to my room and passed out.

I woke up to an orgy. No locks on the door and they picked my room to have a party.

I was flattered.

I believe that I mentioned before that wherever we landed, --- A gaggle of nonsked airplanes also landed.

!!!WRONG!!!

This was an old non-sked ploy.

You partied in someone else's room, cut one of the fillies out of the herd and took her to your room.

Meanwhile, the host of the party got drunk, fell down and threw up. Not necessarily in that order. Which I did.

That night we all went out to the ---

"TEA HOUSE OF THE AUGUST MOON"

---A well appointed brothel with many <u>BEAUTIFUL</u> Geisha Girls---

We weren't there five minutes and Nory Ellis was walking out the door with the pick of the litter.

---BIG SPENDER---

Too rich for my wallet and besides that, I was still a Non-Sked virgin.

Dirty Dan and Nels were acting like two blind dogs in a butcher shop---sniffing every skirt in sight.

Gina put up with this amour for about thirty minutes and grabbed Dirty Dan by the crotch and dragged him back to the hotel.

Nel's girlfriend, Tina, grabbed Nels by the balls and fled the scene, ---leaving me all alone to drink Sake, a Japanese rice wine.

Two Sakes and even the ugly Geishas started looking pretty and there were no ugly Geishas.

I staggered back to the Daichi Hotel and passed out.

Sake and I were never good traveling companions.

The next day we went back to Wake Island, then Honolulu and then on to the "States".

I went home. My wife was still in Oklahoma and I slept for twenty-four hours.

Chief Pilot Captain Bill Butler called me just as I was waking up---perfect timing.

Chief Pilot Captain Bill Butler knew I would need some re-entry time, and he let me re-enter to the maximum, ---"Thanks for taking care of that engine at Travis and the Inverter at Wake Island."

Captain Bill Butler never missed a chance to laud his troops.

"That's my job." How he knew about it already---I'll never figure out.

"The head cheese wants to talk to you. His name is Melvin Ward." and before I could ask why, he switched me over to Mister Ward's office.

The secretary answered, ---"Melvin Ward's Office."

"Yes, my name is Jack Beck and I'm supposed to talk to Mister Ward." I was shaking in my boots figuring that he was going to shit-can me for waking him up in the middle of the night.

"Mister Beck, this is Melvin Ward."

Now I was really shaking in my boots. Other than the TIGER FUNK FIRING, no one had ever called me MISTER before.

"I want to personally thank you for taking care of that engine at Travis Air Force Base and apologize if I was rude to you on the phone."

I WAS STUNNED. All I could say was "Thanks".

I found out later that Mister Melvin Ward was once a Non-Sked Flight Engineer and knew the trials and tribulations of the job.

I called Chief Pilot Captain Bill Butler back, ---"Any trips open?"

"Yes there is. Muldoon just called in sick and said that he and his family are down with the flu. The trip checks in tomorrow night at 2300 hours. It's yours if you want it."

Without hesitation, ---"I'll take it. Oh by the way Bill, I still don't have a uniform."

I worked hard for those two stripes on my sleeve. I wanted to swagger around with them---even if it meant sweating my balls off in the hot and humid South Pacific.

"Go over to Tarpy Tailors, next to the Los Angeles Airport, and get fitted tomorrow. I'll call them now and tell them you're coming."

"Thanks Bill," and hung up.

I arrived at Tarpys early in the morning hoping that I could get my uniform for the flight that night.

No such luck, it had to be "alter-ego-ed."

"How long?"

"Three weeks," the tailor swished as he measured my inseam for the third time.

Never trust a tailor that dotes on your in-seam and forgets to measure your waist.

The uniform was a shit brindle brown. The color was somewhere between baby shit brown and cervasa taco throw up. The material was good for one sit down. When you got up ---it looked like you were wearing Lawrence Whelk's Accordion.

"How much?" I asked, keeping a safe heterosexual distance away from him.

"When Captain Butler called yesterday, he said to charge it to the company," was his sweet response as he went again for my in-seam.

I went home, called Bill Butler and thanked him.

"No thanks necessary, you more than earned it on your last trip."

"Well I appreciate it and by the way, speaking of my last trip, we don't have to long to go on that four month contract."

"Don't you read the bulletin board? Our contract has been extended for another year."

"I didn't know that we had a bulletin board, but that's good news. Thanks again for everything."

"ALLS WELL THAT ENDS WELL"

PRFPACPJM

*****

---One other fishing trip that I have to write you ---about fishing on Wake Island---

One of the Filipinos had a small fishing skiff. I gave him two bucks to take me out fishing.

He did.

His fishing pole looked like a three foot fiberglass broom stick with a reel on it.

He hooked on to a big one and started to reel it in---by using the side of the boat as a fulcrum and manipulating his fishing rod as a lever.

Every few minutes, the line would slacken up for a second---then be taut again.

The Filipino finally got the massive fish---**HEAD**---on the boat.

The Great White Sharks were striking the massive fish and chowing down on it as the Filipino was reeling the fish in---causing the line to slacken.

I took one look at the fish head---I took one look in the clear teal-blue waters of the Pacific Ocean---I took one look at a half-dozen Great Whites circling the tiny skiff. I took one look at the Filipino---**"TAKE ME BACK TO WAKE."**

****

A traveling salesman was motoring through the country. He stopped by a sheepherder's camp, approached a sheepherder and said, ---"I hear a sheep's pussy is just as good as a woman's pussy and I'd like to try one."

The sheepherder said, "Help yourself, sonny, ---there's over a hundred of them out there in the pasture."

He did.

When he returned to the shepherd's camp---the shepherd's were in hysterics with laughter.

"What's so funny---haven't you ever seen anyone screw a sheep before?"---

"Yes we have, but you picked out the ugliest one."
*****

--- CIRCA ---

JULY---I-NINER-5-NINER

I went to the airport, early as usual, fueled up the DC-6 and went into Twentieth Century Airlines Operations.
I met
CAPTAIN BUCK PRENTISS.
Big burly motha-fucka, as Captain Bill Faries used to say.
Wrestle a gorilla with one banana tied behind his back. Sweat like a race horse in heat after a six furlong race.

*****

That's six-eighth of a mile (one furlong=one/eighth mile to you non-gamblers who drive the Santa Monica Freeway at eighty miles an hour---Martin-i-zed.
One furlong is equal to one eighth mile.
"*And there off*" *cried the monkey as the lawnmower ran over his balls.*
"*And there off*"---*like the hired maids pants.*

*****

Captain Buck Prentiss, ---"I just fired the Co-pilot because he pissed me off."
I didn't inquire as to why. I sure as hell didn't want to piss him off. I'm just crazy, not stupid.

*****

Huck lost one of the wheels off his car as he was passing an insane asylum.
Scratching his nuts and looking at the problem, which consisted of all the lug nuts on the befallen wheel had worked loose and were somewhere whence he were.
Huck was trying to figure out how to get back into town.
An inmate of the asylum looked on the situation and said, ---
"*Take one lug nut from each of the other three wheels and put it on the befallen wheel.*"
Huck did---looked at the inmate---
"*That was a brilliant idea. How come you're in there?*"
"I'm just crazy, not stupid."

*****

Captain Buck Prentiss grabbed me by the arm, --- "Let's go."
Hell yea, I'll go anywhere when my feet are barely touching the ground.

We got on a tug, cut across Runway 07/25 without clearance from the tower and went to the terminal.

If you did that now-a-days, you'd be in the same jail as your uncle that nobody ever mentions.

We went into the Burbank Terminal Bar.

MY THOUGHTS---"What are we going to do now---get drunk?"

—ROY WAS THE BARKEEP—

He was a "barkeep-sake" at the Burbank Airport and knew every Non-Skeddar that---**Flew in and flew out of the Burbank International Airport.**

Captain Buck Prentiss got Roy's attention, --- "I need a beer and a Co-pilot."

To be a Co-pilot, in 1959, all you needed was a Commercial Pilot's License and three take offs and landings in the airplane you're going to fly. *Shit, you didn't even need an Instrument Ticket---Me thinks.*

Roy the Barkeep looked at me, ---**"WHADYAWANTKID?"**

I looked at Captain Buck Prentiss---Captain Buck Prentiss looked at me, ---GRIMACING.

"I'll take a beer Sir."

I looked at Captain Buck Prentiss. ---Captain Buck Prentiss looked at me, ---SCOWLING.

"And a Co-Pilot."

I looked at Captain Buck Prentiss---Captain Buck Prentiss looked at me. No longer scowling---No longer grimacing.

Sorta had the look on his face of a man trying to hold back a fart.

I "took the look" as an OK and drank on my beer.

"Roy the Barkeep" pulled a phone out from under the counter and dialed a phone number by memory ---made a few gubernatorial grunts and gestures and hung up.

"I know this nice kid---he's inexperienced--- but eager. He'll be over at Twentieth in thirty minutes."

Captain Buck Prentiss, gruffly, --- "Thanks."

We left and again went back across, Runway 07/25---without clearance to---

---**TWENTIETH CENTURY AIRLINES**---

Captain Buck Prentiss went into Operations.

I jumped off the tug---did a walk around pre-flight inspection of the Mighty DC-6.

I got in the cockpit and got her ready to go.

Captain Buck Prentiss, the "new hire" Co-Pilot and the Stews came on board.

CAPTAIN BUCK PRENTISS introduced me to the crew.
---CO-PILOT DUSTY DRAPE---
---STEWARDESS CONSTANCE LUJAN---
---STEWARDESS SALLY McKIERNAN---

Dusty Drape was the new Co-Pilot's moniker. Seemed like a nice person. Only thing I didn't like about him was that he had a uniform on. *MY THOUGHTS---"He haint been working here for ten minutes and already he's got a uniform."*

Co-Pilot Dusty Drape's wife had crocheted three fuzzy stripes on the sleeves of his uniform that we all snickered at.

Captain Buck Prentiss crawled in his seat and said to Co-Pilot Dusty Drape, ---"You need three take offs and landings to be legal. I'm only going to give you one because we're running late."

We took off and Co-Pilot Dusty Drape called out, ---**"GEAR UP."**

Co-Pilot Dusty Drape leveled off at one thousand feet **AGL.**

(Above Ground Level)

Co-Pilot Dusty Drape made a right turn to the **Crosswind Leg.**

—SMOOTH—

Crosswind Leg---*The first 90 degree turn, right or left, after take off.*

Co-Pilot Dusty Drape aviated a couple of nautical miles,

---then made a right turn to the

Downwind Leg.

—SMOOTH—

Co-Pilot Dusty Drape flew downwind for a few nautical miles.

Downwind Leg--- *paralleling the airport.*

The altitude never wavered an **RCH.** ---*Red Cunt Hair.*

—SMOOTH—

Co-Pilot Dusty Drape turned right to the **Base Leg,** ---

Flew a couple of nautical miles, then turned right to the

---Final Approach---

Base Leg---*90 degree right turn to final*---***Final Approach***---*the approach to landing.*

^^^^^^^^NOT SmOoTh^^^^^^^^^

???Wha hoppan???

All hell broke loose.

We were going through more gyrations---

---Than an "E" ride at Disneyland—

Co-Pilot Dusty Drape looked like a monkey fucking a football.

Co-Pilot Dusty Drape was a light airplane instructor and he had never been in an airplane this big in his life.
We were less than one hundred feet above the runway and going sideways.
I'm not a religious fanatic---but I was saying many---
---"HAIL BLOODY MARYS"---

---BUCK GRABBED THE CONTROLS---
---KICKED IN A RUDDER---
---ADDED POWER---
---ABORTED THE LANDING---
---TOOK UP A HEADING TO TRAVIS AIR FORCE BASE---

We picked up our passengers, which were Servicemen, their spouses and their diapered squalling babies.
The Navigator, *whose name will be withheld to protect the guilty---you'll read why later on,* came on board and we proceeded across---
---"THE GREAT POND" aka ---THE PACIFIC OCEAN---
About four hours out of Hawaii, the #1 engine **LOW OIL PRESSURE LIGHT** started flickering. I checked the #1 oil tank quantity gauge. The needle was in the red---dangerously low.
No problem.
The DC-6 had a **thirty gallon reserve oil tank** in the left wing root.
I nurtured the #1 engine, feeding it just enough oil out of the reserve oil tank to keep the **low oil pressure light** from illuminating.
Thirty Gallon Reserve Oil Tank---15 gallons of oil and 15 gallons of gasoline---mixed. *The gasoline kept the oil from congealing at cold temperatures and evaporated from the heat as it entered the oil tank.*
Co-Pilot Dusty Drape made the landing at the---
---**HONOLULU INTERNATIONAL AIRPORT**---
! SMOOOOOOOOTH!
Very nice---Captain Buck Prentiss made Co-Pilot Dusty Drape hand fly the Mighty DC-6 for a couple of hours on the way to Hawaii. He also made Co-Pilot Dusty Drape make the descent and approach without the auto-pilot.
The hands on flying gave Co-Pilot Dusty Drape a feel for the Mighty DC-6. This, and the fact that a fully loaded airplane is easier to land than an empty airplane, made Co-Pilot Dusty Drape look pretty damn impressive.
Why is a fully loaded airplane much easier to land than an empty one???

All airplanes are designed to take off, fly and land fully loaded. --- Anyhoo---that's what they tell me.

As we were taxiing to the gate at the Honolulu International Airport---the **# 1 engine low oil pressure light** illuminated. I shut down the #1 engine immediately.

We taxied to the terminal and I got off the airplane before the passengers did. I wanted to see where all the oil went.

I found it alright. The #1 & #2 engines and the left side of the airplane were covered with oil.

Looked like it was dipped in Jed Clampett's swamp.

The number one engine's propeller housing was almost separated from the engine. Twenty of the fifty bolts were the only ones still intact.

If the propeller housing had separated from the engine, the #1 propeller, due to its clockwise rotation, it would have taken out the #2 propeller and both of them would have crashed into the fuselage cutting it in half at the cockpit.

Keeping the engine running almost killed us.

I damn near killed a whole plane load of people trying to do a good job.

"ALL'S WELL THAT ENDS WELL"
PRFPACPJM

--- CIRCA ---

THE NEXT DAY ---*me thinks*

The next day we left Hawaii for Wake Island.

About two hours out of Wake Island we had a "run-a-way" propeller on #1 engine. I feathered the propeller immediately, --- then shut off the fuel to the engine.

If the propeller would have broken loose, the #1 engine propeller, due to its clockwise rotation, would have taken out the #2 propeller and both of them would have crashed into the fuselage, cutting the airplane in half at the cockpit. ---Ouch!

All counting's and rotations on airplanes are described as if you were sitting on the tail facing forward.

If you let the propeller run-a-way too long, it will come off the engine and into the airplane.

Through the whole smear, Buck hadn't said a word to me. He would just look at me and scowl.

I didn't know what frightened me the most. ---**Buck or dying.**

We spent the next two weeks on---**THE ATOLL OF WAKE ISLAND** waiting for an engine to be shipped in from the "States" so we could replace the #1 engine.

"What's Wake Island like?" you might ask. ---Sorta like being in hell with water around your campfire.

I fished---played pool--- drank two-bit Asahis---generally fried my brain in the boiling sun.

We finally got the engine replaced and left for Agana, Guam.

Co-Pilot Dusty Drape flew the entire trip---a good part of it with the auto-pilot off---did a helluva job.

---STEWARDESS CONNIE LUJAN---
AND
---STEWARDESS SALLY MCKIERNAN---

Bid our passengers adieu and welcomed the new ones aboard.

I checked the oil and put on some gas.

We had a two hour layover on Guam and then saddled up for our flight to Tokyo.

So much for CAA's crew rest bullshit

We did the before start checklist and I prepared to start the engines.

Just my luck, it was the changing of the command. One General was replacing another General.

There were over one hundred troops standing out on the tarmac in the hot sun with rifles they wouldn't know which way to point if they had to fire them. A lot of wasted taxpayer's money for nothing.

Captain Buck Prentiss, ---who hadn't said two words to me since we left Burbank, turned to me, talking through clenched teeth and sweating profusely, ---"**DON'T BACKFIRE THE ENGINES.**"

This is like telling your brand new puppy dog not to shit on your brand new carpet.

---KAPOW---KAPOW---KAPOW---KAPOW---

Naturally I backfired all four engines.

Each backfire ---Buck would glare at me with narrowed eyes, clenched teeth and sweating like a pig with no pores.

Pigs don't sweat because they haint got no pores---me thinks.
That's why they wallow in mud---to keep cool. ---me thinks.

Each backfire---one hundred troops would jump about two inches in the air in unison.

Hell, it was probably the only thing they ever did as one.

WE LEFT.

As we entered Tokyo's Controlled Airspace---the Japanese Airforce came up to intercept us. The aforementioned, no-name Navigator had us lost.

I was too ignorant of the situation to be frightened. I thought that this happened all the time.

If ignorance was bliss, then I was the world's biggest blister.

Co-Pilot Dusty Drape's teeth were chattering. Muy sweat-balls were coming off Captain Buck Prentiss' forehead. Sorta looked like he was in a rain-storm.

Captain Buck Prentiss, --- "These fucking Nips are gonna blow us out of the sky."

Captain Buck Prentiss had been a Lockheed P38 reconnaissance Pilot during the Big War and had been shot down by Zeros—**Once-Twice.** ---Guess Buck thought---

---THRICE WOULD NOT BE CHARMING---

We finally received the Tokyo Low-Frequency Radio Beacon and got back on course.

The Zeroes waggled their wings in salute---Sayonara.

We arrived in Tokyo and took the usual Hari-Kari Taxi ride to the hotel. **Sort of like riding a skateboard on the Ventura Freeway during rush hour.**

WE LIVED.

I was barely in my room ---**"RING---RI--"**—"Hello". Captain Buck Prentiss, ---**"Get your ass down to my room immediately."** *Sounded like he was still talking through clenched teeth.*
MY THOUGHT--- "Oh man, he's going to shit-can me for backfiring the engines."

I hurried down to Buck's room.

Co-Pilot Dusty Drape, who professed to be very religious, was there with a three piece suit on.
MY THOUGHT---"Oh shit, he's going to fire both of us."

Captain Buck Prentiss took three quarts of Canadian Club out of his bag and placed a bottle in front of each of us.

"I fired the Navigator---he's on his way back to the States. ---**DRINK**," ---Buck said through sweaty jowls and clenched teeth.

I opened my bottle and took a couple of sips. I'd drink rat poison before I'd defy this gorilla---besides that, if he's going to fire me, I might as well get mellow.

Tasted fine, should last a long time.

Dusty stared at the ceiling. Drinking booze was against Dusty's Jehovah.

Buck looked at Dusty, ---**"I said drink."**

Dusty took a couple of swigs---Dusty chugalugged that puppy---Dusty turned into an animal with a wild look in his eyes, ---"I want some action."

Apparently Dusty's wife wasn't servicing him either.

Hallelujah---Religion's a wonderful thing as long as you keep it out of the bedroom.

Buck un-clenched, ---"I'm going out for some action. ---You guys wanna come along?"

Dusty was up, bottle in hand and ready to rock and roll before Buck could finish his sentence.

I said, **"Okay by me."**
MY THOUGHT---*"Better than getting fired"*

We proceeded to the ---**"THE HONEY BUCKET"**.

A Honey Bucket is something that the Japanese peed in and threw out of the window into trench they had dug especially for that occasion.
Didn't sound too appetizing to me

Nice place though---lavishly done.
"THE HONEY BUCKET" had a circular bar that rotated very slowly.
The men sat at the bar. ---The Geisha Girls sat along the walls.
As the bar rotated, you would look them over and motion to the one that suited your fantasy,--er, --fancy.
Sort of like a human smorgasbord.
The Geisha Girl would come over, negotiate the amount of Yen she fantasized,--er, ---fancied and you would be on your way to ---Japanese Buddha Heaven.
Well, I guess that's the game of life. Negotiate— Capitulate— Fornicate.
Who wins the game of life?

---LIFE IS BUT A GAME OF HEARTBEATS---
---AND THE WINNER OF THE GAME---
---THE ONE WITH THE HAPPIEST HEARTBEATS---

CAPTAIN JACK RESLEY BECK---RE-ALLY-TIRED

The "Cock---Tail" Bar hadn't made a full turn and Dusty was already in negotiations. Dusty was Sayonara before the bar had rotated a complete circle. Dusty was definitely in heat. Dusty had found a new Jehovah.
Buck and I sat there, drank Sake and chatted.
Nice guy---just looked meaner than a junkyard dog.
Captain Buck Prentiss even complimented me on the way I handled the number one engine going into Honolulu. I didn't tell him that I damn near killed us by keeping the engine running.
Every once in a while Buck would look over his shoulder at the Geisha Girls. Buck's peepee had a mission that night and it wasn't going to the Mission.
Finally Buck motioned to a good-lookin' Geisha.
She came across the room and said to Buck, "Mushy-Mushy."
---They Mushy-Mushyed---
Translation---
They negotiated her pussy. ---As Bob BarYing says, "The Yen is Right".
THEY LEFT.

I finished my Sake and left. I wasn't ready for that kind of action yet. I had my own Religion.

We left Tokyo for Clark Air force Base in the Philippines at O'dark-thirty.

Buck had a grin on his "kisser" that if he should die, it would take twenty undertakers to take the smile off his face.

Dusty was purring like a "pussy" cat.

Amazing what that mayonnaise maker can do for a man.

Me? ---I was nursing a Sake hangover.

We stayed just three hours at Clark Air Force Base and then went on to Wake Island.

So much for CAA crew rest.

We got back to the Burbank Airport without any further ado.

I went home. My wife was there.

"How come you're not at work?" I asked.

"I quit because I'm pregnant."

She hadn't even started to show yet and she quit a job that consisted of sitting on her butt.

I propositioned her for some knooky.

"I can't do that, I'm pregnant, and besides that, what will the neighbors think?"

She went shopping.

I took another warm-soapy shower and went to bed.
AMEN & GOODNIGHT

"ALLS WELL THAT ENDS WELL"

PRFPACPJM

*****

Some quotes from
CAPTAIN LELAND
HOORAY-HOORAY---IT'S THE FIRST OF MAY
OUTDOOR FUCKING STARTS TODAY

When a new-hire Stew was sitting in the Jump Seat---
CAPTAIN LELAND

Would turn around in his seat and in the most effeminate voice and ask, ---"Would you like to hear a poem that I've composed and dedicated to the **Month of May?**"

The young Stew Lady's thoughts, ---"What a **NICE** Captain."

The young Stew Lady's words, --- "Oh, yes, Captain Sir."

Then
CAPTAIN NICE
WOULD SAY
**HOORAY HOORAY
IT'S THE FIRST OF MAY
OUTDOOR FUCKING
STARTS TODAY**

Young Stewardess Lady would look and smile.
Young Stewardess Lady would look perplexed.
Young Stewardess Lady would look in disbelief.
Young Stewardess Lady would look back.
As Young Stewardess Lady would leave the Cockpit flipping---
**CAPTAIN LE"Nice"LAND
"THE BIRD"**
Hence the nickname
CAPTAIN NICE

CAPTAIN LELAND

I flew Flight Engineer and Co-Pilot for Captain Leland. He was probably the sharpest and smartest man that I have ever known.

Smart man, ---Mind like a steel trap and fast on the trigger.

Captain Leland was an ex cat-skinner---tough and rugged---gap between his two front teeth.

The ladies loved him---even the ones that were repulsed over his drinking and vulgarity.

He drank a lot---not because he was an alcoholic, ---But because his mind was so active that he had to drink to calm it down.

When he was in his mid-fifties---PSA retired him.

Captain Leland would call in sick, apparently drunk on his butt and say to the schedulers---"Hey baby---I can't make my flight today."

"Why---what's wrong?"

"I broke my leg baby."

"Oh---that's terrible. Are you ok?"

"Oh yea---I'm fine baby. I can make my flights tomorrow though."

Well---this went on for several months and Pacific Southwest Airlines retired **CAPTAIN LELAND** to the tune of 300 bucks a month.

Seemed shitty to me because Captain Leland started with PSA in the late fifties.

He worked his as off, like we all did in those days, for slave labor wages.

I felt sorry for him till I found out that his mother had left him an acre of land in Riverside, California. And that didn't seem like a big deal till I found out that the acre of land that Leland's mom had left him was right smack dab in the middle of the City of Riverside.

I miss Leland, ---he was quite a man.

Some quotes that I heard from many Co-Pilots, ---"I'd rather fly with Leland when he's hungover than a lot of these egotistical Captains."

Some more of CAPTAIN LELEND'S---
Sayings&bullshit.

"I don't mind you shitting on me."
"I don't mind you wiping your ass on my shirt."
"But when you complain because I stink."
"That's where I draw the line."

---More---

"Leland---why are you dating that girl? ---she is duuummmb."

"Ya ever get a piece of brain---baby?"

THERE IS NO SUCH THING AS LUCK---GOOD OR BAD

TIMING
THAT'S THE NAME OF THE GAME

GOOD TIMING---BAD TIMING

You are at the right place at the right time-??GOOD LUCK??

You are at the right place at the wrong time---??????????

You are at the wrong place at the right time---??????????

You are at the wrong place at the wrong time-??BAD LUCK??

!!!YOU GET THE GREEN WEANIE!!!

SO TO YOUR GOOD TIMING FRIENDS---SAY

"GOOD TIMING"

TO YOUR BAD TIMING ENIMIES---SAY

SAYONORA
SEE YOU LATER---AGITATOR

CAPTAIN JACK RESLEY BECK---
REallyTIRED

"ALL OF LIFE OR DEATH IS A MATTER OF TIMING"

--- CIRCA ---

FEBRUARY 2---1-NINER-6-ZERO
My four-month job had turned into a year's worth of flying.
We had a nose gear collapse upon landing on Wake Island.
I was there for two weeks. **—ONEMOTIME—**
--MY FIRST SON, MARK, WAS BORN JANUARY 29, 1960 --
---WHILE I WAS ON THE ATOLL OF WAKE ISLAND---

I had already been gone for five weeks and I still wasn't near the sanctuary of home.

I called Captain Bill Butler on a Wake Island Ham's Short Wave radio. I told Captain Butler that I was quitting and wanted to come home to see my baby boy.

Chief Pilot Captain Bill Butler was very understanding.

"Okay, come on home, but you still have a job here if you change your mind. Will you work a trip to Honolulu tonight and deadhead home on the same airplane back to the "States?"

"SURE---Over and Out"

I checked in at the Wake Island International Airport at 2300 hours.

---CAPTAIN BUD MILLIGAN---
---CO-PILOT RALPH PADILLA---

---NORY ELLIS---
the orange eating, side mouthed grinning lecher
---THE NAVIGATOR---

---STEWARDESS IDELLA BROWN---
---STEWARDESS MARCELLA PADILLA---

Were already on the airplane.

I told them about my conversation with Bill.

Captain Bud Milligan, ---"You're not too bright, are you? You're quitting a good job."

Then Captain Bud Milligan light bulbed, ---"If you're going to stay on this bird all the way to the States---let's take some booze back."

Captain Milligan had done this before and knew where to hide it.

We each bought a case of Canadian Club at the Wake Island PX.

When you bought Canadian Club by the case---it was only ninety cents a fifth---compared to one dollar and ten cents a fifth when bought individually.

Captain Bud Milligan took me to the aft baggage compartment and showed me where to---

"Snuggle the smuggle".

I grabbed a screwdriver, climbed into the aft cargo compartment and opened the aft vent. ---

"Snuggle-smuggle" city.

Some peoples, ---I suspect the Twentieth Century Airline owners in cahoots with the mechanics, were smuggling transistor radios back to the States.

There looked to be at most---one hundred of them.

I could have cared less except that they were on the cables that were attached to the rudder and the elevator.

I moved the transistors off the cables and secured our booze to a bulkhead with the wire that one of the Wake Island Airport Mechanics had given me.

I swiped four of the transistors, secured the vent and went back up into the cockpit.

I told the crew about the contraband.

Captain Bud Milligan---looking at the four transistors under my arms, ---"If the bosses find out about this---they'll fire you on the spot."

"I've already quit so they can't fire me."

"Oh, -Oh---Oh yea" was Bud's reply and he said no more.

We flew to Honolulu.

Captain Bud Milligan and crew went to the Honolulu Biltmore Hotel.

"PARTY TIME"

I went through Customs.

The Customs Agent, ---"How come four transistor radios????"

"One for me--One for my wife--One for my folks-One for my wife's folks."

"OK"

I got back on the DC-6---disguised as a passenger---almost. I sat on the floor in the back cabin of the DC-6, whiffing puke and baby doo-doo.

We flew to Travis Air Force Base. Deplaned the passengers---then ferried to the Burbank International Airport.

We landed at 0100 hours.

I waited for everyone to leave, crawled into the aft cargo pit and retrieved our booze.

I also **STOLE three more transistor radio**s.

What the hell---if you're gonna steal---**steal in BOLD TYPE.**

I put all the loot in my car and was about to drive away when a pick-up drove up to the aft cargo pit.

Three guys got out of the pick-up. I recognized them as mechanics.

Two mechanics got in the aft cargo pit and one mechanic stood on the truck bed. They formed an assembly line. One mechanic was retrieving the transistors and tossing them to the mechanic at the pit's entrance---who in turn tossed them to the mechanic in the pick-up.

I waited.

The whole process took only thirty minutes. I laid down on the car seat---feigned sleeping.

They drove right by me and I went home with my loot. It was three in the morning.

I was carrying in all the contraband and my wife awakened, ---"What are you going to do with all that liquor?" She didn't drink booze and couldn't understand why I did.

I was tired, ---"I'm gonna drink it and if you don't get off my back, I'm gonna drink it all right now."

She went back to bed.

I had a couple of drinks---went to my couch---passed out.

I didn't want to get too romantic, after all, I was only away for five and a half weeks.

I got a wake up call early in the morning by a terrible howling. Shoot, it was my newborn son, ---

---MARK RESLEY BECK---

I went into the bedroom and picked him up out of his crib. He was beautiful and I was one proud father.

I found a bottle for him and a bottle for me. Marky's was white---mine was amber.

We had our fill and both fell asleep on the couch.

LOVED MARKY THEN---
LOVE CAPTAIN MARK RESLEY BECK NOW.

Except for feeding, diaper changing and Mark pissing in my face---
I slept the entire weekend.

"ALLS WELL THAT ENDS WELL"

PRFPACPJM
****

**My son
Mark Resley Beck**
Nka
CAPTAIN MARK RESLEY BECK

Decided that he wanted to become a pilot---at the age of fourteen.
"How come Marky? ---I thought you were scared of flying."
"Not anymore---the big titted Stewardesses changed my mind."
"OK Marky---I guess that's a good enough reason."
I decided to instruct him in a very small airplane.
**---FLIGHT SCHOOL OPERATER DARYLE BURGER---
---Nka CAPTAIN DARYL BURGER---
Decided to---instruct me to instruct---MARK RESLEY BECK in a light airplane.**
!!!WRONG!!!

Mister Daryl Burger and dad Beck got in a puddle jumpin' light aircraft---taxied out, ---"Gee-whiz Captain Beck---I feel funny giving you flight instructions---you being a Captain."
"We'll SEE---**WE'LL SEE**"

"Daryl---I haint got much time in one of these "kites". Actually the only hours I have in light airplanes is enough to get my Commercial License and Instrument Rating---somewhere below three hundred hours."

Mister Daryl Burger ---**"SAW"** ---became scared "shitmore". *As opposed to "shitless"*

I never got close to the ground. I would flare for landing and Daryl would calmly say, ---"Bring it on down Beck---Bring it on down."

ONE HOUR "FLEW" BY. ---I never got close to the ground. I would flare for landing and Daryl would SHOUT, ---!!!**"BRING IT ON DOWN BECK---BRING IT ON DOWN"**!!!

Finally---**MISTER DARYL BURGER** became **CAPTAIN DARYL BURGER** ---took the controls and landed the fuckin' "kite".

We taxied back to Daryl Burger's Flight School Operations.
Marky was jumping up and down---waving his arms.

Mark came to the side of the airplane---ready to jump in---get his first flight lesson from his old man.

!!!WRONG!!!
I deplaned.
"Where ya going---dad???"
"To get a beer."
"HUH"
"I'm gonna go get a beer. Get in the car."
"OK---what about my flight lesson?"
"Get in the car and I'll tell you all about it."
"OOKAAAY---DAD."
"I couldn't land the dad-blamed kite Markie---just couldn't get it close enough to the ground."
"Daryl's gonna get a flight instructor for you tomorrow."
"OK---Dad---thanks for trying."
**Daryl did and they are both flying as Captains for---
PACIFIC SOUTHWEST AIRLINES "PSA" nka US AIRWAYS
---"GOOD TIMING"---
---CAPTAIN MARK RESLEY BECK---
---CAPTAIN DARYL BURGER---**

"ALL'S WELL THAT ENDS WELL"

PRFPACPJM

****

CAPTAIN DON STEVENSEN
After I had missed my umpteenth radio call of the day
"I'm gonna get you a Plexiglas stomach Beck."
"Why Don?"
"So you can see out because you always got your head up your ass."
*****

CHIEF PILOT CAPTAIN BILLY D RAY

"I have a complaint here from a stewardess saying you're taxiing too fast. She says she has bruises all over her body from it."
"Want me to slow down Bill? ---I'll be glad to slow down."

"Chompchompchomp"---another pipe stem bites the dust, ---
"I didn't say that Jack."
"I'll be glad to slow down Bill."
"Chompchompchomp" another--- pipe stem, ---
"I didn't say that Jack."
"Whatja call me in here for?"
"Get out of here Beck."

Captain Billy D. Ray and the other Chiefs knew that if they told me to slow my taxi speed down that they would have to clock my taxi speed with a calendar.

Funny---of the maaaany times that I got called on the blood red carpet for taxiing to fast---no one ever told me to slow down. The only airports where I would taxi fast were outlying airports such as Fresno Airport in central California---and never on a wet taxiway.

The taxiway in Fresno parallels the runway except for a slight dogleg about halfway down the taxiway---which I would slow down for.

The airspeed indicator on the airplane does not start indicating till the aircraft attains 60 Knots.

I was doing about 75 Knots one sunny day and some one in the Fresno Tower laughingly said **"ROTATE".**

From then on---every body, including other airliners would say **"ROTATE"** *when I was taxiing out for take-off.*

I would get the airplane back on schedule and everyone, including the passengers, thought it was great.

I have a story about getting written up for taxiing too fast at Fresno by another Chief later on in Volume 1.

--- CIRCA ---

14 FEBRUARY 1-NINER-6-ZERO

CUPID & AMOR & EROS

VALENTINE DAY

MONDAY MORNING WAKE UP CALL---

I didn't have a job and now I had a family to support.
Thank God I didn't tell my wife. She would have ragged on me the entire weekend.
I panicked.
---Didn't know what to do or who to turn to---
I suited up in my pastensed grey flannel suit---went out to the--- **BURBANK INTERNATIONAL AIRPORT BAR** and talked to **ROY THE BARKEEP.**
I was hoping that he'd remember me.
"Yea, you're the punk kid that was in here with Buck a while back."
Well, at least he remembered me.
He knew what I wanted and before I could open my mouth, he said, ---"Los Angeles Air Service is hiring. I'll let you out the back door---walk across Runway 33. It will be the first hangar that you come to. Ask for Doc Schnitter---he's the Chief Pilot."
I walked across Runway 07/33.
Try walking across a runway without a clearance now and some one will Burp Gun your butt.
I entered the first hangar that I came to. I saw a guy dressed in dirty torn coveralls sweeping the floor. I went up to him, ---"Do you know where Captain---er-a---Doc Schnitter's office might be?"
"I'm Captain Schnitter."
I looked at Captain Schnitter somewhat dubiously---torn coveralls---broom in hand.

"I also do windows," **CHIEF PILOT CAPTAIN DOC SCHNITTER** said---chuckling and shaking my hand at the same time.

"My name is Jack Beck. I've been flying Flight Engineer for Twentieth Century Airlines across the airport over there for almost a year. ---*Pointing toward the Trans American hangar.*

"I have over 1,500 hundred hours of Flight Engineer time on a DC-6. I also have a lot of right seat time. The Captains would let me hand fly it in cruise a lot when the Autopilot was inoperative. I have even made a few descents but never have made a landing. Actually I'd like a Co-Pilot job if you have one open. I have my Commercial and Instrument rating---and---oh---yes--I was a Flight Line Mechanic for Flying Tigers for over two years."

I told Captain Schnitter about quitting Twentieth Century Airlines.

"We have a Co-pilot /Flight Engineer slot open."

This took me aback, ---"What kind of animal is that?"

"We found out by hiring Flight Engineers with a Commercial Pilot's License that we can eliminate one crew member when we multiple crew."

"Well Captain Schnitter, I believe I qualify for the job" as I showed him my "Tickets to fly".

"Good, --- be out here tomorrow at 0900 hours---we'll give you three take offs and landings and get you qualified. We're going to send you to Spain for three months."

!!!GULP!!!

All of a sudden being gone for five weeks at a time didn't seem so bad.

I took Doc's phone number and left.

I stopped back by the Burbank Airport Bar---had a beer---thanked **ROY THE BARKEEP.**

MY THOUGHT---"Well, it's either being gone for three months or its Bill Butler ass kissing time."

I finished my beer and walked diagonally across Burbank Airport's Runway 07/25 where it intersects Runway 15/33 to Twentieth Century's Hangar.

Baby how things change.

Captain Chief Pilot Bill Butler was walking around a DC-6, saw me and motioned me over, ---**"Want your job back?"**

I didn't get a chance to say nuthin'.

"Do a walk around and let's get going."

"Where?"

"We're going to ferry this DC-6 to Travis Air Force Base---pick up a broken one and bring it back."

"Who's the Co-Pilot?"

"My brother Bob."

I did a fast walk around exterior preflight and boarded the creaky DC-6. Captain Bill Butler, already strapped in the left seat, bade me to sit in the right seat. Brother Bob sat down in the Flight Engineer's seat.

Captain Bill Butler looked at me, ---**"You fly this old DC-6 to Travis. I'll fly the wounded duck back here to Burbank."**

I was nervous but not a stranger to the right seat of the **MIGHTY DC-6.**

A lot of pilots had let me steal right seat time once we got to cruise altitude, particularly when, no, always when the auto-pilot wasn't working. I know I wrote that before---but what the hell---I was proud of any right seat time that I could steal at that point in time.

This would be my first take off and landing though. The take off was shaky-smooth.

The landing was a litta shaky-smooth—actually---a lotta shaky.

Bill just sat there with his hands on his lap. Calm as could be. After all, we had more than two miles of landing runway to work with. He knew that sooner or later we'd get on the ground ---**even if they had to shoot us down.**

We finally got on the ground and taxied to the gate.

On the way to the gate---Travis Ground Control called us, ---**"What were you guys practicing out there? I've never seen that many gyrations, all at one time—in my life."**

Captain Bill Butler, ---"We were just trying to see how long a landing we could make and still be safe."

Ground Control snickered, "Sure. ---I hope I'm still here for your take-off. Its guys like you that make my job fun."

I was mortified and felt like crawling under the seat.

Chief Pilot Captain Bill Butler ---sensed my chagrin, grabbed me by the shoulder, "Don't worry about it Beck, ---you'll do a lot worse than that before you retire."

CAPTAIN BILL BUTLER was right---as usual.

I DID---more than once, as a matter of fact---a whole shitpot full of times.

We found the broken DC-6 with a broken engine---a three engine ferry.

No big deal to get a ferry permit in those days. Now it takes ten mechanics and an act of Congress to get a ferry permit.

Captain Bill Butler flew us back.

Co-Pilot Jack Beck keyed his mike and said, ---"Burbank Tower---this is Twentieth Century Airlines ferry 169. ---How do you read?"

"Five by five Butler, ---where you is?"

Captain Bill Butler picked up his mike and said, ---"We're over Simi Valley---about ten miles out at five thousand feet."

"Oh yea---we see you guys out there. You're cleared to land Runway 25. Wind is out of the northwest at twenty five knots---gusting to thirty five knots. All the light airplanes are grounded. A Santa Ana wind is kicking in big time. It's supposed to get worse. Better hurry on down."

Co-Pilot Jack Beck, ---"Roger---Twentieth Century Airlines Ferry 169 is cleared to land Runway 25. You're right about it kicking up some. Ya can't see Palmdale for the blowing sand."

*****

SANTA ANA WIND---Blows hot and dry out of the desert---fastly. The Native Americans call it---"DEVIL WIND".

*****

The approach was a tricky one. ---You had to skirt the mountains that are east of the Burbank Airport and get the holybejesus kicked out of you from the updrafts of the wind blasting up and down and around the San Gabriel Mountains.

I glanced over at **Captain Bill Butler.**

Captain Bill Butler had a cup of coffee in his right hand and the yoke in the other. He was manipulating the throttles with his right elbow, calm as a cucumber.

Come to think of it, I have never seen a nervous cucumber.

I was shaking like a dog shittin' razor blades.

When we were one hundred feet above the runway, Captain Bill Butler put down his coffee, kicked in full left rudder, lowered the right wing and greased the Mighty DC-6 right on the numbers.

Captain Bill Butler picked up his coffee mug, took a sip, ---taxied us to the gate.

CAPTAIN BILL BUTLER---Spilt nary a drop. ---**WHATAGUY.**

I looked back at Bob Butler to make a comment about what a great approach and landing his brother Bill had made. I had never seen that shade of burple on anyone's face before, as a matter of fact, I had never seen that shade of burple anywhere before.

I said nothing---turned back around.

I went into Chief Pilot Captain Bill Butler's Office and phoned Captain Doc Schnitter, ---"Captain Schnitter, Sir, ---I'm going to stay with Twentieth Century Airlines. My wife just had a baby boy and I have a need to be home."

"I understand Jack---figured that much. I saw you over there consorting with the enemy." ---Doc laughed and hung up.

Came to find out that Captain Bill Butler and Captain Doc Schnitter were the best of buds and that they had started out together as Flight Instructors at Grand Central Airport in Glendale, California.

I started to leave---

Chief Pilot Captain Bill Butler, ---"Whatever happened to that uniform that you got at Tarpy Tailors? You seemed so anxious to get it. Didn't you like the color? *Chuckle---chuckle*"

"Oh shit---guess that I forgot about it. I'm sorry---you were so nice to buy it for me. I feel like a schmuck."

"Not a problem for me Jack---I've kept you pretty busy. Oh and by the way---all the Captains have given me good feedback on how you handle your self on the airplane---and on the ground. They tell me that you keep 'em flying with your mechanical know how."

"I'm proud of you Jack. Makes me happy that I took a chance on you and hired you."

"Thanks," ---I turned my head to hide my teary eyes and started to my car.

CHIEF PILOT CAPTAIN BILL BUTLER---walked with me to my car with his arm around my shoulder---shook my hand---patted me on the back.

I LEFT

I rushed on over to Tarpy Tailors near the Los Angeles International Airport and picked up my two striped, shit-brindle brown, taco-throw-up-accordianated uniform from **Tailor Tarpy at sleeves-length.**

I entered Tarpy Tailor's bathroom---**LOCKED** the door---put on **MY UNIFORM.**

The shit-brindle pants were tight in the crotch and loose in the waist.

The jacket fit just right.

I looked in the mirror at the two stripes on each arm.

I left Tarpy Tailors with my uniform on---wasn't ever gonna take it off---probably sleep in it.

I was walking tall.
I went home and opened the box of wings that **Chief Pilot Captain Bill Butler** had given me on **the day** he hired me and gave me the break of my life time and a wonderful flying career.
???HUH???
The hat wing's logo ---
---TRANS AMERICAN AIRLINES---
The Uniform Jacket wing's logo ---
---NORTH AMERICAN AIRLINES---
I motored back to Twentieth Century Airlines at the Burbank International Airport.
I asked **Chief Pilot Captain Bill Butler** for some---
---TWENTIETH CENTURY AIRLINES WINGS---
"These are the wings we use--the owners go IRS Bankrupt---start another airline---use the same wings---save bucks for gasoline.
You are flying for ---
"NORTH AMERICAN"
"TRANS AMERICAN"
"TWENTIETH CENTURY AIRLINES"
I left

*****

According to Honest Abe, ---"All men are created equal"— Then the umbilical cord is cut & then it haint necessarily so.

Heard outside the Ford Theater, ---"Other than that, Misses Lincoln, how was the play?"

*****

Ya never know whatcha have till ya lose it---ask some ex-spouses.

*****

--- CIRCA ---

FEBRUARY 29---1960
Leap Day

I went home and there was a telegram from Continental Airlines.

IF YOU ARE STILL INTERESTED IN EMPLOYMENT WITH CONTIENTAL AIRLINES STOP CONTACT CONTINENTAL AIRLINES CHIEF PILOT'S OFFICE AT 303-485-2752 IMMEDIATELY STOP CHIEF PILOT CAPTAIN SKIPPER MAKELY STOP

I telephoned the next morning,.
"RING---RING---RI--"
"Chief Pilot's Office---Captain Makely here."
"Sir, this is Jack Beck---I received a telegram from you yesterday about employment with Continental Airlines."
"Yea, hang on. -----Yea I got your application right here--let's take a look----------------Hummm-OK. Is it true that you have a Commercial Pilot's License and Instrument Rating along with fifteen hundred hours of Flight Engineer's time logged?"
"Yes sir---I do."
"Can you come to Denver tomorrow for a couple of days? We need you to take a battery of tests and a physical."
"Sure, I'll be there."
"Good, I'll have a ticket waiting for you at the Continental ticket counter at the Los Angeles Airport---0700 hours departure time."
I called Captain Bill Butler and told him what had transpired.
Chief Pilot Captain Bill Butler, ---"Good luck to you. Call me when you get back---I may need you for a trip next week."
"Yes Sir---I'll do that."
I arrived at the Los Angeles International Airport at 0500 hours the next morning and went to Continental's ticket counter.
The ticket counter was dark; in fact, I was the only living soul around.
A ticket agent finally showed up. He gave me my tickets to ride muy pronto.

MY THOUGHT---Pretty snazzy service---of course---I was the only one in line.

I boarded the mighty Boeing 707---first one on.

We landed at Stapleton Airport in the "Mile High City" by the name of Denver, Colorado.

I deplaned---called---**Chief Pilot Captain Skipper Makely.**

"Stand out by the baggage pick-up and I'll send a Continental marked car for you. I'd come get you myself but it's a zoo over there at this time of the morning and I might miss you."

Ten minutes later ---I was in a car and on my way to be a Continental Airline employee, or so I thought.

The driver directed me to the Chief Pilot's Office, which was in Continental Airline's Overhaul Hanger.

I met Chief Pilot Captain Makely for the first time. Nice old guy, a little grey around the temples but other than that, he looked like he was in pretty good shape.

"Good Morning, Chief Pilot Captain Snakely—er--Makely, ---SIR."

"People call me Speedy. I prefer Speedy over SIR."

"OK—er—SIR—er—Speedy."

I showed him my licenses, first class medical certificate and my **LOGBOOK**---which was as phony as a Three-Dollar Bob.

"I understand you've been flying the South Pacific for Bill Butler."

I was taken aback, ---"How do you know that?"

"We're old Non-Sked buddies. Bill called here and put in a good word for you."

Speedy walked me over to the infirmary, which was just across the street from his office--- introduced me to the nurse and told her that I was a new hire.

"Come back to my office when you're through with this bullshit."

"OK—er—sir-Speedy."

He left

Nancy Nurse started out by drawing a couple of gallons of blood out of my scrawny bod and then put me on a treadmill for thirty minutes.

Then Nancy Nurse made me lie down and put electrodes---

---**"ALL OVER MY BODY"**---

I had never seen an EKG performed before and inquired, nervously, ---"Is this thing gonna shock me?"

"You'll feel no pain." ---She said with a laugh of the Wicked Witch of the North as she eagerly pushed the execution button.

Hmmm.

After that Nancy Nurse gave me a series of written tests.

Some psychological and some to test my knowledge.

It was called a **STANINE TEST**---two hundred questions.

Nancy Nurse explained to me, that in order to pass, I had to fall into a certain

---**GREY AREA**---

Above it, the **BLACK AREA**---meant that I was too smart to fly airplanes.

Below it, the **WHITE AREA**---meant that I was too dumb to fly airplanes.

Didn't make any sense to me, at that time, but I found out over the years: ---

The geniuses---the Pilots in the **BLACK AREA**---the Pilots who knew more about the subjects in ground school than the instructors---sweat a lot---couldn't cut the airfoil---went and sold shoes at Kinney's.

The dummies, the Pyluts in the WHITE AREA, didn't sweat a lot, couldn't cut the ayrfoyl and went and sold shoes at Kinneys.

Some of the questions ranged from **did I like my mother's tits to how many gears went this-a-way and that-a-way.**

Seemed to me that the guy who made it up must have been a **combination of a pervert and a mechanical freak.**

Chief Pilot Captain Makely---Er---Speedy arrived at five to pick me up.

"Mister Beck's not finished with his tests yet Speedy."

"Uh---uh---okay. He can finish them manana---its Miller time."

"I'm going to drop you off at your motel and you can finish up the tests tomorrow. I'll pick you up at 0900. I have "**The Box**" scheduled for you at 1400 hours.

*****

---"**THE BOX**"---

---**A CHARLES LINDBERG ERA FLIGHT SIMULATOR**---

A LINK TRAINER WITH PHONY WINGS & NO WINDOWS THAT MAKES YOUR ASSHOLE PUCKER AND YOUR SWEAT GLANDS OVERACTIVE FROM THE TIME YOU SEE IT TILL YOU GET BACK HOME. ---*and have a couple of beers down your gut.*

"Thanks for the ride. I'll see you at 0900."

The next day I finished the rest of the written tests---wandered over to Speedy's office.

He was not there and I had one hour to waste before I took my check ride. I did a fast walk-about to try to get rid of the jitters.

It helped a little---damned little.

Speedy found me and walked me over to where the Link Trainer was located.

Captain Skipper Makely—er---Speedy introduced me to the instructor. He left.

I got in the "Box" and proceeded to take my check ride.

It was the, now obsolete, ---**LOW FREQUENCY AURAL RANGE.**

This consisted of making an approach entirely by sound---without visual clues.

It consisted of a big X with the A quadrant being East and West and the N quadrant being North and South. The N section would sound a dah-dit and the A section would sound a dit-dah.

You would take up a heading and when you intercepted a leg of the X, the dah-dit and the dit-dah would sound as one and then you would take up the published heading of that leg. If the signal got weaker it meant that you were going the wrong way.

$$N$$
$$A \quad X \quad A$$
$$N$$

You would then make a one hundred and eighty degree turn and track inbound on the leg you went out on. Now the signal should be getting stronger until you get to the "Cone of Silence," where the signal quits. At this point you would descend to your published altitude, fly the published heading and commence your approach and---

Pray that you would see the airport in time to land.

The minimums for getting below the clouds and above the surrounding terrain were very high---thus when you descended below the clouds and saw the airport---you were assholes and elbows getting down to the airport.

I did all of these procedures with ease and got out of **THE BOX.**

I FLUNKED.

According to the Check Airman's charts---I bounced off every mountain west of Denver.

I was mortified. ---I didn't even go back to see Speedy.

I skulked over to the terminal and boarded a Continental Boeing 707 bound for the---**Los Angeles International Airport** ---sobbing.

!!!UPON OUR DESCENT INTO LAX!!!

It was apparent that we were a little high on approach coming into the Los Angeles Airport because the crew reversed the inboard engines. --- *#2 engine and #3 engine*

I never had experienced an in-flight reversal before. Strictly against FAA law. *Me thinks*

Talk about shake, rattle and roll.

I thought we had skimmed off a mountain or the Boeing 707 was disintegrating.

Sorta felt like a Mack Truck slamming on his airbrakes at 80 MPH.

All the coffee pots and miniature booze bottles came hurtling down the aisle.

I leaned out in the aisle and commandeered a handful of Mister Jim Beams.

I sloshed them down---I stopped sobbing. **I started bawling.**
*****

Amazing how a little amber elixir can turn all those little nagging problems into------ONE BIG BACK-BREAKER---
PER CAPTAIN LELAND
*****

As I look back on it now, it was a blessing in disguise. I would have been working for that egomanYical *$!*%&*^%% Lorenzo, who has ruined the careers and lives of so many airline employees ---and he probably would have ruined mine.

You never know, pilgrim---you just never know.
********PARTICULARLY IN THE AIRLINE TRADE********
I would have been Continental Airlines first pilot/flight engineer
One day you're sitting in the LEFT Seat---making beaucou bucks.
Next day you're selling shoes at Kinney's---looking up women's skirts.
OR
One day you're selling shoes at Kinney's---looking up women's skirts.
Next day you're sitting in the Co-Pilot's seat. ---
???Wondering what that asshole sitting next to you is doing---
Sitting in your chair???

I called Chief Pilot Captain Bill Butler the next day and told him what had transpired in Denver.

I thought Bill would chastise me or at least call me a dumb shit.

All Bill said was, ---"No problem. By the way, I need you for a trip on Tuesday."

"Where to? ---How long?"

"This one is stateside. You'll be back in a week.
Check in is at 0900 HOURS."

"Who's the Captain?"

I knew most of the Captains by now and had my favorites, ---
CAPTAIN DIRTY DAN TIBBETTS ---being #1---atop of the list.

Bill, ---"Ronnie May"

Beck, ---"He's a great guy to fly with."

Bill, ---"Good---glad you like him."

Beck, ---"Never heard of him."

Bill, ---"Okaaay Beck, guess you've had too many trips with Dirty Dan."---
-*"chuckle---chuckle"*

Beck, ---"Thanks"---I hung up---went and did my laundry.

--- CIRCA ---

MARCH 3---1NINERSEXZERO

I checked in early Tuesday morning, at
---TWENTIETH CENTURY AIRLINES OPERATIONS---
---BURBANK INTERNATIONAL AIRPORT---
Introduced myself to ---
---CAPTAIN RONNIE MAY---

I did my Pre-flight walk-around and Cockpit pre-flight of the ---
---MIGHTY DC-6 SILVER WINGED AIRLINER---
We did all the fundamental checklists necessary to take wing---taxied out to Runway 15.

We were number five in line for take off. There were four other DC-6s in front of us---all of them flying to the same airport that we were flying to.

The first DC-6 took off and, as we watched its path of flight, saw all four engines quit just as it lifted off. The DC-6 flew head on into a Mausoleum that was in a grave yard off the end of Burbank Airport's Runway 15.

Captain Ronnie May talked to the pilots of the other airplanes and suggested that we all go back to the gate and run up our engines.

Captain Ronnie May told them that we had seen all four engines quit on the airplane that crashed.

Everyone ranted and raved thinking Ronnie May was trying to pull a fast one and be number one for takeoff.
An old non-sked trick

Finally Ronnie May said, ---**"I don't give a shit what you guys do---I'm going back to the gate."**

Now there was a mad scramble to go back to our respective ramps.
We taxied to our ramp.

Captain Ronnie May pointed the Mighty DC-6's tail toward the blast fence---set the parking brakes---gestured for me to run up the engines.

I DID
I ran up all four engines at maximum power.
!!!ALL FOUR ENGINES QUIT WITHIN TWENTY SECONDS!!!

I put the mixture controls to cutoff---got out of my seat---went back into the passenger cabin---pulled out the right over-wing emergency exit---climbed out on the wing.

I opened a fuel cap and took a whiff.

Smelled like gasoline. ---

Looked like gasoline. ---.

Tasted like gasoline. ---

Just like 115/130 Purple Gasoline should smell-look-taste like.

I slid down a ladder that a Mech had put up to the wing---unbuttoned the cowling on #3 engine---pulled a spark plug out of a cylinder---examined it.

Looked like oil---smelled like oil---tasted like oil ---**IT WAS OIL.**

I clambered back up on the wing.

I took the caps off the **ADI TANKS.**

The ADI liquid looked like oil---smelled like oil---tasted like oil --- IT WAS OIL.

*****

ADI
ANTI-DETONATING-INJECTION

Sounds like something you'd like to give to your ex-wife.

ADI is a fluid made up of Isopropyl and other assorted alcohols. It is injected into the cylinders at take-off power to cool the engines so more horsepower can be extracted from the engines. Without the ADI---the engines would disintegrate at higher power settings due to excessive heat. Nuts and bolts a.nd aluminum all over the numbers at the end of the runway.

So much for ground school---Whew---sorry I started that bullshit.

*****

When the ADI fluid was called for at take-off power, the oil entered the cylinders and fouled the spark plugs.

THE ENGINES QUIT INSTANTLY.

The Mechs and I drained and flushed all the ADI tanks and changed all the spark plugs.

Captain Ronnie May and I took the DC-6 back over to the blast fence and ran each engine individually up for five minutes at full power.

Works fine—Lasts a long time. ---*I pray a lot*

Captain Ronnie May was satisfied that we had a sound airplane.

We left for all the Metropolises in the United States.

Flat Rock, Kansas---Bumfuc, Idaho---Clive, Iowa---Podunk, Texas--Intercourse, Pennsylvania.

We landed one place where half of the town came out to greet us. There was a horde of twenty, including children, cats and dogs. The place was so small that the town prostitute was still a virgin.

The highlight of the trip was a layover in New York City. I went to my first, last and only Broadway Play ever.

The play was on Broadway and was titled---
"THE SWEET BIRD OF YOUTH"
Starring an aspiring young **Salad Dressing** maker by the name of **MISTER PAUL NEWMAN.**

Captain Ronnie May saved a lot of lives and aluminum that day in Burbank. Ronnie didn't like mausoleums or graveyards and it was not his day to visit them.

Ronnie got killed a few years later taking off out of La Garbage, oops, I meant La Guardia Airport in a Stretch DC-8.

Captain Ronnie May rotated on take off and a chunk of concrete flew off of one of the tires and jammed itself between the elevator and the horizontal stabilizer.

The hunk of concrete froze the elevator in a nose up position.

The Stretch DC-8 went straight up for as long as its engines could sustain lift, stalled, turned over on its back and crashed.

The crew was the only souls on board. ---They all perished.
"FATE IS THE HUNTER"---ERNIE GANN

*****

OLD PROVERB
---MONEY IS THE ROOT OF ALL EVIL---
NEW PROVERB
--NOW IT'S THE WHOLE FRIGGIN' TREE--
*****

I would crawl through a mile of broken glass just to smell the exhaust of the laundry truck that takes Shania's undies to the cleaners.

*****

This question I ask my kids:
Are you as happy or happier now--- than you were last year at this time?

And the Answer is:
Yes---You're on a good horse---ride it well.
No---Cut across the grass and take another route.
Down the road of life on a different horse-course.

*****

PURGATORY
WEBSTERS NEW WORLD COLLEGE DICTIONARY
"Any state or place of temporary punishment, expiation, or remorse"

PURGATORY
BECKSTERS OLD WORLD SCHOOL OF HARD KNOCKS DICTIONARY
*"Any state or place of temporary punishment, **expiation**, or remorse between*
"IDO&IDONT"
Expiation--- *to pay the penalty of & make amends for.*

*****

Here's something that I want to ask you folks that are reading this bullshit—

???ARE WE IN PURGATORY AT THIS POINT IN TIME???
"OH---I LOVE HER/HIM SO MUCH--I'M IN "HEAVEN".
---*TEN YEARS---IN PURGATORY*---
"HE/SHE MAKES MY LIFE IS A LIVING "HELL".

CAPTAIN JACK RESLEY BECK---REallyTIRED

--- CIRCA ---

A DAY IN APRIL---1-NINER-6-ZERO

We arrived back in Burbank a week later. The month was April and there was nothing on the bulletin board about a new contract.

I called CHIEF PILOT CAPTAIN BILL BUTLER the next day and inquired if a new contract was in the offing.

"Haven't got a clue as to what is happening, but if I hear anything, you'll be the first to know."

"Thanks---Thanks for everything Bill---
I really appreciate everything.
I'll always remember you and what you have done for me.
Thanks again. ---So-long."
Well---I do remember
---WITH TEARS IN MY EYES---

*****CHIEF PILOT CAPTAIN BILL BUTLER*****

I DEDICATE THIS BOOK TO YOU BILL
THANK YOU

"ALLS WELL THAT ENDS WELL"

PRFPACPJM

*****

Twentieth Century went tits up in the latter part of Nineteen-Sixty.
Los Angeles Air Service became Trans International Airlines –
Based at Oakland, California.
CAPTAIN BILL BUTLER BECAME CHIEF PILOT AT TIA
(TIA---pronounced Teeya)
TIA lasted until the end of the seventies.
The Chiefs took their "Golden Parachutes", ---
Bailed out and landed in Beverly Hills.

The Indians also bailed out and landed in Beverly Hills, ---selling shoes to the Chiefs at Kinneys.
*****

$$$"Golden Parachutes"$$$
The Scourge Of The Working Man
Not So Very Long Ago---
OOOOO Airlines Was Going To Buy XXXX Airlines. The Ceo of XXXXX Was Going To Bail Out Of XXXXX with His Golden Parachute ---To The Tune of 250 Million American Dollars.
No Shit---Ladies and Gentleman---
$250,000,000$

Just thought that maybe you stockholders might want to know where your money goes.
*****

XXXXXX just went through its second bankruptcy.
I understand that the CEO still has a golden parachute.

--- CIRCA ---

1 MAY---1-NINER-6-ZERO
*Hooray---hooray---it's the first of May
Outdoor fucking starts today.*
CAPTAIN LELAND

MAYDAY---MAYDAY---MAYDAY
**I was starting to get antsy about my future income making.
I HAD A FAMILY TO SUPPORT.**
I went out to the Burbank Airport, ---saw **ROY THE BARKEEP.**
Roy poured me a beer, ---"What dya want now, Kid Beck?"
I stammered-blushed-blanched---could not speak.

Roy the Barkeep laughed---went over by the phone---wrote something down---handed the note to me, ---"That's Captain Russ Kreig's phone number---he's the Chief Pilot for Aero Americana---or somthin' like that. He called over here a few minutes ago and is in desperate need of a DC6 Flight Engineer."

"He's so hard up for one that he might even hire you," ---**Roy the Barkeep** said with a sly grin.
Thank you,
---ROY THE BARKEEP---
OF THE
---BURBANK AIRPORT TERMINAL BAR---
I LEFT.
I called Russ Kreig and asked if he was in want of a Flight Engineer.
"Yes---YES---**VERY MUCH SO**. Do you have a Flight Engineer's License?"

"Yessir, and a Commercial and Instrument tickets also."
"Well---do you have any DC6 time at all?"
"Yessir---over fifteen hundred hours, ---I've been flying for Twentieth Century Airlines out of Burbank Airport for the last year."
"You've been flying for Butler???"
"Yes sir"
He sounded impressed, ---**"CAN YOU BE OVER HERE AT 1700 HOURS TODAY?** We have a test hop scheduled at that time and we'll take a look at you. Aerovidas Sud Americana is based at the freight terminal on the south side of the Los Angeles International

238

Airport. We have a test hop scheduled today and we'll have a look at you."

"Aerovious what???"

"AEROVIDAS SUD AMERICANA"

"There's a guard at the freight entrance gate---ask him. He'll point you our way."

"Thanks, I'll be there---bye."

I left early to avoid the rush hour traffic and got there two hours ahead of time.

I found the **Aerovidas Sud Americana** Chief Pilot's office and met---**CHIEF PILOT CAPTAIN RUSS KREIG.**

Handsome man with curly black hair.

He was sitting at his desk with a good-looking blonde on his lap.

"Mister Beck---I'd like for you to meet my wife, Jeanie."

Which I took for bullshit

"Nice meeting you---maam."

Came to find out later, that in fact, she was his wife.

YOU NEVER KNOW---PILGRIM---YOU JUST NEVER KNOW

"You're a little early. Anxious?"

I nodded my head "yes"---couldn't speak---had a lump in my throat. ---

My Adams Apple had turned into cider.

"We're in luck. The mechanics finished early and the airplane is out on the tarmac waiting for us. Let's go out to the airplane. I'll watch you do a pre-flight walk around and a cockpit preflight. The mechs replaced all the control surfaces pushrods and we have to do a test flight. We'll just do an engine shut down---start her up and come right back. It's almost Miller Time."

We eventually made our way into the cockpit.

I did a before start checklist and only then did it dawn on me that we didn't have a Co-pilot.

About that time, Jeanie tapped me on the shoulder, ---"Excuse me---I have to get by you."

I wondered where she thought she was going. I got up and put my seat up so she could get by.

She deftly slid into the right seat and buckled up.

All the while, Captain Russ Krieg was watching my face to see my reaction.

My jaw dropped and Russ broke out laughing, ---"She's got all the ratings and is a damn good pilot."

I shrugged my shoulders, --- "Fine with me."
We took off and I shut down an engine and restarted it.
Russ, ---"I've seen enough---let's go home."
We went back to the airport---landed---deplaned---went into Captain Russ Kreig's 8X8 office.
"You're hired. Be here tomorrow at fifteen hundred hours."
"I can't make it. I've got to give Twentieth Century Airlines two weeks notice."

Captain Russ Kreig shrugged his shoulders, picked up the phone and dialed a number by memory, ---"Bill, I have a Flight Engineer of yours that I need for tomorrow and he insists on giving you two weeks notice---Yea, it's Beck---Okay, I'll tell him."

Captain Russ Kreig turned to me, ---"You're off the hook Jack. Be here tomorrow at 1500 hours."

All of a sudden it occurred to me that I had no idea where I was going to be flying to. With a name like Aerovidas Sud Americana, only God and Russ knew where we were going. *And maybe Jeanie*

"Where are we going tomorrow?"

Russ and Jeanie both laughed.

Russ, --- "Cape Canaveral. ---The trip is a piece of cake---we get to Cape Canaveral, Florida early Thursday morning and get back home Saturday afternoon at fifteen hundred hours.

I'll explain it all to you tomorrow. In the meantime, we're going to go have a couple of beers and wait for the traffic to ease up. ---Want to come along?"

"Sure"---sounded better than sitting on the San Berdoo Freeway at rush hour."

*****

**I called CAPTAIN BILL BUTLER the next morning.
"Thanks Bill ---thanks for giving me a start in life."
"Good luck Jack ---See you around."**
*****

--- CIRCA ---

2 MAY 1960

Hooray---hooray---It's the second day of May
Outdoor fucking started yesterday.

I checked in Wednesday afternoon a little early. Russ and Jeanie, our female Co-pilot clad in a tight sweater and mini skirt, were already there and rarin' to go. Come to think about it, she was probably the only Commercial Woman Pilot in the world in nineteen-sixty. *Confucius say---"Woman who fly upside down have clack-up."*

We had no Stewardesses on board, ---so Russ, using his good old Yankee know how, brought along his own Stew.

We took off, headed south at two hundred feet **AGL** and went along the shoreline. Jeanie was flying and doing one helluva job.
AGL--Above Ground Level--But in this case A-S-L--Above Sea Level.
Russ was enjoying the scenery, both inside and outside the cockpit.

All of a sudden it hit me.

We were going south toward Mexico.

The name of the airlines translated to Airlines of South America.
---me thinks

Cape Canaveral was ninety degrees to the left.

I got a litta, no a lotta anxious and tapped Russ on the shoulder and inquired, ----**"How come we're not heading East?"**

Russ sensed my concern, laughed, ---"I'm sorry. I promised you our routing. It's very simple---we go to San Diego first---then Denver---then on to Cape Canaveral---lay over for thirty hours and return back to Los Angeles by the same routing."

"Starting today, we have a contract with NASA for one year. We haul rocket parts both ways. We take the new parts out and bring the used parts back."

My qualms dissuaded, I then could concentrate my juices on Jeanie's mini skirt.

We took on part of our cargo at San Diego and continued on to the mile high city of Denver where we took on the remainder of the cargo ---then left for Cape Canaveral.

When we got to our cruising altitude, Jeanie excused herself and went in the back to lie down on a palette that she and Russ had made up before we took off.

Russ motioned for me to get in the right seat, ---which I did in a heartbeat.

Captain Russ Krieg clicked off the auto-pilot and motioned for me to hand-fly the DC6.

I was awesome.

I kept that puppy at exactly fifteen thousand feet. Didn't waiver an RCH. *red cunt hair*

Russ watched me for a while, ---"Nice job."---

Then Captain Russ Kreig got out of his seat and went to the back to join Jeanie.

I was alone---I was in command. ---The ace of the base and doing one helluva job.

Russ and Jeanie came back to the cockpit when it was time to start our descent and I begrudgingly got back in the Flight Engineer's seat.

--- CIRCA ---

3 May 1960
Hooray---hooray, it's the third o---
Forget it, that's enough of that bullshit for now.

We landed at Cape Canaveral early Thursday Morning ---
---Taxied to the loading docks---
I opened the forward cargo door and slid down the emergency escape rope. ---Found a ladder and put it up so Russ and Jeanie could deplane. Couldn't help but notice Jeanie as she came down the ladder. Nice wheels.

She saw me looking and smiled. Proud woman she was.

I did a post flight of the airplane to make sure it would be ready to go on Friday.

We went into the town of Coco Beach and got our rooms. --- then went to a bar and had a couple of beers.

I got up to leave and Russ grabbed me by the arm, ---"Be in the lobby at eight. We're gonna party hearty tonight."

I was---we did and I woke up Friday afternoon with an excruciating headache. It was gonna be a long trip home.

---HEADWINDS AND A HANGOVER---
We landed at the Los Angeles Airport Saturday morning.
This was the job that I was looking for.

Sunday through Tuesday and the better part of Wednesday off, a thousand bucks a month, a great guy to fly with and a mini skirt to ogle.

!!!LIFE WAS GOOD!!!
*****

A man & his wife were walking down a corridor at the Burbank (BUR) Airport---they discovered they had gone the wrong way.

This is what I heard as I was passing through the boarding lounge, ---"%& *#$^^& *Harry, you led us the wrong way."---
*"**Shit Martha**, how was I to know this was the wrong corridor?"*
***And** that, gentleman, is the American way---*

A married couple going the wrong way in a place that's new to both of them and the old man's getting his ass chewed for a mistake they both made.

Haint no fuckin' justice, guys.
*****

These two Afro American ladies were having their pictures taken at a photo studio.
　When the photographer went under his hood, ---
The one lady asked the other lady, ---"What's he doing?"
　"He's gonna focus."
　"Bof of us?"
*****

Pat and Mike were drinking buddies that worked as airplane mechanics in Pittsburgh, Pennsylvania.
　One day the airport was fogged in and they were stuck in the hangar with nothing to do.
　Pat said, --- "Man, I wish we had something to drink!"
　Mike said, --- "Me too, y'know, I've heard that you can drink jet fuel and get a buzz."---
　"You wanna try it?"
　They poured themselves a couple of glasses of high-octane hooch and got completely smashed.
　The next morning---Pat wakes up and is surprised at how good he feels. In fact he feels great.
　NO hangover---no bad side effects. Nothing!
　The phone rings---
　It's Mike---"Hey Pat---I feel great. How do you feel this morning?"
　Pat says---"I feel great also---You don't have a hangover Mike?"---
　"No that jet fuel is great stuff---no hangover---nuthin---we ought to do this more often."---
　"Yeah---well there is just one thing."---
　"What's that?"---
　"Have you farted yet?"
　---**"NO"**---
　"Well don't---I'm in **PHOENIX.**"
*****

--- CIRCA ---

ZERO NINER-MAY---1960

We took off from Denver one night heading for Cape Canaveral.
I couldn't get the Douglas DC-6A to pressurize.
I tried everything that I knew. No luck. I even read the airplane's manual, which was unheard of at that point of Aviation Time.
No luck.
*****

DC-6A---cargo configuration---DC-6B---passenger configuration---I believe that's the case in all airplanes---me thinks---but who knows--- ***"Only the shadow knows"****---remember that old radio program?*
*****

We flew to Cape Canaveral unpressurized at fifteen thousand feet.

Russ wasn't real happy with my performance. Breathing rarified air at fifteen thousand feet for six hours tends to make a "man a little of woozy and a lot of cranky".

No palette time with Jeanie magnified Russ's pissoffidism.

We landed at Cape Canaveral and taxied to the loading docks.

I knew there was something wrong and I was determined to find out what.

I opened the forward cargo door. I didn't even use the emergency escape rope. **I just jumped out of the forward cargo door and hit the ground running.**

I didn't go fifty feet and I found the culprit. Some bozo had driven the forklift's tines through the fuselage---a couple of inches below the aft cargo door ---never bothered to tell us.

There were two holes about six inches by twelve inches that were leaving the air out of our aluminum balloon.

I got a ladder and helped Russ and Jeanie out of the airplane.

I grabbed Russ by the arm and showed him our gaping holes.

Russ was smiling and pissed at the same time.

Captain Russ Krieg, ---"It's a good thing the forklift tines didn't hit anything structural or we wouldn't be standing here right now."

I was vindicated.

"Sorry I doubted you."---Patted me on the back.

We found a mechanic and showed him our problem.

"I can fix it in a couple of hours if I can use **scab patches**."

*****

SCAB PATCH

So named because it looks like a scab on your skin.
*Scab patches are fastened with **cherry** rivets, so named because you don't have to **buck** them.*

*****

Cherry rivets are so called because you can put them in a blind "hole" and plug it up without anyone "bucking" it on the other side.

A mechanic told me that there was/is a sexual connotation to the cherry rivets so you are going to have to use your imagination. My virgin mind never could figure it out.

Come on you guys ---use your imagination.

Scab patches cause drag and are usually temporary so you can get back to your home base and get the injury fixed properly.

*Not so in the case of this old freighter---she had so many scab patches on her that she looked like a heavyweight that just went 15 rounds— **and lost**.*

*****

"Fine with us," Captain Russ Krieg said and we departed for our favorite watering hole.

Came the next afternoon and we went to the airport. I was hung over and feeling awfully burpee.

Russ sat down in the right seat and motioned for me to get in the left seat.

Jeanie sat in the Flight Engineers seat with her mini skirt at half-mast. She sure liked to show off what she had and I will have to admit---she had it.

I taxied out to Runway 19 and put the parking brakes on. I started to get out of the seat. Captain Russ Krieg grabbed me by the shoulder and sat me back down, ---**"MAKE THE TAKE OFF."**

I started shaking like the leaves on an Aspen Tree in the Rockies in September.

All I could think of was that I was going to fly this monster off the ground from the left seat. Every thing that I had learned went down the tubes. I had tunnel vision. All I could focus in on was one instrument. The rest of the instruments were a blur. *Just like this paragraph.*

I locked in on the airspeed indicator. I knew I would need that one over all the others.

I turned to my right and asked Jeanie for take-off power.

Jeanie leaned forward and set the power, which hiked her mini skirt up even higher. My myopia went from the airspeed indicator to Jeanie's legs.

I forced myself to look at the instrument panel and by that time we were at take off speed.

I pulled back on the yoke and we lifted off. I sat for a moment, astounded by my accomplishment.

Russ tapped me on the shoulder, ---**"Do you want me to bring the gear up?"**

!!!CARDINAL SIN!!!
I FORGOT TO RETRACT THE LANDING GEARS.
Or in this case---The take off gears
Some pilots have forgotten, ---some pilots have wished that they hadn't forgotten.

"Yes, please."
I didn't even try to hide my embarrassment.
Russ chuckled, but said nothing. He knew that I had **tunnel vision**.

*****

Let me explain tunnel vision. ---It's like looking up a ladies skirt. You can't see the forest for the pubes. You forget to look around and see the other things necessary to flying and living.
*****

I hand flew The Mighty DC-6 to cruise altitude---engaged the auto-pilot---started to get out of the left seat.

Once again Captain Russ Krieg put his hand on my shoulder and pushed me back down, --- "You're doing fine Jack. Jeannie and I are going to get some naptime---ring us if you get sleepy."

Captain Russ Kreig disengaged the auto-pilot and went back in the cargo compartment with Jeannie.

I hand flew the Mighty DC-6A for a couple of hours and put it back on auto-pilot. I was one tired hombre.

"ALLS WELL THAT ENDS WELL"

PRFPACPJM

--- CIRCA ---

NINER JUNE 1NINER6ZERO

HAPPY AEROVIDAS SUD AMERICANA BIRTHDAY TO ME

"RING---RING---RI--"
"Hello"
"Hey Beck, this is Muldoon. ---Beck, I quit Twentieth Century. I'm flying for PSA. They're in need of another Flight Engineer. I told the Chief Flight Engineer about you and he wants to interview you."
"What's a PSA?"
"Pacific Southwest Airlines"
"What are you flying?"
"Lockheed Electras"
"Not the same kind of Lockheed Electra that Amelia Airhead, oops, I mean Airheart tried to fly around the world in I hope. She should have stayed in the kitchen."

Muldoon laughed---then said, ---**"WELL???"**
"I'll give it some thought. I'm pretty happy with what I'm flying right now. I'm flying for Aerovidas Sud Americana. We leave Wednesday afternoon and come back Saturday. Got a great Captain to fly with ---his name is Russ Krieg. You're not gonna believe this ---his wife is the Co-Pilot."

"Airovia---what?"
"A-E-R-O-V-I-D-A-S---S-U-D AMERICANA.
I have no idea where their home base is. All I know is that they have a year contract that started with my first trip."
"That sounds good---but I think you'll have a better deal here."
"Where does ---uh---PSA---is it---fly to?"
"Just up and down the coast Beck---just in California. They started out flying San Diego to Burbank to Oakland and now they've expanded to include Los Angeles and San Francisco."
"Wow---that sounds great. How long are you usually away from home?"
"Day trips---we go out in the morning and come back at night---except of course if we get fogged out."
"YOU COME BACK ON THE SAME DAY YOU GO OUT ON?"

"**Yep**---pay is two and a quarter cents a mile. Right now I'm salaried at four hundred bucks a month---for a year---then I go on mileage pay."

"Shit---Muldoon, ---I'm making twelve hundred bucks a month now. I hate to give that up. My wife and I just had our son a few months ago---he's expensive."

"Yea---I know what you mean Beck---my wife Joanne had our baby boy in November. He's eating up most of those four hundred bucks by himself."

"What's his name?"

"Mikie---Mike."

"We named our son Mark Resley---that's my middle name."

"Yea I know. Can't figure out why you're so proud of that name."

"When I was a kid---it was fighting words---now I'm sorta proud of it."

"Yea---*sigh*---what dya want me to tell the Chief Engineer?"

"I don't know Muldoon."

"Dya want his phone number?"

"Yea---give it to me and I'll talk it over with my wife. She's pretty well entrenched here. I don't think she'll want to move. We'd have to move there if you just have day trips."

"Oh yea---you can't commute---that's for sure. His home phone number is 714-789-6884. Got that?"

"No---let me get a pencil---go ---**ROGERRRRR---ready to read back.**"

"*OOOOKAAAAY---sigh*---714-789-6884"

"Muldoon, what's the Chief Flight Engineer's name?"

"Bob Lefty."

"Bob Lefty at **714-789-6884**---Okay---Thanks for thinking of me---bye."

I talked to my wife about it and she was not at all happy with the idea.
"I'm not moving to San Diego. All my friends are here---and besides that, San Diego's a Sailor town."

So much for talking it over.

*****

Richard Carlyn---

"*If everything is improved & brand new this year, what the fuck were they selling us last year?*"---

Also from Richard Carlyn---
   "Did ya ever notice that the women that are against abortion are so ugly that you wouldn't fuck them anyway?"
*****

*Do you know why women have periods? ---
Because they deserve them.*
*****

*Why do women have yeast infections???
So they know what a miserable cunt feels like.*

*****

A Captain, Co-Pilot & Flight Engineer were discussing the merits of sex---
   The Captain, an older man, said--- "Sex, to me, is 70% work & 30% pleasure."
   The Co-Pilot, a younger man, said--- "Sex, to me, is 30% work & 70% pleasure."
   The Flight Engineer said--- "Sex, the way I see it, is all pleasure---if there was any work involved, you'd have me doin' it."
*****

*Two kids were talking---
"My dad eats light bulbs."---
"How do you know that?"---
"Last night I heard him say to my mother---
turn out the light and I'll eat it."*
*****

*Do the name Quasimodo ring a bell???---
Do the name Ruby Begonia ring a bell???*

--- CIRCA ---

LATTER PART OF JULIO 1-NINER-6-0

I'm gonna give PSA a call anyhoo.
Where did I put that dad blamed number that Muldoon had given me?
Oh---yea---here it is---right under my beer can---714-789-6884.

"RING---RING---RI--"
"Hello"

"Yes---hello---my name's Jack Beck. I'm looking for the Chief Flight Engineer's Office. Guy by the name of Beauleftee---or something like that."

"This is **Bob Lefty**."

"Oh---yea---Beauleftee---I think that's the name. Is this the office of the Chief Flight Engineer for Pacific South---uh---er---Southern Airlines?"

"This is **B-O-B-L-E-F-T-Y** and yes I am the Chief Flight Engineer for Pacific **S-O-U-TH-W-E-S-T** Airlines. You have dialed my home phone number."

"Oh---I'm sorry---that's the number that Muldoon gave me---uh---Muldoon told me that you were in need of a Flight Engineer."

"Yes I am. Have you any Flight Engineer time on a Lockheed Electra 188?"

"No sir---I do not---as a matter of fact, until Muldoon told me about PSA ---I never heard of the Airplane or the Airline. I do have close to two thousand hours Flight Engineer time on a DC-6 though---and most of that time is over the Pacific and the Atlantic Oceans---I also have an A&E License. I was a Flight Line Mechanic for Flying Tigers at the Burbank Airport for over two years."

"How old are you?"

"Twenty-six---sir"

"Well---okay---I was looking for someone with Electra experience. That Flight Line Mechanic experience will do. Where are you now?"

"I'm in my apartment in Glendale, California."

"OH---oh, I thought you were here in San Diego. I'd like to at least meet you---uh---when can you come down to San Diego? **I'd like to interview you as soon as possible."**

This caught me by surprise, ---"Sure---uh---whenever."

"Mister Beck---I'll meet you in the San Diego Airport Terminal Coffee Shop about nineteen hundred hours. Can you be there?"

"Today---uh---tonight?"

"Yes---it's only fifteen hundred hours now. That'll give you four hours to get here."

"Yes sir. I'll be in the San Diego Airport Coffee Shop at nineteen hundred hours---right."

"That's right Mister Beck---1900 hundred hours in the airport coffee shop."

"Okay---see you then---thanks---Goodbye Sir."

MY THOUGHT--- "He called me mister twice---I hope he isn't gonna fire me before he hires me."

I drove to San Diego---without my wife's knowledge---chicken shit Mister Beck.

I met Chief Flight Engineer Lefty in the---

---San Diego International Airport Terminal Coffee Shop---

Unlit stogie in mouth---

Coffee cup in one hand---

I shook hands with the other.

I sat down and took my Flight Engineer's License and my First Class Medical Certificate out of my wallet---handed it to Chief Flight Engineer Bob Lefty.

Chief Flight Engineer Lefty perused it with a smile.

Then I proudly showed Mister Lefty my Commercial Pilot Certificate and my Instrument Rating.

CHIEF FLIGHT ENGINEER LEFTY, ---Scowled---frowned---snarled---squirmed---farted---blanched and finally turned scarlet.

"I can't hire you."

"HUH???"---I was surprised. ---"WHY NOT?"

"You have a pilot's license and I hate pilots."

This stupid schlemiel hated the people that were taking his fat ass from A to B.

I got up and walked out. ---Didn't even bother to say goodbye. I was used to dealing with people that had some common sense and wasn't about to work for this ignoramus.

I left
*****

Lefty was a ground school instructor on the Electra at Lockheed Aircraft Corporation when PSA bought the Electras. PSA hired him and gave him the title of Chief Flight Engineer.

PSA didn't know what a Flight Engineer was supposed to do, be or look like and after talking to Lefty, I didn't think he did either.

Up to that point of time---PSA had DC-3s and DC-4s, which did not require a Flight Engineer.
*****

I called Muldoon. ---"Sorry Muldoon, but that guy is an asshole---Thanks for trying to get me hired. I do appreciate it."

"You're welcome Beck, but quit being such a hot head."

"Fuck you---bye."

Wednesday rolled around again and Russ, Jeanie and I landed at San Diego. I opened the forward cargo door, slid down the emergency escape rope and got a ladder for Russ and Jeanie. She had slacks on.

Ruined my day.

I was checking the tie down straps on the rocket parts that we had picked up in San Diego when someone tapped me on the shoulder.

It was "Boob" Lefty.

Now my day was really ruined.

I had told him, at my so-called interview that I was flying for Aerovidas Sud Americana and came through San Diego every Wednesday evening on my way to Denver.

We sat on the Aft Cargo Compartment door floor with our legs dangling out of the airplane.

"Why don't you come aboard?"

"HUH?"

MY THOUGHT---"I'm already on board you ignoramus---even though I knew what he was alluding to."

"Let's go have a cup of coffee."

"Okay---I'm all through here."

We went into the coffee shop, sat down and ordered some "Joe".

I knew Lefty was FAA material then. The FAA can't talk or think without groping a cup of coffee.

I was right, Lefty became an FAA Inspector later on in life.

Lefty was staring at his cup of coffee like a man staring at a couple of tits, ---"If you promise me that you'll never become a pilot with PSA---I'll hire you."

Aerovidas Sud Americana's contract was getting a little rocky and I needed a new job bad, even if I had to kiss this mongoloid's ass to get one.

"Sure---I don't want to be a pilot," ---with my fingers, legs, arms and even my eyes crossed.

That wasn't enough for this ignoramus.

"I want a written statement to that effect."

I took a napkin and scribbled, ---"I, Jack Resley Beck, will never become a pilot with PSA."

I didn't even sign it and handed it to him.

He was happy with the note, ---"I need you desperately to attend ground school this coming Monday morning."

This dipshit was hard up for a Flight Engineer and I had to kiss his ass to get the job.

"I'll see if I can make it. I'm obligated to give Aerovidas Sud Americana two weeks notice. If you give me your phone number---I'll call you Saturday afternoon and tell you if I can make it."

I knew that I'd be there, come hell or high water, but I wanted to see the "worm squirm".

Lefty wrote his office phone number on the back of the napkin that I had written my promise on --- handed it to me.

I shook his coffee clutching hand and went to fly.

On the way to Denver, I told **Chief Pilot Captain Russ Kreig** what had transpired.

Chief Pilot Captain Russ Krieg was not happy with me---matter of fact---he was a little bit P-Oed.

"Beck, you're only twenty-six years old and you're on your way to becoming an airport bum. PSA will be your third airline job in two years. I've watched guys like you. They bounce around from one airline job to another and never have a steady life."

He ranted on and on.

"PSA is just another non-sked and will probably fold in six months."
I flew for PSA for twenty-eight years, until US Airways bought PSA.
Then USAirways for another six years for a total of thirty-four years.

YOU NEVER KNOW, PILGRIM---YOU JUST NEVER KNOW.

After Russ cooled down a little---I said, "They want me to start Monday morning."

Captain Russ Krieg came down off his high horse, ---"I'll make you Chief Flight Engineer if you remain with Aerovidas Sud Americana."

"How much more will the job pay?"

"No more money, but you'll have a title."

Chief Pilot Captain Russ Krieg saw the "No way Hosay" look on my face, ---"Go and Good luck to you."

Nice man---Never will forget---

---CHIEF PILOT CAPTAIN RUSS KREIG---
&
---CO-PILOT JEANNIE---
*****

I found out fifteen years later that Russ had retired and resided in San Mateo, a suburb of San Francisco. I obtained his phone number and gave him a call. He was happy to hear from me and that PSA was still in existence.

*****

I called Lefty Saturday and told him that I'd be in ground school Monday morning.

"Fine, glad you can make it."

--- CIRCA ---

2 AUGUST 1-NINER-6-ZERO

Sunday morning I rented a trailer and packed all my worldly belongings in it.
I headed for San Diego with a very bitchy wife and a very squalling baby.
2 hour drive---2 hours of pissin' and moanin'.
I kept my response to a minimum, ---**"YES DEAR."**
TRANSLATION---*"Please shut the fuck up---you're driving me bonkers."*

*****

*"You pass this way only once. ---
If you do it right---You don't have to come back."*
CAPTAIN JERRY HOLLY

*At Christmas Time---We Would Sing, ---
"Deck the halls with* **BALLS OF HOLLY."**

*****

--- CIRCA ---

Nah---it haint "on or about"---I know the exact date---

03 AUGUST---1-NINER-6-ZERO

I reported in at PSA Monday morning.
Lefty introduced me to the Chief Pilot by the name of Righty.
After listening to him for a while I could see he was of the same brain waves as Lefty. He let me know in no uncertain terms that he thought Flight Engineers were excess baggage.
One of Righty's comments was that he was trying to get approval from the FAA to rotate the Flight Engineers's seat one hundred and eighty degrees---so it was facing the passenger compartment.
This would enable the Flight Engineer to do public relations work in flight.
The cockpit door was locked open then and it was not uncommon to have five or six passengers in the cockpit during flight.
MY SENIORITY NUMBER WAS TWENTY-SEVEN.
PSA had twenty-seven crew members including a Chief Pilot, Assistant Chief Pilot and a Chief Flight Engineer---a DC-4 and---
---TWO LOCKHEED ELECTRA L-188s---
A lot of Chiefs--- better known as the deadwood gang--- and so few Indians.
I was hired for the third Electra that was due the latter part of August 1960.
Lefty took me to a room on the side of the hangar and commenced ground school.
Black, no Blank Monday---
I call it. ---The longest, most boring day of my life.
Lefty was actually counting rivets on the airplane. He counted rivets till 1800 hours.
I couldn't wait to get out of Ground School.
I was about to leave when Flight Engineer Muldoon walked in.
I shook Muldoon's hand and asked, ---**"What the devil are you doing here?"**
Muldoon whispered, ---"I've been checked out for two months now and this bozo keeps me coming back to ground school. I've made two

round trips between San Diego and San Francisco today. I'm tired and don't need this bullpucky."

Muldoon was a little testy which was out of character for him. ---*at that point in time.*

Guess he was tired. ---I was soon to find out why.

Lefty continued on with his so called ground school, ---"The bulkhead behind the cockpit has eight hundred and fifty four rivets and is at station ninety-two."

I looked at Muldoon—whispered, ---"Who cares?"

Muldoon shook his head, ---"I certainly don't."

Rivet counting lasted till **0200 hours.** *(two o'clock in the morning).*

Lefty finally dismissed us.

I was on the way out the door when Lefty caught up to me,

"Beck, I need to talk to you."

MY THOUGHT---*"What the hell did I do now?"*

"HUH?"

"Be back at the hangar at 0600. We'll do a preflight together and you can make a round trip with me."

Well, no beers tonight. It was going to be a short night.

I showed up at O'dark thirty as ordered.

Lefty and I did a walk around preflight of the Lockheed Electra together.

We got in the cockpit and turned on the APU. (*Auxiliary Power Unit*) We did a cockpit preflight, warmed up the Lockheed Electra and made sure all systems were A-OK.

Lefty was in the Flight Engineer's seat. I sat in the Captain's seat watching him do his dog and pony act.

There was a thump, thump on the side of the aircraft. I looked out and saw a mechanic signaling me to release the brakes by making a fist and than opening his hand---again & again.

I looked back around at Lefty in askance, --- "Get out of that seat---you're not checked out yet."

Lefty slid the Flight Engineers seat back and a few inches to the right so I could get by him.

I did and he jumped into the Captains Chair.

I started to sit in the Flight Engineer's seat.

"Don't sit there---you're not checked out yet."

MY THOUGHT---*"What the hell???"*

The Mechanics towed us over to the terminal which was on the other side of ------**San Diego International Airport's Lindberg Field.**

When we arrived at the boarding **"GATE"**, the same mechanic signaled Lefty to put the parking brakes on by opening his right hand and then making a fist.

Lefty responded by setting the parking brakes by using the toe brakes on top of the rudder pedals and pulling a lever on the center pedestal.

Lefty then showed a clenched fist to the mechanic indicating that the parking brake had been set and the mechanic could remove the pin from the tug's tow bar that was attached to the aircraft.

The boarding "GATE" was merely a five-foot chain link fence with an open patio that seated about twenty people.

I went into the cabin so as to open the forward cabin door and put out the integral passenger boarding stairs, ---only to hear---

Lefty shout, ---**"DON'T TOUCH ANYTHING BACK THERE---YOU'RE NOT CHECKED OUT YET."**

I came back up into the Cockpit and sat in the Jump Seat hoping that was okay with ass-eyes.

The Jump Seat is directly behind the Captain's seat on the Lockheed Electra L-188---as it is on every airplane that I've been on.

Why it's called a Jump Seat is a mystery to me 'because I've never even seen it skip or hop---let alone jump. *Just Josh---ing*

**The "JumpSeat" is the place where the FAA and Check Airman sit ---
---and watch you, ---squirm---sweat---pucker up your asshole---**

*The Flight Engineer's seat on the Lockheed Electra L-188 was built just like your favorite living room chair---with the sweat stains on the arm rests. The Flight Engineer's seat reclined and had up and down armrest---jut like the two SKY GOD's chairs. After sitting in the ass bustin'---back-breakin' DC-6's Flight Engineer's chair for over two thousand hours---This was---in one word--- **FIRSTFUCKINCLASS.***

The Pilots---
**---CAPTAIN DOUG FAULKNER---
---CO-PILOT CAPTAIN JOHN POWELL---**

Boarded---sat in their respective seats and we took off for the Burbank Airport without any further to-do.

We arrived at Burbank---**Deplaned and emplaned ninety-eight passengers in ten minutes.**

That was PSA's bailiwick at that time--**Fast turn arounds and mini-skirted-hot pantsed stewardesses.**

Some one tapped me on the shoulder. It was one of those mini-skirted hot pants Stews, ---"We're gonna fill up and I need the jump seat."

I looked at Lefty in askance???

"Yea, ---when the airplane fills up---the forward Stew has to give her seat to a passenger and take the Jump Seat. There's a Flight coming through here in a couple of hours on the way to San Diego. You can catch that flight and go on home."

"I'll see you in Ground School at 1800 hours tonight---Do not---I repeat DO NOT be late."

I left

I went into the Burbank Airport Terminal Building and went to the one man---oops---one woman ticket counter.

I showed the lady my paper PSA Identification tag that was pasted to my lapel by Lefty when I arrived that morning, --- "I'm a new hire Flight Engineer. I'm in training and I just got bumped off of Flight 749. I need to get back to San Diego."

I asked her about getting a Jump Seat ride on the next southbound flight.

"Flight 704? Let me check---hummm---1030 departure. Flights booked full with standbys and the FAA has the Jump Seat. Next one coming through---hummm---Flight 304 is at 1630. That one's---hummm---full also. The Jump Seats open. I'll---hummm---book you on it. You'll probably get bumped---hummm---by the FAA. They've been on almost every flight out of here---hummm---since we got the two Electras. What's a---hummm---Flight Engineer?"

"I'm the third man in the Cockpit---I take care of the fueling, pressurization and fix the airplane when there's a mechanical."

"Oh---hummm"

"Yea---I used to fly Flight Engineer for Captain Bill Butler at Twentieth Century Airlines across the airport over there."

"Oh---humm"

"Yea---I just hired on with PSA yesterday."

"Oh---hummm---here's your Jump Seat pass."

MY THOUGHT--- *"I think she's a hummer---Guess I impressed the dogshit out of her."*

I left.

I waited at the boarding gate until Flight 704 arrived---filled up---a Stew took the jump seat---the Electra departed---without me.

So far---this sojourn with Lefty and PSA was nothing but m-i-n-u-s-e-s.

I walked across Runway 15/33 looking for Doc Schnitter---found him---sweeping the hangar floor, ---"Job's still open Jack. I hire a Flight Engineer---he flies one three-month trip to Spain---comes back---quits."

"Oh"

"Wanna try it?"

"Oh---no---I just hired on with PSA. I just started yesterday."

"You have? Great---stay with them. They're lookin' good since they got those Electras. It appears from here that every flight in and out of Burbank is full."

"Yea---looks like they're doin' real good. This was my first observation flight this morning and I got bumped out of the Jump Seat."

"Yea---I know that the FAA has been hawk-eyeing PSA since they got the Electras---mainly because of the new Flight Engineers. I guess you know by now that your Chief Pilot is trying to get a waiver so the Electra can be a two man Cockpit."

"No---I didn't know that. I've only met him once and he let me know in no uncertain terms that Flight Engineers were excess baggage. He's trying to get FAA approval to turn the Flight Engineer's seat around so it faces the passengers---so the Flight Engineer can do Public Relations work in flight."

"HE WHAT???"

"Yep---that's what he told me---the one and only time I met him."

"Well---I know him personally. There's no way that the FAA is gonna condescend to his wishes---so put it out of your mind and do your best. Captain Butler has nothing but praise for you Jack. When Bill tells me something---I listen."

"Thanks Doc---I need those kind words right now. PSA doesn't have a flight coming through till four-thirty. I've got some time to kill. I'm gonna walk across the Runway and say hi to Captain Butler."

"Don't waste your time Jack. Twentieth went down the tubes last week. Captain Butler went up north to honcho Teeya."

"TEEYA????"

"Yea---**Trans International Airlines**, T-I-A---they're based in Oakland. TIA is an offshoot of my outfit---Los Angeles Air Service. I'm the only one that stayed in Burbank I'm Chief Pilot of a one airplane airline."

"**Captain Butler is Chief Pilot at Teeya---in Oakland---now?**"

"Yea---Jack---PSA goes to Oakland. ---Stop in and see him when you go through there. He'd love to see you. Bill always asks if I know if you're still with that Mexican Airlines---what's the name? ---Aerosod American."

"Aerovidas Sud Americana---The Airline is South America based, ---I think in Argentina. I had my last flight with them on Saturday."

"Oh---where did you fly to?"

"Los Angeles International Airport to Cape Canaveral. We stopped in San Diego and Denver. It was a great job. We'd take off Wednesday afternoon and come back to LAX on Saturday afternoon."

"Who was your Captain---Maybe I know him."

"Captain Russ Krieg---really a nice man to fly with. His wife Jeanie was the Co-Pilot."

"I know Russ and Jeanie well. We got our Commercial Pilot Licenses at Grand Central Airport over there in Glendale together---at Ryan School of Aeronautics. Jeanie could out fly both of us. We had a lot of fun together."

"Wow---I got my licenses at Ryan's too."

"That's nice---when did you say that deadhead of yours was coming through?"

"Uh---1630."

"Good---let's go see Roy and have a beer---I'm buying. I need a Flight Engineer for a trip on Friday---maybe Roy can find one for me."

"I'll go with you Doc, but I'll just have a cup of coffee. If I got it figured right---that ass-hole Chief Flight Engineer that hired me will be working that flight. I want to be completely sober if he is."

"The Chief Flight Engineers an asshole? ---What's his name?"

"Lefty"

"I don't know him---I've heard that PSA hired him for the Chief Flight Engineer's position out of Lockheed. He was a ground school instructor there on the Electra---I think."

"Yea---I believe that's what Muldoon told me."

"Is Muldoon working at PSA too?"

"Yea Doc---he got me my job there."

"I met Muldoon on Wake Island once. From all the feedback--- from all the Captains that I have talked to---you and Muldoon are the best. The most conscientious Flight Engineers that they have flown with in a long time."

"Thanks Doc---after dealing with Lefty---I needed that."

"What's with Lefty Jack?"

"I don't know. All I know about him is that he hates pilots and always has a stogie in his mouth."

"HE HATES PILOTS???"

"Well---yea---that's what he said at my interview. Made me sign a statement that I'd never become a pilot at PSA---or he wasn't gonna hire me."

"Did you sign it?"

"Yea---I had to or he wasn't gonna hire me."

"Well---Jack---you don't have to honor that. ---That's stupid."

"Yea---I know that Doc. I just signed it because he wasn't gonna hire me if I didn't. I wanted the job cause I could be home with my family every night."

"You're home every night?"

"Yea---that's what Muldoon said, ---Two or three round trips between the Bay Area and San Diego. Muldoon said that he's home every night---unless he gets fogged out or has a mechanical."

"Well---looks like that's the job you're looking for Jack. Stick with it. Guys like Lefty come and go. He won't last. Just say yessir to him when he talks---then go out and do your job."

"Its called eating shit pills. You take them and once the asshole is out of sight—they dissolve."

"Okay Doc---thanks."

We sat down.

Roy the Burbank Terminal Barkeep brought us two beers.

So much for drinking coffee

"Hi Doc. How ya doin' kid---you still flying with that South American Airline? ---How are Captain Russ Kreig and Jeanie doing? They haven't been in here for a long time. Tell them Roy said hi."

"I'm a Flight Engineer for PSA now Roy---I just started yesterday."

"That's great kid---heard PSA could use a few more Electras. I hear that they are turning away more passengers than they're hauling."

"Yea---I guess so---I just got bumped out of the Jump Seat this morning. ---It was my first observation ride. I'm gonna spend the whole day here for just thirty-five minutes of flight training time."

"Yea kid---I hear the FAA is on just about every flight."

"Not the Fuzz Roy---a stewardess bumped me out of the Jump Seat."

DOC---"HUH"

ROY---"HUH"

"Yea---when the airplane fills up---the forward stew gives her seat to a passenger. She then sits in the jump seat for take-off and landing."

DOC---"You're kidding me!"

ROY---"You're kidding me!"

"No kidding---that's the scoop for sure."

"How in the world did they get the FAA to approve that?"

"I have no idea---all I know is that the forward stew came in the Cockpit and Lefty told me to leave---go home."

Roy, ---"Never heard of that before, ---have you Doc?"

"No I haven't. ---I need a Flight Engineer Roy---know of any needin' some work?"

"Yea---matter of fact I do. Dick Greenberg lost his job when Twentieth went tits up. He's been in here every day since asking me if anyone was hiring. Greenberg's out in the terminal someplace wandering around hoping someone will need him. He's got his uniform on so ya can't miss him."

"Do you know him Jack?"

"Yea I do---nice guy---talks a lot."

"I'm gonna go try to find him. If I can't Jack---I'll come back and get you. You know what he looks like."

"I'll go with you Doc---Thank you for the beer. Probably see ya manana Roy."

As I slugged down the last precious drop of the golden elixir.

Chief Pilot Captain Doc Schnitter and Self left the bar looking for---

---**FLIGHT ENGINEER DICK GREENBERG**---

Found him.

We didn't have to go too far. ---Greenberg was seated at the entrance to the bar.

I introduced Flight Engineer Dick Greenberg to Captain Doc Schnitter.

I left.

I went and bought a roll of LifeSavers to hide my beer breath. ---

Waited for Flight 304.

I was right---Lefty was on it.

I crammed some LifeSavers in my mouth and went out to the airplane and did a walk around with him.

"It looks like we're gonna fill up---you'll probably get bumped out of the Jump Seat again."

"How am I gonna get home---this is the last flight to San Diego tonight."

"Get a motel and come down in the morning."

"I can't do that. My wife and son are in a motel in San Diego. Besides that, ---I haven't got any money for a motel."

"Use your American Express."

"Lefty---I'm going to San Diego in the Jump Seat on this airplane---whether you fuckin' like it or not."

"Well---apparently you don't like working here."

"You can fuckin' fire my ass if you want, ---**I'M GOING HOME ON THAT AIRPLANE."**

Lefty bit his unlit cigar in half and said**, ---"YOUR CHOICE."**

Captain Doug Faulkner just happened to walk by---overheard the conversation.

"Lefty---go into PSA Ops and list this man in the Jump Seat---NOW."

Lefty left.
BECK---1   LEFTY---0
I boarded.

The forward Stewardess was already in the jump seat.

I went all the way to the rear of the airplane and took a seat by the window before the passengers started boarding. I figured that when the Stewardesses made their head count and the Electra was filled to capacity; ---the Stewardesses would just count me as a passenger.

I didn't have a uniform on---just my pastensed Grey Flannel Wide Lapelled Suit."

This went on for the next twenty-seven days; ---work six days---one day off.

Each and every morning I'd get to the airport at 0600 hours---sit in the jump seat and watch Lefty do his Flight Engineer act.

We'd get to Burbank---the airplane would fill up---a Stew would bump me out of the jump seat. I'd sit and wait for the next flight southbound---it would fill up.

I'd go have a beer---chat with Roy---wait for the next southbound flight---eat some Lifesavers---deadhead back to San Diego.

If I caught the 1030 flight---I'd go home---take a nap---then go to ground school at 1800 hours. If the 1030 flight filled up---I'd catch the late one with Lefty---go to the soup can machine---have a Lipton's Gourmet Chicken Soup Meal with Lefty and Flight Engineer Muldoon. ---go to ground school.

This is how I caught one of the 1030 flights back home.

I took the dispatch and manifest papers from **MISTER KEN HODGES.** ---A Burbank PSA Operations Agent as he was walking to the plane, ---"I'll take them on board for you Ken---save you some steps."

"Thanks Beck---I appreciate it."

Later on in life Ken Hodges went on to being---

---**MISTER KEN HODGES**---
---**STATION MANAGER**---
---**PACIFIC SOUTHWEST AIRLINES**---
---**HOLLYWOOD BURBANK INTERNATIONAL AIRPORT**---
---**THE BEST OF THE BEST**---

I waited till the last passenger boarded---went up the boarding ramp---handed them to the forward stewardess by the name of **Miss Nancy Marchand**.

She thanked me and took the papers to the cockpit.

I waited till Miss Nancy Marchand's back was turned to me and slipped into the forward biffy---sat down on the toilet and held my breath. I didn't lock it---because the Stew, as part of her pre-flight activities, would see the **"OCCUPIED"** sign and attempt to see who was in there.

When the Electra started to taxi out---the forward stew opened the biffy door, as part of her pre-flight duties, to ascertain that it was indeed **"VACANT"**.

I put my index finger to my mouth in a shush gesture. She smiled---closed the biffy door.

I heard Miss Nancy Marchand put the ---**"OUT OF ORDER"**---sign on the door and I breathed a sigh of relief.

While taxiing to the gate in San Diego, ---Miss Nancy Marchand opened the biffy door---grabbed my hand and put me in the forward gallery.

The Electra stopped at the gate and Miss Nancy Marchand opened the forward passenger door---lowered the stairs and literally pushed me out the door saying---**"HURRY-HURRY---before any one sees you."**

I did.

I "borrowed" a tug and was on the other side of the San Diego International Airport before the last passenger walked down the boarding ramp.

*****

De-clawing a cat is like disarming a soldier.

So funny----everybody else's farts stink & mine don't---me thinks.

Read your daily newspaper or do a X word while gruntin & groanin on the Crapper & you'll never be constipated----weeeelll---almost never.

Why did I capitalize Crapper.
A man named **CRAPPER** *invented the toilette.*

Who invented woman? ---A Pollack
Who else would have placed a lunch counter next to a shithouse?

Here I sit broken hearted---came to shit---only farted.

Well---that's enough shitty jokes for now.

*****

At one time in my life---I could drink a quart of whiskey and not even stagger---Hell---I couldn't even move.

We all live in glass houses
Some are just a little less shatterproof than others

---CAPTAIN JACK RESLEY BECK ---RE_{ally}TIRED---
How's that old saw go???
"The hand that rocks the cradle---rules the world"
And that was hep before women's lib.

*Men---we are mashed potatoes without the gravy---chopped liver---the last of the Mohicans---up shit creek without a paddle—haven't got a pot to piss in, but at least we got a window to throw it out of--- **doomed.***
*****

An airline pilot wrote that on this particular flight he had hammered his ship into the runway really hard. The airline had a policy which required the first officer to stand at the door while the Passengers exited, smile, and give them a "Thanks for flying our airline."

He said that, in light of his bad landing, he had a hard time looking the passengers in the eye, thinking that someone would have a smart comment.

Finally everyone had gotten off except for a little old lady walking with a cane. She said, "Sir, do you mind if I ask you a question?" "Why, no, Ma'am," said the pilot. "What is it?" The little old lady said, "Did we land, or were we shot down?"

*****

*****

Ebecaneezer, King of the Jews.
*Spell **THAT** in four letters*
And I'll give you my shoes.
*Remember **T-H-A-T** one???*
*****

This one black lady asked another black lady---
"Have you ever been picked up by the fuzz?"---
"No---but I'll bet it sure do hurt."

*****

--- CIRCA ---

One zillion rivets later.

We got two new hires in our class---**PILOTS.**
---CAPTAIN RAYNOR EUGENE KEOUGH---
---THE BEST OF THE BEST---
&
---CAPTAIN BILL JOLLY---
---THE BEST OF THE REST---

I know that haint the best way to pay tribute to two of the bestest people that that I have known---so if you don't like it---write your own book---or as---

Captain Denny used to say, --- *"If you don't like my face---fuck it"*
Lefty started his rivet counting over again.
---Co-Pilot Bill Jolly & Co-Pilot Raynor Eugene Keough---
Looked at each other wondering what he was talking about. I had been attending ground school for well almost a month now and hadn't learned a thing about the engines or propellers---except for what I had learned on my own.

Did you know that some jellyfish have tentacles 120 feet long?
*That's what Alex Tru**bec** "Jeopardizes."*

When I was marooned on Wake Island for a couple of weeks---
A Filipino was out diving for clams.
When he was coming up to surface---he came up inside of a large
PORTUGESE MAN OF WAR
Instant death
*****

"Money doesn't buy happiness."
But if you're unhappy---it sure is nice to have around.

--- CIRCA ---

1 SEPTEMBER---1-NINER-6-ZERO

I showed up at 0600 hours---Lefty was no where to be found---**AWOL**.
I called PSA Operations and informed them that the Flight Engineer hadn't showed up.
"Who is it?"
"Mister Lefty"
"We'll give him a call."
"Thanks"
The mechanics towed the Electra. ---I rode the brakes from PSA's Hangar on the West Side of the San Diego International Airport to the Terminal on the East Side of the San Diego International Airport.
I set the brakes and went into PSA Operations---asked if they had made contact with Lefty yet.
"We've been trying to call him for thirty minutes with no response."
I went back out to the airplane and did a walk around pre-flight and a cockpit pre-flight so we would be ready to go when Lefty showed up.

SCENARIO

AIRPLANE---LOCKHEED ELECTRA L-188
AIRPORT OF DEPARTURE---San Diego International Airport
AIRPORT OF DESTINATION---BUR---OAK---LAX---SAN---
                              LAX---SFO---SAN
CAPTAIN---DOUGLAS FAULKNER
CO-PILOT---CAPTAIN RICHARD DOLL
FLIGHT ENGINEER---MISSING
PSEUDO FLIGHT ENGINEER---BECK
STEWARDESS---MISS MARY MASON
STEWARDESS---MISS NANCY MARCHAND---Chief Stewardess
DEPARTURE TIME---NOW---NO LEFTY-YETTI.

ACT I

I sat in the Flight Engineer's seat and did the required checklists with the Pilots.

Captain Doug Faulkner looked around at me, ---"I hope you're checked out because it looks like we're going to need you today."
"Sure am."
On the job training--- Sorta like an attorney practicing law..

ACT II
And as Jackie Gleason used to say on "The Honeymooners"—
-"AWAY WE GO."
---TO BURBANK---35 MINUTES FLIGHT TIME---
---10 MINUTES GROUND TIME---
---TO OAKLAND---59 MINUTES FLIGHT TIME---
---20 MINUTES GROUND TIME---
---TO LOS ANGELES---58 MINUTES FLIGHT TIME---
---10 MINUTES GROUND TIME---
---TO SAN DIEGO---21 MINUTES FLIGHT TIME---
---45 MINUTES GROUND TIME---
---TO LOS ANGELES---21 MINUTE FLIGHTTIME---
---10 MINUTES GROUND TIME---
---TO SANFRANCISCO---55 MINUTE FLIGHT TIME---
---90 MINUTES GROUNDTIME---
---TO SAN DIEGO---90 MINUTES FLIGHT TIME---
---GROUND TIME---I'M OUT OF HERE---

ACT III
We landed at San Diego
Captain Doug Faulkner shook my hand, ---"You do a helluva job for a new hire. Lefty has trained you well."
"Thanks---I know every rivet on this airplane."
Captain Doug Faulkner looked at me kind of puzzled---dropped the subject.
I went home---went nappy bye—on my couch.

ACT IV
"RING---RING---RI--"
I looked at the clock through blood shot eyes---yikes---**2100 HOURS**.
It was Lefty---He sounded a litta-no-a lotta pissed.
"Do you want to work here or not? You were supposed to be here at 1800 hours."
"I'll be right there."

ACT V

I got to the classroom---Lefty was still seething.
MY THOUGHT---When Lefty finds out that I flew his trips---he's going to look like Mount Fuji when she popped her cork.

Lefty started counting rivets.

"RING---RING---RI--"

Lefty answered it---listened to the voice on the other end and said, ---"Beck hasn't had a check ride yet and isn't qualified to fly the line."

I hawk eyed Lefty.

His face turned crimson, then white and then burple. By the look on his face, I could tell that he had found out that I had flown his trips.

Lefty approached me with a look on his face of a rabid dog with a stogie in its mouth.

"Did you take a trip today?"

I stood up and got about six inches from his face, ---"Yes I did you flaming asshole."

I was fed up to here with his rivet counting bullshit.

I was prepared to quit---duke it out---or both---if he gave me any static.

Thus far, I had over 300 hours of duty time in less than a month. ---Less than 30 hours of flight training and that was in the jump seat.

The room "sounded very silent".

Flight Engineer--- Muldoon **---Captain Raynor Eugene Keough ---Captain Jolly Bill---oops---Bill Jolly---**all looked at me like I went crazy.

Hell, you had to be a little whacky to fly airplanes in those days.

Lefty went to the phone and called PSA Operations back.

Lefty listened and listened and listened.

Lefty nodded and nodded and nodded.

Lefty had his back to the wall and he was facing it.

I should have been checked out two weeks ago and Lefty knew it. The third Electra was on the line and they needed crews for it. Lefty slammed the receiver down and started toward me.

There was no doubt in my mind that he wasn't happy.

I stood up, ready for combat. I was not going to take any more of his bullcrap.

I was going to deck his ass.

Lefty sensed it, stopped, ---"Check in time is at 0615 tomorrow."

"Okay by me," I said and turned around to leave.

"Where are you going? ---Ground school isn't over yet."

"It is as far as I'm concerned, I need some rest."

Flight Engineer Muldoon---who had been putting up with counting rivets for over three months---got up and left with me.

Flight Engineer Muldoon also had an early check in.

I glanced back at Keough and Jolly. Their eyes were as big as saucers. They couldn't believe that this exodus was happening.

Lefty was in shock. He knew that he couldn't fire us because they would have to ground an Electra if he did.

We had him by the balls and he knew it.

BECK---2   LEFTY---0

On the way home Muldoon and I stopped by a watering hole named,

---THE SOUTH SEAS BAR&GRILL---

It was PSA's home away from home. You could stop by the bar any time of the day and find at least a half dozen Crews&Stews there.

We closed the South Seas Bar&Grill---staggered out. Not real smart, ---now we were not only going to be tired but have a hangover too.

ACT VI

I arrived at the hangar at 0615---guess who was there? ---

You're right, my man Lefty.

"I'm going to ride in your Jumpseat all day to make sure you're safe enough."

"Fine by me," and I proceeded to do an exterior pre-flight walk around.

Lefty followed me everywhere I went. He was on me like stink on a civet cat. He was trying to unnerve me. He wanted me to screw something up so he could ground me. This way he could tell the bosses, ---"I told you so" and fire my scrawny ass and thereby save face.

ACT VII
AIRCRAFT---LOCKHEED ELECTRA L-188
AIRPORT OF DEPARTURE---San Diego International Airport
AIRPORTS OF DESTINATION---BUR-SFO-BUR-SAN-LAX-
OAK-LAX-SAN
CAPTAIN---CAPTAIN DOUGLAS FAULKNER
CO-PILOT---CAPTAIN BILL LAKE
CHECKED OUT FLIGHT ENGINEER---*me thinks*---BECK
Pissed Off Jump Seat Check Flight Engineer---Lefty
STEWARDESS---ANN GARAFALO
STEWARDESS---JILL ZWALEM---

*****

Stewardess Ann Garafalo---beautiful lady---great personality---we called her Ann Garbuffalo---used to piss her off---Sorry Annie. ---I saw Ann not to long ago---She's just as pretty as ever---inside and out.

*****

We were taxiing out for take off. Lefty started asking me technical questions that only he could know the answers to.

The Captain, **Captain Douglas Faulkner,** was the same Captain that I had flown with the day before. Captain Douglas Faulkner stopped the airplane---put the parking brakes on---turned around, ---"What's all the hubbub back there?"

Lefty, ---"I'm giving a check ride."

"The noise is very distracting and if you want to stay in the jump seat---I suggest that you be quiet and observe like you're supposed to do."

BECK---3   LOFTE---0

We left San Diego on time---got to the Burbank Airport ahead of schedule.

The airplane filled up.

Stewardess Ann Garafalo---wanting the jump seat---came into the cockpit.

Lefty got out of the jump seat and told me to get off the airplane, ---"I'll take it from here."

Before I could get my seat belt unbuckled---**Captain Douglas Faulkner**---turned around---looked at Lefty---pointed at me, --- "This man was assigned this trip and he is not getting off, you are."

Lefty stammered, ---"He isn't officially checked out yet."

"He flew with me all day yesterday, did a good job and as far as I'm concerned---is checked out."

"NOW HIT THE BRICKS."

Lefty left with his stogie between his legs.

BECK---4 LEFTY---0

I was smiling---both inside and out.

Captain Douglas Faulkner, ---"I never have respected that man since I went through his ground school. We counted rivets for three weeks. When I went through training on the airplane, I was always playing catch up."

EPILOGUE

I flew Flight Engineer for Captain Douglas Faulkner the rest of the day and most of the night.

---FIFTEEN HOURS OF DUTY TIME---
---STORMS IN THE SAN FRANCISCO BAY AREA---
---FOG IN THE LOS ANGELES/BURBANK AREA---
---SWEAT IN THE ARMPITS---

I was one tired hombre.

I won all the battles but Lefty won the war.

"ALLS WELL THAT ENDS WELL"
PRFPACPJM
*****

"Joe---That guys a fairy."
"He can't be---not the way he kisses."
*****

Overheard on an American Airlines flight into Amarillo, Texas, on a particularly windy and bumpy day: During the final approach, the Captain really had to fight it. After an extremely hard landing, the Flight Attendant said, "Ladies and Gentlemen, welcome to Amarillo. Please remain in your seats with your seat belts fastened while the Captain taxis what's left of our airplane to the gate!"

****

FLIGHT ATTENDANT DEBBIE MCARTHY

"Don't it make my brown eyes blue" is playing on the radio as I write this.

Debbie McCarthy was always singing this song.

Flight Attendant Debbie McCarthy was on PSA's Flight 182 when it went down in San Diego.

When I hear it---I think of her and all the finest of PSA's people that were on Flight 182 and my stomach churns---and I start to cry. Still affects me that way---27 years later.

GOD BLESS you Debbie and the beautiful people that were on that Flight 182. There's a memorial plaque at San Diego's Museum of Flying in Balboa Park to these fine people.

I'll try to get a picture of it and put it in this book.

NO---I'M NOT GOING TO DO IT THAT WAY.

As you might have noticed---this book has went from a "book"---to Volume 1 and so in Volume II, I will endeavor to put anything that you FAX or E-Mail me to put into Volume II about the people on Flight 182.

Anything that will honor the people on Flight 182 on that ill-fated day in September of 1978.

---ALSO---

If you have had any experiences in the Aviation Field, in the Air or on the Ground, good or bad, that you would like to be put in Volume 11, please write me at —

Becksflyinghigh@AOL.com
or FAX me —
FAX 928-754-5319

If I put them in Volume 11 of "Flying "High" —

I will pay you Fifty dollars for each article, or, according to the amount of words that you have written, whichever is higher, when the book, ---Volume 11 of Flying "High" is published.

For your protection---I will destroy any materials not put in the book. —

"Flying High"—Volume II

Please include your E- Mail address or anyway that I can contact you.

I will put the above article a couple of times in this Volume, Volume I.

****

--- CIRCA ---

Probably the next day

For the next six months, Muldoon and I would fly the early morning flights.

One left at 0700 hours and the other left at 0715 hours.

The 0700 flight sequence---

SAN-**SAN**- DIEGO---25 MINUTES to LOS-**LAX**-ANGELES---60 MINUTES to SAN-**SFO**-FRANCISCO---60 MINUTES to LOS-**LAX**-ANGELES---25 MINUTES to SAN-**SAN**-DIEGO

TWICE

This flight sequence was blocked for 5 hours and 40 minutes which usually took 6 and ½ hours of flight time to complete. It consisted of 11 hours of duty time as check in time was 0600 hours.

The 0700 flight sequence landed at 1700 hours, **and** at 1800 hours I would be in Lefty's "riveting" ground school.

The 0715 flight sequence---

SAN-**SAN**- DIEGO---35 MINUTES to BUR-**BUR**-BANK---55 MINUTES toOAK-**OAK**-LAND---55 MINUTES to BUR-**BUR**-BANK---35 MINUTES to SAN-**SAN**-DIEGO

TWICE

This flight sequence was blocked for 6 hours and usually took at least seven hours of flight time to complete. It consisted of 11 hours and 30 minutes of duty time as check in time was 0615 hours.

The 0715 flight sequence would land at 1745 hours **and** at 1800 hundred hours---Muldoon would be in Lefty's "riveting" ground school.

Our flight time, at that point in aviation time, **was calculated** from---

Brake release for take-off>>>→to TOUCHDOWN.

Both trips were worth over 6 & 7 hours, which didn't mean fiddly-doo-doo, because Muldoon and I got a salary of four hundred dollars a month.

EVERYONE ELSE GOT PAID BY THE MILE.

**Captains earned six cents a mile.
Co-pilots earned three cents a mile.
Flight Engineers earned two and a quarter cents a mile.**

Flight Engineer Muldoon and Self would adjust our time sheets to make it look like we were obeying the FAA law. We'd grab a can of chili out of the machine and go to ground school till 2000 hours.

Lefty knew by now that we wouldn't stay any later.

We'd watch the clock and when the minute hand hit 2000 hours, ---we'd get up and leave.

Sometimes Lefty would have his back to us---writing on the chalkboard. He'd be giving some kind of dissertation and wouldn't even know that we boogied.

It was Miller time.

Captain Raynor Keough, Muldoon and Self would hit the South Seas Bar, have a couple of beers and then go home.

Captain Raynor Keough and Captain Bill Jolly finally quit Lefty's riveting ground school ---said in unison as they walked out the do-de do-door, ---"This is bullshit. We haven't learned a daggone thing. This is a waste of time. ---We're out of here."

**Muldoon and Self flew these two sequences six days a week.
FOR FIVE---*count them* ---5 MONTHS
AUGUST---SEPTEMBER---OCTOBER
NOVEMBER---DECEMBER
---6 DAYS A WEEK---EVERY WEEK---**

I'll figure that out for you---just in case you're a real "Airline Pilot" ---and can't add without counting on your fingers.

**4 weeks in a month x 5 months=
20 weeks x 6 days a week=
120 days @ an average of 6hours a day =
720 hours in 5 months---
Averaging---144 hours a month FLIGHT TIME** ---
FROM PARKING BRAKES RELEASED FOR TAKE-OFF
>>>>>TILL TOUCHDOWN<<<<<**

And that doesn't include the time Muldoon and I spent in ground school or---the South Seas Bar&Grill.

*****

That's more than some of you weenies and pussies fly in a year now and you still bitch about it.

"Those were the days my friend---we thought they'd never end."

They did.
"That's when men were men and women were women."
Nowadays ---Nobody knows---till they take off their clothes.
And even then it's still iffy.
****Flight time now consists of ---from the time you release the parking brakes at the gate until you set them again at your destination. This means you not only get paid for flying, but for taxiing and sitting around picking your nose and scratching your ass while waiting for take-off.*
*****

Muldoon and my sequences got back to San Diego at 1700 and 1745. We'd grab a can of chili out of the machine and go to ground school till 2000 hours. Lefty knew by now that we wouldn't stay any later. We'd watch the clock and when the minute hand hit 2000 hours, we'd get up and leave.

Sometimes Lefty would have his back to us and writing on the chalkboard. He'd be giving some kind of dissertation and wouldn't even know that we boogied.

It was Miller time. We'd go to the South Seas Bar, have a couple of beers and then go home.

We did this scenario six days a week. The FAA was in power and just like God gave us the seventh day to rest.

Every week, on our so-called day of rest, the Chief Pilot would have us come in for one of his dissertations. We'd sit there sometimes for eight hours and listen to this guy drone on about nothing.

After three of these bullshit sessions---I quit going to these bullshit sessions. I was home every night and saw less of my son than when I was flying for the Non-Skeds.

As I said before, my salary was four hundred dollars a month and I was flying enough---that if I was getting paid by the mile, ---I'd be making well over one thousand bucks a month.

One hundred hours a month doesn't sound like much time to you landlubbers, but to get this much time you multiply by three. In other words, I was at work over three hundred hours a month and that didn't include ground school and the Chief Pilot's bullshit sessions.

Muldoon and I were each flying well over one hundred hours a month. Max time by FAA law was one hundred hours a calendar month and still is. We'd adjust our time sheets to make it look like we were obeying the FAA law.

DOMESTIC
100 HOURS PER MONTH
1000 HOURS PER YEAR
6 DUTY DAYS---24 HOURS OF REST

INTERNATIONAL
120 HORAS PER MONTH
1000 HORAS PER ANNO
6 DUTY DAYS---24 HORAS 0F RESTO

The Captain that I flew with a lot was---**CAPTAIN DON STEVENSON.**

A litta bald and a lotta fat type of nice guy.

Captain Don Stevenson was the company scheduler. Captain Don Stevensen would take a quart of Scotch off the shelf and make out the **weekly---*Yea---I said weekly*---schedule.**

The more he drank, the more the people he didn't like---got shitty trips.

I was on his good side. I got to fly with Captain Don Stevenson a lot and you know---after he finished that jug---who got the best trips.

One day I told Captain Don Stevenson how much money I was making and that I felt that it was inadequate for the amount of time that I was flying.

Captain Don Stevenson knew that Muldoon and I were flying over a hundred hours a month and agreed with me.

Captain Don Stevenson went to Lefty, ---"Muldoon and Beck are flying over one hundred hours a month. You have to pay them by the mile so they make a descent wage. They are certainly earning it."

"If I pay them what they're worth, I will not have any control over them. I want Beck and Muldoon to do odd jobs for me after they get off their flights. I want the two of them to come in to my office when they land at night and help me with projects that I'm making up for when I teach the pilots their annual two days of required ground school. ---See that uncompleted circuit breaker panel mock-up over there. I asked both of them to come in on their days off to help me with it. I haven't seen either one of the two fuck-offs for two weeks."

Captain Don Stevenson went to Chief Pilot Righty with the same plea.

Chief Righty said, ---"If we pay them by the mile---they will not make enough to live on."

The dumb shit didn't know that Muldoon and I were flying over a hundred hours a month.

Captain Don Stevenson ---exasperated, went to---
---**MISTER KENNY FRIEDKIN**---
---**THE FOUNDER AND OWNER OF PSA**---

He told Kenny of the situation.

Kenny's flat response---

"We'll pay them by the mile, my people deserve the best."

GOOD MAN---LOVED HIS EMPLOYEES AND HIS EMPLOYEES WERE LOYAL AND WORKED HARD FOR KENNY.

My pay check the next month was for twelve hundred dollars. Three times the amount that I had been making. Of course my income taxes increased four times the amount that I had been paying.

It even impressed my wife, but not much.

How goes the saying? "You can't live with them and you can't live without them and they can't stand up to pee."

****

*****MISTER KENNY FRIEDKIN*****
KENNY---AS HE LIKED TO BE CALLED
WAS THE BEST EMPLOYER/BOSS MAN
THAT ANY PERSON COULD HAVE.
KENNY WAS ALWAYS ON OUR FLIGHTS
CHECKING OUT HOW THINGS WERE GOING
NOT PARTICULARLY TO CHECK ON THE OPERATION
MOSTLY TO SEE HOW HIS EMPLOYEES WERE
GETTING ALONG
KENNY WAS ALWAYS THERE IN TIMES OF TRAGEDY
WITH
WHATEVER IT TOOK TO HELP---
---INCLUDING MONEY---
GOOD BOSS MAN
MISTER KENNY FRIEDKIN

****

CIRCA

NINER-JUNE---1-NINER-61

HAPPY BIRTHDAY TO ME
27 YEARS OLD AND STILL NOT A CO-PILOT

We landed one evening in San Diego---
Lefty was standing at the gate---apparently waiting for me.
MY THOUGHT---"Oh shit, what did do I to piss him off this time?"
I stopped going to ground school when I started getting mileage pay and I figured that he was there to bodily take me over to the classroom.
I deplaned and walked right up to him. I had been with PSA almost a year---my probation period was almost over. I wasn't about to kiss his ass anymore---not that I ever did.
"The FAA is giving Captain Bruno a **check ride** and I'm going to give you one."
"Check ride???---My yearly check ride is not due till September. September fifteenth to be exact. That's the date you put in my records. I know---I went and checked to make sure that I had some record of being checked out to fly the line."
"Doesn't matter---we're going out on the airplane you came in on. Let's go do a preflight and get her ready to go."
"I haven't eaten all day---I'm famished."
"You should have planned your day better. Once you've been in the flying game as long as I have, you'll get the picture."
"I had no idea that I was going to get a check ride tonight."
"That's no excuse."
"Where's Bruno at now Lefty?"
"In the airport terminal coffee shop with Chico. ---Chico's the FAA Designated Flight Inspector for PSA now."
"Can I just run in and grab a hot dog?"
"You're getting a check ride Beck. Do your job---they'll be out here any minute now."
My Words---"Yessir"
MY THOUGHT---"Fuck you lardass."
FAA dude and Captain Bruno finally show up---forty minutes later.

MY THOUGHT---*"Shoot, I could have had a beer, a hot dog and a twenty minute nap by now.*

*****

***A man who knows not and yet he knows not he knows not---
shun him
A man who knows not and yet knows he knows not---befriend him
A man who knows and yet knows he knows---follow him
A man who knows and yet knows not he knows---watch him***

*****

Women---great plumbing---crazy wiring
PER CAPTAIN ZEBRA KITTY
*****

*A man's driving down the road with his "blonde" lady friend ---with his dog in the back seat.
The dog started raising hell ---the dog finally calmed down
The guy turned around in his seat ---said ---
"That's one"
Once again said dog did said raisin' hell ---
"That's two"
Once again said dog did said raisin' hell ---
"That's three"
And pulled him out of the car & shot him in the head.
The man got back in the car & started driving' down the road.
The "blonde" lady friend started ragging on the guy about shooting the dog.
The man looked at her & politely said ---*
"THAT'S ONE"
*****

--- CIRCA ---
Same friggin' day

SCENARIO
AIRPORT OF DEPARTURE---San Diego's Lindberg Field
AIRPORT OF DESTINATION---San Diego's Lindberg Field
AIRPLANE---LOCKHEED ELECTRA L-188
CAPTAIN---BRUNO
CO-PILOT---CHICO---FAA CHECK AIRMAN
FLIGHT ENGINEER---BECK
JUMP SEAT CHECK FLIGHT ENGINEER---LEFTY

ACT I

I read the checklist and double-checked every item. Lefty was hanging on every word that I uttered hoping that I'd fuck up so he'd have a reason to bust me.

I learned early on in my career that you operate an airplane three different ways---

THE FAA WAY---
  THE COMPANY WAY---
    THE SAFE SENSIBLE WAY

When you have the FAA in the cockpit, ---you give them an FAA performance.

When you have a Company Check Airman in the cockpit, ---you give them a Company performance.

When they leave, ---you go back to operating the safe sensible way that you were taught when you hired on.

*****

About the FAA Check Airman and Company Check Airman, When a check airman gets in your jump seat---
  Be very courteous---
    Always say yes sir and that's a great idea sir.
      I'm glad you're with me today sir.
        I have learned so much sir.

!!!TRANSLATION!!!
  The very first minute that you see the Company Check Airman or the FAA check airman---

Zip down his fly.
---Start whacking him off---the entire time that he is with you---
Wipe him off with his shirt tail.
Zip him up.
Shake his hand with the hand that you whacked him off with.
Bid him adieu---
Wash your hands---
Then go back to operating the safe sensible way.
*****

I HAINT KNOCKING THE FAA OR THE COMPANY WAY---
THEY ARE THE BEST AND YOU SHOULD ABIDE BY THEM---
--ALL I'M WRITING IS THAT YOU HAVE---
---THE HUMAN FACTOR ON BOARD---
---CASE IN POINT---

SCENARIO

ACT1-2-3-4-5-6-7-8-9ETCETCETC

AIRPLANE---BOEING 727-100---Overpowered Rocket Sled
AIRPORT---San Francisco International Airport
CAPTAIN---BECK
CO-PILOT---CAPTAIN BILL WALTHERS
FLIGHT ENGINEER---CAPTAIN J.P. LEWIS
STEWARDESS---MISS LORAINE GREEN
STEWARDESS---MISS KAREN FLAGSTAD
STEWARDESS---MISS DENISE HOLCOMBE
STEWARDESS---MISS KAREN ROMAN
JUMP SEAT OBSERVER---PSA CHECK AIRMAN

ONE ACT PLAY
And it's a long fuckin' act.
---NOISE ABATEMENT TAKE-OFF---
"THE SID" --- (Standard Instrument Departure)
---DEPARTURE PROCEDURE---
---FOR NOISE ABATEMENT AT SFO, ---

"Maintain runway heading (280 degrees) for 6 nautical miles---Make a left turn and proceed on course."

We took off. Maintained a runway heading of 280 degrees---accelerated the overpowered Boeing 727-100 to 250 Knots and made a left turn to an "on course" heading of 160 degrees at the 6 mile SFO DME FIX (*DME ---Distance Measuring Equipment*) ---maintaining 250 knots.

I was flying exactly what the Standard Instrument Departure Plate depicted.

EPILOGUE
---AIRPORT---SAN DIEGO INTERNATIONAL AIRPORT------JUMP SEAT OBSERVER---PSA CHECK AIRMAN---

"Beck---when you get to the 6 mile DME fix at San Francisco---pull the nose of the airplane up as you make your turn---slow to 210 Knots in the turn, then accelerate back to 250 Knots when you steady out on your assigned heading. **You will probably shave a minute or two off the flight time."**

!!!TRANSLATION!!!
---And it's a long fuckin' translation---

"Beck---when you get to the 6 mile SFO DME FIX, ---pull the nose up so as to further restrict your visibility in a high density light airplane area which will add on a few extra "G" FORCES to the added "G" forces that are induced by putting the airplane in a bank so as to take some poor old grandmother's already sagging tits and lower them a few more inches."

"This will save you a minute or two of flight time that will be negated when you arrive at Los Angeles too soon for the time slot that you have been assigned."

"Los Angeles Approach Control will then put you in a holding pattern and you will then miss your time slot because you will be on the outbound leg of the holding pattern when that time slot occurs and Los Angeles Approach Control will keep you in that holding pattern till they can find a slot for you."

"As you circle in that holding pattern you will notice that you're running low on fuel because the company told you to take minimum fuel to keep the airplane light so the company can save money on fuel costs."

"Then at this time Beck---*are you listening*???---You will have to 'Declare an Emergency' and write a short 1,000 Page Note to the FAA and PSA as to why you didn't carry enough fuel."

"At this time you are cleared direct to the Los Angeles Outer Marker and---

---"CLEARED FOR THE APPROACH"---

"About this time you will hear on your #1 VHF radio,"---"Los Angeles airport is now closed due to fog. ---PSA Flight 969 cleared direct to the Burbank outer marker. ---PSA 969--- CONTACT BURBANK APPROACH ON 121.9---SEE YA."

"Upon landing at Burbank---you will notice that there is no gate space because every airliner in creation has landed there before you because they took minimum fuel to keep the airplane light so as to save fuel."

"At this time you will be trying to contact Station Manager Ken Hodges on the PSA Company Radio on 130.9 but will not be able to get through because---

---STATION MANAGER KEN HODGES---

Is out unloading baggage because the station is undermanned to save money so the Bosses can have their own private Gulfstream Jet to take the Stews to Acapulco."

*****

I went by the PSA Hangar and espied a Gulfstream Jet Airplane with the PSA LOGO on its tail.
I asked a Mechanic, "What is PSA doing with a small business jet?" thinking PSA might be doing charter flights for the "Rich&Famous."

PSA Mechanic, ---"We're fueling her up now. The Bosses take a herd of Stewardesses to Acapulco every week at this time and stay for a couple of days. Someone told me that they are partying from the time they leave San Diego till they get back to San Diego."

*****

"At this time you will announce over the Public Address System that Los Angeles International Airport is closed for the night due to fog."

"At this time you will hear much pissin' and moanin' from your passengers,"---"Why can't PSA ever be on schedule and at least be at the right airport for once."

"This is your cue---the moment you have been waiting for"---
"LADIES AND GENTLEMAN---
FREE DRINKS FOR EVERYBODY"
"And at this time--the pissin' and moanin' will stop and every Stewardess call button will say,"
---"DINGDINGDINGDINGDIETCETCETC"---
"And about this time the Head Stewardess will come bustin' into the cockpit saying"---"YOU DUMB SHIT BECK---WE'VE BEEN ON DUTY FOR FOURTEEN HOURS."

"And at this POINT IN TIME---the Head Stewardess will leave slamming the cockpit door so hard that the blow out panels in the cockpit door will be knocked out."

"A few minutes will pass by and you will hear the natives growing restless one more time because we have run out of booze."

"At this time you pick up the Public Address Mike and say,"---"LADIES AND GENTLEMAN---THE BUSSES THAT ARE TAKING YOU TO THE LOS ANGELES INTERNATIONAL AIRPORT HAVE JUST ENTERED THE BURBANK AIRPORT."

"This will buy you another few minutes before MUTINY sets in and hopefully by then, ---The passengers will be on the Hollywood Freeway."

"At this point in time---
FLIGHT ENGINEER J.P. LEWIS---
Will show up with a fuel truck that he has commandeered on his own volition."

"FLIGHT ENGINEER J.P. LEWIS---
Fuels the airplane and enters the cockpit reeking of kerosene---trying to get the grease off his hands."

"At this time the SEL CAL goes Avon Lady Ding Dong. It's Company calling us on 130.9---that is the assigned company frequency that the FCC has assigned PSA."

---FLIGHT DISPATCHER KENNETH RICH---
"Captain Beck---San Diego Airport is now closed due to ground fog---I have you and your Crew rooms at the Golden Gate Motel. ---Make sure that airplane is down here at 0600 hours in the morning."

"We're not legal Ken---we checked in at 0600 hours this morning."

"How much flight time did you get today Beck?"

"Shit I don't know---how much time did we get today J.P.?"
"Only five hours Jack."
"ONLY FIVE HOURS???"
"Yea---five hours---they cancelled that Los Angeles round trip on us. Remember that four hour layover?"
"Yea---okay---thanks J.P. ---Ken---we only have five hours of flight time."
"Five hours?---well you need double that for rest time ---so that's ten hours of rest time---it's twenty-one thirty now---we'll call it twenty-one hundred hours---your crew will be legal for a zero seven hundred hour check-in."
"Shit Ken---this place is a zoo---we won't get to the motel until midnight. Can't you make it later? The fog at the San Diego Airport never lifts till ten or later anyway."
"We need the airplane Beck---check in is at zero seven hundred hours."
"Fuck you very much Ken."
"Dispatch out."
"All this time FLIGHT ENGINEER J.P. LEWIS is securing the airplane---making sure that we'll be able to take it back to San Diego manana."
"At this point in time---
   ---CO-PILOT---CAPTAIN BILLWALTHERS---
       ---Cap'n BECK---
            AND
   ---FOUR VERY BITCHY STEWARDESSES---
       DEPLANE ---SAYING IN UNISON---"
"Beck---you dumb shit---why did you order free drinks for a full airplane when you knew we would run out of booze before we got halfway through the airplane. All you did was wake up the drunks that were already passed out and by that time---the booze was gone."
"We are tired---Beck---tired---Beck---T-I-R-E-D and our panty-hose are sagging down to our knees."
"Sorry---S-O-R-R-Y---Sorry"
FLIGHT ENGINEER J.P. LEWIS---Shuts down the Boeing 727-100 and we proceed to curbside to find a packed hotel van. The van departs---the van comes back---the van departs---the van comes back---etcetcetc.

We check in at the---Golden Gate Hotel---At midnight.
We all went to our rooms.

I told everyone NOT to set their alarms and that I would call them when I made sure that the fog had lifted at the San Diego Airport.

I waited till everyone was settled in and went back to the check-in desk to get another room because I knew that the phone in the room that had my name on it would be ringing off the hook at 0'dark thirty.

"MY ROOM IS NOT MADE UP---MAY I HAVE ANOTHER ROOM PLEASE?"

I bought a couple of brews and went to my newly acquired room. Set the alarm for 1000 hours---drank the brews---went to sleep.

"AND NOW FOR THE TEN 0'CLOCK NEWS"

Oh---yea---10 o'clock---where---oh yea---better call everyone---get going.

I called the front desk, ---"This is Captain Beck. ---Will you please call my crew and wake them up?"

"What's the flight number?"

"PSA Flight 969---we checked in at midnight."

"Flight 969---Yea got them---right---they checked out hours ago."

"Huh"---"Thanks"

"I've been calling Captain Beck's room since four o'clock this morning. ---What room are you in?"

"I don't know---I had to switch rooms---the room you gave me wasn't made up. Bye"

I shit---shined---showered and shaved and was out the do-de-do-door in 10 minutes.

I went down the elevator to the hotel lobby. ---Bodies everywhere.

CO-PILOT---CAPTAIN BILL WALTHERS, ---"Where have you been? Company has been calling here for you all morning. They called me when they couldn't get a hold of you so I called the rest of the crew. Company called me at five---told me to have everyone deadhead to San Diego on the 0700 hours flight.---We've been to San Diego already---circled waiting for the fog to lift---returned to the Burbank Airport---came back to the hotel to wait---the terminal is a zoo---no place to sit or even stand."---"WHERE YA BEEN---BECK?"

"I SWITCHED ROOMS LAST NIGHT---they must have called the other room."

"Did you do that on purpose Jack?"

"Fuck---yea"

"Smart Man---we all should have done that. The fog still hasn't lifted. We might have to bus home with the passengers."

"Not me---let's go rent a car---I haint listening to pissed off passengers for three hours."

"Good---I'll go get J.P. Lewis and let's get going. The Stews have already left---one of their boyfriends picked them up and took them home."

"Oh---that's great." as I searched my wallet for my American Express Card.

And that---
Mister Richard Hughes and Mister Chris Roberts---IS WHAT HAPPENS WHEN YOU DO IT A CHECK AIRMAN'S WAY.

---THANK YOU VERY MUCH---

I am not putting down the FAA or Company Check Airmen. All I'm trying to tell you is this---listen to what they have to say. ---TAKE IN THE GOOD---SHITCAN THE BAD---

And no matter what you think of the bits of wisdom that they have bestowed on you---

---ZIP DOWN THEIR FLYETCETCETC---

In other words---

Shut up---listen---agree

aka

Kissing ass

---TAKE IN THE GOOD---SHITCAN THE BAD---

ACT 1A
NOW BACK TO LEFTY---

That night I was an Academy Award candidate. I gave Lefty a sterling performance---That is until we took off.

We get airborne and the FAA Chico pulls the #1 power lever back to idle.

I put my hand on the **NUMBER ONE ENGINE SHUTDOWN-FEATHERING HANDLE**---looked at Captain Bruno---wait for his command to pull it.

He says nothing and appears to be in a state of shock.

I then look at the FAA in askance. He too looks like he's in a state of shock. I look out the right side window and see why. ---

---WE ARE FLYING SIDEWAYS OVER PSA'S HANGAR---

Captain Bruno has kicked in the wrong rudder.

MY THOUGHT---"Fuck me"

I pull the **FEATHERING SHUT DOWN HANDLE** and feather the propeller on my own volition. I don't want to die---at least not before I have the chance to cram Lefty's stogie down his throat.

The propellers on the Electra engines are massive---not unlike four barn doors. If an engine fails and the propeller is not feathered and streamlined, it will cause a shitpot full of drag and a severe yaw, ---even if you kick in the correct rudder.

The FAA Dude takes over the controls---straightens up the airplane so it can get some lift over the wings.

WE MANAGE TO SURVIVE.

Our recovery was about fifty (50) feet over the San Diego Bay---where there are now high rise hotels on Harbor Island.

LIFE OR DEATH IS A MATTER OF TIMING.

I unfeather the propeller---start up the engine---we fly back to the San Diego Airport.

MY THOUGHTS---"This is over. We survived and it's cervasa time.

Guess again.

Bruno and the FAA dude are old fuck buddies. He wasn't going to give Bruno a down, even if it takes all night and drowns an innocent airplane.

Lefty taps me on the shoulder, ---"Don't ever shut down an engine without the Captain commanding you to."

I retort quite haughtily, ---"If I hadn't shut down that engine and feathered the propeller, ---we'd be drinking sea water right now." "Doesn't matter, it's at the Captains discretion to shut down an engine." *MY THOUGHT---"Fuck you lardass."*

ACT II
We take off again.

Second verse, same as the first---

FAA dude shuts down number one engine---Captain Bruno kicks in the wrong rudder---the airplane unflies sideways over the PSA hangar.

This time I don't hesitate. I pull the number one engine shutdown-feathering handle.

The FAA Dude kicks in the correct rudder.

We level off one hundred (100) feet above the San Diego Bay. *Hell, if you think about it, that's a one hundred percent improvement.*

We fly back to the San Diego Airport and land.

Lefty taps me on the shoulder, ---"Don't ever shut down an engine without the Captain's command."

MY THOUGHTS---*"Fuck you lardass."*

MY WORDS---"FUCK YOU LARDASS."

ACT III

We take off again.

Third verse, same as the first---only not as "wurst", --- and I'm not talking "sausage".

This time the FAA Dude didn't shut down an engine. Bruno still kicks in a rudder thinking we're losing an engine.

Sort of like Pavlov's dog. ---On a CHECK RIDE if you take off with the FAA in any seat---you start salivating---assume that you are going to have an engine failure. You are hot-wired to kick in a rudder.

We fly over the hangar again, only this time we were going more forward than sideways.

We are a good thousand feet over the San Diego Bay.

We're squattin' in tall cotton and my armpits are starting to dry up.

ACT IV

We climb to eight thousand feet to do some air work.

First we do steep turns to a forty-five degree bank.

*****

The steepest turn we ever do in normal operations is 30 degrees of bank.

*The reason for the 45 degree bank---**pilot coordination***

With every degree of bank---the airplane loses lift. The more the bank---the more lift the wings lose.

*To compensate for this---you must either add power or pull back on the yoke---or both---**mostly both**. The pilot is not allowed to trim out the backpressure on the yoke, which starts to get pretty damn heavy in a 45-degree bank.*
---*Hernia hurtin' time*---
*****

The steep turn maneuver requires plus or minus one hundred feet, meaning you have to do a 360-degree turn and not climb or descend over one hundred feet from your entry altitude. Also a plus or minus of 10 knots is maximum loss or gain of airspeed from your entry into the maneuver.

Bruno does the maneuver.
Bruno climbs five hundred feet.
Bruno is out of control.
Bruno descends a **THOUSAND** feet.
I'm getting airsick and am about to toss my tacos.
The FAA Dude takes the controls and gets us back straight and level.

ACT V
Now we're going to do stalls.

A stall is where you retard the power levers to flight idle---pull the yoke back slowly into your lap---lift the nose of the airplane up until the wings lose their lift.

The airplane will shake and shudder, ---*like a wife faking an orgasm,* and then nose over. ---*like a wife faking a blow job*

At this time you're supposed to add maximum power---relax the back pressure on the yoke---**Recover.**

Captain Bruno does all the above---except adding power.

Bruno adds Max Power on the #1 engine and #2 engine and #3 engine, ---missed the #4 engine power lever.

We go into a secondary stall---I think---then the Mighty Electra flies into a fit of contortions that I have never experienced before---or since.

I'm looking up---no down---no sideways at the ocean coming up to say hello.

I reach up and push the #4 power lever forward as far as I could as I am being G-forced to all sides of the cockpit.

The Electra levels off all by its lonesome.
Not my day to go to the big airport in the sky.

ACT VI

We go back to San Diego, land and go into Lefty's office to debrief.

The FAA Dude is writing a synopsis of the check ride. I can't help but notice what he was writing, ---**"The check ride was well done---and at times---Captain Bruno borderlines on genius in an airplane."**

I am more nauseous after reading that bullpucky than I was when Bruno was doing his suicidal acrobatics. The dipshit almost killed us and now he was the ace of the base.

Nice to have friends in high places.

I have friends in high places too but didn't feel like joining them that night.

Then Lefty, the FAA and Bruno start ragging on me for feathering the propeller and adding power on my own volition.
MY SOUTHERN THOUGHT--- *"Fuck you all."*

It is midnight and these yo-yos are going to sit around and pat each other on the ass till sun-up.

I excuse myself on the premise that I had to give a shit.
---FINALEEE---
I LEFT.

I go to the **SOUTH SEAS BAR&GRILL**---I have a couple of beers.

I wonder if I was missed or if they're still whacking each other off with that genius bullshit.

Who cares? I'm still alive.

ALL'S WELL THAT ENDS WELL.

PRFPACPJM

--- CIRCA ---

APRIL---1-NINER-62

!!!PSA FINALLY SHITCANNED LEFTY!!!
LEFTY LEFT---Hired on as a Maintenance Inspector with the FAA. Good fuckin riddance.

I saw Lefty a few years later---coffee cup in hand---stogie in mouth---lard on the ass.

Baby---some things don't change.

MISTER NORM WATERS took over as---
---CHIEF FLIGHT ENGINEER NORM WATERS---

Chief Flight Engineer Norm Waters was/is a sharp man ---with a lot of savvy.

Chief Flight Engineer Norm Waters was the foreman of PSA's machine shop when PSA closed the machine shop down.

They Fired Lefty and Hired Norm Waters as Chief Flight Engineer.

Up till then, Norm didn't even know there was such an animal as a Flight Engineer. None the less, they tutored him day and night and he got his Flight Engineer's License within a month.

Norm Waters was easy to work for and really didn't care how many rivets the Electra had.

*****

A POSTCARD THAT I SAW WHEN I WAS A LAD

A newly wed couple had finally made it to their hotel room.

On the left half of the postcard---
The bride was gazing out the window at a full moon with her petite behind being observed by the groom lying on the bed.

On the right half of the postcard---twenty years later---
The bride was gazing out the window at a full moon with **Un-petite** *behind being observed by the* **Un-groomed** *man lying on the bed.*

Un-petite---*Big fat dumper*
Un-groomed---*Big Fat dumper gut.*

CAPTION
It's the same old moon---but it's getting bigger every year
*****

One more puberty memory---An advertisement in a magazine
　　An Indian buck was lying on a sheet made into a hammock. ---Looking a litta---no---a lotta frazzled. --- (fucked-flat)
An Indian maid was walking away---with a smile on her face.
CAPTION
"A BUCK WELL SPENT ON A SPRINGMAID SHEET"
Very risqué for the forties.

--- CIRCA ---

NINER JUNE—1-NINER-62

HAPPY BIRTHDAY TO ME
28 YEARS OLD AND STILL NOT A CO-PILOT

Our Twins—
Kevin Shaun Beck and Shelbi Daun Beck were born.
!!! I'M STILL NOT A FRIGGIN' CO-PILOT!!!
Captain Righty departed the Chief Pilot's Office.
ENTER
Chief Pilot Captain Smith
Great Pilot---Great Guy
A good man to sit in a Cockpit of an Airplane with.

Captain Smith had an office in the hangar like Righty---the Chief Pilot before him---but his real office was in the **South Seas Bar&Grill.**

Whenever you had a problem or was/were in deep horse pucky---you went to the South Seas Bar&Grill to do your groveling.

Chief Pilot Captain Smith had his own "private" booth there.

Whenever I say private, ---I mean that nobody else would sit there because they knew it was Smith's "Office" and wanted to keep their jobs.

Firing people was easy in the early sixties. All they had to do was write you your final check. ---
Give you a pink slip---pat you on the ass---boot your butt out the door.

A---If a Stewardess put on weight
B---Got married
C---Pregnant
D---Any of the above
The stewardess was out the do-de-do-door.

Now a day it takes an act of congress to fire a crew member and that includes stews---er---sorry, ---Now addressed as **Flight Attendants.**
*****

For instance, PSA had a Captain check in at the Burbank Airport---drunk on his ass. If he had gone up in the cockpit and kept quiet, he would have been home safe. Not this guy ---he had to give the mechanics a ration of shit.

Well nobody likes to have their ass reamed out at any time---particularly at O'dark thirty.

The mechanics smelled the booze on him and called the FAA.

The FAA met the Captain at the San Jose Airport and gave him a blood test. ---**He tested at .07.**

The Fuzz figured that he was well over .10 when he checked in at the Hollywood Burbank Airport.

PSA fired him on the spot.

The Pilot went to Alcoholics Anonymous for a year---got a gold coin for being a good boy and got his job back.

I haven't the slightest clue why a Chief Pilot would rehire a Captain "**that got caught**" coming to work drunk to fly an airplane.

Ah yes---nice to have friends in high places.

It is written---God takes care of Angels and drunks. ---Right Bill A.?

--- CIRCA ---

APRIL---1-NINER-63

I was flying a lot with---**CAPTAIN DONG SEVEN.**
We would fly all day---hit the **SOUTH SEAS BAR&GRILL** at night.
Dong's girlfriend, Emma usually showed up around midnight.
Emma worked the swing shift at Ma Bell. Real pretty lady---Blonde Hair---Blue Eyes---Nice Bod---A real lightweight when it came to the "sauce".
Two drinks and Emma became Suzy Round Heels.
Miss Emma would start nagging at Dong to bounce her bones.
One night Dong told her, ---"If you don't shut up---I'm gonna fuck you right here on the dance floor."
That's all the foreplay Emma needed. In about ten seconds, Emma was lying on the dance floor---panties on one ankle.
Well, I guess that was all the foreplay that Dong needed. In ten seconds Dong was on top of her---humping away.
They finished their two person orgy---got a sitting ovation from the bar patrons and came back to the booth and sat down.
Emma took Dong by the hand---looked him in the eyes, ---"Isn't that the best you've ever had?"
Dong's retort, ---**"Better than a screwdriver in the eyeball."**
I drank a little more than I should have that night. I guess watching people fuck stimulated my appetite for alcohol.
I got to bed at two in the morning and got back up at five---went to the **SAN DIEGO INTERNATIONAL AIRPORT.**
I felt like I was Non-Skedding again.
The Electra was in the hangar and I had to "ride the brakes" while the mechanics towed the airplane to the terminal. *Ride the brakes???---Sit in the Captains chair and be prepared to slam on the brakes if perchance the tow-bar separates from the airplane.*
I saw a couple of mechanics that were friends of mine and stopped to chat with them.
I was still half in the bag and very talkative. Their eyes began to tear and they backed away from me. They had been working since midnight and stale martini breath was not welcome at six in the morning, ---"Are you okay?" Mechanic Jaye inquired.

"Fuck yea, never felt better in my life."
MY THOUGHT---Hell, when you're three sheets in the win--- you always feel good.

Wale and Jaye took me over to the candy machine.

Bought me some breath mints--- shoved them in my mouth.

Didn't work. 1 still smelled like an uncorked bottle of gin.

We got to the terminal and I went into PSA Operations.

Captain Spike took one look at me, ---"Are you alright?"

Shoot, I was feeling no pain, ---"I feel great."

Co-Pilot Captain Bulke came over to me---pulled a pack of breath mints out of his pocket---shoved them down my throat.

Dispatcher Bill Gosselin brought me a cup of black coffee. I drank it---Dispatcher Bill Gosselin brought me another.

Now I'm not only half drunk, ---I'm on caffeine and sugar high.

They had my heart so fucked up that it didn't know whether to beat hard or mellow out.

I went back to the Electra---walked around the airplane several times trying to get my head clear.

It worked. I became lucid---sober.

One of the station agents, ---**MISTER CLIFF GREGORY laterka CAPTAIN CLIFF GREGORY nka REVERAND CLIFF GREGORY c**ame up to me.

I backed off so he couldn't smell the booze.

I had enough candies shoved in my kisser for one morning.

"Beck, you're the best Flight Engineer that PSA has."

I was taken aback. ---"What do you mean by that? I inquired as to the reason he said that thinking he was being facetious.

"You're the only Flight Engineer that walks around the airplane more than once."

I didn't have the heart to tell him that I was merely trying to sober up.

*****

Cliff Gregory went on to become one of our Captains, retired early and is now a Reverend in Salt Lake City, Utah. ---Say a prayer for me Cliff.

*****

We took off---got to cruising altitude.

Captain Spike looked around at me, ---"Son, you're lucky that you're flying with me today---no other Captain would have let you in the cockpit in your condition."

I set cruise power and said nothing. Even in my debilitated condition---I knew when I was well off.

We had three round trips between San Diego and San Francisco that day. I drank coffee all day long trying to stay awake. My armpits were wet down to my waist and my hands were shaking so much that I couldn't hold a cup of coffee without spilling it all over the place.

I went to the **South Seas Bar&Grill**---had a beer---hoping to shake the shakes. I downed three Coors and started to come back to the land of the living.

Captain Dong Seven walked in---sat down beside me, --- "How did your trip go today?"

"Piece of cake," I lied.

"I was supposed to have that trip with you, but I overslept. I'm going to quit drinking," Captain Dong Seven said as he ordered a double martini.

I left.

I went home and got a good nights sleep.

I showed up the next morning---went into PSA Operations.

There stood Captain Dong Seven.

Dong looked worse than I did the morning before--if that was possible.

Dong said something to me and my eyes started watering. Apparently Dong had eaten a bunch of garlic cloves trying to hide Dong's booze breath.

Dong's breath was so repugnant that it would have brought a tear to a glass eye.

We get in the cockpit and in comes a Check Pilot, ---"What is that foul smell?"

"We don't know, it was like that when we got here." I said trying to suppress a laugh.

Captain Dong kept his head looking forward---talking out of the side of his mouth when necessary to respond to the checklist.

We landed at the San Francisco International Airport.

The Check Pilot stood up---patted Captain Dong on the back, ---"Nice job Dong."---left.

I patted Dong on the back, ---"Nice job Dong---but I'll like it even better if you quit breathing."

When we got in that night, Dong and I hit the **SOUTH SEAS BAR&GRILL** for a beer.
The garlic was still with Dong Seven.
Needless to say, I sat several stools away from Dong.

*****

A couple of---
Captain Spike
*Unmemorable Corn-dog jokes
A Priest asked a Nun if he could kiss her---
"You can kiss me but don't get into the Habit."
I forgot the other one*

*****

*Ooooops---I just remembered it.
The teacher told little Johnny to give her a sentence with the word* **PROBABLY** *in it
Johnny said, ---"I was watching my sister and her piano instructor through a keyhole. They had both taken off their pants."
"They were* **PROBABLY** *going to shit in the piano."*

*****

*Say this to your young old lady when she gets up in the morning complaining how shitty she looks---
"You sure are pretty---no matter how bad you look."
She will think it over and depending on how she interprets the underhanded compliment---
She will either whomp your butt or kiss you---or both if she's kinky.*
*****
Life doesn't always appear as it seems---do it?
*****

---Overheard at an Airport Security Checkpoint---

"HEY JOE, HEAR YOU NABBED A COUPLE OF PILOTS WITH WHISKEY BREATH YESTERDAY."

"YEA MIKE---THAT'S THE SECOND TIME THIS MONTH THAT I TURNED A COUPLE IN."

"GUESS IT TURNED OUT THAT IT WAS ONLY LISTERINE THAT YOU SMELLED, JOE. I HEAR THAT THE TERRORIST THAT THEY NABBED CAME THROUGH YOUR STATION WHILE YOU WERE TURNING IN THE PILOTS."---
"SEEMS TO ME JOE THAT YOU'RE DOING THE FAA'S JOB AND NEGLECTING YOUR OWN."

"YEA MIKE, I KNOW ---BUT TURNING IN THE PILOTS IS A HELLUVA LOT SAFER AND MUCH MORE FUN."

CAPTAIN JACK RESLEY BECK---REallyTIRED

--- CIRCA ---

6-9

ZERO-NINER JUNE---I-NINER-6-3

HAPPY BIRTHDAY TO ME

29 YEARS OLD AND STILL NOT A CO-PILOT

CAPTAIN DON STEVENSEN
Liked to fly
"Balls to the wall"
"Pedal to the metal
"Max gas Jack"
I loved it.

SCENARIO

LOCATION---IN THE SKY---Somewhere over the state of California.
CAPTAIN---DON STEVENSEN
CO-PILOT---CAPTAIN FAYE DENNY
FLIGHT ENGINEER---BECK
STEWARDESS---NANCY MARCHAND---CHIEF STEW
STEWARDESS---LORETTA COPPNEY

ACT I

We had a lot of fun passing Boeing 707 Jet Aircraft and anything else that had wings.

The reason that we could pass the Jet Airplanes was that we could go, when the weather permitted, VFR *(Visual Flight Rules)* --- simply meaning---BEELINE---**A to B** with no turns---
---DI-fuckin-RECT---

The Boeing 707 Jet Aircraft had to go IFR *(Instrument Flight Rules)* ---Flying the Airways. ---Sometimes having to slow down for inbound traffic from all directions.

Captain Don Stevensen would merely get in the flight pattern at our destination airport and the tower would have no choice but to clear us to land.

We had a ball---listening to **United Airline Pilots** with their **SUPER JETS** pissin' and moanin' because we landed before them and they had taken off before us.

Captain Don Stevensen always kept the Electra up against the--- "Barber Pole".

*****

"Barber Pole", a red and white striped indicator on the airspeed instrument which showed us our maximum airspeed. If the airspeed indicator exceeds this "Barber Pole"---A VERY LOUD CLACKER sounds---much like a woodpecker on the side of your house---and that VERY LOUD ANNOYING WOODPECKER will not stop clacking until the airspeed indicator drops below the "Barber Pole". "Listen to the Mockin' Bird---peckin' on a wooden turd." 'member that one???

*****

ACT II

One day we got word that a Lockheed Electra had crashed some where in the Rockies.
An eye witness said that the Electra "had just fallen out of the sky".

The FAA and CAB descended on the crash sight. After intensive investigations, they found nothing that caused the crash.

Captain Don Stevensen was not satisfied with the results of the investigation, ---"We're going to back off on the airspeed to **two hundred and twenty-five knots."**
"Our maximum altitude is going to be **twenty-three thousand feet**."

I scoffed at Captain Don Stevensen---wondering how he thought he was smarter than the CAB investigation team.
Under my breath.

Now every one was passing us---including our own company Electras. This made me antsy and I would squirm in my seat when one passed us. I wanted to go back to our old modus-opperendi.

After all--- we were getting paid by the mile, ---not by the hour.

ACT III
About a week later another Electra crashed.

An observer that witnessed the accident, ---"The Electra just simply fell out of the sky in two parts."

Now the investigation became even more intensive.

EPILOGUE

THE RESULTS---
"EXCESSIVE AIRSPEED---COUPLED WITH TURBLENCE AND INADEQUATE ENGINE MOUNT PADS COULD RESULT IN THE PROPELLERS CAUSING A GYROSCOPIC RESONANCE THAT WOULD CAUSE THE WINGS TO SEPARATE FROM THE FUSELAGE OF THE LOCKHEED ELECTRA L188."

THE SOLUTION---
"MAXIMUM AIRSPEED WILL BE TWO HUNDRED AND TWENTY-FIVE NAUTICAL MILES PER HOUR AND MAXIMUM ALTITUDE WILL BE TWENTY-THREE THOUSAND FEET UNTIL LOCKHEED TAKES EACH AND EVERY ELECTRA AND BEEFS UP THE WING SPARS AND ENGINE MOUNTS."

FINALE

I will always wonder how---**CAPTAIN DON STEVENSEN---HAD THE INSIGHT TO KNOW WHAT UMPTEEN TRAINED INVESTIGATORS TOOK TWO CRASHES TO FIND OUT.**

"ALLS WELL THAT ENDS WELL"
PRFPACPJM

--- CIRCA ---

AUGUST 1-NINER-63

I got blocked with Captain Bluud and Co-pilot Rock for three months. Most boring time I've ever had on an airplane. They were good friends and talked about their golf games --- excluding me from all conversations.

*****

Captain Spike had just taken over the scheduling duties and came up with the "bright fuckin' idea" of blocking a crew together for three months.

I think at that time he also came up with the "bright fuckin' idea" of that same crew flying the same fuckin' block of flights for three months. And that ladies and gentleman is fuckin' ridiculous.

Try planning your life out three months in advance and getting blocked with people that you have nothing in common with--- let alone sit in a 6X6 aluminum box with.

*****

SCENARIO

AIRPLANE---LOCKHEED ELECTRA L-188
CAPTAIN---BLUUD
CO-PILOT---ROCK
FLIGHT ENGINEER---BECK
STEWARDESS---MISS ANN GARAFALO
STEWARDESS---MISS LORETTA COPPNEY
LOCATION---5,000 FEET OVER SAN FRANCISCO BAY

ACT I

We were on approach to the San Francisco International Airport one afternoon---

I noticed an increase in the---**#3 ENGINE'S PROPELLER GEAR BOX OIL PRESSURE.**
This is an indication of an impending propeller gearbox failure.

*****

The Propeller Gear Box is the drive gears that reduce the engine's constant speed of 10,000 R$_s$PM. (Revolution$_s$ per Minute) to

1,000 R*s*PM to drive the propeller. If the propeller goes 10% over 1,000 R*s*PM, --- the PTS (Propeller Tip Speed) would exceed the speed of sound. That would cause the propeller to cavitate---thereby setting up a resonance that would rip the engine from its mounts and rip the silver wing out of its black roots.

Constant Engine Speed of 10,000 Revolutions per Minute
Constant Propeller Speed of 1,000 Revolutions per Minute
How does it go forward if the engine runs at a constant speed???
"PFM"---Pure Fuckin' Magic—no---not really.
The forward speed is controlled by PROPELLER PITCH.
The more the pitch---the faster you go.
Also works backing the Lockheed Electra up.

When we were on the runway and had a few minute hold before we could take off, --- I'd check with tower to make sure that there was no aircraft or vehicles behind us.

I'd taxi forward a few hundred feet---put the propellers in reverse pitch---back up to the departure point---taxi forward a few hundred feet---etcetcetc. Helped pass the time and the passengers loved it.

One thing I had to be careful of when backing up---**Do not put on the brakes,** because if the Electra was a little tail heavy---it would go on its tail.

I would stop backing up by putting the propellers in forward pitch and adding power.

*****

I pointed at the **#3 engines propeller gear box oil pressure gauge** and showed Captain Bluud the **high oil pressure indication.**

Captain Bluud was not impressed.

I advised him to retard the power back on the #3 engine because if we didn't---the propeller gear box might eat itself.

The advice fell on deaf ears.

ACT II

We landed and taxied to the gate. I got my toolbox and was off the airplane before the passengers had a chance to unbuckle their seat belts.

I grabbed a ladder, dragged it over to the #3 engine and opened the cowling. I pulled the oil filter on the gearbox and took a look-see.

The oil filter was full of metal. So was the magnetic plug.

ACT III

I went into **San Francisco PSA Operations**---called **San Diego Maintenance** and advised them of the situation.

They put the head of maintenance on the phone, ---"Whatever you do, don't start that engine. We'll send you a three engine ferry permit and a mechanic to sign it off. We have a flight leaving here for San Francisco in thirty minutes and the mech will be on it."

"I agree," I said and hung up.

I told the SFO Operations Agent to hold up on the boarding because we had a sick engine and went out to the airplane and told Cap'n Bluud what maintenance had said.

ACT IV

Cap'n Bluud got a little huffy, ---got out of his seat, ---went into PSA Operations and called maintenance.

I followed Cap'n Bluud to see what kind of bullshit he was going to feed San Diego Maintenance.

I overheard Cap'n Bluud tell them, ---"Beck's over reacting. I'm going to start up all four engines, load up the people and bring them to San Diego."

Apparently they agreed with him. Cap'n Bluud hung up and told the PSA Operation's Agent to commence boarding the passengers.

Cap'n Bluud turned to me, ---"We're not going to do a three engine ferry. We're going to take the people to San Diego."

ACT V

I stated flatly, **"I'M NOT GOING."**

Cap'n Bluud was shocked, ---"I want to make sure that I understand you right. Are you flat refusing to go on that airplane?"

"Yes sir, I don't think it's safe."

Cap'n Bluud was flustered, ---"You may lose your job over this."

"I don't give a rat's ass---I'M NOT GETTING ON THAT AIRPLANE."

ACT VI

Cap'n Bluud had his back to the wall. Cap'n Bluud told the PSA Operations Agent to hold up on the boarding and called maintenance back. I overheard him say something about a ferry permit.

I went and did a walk around. I went into the cockpit, feathered #3 propeller and did a three engine ferry check list.

Bluud got in his seat and 1 could tell by his demeanor that he was a litta unhappy with me---no actually--- I think he was a lotta pissed off at me.

ACT VII

We landed at San Diego.

Cap'n Bluud turned around in his seat---looked at me, ---"I want you to come with me."

I followed him to the Chief Pilot's office. He's wasn't there ---vacant.

1 followed him to the Chief Flight Engineer's office. He's wasn't there either ---vacant.

I knew where they were, but I wasn't telling. Cap'n Bluud was a teetotaler and didn't know the South Seas Bar&Grill existed.

ACT VIII

We started to leave and a mechanic came up to us, ---"Good thing you didn't take off with the number three engine like it is. You would have had parts scattered all over San Francisco Bay."

Cap'n Bluud walked away muttering to himself.

ACT IX

I went to the South Seas Bar&Grill.

The Chief Pilot and the Chief Flight Engineer were sitting there in Smith's "private" booth.

I had a beer. ---I left.

ACT X

The morning after---

I got a call from Norm Waters, the Chief Flight Engineer, ---"Beck, you did a good job of saving that engine yesterday. Thanks for doing a job well done."

"No problem."

"One thing, before I hang up, maintenance tells us that Cap'n Bluud was wanting to bring that airplane down here full of passengers with all four engines running. Is that true?"

I lied, ---"I don't know. After I talked to maintenance---1 went out and did a preflight."

Chief Flight Engineer Norm Waters, ---"Cap'n Bluud is up in the Chief Pilots Office getting his "buutt" reamed out right now."

I feigned ignorance---which isn't hard for me to do, ---"How come?"

"According to the Operations Agent at San Francisco, Cap'n Bluud tried to coerce you into taking the airplane with passengers. Is that true?"

"I don't remember."

"Nice try Beck and thanks again for saving that engine."

FINALE

I went to work the next morning and ran into Cap'n Bluud, --- "1 heard you lied for me."

"I have no idea what you're talking about," turned around--- went out to the Electra---did a walk around Pre- flight.

"ALLS WELL THAT ENDS WELL"

PRFPACPJM

--- CIRCA ---

196----1, 2, 3, 4,5,6,7
I flew a lot with---

CAPTAIN RAYNOR EUGENE KEOUGH

Captain Ray Keough was one of the pilots that I was in ground school with. Captain Ray Keough got hired on in 1960 and was a Captain before the end of 1960.

On Ferry Flights and Positioning Flights, *no passengers on board*, once we were airborne and out of the light airplane traffic--- Captain Ray Keough would ask **Co-Pilot Captain John Powell---**who always was flying Co-Pilot for Captain Raynor Keough---to get out of his seat.

I'd hand fly the Electra to our destination and land.

Captain Raynor Eugene "Skippy" Keough would rag on me from the time I got in the Co-pilot's seat till I got out. He was a great instructor and by the time he got through with me, I was quite proficient at flying the Electra.

Why "Skippy"???---Captain Raynor Eugene "Skippy" Keough was always eating Skippy peanut butter.

Captain Raynor Eugene Keough and I were talking airplanes one day and he found out that I didn't have a multi-engine rating.

Captain Keough called a friend of his and got us a twin engine Apache---a gutless wonder, but it filled the ticket.

We took off from San Diego's Lindberg Field and flew around for a couple of hours.

"Kug," as we called him, shut down an engine a couple of times and I handled the problems easily.

We landed back at San Diego and taxied to the light airplane terminal.

Captain Keough said, ---"I scheduled the FAA for your check-ride at 1400 hundred hours which is fifteen minutes from now---as a matter of fact---here he comes."

I was stunned and stammered, ---"I---I-I expected at least five practice sessions."

Kug ignored my plea and got out of the Twin Engine Apache.

The FAA inspector got in.
1 shook his sweaty hand and introduced myself.
The FAA Examiner had a "Fear of Flying." He was about to retire and didn't want to die at the hands of a snot-nosed rookie.

"We'll go up for thirty minutes, come back and I'll sign you off." *MY THOUGHT---* "*Piece of cake, I can fly a manhole cover for thirty minutes.*"

We took off and flew around a little.
The FAA did nothing but sit there and sweat.
1 got bored and shut down an engine myself. I wanted to show him what a great aviator I was. 1 did a couple single engine maneuvers and then attempted to restart the engine.

Ah Oh---Wouldn't start---I tried again---No dice.

Now this guy was not only sweating---he was shaking and shouting, **"GET THIS FUCKIN' AIRPLANE ON THE GROUND."**

He was pissed and I was not his hero.

We landed, taxied to the light airplane terminal on one engine, shut down and went into his office.

He was not a most happy fellow.

"You're lucky that I don't ground you for that stunt," he said as he reluctantly signed my Temporary Multi-Engine Certificate. He knew that if he gave me a down that he'd have to go up with me again.

1 shook his sweaty hand and left.

"ALLS WELL THAT ENDS WELL"

PRFPACPJM

I called Kug and told him what had transpired.
CAPTAIN RAYNOR EUGENE "SKIPPY" KEOUGH---Chuckled, ---"What are you trying to do---give the old fart a heart attack?"

I also told Kug that I couldn't get the number one engine started, even on the ground.

"I'll take care of it," and hung up.

When I went to work the next day, I left Kug a check for thirty bucks for the airplane and the instruction period and put it in his box.

When I got back that night, I found the check in my box, --- ripped to shreds.

THANKS

CAPTAIN RAYNOR EUGENE KEOUGH---

FOR EVERYTHING.
*****

We're all in the same boat---lets all row the same way.
Sayeth
CAPTAIN BILL HOWE

Captain Bill Howe---Great Pilot---Great Guy---Native American Heritage---Can't remember the tribe.

I watched Captain Bill Howe land the Lockheed Electra with the yoke in his left hand and a cup of coffee in his right hand using his forearm to manipulate the power levers (throttle levers) ----in a 20 knot crosswind---getting the shit kicked out of us.
(Yoke? ---It's the steering wheel that's attached, by cables or hydraulic mechanisms, to the Ailerons and the Elevator. The Ailerons cause the Airplane to bank causing the airplane to turn and the Elevator causes the Airplane to climb or descend)---

Captain Bill Howe was 58 years of age when I first flew with him. Captain Bill Howe would look around at me in the Engineer's seat and say, ---"You want my job, don't you."

I would always say, ---"After you retire, Sir."

Captain Bill Howe was a soldier of fortune at one time. --- While married to a Peruvian Princess---Captain Bill Howe hand dropped bombs out of open cockpit bi-plane in Peru.

Captain Bill Howe told me that he was married thirteen times. I reckon Captain Bill Howe is up there in his Happy Hunting Grounds with all his 13 wives?????

Does that sound like heaven or hell???
*****

--- CIRCA ---

1982---OR THEREABOUTS

I just happened to remember this event---so I'm gonna put it in here.
While walking through the PSA's Boarding Lounge in Las Vegas---I stopped to talk to one of our new hire Co-Pilots. I can't remember his name---a super nice man.

He told me that he couldn't get back to San Diego because all the flights were full and that he had been there all day long with his two young sons trying to depart---anywhere.

I went and checked with **Gordon---PSA's Las Vegas Station Manager**---also a super kind of man."

"Flight is way over booked---he and his sons will never get on---it's the last one out."

"Well Gordie---if it's okay with you, I'm gonna take his sons on board and show them the Cockpit."

"Thanks Beck---that's really nice of you."
With a winking eye---Gordie knew of my intentions.

I walked over to the Co-Pilot and took his sons by the hands---"I'm gonna take your boys and show them the cockpit---why don't you come along too."

"Uh---okay---thanks."

We got in the very small cockpit of the MD-80 *(A stretched DC-9)* and I locked the door.

"Okay---here's the game plan. ---When the Stewardess dings us to come in---put your sons in the coat closet and cover them up with our coats---got it?"

"Thank you so much---I really appreciate it."
"You're welcome."
She dinged---
They hid---
She came in---She left---
We left.

--- CIRCA ---

1-NINER-63

---My next block of flights were with **CAPTAIN BILLY D. RAY**---

We deadheaded up to San Francisco to pick up an airplane and start our sequence of flights for the day. We had two hours to kill and decided to do lunch. Our airplane had already arrived and 1 decided to read the log book before 1 ate.
There was only one squawk ---but it sure caught my eye---

LOG BOOK
AIRCRAFT 174
ELECTRA L-188

#1.---On take-off the #2 engine's fire warning light comes on and the fire warning bell rings. Retarding the #2 power lever extinguishes the fire warning light and shuts off the bell. SUSPECT FAULTY FIRE DETECTOR	Ground checks OK Rube Goldberg A&P6969696969

I decided to forego chow and look the #2 engine over. I felt that there was something definitely wrong and started opening inspection plates on the #2 engine, which were the size of a medium pizza pan--- looking for the culprit.

I had most of the inspection plates off and lying on the ground.

Captain Bill Ray came back from lunch and saw the mess, ---
"What in the devil are you doing?" he asked with a tone of pissedoffiness in his voice. ---"Do you know we have less than thirty minutes before departure?"

I looked around at the havoc that I had created. Sort of looked like Humpty Dumpty. All the King's Men and Four Mechanics couldn't put it back together again for an on time departure.

"Bill, there's something amiss with this engine and I'm going to find it."

With this in mind---I got in the wheel well---unscrewed the last inspection plate---threw it on the ground.

I heard **Captain Billy D. Ray** wince when it rattled to the ground.

I took my flashlight and looked where the compressor section bolted on to the turbine section.

!!!I FOUND THE PROBLEM!!!
"Bill come look at this."

"What did you find?" Bill asked dubiously as he ducked into the wheel well.

I shone my flashlight on the problem.

All the bolts and nuts were missing where the aft compressor section was attached to the forward turbine section---except for twelve.

There were forty-five bolts missing from the circumference of the two assemblies.

CAPTAIN BILLY D. RAY, ---"Damn"

!!!THIS WAS HAPPENING!!!

With high power settings, the **COMPRESSOR & TURBINE** assemblies would separate and allow hot compressed air to blow on the fire detectors and set off the fire warning in the cockpit.

Pulling back on the power would allow the **COMPRESSOR & TURBINE** assemblies to come back together, stop the leaking hot air, allow the fire detectors to cool off and extinguish the fire warning in the cockpit.

If the two assemblies would have separated on take off---we would not only have lost the engine, but the left wing as well.

What's the saying? ---When you've had a drink and the barkeep asks you if you want another, you say---"Why not---can't fly on one wing."
Captain Bill Ray and I went into San Francisco PSA Operations

Captain Bill Ray called San Diego Maintenance.

Captain Bill Ray told them of our problem.

Captain Bill Ray listened to what they had to say.

Captain Bill Ray cupped his hand over the mouthpiece, --- "What do you think of a three engine ferry?"

I shook my head no---gave him a thumbs down---left---got cleaned up.

We commandeered an airplane that landed at our departure time so we were only twenty minutes late.

Before we taxied away from the gate, 1 looked over at the sick airplane.

The crew that was taking it out was standing under the number two engine, scratching their heads, wondering if a tornado had come through.

Captain Billy D. Ray---**a**lways a gracious person looked around at me, ---"**Nice job Jack**."

"Thanks."

We flew a round trip to the Los Angeles International Airport.

Taxiing into the Gate at San Francisco---I tapped Captain Bill Ray on the shoulder, ---"There's Aircraft 174. ---Doesn't look like they got it fixed."

"No it doesn't Jack---I hope they don't want us to take it to San Diego."

"I'm not getting on that airplane."

"I'm not either Jack." Captain Ray said as he parked the brakes.

A mechanic approached the airplane waving his arms. Captain Bill Ray slid open his sliding glass window and stuck his head out so as to hear what the mech was all frantic about.

Captain Billy D. Ray listened to what he had to say---turned around to me, ---"They want us to ferry 174 back to San Diego."

"Bill---I don't think that's a good idea. That turbine section is only hanging there by five bolts."

"Not so---the mech said that they replaced all the bolts, ---but the engine still has to be replaced."

"Well---yea---that's fine with me then. I'll hop out and give a fast look-over---just for grandma."

We landed at San Diego International Airport and taxied over to PSA's hangar.

---CHIEF FLIGHT ENGINEER NORM WATERS---

Was standing there waiting for us---came up to me---shook my hand, ---"Nice job Beck, you saved an airplane."

"Thanks"

"ALLS WELL THAT ENDS WELL"

PRFPACPJM

--- CIRCA ---

0'dark thirty---next day---I think.

"RING---RING---RI---"

"Hello"
"Hey Beck---this is Thommy. ---What are ya doin' right now."
"I'm fuckin' sleeping Thommy---what time is it?"
"Pretty close to zero four hundred hours."
"What the fuck ya want Thommy---you just woke up my kids, godamit---I'm fuckin' tired. I just got home a couple of hours ago. We had to ferry an airplane back to San Diego. I'm beat---what the hell you calling me at this hour for?"
Cap'n Thom, ---"Was it aircraft 174?"
"Yea---I don't know---yea---I can't remember. We just landed a few hours ago."

"???WHAT'S WRONG???"

I shouted jumping out of bed and heading for the john---realizing too late that I was attached to the telephone---that was attached to the wall.
"Hang on Thommy---I dropped the phone."
"Calm down Beck---nothings wrong. It seems that you passed your engine on the way down to San Diego."
???HUH???
"Maintenance fucked up. They sent the spare engine for 174 up to San Francisco on Flying Tigers. The mechs were changing shifts and they neglected to tell the swing shift that you guys were bringing the sick airplane back to San Diego."
"Oh---OK---What are you calling me for???"
"Well---uh---Have you been drinking? The logbook shows you landed at twenty-one hundred hours."
"Yea---I stopped and had a couple at the Lost Knight with Captain Crank."
"Just a couple???"
"Yea---that's all. I was tired. I put in a fifteen hour day. So what are you calling me for?"

"I have to ferry the airplane, which you brought in, back up to San Francisco."

"So what the fuck ya calling me for?"

"You---BECK---are the only Flight Engineer in town."

"Not me Thommy---I haint anywhere near being legal. Shit---I won't be legal till this afternoon sometime. Beside that---**I am fuckin' bushed** and I haint gonna be on that airplane with you."

!!!"I'LL LET YOU FLY RIGHT SEAT"!!!

"I'M ON THE WAY. Is the airplane still at the hangar?"

"Yep"

"BYE"

--- CIRCA ---

Shit---I don't know. It's still dark out and I'm on the way to the airport and I don't wear a watch.

SCENARIO

AIRPORT OF DEPARTURE---San Diego's Lindberg Field
AIRPORT OF DESTINATION---San Francisco International
AIRCRAFT---3 ENGINE FERRY LOCKHEED ELECTRA L-188
CAPTAIN---THOMAS
CO-PILOT---MISTER ED
FLIGHT ENGINEER---BUSHED BECK
STEWARDESSES---NONE

*****

FAA regulation—only the required crew can be on a three engine ferry---period. *Unless there's some stew meat in the back that you might have overlooked.*

Flying with Thommy was always a mind boggling experience. Never knew what he was going to say or do.

When ferrying or positioning the Lockheed Electra, **no passengers***, he wouldn't even ask the Co-pilot to get out of his seat. He'd just look at the guy and say, "Get out of your seat and let Beck get in."*

I would hand fly the Electra and Thommy would yak at me as to what I was doing wrong---which was a lot of yakking.

ACT I

I arrived at the sick Electra and started to do a walk around preflight inspection.

CAPTAIN THOMAS saw me and hollered out of his sliding glass window, ---"GET YOUR SCRAWNY ASS UP HERE BECK---WE ALREADY DID THE WALK AROUND---COME ON BUDDY---WE'RE PUMPIN' MUD. PULL THE CHOCKS OUT AND LET"S GET GOING."

"OKAY"

I entered the cockpit and started to sit in the Flight Engineer's seat.

ACT II

Cap'n Thom held out his hand---keeping me from sitting down, ---"Mister Ed---get up out of your seat and let Beck sit there."

At first Mr. Ed looked at Thommy in disbelief. But then complied.

I sat in the coveted right seat and looked back at Mr. Ed. He was pissed---to say the most. Mr. Ed was an ex military Captain and the thought of some lowly Sergeant/Flight Engineer taking his seat was below his status in life.

ACT III

Captain Thomas, ---"Start the engines Ed and let's get going."

"Huh---you want me to start---okay---let me see now---okay---turning number four---is number four clear out there Beck?"

I opened MY sliding glass window, ---"Number four engine is clear Ed---go ahead and turn it."

"Turning number four---we have rotation---light off---accelerating---engine stabilized at idle."

"Clear three Beck?"

"Number three is clear."

"Turning number three---we have rotation---light off---accelerating---engine stabilized at idle."

"Clear number two Captain?"

"No Ed---that's our bad engine---you are cleared to start number one though."

"Oh yea---turning number one---we have rotation---light off---accelerating---engine stabilized at idle---hey---I did good for the first time."

A mechanic heard the engines starting, came running out of the hangar, disconnected the APU and saluted Cap'n Thom off with his social finger.

"Yea---call for taxi Beck."

"Lindberg Tower---this is PSA Ferry 174---taxi clearance please."

"PSA Ferry 174---cleared to Runway Niner---taxi on the Runway if you want---when you get to the end---you are cleared for take-off---wind is out of the east at twenty knots---altimeter---two-niner-point eight-two---I'm the only one in the control tower so goodbye."

"Roger---PSA Ferry 174."

ACT IV

"Okay Beck---we're in position for take-off. I'm gonna set the parking brakes---then we'll talk about the take-off---so put your hands in your lap where you can't fuck anything up till I say "YOUR AIRPLANE". ---"Ya understand Beck?"

My words---"Yessir"

MY THOUGHTS---"I'M GONNA TAKE THIS BIG BABY OFF FOR THE VERY FIRST TIME---SHUT UP AND LET ME AT IT."

"This is a crew briefing that I want you to pay attention to Beck---probably the first time that you have ever listened to one."

My words---"Yessir"

MY THOUGHTS---"I'M GONNA TAKE THIS BIG BABY OFF FOR THE VERY FIRST TIME---SHUT UP AND LET ME AT IT."

"Ed---I want you to, when I say the word---advance number one and number four power levers to maximum power."

"Beck---at that time I want you to put both hands on the yoke and your feet on the rudder pedals."

"At this time I will release the brakes and as our speed increases, I will advance the number three power lever towards maximum power."

"At this time---Beck---you will start pushing on the right rudder because the airplane will "head for the barn"---*go to the left*---because of the added power on the number three engine. As the speed increases---you will start releasing the pressure on the right rudder because the slip stream over the vertical stabilizer will tend to keep the airplane on center line."

"BECK---YOU LISTENING???"

My words---"Yes Sir"

MY THOUGHTS---"I'M GONNA TAKE THIS BIG BABY OFF FOR THE VERY FIRST TIME---SHUT UP AND LET ME AT IT."

"BECK---The Key Word Is CENTERLINE---get it? ---I'm gonna put in a few increments of right rudder on the rudder trim knob---it'll help alleviate the pressure on your right leg."

MY WORDS---"YESSIR"

MY THOUGHTS---"I DON'T KNOW WHAT THE FUCK YOU ARE TALKING ABOUT---I'M GONNA TA---."

"Brakes are released,"---"YOUR AIRPLANE BECK."

"Max power number one and number four Ed. I won't start adding power on number three engine till we get about seventy knots. Take it easy on numb nuts over there. He'll be assholes and elbows as it is."

ACT V

Untrue to his word, **CAPTAIN THOM*ASS*** advanced the number three power lever right along with Mr. Ed as he pushed the #1 and the #4 power levers forward. *Did I misspell Thomas? ---"Sorry Thom---never could pay attention to details."*

I was "Assholes and Elbows" trying to keep the Mighty Electra on the centerline. ---Which I didn't--- least not until we got to take off speed. By then we were airborne.

Cap'n Thom said, ---**"POSITIVE RATE OF CLIMB BECK."**

Beck said, ---**"GEAR UP"**---

Cap'n Thom, ---
"LANDING GEARS UP AND IN THE WHEEL WELLS--- RED INTRANSIT LIGHTS ARE EXTINGUISHED."
Beck, ---**"FLAPS UP---CLIMB POWER---ED."**
Mister Ed, ---**"Climb power set."**

At this time---I reached on the center panel for the rudder trim knob and cranked in another four units of rudder trim---then and only then could I take my feet off the rudder pedals and stop my right leg from shaking.

*****

*When I say cranked---that's exactly what I mean. ---**CRANK**--- Because of the high powered engines and barn door propellers on the Electra. ---If you should lose an engine on take-off---the yaw is so great that you have to put in full rudder immediately to the stops.*

The rudder trim knob on the Electra is called a "Coffee Grinder".

Why? You might ask—and even if you don't---I'm gonna write you anyways.

Because it looks like a coffee grinder so that you can crank in a whole lot of trim so very fast. Because if you don't---you are gonna have a very shaky leg and an airplane that's flying sideways.

ACT VI
I was starting to do a good job, even getting a little cocky.

Captain Thommy couldn't stand my demeanor. Captain Thom took his newspaper, cut out holes for my needle, ball, altimeter and airspeed indicator and taped it over my flight instrument panel.

Basic instruments to say the least. ---No problem. 1 just used Thommy's more sophisticated flight instruments to aviate by.

Thommy wasn't about to give me that levity so he took a newspaper and covered up his instruments.

Now I was back on basic instruments and doing one helluva job.

Thommy, not the one to be outdone, reached over and pulled #1 engine's power lever back to idle.

That was the straw that broke this camel's back. I had all the rudder trim in and the airplane was still yawing to the left. Now I was assholes and elbows trying to keep the airplane top side up.

I kicked in right rudder and that helped, only thing is my leg started shaking and so did the airplane.

I reached over and pulled number four power lever back a skosh.

That was the answer. The airplane started to fly straight and level and I breathed a sigh of relief.

All the while, Captain Thom-ass sat with his arms folded with a shit eating grin on his face. He busted my chops and was proud of it.

Once again I looked back at Mr. Ed. He was so pissed that smoke was coming out of his ears. He kept his mouth shut knowing that Thommy would kick his ass out of the cockpit if he said anything.

ACT VII
We continued on to San Francisco.

On approach into the San Francisco International Airport---I looked at Thommy and cried uncle, ---"Can 1 please take the newspaper off the instrument panel for landing?"

Captain Thomass just sat there with his arms folded---gave me a fuck no look.

I then **BEGGED** for all three engines for landing.

Captain Thomas smiled and pushed the # 1 Engine's power lever forward.

MY THOUGHT---"Well---three engines aren't as good as four but a helluva lot better than two."

After a lot of blood, sweat and tears---AND MANY ABNORMAL GYRATIONS, ---I finally got the airplane on the runway.

Captain Thommyass sat through the whole operation with his arms folded and a grin on his face. It was a tough ordeal but it upped my confidence in my aviating ability.

ACT VIII

I deplaned to do a walk around. Mr. Ed followed me, waited until we were out of Thommy's hearing range---started ragging on me.

Mr. Ed, ---"That flight was the most unethical, unorthodox, unprofessional flight that I have ever been on. You and Thommy should be given six months "on the beach".

Mr. Ed also told me that he was going to go to the Chief Pilot and the FAA about the situation.

I listened to his ranting and raving all the way around the airplane.

Mr. Ed departed and went into operations to fill out the flight plan.

I was a litta---no---a lotta clanked up over his dissertation and figured that I had better tell Thommy about it.

I went into the cockpit. Tom was sitting there reading the newspaper that he had poked holes through and put on my instrument panel.

"Thommy, we have a problem."

"Is the airplane okay?"

"Yes"

"Then I guess we don't have a problem, do we?" and went back to reading his newspaper.

I went to the galley, got a cup of water and threw it on him.

Now I got his attention.

Captain Thomas, ---"What the fuck is so important? Can't you see I'm busy?"

I had to laugh. I even soaked his newspaper, --- "Thommy, you have to hear this."

"Alright, but it better be good." he said as a drop of water fell off his nose.

"Mr. Ed is using the "un" words."

"What in the fuck do you mean by that?"

I reiterated what Mr. Ed had said to me.

"1 don't recall anything out of the ordinary. Do you?"

I was shaking my head no when Mr. Ed walked into the cockpit. He started to get in the Co-pilot's seat when Thommy tapped him on the shoulder.

"Hu-uh, you're in the flight engineer's seat, as a matter of fact, plan on spending the rest of the trip there."

I sheepishly crawled into the Co-pilot's seat.

I looked back at Mr. Ed. He was staring daggers at the back of Thommy's head and if looks could kill, ---we would have been without a Captain.

Thommy must have felt the knife wounds because he abruptly turned around and stared at Mr. Ed, ---"I'm given to understand that you don't like the way I operate an airplane."

Mr. Ed's daggers turned to rose petals and he got on the defensive, --- "I just inferred that the flight here was a little rougher than normal."

"Do you have another job in mind to go to?" Thommy asked.

"Well, no, I'm happy here," Mr. Ed stammered.

"Then you better mind your own business and keep your fuckin' mouth shut."

Mr. Ed uttered a very weak "okay" and that was the end of that.

We deplaned and the mechs towed Aircraft---Tail Number PS174 over to PSA's San Francisco Maintenance Hangar to replace #2 Engine.

Later on that day we had an hour layover in Los Angeles. I was sitting in the Co-pilot's seat half asleep. I sensed something and looked behind me.

There was Captain Thommy with a cup of water in his hand.

Cap'n Thom never let anyone get the best of him and I was about to get watered down.

I started back pedaling. Trouble was there was no place to back pedal to.

I apologized emphatically telling him that I would never throw another cup of water on him again.

"If you mean that, shake," he said as he put his hand out.

I ignored his hand and shook my body.

Captain Thomas threw his head back in laughter.

---Big mistake---

I hit the cup of water and it not only went all over him, but all over the cockpit.

It was the only time that I had ever bested Thommy.

THANKS ---
---CAPTAIN THOMMAS FRIEDKIN---
FOR
EVERYTHING
*****

PSA's ELECTRA---PS-174 tail number
Was bought at a "bargain sale".

PS174 was Lockheed's first Electra off the production line.

PS174 was used for the initial training of Lockheed' Test Pilots & Flight Engineers. ---Who in turn did all the flight testing on poor old PS174.

So when PSA procured the beat up Electra PS174---she had already lived a life time.

Scab Patches all over her poor twisted beat up young body and she handled like a Mac truck.

Even the engine cowling didn't fit just right---working on her was nothing but a pain in the ass.

Needless to say---when PSA started phasing out the Electras— PS174 was the first one out the hangar do-de-do-door.

--- CIRCA ---

1964

I HAD A LOT OF FLIGHTS WITH

---CAPTAIN STU CARSON---
---GREAT GUY AND ONE HELLUVA PILOT---

Captain Stu Carson knew of my aspirations to become a Co-pilot and whenever we had a ferry flight or a positioning flight---

Captain Stu Carson would put me in the right seat and let me fly the trip.

*****

Positioning Flight; *---positioning an airplane, no passengers, from one airport to another to fulfill scheduling requirements.*

Ferry Flight; *---ferrying an airplane, no passengers or flight attendants, from one airport to another for maintenance or to fulfill scheduling requirements.*

Captain Stu Carson never said much until we were on final approach.

Captain Stu Carson was always calm, never raising his voice nor threatening me.

On **every** approach---**Captain Stu Carson,** ----"Jocko, I don't care what you do---just make sure that you scatter the wreckage on the **CENTER LINE** of the runway."

For some reason, I usually was a little low on final approach. *A bad habit to get into.*

At this time---**Captain Stu Carson,** ---"Jocko, get this airplane back up on the glide slope."

I would respond by adding too much power and getting too high.

Then **Captain Stu Carson** would calmly say, ---
!!!"**SHUT HER DOWN, PAPPY, WE'RE PUMPIN' MUD."**!!!

Sometimes---ACTUALLY MOST OF THE TIME--- the landings were hard ---**but always on center line.**

Thank you ---**CAPTAIN STU CARSON** ---For everything.

--- CIRCA ---

NINER JUNE---1-NINER-64

HAPPY FLIGHT ENGINEER BIRTHDAY TO ME
THIRTY YEAR OLD---OLD MAN
STILL NOT A CO-PILOT
AND
GETTING OLDER BY THE CHECK RIDE

I felt doomed and destined to be a Flight Engineer forever. Not that flying Flight Engineer wasn't fun, but to me, being a Pilot was even funner.

I started putting out resumes one more time. I loaded up the postal service with them.

NADA

TRANSLATION---Not a Damn Thing Anyway

The year passed by quickly, the twins, Kevin and Shelbi, turned two and I could communicate with them.

*****

Mark was four and we did a lot of hunting and fishing together.
Just a little note here on hunting and fishing with Markie---
Markie and I were fishing for mud catfish in a pond near his grandfathers, Bert Wright, farm house in Webbers Falls, Oklahoma.
The pond was full of water moccasins---about every minute or two a water moccasin would swim across the pond. I'd shoot at them with Marvin Wright's, my brother in law, 22 rifle.
This one water moccasin decided that he had enough of being shot at---made a screeching ass halt in the pond---swam toward us---pissed.
I finally got the water moccasin in my sights and about that time Markie got afraid of the gun and pushed on my leg causing me to miss the pissed off snake.
The water moccasin came to the bank that I was standing on but it was too high for him to jump up on.
There was a tree limb right above the snake and he jumped up on it figuring that he could get to us that way.
I kicked Markie away---shot the snake coming at us on the tree branch.

Brother-in-law Marvin Wright showed up about that time---said,—"Don't you be messin' with those water moccasins in this chere pond, —they're the Stubby Tailed Water Moccasins and they are aggressive and poisonous as hell."

No shit Sherlock---We Left

*****

1964 was almost history and still no Co-pilot job had come my way.

I was panic stricken. I had turned thirty in June, an old man in the flying game at that point in Aviation time.

I went to the **South Seas Bar&Grill** looking for---

---CHIEF PILOT CAPTAIN SMITH---

Captain Smith was in his "Naugahyde office" with a blonde on one side of him and a redhead on the other side. I crawled in Captain Smith's "office" and sat next to the blonde by the name of Mary Matteus. *We called her Merry Mattress because she was in bed most of the time.*

All the other crewmembers, in the bar, first looked to see what was happening and then stared at their drinks.

This was not good. Pissing Captain Smith off was not a good idea when asking for a Co-pilot job.

I finally got Captain Smith's attention, ---**"I WANT TO FLY AS CO-PILOT,"** I shouted over the hubbub of the bar.

"Huh," Was his response.

I repeated my request, this time shouting even louder.

"I WANT TO FLY AS CO-PILOT!"

"Huh," was again Captain Smith's response. He just wasn't hearing my plea.

I physically pulled Miss "Merry Mattress" out of the booth---she staggered to the powder room.

This was not too bright as it pissed Captain Smith off.

I slid back into the booth and got as close to Captain Smith as I could without sitting on his lap.

Now there was a hush in the bar and all heads were turned our way---

I hollered so everyone could hear me, ---

"!!!I WANT A JOB AS A CO-PILOT!!!"

He ignored me, ---"Where's Mary?"

"She went to shit and the hogs ate her," hoping to get his attention.

Once again I repeated my plea.

I guess he heard me this time because Cap'n Smith said, -- "You're too lackadaisical to be a Pilot---but you're a damn good Flight Engineer."

"I intend to become a Pilot even if I have to quit."

"God Speed," was his response.

I said no more ---drank my beer.

I left.

****

Just a note here on Captain Smith---He had his office in the South Seas Bar&Grill because that's where most of the Crews&Stews would go to after a hard days work.---ha-ha.

This is the way Captain Smith would get to know their troubles and problems of the day.

As for the Stews---Captain Smith always left the South Seas Bar&Grill---alone.

A real family man

*****

A little boy was pulling his wagon around the block---a little girl approached him---

"I'm a pilot and this is my airplane. Do you want a ride?'

"Yes" she giggled as she climbed into the wagon.

The little boy pulled his airplane with little girl passenger in it around the block. As the little girl "exited the airplane", the little boy noticed that she had no panties on.

"My---that's a pretty thing."

"Do you want to kiss it?"

"No, I'm not a real PILOT."

As told to me---& everyone else that would listen by
CAPTAIN SPIKE

*****

--- CIRCA ---

DECEMBRE---UNO-NEUVE-SEIS-QUARTRO

HAPPY HONAKAH ---1964

MERRY CHRISTMAS
Mark Resley Beck---4   Kevin Shaun Beck---2   Shelbi Daun Beck---2

The next day I was looking at the classified section of the newspaper.

American Airlines was advertising for pilots.

I couldn't believe my eyes. I had never seen a help wanted ad for pilots for a major airline before.

I called American Airlines to schedule an interview.

The female voice on the other end, ---"Come in as soon as possible. ---You don't need an appointment."

"I will be there in about two hours---bye."

This took me somewhat aback. ---I tried to get an interview with American in 1960 and they not only laughed at me---they wouldn't even let me in the door.

*****

Through an intercom---located on the padlocked-10 foot---chain-linked-gate--- **POSTED**

**AMERICAN AIRLINES PERSONNEL
NO TRESPASSING**

"The Guru" in the magic box ANNOUNCED---
"We have four hundred pilots on furlough and do not anticipate any hiring till well into the 70's."

*****

Well, they were hard up for warm bodies in 1964 and mine was hot to trot.

**"ALL OF LIFE OR DEATH IS A MATTER OF TIMING."
"HAINT NOBODY KNOWS NUTHIN"**

I put on my antiquated single-breasted, draped gray flannel suit that I got when I graduated from high school, hopped a **PSA** flight to Los Angeles---went to American Airlines Personnel.

I figured that there would be a couple hundred pilots trying to get in the front door.
!!!WRONG!!!
There was nobody around except the secretary. I introduced myself---told her that I was there for an interview, ---"Go right in Mister Beck, ---the head of personnel is awaiting your arrival."

Now I'm starting to wonder. Four years ago these people thought I was a clown for asking for a job and now they're calling me Mister.

The personnel person was an Oakie from Muskogee by the name of --- **JIMMY DON.**

Nice guy with the typical down to earth, relaxed Midwestern demeanor. He liked me, my phony log book and my un-phony Flight Engineer time.

After a two-hour interview, Jimmy Don told me that I was hired as far as he was concerned.

I was still curious as to why I was the only applicant there and asked, ---"Why?"

Mister Jimmy Don pulled out a newspaper from a desk drawer---showed it to me, ---"**THIS IS WHY.**"

There in living, loving black and white was the reason for my solo appearance.

United Airlines had run a full page advertisement in the Los Angeles Times literally begging for pilots.

The requirements for an interview were so low that a person with a Student Pilot's license wearing coke bottom glasses and a high school diploma "could get a foot in the door".

"United also has run a similar advertisement in the Dallas and Denver newspapers," ---Jimmy Don added.

MY THOUGHT--- *"The demand has finally exceeded the supply."*

The next day, every major airline in the country was running full page advertisements in the papers requesting pilots.

I had become somebody.

It was even rumored at that time that United Airlines was actually going around to colleges recruiting any-**BODY** that was walkin' upright to train as future United Airline Pilots.

We "was" in demand. ---We "was" somebody.

Jimmy Don scheduled me for a battery of tests and a physical the next day at eight in the morning.

"I'll be here." ---I left.

I checked into the Airport Marriott. I needed a good nights rest if I was to perform "on the morrow".

I slept---restlessly.

I arrived back at American Airlines. The testing room was crammed with **Pilot Wantabees.**

The **WORD** had spread about the pilot hiring boom and everyone that had even a Student Pilot's license had come out of the woodwork.

The word for today is legs. ---Spread the word.

The test was the same as the one that I took at Continental.

--- STANINE TEST---

"Did you like your mother's tits and "winch" way a gear will turn at the end of umpteen turning gears?"

Seems like the kook that "invented" it was somewhere between a pervert and mechanical freak.

We finished up at 1800 hours. ----I went back to the Airport Marriott.

Best one on the Cahuenga Boulevard Strip. ---5 * * * * *

My mind was comatose and badly in need of some beer and some rest---in that order.

*****

Stewardess Flight Attendant Miss Muffie Burke---"How do you rate a hotel, Beck?"

"Quiet-necessity and if I can watch TV while "giving" a shit."
*****

I took a seven hour physical the next day and went back to see Jimmy Don as ordered. Jimmy Don called over to the hangar and got me an interview with the Chief Pilot.

Jimmy Don laughingly, --- "His name is Mannex. They used to call him "Mad Dog Mannex" because of his antics on the overnights. Streaking up and down the halls bare assed was his forte."

Jimmy Don got me a company car that took me over to the hangar.

I went into "Mad Dog's" office and introduced myself to Captain Mannex. He was a pleasant looking man with laughter in his eyes. He was pleased with the results of my written and physical examinations.

He then looked at my employment application and frowned, ---

"**You don't have a college education?**"

"No sir, all I have is a high school diploma."

"We can't hire you without at least two years of college or **equivalent**."

I hid my disappointment, shook his hand and left.

I was heartbroken. I went through two days of rigorous tests and a whole lot of dreams, only to be rejected.

I was used to rejection by now, both in the pilot job market and at home. On the flight back to San Diego, I started wondering what he meant by---

---"**TWO YEARS OF COLLEGE OR EQUIVALENT**"---

When I arrived back home, I went through my archives and dug out the Two Year College **GED** that **Sergeant Dale Jones** insisted that I take when I was in the U. S. Army 18th Airborne Corps.

I called Captain "Mad Dog" Mannex and asked him what he meant by "**EQUIVALENT**".

Mad Dog, ---"Any written document that says you have passed a two year college exam."

"**Does a GED test that I took and passed when I was in the army carry any weight?**"

"Sure, that's all we need, ---when can you come back?"

"I'll be on the first flight in the morning."

"See you then Mister Beck."

The Major Airlines were hard up for pilots and would take any warm body under any pretense.

Prior years a Pilot wantabee would have to be---

26 years of age or younger

Possess a Commercial Pilot's License

Instrument Rating

Multi-Engine Rating

2,000 hours of Multi-Engine time

First Class Physical---no waivers

20-20 vision---uncorrected

—**THE ABILITY TO JUMP OVER A TEN-FOOT LOCKED BARBED WIRE GATE**—

I arrived at American Airlines Personnel the next morning---showed Jimmy Don my GED Test results.

Jimmy Don was happy with them, ---"Go see "Mad Dog", oops, I mean Captain Mannex and show him your so called "two year college diploma".

"I saw that you didn't have any college when we had our initial interview. ---I was hoping to slip you by,"---Jimmy Don said with an Oakie twinkle in his eye.

I commandeered a tug---drove over to the American Airlines Hangar---found Mad Dog.

Captain Mannex was also happy with my papers---took me to the Simulator Building that had the new-fangled simulators that had **aural, motion and visual complements**---all at the same time.

Captain Mannex gave me "a piece-of-cake-honey-coated-icing-on-the-pudding" simulator Co-pilot check ride---hired me on the spot, ---
 "When can you be in Dallas for training?"
The "Mad Dog" caught me by surprise.
"I'll need at least a month to get my life in order."
I was buying time. ---I wanted one last shot at flying Co-pilot for PSA.
"Well, we needed you yesterday, but---if you need a month, you've got a month. The negative thing about a month is that you'll lose about forty seniority numbers."
"We're trying to hire about ten pilots a week."
Chief Pilot Captain Mad Dog Mannex scribbled a note---handed it to me, ---"Give this to Jimmy Don and tell him I've reformed and am no longer called "Mad Dog".
MY THOUGHT---"Horse-doo-doo."

He chuckled at the look on my face---my kind of people---nice guy and a hell raiser.

I stopped by the American Airlines Personnel Office and gave the note to **Mister Jimmy Don.**

Mister Jimmy Don read it, shook my hand**,** ---"Welcome aboard, I know you'll do well."
"Thanks" ---I left

*****

Legend: ---The custom of shaking hands began in the "Stone Age." When two men approached each other, they held out their right hand to show that they were not carrying a weapon.

Some "Sophistication Age" later, a "High Society" "Bronze Age" dude introduced the shaking of hands.
THE BEGINNING OF THE "SPREADING OF COLDS" AGE.
*****

--- CIRCA ---

ONE---JANUARY---ONE-NINER-SIXTY-FIVE
HAPPY NEW YEAR EVERYBODY

When I got home, my wife handed me an opened telegram, which read ---

MR. JACK R. BECK
PLEASE REPORT TO AMERICAN AIRLINES DALLAS BASE OPERERATIONS FEBRUARY FIRST 1965 FOR COPILOT FLIGHT ENGINEER TRAINING STOP PLEASE CONFIRM BY TELEPHONE ASAP STOP CHIEF PILOT OFFICE 817-379-6143 STOP

I called---confirmed.

The reporting date was exactly one month away from my initial interview. Like I said, the airlines were hard up for aviators/warm bodies and they needed them yesterday.

My wife, who was always the last to know, said, --- "I didn't know that you had applied to American for employment. I have made a lot of friends here and don't want to leave."

"YES DEAR"

I placated her by telling her that it was just a ploy to get on with PSA as a Co-pilot.

She shook her head, "PSA isn't going to hire you as a Co-pilot." Turned around and walked out the door.

As you can see---she was always supportive of me. "Ha."

*****

"Doc---I love my wife. We have been happily married for ten years but our sex life is dull."
"Go home---walk in the house--- rip your wife's clothes off--- Make mad passionate love to her right on the living room floor."
The next day he happened to see the Doc at the Wal Mart check out counter---
"Well---how did it go?"

"I did what you told me to doc. I walked in the house---ripped her clothes off and made hot passionate love to her right on the living room floor."

"Did she like it?"

"No---not at all---but her bridge club got a helluva kick out of it."

*****

*****

And from the pilot during his welcome message: "Delta Airlines is pleased to have some of the best flight attendants in the industry. Unfortunately, none of them are on this flight!"

*****

Heard on Pacific Southwest Airlines just after a very hard landing in Salt Lake City: The flight attendant came on the intercom and said, "That was quite a bump, and I know what y'all are thinking. I'm here to tell you it wasn't the airline's fault, it wasn't the pilot's fault, it wasn't the flight attendant's fault, it was the asphalt."

*****

--- CIRCA ---

2 JANUARY---1965

The next morning I called Chief Pilot Captain Smith at his real office in the **PSA** hangar. I wanted to tell him what had transpired with American Airlines and that I'd stay with PSA if he gave me a Co-pilot job. He wasn't there. I went to the main office.
NADA.
No one knew of Captain Smith's where-a-bouts.

I went to the South Seas Bar&Grill---found his booth empty. I asked Howie, the barkeep, as to his where-a-bouts.

The barkeep told me that Captain Smith was in Seattle doing an acceptance flight on a Boeing 727-200.

The only person that knew where Captain Smith was---was a bartender.
I gave up and went home.

There waiting for me was another telegram from American Airlines.

JACK R. BECK
YOU ARE TO REPORT TO DALLAS BASE OPERATIONS FOR GROUND SCHOOL ON 25 JANUARY 1965 STOP PLEASE ACKNOWLEDGE BY CALLING 817-379-6143 COLLECT STOP ADVISE US OF YOUR INTENTIONS.

I called and told them that I would be there on the twenty-fifth.
A week went by ---I still hadn't found Captain Smith.
Waiting for me at home was another telegram.

JACK R. BECK
YOU ARE TO REPORT TO DALLAS BASE OPERATIONS FOR GROUND SCHOOL ON 18 JANUARY 1965 STOP PLEASE ACKNOWLEDGE BY CALLING 817-379-6143 COLLECT STOP ADVISE US OF YOUR INTENTIONS STOP

Was I in demand or not?
I kicked back, had a beer and wallowed in my newly found popularity.
---DING-DONG-DING-DONG---

Another telegram from American Airlines, ---they didn't even give me a chance to answer the last one.

JACK R. BECK
YOU ARE TO REPORT TO DALLAS BASE OPERATIONS FOR GROUND SCHOOL ON 11 JANUARY 1965 STOP PLEASE ACKNOWLEDGE BY CALLING 817-379-6143 COLLECT STOP ADVISE US OF YOUR INTENTIONS STOP

I drank a whole six pack of Brew 102---wallowed in my newly found demandability.

In reality---I figured one more telegram and **American Airlines** would be asking me to report yesterday.

I called American Airlines back and confirmed the eleventh report date.

It was now the Sixth of January, which gave me just five days to quit **PSA** and report to Dallas, Texas.

I was running out of altitude, airspeed and ideas---all at the same time.

The next day I worked a flight to San Francisco.

Chief Pilot Captain Smith was waiting at the gate and wanting to fly home with us.

The airplane filled up and Cap'n Smith **HAD** to sit in the jump seat.

DRY---dry "Martins" on the Flight to "San Diego Weigo" for Cap'n Smith.

After we reached our cruising altitude of 23,000 feet---leveled off and Captain Lee Thaxton put the auto-pilot on, ---I told Captain/Chief Pilot/ Mr. Smith that I desperately needed to talk to him.

"Meet me in my office," was his very curt reply.

We landed in San Diego and everyone deplaned---except me.

I had to "ride" the brakes while the mechanics towed the airplane to the West Hangar.

✬✬✬✬✬

---West hangar---Airplanes and Mechanics---
East Hangar---Crews&Stews&Booze aka South Seas Bar&Grill
*****

We finally arrived at the West Hangar. I quickly "borrowed" a tug and "sped" back to the terminal. I was in a hurry and wanted to talk to

Captain Smith before he went to the Martini Heaven that circles the Planet of the Apes.
Time was of the essence.
I got to the **"East Hangar"** *South Seas Bar&Grill.*

Captain Smith was in his "Office"---flying solo, ---"Sit down and be brief about it."

News travels faster than jet planes in the airline industry.

Smith already knew that I had a job with American Airlines.

I made it brief, ---"I want you to give me a Co-pilot's check ride and a job as Co-pilot or I'm quitting **PSA**. I have been hired by American Airlines. I can't give you too much notice because I have to be in Dallas, Texas within five days."

Smith was not surprised, ---"I can't give you a check ride in an airplane that you have never flown before. ---It wouldn't be fair to you."

"I don't give a shit. I'm leaving anyway and to me, it's a no lose situation."

I neglected to tell him that I probably had more "stick time" in the Electra in the past year than he did.

"I'll think about it, as for now, get out of here."
End of interview.

"stick time" ---hands on flying ---no auto-pilot

*****

"Opawaitor---give me Twinity Twee-Twee-Twee."
"Oh -you sound so cute little boy. What classes do you take in school?"
"Dictaphone"
???Dictaphone???
"Yea, dictaphone up your ass and give me Twinity-Twee-Twee-Twee."
*****

--- CIRCA ---

08 JANUARY 1965

"RING---RING---RI---"

"Hello"

"This is Captain Smith, ---'Bring your log book and be in my office before noon."

"I didn't know that you had an office," was my caustic reply. After all, I was quitting and didn't have to kiss his behind anymore.

"Just be here before noon," was his even more caustic retort and hung up. He knew that I was jiving him and didn't feel like putting up with my bullcrap.

I got my logbook and leafed through it. It was a work of art that even Rembrandt would have envied.

At this time in life, not counting the right seat time that I had in the Electra---which I could not log because it was illegal, I only had three hundred hours of actual Pilot flight time logged.

I had logged an additional eleven hundred bogus hours of **P-51** time, meaning that I penciled the hours in with a **Parker 51** Ballpoint Pen, giving me a total of fourteen hundred hours in my logbook.

I'd go to an airport, look for an airplane that I was checked out on---or not checked out on--- and using that airplanes tail number---put a few more hours in my log book.

I spent a lot of time on this masterpiece using different pens and even going so far as to spilling coffee on a couple of pages to make it look authentic.

I spent the next two hours dummying in another three hundred (300) hours giving me a total of seventeen hundred (1700) hours.

The last three hundred (300) hours that I put in my log book in those two hours? You might ask –I just dummied in four (4) hours each day in the last few months. I didn't even try to make it look authentic. ---Shoot, I was leaving PSA anyway and I didn't care if Smith believed it or not.

If you're going to lie, **LIE IN BOLD TYPE.**

--- CIRCA ---

Same day---only later.

I got to Chief Pilot Captain Smith's real office at eleven hundred hours. He looked like someone had drug him through a brush heap backwards.

A few martinis with a blonde and a redhead can do that to a man.

I threw him my logbook and he scanned through it. He dwelled on the last three hundred hours that I had penciled in **that morning**, --- not even looking at my Rembrandt creation.

Captain Smith threw my logbook back at me, ---
"YOU SURE FLY A LOT."
I was ready to quit and he knew it.
"When are you leaving for Dallas?"
"Soon"
"I'll think on it."

I left---went to the South Seas Bar&Grill---got shitfaced.

Captain Smith came in with a chick on each arm. Now I know why it was imperative that I saw him before noon.

Like Cinderella's carriage that turned into a pumpkin at midnight, Smith's pee-pee turned into a hard pumpkin at noon.

I left

Fuck 'em. I went home and started packing for Dallas.

I got knee walking drunk and drove to the Caliente Horse and Dog Racing Track in Tijuana, Mexico.

Not too bright. If the cops pull you over in Mehico and you've only had one beer, you're going to spend a very, very long night in the Tijuana jail and maybe a very, very, very long year if you can't find someone to bail you out.

Luckily I got to the track without incident, won forty bucks and was just about sober when I started home.

On the way home I decided to do a little boogying in Tijuana Town. Do a little dancing with some senorita and watch a dog and pony show. This is where the dog tries to mount the pony or vice versa. Never got to see the show nor did I get to rub bodies with a "senor-eater".

I drove down a one way street the wrong way.

The Federales pulled me over.

I stopped and rolled my window down. One of the Federales stuck his head in the window and put his face about two inches from mine. I thought he was going to kiss me. Perchance I was going to be part of a dog and pony show, only thing was, I didn't know if I was going to be the dog or the pony.

"Senor, you've been drinking," he intimated as he smelled my breath.

I lied and told him that I had a beer at the dog track. I didn't think that it was prudent of me to tell him that a few hours ago I couldn't walk and had to drive to get anywhere.

"If you've had a cervasa senor, ---we have to take you to jail. You cannot drink even just one beer in Tijuana and drive."

Here I am in one of the most decadent cities in the world and they're going to throw me in jail for drinking a beer.

I got completely sober real fast. A Tijuana jail was not my idea of the Beverly Hills Country Club.

I inquired as to how much it was going to cost me to get out of jail.

"Forty American dollars Senor."

"Can I give you twenty dollars and you pay the fine for me?"

"Senor, you are going to jail and you are still going to have to pay forty dollars to get out."

Now he has my attention.

El Federale wanted forty bucks and was not about to bargain.

I pulled out two twenties, handed them to him, and again asked him if he would pay the fine for me.

"Do you want a receipt Senor?"

"No, Senor." ---I just wanted out of there so I could go back to the "States" where I was familiar with the jails.

El Federale methodically crumpled up the twenties into the size of a marble while his hand was still in the car.

El Federale stood up---pointed down the road---pretended to give me directions.

I left T-Town and went home. The Federale had taken all my winnings and my head was starting to hurt.

I got home, had a couple of Brew 102's and went to sleep on the couch. The last thing that I wanted to do was wake up my wife.

I'd rather do combat with the Federales in T-Town.

--- CIRCA ---

10 JANUARY 1965

"RING---RING---RI---"
The phone rang at 0600 hours.
It was---**CHIEF PILOT CAPTAIN SMITH.**
MY THOUGHT---"This guy flies with the eagles in the daytime and the owls at night."

I was trying to remember how I got home when he said, ---"If you still want me to give you a check ride, ---be down here at 2100 hours tonight." He was brisk.

"I'll be there," was my very courteous reply.

Now it's back to square one, aka ass kissing time.

I called Muldoon and told him what Smith had said. Muldoon and I were going to take our wives out to dinner that evening and I wanted to tell him that we couldn't make it.

Flight Engineer Muldoon, ---"Yea, I just got a call for the same flight and was about to call you and cancel dinner. I'll pick you up at eight and we'll ride down together."

"See you then," I said and hung up.

Now I have a whole day to sweat out a check ride that will change my destiny.

*****IF I WIN---I STAY WITH PSA*****
*****IF I WIN---I'M ON MY WAY TO DALLAS*****

Time passed very slowly that day. It's like one of our Captains by the name of Leland once told me, ---"Ten seconds is not a very long time, but hang by your balls for ten seconds and it will seem like an eternity."

Well, I hung for many hours that day and it was a hundred eternities.

Flight Engineer Muldoon picked me up as promised and we went to the airport.

We were walking over to PSA Flight Operations and I was shaking like a leaf on an Aspen Tree during a windstorm in the Rockies in September.

Muldoon sensed my anxiety and tried to calm me down by saying, ---**"Are you cold?"**

"No Mmmmuldoon, I'm just terrified," I stammered.

Muldoon patted me on the back and said, "You'll ace it."

Didn't calm me down any but it was nice to know that someone had faith in me.

We went into operations and there were four new hires that were going up with us for training.

---CAPTAIN ALAN WATSON---
---CAPTAIN JOHN HARDIN---
---CAPTAIN TED BOOTH---
&
WUCO
*****

---CAPTAIN ALAN WATSON---

Captain Alan Watson already had his training and was getting a check-ride.

Captain Alan Watson retired in 1993.

Last I heard ---Captain Alan Watson was flying somewhere in the Orient.

Captain Ted Booth ---- was another trainee.

Many years later Captain Ted Booth went out on a medical--- and was last known to be alive and haunting the casinos in Las Vegas.

Captain John Hardin was another.

Captain John Hardin augured in when he flew up a box canyon near Yosemite National Park.

—CAPTAIN JOHN HARDIN—
—CAPTAIN BOB RIMEL---
---CAPTAIN RON FOX---

Were flying a Navy Twin-Engine S-2 with a **"radome"** on its back

"RADOME" ---*A large dome-shaped housing for protecting a radar antenna*

They were cruising up a canyon looking for deer and ran into a canyon wall.

Captain Hardin, Captain Fox and Captain Rimel had flown over my postage stamp sized ranch a couple of weeks prior to the accident.

They flew a couple of passes back and forth above my place at about one hundred feet AGL.

The last pass that they made was about fifty feet above the ground.

That's when they threw a "shitload" of unwound toilet paper out of the cargo door.

Most of the toilet paper lit in my California Oaks, only to remain there for years.

A grim reminder of ---THREE NICE PEOPLE

WUCO

Wuco, **last and least**, claimed to be the Chief Pilot of Philippine Airlines at one time.

*****

*****

A young lady married a Frenchman and her mother warned her, ---"You gotta watch those Frenchies---sooner or later he's gonna want to swap ends."---

"OK, Mom I'll be careful."

Several months go by and one day the Frenchman says to his bride, ---"Do you want to swap ends tonight?"

"No-No-No--my mother warned me about you Frenchman---I'm not gonna do it."

"Don't you ever want to get pregnant?"

*****

*****

Another flight attendant's comment on a less than perfect landing: "We ask you to please remain seated as Captain Kangaroo bounces us to the terminal."

*****

--- CIRCA ---

JAN 1965---2200 HUNDRED HOURS

We fired up the Electra and took off.
CAPTAIN ALAN WATSON ----Was the first to fly.
Captain Alan Watson passed his check ride with "Flying Colors".

Nice job, ----Captain Alan Watson. ---NEAT GUY---good as any man that strolls down the pike.

Next up was Wuco. ---Wuco claimed to be the Chief Pilot of Philippine Airlines at one time.

I sat in the jump seat for Wuco's training ride. Thought maybe I'd learn something.
!!!WRONG!!!
The Electra could have qualified as an "E" ride at Disneyland.

The only time we were straight and level was when we were going through it. The Electra was going sideways, up and down and doing gyrations that I had never seen or felt before.

It was a beautiful night---and I was getting airsick.

Flight Engineer Muldoon set off a false fire warning on #2 Engine, which illuminated the #2 Engine fire-shutdown handle a mesmerizing GLOWING RED and sounded a very LOUD BELL.
*****

We didn't have the high-tech training boxes on the Electra that we have on airplanes now, so Muldoon just reached up on the overhead panel and pushed the #2 engine fire warning test at Captain Smith's nod of the head which he and Muldoon had done so many times before on training and check rides.

Nowadays we have a "Black Box" that can simulate anything from an engine failure to a biffy overflowing.

For those of you that tuned in late. Biffy---airplane toilette
*****

WUCO ----????Philipine???Airlines?????Ex Chief Pilot?? ---looked at the RED warning light and screamed, ---**"WHATS THAT FUCKIN NOISE? Turn off that fuckin' red light---Stop that fuckin' noise."**

WUCO, after many landing attempts---got the Electra on the ground.
---Hesus lives.

Chief Pilot Check Pilot Instructor Pilot Captain Smith had enough of Wuco---told him to get out of the seat and go back into the cabin.

Chief Pilot Check Pilot Instructor Pilot Captain Smith--- Looked around at me, ---"Your turn in the "barrel."
*****

Our hillbilly forefathers would take a beer barrel and drill a hole in it.

*One guy would get naked get in the barrel and the others would cornhole him--- hence the term your turn in the barrel. The hillbilly that couldn't get his pecker through the hole got to do the host's wife hence the song the---"**Beer barrel pork-her**".*

I think I wrote this hillbilly bullshit before---what the hell---Give you arm chair critics something to talk about.
*****

I craaaawled into the right seat.

My heart craaaaawled into my stomach. ---The rest of my vital organs craaaaawled into my throat.

I was so choked up that I couldn't speak.

As DON HO sang, "This is the moment that I've been waiting for, --- Aloha Aloha."

All of a sudden a sense of calm came over me.

Thanks to all the Captains that let me fly right seat---

!!!I KNEW I COULD DO IT!!!

Check Pilot Captain Smith, ---"Your airplane."

I looked over my left shoulder at Muldoon, ---"Max Power---please."

Muldoon pushed the Power Levers forward to **MAX POWER.**

We went roaring down the runway and the mighty Electra lifted off.

I felt a surge of confidence that I had never experienced before.

I might not pass the check ride, but for the next few minutes, ---I was going to be a **CO-PILOT.**

Captain Smith felt my bravado---started to test me. Captain Smith shut down the #1 Engine.

No problem.

Muldoon feathered the #1 Engine's Propeller.

Feathered the Propeller---Streamlined the propeller into the slipstream for Minimum drag.

I kicked in the right rudder and compensated for the yaw by cranking in some rudder trim. I wasn't even straining.

The Electra's rudder trim knob actually had a handle on it like a coffee grinder because the yaw was so great when an engine failure occurred.

If you experienced an engine failure---you would just start cranking like crazy to trim the airplane. If you didn't, the leg that kicked the rudder in got very tired and would start shakin&quaking---hence---a shuckin'&jivin Electra.

*****

If you want an example of what I am talking about, ----Sit down on the floor---face the wall---put a foot on the wall and push with all your might for five minutes—shake????????

---Shake---
*****

We climbed out over San Diego Bay. ---Captain Smith shut down the #2 Engine.

I didn't even put my foot on the rudder. I just cranked the rudder trim handle like mad and the Electra was flying straight and level.

Captain Smith was a litta amazed and a lotta perplexed. No rookie could be doing that good. Not in the Electra.

Now Captain Smith really started to test me, --- "Slow to ten knots above stall speed and climb to eight thousand feet in a right turn."

I complied with ease.

This maneuver was/is hard enough to do with four engines, let alone two. I had to add extra power because I was turning into the two good engines. *More power meant more trim.*

Alas the trim knob "bottomed out."
---Shaky right leg time---

Now Captain Smith started scratching his head and his balls at the same time. ----*Who says that check captains haint coordinated???*

No rookie could do that maneuver without falling out of the sky.

"Now descend to six thousand feet at the same airspeed."

I complied.

Now here is the trick.

I had been climbing with maximum power on the number three and four engines with the entire right rudder trim in.

I pulled the power off to descend and the Electra yawed to the right.

I cranked vigorously on the rudder trim to the left and zeroed out the rudder trim tabs.

My feet never touched the rudder pedals.

Everything worked out perfect. I was the ass, I mean the ace of the base.

Now Captain Smith was no longer amazed. Captain Smith was flabbergasted.

Captain Smith was not letting up on me. Anyone can get lucky.

"Give me a steep turn to the right." ---commanded Check Pilot Captain Smith.

I cranked the mighty Electra over into a forty five (45) degree bank. ---Added power on #3&#4 Engines.

The more the bank on any airplane, the more power you need.

The more power, the more rudder trim you need.

No problem.

I don't have a drinking problem---I get drunk---fall down---throw up---no problem.

I cranked in the trim that I needed---completed the turn---rolled out straight and level.

I was shit hot that night---the ace of the base.

I never varied in my altitude or airspeed an RCH. *Red Cunt Hair*

I was awesome to say the leastmostleast.

Captain Smith was not to let up on me, ---"Give me a power off stall."

This maneuver is usually done with four engines.

I only had two turning and burning and two un-turning and un-burning.

I complied.

I was assholes and elbows trying to keep the Electra under control, but managed to perform the maneuver successfully. Smith was impressed---but not as impressed as I was of my performance.

I was GODS gift to aviation that night.

Check/Training Pilot Captain Smith, ---"Take us back to the San Diego Airport and land."

I turned the Electra around---headed for the San Diego International Airport.

I looked over my left shoulder at Muldoon, ---"Light on" *(As opposed to "light off")* the number one and number two engines." *Translation ---start the #1&#2 engines*

Captain Smith held his hand over the start switches and would not let Muldoon start the engines.

I looked over at Captain Smith cum grano salis. Cap'n Smith had a shit-eating grin on his face.

Cap'n Smith was going to make me cry uncle even if he had to scuttle an airplane.

I flew downwind---turned base.

Captain Smith got us clearance to land.

I turned on to the final approach---put the gear down---configured to land.

San Diego International Airport Tower said, ---"PSA 174---do a couple of 360s. We have debris on Runway 27 and have to clean it off before you land."

Captain Smith keyed his mike, ---"Right or left."

"Your choice." was the controllers reply. "The airplane that just took off blew a tire and there's black rubber all over the runway."

I started a left turn---called for the gears up.

Captain Smith looked at me, ---"Are you sure you want the gear up?"

"Pull the fuckin' gears up."

Captain Smith flinched. ---Captain Smith smiled.

Captain Smith put the gear handle in the up position and the landing gears locked in the up position in the wheel well.

---*3 landing gears down & locked---3 green lights---*

---*3 landing gears in transit---3 red lights---*

---*3 gears up & locked---3 no lights--- (blank)---*

Captain Smith looked over at me---grinned---nodded.

Captain Smith knew damn good and well that we couldn't maintain our altitude with the gear down and only two engines running.

I had just passed another test.

Jehovah lives---LORD come through the roof---I'll pay for the shingles.

*****We landed*****

Captain Smith booted me out of the seat.

Someone else's turn in the "barrel."

While I was de-SEATING from the coveted right seat, --- Chief Pilot Captain Smith gave me a thumbs up and a nod.

Wasn't necessary, ---**I KNEW THAT I HAD PASSED.**

When you're hot you're hot, and when you're not, you're colder than Ice Station Zebra.

We finally finished up around midnight.

We all migrated to the South Seas Bar&Grill.

I walked in with Chief Pilot Captain Smith**.**

Cap'n Smith invited me into his "naugahyde office."

All the CREWS & STEWS in the bar got silent---looked our way.
Haint nobody got invited into Smith's "naugahyde office", ---
    A---Unless they wore a maximum/minimum skirt
    B---Were getting their ass chewed out
    C---Shit-canned
    D---YEP
    E---ALL OF THE ABOVE
They figured that I had fucked up again---was about to get my ass chewed out---shit-canned. ---
    And---They wanted to hear it.
*****

Crews&Stews are like that.

They love gossip more than a housewife that eats Bon Boris, watches the Price is Right, the Old and the Breastless all day and then sprays everything porcelain with Pine Sol. The house smells as clean as a hospital and she is one helluva home-maker---an old maids ruse.

The bread-winner comes home feeling guilty because he stopped by a bar with his secretary that has legs up to her neck. He then takes his curler-spotted wife out to dinner because she's been toiling the "whole live-long day." Nice job, if you can get it.

Look at it like this.

You have a five-hour flight, it takes about thirty minutes to get to cruise altitude. All this time you're pretty busy and not too much is said. Now you're "cruising in cruise."

The auto-pilot is flying the airplane and all you have is the very hot bright sun and endless sky to look at.

Ennui enters her boring kisser.

Let the games begin.

The three ESSESS are the main topics for the next four and a half hours.

    A; SEX
    B; SENIORITY
    C; SALARY
    D; YOU BETCHUM RED RYDER

You are a captive audience in a small aluminum sardine can and have no choice but to listen to each others bullshit until it's time to

start your descent. You gossip about the wild parties, who's dickin' whom and what a great aviator you are.---
Just part of the job, ma'am.
*****

I bought a round of drinks for the nosey Crews & Stews.

They turned away---concentrated on their **FREE** "toddies for the bodies." Drinking **FREE** booze had its priority with Crews&Stews.
*****

What happened to Wuco???

A few days later CHIEF CHECK TRAINING PILOT CAPTAIN SMITH &Wuco were flying a training mission at ONTARIO INTERNATIONAL AIRPORT California. Smith had the "hood" up --- [No forward vision on the Copilots windshield].

Wuco turned onto final. ---Very Nice.

Wuco commenced his approach---leveled off at 3000 feet doing 250 knots.

Wuco intercepted the Ontario Airport glide slope.

Wuco started his descent flying at 250 knots. ---not nice.

Wuco intercepted the Outer Marker at 2000' --- leveled off---still doing 250 knots. -not fucin' nice at all.

Wuco flew over the Ontario Airport Runway 25 centerline at 2,000 feet and 250 knots. Landing gear up---flaps not extended. –Not very nice at all. ---Not conducive to kissing Ma Earth's butt.

Captain Smith took over the controls of the Electra---Landed the Electra at the————**Ontario International Airport—**

Captain Smith fired Wuco's un-airworthy ass. ---Kicked his butt off the Electra.

Captain Smith flew the Electra back to the San Diego International Airport.
*****

--- CIRCA ---

11 January —1niner65

0100 HOURS

CAPTAIN SMITH
"You did a good job for **NEVER** having flown the Electra before,
---OR---
MAYBE never having flown the Electra before."

Captain Smith knew, for me to do as good as I did, that I had been stealing right seat time.

I said nothing---just nodded my head. I knew that I had passed and didn't want to screw it up with my **BIG** mouth.

Chief Pilot/Captain Smith, ---"If you still want to stay with PSA, you can have the next Co-pilot slot that becomes available."

!!!"I'LL STAY"!!!

"I have a lot of friends at PSA and never wanted to leave in the first place."

"I JUST WANT TO FLY AS A CO-PILOT."

I was now on my third "Tini"---getting muy juiced. The tensions of the day---the relaxing of the alcohol were affecting my brain. I became verbose---started ranting and raving.

It didn't matter though, ---Smith wasn't listening. The blonde and the redhead had showed up and Smith was only hearing through his earless head.

My hands became miniature airplanes showing Smith what a great aviator I was.

Smith's hard on had taken over his soul and could have cared less if I was Charles Lindbergh. Smith had his priorities and my flying skills were not one of them.

I was on my fourth Martini and to say the least/most/least---- I was drunk as a skunk.

*****

Has anyone here ever seen a drunken skunk???-*I have*. One used to come down off the rocks when I lived on my postage stamp sized ranch in Ramona, California.

I would feed him cat food---even pet him.
Then one day I spilled my bottle of Miller High Life. He slurped it up before I could wipe it up.
From then on---I'd always give him a saucer full of Millers.
He'd drink it---fall asleep right on the spot.
All I can write you is that a drunken skunk is not a good drinking companion.

*****

My airplane hands were now in a dogfight shooting at each other---trying to knock each other out of the sky.

My right hand was Captain Eddie Rickenbacker---my left hand the Red Baron.

Captain Eddie Rickenbacker took a pass at Smith's head trying to knock him senseless. Didn't matter though---Smith's brains had descended to his shorts and like **MORAY EELS**---you have to shoot them in the lower part of their anatomy to kill them.

The Red Baron was making another pass at Smith's head when I felt someone sidle up next to me.

"It must be Merry Mattressback," I opined.
Was this my lucky day or not
!!!**WRONG**!!!

I looked around---it was Muldoon---yich---he wasn't even blonde.

Muldoon was pissed because he knew that I was making an ass out of myself and wanted to get me out of there before the Red Baron, Captain Eddie Rickenbacker and my drunken mouth shot me down.

The Red Baron made a pass at Muldoon's head---tried to shoot him out of the booth.

Muldoon was not amused, ---"Get your scrawny ass up. We're going home."

Smith was in pecker-pecker land---I was helter-skelter---Muldoon was PeeOd.

Muldoon physically picked me up by the back of my collar---pulled me out of the booth---dragged me out of the bar---<u>threw</u> me in his car.

I was feeling no pain---I thought that I was a wild & crazy guy.

Muldoon ragged on me all the way home telling me what an asshole I was and telling me that I almost blew the Co-Pilot job that I wanted so much.

Not to worry, mate, ---I was feeling playful and the planet earth was my Frisbee.

SIX MONTHS AGO I COULDN'T SPELL PYLUT
AND
*****NOW I ARE ONE*****

Muldoon was/is only five years older than me but thought he was my father---liked to "rag" on me no matter how hallow the occasion.

Muldoon was straight and narrow---I was a "wild and crazy guy".

Flight Engineer Muldoon is now 59---oops another year down the tubes---60---oops another year down th---61---oops another ye---62---oops another y---63---oops another---64---oops anoth---65---oops ano---66---oops ano---67---an---68---a---69---anoth---70---anoth---71---anoth---72---another—73---74---75 years **YOUNG** and still flying MECHANIC/FLIGHT ENGINEER For the **NON-SKEDS. ---THE LAST OF THE BUFFALO HUNTERS.**

Sixteen years, now make it seventeen, I've been working on this cher book and---you know what---it's still fun.
*****

I called Mister Jimmy Don Wright the next day and told him what had transpired.

"I'm happy for you Jack, but I still think you should have gone to Dallas and become a pilot for American Airlines. Any way---good luck to you."

"Thanks Jimmy Don and thank you for helping me to get hired with American Airlines. It was what I needed to get to fly Co-pilot for PSA. I appreciate all that you have done for me."

"Thank you. Bye"

"ALLS WELL THAT ENDS WELL"

PRFPACPJM

--- CIRCA ---

11 January---1NINER65

0900 HOURS

When I arrived back at work ---**9 hours later,** I stopped by Chief Pilot Captain Smith's real office.

"Any Co-pilot slots open yet?"

"**NAH**" ---Smith said without even lifting his head up from the two inch stack of paper-work.

Smith knew who it was.

Smith knew that this was a preview of coming attractions.

I landed at midnight and went to the South Seas Bar&Grill---walked directly to Smith's "naugahyde office"---asked Smith if they were hiring Co-pilots yet?

"Get the %*(^{A}&)#t& out of here Beck."

I took the hint---I left.

All of January---All of February---All of March---All of the first week in April.

Every day---

Smith would get a phone call from me ---or I would stop by his office every day.

I'd start walking away and Smith, without lifting his head with ears, would shout in a very loud voice, ---**"BECK---DON'T CALL ME---I'LL CALL YOU."**

Talk about the squeaky wheel syndrome.

Every day ----Chief Pilot Captain Smith would get a little more vehement in his answers.

They ranged from---**"NO, BECK---**We are not hiring Co-Pilots today." **Tooooooo "Getoutofhereyou bothersome"** ------- "j*&%^{A}$t_J&*(*$_{COMMA}$+^^()*()&^{A}*)$_{PERIOD}$*%^{A}()_*&%&)_+»*&%^{A}&)j&^{A}) $%$_{PERIOD}$"

I can't remember the rest.

--- CIRCA ---

APRIL---I-NINER-65

I went into **PSA** Operations to check out. I had put in a super shitty fourteen hour day with a super shitty Captain. I was fantasizing how good that first beer was going to taste.

A Check Pilot by the name of Captain Gordie approached me, ---"Smith called me today and told me to give you some pilot training tonight. I'm also giving my young friend Joe some training time."

I was tired---disheveled---smelled like Billy Goat Hill.
Do you know how to keep a fish from smelling? ---cut off its nose.

All of a sudden the thought of flying **right** seat brought my adrenalin level up a couple hundred notches.

I was not a-rose but---I a-rose to the occasion. I was ready---raring to go. I was "game"---in more ways than one.

Captain Gordie, Joe and I got back on the same airplane that I had come in on. Gordie put his friend Joe in the right seat and I sat in the Flight Engineer's seat.

Joe was a hopeful new hire. Joe was a Light-Airplane Instructor-Pilot.

Joe flew the Electra like a Light-Airplane Instructor-Pilot. Joe was all over the sky. Joe flew the Electra like a monkey fucking a football. Joe made several landing attempts, but never quite made it to the runway.

Finally, after two hours of skidding and slewing around the sky, Joe landed the Electra.

Now it was my turn. I got in the coveted right seat and Joe got in the Flight Engineer's seat. Joe was now a Flight Engineer and before that night didn't know that such an animal existed.

We took off and Gordie shut down the #2 Engine.

No problembo.

For the next twenty minutes Gordie did everything he could do to make me look as bad as his friend Joe.

No problembo---formeo.

I aced all the maneuvers that he threw at me. To say the most---I was God's gift to aviation that night.

Gordie booted me out of the right seat---put his buddy Joe back in.

We landed two hours later.

If you're keeping score:

Joe—4 hours   Beck—20 minutes.

Gordie could have cared less if I made it or not and was using my allotted time to pass his buddy Joe.

"Me Worry"---NO---I was good. ---Hell---**I already had over ONE HUNDRED HOURS of Lockheed L-188 Electra training.**

**THANX TO
CAPTAIN THOMMY FRIEDKIN
CAPTAIN STU CARSON
CAPTAIN RAYNOR EUGENE KEOUGH
CAPTAIN LELAND CORPORON
CAPTAIN LEE THAXTON
CAPTAIN LES DELINE
CAPTAIN DICK ADAMS
CAPTAIN JOHN POWELL
AND A SPECIAL THANX-TO
CHIEF PILOT CAPTAIN BILL BUTLER
FOR HAVING FAITH IN ME
AND**
Giving me the chance to have the most wonderful CAREER that---
Any person could ever possibly have.

I knew I could make it. I could have cared less about not getting my allotted time. The only thing that I was pissed off at was that it was 0230 hours and the South Seas Bar&Grill was closed.

I went by the South Seas Bar&Grill anyway---knowing that there was always some Crewmember in the parking lot, or should I say porking lot, with a six pack fondling a Stews-member.

After the Walt Disney ride that I had just experienced---I needed a brewski.

I went into the South Seas Bar &Grill parking lot---got out of my car in hopes of finding a beer.

There were three cars there. They were all bouncing like they were going up a rutty road. The fur was flying.

I noticed a fourth car in the back of the parking lot that was dormant. It belonged to a guy named Herman who was true blue to his wife but got his rocks off by watching other people getting their rocks off.

I tapped on Herman's window. I knew that Herman always had some beer. Herman had a cooler in the back seat that was as wide as his car. It was always well stocked with beer and some hard stuff. Herman didn't hear me. Herman was watching some pimply-butted Crews-member pumping a Stews-member in the convertible next to him. Herman's eyes were glazed over.

Herman was fondling himself. ---**Rapido.**

I opened the back door of his car and swiped a couple of beers out of his cooler. Herman didn't even know that I was there. Herman was in pecker-pecker land which is somewhere between the first half of a blow-job and an orgasm.

I could have taken the whole cooler. Herman would not have known it. Herman finished himself off. Herman screeched out of the "porking" lot. Herman was going home to his wife with a limp dick and pecker-tracks on the car seat. Not a good combination.

*I hope his wife didn't give him the **float test.***

Float test, ---*You come home from a four day overnight and your wife makes you sit in a bathtub full of water--- if your balls float,---she fondles them---with a "ball"peen hammer.*

I went back to my car---drank one of the beers.

The tidal wave of metal in the "porking lot" had subsided. The glow of cigarettes was everywhere. It was/is always nice to have a smoke once you've popped your nuts.

*****

*It's like one blonde said to another blonde,
"Do you smoke after you make love?"
"I don't know---I've never looked."*
*****

I didn't even drink the other beer
I Left

It's was 0400 hours---my wife was asleep. I collapsed on the couch so as not to disturb her.

What's the old saying? "Let sleeping wives and dogs lie."

I got back up at 0530 hours and went back to work. I had a twelve hour day ahead of me and was very tired. My only redeeming feature: ---I wasn't hungover.

We landed that evening and there stood Gordie. The dipshit didn't even tell me that we were having another training flight that night.

Same scenario, ---Joe started out and flew for two hours. I got in the right seat ---flew for twenty minutes and got my carcass kicked out of the Co-pilots seat.

Joe flew the remaining hour and forty minutes.

The only change was that Joe was improving.

It's tough to transition from a light single airplane that flies at seventy (70) miles an hour to a four engine airliner that flies at two hundred and fifty (250) miles an hour.

Next day was the same. ---Fly Flight Engineer all day and Co-Pilot trainee for twenty minutes at night.

Score

Joe—11 hours   Beck—1 hour

I looked up Chief Pilot Smith at the South Seas Bar&Grill. I told Chief Pilot Smith that I was getting fucked out of my training time by Gordie and was afraid that I wouldn't be ready for my check ride.

In those days---if you flunked a check ride, you were on the street looking for the unemployment office---or a job at Kinney's.

"Quit your bitchin' and go home and get some rest. You look like hammered dog shit."

I got a roadie. ---That's a beer to go for you bible thumpers---who supposedly don't imbibe.

I went home.

That bullshit with Gordie---went on for five days. I got a little over an hour and a half of training time.

Finally it was Saturday---my day off. I was so exhausted that I slept till 1700 hours.

The phone woke me up. It was Captain Smith, ----"Be down here at 1900 hours. I have you scheduled for a check ride."

"Smith, I don't have enough training time. I'm not ready for a check ride."

"Bullshit, you've been training for four hours every night this past week."

"Gordie has given his buddy Joe most of the time and I only got about twenty minutes of right seat time each night."

"**No matter, we need a Co-pilot for tomorrow and you're elected.**"

Smith softened a little, ---"You'll do fine Jack, I've seen you in action."

Captain Smith even called me by my first name which I had not heard since I left home.

*****

Just happened to remember this. ---

I met an American Airlines Captain a few years later that hired on with American Airlines the same time that I was interviewing with American. He made Captain the same month that I did ---two years later.

--- CIRCA ---

SOMEWHERE BETWEEN APRIL FOOL'S DAY
AND
THE FIRST OF MAY
1-NINER-65

Hooray---hooray---it's the first of May.

Outdoor fu---Show me a man that doesn't eat pussy and I'll take his wife away from him. ---Per Cap'n Shaft Crank.

I arrived in operations a litta early and a lotta overanxious.

Captain/Chief Pilot/Check Pilot/Training Pilot Smith---FAA Dude---Gordie and Joe---a new hire Flight Engineer ---a Check Flight Engineer were there---all rarin' to go.

After all---this was Saturday night---the mayonnaise would be flowing at the South Seas Bar&Grill.

The "Saturday Night" check ride was just a formality to get out of the house for some carousing.

Horgey and Hosay went first.

Joe passed with ease—did a helluva job---after all—Joe had most of my allotted training time under his belt.

Right—Joe Good--- old buddy—you plagiarizer of my training time.

CAPTAIN JOE
GOOD PILOT---GOOD-WIN

We landed at Ontario Airport, about thirty miles east of Los Angeles, and it was my turn to wing my stuff.

Captain Smith got in the left seat. I got in the right seat---we took off.

After lift off ---Check Pilot Captain Smith shut down #1 Engine---looked over at me ---grinned.

Captain Smith wasn't trying to bust my chops but wanted to show the FAA Dude what a great instructor he was.

We climbed another thousand feet.

Captain Smith shut down number two engine and looked over at me---smiled.

I took care of the problem with ease, after all---I had over an hour and a half of flight training---not counting the 100 hours of Electra right seat time that I was lucky enough to get.

The FAA Dude was impressed. ---Check Pilot Captain Smith was smirking. ---I was the ace of the base.

Training Pilot Captain Smith put the "Hood" up so I didn't have any forward visibility. He instructed me to do an ADF approach [Automated Direction Finder] ---which is now obsolete.

No problembo for me except there was a full moon and a lot of Arkies and Okies had moved to California causing a disturbance in the magnetic field that surrounds the Planet of the Apes.

The ADF needle was skittsying around all over the dial.

I headed toward what I thought was the ADF station, got what I thought was a station passage---flew for thirty seconds---did a right one-eighty---commenced my approach.

Now the ADF needle was really going ape-shit, slewing to the left---then to the right---left---right---left---right---etcetcetcetc..

I got a station passage *me thinks* and turned to a heading of 250 degrees.

Now I was working on the tail of the ADF needle and it was more erratic than it was before.

I put the landing gear down, --- put the flaps down and configured to land.

Now I get a light bulb.

The road between San Bernardino and Los Angeles, known as the San Berdoo Freeway, runs parallel to the approach course and also the runway that we were going to land on.

I had no forward vision because of the "Hood" but could see out of my side window.

I pretended I was flying the tail of the erratic ADF needle---but in reality---I was "keeping my eyes on the road" with my peripheral vision.

I saw the Kaiser Steel Factory which was abeam the touchdown zone of Runway 25.

I shouted, ---**"MINIMUMS!"**

Captain Smith pulled the hood out of the window, ---**"LAND"**.

I was right on the center-line of Runway 25.

I pulled the power back---greased the mighty Electra on the runway. ---got a sitting/standing ovation.

No one could believe that I could shoot that approach as erratic as the ADF needle was and be on centerline.

Thank God for the San Berdoo Freeway and the Kaiser Steel Factory.

We turned off the runway---Smith put the parking brakes on---checked the captain's chronometer on his instrument panel. It was 2200 hours.

Smith knew that bitches with moist britches were ass-itting on it.

Smith turned around to the FAA Dude, ---"What do you want to do now?"

"If you're happy, then I'm happy. As far as I'm concerned, any one that can shoot that ADF approach, as erratic as it was, can do any approach."

Chief Pilot Captain Smith, ---"Let's go home."

The FAA dude also had some action going at the South Seas Bar and Grill and if we stayed out much longer, he would have to go home to his fat old lady who thought the crack in the ceiling was sexual foreplay.

Question---What's the difference between your wife---your girlfriend---and a prostitute?"

Your girlfriend---Are you through already?

A prostitute---Aren't you through yet?

Your wife---I never noticed that crack in the ceiling before.

I got kicked out of the right seat and the FAA Dude took my place.

We took off and flew to San Diego.

Now it's "E" ride time at Disneyland. The FAA Dude was flying all over the sky.---Pukesville---

We landed at San Diego and the FAA Dude pranged. We bounced about four times and finally got stopped.

The FAA Dude looked at Smith and said, ---"At least I didn't kill us."

Smith could care less. Smith's semen level was way above his ears. Smith could not hear anything except---MEOW.

We went to Captain Smith's real office to debrief and hopefully get signed off.

Chief Pilot/Check Pilot/Training Pilot/Captain Smith and the FAA Dude both wrote on a form that looked like it came out of a doctor's office---and not much more legible.

All the paper work bullcrap was over now and it's Tank-hooray Gin time.

I did notice one thing though, ---the FAA dude recorded four landings in his log book.

"Truth is stranger than fiction"
*****

In defense of the FAA Dude's landing---the FAA rarely gets a landing and just to get to the runway with that little flying time is a feat in itself.
*****

We all went to the **SOUTH SEAS BAR&GRILL.**

I got to sit in Smith's Naugahyde "Office." ---*One mo time*

The FAA Dude found his piece of meat and left with her.

Gordie and Joe shared a beer—departed.

The Check Flight Engineer and the new hire Flight Engineer had a glass of water and boogied.

Now it was just Self and Smith---I tried talking Pilot talk to him.

---No dice---

"Get your butt out of here and get some rest. You have a 0600 show tomorrow. This is your first Co-pilot trip. If you screw it up I'm gonna castrate you, and by the way---don't act so cocky. ---I also know about the San Berdoo Freeway and the Kaiser Steel Factory," ---Captain Smith said with a grin.

Me? ---I said nothing ---**I WAS A REAL CO-PILOT.**

Real Co-Pilots keep their mouth shut. ---*if their smart*

The redhead and the blonde were buzzing around the booth like flies around a stable.

I got up---left---even I knew/know when I'm not wanted.

SIX MONTHS AGO
I COULDN'T SPELL PYLUT
AND
NOW I ARE ONE

I got home about midnight and my wife greeted me at the door, —
"Where have you been?"

I had been home a total of 40 hours in the past week and now she was wondering where I had been.

"I have been taking a Co-pilot check ride and I passed."

Now that I've passed---she's pissed.

"You stupid donkey. We can't afford for you to fly Co-pilot."

I always liked the way she greeted me when I got home with all her warmth and love. After all, she hadn't seen me in a week and I know that she had missed me so much she could shit BBs.

"Why are you waiting up for me?"

This was new to me and I couldn't figure out her adulation.

"I'm out of money and need some checks---you have the only checks that we have left."

I gave her my check book and went to my couch. I had four hours sleep coming and wanted to make the most of it.

Actually, she was right. I was making $1200 bucks a month flying Flight Engineer and now---flying Co-Pilot, I would be making $500 bucks a month. Even I knew that was over 110% cut in salary---1% cut in income taxes.

Didn't matter to me though---I finally realized my dream of becoming a Co-pilot.

I went to work the next morning---sober.

I walked into operations and I was greeted by Gordie and Joe, --- "Joe is going to fly right seat today and you can sit in the jump seat---or even go home if you want to."

Gordie had a nasal voice and it was irritating as hell at that/this time of the morning---in actuality at any time of the morning---afternoon---night. Sounded like a Nicholson file being scraped over the edge of a sheet of .020 aluminum.

"Gordie, I was assigned this trip by Captain Smith. He told me that if I didn't make it, he was going to----"**DEBALL ME.**"

"Doesn't matter," he nasaled out. "Joe is my Co-Pilot."

I wasn't going to put up with his bullshit. I called Smith at home---woke him up.

"Captain Smith, ---this is Beck."

"What the devil are you calling me at this hour for?"

Smith was nocturnal---the sun was coming up---It was time to rest.

"Gordie is giving Joe my line time---Gordie told me to leave and go home if I didn't like it."

"Daggone it---let me talk to Gordie."

I gave Gordie the phone---watched. ---

Gordie had bushy eyebrows.

Gordie was getting his ass chewed out.

Gordie's bushy eyebrows were going from---

---Gordie's forehead to almost covering Gordie's eyeballs---

Gordie hung up the phone---went over---talked to Joe.

Joe left

I went out to the Electra---sat in the coveted right seat---put on my seat belt---buckled it so tight that Gordie could not have pried me out of the right seat with a crow-bar.

We only flew four legs that day.

Two round trips---San Diego---San Francisco---San Diego---San Francisco---San Diego.

SAN---SFO---SAN---SFO---SAN.

Gordie was pissed and flew them all. Didn't hurt my feelings.

I was a **C-O-P-I-L-O-T.**

SIX MONTHS AGO I COULDNT SPELL PYLUT AND NOW I ARE ONE

I went straight home—had a Pepsi Cola toast with my three children --- **To my new found success.**

A—MARK RESLEY BECK
B—KEVIN SHAUN BECK
C—SHELBI DAUN BECK
D; LOVED THEM THEN   LOVE THEM NOW
Most of the time

There was a note from my wife. Simply stated, ---"I'm at my friend's house."

I turned on the "idiot tube" and watched it with my children.

"Gunsmoke" came on.

I had a beer in one hand and my kids in the other. ---

My wife was not chewing my ass.

I WAS A COPILOT.

Am I squattin' in tall cotton or not?

My life has always been good but this night was great.

The kids went to bed---I fell to sleep on my couch watching Gunsmoke.

"ALLS WELL THAT ENDS WELL"

PRFPACPJM

--- CIRCA ---

Day 2 of **CO-PILOT** *line time with Gordie.*

"RING---RING---RING---RING---RING---RING---RING---RING---RING---RING---RING---RING---RING---RING---RING---RIN--"

"HELLO"

The phone rang at 0600 hours---It was Gordie.

"Beck---can you be here in thirty minutes?"

"Why?" was my groggy response.

"Joe got in an accident on the way to work. ---You're the only Co-Pilot we have to replace him."

"How is he?"

"Nobody knows---just get down here. We have a 0700 departure."

"Okay"

I got dressed---sans shower and shave---drove to the San Diego Airport---slid into the right seat of the Mighty Electra.

Gordie looked over at me, ---"I'll fly all the legs today---you can watch me and maybe learn something."

"Gordie---you're a Check Pilot. You have to let me fly to see if I can actually do it. I need twelve and one half hours of hands on flying the Electra before I'm legally checked out---and you know it."

Gordie's nasally twang, ---"I'm also the Captain and you will do what I tell you to do."

"I'm also a person and you can go fuck yourself." I slid out of the seat and got off the Electra.

I went into operations and called Captain Smith.

"What the devil do you want now, Beck?" ---Partially comatose. Smith and 0700 hours were definitely not friends.

"Gordie won't let me fly the Electra." ---*horehey won't let me play*

I also told him that I wasn't legal to fly because I had been on duty fourteen days in a row.

*****

After six days you have to have at least twenty four hours of rest. Now-a-days the 24 hour rest-period has to take place from 0001 hours to 2400 hours. ---me thinks.

At that point in time, the rest could start at any time and end at any time, as long as it was 24 uninterrupted hours.
These were called "Mexican 24 hour rest periods".
*****

"Let me talk to Gordie."
I turned around to go out to the Electra to get him. ---Not necessarrio---Gordie was right behind me and pissed off. ---*tosaythemostleastmost.*

I handed Gordie the phone. ---Gordie was getting his ass chewed out again.

Gordie's bushy eyebrows were going up and down like an elevator at a drunken Shriner's convention in Phoenix, AZ.

Gordie handed me back the phone which was wet from his sweaty palms.
Gordie left
"Beck, don't leave, I'll be right down."
I stayed.

Captain Smith showed up in thirty minutes. Captain Smith must have slept with his uniform on to get there that quick because Captain Smith lived over twenty minutes away.

Captain Smith took my time card/sheet out of the book---threw it at me, ---"Make yourself legal and let's get going."

Captain Smith went out to the airplane---sent Horhey home.
I used my ever ready Everhard *(I think that's how you spell it)* Eraser.
Everhard erased the trips that would put me in jeopardy if the FAA got on to it.
*****

Everhard—I like that name. Rings a bell.
Do the name Ruby Begonia ring a bell?
Do the name Quasimodo ring a bell?
*****

Funny how things go.
Now I was erasing flying time. Less than a year ago---I was penciling in P-51 flying time. ---*Parker 51 ballpoint time ---phony time*

We departed thirty minutes late and Smith let me fly every leg.
All "near" perfect approaches. ---The landings were **"nearly"** grease jobs.
*****

Nearly is a state of relativity. --- ask Einstein's Aunt.
*****

I was awesome---To say the mostleastinostleast.

The day passed by quickly---
**CAPTAIN SMITH AND HIS CO-PILOT
WENT
---TO THE SOUTH SEAS BAR&GRILL---
Smith invited his Co-Pilot into his "Office".**
The South Seas Bar&Grill fell silent. –The Crews&Stews looked our way.
I had been in Captain Smith's "Office" tooooo many times lately.
The Crews&Stews opined that either---I was getting fired or we were butt fuckin' each other.
---CHIEF TRAINING CHECK PILOT CAPTAIN SMITH---
Scribbled on a Martini-Stained-Bar-Napkin---

**"Jack Beck has passed all Co-Pilot check rides
and is now authorized to fly right seat."
Captain Smith   Chief Pilot**

"Give this note to my secretary tomorrow and have her put it in your records."

"I don't have the required line time because of Gordie."

"Doesn't matter. As far as I'm concerned, you're checked out and legal to fly Co-Pilot. I'll dummy up all the time you need when I get to work tomorrow. By the way you don't have to worry about Gordie any more---thanks to you---Gordie is no longer a Check Pilot."

"Now I suggest that you go home and get some rest. You still look like hammered dog shit."

"Thanks for the compliment."
I left

--- CIRCA ---

The day after the day after
Hooray-hoo---oops---I'm a pilot now.
Real pilots don't say the F-Word. *haha*

I woke up the next morning to a ringing phone. It was Dave Wright---PSA's one man record keeping department and go-fer.

Mister Dave Wright aka Copilot Dave Wright nka Captain David Wright wanted to become a Co-pilot---also.

I could sense by his voice he was a little jealous that I made it first. Dave Wright didn't have enough flying time and didn't have the balls to dummy in the time like I did---or was too honest.

*****

At one time---when Dave Wright was flying Captain for---**CAPTAIN JACK DODDLE'S---"SWIFT AIRLINES"**---for pay and I was flying Co-Pilot for Captain Jack Doddle for no-pay on the Twin Engine Amphibious Mallard from San Diego to Las Vegas and back---in the middle of the night, ---*to build up my flying hours*---and when I got back to San Diego would suit up and fly Flight Engineer for PSA all day and then un-suit up and fly pay-less Co-Pilot for paid Captain Dave Wright for Jack Doddle's Swift Airlines every friggin' day of the week.---

Dave Wright told me that if I was lucky that someday I would be flying Co-Pilot for him at PSA---Someday---Lo and behold later on---Dave Wright flew Co-Pilot for me. ---At PSA.

Remember the Non-Sked saying, ---

"Be kind to your Co-Pilot, ---for someday he may be your Chief Pilot."

YOU NEVER KNOW---YOU JUST NEVER KNOW—
Not in the aviating business anyway.

One other item---When I went to the Airport to go fly Captain Jack Doddle's Twin Engine Mallard Amphibian to build up time so maybe someday I could fly Co-Pilot for PSA. I would go into PSA's 12X12 Crew Lounge and strut around with a Telex Headset around my neck hoping to be seen by Captain Smith.

Didn't work---never saw him. Reckon he was busy in his *"office"*.

*****

Dave Wright said, ---"We need to know how much time you have for our records."

Well this is the way that I looked at it---they believed seventeen hundred hours---so I doubled it.

"I have three thousand, four hundred hours of flying time."

"You have thirty four hundred hours of flying time?????" --- *Dubusioususpiciously.*

"I'll mark it down but I don't believe it."

My Words; "Believe what you want."

MY THOUGHT---"Believe what you want---file clerk."

At that point in time---at PSA, ---you needed Five Thousand (5,000) hours to check out as Captain. I made Captain in less than two years. Those 3,400 hours that I had told Dave Wright that I had---coupled with the 2,000 hours of "real" time that I had flown in those two years, gave me well over the required time of 5,000 hours that PSA required to check out as Captain.

I went to the Chief Pilot's Office and gave to Captain Smith's secretary the note that Smith had given me.

She "gave me no respect" because of my life style. She thought that---She and Smith were Co-Chief Pilots---And she didn't even have a Pilots license. Right ---**MISS BONNY.**

She read the note, ---"Does this mean that you are now a Co-Pilot?"

"What does right seat mean to you?" was my haughty response.

"I'll go ask Smith," was her even haughtier reply.

My Word, --- "Fine with me"

MY THOUGHT---"Fine with me---lady chief pilot"

I left

CIRCA

ZERO NINER ---JUNE, ---1-NINER-65

HAPPY CO-PILOT FLYING BIRTHDAY TO ME

Hooray---hooray---It's the first of June
Outdoor fucking started last month so we'll have to catch up.
PER---Co-pilot Beck

I flew Co-Pilot on the Electra for the next year. I was one happy right seat mutha campa.

Flying Co-Pilot on a three man airplane meant that all I had to do was fill out the flight plan when we checked in---then my hot pants chased hot pants the rest of the day.

The Captain made all the decisions. The Flight Engineer did all the work.
Me—I was cunt-ent.

I was back up to making twelve hundred bucks a month which made my wife happy.

My children were happy. I was in seventh heaven---where ever the hell that is.

In the meantime---back at the raunch, ---Chief Pilot Captain Smith took another job.

PSA's NEW AVIATION BOSSMAN

CHIEF PILOT
CAPTAIN SPIKE

When Captain Spike became---Chief Pilot Captain Spike. ---Captain Spike also took over the scheduling duties. Captain Spike was everywhere---a real work-aholic.

Captain Spike worked as ---
    A---Chief Pilot
    B---Scheduler
    C---Screened the new hires

D---Fired the old hires and even---
D+---Flew the line.
D++YEPYEPYEPYEPYEPYEPYEPYEP

Captain Spike was at PSA eight days a week---twenty-five hours a day. Captain Spike expected us to be work-aholics also. Haint gonna "work" that way---Spike. Not a smart idea. Crews&Stews only flew airplanes to get from one party to the next.

*****

"Flying is our hobby, baby, partying is our job." Quoth **CAPTAIN LELAND** — Evermore.

*****

Many---Many times---when I went to work---Captain Spike would be there with my time card/sheet---hand it to me, ---"I think you made a mistake on your time card/sheet. It projects out to over a hundred hours this month so you better correct it."

*****

TRANSLATION—

*"**Erase it**---or you'll run out of time and I won't be able to man the schedule."*

*"**Because** we have no reserve pilots."*

*"**Because** PSA is growing so fast that I can't find new hires."*

*"**Because** the Major Airlines are taking anyone out there that can breath and has a Commercial Pilot's License."*

"PLEASE."

One hundred hours of flight time was and is the maximum number of hours you can fly in a calendar month.

*****

I always complied---We got paid "Miley" Not "Hourly".

*****

TRANSLATION---

PSA Stews&Crews were paid by the mile---so the more hours you erased meant the more miles that you could put on your paysheet.

We had no reserve pilots and PSA would have to cancel flights if any of us ran out of time.

*****

Go into real estate ---get a lot while you're young.

*****

"Your seat cushions can be used for flotation; and, in the event of an emergency water landing, please paddle to shore and take them with our compliments."

*****

"As you exit the plane, make sure to gather all of your belongings. Anything left behind will be distributed evenly among the flight attendants. Please do not leave children or spouses."

*****

--- CIRCA ---

1-niner-6???

PSA inaugurated service into **San Jose International Airport**, shit I can't remember---some time in the late sixties.

Captain John Harden flew an Electra, sans pax, with News Media & PSA EXECS from San Diego to San Jose for the "Air to Ground Breaking" Ceremonies.

Captain Al Oranski flew an Electra, sans pax, with news media & PSA EXECS from San Francisco to San Jose for the "Air to Ground Breaking" Ceremonies.

BY "COINCIDENCE"
---CAPTAIN JOHN HARDIN---
&
---CAPTAIN AL ORANSKI---
ARRIVED OVER SAN JOSE INTERNATIONAL AIRPORT
At the same time---eye ball to eye ball with the---
---SAN JOSE AIRPORT TOWER CONTROLLERS---

---Flying in opposite directions---
Captain John Hardin flew on one side of the San Jose tower going north.
Captain Al Oranski flew on the other side of the San Jose tower going south.
---BALLS TO THE WALL---
---PEDAL TO THE MEDAL---
---MAX MUTHAFUCIN POWER---

CHIEF EXECUTIVE OFFICER J. CLOSE
ADDRESSEDTHEPRESS
"THEY'RE GOING TO GET WHAT'S COMING TO THEM."
!!!THEY DID!!!
CHIEF EXECUTIVE OFFICER J. CLOSE
TOOK THEM OUT TO DINNER THAT EVENING
GOOD BOSS ---CHIEF EXECUTIVE OFFICER J. CLOSE
---GOOD PILOTS---

---CAPTAIN JOHN HARDIN---
AND
---CAPTAIN AL ORANSKI---
*****

In The 60s---
Make Captain---
Get divorced. ---
Have A Stewardess Named After You
****

Ya never know what you have until you lose i.

*****

Weather at our destination is 50 degrees with some broken clouds, but we'll try to have them fixed before we arrive. Thank you, and remember, nobody loves you, or your money, more than PSA."

*****

--- CIRCA ---

FEBRUARY---1966

Hooray---hooray, ---It's February.
Outdoor fuckin' starts the first of May.
It haint rhyming but it gets the job done.

"RING---RING---RI--"
I got a phone call from
Check Pilot Training Pilot Captain Billy D. Ray ---

"Be down here at twenty one hundred hours. PSA has just bought another Boeing 727-200 and needs four more Co-Pilots and you're one of them. We'll start your training tonight and hopefully have you done by the time the Boeing 727-200 gets here."

For the next week I flew Co-Pilot on the Electra in the day time--- trained on the Boeing 727-100 at night.

*****

"There may be 50 ways to leave your lover, but there are only 4 ways out of this airplane."

*****

"Thank you for flying PSA. We hope you enjoyed giving us the business as much as we enjoyed taking you for a ride."

*****

As the plane landed and was coming to a stop at Burbank, a lone voice came over the loudspeaker: "Whoa, big fella. WHOA!"

*****

After a particularly rough landing during thunderstorms in Memphis, a flight attendant on a PSA flight announced, "Please take care when opening the overhead compartments because, after a landing like that, sure as hell everything has shifted."

*****

From a PSA employee: "Welcome aboard PSA Flight 245 to Tampa. To operate your seat belt, insert the metal tab into the buckle, and pull tight. It works just like every other seat belt; and, if you don't know how to operate one, you probably shouldn't be out in public unsupervised."

— CIRCA —

1 MARCH, 1-NINER-66

*****

Hooray hooray— it's the first of March
Outdoor fuckin' starts to day
per
CAPTAIN LELAND
*****

Location—San Francisco International Airport
I finally passed my check ride on the Boeing 727-200.
Captain Check Training Pilot Billy D. and I went out on the town.
CeeeeLeeeeBrayTeD. *(Celebrated)*
Captain Bill Ray and Self went to a Japanese restaurant in **China Town in San Francisco.**
Drank many Sakes ---forgot the fish heads and "flied lice".
*****

These two guys were sitting in a Chinese restaurant.
When the waiter came over to take their order---
One of the guys said watch this as he gave his order to the waiter---
"I want to order some **FLIED LICE AND GLOUND LOUND."**
The waiter took offense---
"It is not Flied Lice and Glound Lound---
It is **FRIED RICE** *AND* **GROUND ROUND---**
YOU PLICK."
*****

Captain Bill and I left the bar.
Lo and behold---in front of me was a parking meter, ---"Watch this Bill." ---I said as I leap-frogged over it.
I went up over it okay---"butt" due to my inebriated condition. ---I got disoriented. ---I landed on my side-hip in the street.
Captain Billy D. ---came over---picked me up---saying, ---"You made a nice entry into the maneuver, but your recovery was unacceptable."
My Word---Ouch

MY THOUGHT---Once a training pilot---always a training pilot. ---I still have arthritis in my left hip from that kifikilty & still walk a little kattywampus from it.

*****

Flying Co-Pilot on the Boeing 727-200 was a horrifying experience to me.

To be truthful---I was scared "Shit-more" of it.

Unlike the "Forgivin" Locklieed Electra L188 ---The "Un-Forgivin" Boeing 727-200 would "Bring You Down to Earth"---**HARD.**

You could put the Boeing 727-200 on profile for landing and it would look like a grease job coming up. ---**KABAM.**

*****

Because of the engines being bolted on the tail of the Boeing 727-200 and the wings being bolted further back on the fuselage to give the Boeing 727-200 a safe Center of Gravity much further back than on most Airplanes heretofore thus placing the Cockpit further forward from the center of gravity. ---Putting your eyeballs on a fulcrum that a one inch up or down of your seat height adjustment meant that your depth perception would change by as much as ten feet. I think fuck---I know.

You could/would hit so hard that it would jar your teeth.

Sometimes the landing was so hard that it would drop some of the oxygen masks in the cabin and if it was really hard--- it would drop all of the oxygen masks.

SCENARIO

AIRPORT OF DEPARTURE---SAN DIEGO'S LINDBERG FIELD
AIRPORT OF DESTINSATION---HOLLYWOOD BURBANK
CAPTAIN---LEE CORPORON
CO-PILOT---BECK
FLIGHT EMGINEER---CAPTAIN BUD TROUT
AIRCRAFT---BOEING 727-200
JUMPSEAT---FAA DUDE

My leg---we took off.

The FAA Dude in the jump seat was a very pleasant person. He talked and joked all the way to Burbank.

I landed on Runway 07 with a bone shuddering crunch.

Quite embarrassing but the oxygen masks didn't deploy.

The impressed unimpressed FAA Dude never said another word and when he could, ---Silently left the cockpit, ---'nuff said'.

*****

You have but one **SIMPLE** regulation
&
One **SIMPLE** moral obligation
When **FLYING** an **AIRPLANE**
GO FROM A TO B
SAFELY
ALL THE OTHER RULES HANDED DOWN FROM
    A: GOD
    B: FAA
    C: CHIEF PILOT
    D: ALL OF THE ABOVE
ARE GUIDE LINES.

*****

--- CIRCA ---

APRIL
1-NINER-66

The most terrifying experience that I had on the Boeing 727-200 was on one dark and stormy night.

Captain Spenser Nelsen ---Co-Pilot Beck and a Boeing 727-200 were cruising at 10,000 feet out over the Pacific Ocean---off the coast of Long Beach between San Diego and Los Angeles.

Through my peripheral vision---I happened to notice a red glow waxing on the nose of the "unforgivtn" Boeing 727-200.

This is a common phenomenon known as Saint Elmo's Fire which usually builds up a couple of feet and leaves the airplane with a bang and a blinding flash of light.

I believe Saint Elmo was lying that night because that spear of fire kept growing like Pinocchio's nose after he told his pine-y old lady that he was out in the forest making pine-y young children.

The "spear" of fire grew over twenty feet long and looked like Sir Valliant's lance or a penis in Paul Bunyan's go-go bar.

I became mesmerized as I watched the incandescent glow in the dark night.

Instead of covering my eyes, or lowering my bead, ---I actually plastered my puss against the windshield to get a better look at it.

Not to "bright" if you'll pardon the pun.

Saint Elmo's Fire left the airplane with a noise like a Mack truck hitting a Volkswagen.

I was driving the VW.

The brilliance was like a thousand flash bulbs going off at the same time at Aunt Sophie's Fifth Wedding.

Aunt Sophie was still claiming that she was a virgin. ---Maybe that's why Aunt Sophie was married four times previous.

I became snow blind and could not see anything, ---except red flags on all the flight instruments and a blinking red emergency light which meant that we had lost all electrical power to our flight instruments.

The next few seconds became a life time to me.

There is an old pilot's saying that being a pilot is ten hours of tedium and ten seconds of adrenalin rush or like---

*****
CAPTAIN LELAND---*Used to say.*
"Ten seconds is not a long time, but try hanging by your balls for ten seconds and it will seem like an eternity."
*****

Finally my eyesight returned---one by one the flight instruments corrected themselves.

I looked over at Spence. He was amused at my fright.

Spencer, unlike this dipshit, had enough common sense to close his eyes when he saw Saint Elmo embracing our airplane.

As far as I was concerned---

Elmo was not a Saint, but the very devil himself.

— CIRCA —

1 MAY 1-NINER-66

HOORAY—HOORAY—IT'S THE FIRST OF MAY
OUT-DOOR FUCKING STARTS TODAY
CAPTAIN LELAND

One of the Captains that I flew Co-Pilot for a lot was **CAPTAIN DON STEVENSEN.**

Captain Don Stevensen sensed my anxiety of landing the Boeing 727-200. Captain Don Stevensen told me that I was fighting the controls when we got close to the ground---"to relax a little".

---Easy for him to say---

The Boeing 727-200 had me tied up in "Knots".

Captain Don Stevensen, ---"I'll show you on this next landing."

When we were about a fifty feet above touchdown, Don took his hands off the controls---put them behind his head, --------------------------

!!!"Watch"!!!

I couldn't believe "wha hoppen". The Boeing 727-200 caught the ground effect, ---leveled itself off---kissed the runway hello.

*****

Ground effect is air becoming compressed between the wings and the ground as the aircraft descends to meet the Terra Firma---the more firma--- the more terra.

*****

Captain Don Stevensen looked over at me and grinned, ---**"See how easy it is?"**

I nodded, ---"If I try that---I'll drive the landing gear up through the wing."

Captain Don Stevensen, ---"Try it you'll like it."

!!!I did!!!---***I did***

From that moment forward---I never got clanked up landing the Boeing 727-200 again.

TRANSLATION—*Most of the time—but some were real sphincter puckering experiences.*

Thanx Captain Don Stevensen for all your wisdom.

These are words to live by taught to me by **Captain Don Stevensen.**
    A---US HUSBAND'S ARE A SORRY LOT.
    B---WHEN YOUR PECKER GETS HARDER THAN YOUR HEAD---YOU'RE IN FOR TROUBLE.
    C---THAT MAYONAISSE MAKER WILL GET US ALL.
    D---ALL OF THE ABOVE

---THANX---
---CAPTAIN DON STEVENSEN---
---FOR ALL OF YOUR WISDOM—

— CIRCA —

NINER JUNE I-NINER-66

6-9-JUNE

HAPPY CO-PILOT BIRTHDAY TO ME

I started flying a lot with---**Captain Fried Kin Thomas.**
Captain Thomas and I had fun. I don't care what your Political/Bible-Thumper preferences are---it's nice to be cooped up in a six foot by six foot area for fourteen hours with someone you enjoy flying with.

CAPTAIN F. K. THOMAS---
SELF---
FLIGHT ENGINEER CAPTAIN J.P. LEWIS---
A BOEING 727---

Took off from San Diego one day with two Braniff Trainees in the jump seats. The Boeing 727-200 had two jump seats.

At that point in time ---PSA had a contract with Braniff Airlines to train their Pilots and Flight Engineers and the trainees would go along with us to observe our operation.

Thommy forgot his cigarettes that day---was having a nicotine fit.

We landed at the Los Angeles Airport and taxied to the terminal.

Thommy deplaned---went to a cigarette machine---got a pack of Camels.

Thommy came back on board---placed them on the pedestal between us---started taxing out.

Thommy always taxied with his sliding-side-window open and would close it right before take off.

I reached down---grabbed Cap'n Thommy's unopened pack of Camels---threw them out of his window.

Thommy couldn't believe it. ---The Braniff Trainees couldn't believe it.

I believed it---I was amused.

The Braniff trainees were astounded. ---Thommy was WOXOF---*perplexed.*

The Braniff Trainees couldn't believe that a lowly Co-pilot would treat a Captain like that.

One of the jump seaters gave Thommy a cigar to quell his nicotine fit.

Thommy lit up. ---The Cigar Pacifier appeared to do its job.

!!! WRONG!!!

While sitting on the taxiway, awaiting take-off clearance, Thommy reached over and put his cigar out on my arm. The Braniff trainees were now dumbfounded and in hysterics. *if there is such an emotion*

Captain Thomas put his hand on the power levers to add some power. We were cleared to taxi into position and hold.

I took the flight planning clip board---slammed the edge of it down on Thommy's hand as hard as I could.

The trainees both gasped as one. ---They couldn't believe this act.

I looked at Thommy---laughed.

The tears were actually rolling out of Thommy's eyes from the pain.

When we got up to San Francisco and were walking to PSA Operations, --- Thommy grabbed my shirt pocket, ---"Do you need this?"

"Yea I do."

Thommy ripped the pocket off of my shirt.

I did the same to Thommy's. We were now partly in shreds---the Braniff Trainees---were in a word---dumbfuckinfounded.

We landed at the San Diego Airport where the Braniff Trainees were to deplane.

One Braniff Trainee got off---the other Braniff Trainee stayed on.

Thommy looked around at him---inquired as to why he was staying on.

The Braniff Trainee, ---"I want to see who wins the war."

Later on that day we landed at the Los Angeles International Airport.

We had a two hour layover---then we had a deadhead to the San Diego .Airport---Thommy was walking through the terminal and the Braniff Trainee and I were a few steps behind him.

I said to the Braniff Trainee, --- "Watch this."

I walked up behind Thommy---grabbed the bottom of his uniform coat with both hands and ripped the back of it clear up to the neck. The trainee was in convulsions---patted me on the back.

"You win."

I neglected to tell the Braniff Trainee that this was the last day we were to wear this uniform and we were changing into new ones the next day.

Thommy got a sweater out of his bag---put it on. We caught our flight and dead-headed home to the—

—SAN DIEGO WEIGO AERPORTO—

"ALLS WELL THAT ENDS WELL"
PRFPAPJM

--- CIRCA ---

JULIO 1-NINER-66

SCENARIO

**AIRPORT— SAN FRANCISCO INTERNATIONAL APT.
DESTINATION AIRPORT—SAN DIEGO INTERNATIONAL AIRPORT
AIRPLANE—BOEING 727-200
CAPTAIN—CAPTAIN THOMAS FRIEDKIN
CO-PILOT---BECK
FLIGHT ENGINEER---CAPTAIN ALFRED STEWART --- GOOD MAN---GOOD AVIATOR**

ACT I

The Boeing 727-200 that we picked up had just come off a training flight and we had to ferry it to San Diego—**no passengers or stews.**

Captain Thommy told Flight Engineer Al Stewart to do a thorough walk around to make sure that there were no popped rivets or pulled circuit breakers.

ACT II

We took off for the San Diego International Airport.

We had just leveled off at 33,000 feet in cruise when the fire warning light on the **#1 ENGINE FIRE HANDLE LIT UP AND THE FIRE WARNING BELL SOUNDED.**

I did my Co-Pilot's job which consisted of silencing the fire warning bell. I looked over at Thommy to see if he was going to pull the fire handle and attempt to extinguish the fire.

Pulling the fire warning handle shuts off all the fluids the engine needs to sustain life---then rotating it to the left or right will release a fire retardant chemical into the engine and put out the fire.

ACT III

Captain Thommy just sat there with his arms folded. Watched it burn.
Should have been playing Nero's fiddle

Here is one of the sharpest pilots that I have/had ever flown with about to let an engine burn off its mounts.

I looked at Flight Engineer Captain Alfred Stewart. Flight Engineer Captain Alfred Stewart just sat there with a shit-eating grin on his face.

ACT IV

I couldn't let this happen. ---I put my hand up to pull the fire handle. Thommy pushed it away.

Now I was a litta perplexed and a lotta pissed because **Captain Thomas Friedkin** wouldn't let me pull the **FIRE HANDLE**.

ACT V

ABOUT THAT TIME THE #2 ENGINE'S FIRE WARNING LITE CAME ON.

Now my perplexity and pissoffity went to stark muther-mucking raving panic.

ACT VI

Captain Thomas Friedkin was still sitting with his arms folded.

The #2 Engine is located in the aft fuselage---right under the vertical stabilizer and rudder. If it burns itself off its mounts---it will take the aft part of the fuselage with it---and the only way that you're going to go is down.
That's what she said

ACT VII

I looked at Thommy again.

Captain Thomas was still sitting there like a statue.

At this point in eternity, I didn't give a damn what any body thought. I reached up to pull the #2 Engine fire handle.

ACT VIII

Captain Thomas pushed my hand away again.

I exerted all ray adrenalin---puckered my 'sphincter---went for the #2 Engine fire handle again.

ACT IX

This time--- **Captain Thomas And Flight Engineer Captain Alfred Stewart** ---both---grabbed my arm and kept me from pulling the #2 Engine fire handle.

ACT X
Then
---CAPTAIN THOMAS FRIEDKIN---
AND
---FRIGHT ENGINEER CAPTAIN ALFRED STEWART---
---Broke out in laughter---

ACT XI
I saw no humor in any of this. I again went for the fire handle---this time more vehemently. This time it took both Thommy and Alfred to restrain me by grabbing my body and my arm.

They say that fear and panic will increase your strength threefold---me thinks.

Thommy and Al Stewart knew that they were losing the battle.

As one they shouted, ---**"LEAVE IT ALONE BECK."**
I did

ACT XII
Thommy and Al ---both broke out in laughter again as both fire handle lights went out.

I sat there in a daze wondering what the fuck had happened.

ACT XIII
Well ---**!!!I FOUND OUT!!!**.

We picked up a Boeing 727-200 that had been out on a training flight.

The mechs had left the "**BLACK BOX**", which has the capacity to simulate engine fires and various other emergencies, ---**PLUGGED IN.**

Then good old **FLIGHT ENGINEER CAPTAIN ALFRED STEWART** sat behind us pushing the switches that would simulate engine fires.

EPILOGUE

Thommy and Al were laughing so hard that they were crying.
I joined in on the laughter---tooooo.
After all it is better to laugh than go down in flames.

"ALLS WELL THAT ENDS WELL"
PRFPACPJM

*****

I have asked many people for inputs as to what a great boss man **MISTER KENNY FRIEDKIN** was and thus far I've only received an input from "**retireded**" CAPTAIN ALFRED STEWART.

I was going to edit it, but I might not do it right---so here is Alfred's tribute to

MISTER KENNY FRIEDKIN

A couple of nights ago I called my friend Jack Beck as I had not heard from in quite sometime and as usual we shot the breeze about our flying days at PSA and how fortunate we both were to have such great careers. During our conversation I told Jack how it was that I had been able to advance from being a mechanic into the flight department as a Flight Engineer.

Jack has been writing a book on his experiences and He wanted this particular story because it involved a roan by the name of Kenny Friedkin who was the founder and president of PSA. Jack and I owe a great debt of gratitude to Mr. Friedkin as this little story will show.

I had been a mechanic for three years and during that time I had studied for My Flight Eng. written, the FAA allowed a mechanic to take the written if they had worked on heavy equipment for two years. Upon passing the written I went to the Flight Department, obtained an interview with the Chief Fight Eng. by the name of Bob Lofty and asked for a position as a Flight Eng. As most people familiar with the good old boy system which at the time PSA was; I was not considered one of the above mentioned, I got turned down flat. Bob Lofty was not very well liked and He had little compassion for anyone trying to get ahead.

My next attempt resulted in the same; being turned down this time by the Chief Pilot, who said that it was not his department and that He left the hiring of Flight Engineer's to Mr. Lofty.

As a last resort I decided to try an Interview with the President of the Company Mr. Friedkin. I went to the main office and requested to see Mr. Friedkin, I was told He was out of the country in China, but 1 could see the Vice President Mr. J. Floyd Andrews; this I decided to do,. I went into his office and told Him what My desire was to become a Flt. Eng. and that I had tried with both the Chief Flt. Eng. and the Chief Pilot and was turned down. He patted Me on the head and said they needed good mechanics and sent me on my way.

I still did not give up and waited until I knew Mr. Friedkin was back in the office, and again went to the office and asked to see Mr. Friedkin, I was blessed as He agreed to see me, I sat down an told Him that I wanted a career with PSA and intended to stay with the Company, that I wanted to become a Flt. Eng. that I had tried through proper channels and had been turned down and that I hoped He might make it possible. He said His Son, Thommy Friedkin was getting His ATP on the Electra and that I could check out at the same time. He picked up the Phone and called the Chief Pilot Mr. Leo Leonard and said check out Al Stewart as a Flt. Eng. and that was it. The Flight Department didn't like it but when the President of the Company said do it there was no argument.

Captain Alfred Stewart
Has been married to a beautiful woman named—

MISSES MARILYN STEWART

For over fifty years now.

CONGRADULATIONS

*****
A TRUE STORY

Just happened to remember this incident which happened **CIRCA** *40 years ago.*

Boeing 727-100 ----A Jet airliner with three engines on the rear of the fuselage.

Location---Some where over the Rockies.

Flight Engineer, ---"Captain Sir---we just lost number three engine and I can't get it restarted."

Airliner Captain, ---"Damn, ---FAA regulations say we have to declare an emergency and land at the nearest suitable airport, which is Las Vegas. I'll start descending early so as to keep our speed up like we still have three engines and we will continue on to our destination, which is Los Angeles."

WELL, THEY DID LOSE AN ENGINE. ---**The engine came loose from its mounts and landed somewhere in the Rocky Mountains, a long time before the Boeing 727-100 landed in Los Angeles.**

"LUCY---YOU GOT A LOT OF 'SPLAININ' TO DO."

*****

--- CIRCA ---

AUGUST
1-NINER-66

---"THE PARTY"---
---I REALLY DON'T KNOW HOW I NEED TO PREFACE---
"The Party"

Tell ya what I'm gonna do---

I'm gonna change all the names to protect the guilty and tell you that, ---

Most of the **"PARTY"** is fact. ---Some of the **"PARTY"** is fantasy.

Some of the **"PARTY"** is from other parties that I have wrote in to make it---

"ONE BIG MUTHA HUMPIN' PARTY"
AND A LITTLE BIT OF FICTION
TO REDUCE THE FRICTION ON MY MEMORY

Just remember, ---"Truth is stranger than fiction"

This is my last story on flying Co-Pilot on the Boeing 727-100/200.

It is the last---but not the least ---as ye shall read---

The most

Here's how it goes.

PSA had a big hangar on the southwest side of the San Francisco Airport.
Now read listen to this bullshit—

F. E. Eastcott, Vice President of Something or other, a Wheel and his Lug Nuts, got the bright idea to build the Crews&Stews sleeping rooms next to---

---PSA'S SAN FRANCISCO AIRPORT HANGAR —

To defray the cost of motel rooms.

Now we were not only flying in and out of "Airports all the Live-Long-Day". ---

We were sleeping at "Airports all the Live-Long-Night".

The PSA "Motel" consisted of ten-double/double bedded rooms, a recreation room and a kitchen that we shared with the Mechanics.

And an antiquated Volkswagen Bus---for booze runs.

It was a cold night in August—a full moon.
As Nick Nolte said in the flick 48 hours---"The coldest winter that I have ever spent was the summer that I spent in San Francisco."
All the party people gathered at the PSA "Motel".
Some Crews&Stews were on flights that overnighted in San Francisco.
Some Crews&Stews made their way there from various stations throughout PSA's system.
Some Crews told their lovely wives that they had to fly that day so they could come to the "impromptu" party and chase Stews.
Some Stews told their boyfriends they had to fly so they could come to the "impromptu" party and chase Crews.
Stews could not be married or pregnant or over 30 or fat this time in the fuckin oops flying game.
Well, they weren't exactly lying---most of them flew in.
Almost half of PSA was at the shindig. ---
Crews&Stews&Mechanics&StationAgents
BaggageSmashers&"FrequentFlyingPassengers"
---No frequent flying perks then---
*****
American Airlines started the Frequent Flyer Program as a short-term promo.
That's the "short & long" of it.
The Frequent Flyer Program caught on with the rest of the Airlines and now they're stuck with a costly money making scheme.
*****
I passed my uniform hat around like a preacher at a Phenix City, Alabama Tent Revival and collected money for the needy, which in this case was going to be in the form of booze.
Just like the money in the hat was gonna buy booze at the Phenix City, Alabama Tent Revival.
I commandeered the antiquated VW bus---went to ---
---Rose & Bills Bar & Liquor Store in San Mateo ---
---A Suburb of San Francisco---
I bought eight quarts of assorted hard stuff, two cases of beer and a bottle of wine.
I delivered it back to ---**PSA HANGAR MOTEL.**
It was only 2100 hours.
We all could have a couple of drinks and still be legal to fly the next morning.

*****

We had an 8-hour drinking curfew at that time. Now it is 12 hours and some airlines have a 24-hour sobriety checkpoint. ---Ycch I'm glad I'm not flying nomo.

I've heard recently that some airlines do not allow drinking on the overnights at all.

Ycch, ycch---double ycch, I'm glad that I'm not flying nomo.
*****

Didn't work that way. ---We "d-ran-k" out of booze before midnight.

I did my Saintly Southern Baptist act once again. ---Passed my hat around the woozy rec-room.

This time my hat was a lot fuller of lucre---partly due to the fact of inebriation, but mostly due to the fact that Rose & Bills Bar & Liquor Store would be closing shortly and the party animals knew that this would be my last run.

I got in the Volkswagen Bus. Stewardess Nancy Benne got in beside me and sat as close to me as she possibly could without sitting on my lap.

I was a little woozy by now and figured that she either wanted a little back seat time or Nancy wanted to make sure that I brought the hooch back.

!!! WRONG!!!
On both accounts
We departed.

Stewardess Nancy Benne put her foot on top of mine---which was on top of the accelerator, **---pushed it to the floor.**
---PEDAL TO THE METAL---

We went screeching out of the parking lot---careening off parked cars---went to **Rose and Bill's Bar&Liquor Store in San Mateo.**

Stewardess Nancy Benne was a thrill seeker. She thought that I was Parnellie Jones.

We "car-oomed" into San Mateo.

There was a line of cars waiting at a red traffic signal and we were still doing Mach 2.

I made a hard right turn on two wheels into a gas station to avoid a rear ender.

We barely missed the gas pumps and continued on to---Rose & Bills Bar & Liquor Store.

I pulled into the liquor store parking lot and only then did I think to push in on the clutch---shift to neutral---turn off the ignition key---put on the brakes with my left foot.

Not bad thinking for a guy that was too drunk to walk.

I got the VW Bus stopped and looked at Nancy Benne.

I expected an atta boy or a sitting ovation for my driving skills. I got neither because Stewardess Nancy Benne was passed out.

Nancy Benne had just gone through a zillion minutes of the wildest ride that Nancy Benne had ever been through and Nancy Benne didn't even know it.

I released Nancy Benne's foot from on top of my foot and went into Rose and Bill's Bar and Liquor Store.

*****

CAPTAIN REGGIE BEAN

And self were having a drink at Rose and Bill's Bar & Liquor Store in San Mateo one overnight.

A demure sweet young blonde thang sitting at the bar raised her glass
---shouting---
"HERE'S TO THE KING"
De-bar-mob-as-one---
"WHAT KING?"
"FUC-KING" she shouted.
*****

Written on the shithouse wall---
At Rose & Bills bar in San Mateo, California.
"Wanna know how to blind a Chinaman???"
"Put a windshield in front of him."
*****

I bought twelve more quarts of the deadly love potion and two more cases of beer. I put my cargo in the "Bus"---put Stewardess Nancy Benne who was in dreamland---in the back seat.

One "Mad Hatter" ride in one night was enough for me.

We got back to the PSA "Motel". Nancy Benne was still passed out in the back seat.

I left her there and took my stash into the woozy "w-rec-k" room.

There was one helluva party going on.

About twenty **studs** and twenty **stud** takers were sitting around in a circle playing spin the bottle. Just like we did when we were kids. Only this time it was an empty whiskey bottle and when it pointed at you---you not only got kissed---but had to take off an article of clothing.

Joy, ---the most voluptuous and sweetest of the stew covey was down to her panties and bra.

Earnest, one of our most stoic and staid Captains, was down to his boxer shorts.

Dja hear about the two maggots making love in dead ernest?

Captain Shaft Crank was stark naked with a hard on and playing with it while ogling Joy.

Captain Gill Fish had a smile on his face---that if he would have died at that moment, it would have taken twenty undertakers to erase the grin from his kisser.

It looked to me like the losers in the crowd were still fully dressed.

I was staggering around with two cases of beer and a case of the hard stuff trying to figure out where to put it down.

Flight Engineer Captain Will Fables saw my plight and got up to help me.

Flight Engineer Will Fables fell against me---knocking me into a sliding glass door.

The door and I hit the concrete together. The door smashed to smithereens.

I kept the liquor intact---spilt nary a drop. Nobody even noticed.

They were all watching the spinning whiskey bottle---hoping that when it stopped---it would point to Joy---so she could remove the rest of her laundry.

I sat down---opened a bottle of Canadian Club---passed it around.

It was emptied half-way around the circle and someone put it down---

---**Spun it**---

Now we had/have two spinning bottles.

I uncorked a bottle of Jack Daniels---took a swig---passed it around the other way.

The Jack got devoured before it got halfway around and wound up spinning in the middle of the circle.

I kept opening beer bottles and booze bottles and passing them around.

Every time one got emptied, ---someone would put it in the middle of the circle---

---**Spin it**---

The bottles were smashing into each other and breaking.

Didn't matter, ---everyone was crawling through broken glass---taking off their laundry---swapping spit.

Out of all those spinning bottles, ---only one bottle ever pointed to me.

I got to take off my left shoe.

I did all the work---everyone else was going to **stud.**

Now it was three in the morning. ---We were out of booze and the Noah's Ark syndrome begins.

Two by Two they started leaving the "Rec" room for a PSA "Motel" Room.

Most of them didn't even have to get undressed. All their laundry was already off and they just left their clothes lying on the "Rec" room floor.

Now I'm drunk on my ass---getting desperate. The only thing that I took off all night was a shoe.

All the bottles were smashed to smithereens---except one.

I got it and spun it furiously. It pointed everywhere except towards me.

Now it dawned on me. There were only three people left---Self---
CAPTAIN SHAFT CRANK
aka
BIG DADDY
&
BIG DADDY'S BIG DADDY

Captain Shaft Crank said, ---"I'm going to get some pussy."

"Fat chance of that Shaft---most everyone's paired up and there are only a few Stews left over---and they're Bible Thumpers."

Could be the only kind of stew you'd want to eat at 3 in the morning

Captain Shaft Crank got up---took the last beer---tried to balance it on his Big Daddy. It fell off---hit the spinning bottle---they both shattered. Now we not only had/have glass all over the place but we had/have beer flowing over the carpet.

Captain Shaft Crank walked over the broken bottles like a Mayan Indian over hot coals---left the W~Rec~K room and stomped on the shattered glass door.

Never spilled a drop of blood.

GOD takes care of drunks & Angels---right Bill A.?

I put on my shoe and went to my room. I laid down on the quilt. I didn't even bother to take my clothes off.

I was going to be getting up in a couple of hours.

I was just about to nod off when I heard a pounding on the door next to my room.

It was Captain Shaft Crank knocking on a Stew's door trying to make his hard on—**not.**

A Stew groggily asked, ---"What do you want?"

"I want to fuck you."

"Go away."

"Can you just let me in so I can kiss you?" Captain Shaft Crank begged.

"Get the fuck out of here you drunken son-of-a-bitch."

"If you could just open the door, ---I would just like to shake hands with you."

"Go away you drunken asshole."

I got out of bed and went to my drunken buddy's assistance.

I tried to tell Captain Shaft Crank that we had to go flying in a few hours and we had better get some rest.

Haint nothing more logical---than one drunk telling another drunk---what it's all about.

Captain Shaft Crank never heard a word I said. Captain Shaft Crank was still naked as a Jaybird.

Whatever that means. Has anyone here ever seen a naked jaybird?

BIG DADDYS BIG DADDY---Had gone from **RED to PURPLE.**

Captain Shaft Crank was in heat and wanted some action.

Captain Shaft Crank picked up a brick and threw it through a Stew's room window.

Captain Shaft Crank reached through the hole in the window.

Captain Shaft Crank opened the door from behind.

Captain Shaft Crank went into the stews "ex-sanctuary".

Pandemonium broke out.

TRANSLATION---All hell broke loose.

The Stews---to say the most---were violently pissed.

The Stews started kicking---biting---hitting poor Captain Shaft Crank's crank and calling him every filthy name that they could think of.

Captain Shaft Crank came running out of the room with a barrage of artillery behind him.

The Stews were throwing everything they could find at him.

Suitcases---water glasses---soap---even the clock that was "hopefully" going to wake them up.

Captain Shaft Crank went back into the "Rec" room---walked over the broken glass---made himself a drink out of all the left over drinks that the party-people had left behind.

I went back to bed with my clothes on.

No use to take them off. ---I was getting up anon.

I finally dozed off.

I woke up to someone pounding on my door.

It was Captain Shaft Crank, ---"Let me in, I want to fuck you."

I got up and opened the door, ---"Shaft, if I had a pussy, I would fuck you myself---just to get some sleep."

Captain Shaft Crank stood there grinning.

Captain Shaft Crank still wasn't bleeding from walking over the broken glass.

I think that all of Captain Shaft Crank's blood was in his hard on which had went from---

---PURPLE TO MAGENTA---

Sort of the color you would see on a radar screen when there is an intense storm up ahead.

I walked with and Captain Shaft Crank and tried to get him to his room.

No dice. ---Fat chance.

The MAGENTA hard-on had taken over his brain.

All Captain Shaft Crank could think about was pussy.

I got Captain Shaft Crank almost to his room.

Captain Shaft Crank stopped at another Stew's room door, ---"I think my girlfriends in there fuckin' someone." *Captain Shaft's Crank had a lot of fuckees that he called girlfriends.*

*****

Captain Shaft Crank was a tough mother fucker.
Six foot two and as tough as they come down the pike.
Rugged looking with a big gap between his two front upper teeth.
A nice person until he had a couple jars of loudmouth in him.
MAYHEM
Fists would be flying if you pissed him off.
*****

Captain Shaft Crank knocked on his "girlfriend's" door.

"What do you want?" mumbled one of his alleged girlfriends.

"I want to fuck you."

"Go away you drunken asshole" they all said in as one.

---Sounded to me like they had rehearsed it---

I don't know how many ladies were in that room, ---but it sounded like a "w-hole" covey of quail.

Captain Shaft Crank pounded heartily on the door.

This time there was no answer. A smart covey of quail becomes silent when a hunter gets near their nest.

Once again I tried to get Captain "Shaft's Crank" to his room.

---No way, Hosay---

Captain Shaft Crank took his fist---punched through the screen and window---tried to unlock the door.

No can do.

Unlike the other door---all the locks were on the other side of the door.

Captain Shaft Crank was undaunted.

Captain Shaft Crank took about ten steps back from the door---rushed at it.

Captain Shaft Crank hit the do-de-do-do with his left shoulder like a battering ram.

Captain Shaft Crank and the door are now as one---lying on the floor in the

---Covey of Quail's Nest---

One of the Quail broke silence, ---"Shaft, where have you been? I've been here waiting for you all night."

Captain Shaft's Crank pounced on her like a mountain lion on a wounded deer.

I went to my room---went back to bed---hoping to get at least a few minutes naptime.

Unfortunately---Shaft and his old/new found love were right next door to me.

Captain Shaft Crank and his true love's "Head"-board was slapping on the wall like a "crack" of thunder "getting off" every "suckond".---Not to mention all the moaning and groaning going on.

I got up. ---Took a warm soapy shower. ---Trying to sober up.

I started to become part of the land of the living. I got dressed and went over to the w~rec~k room to "fetch a pail of coffee".

What's the old saying? ---Pour coffee down a drunk and all you get is a wide awake drunk.

The "W-Rec-K" room looked like Normandy Beach on "D" Day. Broken glass everywhere---a sliding glass door that was, to say the most---destroyed.

The stench of stale booze permeated the air---made me nauseous.

I have not had one ounce of sleep and a twelve hour day ahead of me.

I went to the kitchen---poured me some caffeine.

I looked over in the corner---saw two naked bodies lying on the cold linoleum.

Both of them were passed out but still flying "United".

I drank my java---attempted to wake them up.

No dice. ---No Number 7. ---No Number 11. ---**Snake eyes**.

About that time Captain Sal came into the kitchen in his boxer shorts bellowing, ---

"WHERE ARE MY PANTS?"

"I have no idea," was my laughing reply.

Captain Sal walked out cussing.

Once again I tied to wake up the coupled-couple.

No luck.

"Light bulb time" When you want to separate a couple of dogs that are "joined up", you throw cold water on them.

I got a pot from the cupboard and opened the freezer. Lots of ice. We didn't use too much ice in those days---sort of tainted the drinks.

The only other thing in there was a pair of uniform trousers.

Now I knew where Captain Sal's pants were. I vaguely remembered a Stewardess that didn't like Sal picking up his britches after Captain Sal had left.

I emptied a tray of ice cubes and put them in a pot---filled the pot to the brim with water---let it sit for a while---threw it on the coupled-couple.

It did the trick.

The only trouble was that the guy came up swinging---groggily.

I easily dodged his drunken fists and the only thing he made contact with was the air and finally---the wall.

Now---the man---wide awake---pissed---wanted to do combat with me.

The man was a big dude from Pensyltucky, Texas.

I didn't want my face shoved in this early in the morning.

Come too think of it---I don't want my face shoved in at any time of the day.

"Godamit Altoon---calm down."

"We're already late for our check in---I have to get Shaft up and find our other Stews."

Altoon looked at his naked girlfriend lying on the cold linoleum---tried to pick her up. She did not cooperate---pushed him away.

"I want you to fuck me," was her incoherent response.

I went and got another pot of ice water and handed it to Altoon to throw on her.

The fistfucker threw it on me.

"Now we're even mothafucka," he said in his Pensyltucky drawl.

Now I was soaking wet. ---But what the hey---it was August.

Only trouble is I was in San Francisco and it was colder than a ten-year marriage vow.

What did Nick Nolte say in "48 Hours"? "The coldest winter that I ever spent was the summer that I spent in San Francisco." Did I write that already? I think I did---shit, I know I did but I haint erasing it.

I got a litta, no, a lotta cranky with Altoon.

"Get her butt up and get her dressed or we're going to have a late departure."

Altoon sensed my anger, ---"Okay mothafucka."

Some Pensyltuckians have a limited vocabulary. BUT they stick with what they know.

I went to find Captain Shaft Crank.

No problem. ---It was the room without a door.

I didn't even have to knock---walked right in---turned on the light.

In one bed was the covey of quail---three Stews sleeping in various positions.

In the other bed was Captain Shaft's Crank with his "Cunt-Du-Jur"---both sound asleep.

They were still hooked up---doggy style---sort of looked like an Air Force refueling mission.

I shook Captain Shaft Crank by the arm---woke him up.

"What's up baby?"

"Captain Shaft Crank, ---we have forty minutes till departure and we have to get our ass in gear."

"What's up baby?"

This was getting me nowhere and time was of the essence.

This time I reached down---grabbed Captain Shaft Crank by the arm---rolled him over.

You might say that I---**UNCOUPLED-THE-COUPLED-COUPLE.**

Captain Shaft Crank woke up with a grin on his face.

The gap between his two front teeth looked even wider than normal.

Captain Shaft Crank always grinned if he emptied his ball sack---as a matter of fact, ---Captain Shaft Crank would smile all day long if Shaft got his crank.

If not---Captain Shaft Crank was still one happy fellow.

Captain Shaft Crank was still ---**CAPTAIN NICE.**

Now came the dawn---in more ways than one. Captain Shaft Crank looked at his "Pilot's Watch" and realized that we were in Jeopardy and Art Fleming or Alex are not too be found.

Blonde----howdja know he was a pilot---blonder blonde—big watch---little peter.

Captain Shaft Crank bounded out of bed and bellowed at me, ---
"MAKE SURE YOU GET EVERYONE UP ."
---**"LET'S MOTATE"**---

Captain Shaft Crank took off for the showers.

Captain Shaft Crank's hollering woke up the covey of quail in the next bed and they were not cooing. They were pissed and calling me every name in the book.

I shook Captain Shaft Crank's Lady Love of the Night trying to awaken her.

She whispered, ---"Shaft, where have you been? I've been waiting for you all night."

Poor lady got her pussy pumped full of love juice and didn't even know it.

Annie L. ---one of the stewardesses in the other bed sat up, ---**"Leave her alone."**

"I'm trying to wake her up. We have to go flying."

"No you're not. You're trying to fuck her."

I had enough of this early morning bullshit and went over to her bed, ---"Shut your fuckin' mouth or I'm going to break your lips."

Annie L. was one of the few Stews who still had all her clothes on.

Annie L. did some "hooking" in her younger "daze".

Annie L. was a religious fanatic with a face that looked like a pan of worms.

Annie L. couldn't get laid in a rooster coop with ten pounds of chicken feed.

A women's libber she was.

Annie L. was her name. Anti abortion was her game.

*****

It's like Richard Carlin quipped---

"Did you ever notice that the women who are against abortion are so ugly, ---That you wouldn't fuck them anyway?"

*****

"You wake her up."---I started to leave.

Annie L. jumped out of bed---grabbed a hairbrush off the dresser---started beating me with it.

I felt like we were married. ---All this abuse and no pussy.

MY THOUGHT--- "I'm gonna be payin' Alimony 'fore the day is dark."

I got out of the room muy pronto. ---Even I can take a hint.

I walked up and down PSA's "Motel" corridor pounding on every door that was still standing trying to get the rest of the Crews & Stews awake.

Their responses were said in five words, ---
"Go away you drunken asshole."
My response was said in four words, ---
"IT'SIXFUCKIN'THIRTY"
"WEREDUEOUTINTHIRTYFUCKIN'MINUTES"
"GODDAMIT"
"GETYOURFUCKINASSESOUTOFBED"
*****

Did I say the F word? Do you say the F word?
Surprise-surprise Gomer
Fuck is not a word
Fuck is an acronym---
Fornicate????---I don't know the rest---
If you know what it stands for let me know at
Becksflyinghigh@aol.com
So the next time say "F acronym" instead of "F-word".
Me thinks.
*****

PSA had three flights leaving San Francisco (SFO) at 0700 hours. ---
FLIGHT 706---BURBANK FLIGHT—BUR
FLIGHT 710—LOS ANGELES FLIGHT—LAX
FLIGHT 1776---SAN DIEGO FLIGHT---SAN

That's the spirit

Lights started a-turning on---showers started a-humming---sounded like a gigantic beehive.

I gave up my town crier bit and went over to the "Rec" room.

Captain Sal was still a-walking around in his boxer shorts a-looking for his trousers and bellowing like a bull elephant in heat.

I told Captain Sal where his britches were---not out of compassion---but out of meanness.

I wanted to see the color of his face when the crotch of his sub-zero pants hit his ganooches.

It was worth being a nice guy.

I had/have never seen that color of crimson on a person's face before in my life.

I went into PSA's hangar and flagged down Frank, ---a PSA mechanic.

Frank was screeching figure eight skid marks on the hangar floor on a 6-ton tug.

"Frank---I have to get to operations as soon as possible."

Frank reeled backwards from my booze breath.

Frank was an old friend of mine.

Frank decided to help me.

The only available vehicle that we could find was an antiquated tug that PSA had bought from war surplus in 1949 when **KENNY** started **PSA.**

Mechanic Frank proceeded to **PSA O**perations, which was a zillion miles away.

Frank had the "Pedal to the Metal"---we should be doing Mach 2.

Sounds great---only thing is---we were only doing Muck 2 MPH.

The tug was jumping up and down like a guy on a pogo stick.

I was coming out of drunken-ness. Nauseous-ness and hangover-ness were becoming a reality-ness. I leaned over the side of the tug and donated yesterday's lunch to the---

—SAN FRANCISCO INTERNATIONAL AIRPORT—

I looked over at Mechanic Tug Driver Frank.

He was in "hog heaven" watching me doing my "hog heavin".

Frank tried to make the tug go faster. Frank couldn't.

Frank alternately pushed down & up on the accelerator causing the old World War II vintage tug to jump even higher.

Once again I leaned over the side of the tug and gave whatever was left in my gut to the---

---SAN FRANCISCO INTERNATIONAL AIRPORT—

Frank was in hysterics and heavin' laughter while I was heavin' barf.

We got to PSA Operations.

I was almost sober. ---

Jumped out of the tug---

Went around to the driver's side---

Thanked Frank for bringing me to---

Pacific Southwest Airlines Flight Operations.

Frank couldn't hear me. Frank was in laughter-laughter land.

I pounded Frank on the left arm real hard with my fist.

Didn't faze Frank. Frank was laughing too hard.

"Thanks for the ride asshole."

I went into San Francisco International Airport PSA Operations.
The Ops Manager---Don---was in a dither.
"Where is everyone?" ---Don asked in his most effeminate voice.
Don was a tall skinny guy with a receding hairline and a pale ashen face. Don was queer---same as gay. Don was proud of it. Don had emerged out of the closet before they had invented closets.
"Don, they're still over at the hangar and you better send someone over there to get them."
"I'll take care of it sweets." ---Don got up and swished to the phone on the other side of the room.
I started making out the flight plan.
I felt a body next to mine. ---
Someone put their arm around me.
Someone put their hand on my hand.
I looked around, ---"I've taken care of the problem sweets and your boys are on the way over." --- as he tried to fondle my body.
I couldn't believe it, ---a mountain of pussy at the PSA "Motel" and I wind up with a "Gay Guy".
I got out of Don's grasp---took our copy of the Flight Plan, ---"Thanx," and got my flight bag and went out to the airplane. I didn't even kiss him goodbye. Enough of that bullshit for me.
I reverted back to being a Flight Engineer---did an exterior pre-flight inspection of the Boeing 727-200---went up into the Cockpit *"kissed"* the APU and "turned it on." *(Auxiliary-Power-Unit)*
I did a preflight of the cockpit and cabin---got the air conditioning system operating---put the electrical system on so the Wall Street brigade could read their stock reports when they boarded.

I looked out the left window---the passengers were starting to board.
No Stews yet--- okay by me.
I looked out the forward wind-screen---espied 2 airplanes.
---1 Lockheed Electra---Flying to Burbank---
---1 Boeing 727-100---Flying to San Diego "Weigo"---
They were dark.
Neither airplane had any electrical power or air conditioning umbilical cords attached to them.
I called into operations and told my swashbuckling lover about it.
"Hi sailor, do you want company?"
"**NO** *"butt"* you had better get some power on these other two airplanes before someone breaks a leg and sues us."

"Okay sweets"
 I watched as two mechanics butt danced their way to the other two airplanes and powered them up.
Gay was/is the way in the Bay.
 I got in the left seat---opened the side window---looked for my crew.
 Two vans pulled up to PSA Operations---full of Crews&Stews.
 One of the swisher mechanics opened the door to one of the vans and proffered a hand to help Captain Shaft Crank out.
 Captain Shaft Crank declined the help---stepped out of the van---fell flat on his face.
 Two Stews got out of the van---picked Captain Shaft Crank up---helped Captain Shaft Crank to the airplane.
 At this time---Altoon got out of the van---hefted Headie, who was still comatose, out with him.
 Altoon threw Headie over his shoulders like a sack of potatoes and proceeded to the airplane.

*****

One thing to mention here.
 We didn't wear our uniform coats May thru October---only white shirts & shit brindle brown britches. No epaulets
 The people watching Cap'n Shaft Crank do his half gainer on the tarmac had no idea that he was going to be the Captain of their ship.

*****

 I turned around and looked at the passengers. Virtually every/one of them were/was breaking their neck---straining---looking out the left window trying to figure out what the fuck was happening.
 Oops I said the *f* acronym again.
 I got a **light bulb**---
To you stuffed shirts that don't peruse the comics---That's an idea.
 I picked up the PA mike, *(Public Address System).*
 "Welcome aboard ladies and gentlemen."
 "We will be getting airborne here shortly. We are experiencing a "slight" delay due to adverse weather conditions at the Los Angeles Airport."

WOXOF

Weather-**O**bscured-**X**-Visibility-**O**Zero-**F**og
 "Please bear with us. We will still get there on schedule because we will have a one hundred and fifty knot tail wind."

A "fibullshit" because the weather at the Los Angeles Airport was---
CAVU
Ceiling And Visibility Unrestricted
Fibullshit---A white lie

I had no idea what the winds aloft were. I found out early on in my flying career that it was best to tell the passengers something---even if it was "fibullshit".

*Which it usually is anyhoo---because the weather is always **changing** and by the time you get to your destination---the truth becomes fibullshit.*

Once again I looked back into the cabin.

All the passengers were now staring at the overhead speakers---listening to my spiel.

It always has seemed funny to me that the passengers would look at the speakers as though they were expecting a human form to appear.

I saw a Convair 404 sitting at a gate on the other side of the tarmac. It was painted the colors of the rainbow and had no tail or fuselage identification numbers.

Seemed strange to me---even in those days.

I heard a voice calling clearance delivery, ---"San Francisco Clearance Delivery, ---this is Astro zero-zero-seven, *(007)* we need a clearance out over the Pacific Ocean to do some maneuvers."

"LIGHT BULB TIME"

Once again I picked up the PA mike, ---

"Ladies and gentlemen, ---if you look out the right side of the airplane, you can see the airplane that our Astronauts are training on. It's painted the colors of the rainbow because it's equipped with an anti-gravity flight system that causes it to fly like the arc in a rainbow, creating a negative gravity in the airplane so the Astronauts can float around and simulate flight in space."

More bullpucky, or at least that's what I thought.

I came to find out later---that particular Convair 404 was retrofitted with space-age-prop-jet engines for more power and actually flew an arc to---

---SIMULATE SPACE FLIGHT---
FOR
---ASTRONAUT/SENATOR TRAINING---

YOU NEVER KNOW PILGRIM---YOU JUST NEVER KNOW.

*****
July 20 1969
CAPTAIN BOB EBERSOL & SELF---
In "full parade dress uniform"---sat in the
---HOLLYWOOD BURBANK INTERNATIONAL AIRPORT ---
---TERMINAL BAR---
With
---ROY THE BARKEEP---
And watched
---ASTRONAUT NEIL ARMSTRONG---
Do a moon walk---
???Wonder if he was on ASTRO 007???
*****

I went back into the cabin.

All eyes were straining to the right for a sight of my astrological **lie** which after the **fact** was the **truth.**

I looked out the forward passenger door.

Two Stews were dragging Captain Shaft Crank's body up the steps. They entered the airplane.

Captain Shaft Crank looked at me, --- "What's up baby?"

"Everything's done. We had better boogie. We're already late."

I took the curtain that hides the galley and pulled the curtain across the aisle so the passengers could not see the holocaust that was going on up front.

"What shall we do with this drunken son-of-a-bitch?" they unisoned.

These two Stews flew together so much that they said everything "asone".

"Throw him in the right seat and let's get going."

They complied and then went into the cabin to placate the---

—NATIVES who were starting to get **RESTLESS—**

I was still holding the curtain up, waiting for Altoon and Headie to board. Altoon still had Headie's limp body over his shoulder and started to stagger up the steps.

Headie was minus hot pants and minus hot panties.

Altoon looked like Davy Crockett with his Coonskin Cap---only Davy's Coonskin was on Altoon's shoulder.

Use your imagination Jenner.

Altoon entered the cabin and put Headie down in the galley.
I dropped the curtain and it once again hid the galley.
Headie was still comatose. I felt her pulse to see if she was still alive.
Well, I thought there should be a pulse there.
Headie groaned a little and I took that for a yes.
Now Altoon started looking for Headie's pulse with his tongue.
Headie really started moaning and groaning.
Altoon went **SCUBA** diving.
I kicked Altoon in the ribs, ---"Get your butt up and let's motate."
Altoon looked up at me and grinned---sort of looked like a rabid Old Yeller with all the white stuff over his mouth, ---**"I'm gonna kick your ass mothafucka."**
"Altoon, we haint got no time to go to war. We have to get out of Dodge."
Altoon stood up---towered over me with dripping clenched teeth and fists. He was a big powerful dude that weighed well over two hundred pounds.
I was lucky to weigh one hundred and fifty pounds---soaking wet.
Altoon shook his head---finally came to his senses---looked down at Headie, ---"What do you want me to do with this mothafucka, mothafucka?"
"Let's put her in the forward biffy and lock it off."
"Okay mothafucka."
Altoon reached down and dragged Headie into the biffy.
All the while I was pulling the galley curtain back so the passengers couldn't see the action.
Altoon put Headie in the biffy---came out.
Altoon locked the biffy door with his Jack knife. There was/is a little slot on the "**VACANT**" sign that you could/can manipulate with a sharp object and lock the door and the sign---should/could/would read, ---

"OCCUPIED"

Altoon was now cognizant that we are/were in deep horse-pucky and that we had better get our act together and get it "on the road again" or should I say---"get it in the sky again".
Willie Nelsen died---He got killed "playing on the road again".
I said to Altoon, ---"Get in the cockpit---make sure you lock the cockpit door---run the checklists."
"MAKE SURE YOU LOCK THE DOOR"
"Yea---Okay---yea---I'll lock the muthafuckin' cockpit door."

Altoon was no longer a warrior---became aware---complied.

I dropped the curtain and guess who was there to greet me? ---Annie L---the Bible Thumper that beat me with a hair brush.

Annie L. was a prostitute at one time. Annie L. saw the light---got religion---quit selling and went to work at PSA.

"What's happening up here?" Annie L. inquired rather brusquely.

"Nothing much, ---just get an "Inop" sticker and put it on this biffy door."

"Why?" was her caustic retort. This cunt was a pain in the ass. *She needed for someone to put the bowling bowl grip put on her.*

"The turd hearse broke down. They couldn't empty the biffy and it smells like shit---if you will pardon the pun."

Annie L. was not amused. Annie L. went by me and started banging on the cockpit door.

I grabbed Annie L.'s arm and turned her butt-ugly ass around, ---"Go get a fuckin' "Inop" sticker and put it on the fuckin' biffy door or I'm going to fuckin' kick your fuckin' ass off the fuckin' airplane."

"You can't do that," was Annie L.'s snotty reply.

"The fuck I can't," ---was my even snottier response. ---"Listen armpit face, get your fuckin' butt to the back or get it off the fuckin' airplane."

Annie L. reluctantly left---went to the back of the airplane.

I got an "Inop" sticker and put it on the biffy door so Altoon's Coonskin Cap could rest in "piece".

I knocked on the cockpit door---Altoon let me in.

I got in the **left** seat and looked over my right shoulder at Altoon to see if he was at least half-way comatose and knew what the new seating arrangements were.

Altoon said, ---"The mothafuckiri checklist is complete mothafucka."

I looked out the left sliding glass window and saw Don, the Gay Caballero operations agent swishing up the boarding ramp with the manifest in hand.

Altoon let him in the Cockpit and relocked the Cockpit Door.

Don sat down in the forward jump seat. ---

Don read the passenger count to me---all the while massaging my neck.

Don looked at Captain Shaft Crank who was sawing logs.

"Oh my, is he alright?"

Don looked at Altoon who was sawing logs---face down---drooling on the Flight Engineer's desk.

"Oh my, is he alright?"

Don put the paper work on the pedestal and started massaging Altoon's body.

I didn't get jealous.

Don got up, patted me on the shoulder and handed me a note, ---"Have a good day Captain."

---SIX MONTHS AGO I COULDNT SPELL CAPTIAN---
AND
---NOW I ARE ONE---

Don left. ---I read the note. ---
"If you are ever in the Bay Area
and want to have fun
Call me at 415-769-7180.
Love Don."

I added a "na" to Don---making it Donna and slipped it into Shaft's sleeping' shirt-pocket.

I found out later that Shaft made a special trip to San Francisco and called "Donna."

Shaft was not happy with my prank and let me know it.

As Shaft tells it--- "I was driving across the bay bridge to meet Donna and had a fart with lumps in it and everything turned to shit from then on."

I woke up Altoon and we started up the engines.

I got clearance from San Francisco Airport Ground Control and began to taxi out. We rolled about twenty feet and a PSA van pulled up in front of us.

I slammed on the brakes to avoid a mid-ground collision as opposed to a mid-air collision.

I called into PSA Operations, ---"Get this mucking van out of our way so we can get going."

"Okay Stud"

Now a passenger door in the van opened and a familiar figure stepped out.

It was J. Close---El Presidente of PSA.

Don swished out of PSA Operations, jumped in the van and pulled it out of our way.

J. Close stood in front of the Boeing 727 flapping his arms up and down---like a humming bird in flight.

J. Close started jumping up and down---like a kangaroo in heat.

J. Close wanted to get on our airplane and go home to San Diego.

I released the brakes, made a hard right turn and resumed taxiing.
J. Close quit his "Flight of the Phoenix" act and ran for cover.

Too little---Too late!
The Phoenix Shall Become Ashes.

When the tail of the Boeing 727-200 pointed El Presidente's direction, ---I added maximum power on the #1 engine.

When we got turned around---I looked the scene over.
El Presidente was getting up off of the ground and dusting himself off.

Now J, Close was running along side of the airplane shaking his fist at us. Lip reading--even at that distance---I could tell that he was not reciting scriptures from the Bible.

I get another **LIGHT BULB** *in my gourd.*

At this point in time---PSA had a commercial on television showing J. Close trying to get on a PSA flight because he was a minute late, indicating that PSA always left on time and would not even wait for the President of Pacific Southwest Airlines.

I again picked up the Public Address System Microphone, ---"Folks, if you look out your right windows you can see the President of PSA running alongside the airplane trying to catch this flight."

"We are making a television commercial at this time of the President of PSA trying to get on one of our flights and he can't because he is one minute late or the flight is full. You can't see the television cameras because they are mounted on the landing gear struts."

If bullshit was dynamite that morning---I could have blown up Russia that evening.

Dya remember this one? "If brains were dynamite---he wouldn't have enough to blow his nose."

"San Francisco Ground—this is PSA 710—ready to taxi."

"PSA 710—is cleared to taxi to runway Two-Eight Right."

I taxied the Boeing 727-200 out to Runway 28 Right.

I parked the brakes---shook Altoon and woke him up again.

"What do you want mothafucka?"

I was beginning to think that the only four syllable word that this Pensyltuckian knew was the motto of Pensyltucky.

"San Francisco Tower, this is PSA 710—ready for take-off."

"PSA 710—San Francisco Tower---Runway Two-Eight Right—Taxi into position and hold."

I shook Captain Shaft Crank and woke him up.

I taxied on to Runway 28.

"PSA 710—San Francisco Tower—Runway 28—Cleared for takeoff."
"Tower, we need a little time on the runway."
"You have a Problem?"
"No problem, just need a little time."
*****

People think I have a drinking problem.
I get drunk- fall down- throw up-pass out.
---No problem---
*****

I looked over at Captain Shaft Crank, ---
"Captain Shaft Crank ---do you want to swap seats for take-off?"
"Nah---Beck---you're doing okay. Make the take off and let's get going."
"San Francisco Tower---this is PSA 710---we're ready to go now."
"Roger PSA 710---cleared for takeoff."
"Give me Max power Altoon."
No response.
I looked around---Altoon was face-down-slobbering on the Flight Engineer's Table, ---
---Drooling—sound asleep---
I started to wake Alton up but thought better of it. I was tired of being called mothafucka.
I advanced the power levers to take-off power.
The Mighty Boeing 727-200 went roaring down the runway and we became airborne.
When I rotated---I heard a **thump-thump.** ---I thought we had a compressor stall.
I looked around at Altoon to see if he had any indication on the gauges.
Altoon was gone---literally.
The **thump-thump** that I heard was Altoon falling out of the Flight Engineer's Seat and bouncing off the cockpit door.
Captain Shaft Crank selected the flap handle to the **"FLAPS UP"** position---then put the landing gears lever in the **"UP"** detent. The gears locked into the wheel wells.
Captain Shaft Crank put the auto-pilot on and fell comatose.
I called San Francisco Departure Control on 120.9 and asked for a right departure turn to go South over San Francisco Bay instead of a left turn which took about ten minutes longer.

"Turn right---proceed direct to the San Jose VOR---direct to the Priest VOR---direct to the Fillmore VOR---then flight plan route to Los Angeles."

VOR---*Visual Omni Range*

I read back the clearance and about that time---**DING-DING**---indicating that a Stewardess wanted to enter the cockpit.

The DING-DING Woke Captain Shaft Crank up.

I DINGED back ONCE indicating that I wanted to talk on the intercom, ---**"What the fuck dya want? We're fuckin' busy up here."**

It was Annie---the Joan De Arc of the airline industry.

I did not need a Saintress at this time---
All I needed was to get to LAX & throw up.

"Do you guys want any coffee?"

"I fuckin' told you to get your ass in the back cabin where you're supposed to be."

"I heard a noise on take off and wanted to make sure everything was alright."

"You serve the fuckin' coffee and we'll fly the fuckin' airplane."

"Do you have to say fuck every time you say something?"

"FUCK YOU---GOODBYE."

Captain Shaft Crank fell back asleep.

I Auto-Pilot navigated the Boeing 727-200 to Los Angeles International Airport.

I woke up Captain Shaft Crank on final approach. ---

"What's up baby?"

"Do you want to make the landing Crank?"

"Yea---sure---I haven't made a landing from the right seat in a long time."

Captain Shaft Crank did. ---Captain Shaft Crank landed at the Los Angeles Airport. ---**Greased that puppy right on the numbers.**

*****

Actually it was little harder than grease job---but by my standards---any landing that you make without dropping the oxygen masks is a "grease job".

*****

I taxied us to the gate---Captain Crank Shaft fell back comatose.

Some one knocked on the cockpit door.

Figuring' it was Annie L---I woke up Captain Shaft Crank.

Captain Crank Shaft looked over at me, ---"**What's up baby?**" ---Then for some unknown reason said, ---"**Show me a man that, doesn't eat pussy and I'll take his wife away from him.**"

And went back to never-never land.

A mechanic gave me the "two thumbs pointing together" sign meaning that the chocks were in place and that I could release the parking brake.

I did.

I got out of the left seat---helped Altoon get up on his feet. Altoon and I "picked up" Captain Shaft Crank and put him in the left seat.

Altoon got back in the Flight Engineer's seat---looked at me, ---"I'm gonna kick your ass mothafucka." ---Put his head on the Flight Engineer's table and went back to beddy-bye.

I got the cockpit door key out of Captain Shaft's snoring pocket---slithered through the cockpit door so no one could see inside---locked it.

Annie L. was there to greet me, ---"That was a pretty hard landing wasn't it?"

I put my face as close to Annie's face as I could without touching lip organs---whispered, ---"**Fuck you---you're still walking aren't you?**"

I got off the Boeing 727-200 and went into Los Angeles Flight Operations.

Chuck, a prematurely balding Operations Agent met me at the door, ---"Where's Captain Shaft Crank? I need to talk to him now."

This I couldn't let happen.

Chuck was a reformed alcoholic who lived with his mommy.

Chuck was straight as William "Tail's" shaft and didn't partake of anything with alcohol in it.

If Chuck saw Captain Shaft Crank in his condition---
Chuck would call
A---FAA.
B---PSA
C---MOM
D---YEP

I told Chuck, —"**Captain Shaft Crank had to give a shit and is in the biffy.**"

*****

SideBarFly
I used that excuse MANY times in my flying job/play-time/hobby career.

When a Chief something or other called me into his Chief something or other office over something or other asking me where I was at the time of the "INCIDENT", —
I would simply say, ---"I WAS TAKING A SHIT."
Knowing that any excuse that I could conjure up would fall on deaf ears of the designated chief somethinorother. —Except the simple phrase, —
"I WAS TAKING A SHIT."
Haint a thing they could/can do about a guy givin' a shit.
*****

Chuck flinched, ---*Toilet talk was dirty talk to Chuck and his mommy.* ---"I just got a call from J. Close. J. Close is coming down on United Airlines and wants to talk to Captain Crank. J. Close wants Captain Crank to hold the flight till he gets here. J. Close sounded like he was very cranky."

"Do you think he's pissed off, Chuck?"

Chuck did a double flinch. ---*Toilet talk was dirty to Chuck and his mommy.*

I filled out the flight plan, got the Boeing 727-200 kerosened up and ready to go.

I called Captain Spike---Our one man scheduling department told him that we had a sick Stewardess on board that needed to come home. I also told Captain Spike that I checked the loads for the rest of the day--- that our passenger loads were light and all we needed were three Stews.

*****

One Stewardess for each fifty passengers was the FAA requirement in those days--- still is--- me thinks.
*****

"Send her on home"
"Thanks"

I did a fast walk around the Boeing 727 100---went up the boarding ramp---entered the cabin.

I caught Annie L. jiggling the cockpit doorknob trying to get into the cockpit.

I was going to send Headie home but now I get a better light bulb.

I have got to get rid of "Saint Cunt". She was going to cause problems that we didn't need.

I approached Annie L. ---tapped her on the shoulder.

A startled Annie L. turned around---faced me with "cunTempted" eyes.

"Annie L, get your shit together and get off the airplane."

"What?" was her indignant response?

"**YOU'RE OUT OF HERE,**" was my more indignant reply.

"I called scheduling---told them you were being a pain in the ass and a detriment to flight safety."

"Captain Spike told me to send you home."

She left.

I unlocked the cockpit door and sidled in. Captain Shaft Crank and Altoon were still comatose.

I got in the right seat and looked out of Captain Shaft Crank's side window. Chuck and Annie L. were on the tarmac having a "Pow-Wow."

Annie was pointing at the cockpit indicating that there was something amiss with the crew.

My Smirk; "If they knew.

MY THOUGHT--- "If they only knew"

Chuck was scratching his hairy balls with one hand and his bald head with the other.

ANNIE L. WAS STEAMING.

Chuck ---mister straight arrow was one heart beat off a stroke.

Chuck, paper-work in hand came up the boarding ramp.

I once again left the cockpit---

Locked the cockpit door---

Stood in the Galley---

Awaiting the paper-work.

Chuck, Mr. Good-body, walked on by and tried to open the cockpit door.

No can do.

Chuck confronted me, ---"What's going on in there?"

"None of your fucking business," ---I retorted as I wrested the paper work out of his hand.

The **"F~U~C~K" acronym** put Chuck into a state of shock.

I grabbed Chuck by the arm---led him out of the airplane---onto the boarding ramp.

Chuck started gibbering at me as to the fact I had a filthy mouth and couldn't talk to him like that.

I got in Chuck's face, ---"**Fuck You**"

I slammed the cabin door in Chuck's "fucked face", unlocked the cockpit door and went in. Captain Shaft Crank had crawled over into the right seat and was sound asleep. It wasn't even noon and already I had dealt with---

"A reformed prostitute"---

"A reformed alcoholic"---

"A reformed heterosexual".

Gonna change the world these people are---haint gonna happen.

As Dino once sang **"It's still the same old world---you haint-a-gonna change it---As sure as the stars shine above."**

It was gonna be a long **F-ACRONYM** day.

Chuck pulled the boarding ramp away and waved his left hand in a circular motion indicating we could start our engines.

I woke up Altoon, who was still drooling on the Flight Engineers desk.

Altoon started the engines. I got clearance to taxi and awakened Captain Shaft Crank.

I looked down at Chuck for a salute---meaning the airplane was clear of all obstructions. Chuck had his arms up in a big "X" which means not to go anywhere. Chuck was also pointing toward the United Airlines terminal.

Then and only then did I realize what the delay was.

Running across the tarmac from United was El Presidente J. Close doing his "humming bird/kangaroo imitation."

I released the parking brakes to taxi out. If J. Close was going to fire us---it will be another day.

The Boeing 727-200 didn't budge. ---I looked at Chuck in askance.

Chuck was smirking. The bible-thumpin'-reform-the-world-ex-alky-who-later-on-saw-the-real-light-and-started drinking-and-chasing-pussy-one mo'-time---had left the chocks in.

Thought he had us "dead" to rights. "Coronor-ed".

All the while---the huminin bird homo-sapien kangaroo---was getting closer.

I noticed on my walk around that we were chalked with "Piper Cub" wooden chalks which were only about four inches high. *Actually, 2' 4x4s with rounded edges ---with ropes, which were always frayed, ---to drag them away from the landing gears.*

I advanced the power levers to "full ships ahead".

The MIGHTY BOEING 727-200 jumped the chocks.

We taxied out.

I looked out the right side window after we made our right turn. J. Close and Chucky-Yucky were ass-over-tea-kettles scurrying for cover.

Captain Shaft Crank was going to have a lot of, as Desi would say, "splainin to do."

---SECOND VERSE SAME AS THE FIRST---

I taxied the Boeing 727-200 to Runway 25 etcetcetcetcetc.

We got back to the San Francisco International Airport---taxied to the gate.

I set the parking brakes and turned off the seat belt sign indicating to the Stews that they could allow the people to deplane.

Once again Captain Shaft Crank awakened---looked out the windshield, ---**"What's the fuckin' hold-up? How come we haven't left the gate yet?"**

Captain Shaft Crank had made a round trip to Los Angeles---dusted off the "Big Boss"---didn't have to put up with "Angelic" Annie L. or Chuck and.---**Did not remember.**

I got out of my seat and went into the cabin to check on Headie.

I knocked on the biffy door hoping that she was still alive.
I heard a click and watched the---**"OCCUPIED"** sign go to **"VACANT"**.

Headie opened the biffy door and stepped out. Headie L. was a good looking lass and even in her debilitated condition, ---Headie L. was a beautiful lay-dy. Only problem was that her mini-skirt was almost up to her naval and cleavered-beaver was very **out fuckin standing.**

I gently took her by the hand---led her into the Cockpit---sat her in the jump seat.

Captain Shaft Crank awakened.

Crank was breaking his neck, looking around, trying to get a view of ---"Mayonnaise Makin' Heaven".

I inquired of Headie L. as to where her hot pants might be and told her I would go get them for her. I couldn't let her serve the passengers under-dressed like she was.

We'd have a rape mob on our hands.
Headie L said, "I haven't a clue."

Came the dawning---Headie L. was the chick that disliked Captain Sal.

Headie L. was the culprit. Headie L. put Captain Sal's britches in the freezer. Now I knew where Headie L.'s hot pants and panties were.

---Captain Sal got revenge for his blue-balls.---

I left the Cockpit---went outside---waved down Frank who was doing figure eights on **PSA's** newly acquired air conditioned closed cab tug just for something to do and doing it well.

"I need a ride over to the hanger Frank."

"Climb aboard old buddy," was Franks eager response.
Frank took me on a "Wild Hare" ride.

By manipulating the throttle and brakes, Frank would actually get the ten-ton-tug airborne. Frank was the Mario Andretti of the tug drivers.

I reflect on it now and can't remember ever seeing Frank with a wrench or screwdriver in his hand.

Frank was a professional tug driver and damn good at it.

Frank was looking at me and laughing waiting for me to throw up again.

I was a little green around the gills but had nothing in my stomach to upchuck.

We got to **PSA**'s Hangar/Motel.

I went into the kitchen to retrieve Headie L.'s panties and hot pants from the freezer. A half a dozen mechanics were there taking a break.

*****

"Blonde---I had a good time last night."

Blondier Blonde----"You were drunk. How do you know you had a good time?"

Blonde---"I threw my panties against the wall this morning and they stuck."

*****

The Mechanics saw me and broke out laughing.

Fuel Truck Willy, ---"What the devil did you guys do last night? The "Rec" room looks like Hiroshima the day they dropped the Atom Bomb."

I opened the door to the "Rec" room and looked it over. It was---to say the most---not a pretty sight. **It** was in one **word—destroyed.** Make that two **words—**

DESTROYED——————————DESTROYED

"Oh yea, Willy---we had a good time---everyone got laid. ---'Cept me."

I went back to the freezer---pulled Headie L's laundry out.

Now the Mechs were curious as to why we were freezing panties and hot pants.

One of the Mechanics got up and came over to take a look at the garments.

"Did you get her so hot that you had to "Freeze" her "Hot" pants before you put them back on her?"

I was not amused. ---**I left.**

So far it had/has been a long F-acronym day and it wasn't even half over.

I went back into **PSA's Hangar** and flagged down Frank who was doing figure eights in an empty hangar on his beloved tug.

Frank saw Headie L's under/over wear, ---"Is that for your trophy room? You sure work fast."

"Fuck you"

I climbed on Franks chariot, --- "Take me back to the airplane, please. We're due to launch in thirty minutes."

"Hang on old buddy. I'll get you there in plenty of time."

We left the hangar in high gear. Frank no longer was trying to chug-a-lug the ten-ton-tug, but was trying to stand it up on two wheels.

I was on a ten-ton-tug hunk of metal with frozen panties in my hand and holding on for dear life.

If I get killed on this/that mission. I can only imagine what my epitaph will/would read---

----

∧∧∧∧∧∧∧∧∧∧∧∧∧∧∧

KILLED ON A TEN-TON-TUG
WITH
FROZEN PINK PANTIES IN HAND

Frank made a hard left turn and actually got the ten-ton-tug up on its two right wheels for a split second. Frank was laughing like a wild man, ---proud of his driving skills.

We finally got to PSA Operations. ---I went inside with frozen panties in hand.

Don swished up to me. ---Don saw the panties in my hand, ---"Oh my, are those yours?"

"No, Don, these are my girlfriends and she got such a hot pussy that we have to keep her panties in a freezer every night."

That ended Don's romantic interlude. Don threw his head back--- did a 180---walked away. ---Pussy was a dirty word to Don.

I went out to the airplane---passed Captain Shaft Crank getting off the boarding ramp.

Captain Shaft Crank stopped me, ---"**I just got a message to call J. Close and I can't understand why. Have you any ideas?**"

"**Beats my four aces,**" **I replied and went up the boarding ramp.**

I always did like playing cards

I wasn't about to tell Captain Shaft the bad news that he was going to hear over the phone.

I entered the Cockpit and found Altoon and Headie in a position that only two Sumo Wrestlers couldn't/can't get "intwo".

Come to think on it---What position can two fat sumo wrestlers get in/two?

I threw Headie L.'s laundry at them---did an about face---left the cockpit.

Once again I locked the cockpit door. "**Love**" is a many splendored thing. I didn't want **it** disturbed.

I did a pre-flight walk around the Boeing 727-200---went back into PSA Operations and did the paperwork.

Don was very aloof.

Captain Shaft Crank was on the phone with a quizzical look on his face. J. Close was chewing Captain Shaft Crank's ass out and Captain Shaft Crank didn't even know why.

Captain Shaft Crank cupped his hand over the mouthpiece— looked at me, ---"Do you know what he's talking about?"

"Beats my four aces." and walked out of **PSA** Operations. *As I said before --- I always did like playing cards.*

I got back on the Boeing 727-200. I went back up to the cockpit---unlocked the door---went in.

Altoon was doing the checklist.

Headie L, ---with all her clothes on---was in the cabin serving coffee.

Heidi L. looked quite radiant.

A hot cock and the recovery rate of youth. ---Are a many splendored thing for a lady.

I slid into the right seat---in came Captain Shaft Crank.

Captain Shaft Crank got in the left seat and sat sideways---facing me, ---"**I WANT TO KNOW WHAT THE FUCK HAPPENED THIS MORNING.**"---Staring me down.

I shrugged my shoulders, pretended ignorance, which is easy for me to do, and said nothing.

"**Well, J. Close is firing everyone that was up here on the overnight including the Stews & Mechs.**"

MY THOUGHT---"Poor Annie L is going to lose her job and she didn't even get her putang---tanged."
MY SECOND THOUGHT---"Good riddance to the "Psalm Psingin Psaint".

Captain Shaft Crank once again inquired about the morning's events. Captain Shaft Crank wasn't letting up and had a need to know so he can save our jobs.

I gave in and reconstructed what happened, including knocking J. Close on his butt.

Captain Shaft Crank couldn't believe it. ---Captain Shaft Crank was pissed at me.

The vein in Big Daddy's forehead was as big and as purple as Big Daddy's "Big Daddy" was the night before.

Captain Shaft Crank's neck was swollen up bigger than his head and I feared for my life.

"Did you really knock him on his ass?"
"Yep"

That did it. Captain Shaft Crank broke out in hysterical laughter.
Altoon joined in, ---
I grinned
Altoon patted me on the back and said "good show".

Every once in a while in this life you get to be a hero. When it happens---cherish it---because it is a rare occasion.

CAPTAIN SHAFT "BIG DADDY" CRANK, ---

Hand flew the Boeing 727-200 the rest of the day without incident.

We landed at the San Diego International Airport at 1900 hours and headed for the South Seas Bar&Grill.

I waited outside while everyone went in. I figured Captain Smith, Vice President of Flight Operations was inside and was going to fire us on the spot.

I opened the door ever so slightly and looked for Smith. Smith wasn't there, but I was running scared.

I went in---had a couple of brewskies---bought a six pack of Bud.
I left.

Through my tenacity and determination I had elevated my social standing from Brew 102 to Bud---sadder---Budweiser.

My wife was waiting for me and was irate because she was going out with her friends. I was supposed to be home earlier to watch the kids.

"The Vice President of Flight Operations has called here three times in the last hour. He wants to talk to you. He said it was very important and that he had to talk to you tonight."

Now I knew why Smith wasn't in his South Seas Bar&Grill office. Smith was in his real office and calling people to fire them.

My wife left---I uncorked a. Bud.

*****

There was a picture of **Sandy Kofax***'s very large pitching hand in the sports section of the San Francisco Chronicle showing a big blister on the his social fingertip---thereby taking him out of his pitching rotation spot for a while.*

Captain John Powell *showed the picture to* **Captain Leland**--- *and asked him,* ---**"Lee---do you think that small blister makes Sandy Kofax's finger ineffective?"**

"I have no idea---ask Sandy Kofax's wife."

*****

On a Pacific Southwest flight (PSA has no assigned seating, you just sit where you want) passengers were apparently having a hard time choosing, when a flight attendant announced, "People, people we're not picking out furniture here, find a seat and get in it!"

*****

On a Continental Flight with a very "senior" flight attendant crew, the pilot said, "Ladies and gentlemen, we've reached cruising altitude and will be turning down the cabin lights. This is for your comfort and to enhance the appearance of your flight attendants."

*****

On landing, the stewardess said, "Please be sure to take all of your belongings. If you're going to leave anything, please make sure it's something we'd like to have."

*****

--- CIRCA ---

Same day---only later
"RING RING RING - RING RING RING -- RING RING RING"
I looked at the clock---2300 hours. I didn't answer it, after all, it was still the Sabbath and it was against my religion to get canned on a Sunday.
"RING---RING---RING---RING---RING---RING---RING---RING"
It rang for five minutes---finally stopped. ---I polished off the sixer---The phone rang again.
"RING---RING---RI--"
Now I was a lotta drunkawunka & a litta bravawava.

I walked over to it. I picked up the transmitter/receiver to answer it. ---Altered my altered ego and ripped its life lines out of the wall.

No more phone calls that night---I still had a job---I passed out on the couch.

"I woke Up Early Monday Morning."

"With no place to hang my head," as the great Johnny Cash would strum it.

I took my kids to Disneyland---sans wife. It was a fun day but I couldn't help fretting about my job.

*****

We had been at Disneyland most of the day. The kids, Mark Resley Beck, Kevin Shaun Beck and Shelbi Daun Beck--- wanted to do a few more rides---so I told them to meet me at the front gate. Needless to say---I was exhausted from the "EARTHQUAKIN' PARTY" and the "AFTERSHOCK".

Kevo and Shelbs came running up to me as I neared the front gate, ---**"THE COPS TOOK MARK AWAY."**
"HUH"
"The cops took Mark away to Disney Land Jail."
"What the devil for?"
"We don't know."
"SHOOT---let's go find him."
"OK dad---we saw where they took him."

We arrived at "Disneyland Jail" and went inside---found Markie sitting on a chair in the back office---just casually sitting there like it was an every day event.

"???WHAT DID HE DO OFFICER???"
"Calm down sir---he picked a flower for the gal in the boat behind his."
"???HE PICKED A FLOWER??? And you brought him in here for picking a flower."
"Calm down sir---those are the rules of Disneyland---pick a flower and we have to bring the child here till his parents pick him up."
"Seems like a dumb rule to me."
"Well sir, if we left the children pick flowers---we just wouldn't have any---would we?"
I thought about it---calmed down.
"Yea---you're right---let's go gang."
We left.

--- CIRCA ---

---samo dayo---

When we got home that night, I reconnected the phone. I had pulled it out so often that I could have done it blindfolded.
   Green wire---top left terminal
     Red wire---top right terminal
       Yellow wire---bottom left terminal
         White wire---bottom right terminal
I picked up the trans-ceiver and got a dial tone. Alexander Graham Bell and I were geniuses.

I called Captain Shaft Crank who said, ---"Where the fuck have you been? I called you last night and let the phone ring off the hook and I've been calling you all day."
MY THOUGHT---*"Guess it wasn't Smith trying to fire my butt—but good old Shaft."*

"I've got bad news, good news. Which do you want to hear first?"
      —NEITHER—
"Bad news first ---They **fired everyone** that was on that overnight Saturday night."
     "Good news second."
"They had to **hire every one back** because half of **PSA** was at the party and they would have had to shut down the airlines because we have no reserve system."
     "Here's what happened."
"After you left the South Seas Bar&Grill last night, J Close and Smith came in. They were so pissed that steam was coming off their heads. I waited till they had a few drinks and they mellowed out, then went over and joined them. They had simmered down a bit and J. Close's toupee was no longer in danger of catching fire."

"We had a couple of drinks and J. Close told me what happened that morning after the party. J Close, in fact, was "doing business" in San Francisco."

"J. Close got to **PSA** Operations early that morning so he could get home and be with his beloved wife and take her to church. When he was in PSA Ops, he got a phone call from the black maid who cleaned PSA's Motel."

"She said, ---"Mr. Close, suh, this place is a mess and I just can't clean it up."

"J. Close laughed and told her that there were some "wild and crazy people" in San Francisco last night and to get some help."

"She then again said, ---"Mr. Close suh, I can't clean this place."

"J. Close said, ---"I'll be right over"

"J. Close at this point told Shaft, ---"That he was amused because he knew who was in San Francisco that night and they probably had one hell of a time."

"J. Close got on a PSA crew van and went over to PSA MOTEL."

"J. Close's amusement was short lived."

"J. Close said, "I looked at the disaster stricken arena. It made World War II look like a Monday morning at Jack in the Box."

"J. Close put his arm around the black maid, trying to console her."

"She was, to say the most, in hysterics and crying."

"J. Close then told her to go on home and he would have the mechanics clean up the "boars nest".

"Before the maid left, J. Close asked her, ---"Would you want to fly PSA this morning after looking at this mess?"

"No suh, Mr. Close, when I flies PSA, I always flies in the afternoon."

I thanked Captain Shaft Crank for the info and for saving our ass and hung up. I uncorked a beer and went to my couch.

I was exhausted from my journey to Disneyland and my first firing from my flying job.

--- CIRCA ---

Middle of the night ---*me thinks*

"Ring---Ring---Ri--"

I answered it saying, ---"Joe's pool hall---Joe speaking."

It was Captain Spike, --- our one man Scheduling Department and Chief Pilot, ---"Beck, we need you for a trip today. Check in is at 1500 hours."

"Great, I'll be there," I responded, happy to still have a job.

Song---Sit on a happy face

I made me a bowl of Cheerios, but instead of using milk, I used beer. Tasted good and I fell back asleep.

I awakened and went to a local bar that opened at 0600.

The bar was called the Aztec Inn and if you didn't get there before 0630 hours, you couldn't get a seat because it was packed with blue/white/zero collar workers, drunks and alkies having a beer instead of caffeine before they started their day, which always made sense to me.

Why start the day with caffeine that increases your metabolism 25% when you can have a beer and reduce your metabolism 25%?

I commandeered a bar stool and ordered a brewski.

In walked Captain Shaft Crank ---spotted me---took the stool next to mine.

"That fuckin' Scheduling Spike woke me up two hours ago and I couldn't get back to sleep."

"Me too. I thought that maybe a beer would put me back to sleep. I've got a 1600 departure and am legal to have a drink right now," I said, to make sure Captain Shaft Crank knew I wasn't drinking on the job.

"Guess what? I've got the same flight and we're together. Let's have another beer."

We had "another" and we staggered out of the Aztec Bar around noon.

I went back to my couch and grabbed some ZZZs.

I woke up to the sound of my three year old twins, Kevin and Shelbi, making a lot of noise. They had got into my stereo cabinet, found my 78 RPM records and was using them for Frisbees which weren't even invented yet. My wife had left and didn't even tell me.

I called a baby sitter---suited up---went to work. We didn't have the luxury of a parking lot at that point in time at **PSA**. We had to park on a hill overlooking the San Diego International Airport.

I parked my shit-brindle-brown Nash Rambler Station Wagon Aka "Old Red"---got out---surveyed the scene.

Even Rambo was not as wary as I was.

I looked down at PSA Operations ---saw Smith and J. Close walking my way.

Not good.

I ran around the block to avoid them and went into PSA Operations.

Captain Shaft Crank grabbed me by the arm, ---"Let's get the fuck out of here while the gettins good."

WE LEFT

Guess what ---Second verse ---Same as the first.

Only this one was/is "wurst" and I'm not talking sausage.

We flew the rest of the day and arrived at the San Francisco International Airport at 2400 hours.

We went to PSA Motel---our home away from home. Be it ever so crumble.

PSA Motel was rockin-n-rollin & shuckin-n-jivin & tootin-n-hootin.

The Crews&Stews were having one helluva "bash".

There was one of our "frequent flyers pax" at the "bash" with a whiskey bottle in one hand and one of our Stews in the other.

A bush in the hand is better than two birds in the bush

There were PSA Service Agents---Mechanics—Baggage Smashers having a "ball." And last, but not least, a blue hair from the local FAA office sitting in the middle of the room in her panties and bra.

"The "w-Rec-k" room was a shambles already and one "wild and crazy mechanic" was throwing empty beer bottles at the walls and windows.

Almost everyone was stark naked and tantalizing the "fuck" out of each other.

Annie, the religious fanatic, was on the couch getting her peehole pounded by a mechanic that hadn't even bothered to take his coveralls or his tool belt off.

I guess the sound of clanging wrenches gives clinging wenches a new dimension.

Annie L. looked very happy with her newly found convention.

The scene made a Roman orgy look like a Southern Baptist Church picnic.

I didn't want any part of this one. ---getting fired once was enough for me.

I went to my room and fell asleep---awakened by someone pounding on the door.

It was **CAPTAIN SHAFT CRANK ---BELLOWING,—**
"SWEETHEART, LET ME IN SO I CAN FUCK YOU."

I looked at the clock---it was 0200 hours---tried to go back to sleep. ---No can do.

Captain Shaft Crank was going down the row of rooms pounding on every door." ---"**LET ME IN SWEETHEART. ---I LOVE YOU AND WANT TO MARRY YOU."**

I gave up on the sleep mode---got up---wrapped a towel around my endowment---chased Captain Shaft Crank down.

Captain Shaft Crank was in heat again and was starting to break into the Stews rooms. Captain Shaft Crank took a swing at me with his right fist and told me to leave him alone.

"Missed me by that much" per Maxwell Smart

I was more than ten feet away from him.

Captain Shaft Crank looked like Don Quixote battling Windmills.

I gave up chasing Captain Shaft Crank down and went to the "Rec" room to get a beer.

It was a sight to behold.

There were broken lamps and kindling wood furniture everywhere. All the windows were shattered and the sliding glass door was once again on the concrete outside in smithereens.

There were naked bodies everywhere.

Annie L. was still on the couch taking on all available "cummers". The "Mechs" had actually formed a line to bounce Annie's bones.

Sort of looked like a stag line at a wedding reception waiting to kiss the bride.

That night---Annie L. was the star in her own movie.
"ANNIE GET YOUR GUN"

I found a warm beer---guzzled it down---went back to bed. ---dozed spasmodically.

I was rousted by the sound of a very irate person, who was hollering, ---"**WHERE'S THAT *&^%%* BECK?**" ---"**I'M GONNA FIRE HIS ROTTEN ASS.**"

I opened the curtain a scoche---watched the action.

J. Close had all the mechanics standing at attention and was chewing ass.

Sorta reminded me of my drill sergeant when I was a "boot" in the army.

Annie walked "saddled legged" out of the "Rec" room---pussy-pink-naked. Sorta looked like she was rode hard and put away wet.

Annie L. caught J. Close's eye. ---J. Close forgot about firing me.

I dressed---threw my flight bag and suitcase out the bathroom window---followed them---snuck around the hangar---found Frank on his "Cadillac" Tug.

The tug was brand new and even had an air conditioned cab.

"Would you please, please take me over to Ops, please?"

Frank grinned, ---"Hop on old buddy and hang on."

I did.

We did another "Mad Hatter" ride to San Francisco International Airport PSA Operations.

Frank was in seventh heaven waiting for me to throw up my toenails. Frank was actually doing "Wheelies" on a ten-ton-tug and loving it.

The only thing I had left in my body to upchuck was the beer that I had pissed out behind the hangar when I escaped from J. Close.

I went into PSA Operations and Sweet Don was there waiting for the Stews & Crews.

"Hi Sweetie, where is everyone?"

"They're all asleep over at the hangar motel and it is a shambles."

"OH MY," ---Don panicked aloud and got the vans going over to PSA motel.

Don knew J. Close was in the area and he was covering his behind, which normally Don liked to expose.

We only had one leg to San Diego and we got there without any farther ado.

It was nine in the morning and the **South Seas Bar&Grill** was open and waiting for us.

The STEWS & CREWS---including some of the party passengers descended on it.

Once again, life was good. ---We proceeded to get inebriated and party hearty.

Toward nightfall, J. Close and Smith walked into the bar and sat in Smith's Naugahyde Office.

J. Close left his wine---sat in the booth next to Captain Shaft Crank and mine. J. Close looked over at us with daggered eyes. J Close was pissed to say the least/most/least. ----**"WHAT WENT ON UP THERE LAST NIGHT?"** ---was J. Close's furious inquiry.

Captain Shaft Crank threw up his hands feigning innocence.

"All I had waaaas one beer and weeent to bed." ---I stammmmerrrred---could hardly speak.

"I fired everyone that was up there including you two."

I got up, went over and sat in J. Close's booth. I got my face as close to his face as I possibly could without kissing him and shouted, ---

"FUCKYOU".

The bar became very silent. ---Perchance I had too much to drink.

I left

My wife met me as I "de-carred", ---"The Chief Pilot just called and needs to talk to you. I hope you're not in trouble."

I uncorked a Brew 102 and went to my couch.

The phone rang---started to answer it---ripped it out of the wall---passed out.

I awakened to the sound of a motorcycle on my front porch.

I grabbed my vintage Model 94 Winchester and went to investigate. It was Captain Shaft Crank, drunk on his ass on his Harley Davidson.

Captain Shaft Crank saw me and my trusty carbine---sobered up a little. ---**"Don't shoot me baby---DON'T SHOOT ME BABY,"** ---was his outcry.

It was two in the morning and Captain Shaft Crank had his fuckin' hog roaring on my porch and he was asking for "Diplomatic Immunity."

"Shut that mother-fucker down. I have neighbors you know."

"OK baby," was his reply and hit the kill button.

"My old lady locked my ass out and I need a place to lay my head down."

"Come on in."

Captain Shaft Crank parked his hog on my lawn and we went inside---had a couple of Brew 102's.

"Have you got a clean shirt I can borrow? **We** have a 0600 check in."

My mind went to the Lone Ranger and Tonto when they were surrounded by Indians. The Lone Ranger looked around and said to Tonto, ---"I think we're in trouble."

"What you mean **we** white man?"

That's what I said to Captain Shaft Crank, ---"What you mean **WE**, white man? I don't have a job."

Captain Shaft Crank---even in his drunken stupor---grinned with his biggest smile of separated front teeth, ---"They had to rehire us because there was no one to take the flights."

I couldn't believe it. I had been fired and rehired, twice, within four days and my sweet wife didn't even know about it.

"By the way, ---J, Close said he admired your spunk and told me to tell you, ---"**FUCK YOU**".

I laughed, ---El Presidente of PSA that we had roughed up, in more ways than one, and he was a "Good Humor Man".

I found Captain Shaft Crank a sleeping bag and went to my couch---woke up a couple of hours later.

I tried to awaken a snoring Captain Shaft Crank ---wasn't meant to be.

I dragged Captain Shaft Crank's sleeping bag outside with him in it---retrieved a pitcher of ice water from the kitchen---threw it on Captain Shaft Crank.

Let sleeping dogs--- captains--- wives lie.

Captain Shaft Crank came out of that sleeping bag cussing and swinging.

The lites on mucho homes came on.

Captain Shaft Crank and I rode to work on his Murder-Cycle.

Captain Shaft Crank was still half in the bag and I don't mean sleeping bag.

The ride was only twenty minutes, but it sobered me up---fastly.

That day and the next few months went without incident.

The only thing that I noticed that day---

<<<**WAS A BULLDOZER RAZING "PSA MOTEL"**>>>

I think the big bosses figured it was cheaper for us to go destroy a Rose & Bill's Motel in Millbrae, California, a suburb of San Francisco, than to annihilate PSA's "Home, Sweet Home." a couple of nights a week.

"ALLS WELL THAT ENDS WELL"

PRFPACPJM

--- CIRCA ---

FIRST of MAY---------I-NINER-67

Hooray---hooray---it's the first of May.
Outdoor fucking starts today.
PER CAPTAIN LELAND

Flying Co-pilot was a fun job.
The Captain made all the decisions.
The Flight Engineer did all the work.
ME??? ---I made out the paper work.
&
Had a W-hole Lot of Fun.
&
On Top Of That---I Got To Fly Airplanes.

"RING---RING---RI--"
I got a phone call from Chief Pilot Captain Spike, ---
MY THOUGHT---"What the hell did I screw up now?"
"We need four more Electra Captains and you're one of them."
"DO I HAVE TO?" I PLEADED.
---Chief Pilot Captain Spike ---
Was amazed---astounded---perplexed---at sea---
MOMENTARILY SILENCED ---Out of whack---fungoed---pissed.
&
Pissoffidly said,
"EVERYONE WANTS TO BECOME A CAPTAIN---
Even the Flight Attendants." ---Was Spike's boggled response.
"WELL I DON'T, ---I'M HAVING TOO MUCH FUN."
"That's your problem Beck, all you want to do is party and this is serious business."
MY THOUGHT---"Can anything that is this much fun be all that serious?"
*"Don't take the world **seri-ou-es**"--- **Abner Doubleday***
"Get your scrawny butt in ground school on Monday morning."
Spike hung up before I could say, ---"OK"
I complied. ---I went to Electra ground school. I got to class about 0830 hours *(zero eight-thirty hours)*, ---which was only a half-hour late.

The ground school instructor---Mister Bob Rieder---glowered at me with both eyes, ---**"You're a little late, aren't you Beck."**

The whole class of 30 new hires with their 30 new suits and 30 Christmas ties on---looked around at me in contempt.

I had on a sweat soiled tee shirt, Levi cutoffs and a dirty pair of tennis shoes.

I lied-er-fibbed—bullshitted---**"fibullshitted"**, ---"There was a big accident on the freeway and I couldn't get around it."

Ground School Instructor Mister Robert Rieder, ---**"Beck, you have a job to do here and I expect you to do get here on time."**

The whole class of aviator Wantabees was sneering at me. Little did they know that within a couple of months that I would be their Captain. *Maybe*
Shit happens and what goes around comes around.

There were no seats available---so I sat on a long counter in the back of the room.

Ground school instructor mister Robert Rieder started telling the new hires about how great PSA was and how fortunate they were to have a job with PSA.

Now comes the dress code. ---"Black tie---black socks---black shoes."

I said, ---"Wow---we don't have to wear pants anymore."

Bob glared at me, ---**"Mister Beck in the back of the room wears argyle socks to work and thinks he's smart."**

Well, that was the first time I was ever accused of being smart---I reveled in it.

Again the whole class looked around at me to see if I was for real.

Now it was almost **"High Noon"** and Mister Bob Rieder was counting rivets on the Electra.
"Do not foreskin me oh my darling."

I looked under the counter that I was perched on and found a small mattress that we used for emergency evacuation training. We would put the mattress under the evacuation slide so we wouldn't bust our butts when we hit the bottom of the evacuation slide.

I put the mattress on the counter---laid down on it---fell asleep---went to ga-ga-land.

I awakened to someone shaking me. It was one of the new hires telling me it was lunchtime.

To him it was lunchtime. ---To me it was---**MARTINI-ZING TIME.**

I hit the Lost Knight Bar in Pointe Loma and ate a couple of "Martins" and drank an Olive.

I went back to ground school.

I crawled up on my self made nest and went back to sleep. I was awakened to someone shaking me.

It was ----Mister J. Close ---El Presidente himself.

Now he's gonna tell the neophyte want-a-bee-new hires how wonderful a company PSA is/was to work for.

I listened for about five minutes---laid down on my palette---went back to dreamland.

After all—I had been with PSA for seven years and had heard all the "**fibullshit**" that he was going to shovel out of his barn-of-wisdom.

Once again someone jostled me. ---I awakened to a new hire in my face, ---"You are a very rude person. The President of PSA was giving a speech and I could barely hear him because of your snoring."

I sat up and got in his face "**SORRRRRY**."

I Left

I went to the South Seas Bar&Grill. J. Close was sitting there---I invaded his booth.

J. Close bought me a drink and we had a little chitchat about my snoring while he was giving his- ---**Sermon on the Mount.**

I apologized.

"Beck, it was a blessing that you were asleep because I didn't have to listen to your bullshit."

I got drunkey-wunkey.

"ALLS WELL THAT ENDS WELL"

PRFPACPJM

--- CIRCA ---

THE SECOND WEEK of GROUND SCHOOL
MAY---1-NINER-67

"Hooray---hooray---it's the second week of May.
Outdoor fuckin' started last week."
It haint rhyming but it'll piss off the bible thumpers that—supposedly--- "Don't drink or smoke or do sinning".

One morning I really over slept. I got to ground school at ten hundred *(1000)* hours.

Bob's eyes were glowing neon at me, ---"Mister Beck, ---do you know what time ground school starts?"

I was facetious, ---"Ten o' Clock?"

Ground School Instructor Mister Bob Rieder was not amused, nor were the whole class of new hires.

They all neoned at me in unison.

I was not going to be the class valedictorian and could care less what any one thought about me.

I left the class on the pretense that I was going to give a shit.

Urge to purge

Instead---I got in my new gold '67 Camaro and drove by the new hire Stew's classroom to see who was happening.

This gorgeous six foot tall Amazon emerged from the Stew classroom. She looked like she should have been in Hollywood instead of a Stew class, oops, ---I meant---**Flight Attendant Stewardess Co-Captain Class.**

I rolled the window down and asked her if she would like a ride to the outer parking lot where they made the new hires park.

"Sure" as she jumped in my golden chariot, --- "**My name is Joanne.**"

Her mini skirt was up to her crotch and she wasn't doing anything to hide it.

I stared at it as if I wasn't doing anything to hide it.

Joanne smiled. ---Joanne liked to show it off.

I drove to the parking lot "across the tracks" to her car.

"Where are you going?"
"I'm going to go have a couple Martinis and eat lunch."

"Can I go with you, please?"
"Of course you can,"---Was my horned-dog reply.

I was sitting there with a golden haired, blue eyed sex goddess, ---with her mini-skirt at half mast and I had just escaped from Bob's ominous eyes and she wanted to do lunch with me.

Was this my lucky day or not?

Sometimes you eat the bare and sometimes the bear bites you.

I drove us to the South Seas Bar&Grill.

We had a couple of drinks. ---

Forgot to eat---had a couple of more toddies.

I just thought of something---I can't remember ever eating at the South Seas Bar&Grill.

All this L-ass was talking about was how much she wanted to get her peehole pounded. The lady was definitely in heat.

Joanne asked me if I would go to her hotel room with her. Then, and only then, I remembered that I had a date with Polka Hauntus, one of our lovelier Flight Attendants, at 1700 hours and it was now 1600 hours.

I got a light bulb. ---I called my buddy Captain John Bull.

The other half of the "Wolf Pack" as Captain John Folting used to call us.

Misses Surely Bull, Captain John Bull's heifer, picked up the transceiver, ---"Hello"

I tried to disguise my drunken voice, ---"This is scheduling and we need Bull for a flight as soon as possible."

"Hang on and I will get him."---

"This is Captain John Bull, ---What's happening?"

"This is PSA Ops. We have a charter for you and we need you here as soon as possible."

Captain John Bull recognized my voice and I knew he was in high anxiety by the tremor in his voice.

"Okay, I'll be there in thirty minutes," was Captain John Bull's nervous response.

---Nowherecomedejudge---

Joanne pulled the phone out of my hand, ---"Captain John Bull---whenever you get here---I'm going to fuck you and suck you like it has never been done before."

I wrested the phone from her. ---"Bull can you get here on time?"---hoping his wife didn't hear the conversation.

!!!WRONG!!!

Misses Surely Bull was on the upstairs extension phone and heard the "w-hole" story.

The next thing I heard was, ---**"Beck, you miserable conniving son-of-a-bitchin asshole---don't you ever call here again and if I ever see you again, I'm going to cut your balls off."**

Bull's wife, Surely Bull, was not jolly. Surely was very religious and for her to talk like that gave me a slight hint that she was not real happy with me.

I hung up and took Joanne back to the PSA parking lot. ---Lo and behold, Polka Hauntus was sitting there in her Volkswagen Bug that wore the license plate that read TEEPEE.

She saw me drive up behind her.

About that time---drunken Joanne threw her arms around me, put a lip lock on me and wanted some "instant lip-t-on tea-se".
Whatever the fuc that means

I grabbed her by the crotch thinking of the old adage, ---"A bush in the hand is better than two bushes in the parking lot."
I'm not sure if that's the saw---but if it feels good---do it.

Now Polka Hauntus was rapping on the side window wanting to get in.

I finally unwound myself from Joanne and got her out of the car.

Polka Hauntus got in and you might say she was not happy with me after watching the two-person-one-man-orgy.

I took Polka Hauntus up to a bar on top of the hill that overlooked San Diego International Airport, ---"By the San Diego Bay", ---a very romantic spot.

I tried to ply her full of booze to calm her down. ---No can/could do. Polka Hauntus, was---to sum it up---in one word, ---pissedtothemax.

"I want to go back to my car" was the only thing that Polka Hauntus would say.

After hearing that for an hour, ---"**Let's go.**"

We started down over the hill. There was a Police Officer directing traffic at the first intersection.

Guess what?

I sideswiped the poor guy and knocked him on his ass. Even in my condition I knew that that was not in good taste.

I stopped the '67 Gold Camaro---went back to pick him up. I knew I should leave---because if I stay---he's going to throw me in the drunk tank.

I just couldn't let him lying there.

Sort of a drunken tradition among drunks.

I grabbed him by the arm and helped him to his feet. He seemed unharmed and dusted himself off.

I apologized emphatically for hitting him.

"No problem shir, I'm drunk on my ass and shouldn't be out here anyway."

We both staggered to his squad car. I opened the back door and he lay down in the back seat.

He passed out immediately.

I closed the door and went back to a pissed-off Polka Hauntus. Only then did I realize that my drunken cop friend would not be able to get out of his car.

WHY??? ---Because there are no inside door handles on the back doors of cop cars.

How do I know???---Been there---done that.

My drunken buddy was going to have a lot of "splainin' to do Lucy", when he woke up locked in the back seat of his police-mobile.

I took Polka Hauntus to her "Teepee" Bug and kicked her ass out of my Gold Camaro. She was being a pain in the ass and I, not being Mormon; didn't need two wives carping at me.

About that time my Gold Camaro shuddered. Some one had broadsided me in my left rear fender.

This was all I needed. I de-railed two pieces of ass, put a cop to bed and was still drunk on my butt.

Now I was the recipient of a fender bender.

I got out of my Gold Camaro and confronted the guy.

I knew the man. He was a mechanic with PSA and a nice person, or at least I thought he was.

"You ran into my car."

"How in the hell could I run into your heap. --- I wasn't even moving."

He staggered around his car checking the damage. He was as pickled as I was.

I said no more, got in my Gold Camaro and drove over to the hotel where Joanne was staying.

I didn't know the name of the hotel, but we called it "Pussy Heaven" because that's where PSA housed all the new hire Stews/Flight Attendants---but I sure knew where it was.

I was still on my butt---but still had the "horns" and I knew I was not going to "rut" them at home.

I staggered into the hotel—asked the night clerk for Joanne's room number.

He squint-looked at me, ---"Joanne who?" ---with raised eyebrows.

Shit, I didn't even know her last name. I shrugged my shoulders.

"Can't help you without a last name." was his caustic reply.

I said thanx---climbed the stairs to the second floor where they housed the new hire Stews.

I walked down the hall beating on all the doors---hollering, ---
"JOANNE ARE YOU IN THERE?"

I got clear down to the end of the hall---thought I struck out---when a door opened.

It was Joanne, dressed in a blue baby doll nightgown with a drink in her hand. The sight would have brought a tear to a glass eye.

She was still in heat, — "Where have you been?"

"To hell and back. ---I've been down in the hotel bar waiting for you."

She apologized saying she had forgotten we were to meet there.

This lady was one fucked up lady.

I went into her room. ---She lay down on the bed, spread her legs and groaned, ---"I love you"---passed out.

I looked at the situation through drunken eyes.

MY THOUGHT---"What would Captain Shaft Crank do in this situation?"

I stopped by a liquor store on the way home---bought a sixer for the road.

There was this new road *(Navajo Road)* that they were making that was just a little bit out of my way home. I could sneak onto it and put the "pedal to the metal" of my Gold Camaro without worrying about police officers chasing me down.

Hell, they wouldn't have caught me anyway.

Navajo Road was a six-mile stretch that had no stop signs or other cars on it.

The last thing that I remembered, before I blacked out was---**the speedometer was pegged out and indicating one hundred and twenty miles an hour and the Gold Camaro was still accelerating.**

I missed the driveway---drove up on our front lawn---hit the corner of our house.

My wile was still waiting up, ---**"WHERE HAVE YOU BEEN? WE HAD A DINNER DATE WITH MY FRIENDS."**

"Ground school lasted a long time today," I schlurrred.

She left. ---I think that she was a little pissed.

Pissoffindism is a many splintered thing.

I went to my couch---drank the rest of the six pack---passed out.

I awakened at 1000 hours, ---got in my Nash Rambler Station Wagon and went back to ground school.

I knew that I couldn't get in trouble with "**Old Red**", which I nicknamed the Nash Rambler, even though he was shit-brindle-brown.

The fastest "Old Red" could do was fifty miles an hour---floor boarded---downhill.

I got to ground school at lunchtime. This was very convenient for me because I could have ---******My Four Star Martini Breakfast. ****"Gilbeys Gin---Breakfast of Champions"******

Life was good. I left---I went to the South Seas Bar&Grill.

I had my gin breakfast---forgot to eat real food---forgot about ground school---forgot about responsibility---forgot that I was a homo-sapien---reverted back to an "Ape Being".

I called my wife and told her that I was coming home.

"Where have you been all day?"

"Ground school---Where else would I be?"

"The cops have been here inquiring about the damage to the Camaro."

I explained to her that it was just a fender bender in PSA's parking lot.

"That's not what they wanted to know about. They want to know what happened to the front end of the Camaro because it is completely disintegrated."

Now I remembered hitting the barriers at the end of my so-called private road. I mowed them down and turned them into toothpicks and matchsticks.

My Gold Camaro and I kicked ass at one hundred and fifty miles per hour.

I went home and called my insurance agent and told him that someone had run into my car and left the scene of the crime.

"Call the police and then go get an estimate."

I told him the cops have already looked at it and that I would take it into the Chevy maintenance garage where I purchased the car.

"Fine, have them send me an estimate. If it's within reason, I'll cut them a check."

The gold Camaro always ran a little bit kattywampus after that incident.

"ALLS WELL THAT ENDS WELL"
PRFPACPJM

CIRCA

JUNE---1967

Hooray hooray it's we're done with May
Outdoor fu---huh---whatever happened to blow jobs?

Monday morning I hopped in "Old Red" and started to go ground school. I was mucho hungover and I did not feel like facing Instructor Bob Rieder.

I bypassed the airport and went over to Polka Hauntus' apartment---hoping she would forgive me for ALLEGEDY jumping Joanne's bones. After all, Joanne was comatose and wouldn't have known what split---oops---hit her.

I knocked on Polka Hauntus' apartment door. Karmen Meander, her best friend and roommate opened the door.

Karmen, a beautiful buxom blonde, was built like a brick shit-house.

Has anyone here ever seen a brick shithouse???---Does it look like a big titted blonde?

"BIG BAD JOHN"---two story outhouse.

Karmen was just as beautiful in the mind.

I inquired of Polka Hauntus' whereabouts.

"Polka Hauntus had an early morning check in."

Karmen already knew that I ALLEDGEDLY bounced Joanne's bones and was not too friendly.

Gossip travels faster than jet planes in the Airline Industry.

"Come on in and have some coffee with me"

I was surprised. ---Karmen never did like me because she knew that I was married and was having too good time at work.

*****
This is one of the poems that I wrote to Karmen over the next year.

HAVE YOU HEARD THE PLIGHT
OF SEYMOUR THE OTTER
A HORSE FOR A MUDDER
A COW FOR A FODDER
AS BLIND AS A BAT
HE COULDN'T CATCH A FISH
IN ALL OF THIS WORLD
HE HAD BUT ONE WISH
THE EYES OF A HAWK
BEHIND & BEFORE
'CAUSE HE FIGURED THAT WAY
HE OTTER SEE MORE
*****

Karmen poured us a cup of Java. I took one sip---poured it out---went to the fridge---got a beer. After all---who wants to be uptight on caffeine at ten in the morning?
*****
*CAFFEINE---clanked up heart beats 25% faster---**ROAD RAGE**.*
***BEER**---HAPPY heart beats 25% slower---Stay off the road.*
You're only issued so many heartbeats—
-make them beat as happy as you can.
*****

Now strange things were happening. Karmen got up---took a beer from the fridge---uncorked it---sat next to me---started fondling my leg.
I figured it out---I think.
Karmen was in heat and, even though she thought that I was an asshole, it was any port in the storm time.
I had her by the balls and of course---I hoped that she didn't have any.
*****
"YOU CAN'T TELL THE PLAYERS
WITH
A PROGRAM."
PER CAPTAIN DIRTY JOHN FRAZIER
*****

Now I started playing hard to get, which was probably not too bright, but sometimes you have to be somebody.

I told Karmen that I was on my way to Rosarita Beach in Old Mexico and that I had intended to take Polka Hauntus with me.

"Can I go with you?"

This girl's pussy must have been on solar heat that morning, and the skies were overcast, to want to go to Rosarita Beach with me.

"Fuck yes and I watched to see if Karmen blanched. ---

If Karmen did---I was out of there by my lonesome.

Now she even became more intense with her leg rubbing and even touching my pee-pee at times, which had become a prick.

I finished my beer and got up to leave. I was still in the test mode and wondering what was on Karmen's mind. Karmen ran into her bedroom and hollered, ---**"Wait for me."**

After a whole bunch of minutes in the wait mode---I got curious as to what she was doing in her bedroom.

I went in to check it out.

Karmen was packing a suitcase.

Karmen was packing a humungous suitcase.

Karmen appeared to be leaving home—forever.

I went outside looking for a Mayflower Van.

My intent was just to go to the Rosarita Beach Hotel which is about twenty miles "South of the Border, Down Mexico Way", ---lay on the beach---do a little body surfing---have a couple of Margaritas and then go back home.

Karmen was packing for a week's stay.

I grabbed the rest of the six-pack and we took off for Mehico.

It was a little over an hours drive and most of it was pretty scenic, if you can call the cardboard houses that the Mexicans lived in---in Tijuana---scenic.

The last ten miles to Rosarita Beach were along the Mexico Shoreline and very pleasant. ---Not because of the spectacular view, but because Karmen now had my fly unzipped and was fondling me. ---

Karmen was definitely in heat.

We arrived at the Rosarita Beach Hotel, which was adorned (*ceilings, walls and floors*) with Spanish tile---absolutely beautiful.

I rented a cabana, for ten bucks, down near the beach so we could change into our bathing suits. I got a couple of margaritas from the bar. ---We went to our new home.

I was still determined to go lay on the beach---do a little body surfing.

I went into the bathroom---changed into my swimming trunks so as to give Karmen privacy time to put on her bathing suit.

Have you ever tried to put on spandex swimming trunks over a throbber? ---Not an easy task I reckon. I don't know. I have always worn boxer swimming trunks because of my scrawny ass.

I knocked on the bathroom door, ---"Are you decent? Can I come out now?"

"Come on down"

I wondered what she meant by that. ---I found out.

Here was this beautiful girl, with tits as big as cantaloupes, in sky-blue baby dolls that was up to her ass. Really sexy cause it had white fringes around the bottom. Some things will turn a guy on.

I did not get out of that cabana for two days. If it hadn't been for room service, ---I would have died from malnutrition---as opposed to rnalfuckation.

Every time I tried to get out of bed ---Karmen would pull me back in.

Karmen was getting stronger---I was getting weaker.

We left Rosarita Beach and I drove Karmen back to her apartment.

She had to carry her own suitcase up the stairs because I was in one debilitated condition.

We got in the apartment and she arrived aroused again. She bodily dragged me into the bedroom---took my clothes off---leaped on my pee pee again.

No way the Lone Ranger was gonna ride again. Karmen didn't care.

Karmen was having a good time.

I was---comatose.

Next thing I heard was the "Teepee" Volkswagen Bug coming into the driveway. Karmen kicked me out of bed, ---**"You shouldn't be here like this. My roommate is home."**

MY THOUGHT---No shit Sherlock---it's not only her roommate but my devoted girlfriend, Polka Hauntus.

I was in deep horse pucky---grabbed all my laundry---including my shoes---ran into the bathroom---locked the door.

I was putting on my clothes when Polka Hauntus knocked on the bathroom door.

"Are you in there Beck?"
"Yes I am. ---I'll be out in a minute."
"Okay. I can't wait to see you," was her aggressive response.

Now I knew Polka Hauntus was hot to trot and I didn't know if I could walk---or even talk. I put on my clothes muy pronto and exited the bathroom.

Well there was Polka Hauntus in Karmen's Sky-Blue nightie---only Polka Hauntus was taller---everything was showing from Polka Hauntus' Belly Button---down.

Polka Hauntus wasted no time and led me into her bed, which was across the room from Karmen's---who was pretending to be asleep.

Polka Hauntus took off my clothes and wanted me to bounce her bones. I was so weak that sleeping would even be a hard thing to do.

I mustered up all my strength and made "love" to her. She got her gun and immediately passed out. She had been flying for fifteen hours and was exhausted.

Thank god that she didn't ask for "suckonds".

I kissed her gently and put on my clothes to leave. I went over to kiss Karmen good-by. She grabbed me by the collar and pulled me down next to her. Karmen had been watching Polka Hauntus and me humpin' and got turned on again.

I reached down and massaged her clit till she got her gun.

There was no way that Roy Rogers was going to ride again tonight.

I left

It was just barely past midnight and I stopped by the South Seas Bar.

It was filled---with Crews&Stews.

I got a booth by myself because in my condition, I didn't need any company. I needed nourishment in the form of liquor.

I got a beer and drank it. I drank two more and all of a sudden my body was replenished with some of the fluids that had come out of it.

Some people drink water and some people drink beer. I drank/drink beer because fishes fuck in water.

I was just about to leave when J. Close, El Presidente and Smith, El Vice Presidente walked in. I scrunched down in the booth hoping they wouldn't see me.

Didn't work. ---They sat in the booth next to me.

They had a drink and pretended to ignore me, but all the while, I knew that they were going to descend on me for not going to ground school, chew my ass out or maybe even fire me **AGAIN**.

They had a few gin toddies and then they came at me.

---One on one side of me and one on the other side of me---

Shit---I was pinned down by El Presidential machine gun fire.

They sidled in and came as close to me as they could without sitting on my lap. The bar got so silent that you could here a drink drop and that was a happening.

All Crews&Stews were turned my way---watching to see me get fired.

J. Close and Smith came as close to my face as they could and as one---shouted, ---"!!!FUCK YOU!!!"

They laughed, patted me on the shoulder and went back to their "Office".

What goes around comes around.

All the Stews & Crews gave me a sitting ovation. ---I was somebody for the moment.

I had another beer and celebrated my celebrity status.

Once a king---always a king---once a k-night is enough.

The next thing I heard was Captain Shaft Crank being paged by Howie the Bartender, ---**"Captain Shaft Crank---your wife is on the telephone."**

Once again there was silence in the South Seas Bar&Grill.

Everyone wanted to hear this conversation.

Captain Shaft Crank picked up the hand-held-phone-transmitter-receiver. ---*"telephone"*.

By the look on his face and all the "I'm sorrys," ---we knew he was getting his ass chewed out by his old lady.

He put the phone on the hook.

Once again the bar became a giant beehive.

Captain Shaft Crank went over to his booth---grabbed his lady friend---put her in my booth.

"Who's making love to your old lady while you're out fuckin' someone else's old lady?" I think that's how the song sings.

Her name was Arlene and she was one beautiful lady---green-eyed brunette---body you could strike a match on.

The next thing Captain Shaft Crank uttered, ---"Would you please take Arlene to her house? I have an emergency at my home and have to get there as fast as possible."

I nodded my head yes.

MY THOUGHT--- "Yea, an emergency castration if you don't get your ass home."

But like the true gentleman that I was---I said nothing.

Captain Shaft Crank left the bar like he was catapulted from an aircraft carrier. He was in deep horse pucky with his wife and was running scared.
Been there — done that.
The next thing I heard was Howie the barkeep of the South Seas Bar&Grill hollering, ---"**LAST CALL FOR ALCOHOL**"---
Me thinks he was a town crier in his previous life 'cause his voice was rhythmic.
I ordered another beer. Arlene ordered another exotic drink that cost six bucks which was way out of my league. I could barely afford the dollar I had to pay for my beer.
Arlene's drink was a color that I had never seen before. I have/had thrown up better looking fluids.
The waitress came over wanting to collect her money.
I lied
"Captain Shaft Crank said to put these drinks on his tab and to give you a twenty-dollar tip." *Twenty bucks then was like a hundred bucks now.*
She was one happy lady and squattin' in tall cotton. Her name was Alicia, not the beauty Arlene was, but very fuckable. She sidled in the booth---sat next to me---looked me right in the eye or should I say eyes, --- "Would you like to come over to my place? I get off in ten minutes."
If I don't/didn't have a hard/heart attack, this will/would be the luckiest day of my life. ---**So far.**
I told Alicia that I had to take Arlene to her house---but would stop by on the way home.
I knew where Alicia lived because she was a neighbor of a good friend of mine. We had been in her apartment for drinks before.
"I'll be expecting you," ---as she patted me on the crotch and left with her lucre.
The beer had rejuvenated my ball sack. I got heart/hard-palpitations.
I grabbed Arlene by her wasp-waist---took her to her house. I pulled up into her driveway and woke her up. She had fallen asleep the minute she got in my car.
Arlene became coherent, ---"I want to go to a motel."
"You're at home and you can go to bed here."
"I want to go to a motel and I want you to fuck me."
Was this my lucky day or not?
"Why don't we just go to your bedroom?"

"My roommate is a lesbian and she doesn't allow men in the house."

I backed out of the driveway and inquired as to where the nearest motel was.

Now she was wide awake and having fun with me, ---"Dolphin Motel. Go to the second traffic signal, turn left and it will be on your right."

No doubt in my mind that Arlene was a regular customer there.

Probably got **"Frequent Fuckers"** rates.

I espied the Dolphin Motel---Sleazebag City---but for ten bucks a night---you can't complain too much.

We walked in---registered.

One of the clerks came up to us, ---"Hi Arlene, long time, no see, where's Dr J?"

No doubt---No doubt in my mind that Arlene was an ir-regular customer at the Dolphin Motel.

Arlene led me to the room---opened the door---ran inside---did a belly flop on the bed---passed out cold.

She didn't even pull the quilt down. Cost me ten bucks to watch her do a half gainer on the bed.

This is not good---but I have Alicia as a Queen of Hearts as my "hole" card.

If you'll pardon the pun

I left the room and went back down to the front desk.

I inquired if Dr. J ran a tab there.

The clerk nodded, ---"Yes, as a matter of fact, he owes us one hundred and thirty bucks."

"Give me my bucks back and put the room on Dr. J's bill. He'll be here in a few minutes. I'm a good friend of his. I brought Arlene over here as a favor to Dr J. His son is sick and he had to go home for a while."

I got my money under squinted eyes and raised eyebrows.

I left.

Costly night for Captain Shaft Crank alias Dr. J---what with castration---buying drinks---renting a motel room and not being there to enjoy it.

Was it good for your shaft, Shaft?

I headed for home. Arlene could walk to her house---she's gonna need the exercise to get the cobwebs out of her brain.

I drove by Alicia's apartment complex and noticed her lights were on in her apartment. I slammed on the brakes and turned into the tunnel below her apartment.

I illegally parked "Old Red" and knocked on her door.
"Where have you been? I've been waiting for you."
"Arlene passed out on me and I had a hard time getting her into her house."
Which, if you think about it, was the truth?
Alicia grabbed me by the hand and took me to her bedroom that was lit up by over a dozen candles. Now I was wondering if I was in some kind of freaky cult.

!!!NOT SO!!!

Alicia put on some "mood" music, and seductively took off her robe to reveal a slinky pussy-pink nightgown that would make any man's heart go pitter-patter.

I bounced her bones and she went to dreamland.

I blew out all the candles and left. I didn't want her to die of asphyxiation after what she had just done for me.

Arlene & Alicia---AA meeting

I was exhausted---the sun was coming up.

I was driving eastbound on Highway 8 with the sun glaring in my eyes. I laid my head on top of the steering wheel---watched the road from underneath the top of the wheel.

I finally made it home---went to my couch---passed out.

Pussy is a matter of feast or famine.

There would be no ground school for me this day. I knew my classmates would miss me.

Fuck em if they can't take a joke.

I woke up around 1500 hours to the irritation of the telephone ringing. Once again, I ripped it out of the wall and went back to sleep.

I slept till 9:00 AM, ---uncorked a beer ---recorked the phone.

"ALLS WELL THAT ENDS WELL"
PRFPACPJM

*****
All the insulation in the world haint doin any good if you leave the barn door open.
*****
Sign on a country store in Phenix City Alabama
"You can whip our cream but you can't beat our meat."
*****

--- CIRCA ---

NINER JUNE---ONE-NINER-SEX-SEVEN cum eleven

HAPPY BIRTHDAY CAPTAIN CHECK RIDE TO ME

"RING---RING---RI--"

HELLO.

"Beck, this is Bill Ray---where the devil have you been? ---I've been trying to call you for three days now and no one answers the phone."

---CHIEF PILOT CAPTAIN BILLY D. RAY---

Was the new Chief Pilot and sounded a litta pissed off. ---Actually he sounded like he was a whole lotta pissed off.

Once again I stretched the truth, ---"I've been in bed for the last three days and can hardly walk."
True or false???---Si or No???

Bill seethed, ---"The ground school instructor just called me and told me that your behavior is very unprofessional."

"Bill, I've got over eight thousand hours in the Electra as Flight Engineer and Co-pilot. ---I know more about the Electra than ten ground school instructors will ever know."

"Well, if you're so hot---be down here at noon. We're gonna give you a Captain's check ride."

???HUH???
"Don't I get any training flights?"
"Get down here at noon and I mean it."

Chief Pilot Captain Billy D. Ray—sounded a litta pissed---no---sounded a lotta pissed.

Got my attention. I poured the rest of my beer down the sink and made some coffee. I needed some caffeine to bring me back to the real world, ---maybe even get some road rage.

I drank some Java and checked out the house to see who was around. My wife and the twins, Kevo and Chel-Chel, were gone but Marky, my seven year old son was in bed asleep.

I called around for a baby sitter and came up empty.

I took a thirty-minute cold shower trying to revive what I had left of my brain and adrenalin. I got out of the shower---I put on some Levi cutoffs---a tee shirt and my dirty tennis shoes.

Marky was now awake and wanting to go fishing.

I told Mark that I had a check ride and to put some clothes on---that he had to go with me---because I couldn't find a baby sitter.

Marky got dressed and we headed for the airport, ---even got there an hour early.

Fortunately, for me, ---Captain Billy D. Ray had to take a flight and was long gone.

---CAPTAIN DON DOLAN---

A newly ordained Check Airman greeted me at the door of PSA Flight Operations.

Captain Don Dolan—A great guy---shook my hand---inquired, ---
"Why did you bring your son along?"

"I couldn't find a baby sitter and I didn't want to leave him alone."

"Fine---Strap him in the jumpseat and let's get going. We only have the Electra for two hours."

I put Marky in the jump-seat and I got in the coveted left seat. Not my covet, but all the other Co-pilot's covet.

I was a happy cuntented Co-pilot.

Chief Pilot Check Pilot Training Pilot Captain Don Dolan---got in the right seat.

SCENARIO

AIRCRAFT---LOCKHEED ELECTRA L188
LOCATION---SAN DIEGO INTERNATIONAL AIRPORT---LINDBERG FIELD
CAPTAIN---*maybe---keep your fingers crossed***---BECK**
CO-PILOT---CHECK AIRMAN CAPTAIN DON DOLAN
FLIGHT ENGINEER---J.P. LEWIS
JUMP SEAT OBSERVER---MARK RESLEY BECK

ACT I

We departed the San Diego International Airport---took up a heading of northeast and headed for the Ontario International Airport which is where PSA did most of our Flight Training at that point in time.

We were about twenty minutes out of San Diego and the SEL CAL went off. Never could figure out what that acronym stood/stands for but it makes a Ding-Dong, Ding-Dong noise like a nervous Avon Lady.
SEL CAL Ding-Dong ---Translation: ---Call PSA Operations.

Flight Engineer J.P. Lewis called PSA Ops---tapped Captain Don Dolan on his left shoulder, ---"They want the airplane back as soon as possible. They just had a mechanical on one of the Electras and they need this one to make schedule."

Captain Don Dolan, ---"We have to go back."

"Shit, Don we're almost there. Can't we just do a couple of take offs and landings and then go back."

I was enjoying my new status being a Captain. Making decisions. My plea fell on deaf ears---
I flunked decision making 101.

Captain Don Dolan was a company man-imal, not a party animal like me.

ACT II

Captain Don Dolan called Los Angeles Center and asked to be rerouted back to the San Diego International Airport.

Los Angeles Center, ---"**IS SOMETHING WRONG?**"
L.A. Center is located in Palmdale, California.

Los Angeles Center was accustomed to our two/three/four/five/six/etcetcetc hour training missions and--- couldn't understand why we were going home.

"Nah, they need the airplane for a scheduled departure."

Los Angeles Center, ---"Turn left to one hundred and eighty degrees---when receiving the San Diego VOR---proceed direct and then you're on your own."

Aviation was "loose as a goose" in those days and not uptight like it is now. ---Has anyone out there in reader land ever felt a "loose goose"?

I cranked the mighty Electra over into a sixty-degree bank--- ignored the assigned heading. ---Dead-reckoned to San Diego"Weigo". ----Didn't lose or gain ten feet of altitude.

I was shit-hot for someone in my dilapidated/dissipated condition.

We landed at the **SAN DIEGO INTERNATIONAL AIRPORT.**

I taxied the Mighty Electra to the gate.

Flight Engineer J.P. Lewis shut down the engines.

We walked into PSA Flight Operations.

Marky was getting restless, ---"Daddy, can we go fishing now?"

I was fighting for my life and all my son wanted to do was to hook a trout. We all have our priorities.

Captain Don Dolan --- Mister Neat Guy —Hearing Marky's words, -—**"If you want to go home---go ahead on.** If you want to finish up, we have an Electra coming in at seventeen hundred hours that we can use to complete the check ride."

I ELECTED TO STAY.

Captain Don Dolan, Marky and I went to the Lost Knight for hamburgers. Don and Marky chowed down on a couple of hamburgers.

I ate an olive and washed it down with gin.

The Electra was late and we didn't get airborne till 1900 hours.

We departed the San Diego International Airport for the Ontario International Airport.

---Onemotime---

Ten minutes out. Same scenario. Dingdongdingdongdingdong and you know it wasn't the Avon Lady.

"SEL CAL"

Flight Engineer J.P.Lewis called PSA Operations and once again tapped Captain Don Dolan on his left shoulder, ---"Ops needs the airplane back ASAP for a scheduled flight."

Don, —"Dadblame it"

I said nothing and racked the Electra in a turn back to the San Diego International Airport.

Marky said nothing because he was in the jump-seat sound asleep.

We landed and walked into PSA Ops.

Captain Don Dolan talked to PSA Dispatcher Mister George Gosselin.

"Beck---Gosselin says that there's an Electra coming in at 2100 hours. If you want to wait for it, we can do the check ride. I think this time we will be able to complete it as there are no more flights out after it gets in.

I looked at Marky who was on the couch sound asleep.

I was the mostest soberest than I had been in the past week, ---

"Sure, I'll wait Don."

I wasn't that tired, but mostly didn't feel like coming back the next day.

Once again we got into the air.

Instead of going to the Ontario Airport, ---we did the check ride at the San Diego International Airport.

Engine chops—fire warnings—hydraulic failures—smoke in the cabin—smoke in the cockpit—stalls—steep turns—one engine inoperative—two engines inoperative— three engines inoperative—and landed on one engine.

I was awesome and my son Marky---was snoring. **We landed at midnight completing a --- TWELVE HOUR UPGRADE TO CAPTAIN CHECK RIDE.**

Captain Don Dolan made out my temporary ATP (Airline Transport Rating) **Certificate.**

**SIX MONTHS AGO I COULDN'T SPELL CAPTIAN
AND
NOW I ARE ONE.**

Captain Don Dolan shook my hand and made a bee-line for the South Seas Bar&Grill. It wasn't too long before the town crier would be shouting, ---"Last Call For Alcohol."

I picked up my sleeping Marky and carried him to the car. I gently laid Marky down in the back seat so as not to wake him.

Didn't work.

"Can we go fishing now daddy?" ---He mumbled and before I could respond---went back to sleep and dreamed of whatever little boys dream of.

I stopped and got a sixer of Brew 102.

My wife wasn't home---a blessing.

I put Markie to bed and popped open a beer.

Once again I passed out on the couch.

**FLYING A TWELVE-HOUR CHECK RIDE---
MAKES FOR ONE HELLUVA LONG DAY.**

Does that qualify me for the Guinness Book of Check Riding Long Necessity?

--- CIRCA ---

10 JUNE 1-NINER-67

"RING---RING---RI-"
I woke up to a ringing phone at 0600 hours.
Hello.
It was Scheduling Captain Spike, ---"We have a Co-pilot trip for you at noon today."

"I'M A CAPTAIN NOW."
"I don't care if you're the Vice Admiral of the fleet; ---get your scrawny butt down here. You're the only one I have to cover the trip."
I took my Markie out to breakfast---went home----suited up for work.
I dropped Markie off at the baby sitters house and went to the airport.
I went into PS A Operations---PSA Dispatcher Mister Ken Rich came up to me, ---"Bill Ray wants to see you and he sounded a little miffed." *MY THOUGHT---"What the fuck have I done now?"*
Oh well---May as well go face "THE PIPE" Music.
*****

THE PIPE---was what we called Chief Pilot Captain Billy D. Ray. When Captain Ray was a litta pissed---smoke billowed out of his pipe.
When Captain Ray was a lotta pissed---it was rumored that he would bite off the pipe stem.
*****

I left PSA OPS and entered head shit shakin' shed.
Aka
CHIEF PILOT OFFICE.

Miss Bonny, the receptionist, secretary and part-time "Co-Chief-Pilot" greeted me with a smirk on her face.
Miss Bonny "Gave me no respect" and she enjoyed watching/hearing me get my butt reamed out, which was oftener than not, when I went up the---**"IRON STAIRS".**
---*So called because it was the egress to the "Pinko" Chief-Pilot Office---*
****

Actually it was kinda nice. You could stand near the stairs and look up ladies dresses as they "ass-cended" and descended the iron stairs --- that is until they installed the **"BEAVER BOARD".**

This hid all crotch shots. --- **"Al-ass"**
*****

"Go right in Captain Beck," Miss Bonny said sarcastically with a shit-eating grin---knowing that I was probably in deep horse pucky.

I entered Bill Ray's office---nervously, still trying to figure out what I had done wrong which could be many——many——many things.

Chief Pilot Bill Ray and Captain Don Dolan, ---who in one night had graduated from **Check Pilot to Assistant Chief Pilot.** -----And

---CAPTAIN RAYNOR KEOUGH---
Check Airman
—ONE OF THE GREATEST PILOTS---
---THAT GOD EVER PUT SILVER WINGS ON---

They were all sitting at their desks. They all had their heads bowed in silence like a prayer meeting at a wake

Nervously—I ATTEMPTED TO MAKE EYE CONTACT.
MY THOUGHT---"Shoot---I'm at a prayer meeting and I forgot my prayer book." ---Furthermore, I felt that the shit was gonna to hit the fan and it was all going to land on me and worse than forgetting my prayer book---**I forgot the toilet paper.**

*****

You're never too rich---You're never too skinny---
And
You never have too much toilet paper.
*****

FAA Examiner Mister Ed Estes —the designated FAA inspector for PSA---entered the room.

We called him "Whispering Ed" because he had a gravelly voice that sounded like a Nicholson File on the edge of a piece of .020 aluminum.

FAA INSPECTOR MISTER ED ESTES walked straight up to me---got as close to me as he could without touching me. ---**Started raging-ragging on me.**

I looked around the room for help but no dice.

Everyone was staring at their desk like they would at a naked girl.

My thought, ----"I'm going to FAA jail". In two and a half words, I was "Scared Shit more".

After five minutes of jumping up and down---hollering---shouting---foaming at the mouth, ---Whispering Ed **UNWHISPERED,** ---

"Let me see your **TEMPORARY CAPTAIN'S CERTIFICATE that Captain Don Dolan issued to you last night.**"

Once again I looked around the head shed for a friendly head shed face. Now the head-shed heads were buried in their head-shed manuals. ---

No help there.

I pulled my wallet out of my back pocket and took the--- **TEMPORARY CAPTAIN'S CERTIFICATE** out---handed it to **UN-WHISPERING ED ESTES.**

WHISPERING ED WAS A-RAGE. Whispering Ed Estes's neck became bigger than his top head and a helluva lot bigger than his bottom head, --- **"Don't you know---that on your initial Captain upgrade---that I have to be there? What the fuck are you tryin' to pull off here Beck?"**

Whispering Ed was completely out of control. His baldhead was as brown-red as an apple that needed peeling---overipely.

Whispering Ed was jumping up and down like a wild man and calling me all kinds of obscenities.

Mister Ed Estes calmed down a little---
Took my Captain's Certificate---
Put it up under my nose---
Ripped it to shreds.

I was stunned---at a loss for a word---frightened.

About that time the head honchos of the head shed dropped their head shed manuals and broke out in head shed laughter.

MISTER FAA FLIGHT EXAMINER INSPECTOR ED ESTES---
Also broke out in laughter.

Chief Pilot Captain Billy D. Ray was laughing so hard that tears were coming out of his pipe.

THE PRICKS HAD SET ME UP.

I was Captain Don Dolan's first Captain Upgrade check out and he had filled out my ATP Certificate wrong.

Mister Ed Estes had to make another one out for me, so they figured that they might as well have some fun doing it---at my expense.

Then everyone come up to me, shook my hand and proffered congratulations. I don't know how sincere they were because they were still in hysterics.

Mister FAA Flight Inspector Ed Estes gave me my **valid** temporary ATP Certificate.

I left.

My juicy 'pits and I went to take what I thought was going to be a Co-Pilot trip.

I walked out of the Head Shed, ---flipped a laughing Bonny the bird and went to the Electra.

CAPTAIN DON DOLAN—followed me out----walked with me.
"**What the fuck ya followin' me for?**"

I was half-pissed and half-amused. *If there can be that state of mind.*

"You're flying Captain today and I'm going with you to make sure you don't get in trouble, —**when you're OFF the airplane.**"

By FAA Regulations---I had to have twenty-five hours of flight time with a Check Pilot in the right seat. Sort of OJT (on the job training) type thing.
Unlike lawyers who practice solo

--- CIRCA ---

STILL THE TENTH OF JUNE---*it's gonna be a long friggin day.*

My emotions now turned to anxiety.
SCENARIO
AIRPLANE---LOCKHEED ELECTRA L188
LOCATION---SAN DIEGO'S LINDBERG FIELD
CAPTAIN---BECK---*me thinks*
CO-PILOT---CHECK AIRMAN Assistant Chief Pilot CAPTAIN DON DOLAN
FLIGHT ENGINEER---CAPTAIN LEE YOUNG
STEWARDESS---MISS DENISE HOLCOMBE
STEWARDESS---MISS KAREN FLAGSTAD

ACT I

We got to the Electra and I climbed in the left seat and in my deepest voice of command ordered **Flight Engineer Captain Lee Young to**------------**"READ THE BEFORE START CHECKLIST."**

Check Pilot Captain Don Dolan, who was now in the right seat---looked at me like I might have a little bit of brain damage from the encounter in the Chief Pilot's Office, ---"Why the deep voice Beck?"

"I'M A CAPTAIN NOW AND I HAVE TO ESTABLISH MY AUTHORITY."

Captain Don Dolan, a very wise man, ---"You have to earn that respect and a low voice isn't the answer."

Now, just to be a smart ass, I did my Carol Channing talk alike and told---**Flight Engineer Captain Lee Young, ---"Start the engines."**

Captain Don Dolan---looked at me---smiled. Captain Don Dolan knew he had created a monster and had to live with it.

We flew a trip to the San Francisco Bay Area and came back to San Diego without any major incident.

ACT II

Captain Don Dolan got out of the right seat.

I inquired as to where he was going as we had another round trip to do. ---"You're safe enough and I gotta meet the bosses at the South Seas Bar&Grill for a late lunch." *Happy hour is always boss.*

My twenty-five-hour-check-ride turned into a three hour Readers Digest version.

CAPTAIN DON DOLAN ---Left. ---Neat Guy.

ACT III

Huck---a new hire Co-pilot came on and climbed into the right seat like an ape gets on a branch of a babboonana tree.

I won't write his name. His nickname was Huck as in the dumb dog in the Huckle Berry hound cartoons.

If you look in the dictionary under the word "Stupid," Huck's picture will be there. Huck was hired sight unseen because his "daddy" was the head honcho of training for Runoff Airlines and PSA was doing Runoff's flight training.

Huck looked over at me and in his Texas drawl, ---"Ah'm going to fly the next three legs and you can have the last one."

"Not so Hucky Baby, it haint going to work that way. Get your lard ass out of that seat and let Lee Young get in it."

Hucky Baby one more time drawled, ---"Ah'm a Co-pilot and besides that, I don't know how to fly Flight Engineer."

Once again I bassoed my voice and said to Huck, ---**"Get the fuck out of that seat or get the fuck off my airplane."**
I passed command decision 101.

He indignantly complied and got out of the Co-Pilot seat and Lee Young got in.

Lee Young looked at me very perplexed, ---after all, ---he was a new hire and didn't expect to get in the right seat for five to ten years.

ACT IV

Co-Pilot Lee Young asked, ---"What do you want me to do?"
"You are going to fly the airplane the rest of the day."
Lee, ---**"Wow, gee whiz."**

Nice guy, Lee Young ---I was glad to help him. Sorta payback time for all the Captains that had let me steal Co-Pilot time when I was a Flight Engineer a couple of years back.
What goes around comes around and paybacks are not always hell.

Now from the Flight Engineer's seat---I hear a lot of pissing and moaning and groaning. Huck was trying to read the checklist. Most of the words were over three letters and he was having a hard time of it.

Comes the "Daun". ---I was not expressing myself well to him and he was from Pensyltucky, Texas.

Altoon, the Flight Engineer from PSA Motel fame had taught me how to talk Pensyltuckytexianan.

I looked around at Huck, ---"Read the mothafuckin' checklist, mothafucka or I'm going to kick your mothafuckin' ass off of the mothafuckin' airplane."

'Nuff said---The Pensyltucky language is basic---but it gets the job done.

Lee Young flew all four legs and did one hell of a job. I was impressed by his aviator's skills because he had very little flying hours and it was all light airplane time.

ACT V

We landed about midnight and **"Co-Pilot Lee Young"** invited us to the South Seas Bar&Grill.

Lee Young averred exuberantly, ---"The drinks are on me and I appreciate the dogdoodoo out of you guys letting me fly all day."

Huck, the bible thumping mothafucka declined saying, ---"I have a wife to go home to and she loves me very much."

*****

A couple of years later she divorced his ass & cleaned his Texas plow. From thence Huck walked around with his Bible in one hand and his dick in the other trying to fuck anything--- No way José--- If Huck was gonna get laid---he had better go back to the best little whorehouse in Texas with his pay check wrapped around his pee pee.
We walked by Huck's motel room one night. Huck had his Bible in one hand and was preaching to a Bible thumping stew. ---Someone shouted---"When ya gonna fuck her Huck?"

*****

ACT VI

Lee Young and I arrived at the South Seas Bar a little after midnight.

Captain Don Dolan, my Check Captain, was still there.

Lee Young and I slid into his booth.

The place was packed and sounded like a giant beehive.

Captain Don Dolan climbed up on the table of the booth---stood up---called for silence.

The Drones and the Queen Bees ceased their Buzzing.

"Sitting next to me is Captain Beck." ---Captain Don Dolan declared.

Now the place became really quiet. Not one person in there thought I would still be with PSA---let alone be a Captain.

They all raised their glasses in a toast to me.

I grabbed Dolan's Martini and toasted them back---gulped it down.

Don was not amused. Don grabbed it back and looked at his empty glass, ---**"You drank my drink."**

"I'LL BUY YOU ANOTHER ONE DON," ---I responded hastily---lest he revoke my Captainship.

About that time, the drinks started coming over to our table.

Everyone in the bar was buying me a drink

At one time---while I was still coherent---I counted ten drinks in front of me. **Being a frugal and a waste not-want not type of guy---I drank them all.**

ACT VII

The bar closed and I started home. I got about halfway home on the Freeway and the lights of a police car and a siren started blaring at me.

I pulled over and got out of "Old Red", ---"What are you shtopping me fer? ---I wasn't speeding." **I indignantly asked.**

"You were only doing seven miles an hour and you were all over the freeway." was his indignant response.

The Police Officer gave me a curbside drunk test.

I flunked with flying colored puke.

The Police Officer handcuffed me---tossed me in the back seat of his PoliceMobile---took me to the San Diego Jail---unceremoniously threw me in a vomitsville-pissed britches cell.

I look back on it now and think he probably saved my life, or better yet, ---someone else's life.

There was a telephone in the drunk tank cell. I called my wife and told her that I was in jail and asked her to come down and bail me out.

She ragged on me for a while as to what a drunken butthole I was and that all my work had been in vain and that I would never be a Captain with PSA---then hung up on me.

I had just spent my last dime. Now I was desperate---a night in the drunk tank with everyone spewing vomit all over the place was not my idea of being in Shangri La.

I went around to all the drunks that were awake and begged for a dime. ---No luck.

I went around to all the passed out drunks and checked their pockets for a dime.

Zippo---N-A-D-A

I then espied a dime in a mountain of puke in the corner. I deftly procured the thin dime---wiped it off on a sleeping drunk's shirt.

*****

I don't mind you shitting on me.
I don't mind you wiping your ass on my shirt, —
But when you complain because I stink.
That's the last straw
Per ---Captain Leland

*****

ACT VIII

I called Captain Shaft Crank

It was 0400 hours. Captain Shaft Crank was groggy from sleep, but obliging, ---"I'll be right down to get you. Don't leave till I get there. *Ha-ha*"

Captain Shaft Crank bailed me out and drove me to my house. I figured I was gonna get a real ass chewin' on the way home. ---Never happened.

Captain Shaft Crank's only remarks, ---**"You haint done nuthin' that any of us have done. You just got caught at it."**

EPILOGUE

Sigh of relief. Thanx Captain Shaft Crank.

"ALL'S WELL THAT ENDS WELL"

PRFPACPJM

— CIRCA —

11 JUNE—1NINER-67

O'dark thirty. ---Throbbing upper head. ---Blaring telephone.
"RING—RING—RI–"
Scheduling Captain Spike, —"Howdy Do"
"Howdy-do" was Spike's trademark in those days.
"Can you be down here in twenty minutes? I need you for a trip. The Captain that was on the trip showed up and was so "sick" that I had to send him home in a cab."

I looked at the clock. ---I only had two hours of sleep.

"I'll be there as soon as I can." ---I was already dressed and could be there in fifteen minutes. I had slept in my uniform and stunk like a multi skirted woman on a Conestoga wagon going across the prairie.

I got to the airport---guess who my crew was. ---Huck and Flight Engineer Lee Young.

Lee Young became instant Co-pilot---Huck became instant Flight Engineer.

Lee Young flew the airplane all day and Huck was starting to like his new job.

I was wiped out---one tired hombre.

We overnighted in San Jose

Lee, Huck and I went out for a couple of drinks. We got back to the motel and found a couple of our Stews wandering around the hallway.

I grabbed one of them and took her to her room.

Young went to his room.

Huck followed us like a Cooper Hound follows a Possum in heat.

Huck sat on a chair across the room---watched the whole operation for over two hours---got up---left.

We checked in the next morning and I asked Huck why he left.

Now this is Texas talking, ---"Ah sat and surveyed the situation and ah didn't think there was anything there for me."

"No shit, Solomon and you fucked it up for me by sitting there for two hours."

"Ah went to my room and ah read my bible and prayed for you people."

"The next time you pray for me---pray that I get laid, which I didn't because you were sitting in that fuckin' chair like a fuckin' vulture half the night."

I decided to let Huck get in the right seat and fly a couple of legs.

We were landing at the Los Angeles International Airport.

Flight Engineer Lee Young read the before landing checklist.

Lee called out an item we had to respond to.

Huck didn't respond---turned around to Lee Young, ---"Ah don't remember that on the checklist."

Lee Young was sitting behind and betwixt us.

When Huck turned around, ---he also took the flight controls with him and put us in a thirty-degree bank less than one thousand feet (1000') above the ground.

I grabbed the yoke and leveled the wings.

Lee once again read an item on the checklist that required our response. Once again---Huck turned around to Lee, ---"Ah don't remember that item on the checklist."

Again Huck put the Electra into a thirty-degree bank, ---only this time we were less than 500' above the ground.

I shouted, ---"I'VE GOT THE AIRPLANE," ---grabbed the yoke---got the airplane under control---I landed.

We taxied to the gate.

Huck was pouting, ---"Ah could have landed it and ah don't like it when someone takes an airplane away from me."

I'm not pouting---but pissed, ---"How in the fuck can you land an airplane when you're not looking at the runway?"

"God saved Daniel from the lion's den."

"Well, you can consider me God and also the Captain of this airliner. ---I saved our ass from crashing in the grass."

We left Los Angeles for San Francisco and once again I let Huck fly.

Everything went well until we were on approach at San Francisco.

I looked at the airspeed indicator and noticed that we're twenty knots slower than we should be for the flap configuration that we were in.

I said to Huck, ---"**You're low on airspeed and you better add some power.**"

Huck's retort, ---"Well if ah can remember right---this chere airplane can fly at this airspeed."

"Huck, you're only ten knots above stall speed."

"Ah know what ahm doin', ---ahm a Co-Pilot."

Well---just about that time---we hit some turbulence from a Boeing 747 and we get the shit kicked out of us. The airspeed decreases and we go into a preliminary stall.

I firewall all four power levers--- (*max gas---pedal to the metal*) ---grab the yoke---get the Electra under control---land.

We taxied to the gate and Huck was pouting again, "Ah was in control of the airplane at all times."

"You've almost killed us twice in the last two hours and you'll never fly my airplane again."

"My pappy told me that I was a good pilot and God would take care of me."

"Fuck your pappy and fuck you, --- **"Do not, and I repeat, do not, ever get in the same Cock-pit with me again."**

He didn't.

I put Captain Lee Young back in the right seat and he flew us home.

"ALL'S WELL THAT ENDS WELL"

PRFPACPJM

*****

*That was the last time that I flew with Huck and I thank my God. The incidents with Huck happened 21 now 22 now 23, now 24 etcetcetc and now in the year 2005---38 years ago and I can't remember what I ate yesterday. Huck is now an airline captain flying big airliners. I suppose he does have a god or he wouldn't be alive today. I know what he looks like, but you don't, so you white knuckled passengers, when you get on an airplane, ask the flight attendant if Huck is the captain and if he is, pray to your God. ---**Your prayers have been answered—Huck retired.***

--- CIRCA ---

END of JUNE---1-NINER-67

SIX MONTHS AGO I COULDN'T SPELL CAPTIAN
---er---captain.
AND
NOW I ARE ONE

I was enjoying my newly found status as a Captain---I even learned how to spell it. Actually, the job was easier than I had imagined it would be and I even had more time to pursue my hobbies.

The Co-Pilot did all the paper **work**
The Flight Engineer did all the **work**
I showed up for **work.**
PEOPLE WERE ACTUALLY CALLING ME SIR
---INSTEAD OF SHITHEAD---
I WAS SOME BODY
MISTER BIG
THE COCK OF THE WALK
THE ACE OF THE BASE
MY CHEST SWELLED SO BIG THAT THE BUTTONS WERE POPPING OFF MY SHIRT.
I looked like Popeye's Wimpy.
EgomanYical MOTHER FUCKER I was.
This lasted all of two weeks

Dispatcher Ken Rich, ---"Captain Bill Ray wants to see you in his office before you go out today."

"Captain Bill Ray???"

"Yea---haven't you heard? ---**Captain Bill Ray** is the new Chief Pilot."

"Oh yea---I forgot ---OK---I'll go on up to his office right now."

I made my way up the iron stairs to the Chief Pilot's Office. ---

First time as a Captain. ---Broke my Captain ego's Cherry.

Chief Pilot Captain Billy D. Ray---

"CAPTAIN BECK---IT APPEARS THAT---*puff-puff on his pipe***---**
ON YOUR FLIGHT ON THE TWENTY FIRST OF JUNE"

"---*puff---puff*---"

"IT IS ALLEGED THAT YOU-----------",
"puff---puff---puff---puff---puff---puff---puff---puff---puff---puff---puff---puff---puff---puff---etc---."

Well so much for the Mister Somebody bullshit---deflated that egomanYiacal attitude in just about ten minutes & twenty puffs. ---SAME OLD SHITHEAD---HAINT NUTHIN' CHANGED---
I left.
From that day forward, ---I always made sure that the egomanYical bullshit didn't become part of my simple job---
---FLYING PASSENGERS FROM A TO B---SAFELY---

*****

Hence the phrase I coined---
"NO MATTER HOW MANY STRIPES YOU PUT ON A JACKASS" "HE STILL HAINT A ZEBRA."
Late that night---I came home and found the place vacated. A note on the refrigerator door read me that the misses had taken the kids to Oklahoma to visit her folks for two months.
I'll miss my children but---**"OH HAPPY DAY---OH LUCKY ME."**
I spent twenty seconds reading the note and went out and hit the bars. If I was to be without my children---I might as well try to enjoy myself.
You've gotta make hay while the sun shines and at this time in my life---I packed one hell of a haymaker.

*****

Worth A Smile
The Blind Pilots
Two men dressed in Pilots' uniforms walk up the aisle of the airplane. Both are wearing dark glasses, one is using a guide dog, and the other is tapping his way along the aisle with a cane. Nervous laughter spreads through the cabin, but the men enter the cockpit, the door closes, and the engines start up.
The passengers begin glancing nervously around, searching for some sign that this is just a little practical joke. None is forthcoming The plane moves faster and faster down the runway, and the people sitting in the window seats realize they're headed straight for the water at the edge of the airport territory.
As it begins to look as though the plane will plough into the water, panicked screams fill the cabin.

At that moment, the plane lifts smoothly into the air. The passengers relax and laugh a little sheepishly, and soon all retreat into their magazines, secure in the knowledge that the plane is in good hands. In the cockpit, one of the blind pilots turns to the other and says, "You know, Bob, one of these days, they're gonna scream too late and we're all gonna go swimming."

*****

I have seen many commercials on television lately advertising pills to alleviate the illnesses that people might have.
Seems to me that some of the side effects are worse than the illness
So I have discovered/invented a **pill** that will---

---CURE YOUR HANGOVER---

Consult your doctor before taking.
Prescription required.

SIDE EFFECTS
Nausea
Throwing up
Headache
Bloodshot eyes
Irritability
The Shits
The Shakes

--- CIRCA ---

---Very early---Morning after---

I got back home at zero-two hundred hours.
"RING---RING---RI---"
It was Joanne, the new hire Stew that I had tried to set Captain John Bull up with.

"Where have you been? I've been calling you all day. I know that your wife is away. I'd like to see you. Are you trying to get rid of me? I don't like the way you're avoiding me."

Now this one I couldn't figure out. I didn't know till a few hours ago that my wife was away and was in awe as to how Joanne knew.

I inquired as to her knowledge of my family's departure.

"I was in my surveillance car---watching your house. When she left---I followed her. She went to the airport and boarded Flight 389 to Tulsa, Oklahoma with your kids. Your wife's parents live in Webber's Falls, Oklahoma and that's where they were going."

Now, I recalled an old grey Cadillac with **DARK TINTED WINDOWS**, sitting across the street---night and day. **The crazy-cunt was spying on me.**

Now I was getting a little concerned as to how this woman knew all this or was she bullshitting me, ---"What airline did they get on?" I asked, hoping to call her bluff.

"American," was her immediate response.

Now I was getting a little more concerned. This was a person that I had a couple of drinks with and she knew everything about my family and me.

I hung up on her and went back to sleep.

--- CIRCA ---

IT'S MAYBE JULY OF 1967

"RING---RING---RI--"
I awakened to a ringing phone at six in the morning. I figured it was "Scheduling Spike" wanting me to take a trip.
Not so. ---It was Joanne again.
"Would you please come over and help me put up a spice rack?"
"Well, when your pecker gets harder than your head---you're in for trouble."
I grabbed my tool box---a six pack of beer---not in that order and went over to Joanne's apartment to put up the spice rack and whatever else I could put up into something spicy.
I walked into Joanne's apartment and was dazzled. Joanne was dressed to the nines.
!!!Black bra---black hose---black garter belt!!!
I could see it all because the white negligee she had on---**WASN'T**.
High heels and all, she looked like she was seven feet tall and very stunning. The sight would have brought a tear to a glass eye and a lesser man would have had a coronary, but I was tough, particularly when I had a hard on---and a six-pack of beer. *Not necessarily in that order.*
We hit the sack and did the "dirty deed".
I tried to get up but she wouldn't let me.
She got up and walked around the bed tantalizing me with her female paraphernalia.
In my haste, I had forgotten to seduce her. *same as taking off her clothes* She still had all her laundry on including her high-heeled shoes.
"I NEED A BEER."
She obliged and brought me one.
I needed nourishment and a replenishment of my ball sack. I gulped it down without breaking continuity of the amber fluid---she brought me another.
This beer I nursed trying to get my libido back.
Once again Joanne strut her stuff around the room. ---
Once again I bounced her bones---passed out.
I woke up around noon and tried to figure out what part of pussyland heaven that I was in.

I did.

I jumped out of bed and called Scheduling Spike, figuring that I was in deep horse pucky. Because---in my haste---I did not let Cap'n Spike know where I was.

Cap'n Scheduling Spike, ---"There's nothing happening here. I got a dozen reserves ahead of you. Take the day off."

I uncorked another beer and relaxed.

Joanne was still asleep and I was one tired puppy.

I watched television for a while and I was going to go home when I finished my brew.

---TOO LATE---

The departure of my choice was negated when Joanne walked out of the bedroom.

Mini skirt and low, low, low neck line sweater.

I had never seen a person who could come alive and change costumes that fast in my life.

When I left her work-stand-bed, she was spread eagled, comatose and in her 100% visibility negligee.

"I'm going to make breakfast for us. Come into the kitchen with me."

I followed like an obedient puppy dog.

When we got into the kitchen---Joanne opened a drawer and pulled out a butcher knife that was so big that it made Sir Lancelot's Lance-a-lot look like a pocketknife.

She started chopping away with the **butcher-er** knife at potatoes and onions.

Not like your thinking. ---She was coming from over her head with **super knife** and slashing them like she wanted to destroy them.

All this time she was looking at me with a grin on her face which was to say the most—**!!!UNFUCKINATURAL!!!**

I started to get a litta nervous, no, a lotta nervous---all of a sudden, ---

---"I'M OUT OF HERE"---

I went to the fridge---got another beer.

If you are going to get stabbed to death---you might as well do it drunk.

Joanne came up behind me and put the knife in my back, ---

"Where have you been?"

I grabbed a whiskey bottle from off the counter and chug-a-lugged it. I wasn't drunk enough to die.

I turned around to a weird sight.

Joanne's eyes were glazed over and she was passing the knife from one hand to another---glaring at me.

Now my being went from nervous to scared shitmore.

Joanne took the knife and put it under my nose, ---**"I want you home here every night." she rasped.**

I was still shaking but was getting some bravado from the whiskey, ---
"I dddddon't live here."

Now Joanne had the knife down near my throat, ---"This is your home and I want you home here every night."

I had visions of my body looking like the potatoes and onions that Joanne had shishkabobbed.

I scarffed down some more whiskey. It helped. I became lotta-bitta-numba & a litta-bitta-brava.

Now she had the knife pointed at my balls and digging into my Levis.

So much for numbness and bravado.

I became stone cold sober and stone cold scared.

When life gets to the nitty-gritty and your balls are in trouble, you had better start thinking ---etcetcetc.

As you are now trying to figure out what the fuck I just wrote???

I said to Joanne, ---"I love our life together and I hope you love me as much as I do you."

That was all it took---Joanne spun around---threw the butcher knife with precision into a kitchen cabinet that was twelve feet away. It shuddered and shook and twanged and finally quit vibrating.

As scared as— I was---impressed. Jim Bowie couldn't have thrown a knife any better.

I feigned interest---went over to the cabinet---pulled out the knife---hoping to keep it away from her, ---"Pretty nice throw."

I looked at the cabinet. ---The kitchen cabinet was riddled with knife holes.

I reckon Joanne had been practicing.

I took the knife and put it in a kitchen cabinet drawer hoping that she wouldn't take offense to me wanting to save my hide.

I went over to Joanne and whispered in her ear, ---"I want to make love to you again."

Joanne was very receptive and started purring---**not like a pussycat, but like a lioness in heat.**

Once again I got scared and told her that I loved her and we would have a wonderful life together.

This calmed her down to pussy purr idle.

Joanne departed to the bedroom to prepare herself for the promised love.

I ran to the door---

Tried to let myself out---

Was running scared---

I wanted to get away from this whacko.

!!!THINK AGAIN!!!
No can/could do.

The door had more locks on it than the Chase Manhattan Bank in New York City.

I could have gotten into their vault easier than getting out of her apartment.

I was like a rat trapped in a laundry room with a cat.

I became desperate---

Opened a window---

Kicked out the screen---

Jumped out.

Good news---Bad news---Good news.

Good news---I was out of there.

Bad news---I was jumping out of a second floor window.

Good news---I landed on top of "Old Red".

He broke my fall. ---I caved in "Old Red's' roof.

What the fuck, he owed me one---after all---I gassed and oiled him all the time.

I slid down the windshield on to the hood---jumped to the ground.

I got in "Old Red", but before I did---I looked up at the window that I had jumped out of.

There was Joanne---white nightie---butcher knife---shouting like a crazy woman.

I took both hands and pushed the "dent" up where my feet landed when I jumped out of the window. ---Not because I cared about the cave in---but because I would have to drive with my head outside the window to drive home---because there was no headroom inside of Old Red.

Head---did you say head?

I put the key in the ignition and "prayed" to "Old Red". "Start now motherfucker or we're both going to die."

"Old Red" started immediately. He felt the anxiety in my voice and knew it was time to get out of Dodge.

I put the pedal to the metal and Old Red and I left the scene.
I felt relieved to get out of the grips of---**"JOANE D' HELL"**.
      ---**Bad news---again---one-mo-time---**
I had driven to a dead-end in the apartment complex and the only way I could get out was to go back the way I came in which was by Joanne's apartment.

I sat for a moment---pondered my fate, ---"How do I get out of here in one piece?"

I locked all the doors and rolled up all the windows, except for one that I couldn't get up. It was the driver's side window. ---Now I remembered that Kevin, my youngest son, had shot it out with a BB gun the week before.

I turned "Old Red" around and once again put the accelerator to the floor, which was like---

---**"PISSING IN THE PACIFIC OCEAN AND HOLLERING FLOOD"**---

I had accelerated up to fifteen miles an hour by the time I got to Joanne's apartment.

Joanne was standing there with butcher knife in hand.

She tossed it at me and it bounced off "Old Red", a life line below my open window.

As Maxwell Smart used to say holding his finger and thumb about one inch apart---"You missed me by that much."

I now had "Old Red" up to twenty---leaving the apartment complex post haste. *I don't know what that means but I was hauling ass.*

I drove down the street about a half mile and a Police Officer pulled me over. He approached the driver's side of the car with gun in hand.

MY THOUGHT---I escaped the crazy woman with a butcher knife in her hand only to get blown away by a snubbed nose Smith&Wesson .38.

The Police Officer walked up to my car door---took one look at me---saw I was harmless---put his gun back in its holster.

I inquired as to why he stopped me.

"I'm Officer Dan and I have been a Police Officer for forty years. I was on a surveillance job watching the apartment complex that you just came out of in a hurry. I thought I saw someone in a white nightie throw something at your car, ---**Just out of curiosity, ---What and Why?**"

I told Officer Dan of kooky Joanne.

Officer Dan, ---"I've been married four times and I've seen a lot of violence, but nothing like that. Get out of the car and get in the squad car. You smell like a Milwaukee Brewery."
   "I can't let you drive in your condition."
"Are you taking me to jail?" I inquired---which all of a sudden seemed like a better alternative than being in Joanne's apartment.
"Nah, I'm going to take you home. I think you've had enough fun for one day."
I got in the front seat of Officer Dan's PoliceMobile and gave him directions to my house. Officer Dan knew where it was because he lived a half a block away from me.
We chit-chatted---I found out that this was Officer Dan's final day on the job.
   !!!OFFICER DAN WAS RETIRING THIS/THAT DAY!!!
Officer Dan also told me that his four ex-wives were taking most of his retirement pay and he had to take a night job at Boney's Supermarket in Ramona, California as a security guard to make ends meet.

*****

This was California Law my friends--- It allows the housewife to sit around the house and eat Bon-Bons and watch Days of our Lives while Officer Dan was out risking his neck. The California judges had awarded most of his pension to them. ---
Alimony--- the fuckin you get for the fuckin you got.

*****

We started down the street that I lived on.
There it was. —
—The grey Cadillac with the DARKENED WINDOWS—
Joanne's surveillance car.
I grabbed Officer Dan by the arm, ---**"STOP"**
Officer Dan pulled over to the curb.
I pointed out the grey Cadillac with the **DARKENED WINDOWS** that was parked a half block down the road.
Joanne had actually beaten us home.
Officer Dan mapped out a game plan---pulled his "38" out of its holster, ---**"This is what we're going to do.** I'm going to pull up behind her and when we stop, I want you to make a bee-line for your house. I want you to go inside and lock every door and window in the house."
   "OKAY BY ME"

Officer Dan put on the siren and every light that a police car can illuminate and we cruised up behind the grey Cadillac with the **DARKENED WINDOWS.**

I started to jump out and then hesitated.
MY THOUGHT---What if she's in the house?

I stayed in the security of the squad car and watched Officer Dan approach the Cadillac on the passenger side. Officer Dan's gun was poised and he was ready for combat. He didn't want to die on his last day on the job.

Joanne emerged from the passenger's side of the car with her hands in the air and spread-eagled her anatomy parts on the PoliceMobile.

Apparently she had been through this before and knew the routine.

I jumped out of the car---ran to my house---got inside---locked everything that had a lock on it.

I peered through a crack in the drapes and watched Officer Dan and Joanne talking.

Joanne was pointing toward my house and was screaming. Officer Dan was making gestures like an umpire at first base indicating,
---"YER OUT"---

Officer Dan was down to his last hours on the police force and was still fighting for his life---sanity.

All my neighbors were out on the sidewalk trying to figure out what was happening.

Joanne got back in her surveillance car with the **DARKENED WINDOWS.**
She left.
Officer Dan came to my front door and I let him in.

Officer Dan took a seat on the couch, ---"That's a beautiful woman---but she's loony as a loon."
Whatever that means

"For a minute, when I was in her apartment trying to find an exit, I thought that she was going to butcher knife me to death."

"I would like to know all the events leading up to the incursion for my report."

I reiterated all that happened from picking her up at ground school till the butcher knife shootout.

Officer Dan's bushy eyebrows went from deep furrows to hysterical laughter.

I had just got through fighting for my balls and Officer Dan thinks it's funny.

All the time I was talking---Officer Dan was filling out his report---laughing—hysterically.

I looked at the clock and it read five minute past four.
OFFICER DAN WAS OFFICIALLY A RETIREE AND A CIVILIAN.

I got up and asked **OFFICER DAN,** who had now become **MISTER DAN**, if I could read the report.

"Sure," ---He said and handed it to me.

I ripped it to shreds.

MISTER DAN's Bushy eyebrows went from laughter---back to deep furrows---back to laughter.

"Officer" Dan dropped the laughter part, ---"What the fuck did you do that for, you dumbshit?"

It was nice to know that we were on a first name basis.

"Look at the clock you fuckin' asshole."
At least I gave him a first & last name
MISTER OFFICER DAN---"!!!I'm off duty forever!!!"

"You betchum Red Ryder---Party time."
Little beaver said

I opened a couple of brew 102's and gave Mister Dan one of them.

Mister Dan took a swig and spat it out, ---**"This tastes like dog piss. Let's go get some real beer. This is my retirement party and I'm buying."**

"Fine with me,"

As Hank Williams's saaang, ---*"If you got the money honey---I've got the time."*

I had the time---was broke---wasn't proud---drank both of the Brew 102s.

We got in Officer Dan's PoliceMobile and proceeded to the liquor store.

**---OFFICER DAN GOT A WILD LOOK ON HIS FACE---
---TURNED ON THE SIREN AND ALL THE LIGHTS---**

Officer Dan finally figured out that he was no longer a police officer and that this was his last hurrah.

We were in a residential section doing seventy miles an hour in a thirty-five mile an hour zone. Cars were pulling over---getting the fuck out of our way.

Mister Dan was doing something that he always wanted to do.

Me---I was alive---for the time being.

We skidded into the Safeway parking lot where the liquor store was located.

Officer Dan drove his blaring squad car right up to the front door of the liquor store.

The owner of the liquor store, a nice guy by the name of Hank, who, as you might have guessed, I knew very well---came running out of the liquor store with his hands in the air.

I jumped out of the squad car.

Hank saw me and put his hands down, ---"What the fuck is happening Beck?"

I explained to Hank about Officer Dan's retirement of forty years and to the fact that we were celebrating.

Hank relaxed and laughed, ---"What do you need, Beck?"

"How's about a case of Beck's Beer and a quart of Jim Beam?"

Actually I slurred the words out but he understood becksbeeralese and put the hooch on the counter.

Officer Dan came walking in, wallet in hand, ---"How much do I owe you Sir?"

"You don't owe me anything Officer. The booze is on the house. Anyone that can spend forty years on the Police Force and still be walkin' deserves a free drink."

MISTER OFFICER DAN said, ---"Thank You."
We left.

MY THOUGHT---The only time I ever got a drink on the house was when I brought a ladder.

Once again we went with sirens ablarin and lights aflashin.

I opened a couple of Beck's Beer and the bottle of Jim Beam. We took a couple of swigs of whiskey and washed it down with the brew.

We turned on to Renkrib Drive. ---The street that housed my house.

I espied it first.---The grey Cadillac surveillance car with the **DARKENED WINDOWS---**

I pointed it out to Dan.

Officer Dan said, ---**"Watch this."**

Officer Dan pulled up behind the mysterious grey Cadillac.

Officer Dan turned on the Police Mobile's loud speaker, ---**"Will the owner of the grey Cadillac please move their car or I am going to have it impounded."**

I saw movement in the car and heard the engine start up. The car pulled away and Officer Dan followed with the siren ablarin' and lights aflashin'.

Meanwhile, every neighbor in the neighborhood was on the sidewalk---watching the action.

I have seen fewer people at the Pasadena Rose Parade.

Dan followed the grey car for a few miles---till the beer can well ran dry.

Mister Dan said, ---"Shall we go home?"

Dan knew he was getting a litta---no---a lotta tipsy and didn't want to roll his PoliceMobile on his last day on the force.

I nodded

Officer Dan headed for my house. I reached over and turned off the siren and all the lights. I had enough attention for one day.

We got back to my house and there was still a large crowd on the sidewalks.

When you live in the "Burbs"---any excitement is better than none.

I instructed Mister Dan to pull into the garage, which was open.

I jumped out and closed the garage door.

So much for nosey neighbors. I will always wonder what they thought that day.

Dan grabbed the quart of Jim Beam and I got the case of brew.

We went into the house. ---We consumed most of the alcohol.

Mister Dan passed out on the couch.

The phone rang and I answered it because I thought it was scheduling.

No answering machine=no call screening

It was Joanne, ---**"WHY AREN'T YOU HOME?"**

Once again I explained to her that I was at home in my own house and that I lived in with my family.

Joanne shouted, ---**"THIS IS YOUR HOME." ---"GET YOUR ASS OVER HERE OR I'M COMING OVER THERE."**

I hung up.

I got a litta---no---a lotta scared.

I tried to awaken Dan, which wasn't about to happen. He was somewhere between the La Brea tar pits and the Carlsbad's Caverns.

I called scheduling which had now become a three man operation.

I got a hold of "Big Fred" ---as opposed to "Little Fred", who was the other scheduler for the night.

I don't know why they called them "Big Fred" and "Little Fred" as they were both the same build, but you can't "tell the players **with a** program" ---unless they're upside down and naked. ---And even then---you can't be sure.

*****

Just like **CAPTAIN JOHN FRAZIER**
Used to say,
"You can't tell the players **WITH** a program."
*****

Big Fred questioned my call, ---"What do you need?"
"I was wondering if you needed any Captains for tomorrow. I would like to take a trip because I'm short of time for the month."
BIG FRED, ---"I thought you were sick."
"What the fuck made you think that?" I said in astonishment.
"We got a call from your wife about two hours ago telling us you were down with the flu and would be out for at least a week. I had a Captains trip all set for you and was about to call you when she called."
"Fred, I'm alive, hale and healthy. My wife is in Oklahoma and she doesn't know if I'm sucking air or not and she could care less."
"Someone's playing a joke on me and I don't think it's a funny one."
"Well I agree with you. The Captain's trip has been assigned to Captain Bull Lett."
"All we have is a Co-pilot trip open that we were going to have to cancel because we have no Co-Pilots. If it's not beneath your Captainship, Your Royal Pain in the Ass Highness, I need you for the trip."
"Do I get Captains pay?"
"Sure, we have no choice," was Big Fred's response.
"I'll take it."
Anything to get away from the raving maniac that was haunting me.
"Be here at 0600 hours. ---I'm signing you in now."
"Thanks," and hung up thinking why does everything have to be at the "Crack of Dawn".
*I once knew a girl named Dawn and she had a pretty nice crack---hence the expression "**The Crack of Dawn.** ---me thinks.*
The phone rang as soon as I put the transceiver in its cradle.
It was Joanne.
"I've been calling you for the last ten minutes and your phone has been busy. Who have you been talking to?"
"ARE YOU CHEATING ON ME?"
"I WANT YOU HOME HERE IMMEDIATELY."

I told her I was talking to scheduling and had an early morning trip. Again I "splained" to her that I was at home in my house and that I wasn't going out for the night because I had an early morning check in.

Joanne shouted, ---**"I'M COMING OVER THERE. I INTEND TO SPEND THE NIGHT WITH YOU. IF YOU DON'T OPEN THE DOOR I'M GONNA KICK IT IN."**

I hung up---scaredly---got my uniform and hat---called a cab---that took me to "Old Red"---boogied to Captain Bob Berson's apartment---that was only ten minutes from the San Diego International Airport.

I pounded on his door.

Bob opened the door as far as the safety chain would allow it, --- "What the devil do you want, Jackie? Do you know what time it is?"

I explained to Captain Bob Berson my predicament and that I was running scared.

"I need a place to lay my head down because I have a 0600 hours check in and that I was out of bucks---that I couldn't afford a motel."

Captain Bob Berson became sympathetic, "Come on in Jackie and let's have a drink---You can sleep on the couch."

*****

Captain Bob Berson---a tall good looking man who all the chicks were after, even pretty lady movie stars, one of which captured Bob, fucked his brains out and then left the party. Who said that all men are created equal?

The movie star left the scene of the "accident" and created another one. The next morning, the Los Angeles Times carried a picture of her face on the front page of their rag. Only trouble was that her face was attached to her head which was "sitting" on top of the hood of her Rolls Royce.

Still a pretty lady.

*****

We had a Scotch and Water.

I told Bob Berson about Joanne.

"Where's she at now?" Berson nervously inquired.

"Probably out in your parking lot watching us," I jokingly said.

Captain Bob Berson was not amused. Captain Bob Berson got up and peered through the drapes, --- "Does she own a grey Cadillac with darkened windows?"

"Yes, that's her." I retorted as the neck hairs on the back of my head bristled. Now I'm not only scared---but scared shitmore, ---"Is she really out there?"

Bob laughed, ---"I know who she is. She used to call here night and day and tell me to come home. Then when I'd hang up on her, she would come over with what she calls her surveillance car and park in my driveway. It got spooky for a while but she finally left me alone."

"I guess I donated her to you."

"Thanks for nothing motherfucker."

Actually, though, that's one of the two reasons that I ran around with Bob Berson.

#1---I'd inherit the ones that he crippled or spurned. ---

The other reason, ---Captain Bob Berson was/is one of the nicest persons that I ever had the pleasure to be around.

I called Scheduling and told Big Fred that I was staying at Berson's for the night and gave him Bob's phone number, ---"Please give me a piss call at zero five hundred hours."

I went to the couch and fell asleep.

--- CIRCA ---

NEXT DAY---??? HOURS

"RING---RING---RI—"

"Hello"

"Yea ---this is Little Fred in Scheduling. **It's ten past six o'clock**. You were supposed to be here at six."

"Oh shit---ok---I'll be there---I'm on the way. I'm at Berson's house---only ten minutes away. I'll be there in fifteen minutes."

"Calm down Beck, ---it's only five thirty. See ya."

Little Fred hung up before I could call him a prick.

I arrived at PSA at 0600 hours.

I flew Co-pilot for a guy named Dan, ---a nervous person who should have been selling shoes at Kinneys and looking up women's skirts instead of flying airplanes.

Not a bad occupation either---Did you say head?

All we had was a trip to San Francisco and back to San Diego, but it seemed like a very long day because this nervous dipshit drove me nuts.

Dan ranted and raved about everything. He was more scared of flying than I was of Joanne.

If that was/is pos-sibley. Dan went out on a medical shortly thereafter. There is a GOD because he would have driven a lot of Co Pilots nuts.

We went into scheduling---

Big Fred, ---"I've got you two scheduled for the same sequence tomorrow."

"Huh-uh, no way Uncle Freddy---haint going to work that way. I've just flown my last Co-Pilot trip and I haint going to do no more."

"Beck, if you don't take the trip, ---we're going to have to cancel it."

"I don't care what you **have to do,** but I'm not flying with this old fuddy-duddy again."

"I'm going to have to report you to the Chief Pilot."

"I don't care if you report me to the President of Fuckin Brazil; I'm not flying with this fuckhead again,"---turned around---went to the-

--South Seas Bar&Grill.

I needed a drink to calm me down because I had become as nervous as Dan was.

That was my last Co-Pilot trip.

In twenty eight years of flying Captain, I never flew Co-Pilot again.

I went into the South Seas Bar&Grill and there was Joanne---all snuggly and cuddly with a "Civilian."

Civilians are non-airline people.

I walked by her booth and she ignored me.

Hallelujah---Jehovah lives.
Lord come through the roof, I'll pay for the shingles.

I had a beer---bought a six pack---went home---walked in the do-de-do-door.

---Went night-night---

--- CIRCA ---

Somewhere in outer space.

"RING---RING---RI--"

I answered Ma Bell---figuring it was Chief Pilot Captain Billy D. Ray---wanting to chew my ass out for not taking that flight.

"Why aren't you home? I'm here waiting for you."

It was Joanne. She was either Houdini or had a twin sister because nobody could have gotten home that fast.

I "fibullshitted", ---"I'm very tired and I am going to take a nap---I'll come over when I wake up."

"Oh, that's wonderful---I can't wait to see you. I love you and miss you very much."

That did it.

I got "Old Red" out of the garage and took him around the block and parked Old Red in my neighbor Jim's driveway which was behind my house and down a small hill.

Jim saw me pull in and came out to greet me.

Nice guy by the name of Jim White---had a pretty wife named Jan White.

"What are you doing here?"

Jim White was curious as to why I drove down to his house because I usually jumped the fence and slid down the ice plant and went to his place when I was out of booze and needed a free drink.

"I just need to park my car here for a while, if it's all right with you."

"Sure, fine with me, but I can't understand why."

Jim White became aware of my nervousness, ---"Come on in the house and I'll fix us a drink and you can tell old daddy Jimmy all about it."

We went into Jim White's house---had a couple of bourbons. I told Jim White of my plight.

Jim White was amused.

Here I am running scared and everyone thinks its fuckin' funny.

I left Jim White's house---crawled up over the slimy ice plant.

Climbed over the fence---snuck in the back door.

I walked in. ---**"RING---RING---RI--"**

I answered it figuring it was scheduling---hoping they were going to give me a trip so I could get out of Dodge.

"I THOUGHT YOU WERE COMING OVER"

It was Joanne. She was irate as hell.

"Oh, I'm sorry my love, I just woke up and was about to call you."

"Bullshit---you fuckin' cheatin' asshole. ---You've been over at your neighbor Jimmy's drinking' bourbon."

She not only knew where I was---but she knew what I was drinking. This woman was getting spookier and spookier.

She not only knew that I was at my neighbors---but she knew his name.

"How come your car is in Jim and Jan's driveway? ---Are you trying to hide from me?"

"Jimmy's a mechanic and he's going to replace my spark plugs."

"BULLSHIT, he's an accountant at the May Company. He doesn't even know what a spark plug wrench looks like."

So much for that lie.

"I'll be over as soon as I can, sweetheart---I've missed you so much."

This calmed her down a bit and she quit screaming in my ear.

"If you're not over here in thirty minutes, I'm coming over there."

Now the words scared shitless went to colon cancer.

I grabbed my uniform---jumped the fence---slid down the ice plant---got in "Old Red".

I drove to Captain Bob Berson's apartment. I was getting away from this crazy woman no matter where I had to go.

Bob opened the door with a shit eating grin on his face, ---"Anything wrong Jackie?"

"You know what's happening you prick---I'm spending the night here whether you like it or not."

Bob knew I was running scared because he had just been through it.

"Come on in Jackie, and we'll have a Scotch and Water and discuss your problem."

"Fuck you. I don't need any bullshit. ---I need a fuckin' drink."

I went into Bob's kitchen and started pouring before he changed his mind.

We had a couple of Scotches and I finally started to relax.

All the time Bob was grinning, because, like a rat, I was caught in the same trap that he had experienced.

"How did you get rid of her?"

"I don't know, one day she stopped calling. ---I never saw her surveillance car outside my window again. I think that's when she came after you."

All of a sudden Bob put down his drink---went over---peered out the window. Bob sensed something that I had no perception of.

Bob turned around---looked at me, ---"She's here and parked behind your car."

Berson was blanched and as white as the tee shirt he had on. By the look on his face I could tell he wasn't fibullshitting me. Now it was obvious that he was as scared of her as I was.

I took a look-see through the window and there she was in loving, living color of grey with **darkened windows** in her surveillance Cadillac.

Bob turned out all the lights---locked all the doors---had us both scared.

We sat down---finished our drinks in **darkness**.

I passed out on the couch.

"RING---RING---RI--"

I answered it figuring it was one of Bob's putang mates that wanted to get serviced.

!!!WRONG!!!

It was Scheduling Big Fred, ---"Beck, we need you here for a trip that leaves in thirty-minutes. Can you make it?"

"How did you know I was here?"

"Your wife called us and told us you were at Berson's and you wanted a trip."

Once again I explained to him that my wife was in Oklahoma and could care less if my lungs were sucking air or not.

"I'll be there."

I put on my uniform which was a white shirt with epaulets and a pair of dark blue trousers and a Captain's cap with enough lightning bolts on the brim to make Thor jealous.

****

Thor was in the heavens---got horny---flew down to earth---found a young lady---fucked her brains out.

Thor became remorseful as to what he had done---

Thor flew back down to earth to apologize to the young lady.

"I'm Thor and I'm sorry for what I did."

"I'm thore too but leth do it again."

I checked outside---The grey Cadillac with the **darkened windows** was gone.

I saddled up "Old Red" and went to work. I didn't even say goodbye to Bob.

I arrived at work and the only parking space I could find was beside the ominous grey Cadillac with **darkened windows**.
Only then did I realize why I got the trip.
Joanne must be on it too and she talked scheduling into giving it to me.

I walked in to scheduling and sure enough, there was Joanne---coffee clutching with a bunch of other stews. ---**"Hi sweetheart,"** she called out to me, "I had a wonderful night with you and it was so nice to have you home."

The Bevy of Quail/Stew looked at me in a state of shock wondering what she was talking about.

I shammed nonchalance---checked in at scheduling---got on the crew bus---went over to the terminal to my airplane.

Co-Pilot Dull Rapper and Flight Engineer Captain Bud Trout were already there---raring to go.

We got in the cockpit and did the before start checklist. A few seconds later the cockpit door opened and there stood Joanne. She looked even taller and more ominous than ever.

"I'm making you fresh coffee my darling, ---just special for you." --She left.

Co-Pilot Dull Rapper and Flight Engineer Captain Bud Trout started grinning and snickering.

Flight Engineer Captain Bud Trout closed the cockpit door, ---"Who is that woman? When I checked in this morning she told me that the Captain was her husband and I know that's not your wife."

I lied to my crew and told them that I had a few drinks with her in the South Seas Bar&Grill and that she just liked to kid around. I neglected to tell them that she threw a butcher knife at me, ---that she was crazy and should be in a loony bin.

The day continued on like this. ---About every ten minutes the cockpit door would open and Joanne would come in and say, "Darling, can I get you some more coffee?"

We didn't lock the cockpit door in those days so all she had to do was turn the door knob to get in the cockpit ---and she came in constantly.

Each time---Co-Pilot Dull Rapper and Flight Engineer Captain Bud Trout would sit there snickering.

I thought about telling them about the butcher knife throwing incident---but declined to do so. They would have went to hysterics and be useless. It was going to be a long day at most.

We were winging our way to San Francisco on the last leg and the whole Bay Area got socked in. We circled for a while and then flew over to Sacramento, which was our alternate, --- about fifty miles away.

We landed---deplaned our passengers **who were in for a long bus ride to the** San Francisco International Airport---**in the Fog.**

I went into Sacramento Operations and pretended that I was making out paper work.

The Crew went to the hotel which was only a short walk---about a half block away.

*****

As
CAPTAIN JOHN FRAZIER---
Used to say---
"Around the corner and up your block"
You figure it out---I never could.
*****

I didn't want to check in with Joanne where she could see my room number.

I gave them plenty of time to check in and went to check in myself. It was close to midnight and the end of a fifteen hour day, which was not uncommon in the 60's.

I keyed the lock and let myself in my room.

In the darkness I could see a human form sitting on the bottom of the bed.

I hurriedly groped for the light switch---turned it on.

!!!JOANNE!!!

How she knew what room I was going to be in or how she got in there, ---I will never figure out.

"Darling, I'm so glad you're home, I've been waiting for you," ---as she took off her coat to reveal a very sexy pussy-pink nightie.

MY THOUGHT--- *"Whatthefuck"*

I hopped into bed with her. If I was going to wake up dead---I may as well do it with an empty scrotum sack.

The next day, on the way home, 1 stopped by a hardware store and bought some more chain latches. I installed them on everything that could be opened---including my fly.

Every once in a while I would peer through the drapes and see the grey Cadillac with the **darkened windows**. I'd look out---it was gone, ---
"RING---RING---RI--"
"WHERE HAVE YOU BEEN AND WHY AREN'T YOU HOME?"
I'd hang up on her with the hair on the back of my neck bristling.
Second verse same as the first---
Car was there---car be gone---ring---ri---
"Where have you been and why aren't you home?"etcetcetc.
Joanne was one spooky lady.

We played cat and mouse for the next month and I was the little grey thing with the long tail.

When I was at work---she was at work---when I was at home---she was parked outside my house with her surveillance Cadillac with the **darkened windows**. When the car was gone---the phone would ring off the hook.

Every once in a while I would get curious and answer it hoping it was scheduling assigning me a trip.

"Darling, why aren't you home, I've missed you so much?"

I'd hang up on her and about ten minutes later the grey Cadillac with the **darkened windows** would show up outside my house. Never could figure that out because it was a twenty minute drive from my house to her apartment and cellular phones---weren't celluring.

My wife and kids came home a week early and I was trying to figure out how to tell her about the phone calls and the grey Cadillac with the **darkened windows**, but before I could, ---
"RING---RING---RI--"

My wife answered it, ---"Hello," she said and got a quizzical look on her face.

I stood there knowing I was in deep horse pucky and going to have to face the music.

"Wrong number,"—Hung up and proceeded to call her girlfriend to go out to lunch with her.

Once again I could visualize the umpire at home plate with outstretched arms, ---!!!SAFE!!!

She left.

No need to service me because as far as she knew---I hadn't been laid in over two months.

Why push things?

I took Mark, Kevin and Shelbi to Disneyland. I hadn't seen my kids in almost two months and I wanted to enjoy them. We had a great time for three days, but I was always looking for Joanne's surveillance car with the **darkened windows**.

We got back home. My wife had made a dinner date with her friends.

"I have to be to work in twenty minutes. I've got to get dressed and get going."

I suited up and went over to Bob's apartment because I still had another three days off on my vacation and no where to go.

I pulled into Bob's parking lot and there it was---the gray Cadillac with the **darkened windows**.

I very silently put "Old Red" in reverse and backed out of the driveway and halfway down the street, ---**"Around the corner and up your block"**---before I turned around.

Apparently, Bob, like a good Australian Aborigine had a boomerang by the name of Joanne and no matter how far he threw her--- she would always come back.

I WAS FINALLY FREE OF HER.
I never saw nor heard from Joanne again.
Puff---the Tragic Dragon Lady
Pissadeared
Quoth the raven ---
"NEVERMORE"

"ALLS WELL THAT ENDS WELL"

PRFPACPJM

*****

"Fatal Attraction"
A movie with Glenn Close and Michael Douglas
I could have written the script from my macabre encounter with Joanne and the grey Cadillac with the **darkened windows**.
*****

--- CIRCA ---

3 AUGUSTO   1NINER67

CELLABRATING SEVEN YEARS WITH PSA

I called **CAPTAIN BERSON** ---let the phone ring forever.
Berson thought it was Joanne and he "wont" about to answer it.
I called Polka Hauntus---called Karmen---with one dime.
I called a few other numbers.
NADA
Not A Damn thing Anyway.
Screw it. ---I put my uniform on the back seat of "Old Red" and we headed for Rosarita Beach in Old Mexico by ourselves.
I stopped in Tijuana on the way---bought a bathing suit.
I went to a local bar where I found out that they hated "Gringos."
*****

T he word "Gringo" ---*originated when cowboys sat around campfires---singing the ballad---"**Green Grows** the Roses"—me thinks.*
*****

The barkeep told me to get out because the natives were getting restless and about to do me bodily harm. ---The barkeep walked out with me and pointed to a bar down the street where touristas were welcome.
I got the hint---went to the other bar---ordered a Margarita---after all, ---**I just didn't fall off the taco truck and I wanted to keep my juevos.**
A young lad about ten approached me and in very poor English, ---"Would you like to fuck my seester, she's a virgin? Only twenty pesos."
"No Senor"---I got up---**I left.**
I had enough excitement for the last two months and getting some kind of venereal mung on my penis would put me in a booby hatch.
I got to the Rosarita Beach Hotel in less than an hour---rented a ten dollar cabana.
I ordered two double margaritas, ---drank them---passed out.
I awakened to a lot of noise around midnight---turned off the lights---carefully pulled back the tattered drapes---looked out the window for the Cadillac with the **darkened windows**.
Talk about paranoia.

The Federales were kicking ass---taking names. They had their burp guns drawn and were herding up all the people that were "laying" on the beach---taking them to jail.

I opened the window a crack to hear what was going on. The Federales were near my cabana and I could hear them clearly, ---"Senor naked guy, we are going to take you to jail."

Senor naked guy, ---"Can I give you the dinero for the fine?"

The Federale, ---"Si Senor---the fine is Eighty American Dollars." *MY THOUGHT---"Shit, fuckin' costs twice as much as driving up-way down a T-Town one-way street." "Shit, how much does the driving up-way down a one-way street fine cost now?" I can't figure out what the fuck I wrote here---I hope you can.*

The naked guy retrieved his trousers---reached in his pocket and took two Jackson's out---handed it to the Federale, ---**"This should take care of it."**

Apparently the guy had been through this before and knew how to bribe these extortionists.

The Federale took the two "score".

"Senor, you don't understand---we are going to take you to jail and it is going to cost you eighty American Dollars."

Now the naked guy was getting a "little panicked". If there is such a state of mind. Spending the night in a Mexican T-Town jail---was---in a word---downrightfucinugly.

Naked, now britches up---fly undone, guy gave the Federale another forty bucks, ---"Will this cover the cost of the fine?"

The Federale took the four twenties and wadded them up into a very small ball so no one could see him take the bribe, ---"Do you want a receipt senor?"

"No Senor,"---the naked guy said, shoes and socks in hand, shirt half on and feet kicking up sand on the way to his car.

Half-naked guy had saved a ten dollar cabana bill but it cost him four "score" to pound sand up his senor-eaters pee-pee on the beach.

The Federale went down the beach looking for new meat and more "scores".

I checked out the back window of my cabana. I was looking in the parking lot for the grey Cadillac with the **darkened windows**. ---

Paranoia had overcome me.

I saw the now un-naked guy get into his souped up '65 Chevy and screech out of El Parkinolotto into the moonlit night.

I reckon that it was his way of telling the Federales to go piss up a rope. He knew that all the Federales had to drive was a worn out World War II Jeep that could barely make thirty miles an hour and that they could/would never catch him.

I lie on the beach for the next three days and body surfed---**RELAXED.** ---Drank margaritas---slept---body surfed---drank Margaritas---slept---body surfed---etcetcetc.

THE CURSE OF JOANNE WAS GONE.
LIFE WAS GOOD---I WAS IN MARGARITVILLE.

I should write a song about that.

I tried to call scheduling. ---NADA

Calling the "States" from "Mehico" or vice versa was an act of God if you could get through. You had to have all nine planets lined up in a row---fifty two Aces up your sleeve and time to siesta.

After two hours of having my ear plastered against the phone, trying to get through to scheduling---**I gave up.**

I put on my uniform---got in "Old Red" ---**I left.**

Adios mothafucka

I had a two hour wait trying to get across the United States/Mexican border. I finally got to PSA a long time after the sun had disappeared out over the Pacific Ocean.

I arrived at scheduling---Chief Pilot/ Scheduler Captain Spike, --- "Where the devil have you been? I've been trying to get a hold of you for three days. I have a charter for you that leaves in thirty minutes."

Captain Spike was pissed---to say the most.

Never did trust a Chief Pilot who was still at work at nine o'clock at night.

I spelled it out for Chief Pilot--- Scheduler---Line Captain Spike or whatever the fuck his pseudonym was. ---**V-A-C-A-T-I-O-N —I've been on vacation.**

"When you're on vacation I still want to be in contact with you in case we run out of Captains."

My Word---"Okay"

MY THOUGHT---"Fuck you"

"Who's the Flight Engineer?"

I didn't care who the Co-Pilot was. If necessary, I could do all the flying, but if you are gonna fly to all the Podunk Airports in the U.S. of A., where the whole town comes out to see you land---you need a good Flight Engineer to keep the airplane in the sky.

"Muldoon"

"Muldoon?"

"Yep, Muldoon"

MY THOUGHT---At least I have the best and we won't get stuck in Bumfuc, Idaho with a---Hemor-hagged-hunk-of-aluminum. Muldoon could fix the hemorrhoids on a gnat's ass with a small screwdriver and a big hammer.

I finally got to the airplane ten minutes before departure. The Co-pilot---name of Ray was in the left seat doing the checklist.

MY THOUGHT---"How nice of him doing my job," because as usual---I was late.

I introduced myself and politely asked him to get out of my chair and to get in the right seat so we could get going.

No way, Jose.

"I'm the Chief Pilot of King's Ranch Resources in the **GREAT STATE OF TEXAS.** My Grand-pappy owns King's Ranch. He told me that ah was supposed to be the Captain on this cher charter.

MY THOUGHT--- "Fuck me---it's almost midnight and I have already encountered two Chief Pilots who should be at the bar drinking moist and chasing moistness."

I slid into the right seat, ---"How much time do you have in the Electra?"

"None, but I have two thousand hours in a Cessna 172."

The Cessna 172 is a four passenger plane with one engine and this "Chief Pilot" was going to be a Captain on a four engine prop-jet airliner without even being checked out on it.

In reality---"Captain" Ray wasn't even qualified to fly Co-pilot on it.

Once again I inquired of his credentials because I thought I misunderstood what he told me.

"I have eight thousand hours as Captain on the Electra and two thousand hours flying a Cessna 172."

Stunned me---This guy had the equivalent of eight years flying the Electra and didn't even know where the "ignition switch" was located.

I slid out of the right seat as gracefully as I slid into it.

I didn't care who flew Captain---but I didn't feel like dieing that night.

I went into San Diego PSA Operations and phoned Chief Pilot Spike.

He was still there.

All work & no pussy makes dick a dull tool.

I told Spike what had transpired.

Spike said, ---"I'll be right over."

I waited in San Diego PSA Operations for Chief Pilot Spike.

"What the heck is going on here? If you don't get out of here in twenty minutes---the curfew sets in and I need you to get to Los Angeles to pick up those passengers and get them over to Phoenix tonight."

Curfew at an airport??? Caused by Vice Admirals in Point Loma that moved there long after the airport was cemented/created.

Brass is ass

Captain Spike was **Pee-OD**.

"Spike---I do not fly Co-Pilot anymore, and for shit-sure----**for someone that isn't even qualified to fly the Electra from any seat.**"

Spike said, ---"His grand-pappy owns King's recourses."

"Fuck you and if you don't get him out of my seat---I'm out of here."

We went up the boarding ramp and into the Electra---Chief Pilot Spike went into the cockpit.

Chief Pilot Ray was still in the left seat and he wasn't about to leave it.

I placed myself strategically in the passenger compartment so I could watch the action.

Now I was watching two Chief Pilots flapping their wings like a covey of quail does when a Red Haired Irish Setter scares them out of the brush.

I watched Ray get out of the left seat and reluctantly slither into the Co-Pilot's seat.

So much for Cessna 172 Chief Pilots Captain-ship-shit.

I got in the "my" seat and looked around at Muldoon who had a shit eating grin on his face.

Muldoon was amused by all the bullshit that had happened.

"Muldoon, have we got enough fuel and is the checklist done?"

Muldoon was in hysterics and couldn't respond---Muldoon could only nod his head.

I took it for a yes and we fired up the engines and got the mighty Electra ready to taxi out.

I told Ray, ---"Ask for taxi clearance and tell them we want to taxi down the runway."

We had to expedite our takeoff because we were only five minutes from the San Diego Airport curfew and we would have to go back to the gate. Then I would have to face the wrath of Chief Pilot Spike if we couldn't get out of Dodge.

Ray was pouting. ---Ray's lower lip looked like it belonged on a pelican. Ray was no longer a Chief Pilot but a lowly Co-Pilot which to him was one notch above a pimple on a well digger's ass.

Ray did not respond, but looked at me with a fuck you look that said, ---"I'm a Chief Pilot and I don't do menial tasks like calling ground control."

I picked up the mike---bypassed ground control---dialed in the tower---told them that we needed clearance for take off.

San Diego International Airport Tower, ---"You have three minutes to get out of here. We're about to close the airport---but for now---you are cleared to takeoff."

I waved off the agent and taxied out at "Mach 2".

I got out on the first intersection which is only half the length of the runway and took off.

Hell, I was taxing so fast that I was almost airborne anyway.

We flew over the Point Loma Vice-Admirals houses about fifty feet above the rooftops.

I looked back at Muldoon and the shit eating grin was gone from his kisser. He knew that I threatened him with death and he wasn't too happy about it.

Flight Engineer Muldoon was always serious about his job and his life---not necessarily in that order.

I looked over at Ray who was a little green behind the gills. He was scared shitmore.

In less than one hour he had shrunk from Chief Pilot status to shriveling wimp Co-pilot unstatus.

We flew on to the Los Angeles International Airport, picked up our human load of cargo and took them to Phoenix, Arizona.

Before we deplaned, ---the head honcho of the charter expedition came into the cockpit and told us that we would depart at 1600 hours the next day.

He left.

---**Party time**---

"Me thinks it's Martini time Muldoon."

Muldoon and I raided the liquor cabinet and took all the litta bottas we could get our grubba litta hands on.

Chief Pilot Ray was in shock and told us that we were stealing from <u>his</u> company.

I looked at Chief Pilot Ray and told him to go fuck himself and that I was the Captain and could do anything I wanted to do on my airplane.

We took a taxi to the Phoenix Marriott Hotel---checked in.

Muldoon and I started chowing down on our contraband in the Marriott Hotel Lobby.

Muldoon looked over our booze stash, ---"Maybe we should invite Ray over to have a drink with us."

That's when I knew that we had plenty of booze because Muldoon never was one to short change himself on the hooch ---or food.

Muldoon called Un-Chief Pilot Ray and invited him to our "party".

Un-Chief Pilot Ray was in the Marriott Hotel Lobby in a matter of minutes. Stealing the booze was against Un-Chief Pilot Ray's moral fiber, ---but drinking it was---AOK.

We partied hearty till dawn.

The last thing I remembered was counting those empty little booze bottles that we finished off. I believe I counted twelve of them ---and all dead soldiers.

To you teetotalers, that means that they were kaput---gone---empty.

We got to the airport at 1500 hours.

UnChief Pilot Ray went into operations to make out a flight plan.

I got into the Electra and secured myself in the coveted left seat before Un-Chief Pilot Ray got in the plane and tried to take it.

I didn't want to ground an airplane in one hundred and fifty degree heat in "Aridzona".

Muldoon did a walk around the Electra and came into the cockpit with a list of squawks as long as his arm and started reading them to me.

I had a hangover as long as his list of squawks and was "hertin fer certin".

I looked around at Flight Engineer Muldoon. ---Muldoon was adorned in a snow-white doctor's smock.

I had never seen a Flight Engineer with a doctors smock on before or since.

I burst out in laughter---told Muldoon that he looked like a DOCTOR.

He got pissed, ---"Do you want to hear these squawks or not?" Muldoon brusquely asked.

"Sure,"---Trying to maintain my composure.

Muldoon read them to me.

I was laughing so hard I was crying.

Have you ever tried to stifle a laugh ---when someone was pissed? Why am I asking? ---Sure ya have---Big Mountain to climb.

We finally got some power on the Electra.

Flight Engineer Muldoon tried to cool it down before our passengers got on.

This didn't work too well because it was one hundred and thirty degrees outside and what with the wind howling at fifty knots---the wind chill factor brought the temperature down to one hundred and twenty nine degrees.

I scanned the instrument panels.

Every red light that pertained to overheat was on.

The hydraulic overheat lights were on.

The engine oil overheat lights were on.

The pressurization overheat lights were on.

The Cockpit looked like a giant RED pin ball machine.

Most of these lights would not illuminate unless the temperature was above 200 degrees Fahrenheit.

Our Electra had sat in the "Aridzona" sun all day and was definitely in heat.

In the words of a Southern Baptist Texan that I know---it was one hot mothafucka.

The passengers boarded and I checked out the cabin. They were fanning themselves with the emergency instructions.

MY THOUGHT--- *"Comes the revolution."*

One passenger started shouting, ---"Cool this mothafucka down."

That's all it took. ---Everyone in the plane started shouting in unison, ---**"Cool this mothafucka down."**

Sort of sounded like the Mormon Tabernacle Choir---only the language was a little different.

Mutiny was eminent---lest we do something.

I looked over at Unchief Pilot Ray for help---Ray was passed out and sweating like he was taking a check ride.

I turned around to Muldoon to see what he had to say about the situation.

Muldoon still had his doctor's smock on and I start laughing again.

Muldoon was not amused.

Muldoon RX smock was soaking wet with sweat and he wanted out of there.

Flight Engineer Muldoon said, ---"If we take off and actually have an overheat in one of the systems, ---we will not know it because all we have are overheat indications. **Let's start 'em up and go---the red warning lights will go out at eight thousand-three hundred feet."**

Now the doctor's smock was no longer funny to me and I started to wonder if Muldoon was "clara-voyant" or maybe some kind of "which" doctor.

We started them up---put the pedal to the metal---left Phoenix, below and behind us.

As we climbed out of 8,300 feet---**Every red overheat warning light extinguished simultaneously**.

I looked around at Muldoon. ---His shit eating grin had turned into a shit eating smirk---that said, "I told you so."

To this day I still think Muldoon made a WAG but I could never get Muldoon to admit it.

WAG---Wild Ass Guess.

We finally got the plane cooled down and flew to Bumfuc, Idaho.

We landed about midnight and the whole town was at the airport watching us taxi in. Of course the population of Bumfuc' Idaho was fifty people---including dogs and kids.

I swaggered out of the airplane like a celebrity and Muldoon followed me.

For just a small moment in history we were somebody.

Muldoon and I got curbside in front of the terminal and commandeered a taxi.

I then realized that something was missing and it wasn't the shit eating smirk on Muldoon's face.

We forgot Un-chief Pilot Ray.

Un-chief Pilot Ray was comatose when we took off.

Un-chief Pilot Ray was comatose when we landed.

We couldn't forget Ray---after all, he had the cab fare and the credit card which was going to pay for our rooms for the night.

Muldoon and I returned to the Electra and dragged Ray out of the cockpit. Ray had been flying four hours and was still incoherent. Ray could have never been a Non-Skeddar.

Ray was somebody and didn't even know it.

We got Ray to the bottom of the ramp.

I looked at Muldoon-- told him that we had forgotten something.

Muldoon looked at me with a question marked face, ---"There's only three of us, who did we forget?"

"We forgot to raid the liquor cabinet."

Muldoon's shit-eating smirk went to a dumb shit look.

Muldoon had forgotten the cardinal rule of Non-Skedding which was that you always borrowed the booze.

Muldoon recovered in a heartbeat. Muldoon went back into the airplane taking three steps at a time up the boarding ramp.

Now Ray was starting to upchuck yesterday's lunch. Ray was lying on the tarmac and wallowing in his own puke.

MY THOUGHT--- *"Ray's a Chief Pilot and he can walk on water---I'm sure he can hop **Scotch** over yesterdays purple hamburger."*

Once again I became Saint Beck, picked him up and leaned him up over the rail of the boarding ramp so he could throw up with style.

Ray passed solid gas. ---Farts with lumps.

I LEFT

Muldoon came out of the airplane with all the booze—in burp bags. They were white and he had so many---along with his white "Doctor Smock"---he looked like Frosty the Snowman.

*****

In case you're wondering what a "Burp Bag" is, it's that little white bag in the pocket of the seat in front of you. If you get a little urpy in flight, you are supposed to toss your tacos in it. Unfortunately, you never have time to grab it when nature calls for you to get rid of unwanted fodder so you just upchuck in the lap of the person sitting next to you.

Now spontaneous combustion sets in--He upchucks in the lap of the person next to him and that person passes it on.

It's like a nauseating chain letter.
!!!!Just kidding!!!
*****

We finally got Chief Stinky Ray in the taxi and proceeded to the hotel.

I got Ray's wallet out of his pocket---found a twenty---gave it to the cabbie. It was a ten minute cab ride and the fare was only three bucks.

---**"Keep the change"**---

After all we were flying for King's Resources which was one of the wealthiest companies in TEXAS, USA at that time, and they could afford it.

*****

Come to think of it, King's Recourses went belly up a couple of years later. I think all their living high on the hog and chartering four engine airplanes and having a Chief Pilot was their demise. I opine---or better yet---me thinks.

*****

Muldoon and I got to the hotel, dragged Un-Chief Pilot Ray into the lobby and threw him on a couch. He curled up into a fetal position and passed out.

Even Chief Pilots need their beauty sleep and for as much as Ray had been snoozing, he should/could be quite gorgeous in the morning.

Once again I borrowed Ray's wallet---took out the company credit card---paid for Muldoon and my Queen Suites. ---and Ray's room.

We woke up Ray and took him to his room.

Once again Muldoon and I partied hearty. Muldoon, being the nice guy that he was/is, ---"What about Ray?"

I told Muldoon that I thought that Ray had joined the Church of the "Later" Day Saints and that he had taken the pledge against drinking.

*****

Dja ever notice that the sins of religions that feel the best are the sins that are sinned the most.

"FORGIVE ME LORD FOR I HAVE SINNED."

*God haint gonna buy that---**we're gonna pay our dues.***

*****

Flight Engineer Muldoon checked out all the miniature booze bottles we had left.

In a heartbeat---Muldoon calculated we had enough for two more nights. Muldoon was always a genius when it came to portion control with the booze---or food.

Muldoon said, ---"Yea, Ray's probably asleep anyway. And besides that, when he's awake---he's a pain in the butt."

We had an "0" dark thirty check in. We went down to the lobby of the hotel before dawn.

Ray was already there, wide awake and not stinky anymore.

We took off and went to Podunk, Texas.

*****

Texans are living proof that Indians fucked buffalos.
I just write what I have heard the Okies say.

*****

After we spent the night in Podunk, we went on to a bunch of Podunk Cities throughout the ---**United States of America.**

Ray was coherent, the weather had finally cleared up and I decided to let him fly a few legs. Before I did, I asked to see Un-Chief Pilot Ray's "Tickets to Fly" and his Medical, not that I really gave a shit, but was curious as to what his credentials were.

	---PRIVATE PILOT SINGLE ENGINE LAND---

Is what it read and Chief Pilot Ray claimed his Medical Certificate was in a dresser drawer back home. This Chief Pilot of King's Ranch Resources didn't even own a Commercial Certificate to fly for hire.

I let "Private Pilot Single Engine Land" un-chief Ray fly anyway. MY THOUGHT---What the fuck, all he was going to do was shake-up a bunch of drunken reality agents. I knew this because one time in flight, I put the auto pilot on and instructed Ray to leave it on and I went back in the passenger compartment to do a little PR work.

The idea of this charter was to look over the North American Landscape and look for real estate to buy or sell. It was 1400 hours and all these guys were either on their ass or passed out. This whole venture was to get away from their wives and try to fuck something in every city we landed at.

	Not to worry. I was getting paid and drinking free booze.

We got to Flat Rock, Kansas and Chief Pilot Ray was flying the Electra from the right seat. It was like an "E" ride at Disneyland. The last time I had felt this many "bumps" was in a bumper car at an amusement park.

The wind was calm and the weather was CAVU, an acronym meaning,

	---"Ceiling And Visibility Unrestricted"---

Which means you can see from Pasadena to Catalina Island when there is no smog, which is rare.—ACTUALLY NEVER—

Chief Pilot Ray was "kicking" in hard left rudder. ---

	Chief Pilot Ray was "kicking" in hard right rudder.

The Electra was sashaying around like a box kite in a gusty wind.

Chief Pilot Ray was pulling back on the yoke and approaching stall speed.

	I looked around at Muldoon.

Flight Engineer Muldoon's eyes were as big as saucers because he knew it was his day to die.

I gently put my knee against the yoke and pushed it forward. We got enough airspeed to maintain flight.

	We landed---

	Chief Pilot Ray greased it on.

Chief Pilot Ray looked over at me, ---"I hope you learned a lesson in flying. ---I can fly rings around you."

Never could figure out what he meant by that, but if I hadn't pushed forward on the yoke, we would have all been pushing up daisies.

The Electra would have been "gears up" in the Sears's parking lot that was on the approach end of the runway that Private Pilot Ray "greased" the Electra onto.

I put Chief Pilot Ray in the left seat.

We departed Flatrock, Kansas and flew to Dallas-Fort Worth, Texas.

Now Ray was doing a hell of a job and flying one Great Electra and I was an awesome instructor.

We landed at Dallas-Fort Worth and once again Ray greased it on.

Luck and God were on our side that day and we survived.

We taxied to the terminal.

Chief Pilot Ray got out of the left seat, ---"I think I've given you enough lessons for one week and I hope you've learned something."

"Where the fuck are you going?"

"I live here and I'm getting off. I've given you enough instruction."

I looked at Muldoon for help.

Muldoon had that shit eating grin on his face because he knew that I was "behind the power curve" because we had to get the Electra back to San Diego before midnight.

The Graveyard Shift Mechanics needed the Electra for a "C" check.

The Electra was scheduled for an early morning departure.

1 told Muldoon to get in the right seat---I sidled into the left seat.

Flight Engineer Muldoon's shit eating grin went to a shit eating grimace.

"I'm not a Co-Pilot and I'm not legal in this seat. --I'm a professional Flight Engineer."

I looked at Muldoon with blood in my eyes, ---"I, as Captain of this chere *(Texan)* airplane am giving you a battle field commission. You are now a Co-Pilot and you're going to fly this chere *(Texan)* hunk of aluminum back home or I'm gonna lie you in state in this chere *(Texan)* Lone Star State. Get the motha-fucka *(Texan)* ready. I gotta go into Ops and make out some paper work. I'm too tired to argue about it."

I heard Muldoon muttering something about being a Professional Flight Engineer.

I left

Muldoon was still muttering about it when I came back on board, as a matter of fact, Muldoon is 60—61—62—63—64—65—66—67—

68—69—70—71—72---73---74---75 and still muttering about it.

Muldoon was 59 when I started writing this chere bullpucky and every time I go back over it we're getting older---he will be 76 in June 2005.

Muldoon flew the Electra and did one hell of a job. At least I think he did because I fell asleep when the landing gears hit the wheel well.

We got the Electra back to the San Diego International Airport and hit the South Seas Bar&Grill.

Chief Pilot Spike was boothed there---waiting for us. Chief Pilot Spike was not a happy camper.

To say the most ---he was one pissed off Spike, ---"Where the devil have you been? I got a call from the Chief Pilot of Kings Resources, name of Ray---he told me that you had departed to San Diego without a Co-Pilot."

"I had a Co-pilot."
"Who?"
I pointed at Muldoon.
"Who flew Flight Engineer?"

"We had a Non-Skeddar that was commuting to San Diego with us and he filled in the blanks."

Spike was grimacing. Spike didn't believe me, ---"Where is this so called Flight Engineer now?"

"How in the fuck should I know? It's not my day to baby sit Flight Engineers."

I glanced at Muldoon.
Muldoon had a shit-eating grin on his kisser.
Muldoon had a shit-eating smirk on his kisser.
Muldoon had a shit-eating laughter on his kisser.
Muldoon had shit-eating tears falling from his kisser.
Muldoon was being a shit-eating butthole.

Muldoon knew that I was back pedaling on a bicycle with stripped gears and treading water in a cesspool.

Spike became more pissed, ---"I want you in my office at 0900 hours tomorrow and we are going to consult the FAA of your actions."

"Fine with me---We are also going to tell them that you are sending out Charters without a qualified Co-Pilot. Ray, the so called Chief Pilot of King's Resources does not have an Instrument Rating, Multi-Engine-rating or even a Commercial Pilot's Certificate. All he has is a Private Pilot's License and the only reason he was flying on a four engine airliner is because he's the owner's grandson. ---Chief Pilot Ray has been on all these charters as Captain and every crew you have sent out on these charters for the last three months will be in violation of FAA Regulations."

Now Spike was starting to smell the stench from the cesspool and became defensive. Spike knew that I had him by the balls and by the look on his face, it was starting to hurt.

One of the Chief Pilot's duties is to make sure everyone is qualified on the airplane and he had simply fucked up by not checking Ray's ratings.
Spike knew he was in deep horse pucky.
Spike was on the same ten speed that I had ridden in on.
Spike was back pedaling it as fast as it could/would go.
Unfortunately, on a ten speed---there are no reverse gears.
Spike uttered, ---"I'm willing to forget this if you are."
I left

"ALLS WELL THAT ENDS WELL"

PRFPACPJM

*****

Private Pilot Single Engine land Chief Pilot Ray's luck in life. He got killed in a Cessna 172 when he ran into a mountain outside of El Paso a few months later.

The NTSB's report, ---"Pilot was apparently getting oral sex and lost control of the aircraft when climaxing and crashed. Parts of the pilot's remains were found in the woman's mouth."

Sorta like coming and going at the same time. ---Use your imagination
*****

*****

—A Muldoon Story—

Flight Engineer Muldoon started out flying Flight Engineer on a **PBY FLYING BOAT** that took off on the Pacific Ocean out of Long Beach and landed on the Pacific Ocean at Avalon Bay at Santa Catalina Island which was---"Twenty Six Miles Across the Sea".

The PBY would fly back and forth between Santa Catalina Island and the Mainland and eventually end up in Long Beach at midnight.

Flight Engineer Muldoon and his wife Jo Anne would work on the PBY in total darkness.

Did I spell Jo Anne right this time Jo? ---probably not.

The prior day's landings on the ocean were like a fat lady doing a belly flop from the high diving board.

The PBY Flying Boat had popped some rivets in the PBY's belly and water was seeping into the bottom of the airplane.

JO ANN would take a flashlight and shine it through these holes. *How's this spelling look? --- Probably not---I'll try this ---***JOANNE**. *One of thems gotta be "write".*

Flight Engineer Muldoon would take a handful of rivets---dive in the Pacific Ocean---swim under the PB Y Flying Boat---see the light--plug them up.

One night, as Muldoon tells the story for the 34-no35-no36-no34etcetcetc time, ---"I gulped a lung full of air and dived under the PBY, put in a few rivets and started to surface for air."

Unfortunately the wind slewed the gigantic aluminum weather vane with wings around.

Because of this---Rivet Buckin' Mechanic Muldoon had got disoriented.

When he tried to get to the surface, ---he couldn't because he was swimming length wise of the PBY. Every time he tried to come up for air, he would hit his head on the bottom of the PBY.

Somehow he figured out where he was and managed to survive the ordeal.

Flight Engineer Muldoon—is 70---NO---71---no---72---73---seventy-four years old now and still flying Flight Engineer for the Non-Skeds. Shoot---Roy Muldoon will be 76 years young this June 2005.

And still flying for the Non-Skeds.

Muldoon is the last of the Buffalo Hunters because all the airplanes being manufactured today are a two man cockpit and the Flight Engineer has virtually became extinct.

FLIGHT ENGINEER BOB JOHNSON
A friend of ours and approaching 70---no71---no---72---no---seventy-three is still flying with the Non-Skeds.
---LAST OF THE BUFFALO HUNTERS---
*****

Now for the big Jeopardy question
How many buffalo roamed the plains of North America in the first years of the eighteen hundreds?

Tell Alex Trubec **eighty million** buffalo & you'll win the bison fur lined shitpot.

So much for buffalo shit which weighs about 20 pounds when it hits the ground.

Any wonder why our land is so fertile & that haint no shit.
*****

"Doc---I want to live to be 100."
"Stop doing Wine Women & Song."
"Will I really live to be 100?"
"I don't know but it's sure as hell gonna seem like it."
*****

For some reason I can't get this page to take some of this bullshit in sequence

So I'm gonna put in some real good stuff on this chere page.

Somewheres at the end of the "Whoring Sixties" and the beginning of the "Sexual Seventies", ---
---PSA was making **BIG BUCKS**---

SCENARIO

"THE IVORY TOWER"

"Hey Joe---what the hell are we gonna do with all the money we're making this year?"

"Shit Mike, ---I don't know. I do know one thing though. If we don't hide it---we are going to pay a whole lot of taxes."

"What say we give our employees a Christmas Bonus Joe?"

"Yea---that's a good idea Mike. How about one hundred bucks for each employee?"

"Yea---let's do that."

SCENARIO

"THE IVORY TOWER"
A few years later.

"Hey Joe---what the hell are we gonna do with all the money we're making this year?"

"Shit Mike, ---I don't know. I do know one thing though. If we don't hide it---we are going to pay a whole lot of taxes."

"What say we give our employees a Christmas Bonus Joe?"

"Yea---that's a good idea Mike. How about one hundred bucks for each employee?"

"Nah---that didn't work last time, ---we still had to pay mega-bucks in taxes."

"I HAD A VISION LAST NIGHT JOE."

"HUH? ---what do you mean by that?"

"FLY---DRIVE---SLEEP"

"WHAAAT?"

Well they did.
PSA bought Hotels and Motels and Rent-a-Car Agencies.
PSA even bought a Hotel on the Hollywood Park Race Track grounds.

---BIG---BIG---BIG losses---
---BIG---BIG---Tax write off---

SCENARIO

"THE IVORY TOWER"
"A few more years later and deeper in debt."
"Saint Peter don't You call me 'cause I can't go."
"I owe my soul to the Company Store."

"Hey Joe this aint working too well."
"Yea ---I know Mike."
"I had another vision last night Joe."
"HUH? ---what do you mean by that Mike?"
"What do you think of a Jumbo Airliner with a Cocktail Bar in the forward baggage pit Joe?"
"HUH?"
"Yea Joe---a Jumbo Airliner with a bar in the forward baggage compartment."
"How will the passengers get down in the forward baggage compartment Mike?"
"I had that in my vision too Joe. ---A spiral staircase."
"What are you gonna do with the passengers baggage Mike?"
"I had that in my vision too. ---Our longest flight is just over an hour long and most of our passengers only have carry on bags---so we'll put all of the baggage in the aft baggage pit."
Well, they did.
PSA bought two Jumbo Jets and put a Cocktail Bar with a spiral stairway in the forward baggage compartment.
Mike and Joe got their wish.
The few months that the two Jumbo Jets flew---PSA got humongous tax write offs.
PSA parked the Lockheed 1011 Jumbo Jets in the desert, after a few months, to the tune of one million dollars a month.

And that ladies and gentleman, boys and girls, is what I call one helluva tax write off.

Shortly after this event---a great gas crunch came upon PSA and PSA was about to go tits up. *Or should I say gears down.*

I talked to the CEO of PSA at that time and he was happy that he was gonna get his golden parachute while the rest of us peons went out looking for jobs.

Stockholders---
You better start looking at these golden parachutes.

I still can't figure out what is happening on this page cause every time I type on it---it goes tits up.

Anyhoo---I'm gonna try writing something on it.

Blonde talking to Blonde, ---"When he said that he wanted me to be the "head of the household", ---I didn't know that it meant that he wanted for me to be giving him head all the time."

*****
Just a little note here on one of our Chief Pilots.
Chief is on an overnight---at the Marriott Hotel---near the Los Angeles Airport.
Chief has a few drinkey-winkeys---Chief gets a little drunkey-wunkey.
Chief is cold---decides to build a campfire.
Chief rips the toilette off of its mounts---builds a campfire in it.
Chief is kicked out of wigwam.
Chief is back to flying airplanes like the rest of us Indians.
*****
---BE KIND TO YOUR CO-PILOT—
---FOR SOMEDAY HE MAY BE YOUR CHIEF PILOT---

CIRCA

A cold night in December.

We landed at Las Vegas one night in a blowing **SNOW STORM.** Yea, you read me right, a friggin' **BLIZZARD.** ---First---last and only time that I have ever seen Las Vegas with snow on the ground.

We deplaned and went curbside to get a taxi. HUH---none there!!!

I went back to PSA's ticket counter and asked the Station Manager by the name of Gordie to call me a cab.

"OK" Gordie said, "You're a cab ---Ha-Ha."

"Just call a taxi for us please."

Gordie went into his office---Came out a few minutes later saying, ---"The taxi is on its way Beck."

"Thanx Gordie---see ya manana."

I went back curbside, got my crew and took them back into a very crowded terminal, saying, ---"Gordie called a taxi for us. Let's wait inside but keep a look out for him. There are a zillion people in this terminal that are wanting a taxi."

Well, we waited and we looked and we waited and looked and we waited and we looked---for two friggin' hours.

We finally got a taxi and motored to the Tropicana Hotel and Casino.

WE FOUND OUT WHAT THE DELAY WAS.

Normally in Las Vegas, all you have to do is walk out the door and two or three taxis are sitting there waiting for your last buck.

The reason for the delay???
THERE WERE ONE OR TWO TAXIS---
PARKED ON EVERY BLOCK ---
ON THE SIDEWALK ---
ON FRONT LAWNS---
---STALLED IN THE GUTTERS WITH WHEELS-A-SPINNIN' ---

Most Las Vegas Cabbies had never driven in snow before, and some had never even seen it up close. The closest they ever came to be around snow was snow capped Mount Charleston ---twenty miles to the west.

--- CIRCA ---

OCHO OCTOBRE---UNO-NINER-SEIS-SIETE

"RING---RING---RI--"
"HOWDY-DOO"
  Captain Spike, ---"Be down here as soon as you can. ---We have a Charter for you."
  "I'm on the way."

SCENARIO;
AIRPORT OF DEPARTURE---San Diego International Airport
AIRPORT OF DESTINATION---San Diego International Airport
AIRCRAFT---LOCKHEED ELECTRA 188
CAPTAIN---BECK
CO-PILOT---CAPTAIN LEE YOUNG
FLIGHT ENGINEER---CAPTAIN DOUGLAS LINEER

---MISSION---
  Fly a bunch of "drinkin" Real Estate Agents from King's Resources around the San Diego, California countryside."
  "**Can't do it Spike**. We have 1,000 foot overcast and the only real estate these people are gonna see are the tops of the clouds. **The only "lots" that they are gonna see are---"lots of booze".**
  "Go anyway, ---they're already half in the bag."
  "OK by me."
  We left. ---We flew.
  As advertised by your local FAA weather-guess-casters, we entered the overcast at 1,000 feet.
  We couldn't fly below the overcast. ---
---FAA REGULATIONS---
  We had to be 1,000 feet above any congested area.
  The terrain in the San Diego Area rises sharply to 200 feet at Torrey Pines Beach Cliffs and as high as 400 feet at Mount Helix and "S" Mountain.
  Both mountains are located about twelve miles from San Diego Airport's Lindberg Field.

We cruised over the overcast for awhile and the Real Estate Agents seemed to be content with their drinky-poos and an occasional visit to the Cockpit with booze in hand.

We **LOCKED** the Cockpit to Cabin door **OPEN** in those days.

The natives grew restless, ---

"I can't shee nuthin' but white. What ish it?"

Thirty minutes flew by---Let the choruses begin, ---

"Wheresh the fucksh the ground? Goddam airline can't get your fuckin' baggage there and I can't shee the fuckin' ground. ---Whatdya do witsh the fuckin' bottle?"

We proceeded out over the Pacific Ocean and let down through the overcast to 500 feet where we were legal by FAA Regulations. --- *500 feet above the water---FAA law---me thinks.*

"Whatsh all this fuckin' water? ---I can't shee anything but water."

I looked at Co-Pilot Captain Lee Young and Flight Engineer Captain Doug Lineer, ---"Fuck it---they paid for real estate and I'm gonna give 'em some."

I cranked the Mighty Electra around in a 60-degree bank---put the standing drunken Real Estate Agents on their ass---proceeded back inland over the La Jolla shoreline.

"Where ya going---Beck?"---Co-Pilot Captain Lee Young and Flight Engineer Captain Doug Lineer said as one, ---**"We're not legal to fly overland."**

"We are if we're going too fast to get the tail number."

"Lineer---give us enough power to maintain 250 knots."

"Young---watch out for light airplanes."

"I'll keep us clear of the high terrain," as we **SPED** over the San Diego

---**"REAL ESTATE"**---

We flew another forty-five minutes.

We landed. ---went into PSA Operations.

Captain Spike was waiting for us**, ---"What the devil have you guys been doin' up there?** The Tower just called me and said that they've got half dozen phone calls from people about a low flying airplane---**AND---AAAAND."**---

!!!**"ONE FROM THE TIJUANA AIRPORT TOWER."**!!!

"DID THEY GET THE TAIL NUMBER?"

"NO"

I left.

"ALL'S WELL THAT ENDS WELL"

PRFPACPJM

*****

Help stamp out prostrate cancer---whack your meat a few times a week.
Help stamp out colon cancer---take a dump once a day.
Help stamp out drunk driving deaths---legalize Mary-juanna.
Help stamp out road rage---ban caffeine.

*****

--- CIRCA ---

9 December—Ininer67

6 MONTHS HAVE FLOWN BY AND I STILL ARE A CAPTAIN

I got a call from Captain Rod Crank---Captain Shaft Crank's brother, ---"Beck, PSA is flying company employees to **LAS VEGAS** for nothing tonight."

"There are three departures."
"One out of San Diego"
"One out of Los Angeles"
"One out of San Francisco"
"I'm flying the trip out of Los Angeles."
"Captain Leland is flying the flight out of San Francisco."
"I'm working the trip out of Los Angeles so I can get out of the house. I signed you up for the trip out of San Diego Weigo."

"What time Rod?" I whispered

"Party time Beck---After the last scheduled flights arrive. We don't get paid for it, but at least we'll have a seat. ---Get out of the house. ---Maybe even get laid."

"OK, SPIKE, I'LL BE THERE. I'M EXHAUSTED BUT IF YOU HAINT GOT ANY ONE TO TAKE THE TRIP, I'LL TAKE THE DAMN THING."---I shouted

Wifey-poo, ---"Who was that?"

"Ahhh, that dad blamed Scheduling Spike. They need a warm body for a Charter tonight and I'm all they got. Damn it, I'm done in. I'm gonna have a couple of beers and go back to bed."

I did.

I checked in a lotta early---just to get out of the house. --- Nobody home 'cept me anyhoo.

I figured that there would be mucho P-S-A-N---S there for ---
---PSA'S FUN FLIGHT TO LAS VEGAS---
Pilots-Stews-Mechanics-Reservation Agents-Station Agents-Baggage Smashers-Ticket-Sellers-Chief Pilots-Check Pilots-FAA Dudes.

NO
---WIVES-HUSBANDS-GIRL FRIENDS-BOY FRIENDS---.

ALL
"LEAVING FOR LAS VEGAS"
I actually had to muscle my way through the crowd.
Full Parade Dress Uniform and Lightning Striked Cap on to get to the front of the crowd.

One Wheel, F. E. Eastcott and his Lug Nuts, would not let me get in a position where I could board first so I could do my job.

I got pissed---The crowd became a mob.
I finally got to the head of the line.
Did you say head???
THE ELECTRA ARRIVED
We left.

Free booze flight---need I say more.
We landed in Las Vegas at 2200 hours.

A---Captain Rod Crank---brought the flight in from LAX.

B---Captain Leland---brought the flight in from San Francisco.

C---Captain Beck---brought the flight in from San Diego.

D---All——Party Time—the above.

My **plan** was to have a Martini and go to bed because we had to get the Electras back to their respective bases by 0600 hours.

---The best laid plans---

Captain Rod Crank and I---aka---"The Wolf Pack"-dubbed on us by Captain John Folting---went hunting.

We baited the traps with Martinis.

Rod ordered the drinks; ---Great---Rod was in heat.

Great---Rod's "pipe" was wanting to get "layed".

Great---"Double martinis for everyone."

Ah yes, they tasted so good---particularly the first one. ---
Who knows after that?

At 0300 hours, someone reminded me that I was supposed to be at the airport.

Time sure flies when you're having fun.

Rod never did get laid---I wasn't drunk---just a little tipsy.

Fortunately---Stewardess Muffie Burke found me wandering around the Marina Hotel Lobby.

Cocktail Waitress Bar Maid Stewardess Flight Attendant Miss Muffie Burke was one of the Stews on my flight and was on her way to the Las Vegas McCarran Airport. Muffie literally poured me into a cab.

*****

Muffie Burke was a cocktail/bar maid/waitress at the Lost Knight Bar & Grill in Point Loma near the San Diego Airport when we first met. Muffie gave me a ration of shit then and never stopped, even when I made Captain. **Right Muffie?**

*****

We arrived at the Las Vegas McCarran Airport around 0500 hours. The cabbie dropped us off at PSA's Terminal. **Nice**---Except the Electra was at the Las Vegas Airport Cargo Ramp which was a Texarkie Mile away.

Muffie pushed and pulled me to the Electra.

I finally staggered into the cockpit---*Now we call them flight stations*-and there was this Co-pilot---*Now we call them 1st officers*---in my seat.

I was pissed.

The Co-Pilot had the Flight Engineer in the right seat---*Now we call them 2d officers*---and he had recruited another crewmember in the Flight Engineers seat.

This Co-Pilot was going to take the Electra back to San Diego without me.

I was starting to become coherent and got halfway pissed, ---

"Hey asshole, get your ass out of my seat—now."

He hesitated momentarily, and then moved his butt where it belonged.

Thank God it was his leg back to San Diego.

When we arrived back to San Diego, ---a pilot friend of mine came up to the cockpit, ---**"Beck, I want to talk to you."**

He was on the flight and saw me staggering across the tarmac.

He followed me out to PSA's parking lot, chewing my ass all the way.

By now, I was sober and the hangover was creeping in. *MY THOUGHT*---Once I get rid of this guy. ---I'm gonna go to the South Seas Bar&Grill and get drunk.

!!!WRONG!!!

He was a tenacious #(*(&^{A}o%%&(

I got in Old Red---
%$*) He got in Old Red---
I got out of Old Red---
$^A&#&% He got out of Old Red.
I started walking---
#%^A&*$&(* He started walking---
I stopped walking---
&(*%^A*())&%%$&()^&%*%$##^A*He stopped walking.
"Where ya goin', Beck?"
"None of your fuckin' business."
"Where are you going, Beck?"
Now I was trying to figure out how to get rid of the mutha&$%*.
"To my girl friend's house."
He was a true blue family man and didn't agree with my happy go lucky ways.
Well I figured that would get rid of him.
---NOPE, NO WAY HOSAY---
"We" arrived at my girlfriend's house and went in.
Then and there in front of her and her roommate---He seemed to take pleasure in---
Reading me the riot act aka reaming my ass out.
He Left.
A---Drinking's fun
B---Partying's fun
C---The I'm sorry for what I said/did last night hangover is not fun.
D---All—oh my fuckin' achin' head—of the above.
And that's my side of the story ---
"I was taking a shit when all this happened."
---CHIEF PILOT SIR---

"ALLS WELL THAT ENDS WELL"

PRFPACPJM
****

*My wife and I were happy for twenty years----**Then we met.***

--- CIRCA ---

FEBRURY 14---1NINER68
HAPPY VALENTINES DAY---GOBBLE-GOBBLE

SCENARIO

AIRPLANE---LOCKHEED ELECTRA L188
CAPTAIN---JACK RESLEY BECK
CO-PILOT---CAPTAIN DOUG LINEER
FLIGHT ENGINEER---CAPTAIN J.P. LEWIS
STEWARDESS---ANN GARAFALO
STEWARDESS---JODIE BRASS

*****

Why do we call Co-Pilots first officers now?
Co-Pilots fly airplanes.
First Officers stand on the bow of the Titanic---inquiring of no one in particular---"What's all that white stuff up ahead?"

*****

AIRPORT OF DEPARTURE---SAN DIEGO
AIRPORT OF ARRIVAL---SAN FRANCISCO

We were about to depart when a Female Boarding agent came up to me, ---"We have an infant in an incubator that has to get to Stanford University Medical Department near San Francisco in a hurry or she's gonna die."

Me---figuring that the Incubator was only a little larger than the infant, figured we could strap the incubator in the frond row seat, ---
---"BRING IT ON BOARD"---
!!!WRONG!!!

We were doing the before start check-list and I happened to glance out my side-sliding-glass-window. The incubator was 4X4X4 and coming up the integral stairs of the Electra along with Doctor and Nancy Nurse.

This was not good. Even in the "Whoring Sixties" it was illegal to put any kind of cargo, large or small, into the passenger compartment.

"Finish the check-list guys, I'll be right back."

I went into the passenger compartment, kicked the people out of their front row seats, took out the removable armrests and directed the infant's small **bedroom** into the allotted space.

It fit ---Snug.

The back of the incubator was tight against the seat backs and the front of the incubator fit tight against the forward bulkhead.

Illegal as hell, but effective.

WE TOOK OFF---GOT AIRBORNE

Somewhere over the skies of Los Angeles the Cockpit door opened. ---**Swiftly**.

It was Nancy Nurse---excitedly, "The incubator has quit working and we have to get to an aid station immediately." She left.

MY THOUGHT---"Oh, shit, I'm in deeeeeep horse pucky."

I started to key the mike to declare an EMERGENCY to land anywhere in the Los Angeles area.

The Cockpit door opened---Un-swiftly.

Nancy Nurse---un-excitedly, ---"You don't have to land. The Doctor got the incubator going again and the baby is gonna be alright."

I put the Mike back in my lap.

They had a helicopter waiting at the San Francisco International Airport for the baby. They got the baby off the Electra before the people started deplaning and were rotoring on their way to Stanford before the last passenger had deplaned.

Very efficient! ---You might say that PSA was the first "Life-Line" Airlines.

A Female Boarding Agent, that didn't like me worth a shit, came up to me with tears in her eyes, --- "That was a wonderful thing that you did. Did you know that what you did is illegal?"

She hugged me and left.

Every time that I arrived at that same boarding gate for the next few months, the same Female Boarding Agent would come out, --- "That was a wonderful thing that you did. Did you know that what you did is illegal? I live near Stanford. ---Every day, on the way home from work, I go into the hospital and check on her."

"She is a beautiful baby and doing well."

Six months fly by---I arrived at that same boarding gate and the same Female Boarding Agent came up to me, with tears flowing down her cheeks.

"The baby died."

I left

alls not well that does not end well

Per me

*****

A TWA STORY

There is a trap door in the cockpit of the Lockheed Super Constellation that leads into the **E&E** Compartment.
(Electrical&Equipment)
The Flight crew decided to play a trick on the Stewardesses.
They put the auto-pilot on, dinged the Stew's call button and crawled down into E&E Compartment.
The Head Stewardess came into the cockpit only to find the cockpit vacant.
Screaming---she ran out of the cockpit---back into the cabin to tell the other Stews.
No big deal---right?
All the Flight Crew had to do was open the trap door and get back to their respective stations before the other Stewardesses came into the cockpit.

!!!NO CAN DO!!!

When the Stew left the cockpit---she left the cockpit door open---
---WHICH WAS OVER THE TRAP DOOR---
Talk about getting **trapped.**
I do not know the rest of the story.
I guess they got out or we would have heard about it on the news.

"ALLS WELL THAT ENDS WELL"

PRFPACPJM

--- CIRCA ---

NINER June---I-niner71
---HAPPY CAPTAIN BIRTHDAY---
Going up the iron stairs---getting my ass chewed out a zillion times
---TO ME---

A CAPTAIN JOHN FRAZIER *story*
AIRPLANE---BOEING 737-200
---One sunny day in June---
Dirty John Frazier and I were flying between the Bay Area and LAX.
To you easterners, ---THE BAY AREA--that's San Francisco (SFO)--San Jose (SJC) and Oakland (OAK).

We had this new Stewardess who was just as nice and sweet as could be. My marriage was pretty much in the dumps by now, so I was being extra nice to her, hoping I might date her sometime.

She was the epit-0-me of sweetness and innocence.

It was the last flight of the day and we had an hour layover.

Dirty John Frazier and I were sitting in the cockpit bullshitting when up comes up this lovely young lady.

"Anything I can do for you two gentlemen?"
Well, you know she's naive when she calls pilots gentlemen.

I, of course, using my best "gentlemanly" smile, ---"Coffee with cream for me please."

Well, good old Dirty John, in only the way he could do it, looked her square in the tit, ---**"Can I stick it your ass for a quarter?"**

She appeared to be in a sate of shock. She looked like someone hit her between the eyes with a 2x4, "What did you say"?
"Can I get a glass of water?"
Very calmly she replied, ---"Oh, that's what I thought you said."
She left the cockpit.

I looked at Dirty John, ---**"Do you have to fuck everything up?"**
Then Dirty John went in to his little song & dance saying, ---
"NEAT—NEAT—NEAT"
Bouncing his seemingly "boneless rubberized" social finger on everything in the cockpit.

—CAPTAIN DIRTY JOHN FRAZIER—

Was real proud of himself---I was a little pissed. ---All that ground work for nil.

Then, this very sweet young thing came back into the cockpit with our drinks. She handed me my coffee and turned to Dirty John---handed him his water, ---

**"JOHN, IT'S NOT WHO YOU FUCK AND SUCK, —
IT'S WHO YOU KNOW AND BLOW."**

Turned around, briskly---left the cockpit---the last that I saw of her.

Oh well---

—YOU NEVER KNOW, YOU JUST NEVER KNOW—

--- CIRCA ---

11 JUNE—1NINER6NINER

And another **CAPTAIN JOHN FRAZIER** *story*
The next day we had a different bunch of stews.
*****

*PS A did not keep the same stews with us for the whole sequence of flights. Sometimes we would fly with 20 to 30 of them on a three or four day trip---***Sorta like a Stew Smorgasbord.**
*****

We had a layover and Dirty John and I were in the cabin talking to three of them.

Well---here comes more bullshit, ---"Hey Beck, are we going to Acapulco tonight or tomorrow?"

After three days with Dirty John, my mind was always a little fried. I was groggy and on the ropes---trying to figure his next words---which even with a clear mind---I could never anticipate any way.

Now Dirty John's got the ladies attention, ---

"My buddy down in Acapulco needs three models and wants me to bring them with us."

Now, he's really got their attention.

Well, I had to play the game.

"Where could we find three models this late?"

Now these three Stews were really getting moist and started to fidget around in their seats.

They were three very pretty ladies. Any one of them could have been a model in her own right.

They all chimed into together, --- "We would be interested in going with you guys."

Now Dirty John gets on a phony defensive, ---"Oh, we couldn't take you into Mexico. You're too young."

This was more bullcrap.

Once again they insisted we take them with us, ---this time more vehemently.

Dirty John, now went on the defensive, --- "If we take you to Acapulco---we can't touch pee pees."

Now, they were really getting excited, thinking we would take them to Acapulco and not try to get into their panties.

One of the Stews, ---"Are we going to be modeling bikinis or gowns?"

Dirty John got this look on his face. ---Which was why he was called Dirty John. ---Which was a very evil leer, ---**"No, little sis—you're going to be modeling gloves."**

I thought that this would piss them off.

No way, Hosay. ---Now they were even more interested.

Now these three stews started looking at their hands---turning them sideways---palms up—palms down.

Dirty John started to chuckle. He was having a field day.

"NEAT---NEAT---NEAT"

Thank goodness, it was time for departure and we had to board the people.

I don't think that even Dirty John could have got out of that one.

"ALLS WELL THAT ENDS WELL"

PRFPACPJM

--- CIRCA ---

HALLOWEEN---1 NINER 6 NINER

One mo **CAPTAIN JOHN FRAZIER** *story*

I found a very hideous, various shades of green---cover the head type, mask on the Boeing 737-200 one dark October night after we landed in San Francisco.

It would have made the kid in the "Exorcist" look angelic.

I donned the mask on the way flying back to San Diego and shone a portable hand held red lens **Aldis Lamp** on it.

I turned my head toward Frazier on that dark October night.

"HEY DIRTY JOHN---LOOK."

Beck you scared me."

"NEAT---NEAT---NEAT"
—**"DING-DING"**—
---**"CLICK-CLICK-CLICK"**---

*****

What is DING-DING???---You might ask.

A button on the overhead panel to call the Stews---One ringy-dingy---pick up the intercom phone---two ringy-dingys---come in the cockpit door.

What is CLICK, CLICK, CLICK???---You might ask.

A button on the center pedestal that locked or unlocked the cockpit door on the Boeing 737.

One click-**unlocked** the door---

Two clicks-**unlock** door-**lock** door---

Three clicks-**unlock** door-**lock** door-**unlock** door.

Most of the time---we didn't have to exert ourselves to reach up to the over head panel to push the ringy dingy button.

We would just hit the **CLICK-CLICK-CLICK-CLICK-CLICK** button on the center pedestal several times and the Stews would come on in the cockpit.

ALDIS LAMP

Aldis Lamp---Def: Actually I don't know what the "Def" is but it was a small hand held flashlight with a curlicue umbilical cord that was connected to the aircraft and had a retractable red lens cover on it.

*****

"Frazier---what the fuck ya doin' calling the girls up here for?"
"Turn your head, Beck," Frazier said as he retrieved his Aldis Lamp out of its socket.
I did.
"What do you guys want now---we're busy?"
Inquired Kathy Lesse as she "slammed open" the Cockpit Door.
!!!"LOOK-LOOK-LOOK."!!!
Frazier shouted, as I turned my head toward Kathy Lessa and Frazier turned the Red Lens Aldis Lamp on my grotesqueness.
STEWARDESS KATHY LESSA
!!!STARTLED!!!
"YOU ASSHOLES"
Turned around and "slammed shut" the Cockpit Door.
"NEAT NEAT NEAT"

SCENARIO:

When? ---The next few months.
Where? ---In the sky.

"NEATNEATNEAT"
"DINGDING"
"CLICKCLICKCLICK"
"YOU ASSHOLES"
"NEATNEATNEAT"

FINAL ACT
"NEATNEATNEAT"
"DINGDING"
"CLICKCLICKCLICK"

---STEWARDESS KATHY COTTON---
Pretty lady
---SCREAMING---SCREECHING---
Jumped backwards---knocked open the Cock-Pit Door with her back side.
Which Frazier forgot to lock with the fourth click.
She bounced fours rows down the aisle on the same backside that---
Kathy Cotton opened the Cockpit Door with.

"NEAT-NEAT-NEAT"

Closing Curtain

No Encore

Another Dirty John story

Dirty John says to a new hire teeny bopper Stewardess, ---"Little Sis---the company wants to know if a Mister Me Hoff is on board."

New teeny bopping Stew says, "What's his first name? I'll see if I can find him."

Dirty John, ---"Jack, his first name is Jack."

The next thing we hear on the Public Address System, ---

"Will Jack Me Hoff please ring his Stewardess call button."

"NEAT---NEAT---NEAT"

*****

I spent all my money on wine, women and song.
*I wasted the rest---***on the stock market***.*

--- CIRCA ---

9 JUNE 1975

HAPPY
PUTTING BIG JIM OWENS IN THE RIGHT SEAT
BIRTHDAY TO ME

SCENARIO

AIRPLANE---BOEING 727-200
DEPARTURE AIRPORT---San Francisco Airport
DEATINATION AIRPORT---Hollywood Burbank Airport
CAPTAIN---BECK
CO-PILOT---GARY "VOLKSWAGEN" VAN WAGNER
FLIGHT ENGINEER---BIG JIM OWENS
STEWARDESS---MISSIS JODIE BRASS
STEWARDESS---MISS NANCY MARCHAND
STEWARDESS---MISS DENISE HOLCOMBE
STEWARDESS---MISSES CAROL CISCO

ACT I

We were ferrying (*no passengers*) from the San Francisco International Airport to the Burbank Airport one **CAVU** day on the Boeing 727-200.

*****

*CAVU---Ceiling And Visibility Unrestricted----Same as **CFS**—Clear Fuckin Skies.*

*****

Twenty minutes out of San Francisco---Co-Pilot, ---Gary "Volkswagen" Van Wagner looked at me, ---"Why don't you let Big Jim land this time?"

Big Jim Owens---our Flight Engineer---was in the process of upgrading to Co-pilot.

I wasn't too keen on letting a rookie land at Burbank. ---
---Short runways and not much room for any screw ups---

ACT II

I looked around at Big Jim, ---"Where are you at in your upgrading to Co-pilot training?"

"I've passed all my simulator check rides and am currently doing line-training."

Line-training is on the job training,--- simply means you go out and fly passenger flights with a Check Airman.

"How many line-training hours have you got Big Jim?"

"Seventy five and I'm still not checked out."

"???SEVENTY FIVE???" ---making sure that I heard Big Jim right.

Eight to sixteen hours of line training was the normal check out time for a Co-Pilot at that time and still is. me thinks

"Seventy Five," was his positive response.

MY THOUGHTS---"Fuck, this guy can't hit a barn door with a bazooka from twenty feet and I'm going to let him fly into the Burbank Airport."

!!!This was no good!!!

ACT III

I looked over at Gary "Volkswagen" Van Wagner hoping Gary "Volkswagen" Van Wagner would show me a head-rotating **NO.** ---A gladiator thumbs down, as to give me some assurance.

NADA.

Not a damn thing anyway

"Switch seats," was my unsure response.

MY THOUGHT---"I'm fucking up."

We were about twenty minutes from the Burbank Airport and I was starting to wonder what I got myself into.

ACT IV

I looked over at Big Jim.

Big Jim Owens was about six foot four and looked like he could wrestle a gorilla and win.

MY SWEATY THOUGHT---"If this big lummox clanks up and freezes on the controls---I'll never be able to take over and land the airplane."

ACT V

I started making ground rules or should I say air rules.

I turned to Big Jim Owens, ---"I'll let you fly us down to fifteen-hundred feet above the ground and then I'll take over and make the landing, ---**Do you understand?"** I asked trying to "cloud" my nervousness.

"Sounds great, thanks for letting me do that much," was Big Jim Owens's response.

I was starting to fidget somewhat.

MY SWEATY PITS THOUGHT--- "If this man can't pass a check ride in seventy five hours, he'll never get us anyway near the airport."

MY THOUGHT---"You can teach a gorilla to fly an airplane if you got a big enough baseball bat and a bunch of bananas."---My problem--- No baseball bat and no bananas.

MY SOLUTION; ---"Jim Owens---I've changed my mind---I'll take over at ten thousand feet."

Big Jim Owens---looking at the endless sky, --- "You're the boss."

I knew that I had hurt Big Jim Owens feelings, but he was being a gentleman about it.

ACT VI

Big Jim Owens clicked off the auto-pilot and commenced our descent.

I expected the airplane to be all over the sky. ---Everything was nice and smooth.

Big Jim Owens descended to ten thousand feet and commenced slowing to 250 knots.

Two hundred fifty (250) knots is maximum speed below ten thousand feet. FAA Regulations.

Big Jim Owens looked over at me, ---**"Your airplane."**

"Continue on Jim, you're doing all right."

Big Jim Owens was doing a damn good job, <u>so far,</u> and I didn't want to destroy his confidence.

ACT VII

We were on approach to Runway 07 at the Hollywood Burbank International Airport---landing to the East---cruising at three-thousand feet.

Big Jim Owens had all the pegs in the right holes making a very nice approach.

Big Jim Owens was plugged in.---*AOK*

I was starting to relax.

ACT VIII
BURBANK TOWER, ---
"PSA 736, break off your approach and circle to land on Runway 15."
???"WHY???" Pissed me off.
Burbank Tower's even more pissed off response, ---"We've got some repair work to do on Runway 07. ---**GO to Runway 15 NOW.**"
Fuck me—"OK"

ACT IX
"Roger, PSA 736 breaking off the approach for Runway 07---Proceeding to Runway 15."
Big Jim Owens looked over at me and said, ---"Your airplane."
"Continue on Jim—You're doing fine."
We had come this far and hadn't dented any aluminum. ---Might as well finish it.

ACT X
Big Jim Owens added power, leveled off at twenty-five hundred feet, made a left turn and headed for the "four stacks". ---A big laundry cleaning plant that was our twenty-five-hundred foot check-point when landing Runway 15.

*****

We would cross the four stacks at twenty-five hundred feet, "as published," put the gear down, put the flaps out and configure to land.

We would then descend to fifteen hundred feet and cross over an "intersection" that consisted of four gasoline stations, turn to a heading of 150 degrees, start a thousand feet a minute rate of descent and land.

We had this down so well that we could do this visual approach when the airport was fogged in and closed to instrument approaches.

I don't know how legal it was, but it worked for us.

Some kind of FAA approved **CONTACT APPROACH** that everyone---

---Including the FAA, interpreted differently for their own convenience---

*****

ACT XI
We were over the intersection.

Big Jim Owens had descended the Boeing 727-200 to fifteen hundred feet---turned to a heading of 150 degrees.

Big Jim Owens, once again said, --- "Your airplane."

"Continue on Big Jim, ---"YOU'RE DOING DAMN GOOD."

My asshole wasn't gnawin' chunks out of the Captain's chair any more and I relaxed.

FINALE
Big Jim greased it right on the numbers.

RUNWAY 15
Big Jim Owens did one helluva job.

I was impressed.

If you can land the Boeing 727-200 at Burbank, you can land it anywhere. ---*that there is a runway*

We taxied to the gate and shut down.

I was a litta perplexed and a lotta upset, ---"How can you sit there and tell me you can't pass your line time check ride and do as good a job as you did coming in here?"

BIG JIM OWENS, ---"Booboo, the check pilot, won't let me land the airplane. We get to the outer marker and he takes the airplane away from me."

"JIM---IT'S TIME TO GET ANOTHER INSTRUCTOR."

I let Big Jim Owens do all of the take offs and landings that day.

Helluva of a job

Big JIM OWENS was/is a good PILOT.

When I got back to San Diego the next afternoon, I stopped by the Chief Pilot's Office and told the Chief Pilot to get Big Jim Owens another instructor/check pilot. I told the Chief Pilot that Jim Owens was a competent pilot and should not be going through all this bullshit because of an egomanYical check pilot.

Chief Pilot, ---"How do you know that Jim Owens is a competent Boeing 727-200 pilot?" ---knowing that I allowed Flight Engineers that were upgrading to Co-Pilot steal some right seat time.

"I know---I just know. Get Jim another instructor ---please."

"I'll think about it Beck---get out of here and go home and get some rest. You look like hammered dog shit."

I left

Big Jim Owens got another check-pilot instructor by the name of Chim.

*****

When Chim was a Co-Pilot, we had a few trips together. He flew an airplane as if he was driving a Mack truck without power steering. He had the finesse of Captain Hook fingering a virgin. Looked like a monkey fucking a football.

Chim & Booboo, --- Big Jim Owens' original check pilot, were buds. They flew in the Military together prior to coming to PSA.

*****

Chim and Big Jim flew eight legs the next day.

Chim let Big Jim land the airplane.

Chim knew he had to pass Big Jim.

Chim was perplexed.

His buddy Booboo had been downing Big Jim seventy-five hours worth and now he had no choice but to pass him.

Chim's words, ---as he signed Big Jim Owens's "ticket to fly", --- "You did a good job today." ---"I don't want to do this but I have to pass you. Booboo told me you were marginal."

That rucking Chim would have ruined Big Jim's career to save face for a "Booboo".

---BIG JIM OWENS EMERGED AS A CO-PILOT---

"ALLS WELL THAT ENDS WELL"

PRFPACPJM

--- CIRCA ---

JUNE 16---1975

ONE WEEK LATER

ONE STORMY MORNING

The Co-pilot hadn't showed up.
I called scheduling and told them we didn't have a Co-pilot.
Scheduling Dale, ---"Big Jim Owens is here in civilian clothes. Do you want him as is?"
"Fuck yea, I'd take him if he was naked."
Who cares what you're wearing as long as your body is warm.
Big Jim arrived and slid into the Co-pilot's seat. Big Jim had a shit eating grin on his face.
Six months ago Big Jim couldn't spell "Co-pylut" and now he are one. By the way, shit eatin' and grin just doesn't seem to jive.
Big Jim was one happy camper.
I looked over at Big Jim, --- "Your leg."
"Thanks, I appreciate your confidence in me."
We were going to San Francisco and the whole Bay area was shitin' and gittin'. Raining and "helling" with a fury. Blowing manhole covers.
Captain Don Stevensen was in the jump seat behind me---commuting home.
Captain Don Stevensen tapped me on the shoulder, ---"Are you aware of what the weather is like in San Francisco?"
"Yep" was my gruff retort.
I knew what Captain Stevensen was getting at. He didn't want the rookie flying in the storm.
"You're still going to let him fly?"
I turned around and looked at Don, ---"Read your fucking newspaper and mind your own "rucking" business."
Never could tolerate anybody in the jump seat telling me how to operate. Some tried and some got kicked out of the cockpit and sat in the back with the passengers.
We arrived in the San Francisco Bay Area.

As advertised, it was blowing manhole covers.

I looked at Big Jim. He was working his ass off---but doing one hell of a good job.

We got cleared for an approach to Runway 19 left---which meant our heading on approach should be one hundred and ninety degrees.

We were still in the clouds.

We locked onto the Runway 19 left approach course.

Our heading to maintain a 190 degree course was 160 degrees. We were crabbing into one hellatious crosswind with a 30 degree correction.

Big Jim was calm---I was smiling---the jump seat rider was not reading his newspaper any more.

We broke out of the clouds at minimums, ---**"There's the runway Jim."**

Big Jim looked out straight ahead, —**"I don't see it."**

"It's at your two o'clock position."

Big Jim looked out his side window---saw the runway---turned toward it.

Not a good idea.

The wind blew us off course and over to Runway 19 Right.

"San Francisco Tower, can we have Runway 19 Right?"

"Roger, PSA 436 is cleared to land on Runway 19 right."

San Francisco Tower had no choice. ---We were only fifty feet above the ground.

Big Jim kicked in full right rudder and put in full left aileron and squeaked it on.

We taxied to the gate.

The jump seater---**Captain Don Stevensen** was telling Big Jim what a good job he had done.

I WAS PROUD AND MY FAITH IN BIG JIM WAS PAID OFF IN FULL.

CAPTAIN JIM OWENS
Is now the
CHIEF PILOT AT USAIR'S LOS ANGELES BASE.

Captain Big Jim Owens is doing a great job and I'm still proud of him.

One other thing, ---I found out later from one of his old girlfriends, that he wasn't called Big Jim because he was tall.

*****
CAPTAIN GARY VAN WAGNER
The Co-pilot that was with Big Jim and me, the day Big Jim landed at Burbank, quit PSA a couple of years later to become a missionary in Africa. The last time that I saw Gary, he was back at PSA trying to get rehired. The last I heard of Gary was that he was flying Co-pilot on a commuter airline somewhere around the Denver area. Good luck---Gary---you're good people.
*****

FLIGHT 182

September 28, 1978

BLACK MONDAY

I was at the San Jose Airport. It was 0600 hours---I had a hangover.

I was down in San Jose PSA Operations talking to Captain Spencer Nelsen and His Crew.

They were flying to the Los Angeles International Airport, and then deadheading home to the San Diego International Airport on PSA FLIGHT 182.

Captain Spencer Nelsen's last flight. ---Captain Spencer Nelsen was retiring that day.

Captain Spencer Nelsen was telling me that he was on his way to a place where he was going to spend his retiring years on the Sea of Cortes in Mexico.

Captain Spencer Nelsen jump seated home on Flight 182.

I had deadheaded from LAX TO SAN on Flight 182 four Mondays prior to and four Mondays after this sad day.

This Monday I was flying through Burbank. *Not good luck---just good timing.*

I left PSA San Jose Operations and boarded my Boeing 727-200 that was going to---

---SAN JOSE—BURBANK—SAN DIEGO---

Per usual---I was late.

I tried to enter the Cockpit. A person was blocking my entry. He was standing in the Cockpit Door with a cup of coffee in his hand. The coffee cup should have told me that he was an FAA dude, but I was sober and wasn't thinking straight.

He was bullshitting with my Crew---

---CO-PILOT CAPTAIN STEVEN SALMONSEN---
&
---FLIGHT ENGINEER CAPTAIN GREG LINDAMOOD---

I thought he was a paying passenger so I was courteous to him. I finally got by him and slid in my seat---asked for the Before Start Checklist.

The dip-shit put his butt in the jumpseat, ---"I'm with the FAA and I'm giving you an en-route inspection."

Great, I'm hungover and I have to put up with this bullshit.
Well now I tried to be professional.
We ran the Checklist according to Checklist Hoyle and we were waiting to push back.
FAA Dude said, **"I want to see your medicals."**
I said, "What the fuck do you want to see our medicals for at 7:00 in the morning? We have a job to do."
---CO-PILOT CAPTAIN STEVE SALMONSEN---
&
-FLIGHT ENGINEER CAPTAIN GREGORY LINDAMOOD-
Showed the FAA Dude their medicals right away
MY THOUGHT---"Fuck you---I'm busy."
On taxi out —thought better of it — reached in my shirt pocket —took my plastic filler wallet out, ---"It's in there."
FAA Dude finally found it, **"This medical is three years old."**
A captain's medical expires after 6 months.
Now, I'm irate. I know I have a current medical---don't know where it is. ---I have to go back to the gate.
I stopped the Boeing 727-200---put on the parking brakes.
Now my iration has gone to pissation. I turned around and asked **Flight Engineer Captain Gregory Lindamood** to look in my coat pocket.
My coat was hanging on the aft side of the Flight Engineer's panel and out of my reach.
Greggy searched my pockets and found my current medical. Greggy handed it to the flaming pain in the ass FAA Dude.
I turned around in my seat, ---"Are you fuckin' happy now?"
FAA Dude nodded but said nothing.
This incident cost us a thirty minute delay. The Wall Street Journal brigade in the cabin now have their papers on their laps, looking over their reading glasses---wondering what was going on. We were the first flight out of SJC and there was normally no delay.
"Is there anything else you want to check?"
"No, I have a meeting at Van Nuys Airport and now I'm going to be late."
The FAA Dude was using the excuse of giving us an enroute check ride just to get to his meeting and then delayed the flight. The FAA Dude felt that checking our medicals was his ticket to ride. It was the FAA Dude's way of justifying him being in the jump seat.

All he had to do was keep his mouth shut. We would have got him to his meeting on time, ---we would have got the Wall Streeters to their meetings on time and I would not have started my day pissed off.

The rest of the flight was uneventful.

The FAA Dude chatted with Greggy & Stevie and was congenial. I was pissed---said nothing.

The ten minute delay had turned into a thirty minute delay--- due to other departures that were normally behind us.

We got to the gate at Burbank and started deplaning.

The FAA Dude got out of the jump seat and headed for the cockpit door. The FAA Dude wasn't even going to say good bye.

Me, ---"Where are you going?"

FAA Dude, ---"I'm going to my meeting."

"You're not doing a complete job. We're going on to San Diego and I want you to go with us."

"Why"? He retorted.

"**PSA** has a record of all our current medicals on file."

One time PSA got in trouble because one of our crewmembers said that he had a medical and didn't. Since that time, the company required that they had a copy of our medical certificate, on file, by the 25th of the month in which we were due.

I then told FAA Dude, "I feel that if you are this interested in medical certificates, ---you should go to San Diego with us---check out PSA's records and make sure everyone is current."

"I'm sure everyone is up to snuff."

"Why in the fuck did we have to go through all this bullshit this morning?"

FAA Dude never answered---FAA Dude shrugged his shoulders---FAA Dude got up and left.

FAA Dude was a Maintenance Inspector. FAA Maintenance Inspector Dude never got in my jump seat again, not by my choice, but by his.

The moral of this story

"Don't piss off a hungover Captain at 0700 in the morning in San Jose." ---FAA maintenance inspector dudes are supposed to sit in the cockpit & keep quiet.

We left Burbank---flew to the San Diego Airport, sans FAA Inspector.

We landed and went over to the crew lounge to check out. I was walking out to my car when this male Flight Attendant in the parking lot started jumping up and down, hollering, ---

!!!"OH-NO OH-NO OH-NO"!!!

I thought he flipped out.

The Flight Attendant had watched PSA Flight 182 going down.

I looked up to the East toward Hillcrest. There was a plume of smoke to five thousand feet.

About this time, everyone was coming out of PSA Dispatch, Scheduling and Crew Lounge, ---

SHOUTING AND HOLLERING.

One of our Crew Members was banging his head against a building. His fiancée was on Flight 182.

A lot of PSA people went up to the wreckage, only a few miles away.

Too traumatic for me to cope with, ---I started home---I had a 45 minute drive.

I stopped off at a liquor store and got some brews---called my wife.

"Why are you calling me?"

"Just to let you know I'm home."

I wanted to save her the trouble of looking for the insurance policies when she heard of the crash. This marriage, my second, was about to go tits up any way. *Actually--- tits down*

By the time I got home, she had heard of the crash from my oldest son, Mark.

Mark lived in a trailer out behind the house and was listening to the radio.

When Mark heard the news, he came into the house, ---

"Have you heard from dad?"

"He just called about ten minutes ago."

Mark then related to my wife about the crash.

When I got home, I proceeded to inebriate my sadness with brew-skies.

About an hour later, **FLIGHT ENGINEER CAPTAIN GREGORY LINDAMOOD** came to the house.

Captain Lindamood was the Flight Engineer on my flight that morning. Greggy started to tell me the names of the people that perished.

I told him that I didn't want to hear it and went into the bathroom and cried.

One of the names he mentioned was **Captain Bill Jolly** --- my best friend.

That hurt.

I found out later that day that Captain Bill Jolly was still alive.

And this is why.

(Next page, please)

--- CIRCA ---

28 September 1978

CAPTAIN---BILL JOLLY
CO-PILOT---CAPTAIN JIM VAN VRANKEN
FLIGHT ENGINEER---CAPTAIN BUD TROUT

Were scheduled to deadhead on Flight 182 to San Diego when they got to the Los Angeles Airport.

They were on push back in San Francisco when Flight Engineer Bud Trout heard something snap in the nose wheel well and said to Captain Bill Jolly, ---"Bill, I don't like the sound of that."

Bill shrugged it off saying, "It's nothing."

Flight Engineer Bud Trout was adamant, ---"I want to go back to the gate and look at it."

Jolly looked at Bud and Vranken, ---"If we go back to the gate, --- we're going to miss our deadhead on Flight 182."

Flight Engineer Captain Bud Trout stood his ground, ---"I want to look at it."

Captain Bill Jolly respected Flight Engineer Bud Trout. Captain Bill Jolly had the Mechanics hook the tow bar back up and pull the Boeing 727-200 back into the gate.

Now all four Flight Attendants were in the Cockpit chastising Flight Engineer Bud Trout because they were going to miss their dead head home on Flight 182.

Flight Engineer Bud Trout didn't even wait for the boarding ramp to be pushed up to the passenger door---jumped---deplaned— went into the nose gear wheel well—found a broken trunion bolt.

If the Boeing 727-200 had taken off and the gear was raised—the nose gear tires would have become kattywampus—stuck in the nose gear wheel well—stayed there for landing.

---WHAT A MAN---FLIGHT ENGINEER BUD TROUT---
Saved his Crew and a Boeing 727-200
DEVOTION TO DUTY
WHAT SAY YOU
*****

An oriental flight attendant had fallen asleep in PSA's Los Angeles Crew---lounge---missed her deadhead home on Flight 182.
All of life or death is a matter of timing.
*****

This was not the only time that
---FLIGHT ENGINEER CAPTAIN BUD TROUT---
Saved
---CAPTAIN JOLLY BILL'S BUTT---
Captain Bill Jolly and Professional Flight Engineer Bud Trout were training Japanese Airlines (JAL) Pilots at PSA's training base at BLYTHE AIRPORT, CALIFORNIA.

SCENARIO

AIRCRAFT---BOEING 727-200
AIRPORT---BLYTHE---IMPERIAL VALLEY, CALIFORNIA
CAPTAIN---"BIIIIILLL" JOLLY
CO-PILOT---CAPTAIN SUMO WRESTLER
FLIGHT ENGINEER--- CAPTAIN BUD TROUT

ACT I

"Trout---turn off the guarded red flight boost switches and let's go on manual reversion. This guys big and we're gonna find out how strong he is."

Turning off the hydraulic flight boost switches puts the airplane on manual reversion likened to driving a Mac truck without power steering.
"OK Bill"

ACT II

Flight Engineer Bud Trout turned off the boost switches.
Captain Japanese Sumo Wrestler put Boeing 727-200 into a right bank.
Good Show

ACT III

Captain Japanese Sumo Wrestler kept Boeing 727-200 in right bank.
Not good show

ACT IV

Boeing 727-200 was almost sunny-side down—on its back.

Shitty show

ACT V
Captain Bill Jolly —
"I CAN'T OVER RIDE HIM BUD— DO SOMETHING"

ACT VI
PROFESSIONAL FLIGHT ENGINEER
CAPTAIN BUD WINNER TROUT
DEFTLY---
Reached up and put the RED guarded hydraulic flight boost control switches to ON.

ACT VII
Only then was Captain Bill Jolly able to override Man Mountain Moto---Put the Boeing 727-200 back to Sunny Side Up.
You're a good man
---PROFESSIONAL FLIGHT ENGINEER ---
---MISTER BUD "NOODLE" WINNER TROUT---
If I were Cap'n Jolly Bill---I would hand cuff myself to you for life.
"ALLS WELL THAT ENDS WELL"
PRFPACPJM

---THE NEXT DAY---I WENT TO WORK—SOBBING---
---SAT IN THE LEFT SEAT—SOBBING---
---LOOKED OUT MY SIDE WINDOW—SOBBING---
---SAW A LITTLE BLUE EYED GIRL KISSING MOMMY AND DADDY GOODBYE---
---GOING TO VISIT GRAMMY---
---ENTRUSTING THAT LITTLE BLUE EYED GIRL TO A---
???PROFESSIONAL AIRLINE CAPTAIN???
---FOR THE FIRST TIME IN MY LIFE I REALIZED THAT I WASN'T AT A PARTY.
I WENT TO WORK---I QUIT DRINKING FOR FIVE YEARS.
---Thank you GOD---

--- CIRCA ---

1-NINER-80

---PSA SCHEDULARS---
---DALE & BIG FRED & LITTLE FRED---
---ASONE---

"You should know that, Beck---you're an Airline Captain."
"I am living proof that that you don't have to be smart to fly airplanes."
"And you guys can go fuck yourself. If you want me to know something---put it in my folder---not on the fuckin' bulletin board."
"I'm on a two man airplane and I don't have time to read the bulletin board when I check in for a flight---and I'm sure as hell not gonna take the time to read the bulletin board when I check out to go home."

*****
Dja ever have a fire ant bite you on the tongue???
*****

Stewardess May B. Stillborn burst into the cockpit---visibly shaken.
"What's wrong?" *I hastily inquired, thinking we may have a major problem.*
"There's a couple fucking underneath a blanket in the last row."
"How do you know they're fucking if they're under a blanket?"
"By the smell---I can tell by the smell."
I pulled a pack of Pall Malls out of my flight bag---handed them to her.
"Give them these when they're through."
Pissed her off---threw the cancer sticks at me---left---slammed the do-de-do-door.

--- CIRCA ---

NINER JUNE---1-NINER-79

SCENARIO

"RING---RING---RI--"
"HELLO"
"HAPPY BIRTHDAY DAD"

ACT I

"Hi dad---this is Mark."

"Yea Mark---What do you need? ---What time is it?"

"Dad---Dya still want to go over to Don and Betty Laughlin's Riverside Casino there along the Colorado River?"

"Yea---I'd like to---What's it gonna cost me? What time is it?"

"Nothing Dad---not a dime---really. ---It's nine thirty."

"Well---this will be the first time. ---What's the deal? What are you waking me up so early for?"

"I have a student that needs some cross-county time."

"**So**---what's that got to do with me?"

"They won't rent him the airplane because he doesn't have enough time for insurance purposes."

"That doesn't make sense---What kind of airplane is it?"

"Twin Engine Comanche."

"Oh---okay---I guess that makes sense. So what you're saying is he needs a warm body with five hundred hours of twin engine time and I'm it."

"Exactly Pops."

"How much twin engine time does he have Markie?"

"Hang on." ---Hey Mark, ---"How much twin engine time ya got?"

"His name's Mark too? ---Good---I might be able to remember it."

"Three hundred and twenty hours Dad---all in a twin Comanche."

"Okay. Where ya gonna pick me up? Do ya want me to come on down to Gillespie Airport?"

"No Dad---we'll pick you up at the Ramona Airport. That way you don't have to drive down the mountain."

"Oh good---yea---that's a great idea---thanks."

"Yea Dad---I figured you like that part of the trip. Same thing coming back. You can get off at the Ramona Airport. I'll come over and go back down to Gillespie with Mark. Just make a pass over the house when you get back and I'll be at the Ramona Airport about the time you taxi in."

"What time do you want me at the **RAMONA** airport for this shindig?"

"Well---by the time you get cleaned up and work your way over there---we should be landing. The airplane is pre-flighted and ready to go. We just have to top off the fuel tanks."

"Okay Mark---see you in a bit---love ya son---bye."

ACT II
RAMONA AIRPORT

"Hey dad---this is Mark Landau. Mark---this is my Dad."

"Nice meeting you Captain Beck---I sure appreciate this."

"You're welcome Mark. ---You can drop the Captain bullshit---just plain old Beck is plenty good. Who's the young lady in the airplane? Is she going with us? I haint sitting in the backseat."

"It's a good friend of Marks, Dad. Her name's Julie. She's very religious so watch your language if you will Pops."

"What the hell dya mean by that Mark? Just kidding Mark Landau---I'll be good."

ACT III
CLEAR #1---C-CHUG-C-CHUG-C-CHUG---VROOOOOM
CLEAR #2---C-CHUG-C-CHUG-C-CHUG---VROOOOOM

"Do you want to fly over to the Bullhead City Airport and I'll fly us back Captain Beck?"

"No Captain Landau---I can't fly these fu---oops---puddle jumpers worth a sh---oops---darn."

"That's okay Captain Beck---say what you want---she's already asleep back there."

"Okay---in that case---drop the fuckin' Captain bullpucky."

"Okay Beck---and away we go."

ACT IV
DON AND BETTY LAUGHLIN'S

"RIVERSIDE RESORT HOTEL & CASINO"

"Here's twenty dollars for you Julie and here's twenty for you Mark---I'm gonna go play some blackjack."

ACT V

"**Where in the devil have you guys been?** I thought you told me that you wanted to be back to the Ramona Airport before dark."

"Well---I did Beck---but guess what---I hit a Royal Flush on the first hand and we took it up to the Racing Book and played the ponies at the race track. We have been there ever since."

"We sorta lost **track** of time---if you'll pardon the pun."

"How dja do at the track?"

"Great---we won another couple hundred---Here's your forty bucks back."

"Thanks---you won big bucks! ---In that case---I'll take it back. Did you have fun Julie?"

"Well---well---it's against my religion. Yes I did have a great time. We're coming back next week. I can't wait---this is a fun place. It seems more like a family place than a Gambling Casino. Seems to me that Betty and Don Laughlin made this place for a family to have fun in more than a Gambling Casino."

"Yea---I like the atmosphere here too. Doesn't seem like the other Casinos that just want to take your bucks and kick you out in the street. I came by here in nineteen seventy-two. All that was here then was a house that Don and Betty Laughlin converted into this Casino. I felt that same homey atmosphere even then. I believe that house is still standing somewhere in the Casino.

ACT VI
BULLHEAD CITY AIRPORT

CLEAR #1---C-CHU-----
CLEAR #2---C-CHU-----

"DAMN IT. Captain Beck---we have a dead battery."

"**I have to get home Mark---I have a zero six hundred check-in in the morning.** Can you hand prop these engines?"

"I don't know---never tried."

I groped under the seats looking for a flashlight, ---"**Look here Mark---a set of jumper cables. What the devil are they doing under the seat? Dead batteries must be a common occurrence with this airplane.**"

"I don't know---this is the first time that I've rented an airplane from this Fixed Base Operator. Your son, Mark, told me that the guy gets his repair work done by an automobile mechanic."

"**Dadblame it Mark---that haint legal.**"

"Yea I know---well---what are we gonna do. Have you ever jump started an airplane?"

"No I haven't. I've hand propped a few before when I started flying. I'm not about to even try hand propping this Comanche.

Look at these jumper cables Mark. They have some sort of cannon plug on one end."

"Yea---I see what you mean---let's get out and see if we can find a receptacle for it Beck."

"**OKAY**"

"**Here it is Mark---right on the nose of the airplane. How convenient. There are some people getting in their car over behind the hangar Mark. ---I feel funny doing this but I'm gonna go ask them for a jump start.**"

ACT VII

"Sir---I hate to ask you this---but can you give us a jump start."

"Sure---no problem---Where's your car."

"Uh---well---uh---Sir---it's not our car---It's our airplane."

"**YOU WANT ME TO JUMP START AN AIRPLANE???**"

"Uh---yes sir---here are the jumper cables made especially for this airplane."

"WOW---Where does that plug fit into?"

"In the nose of the airplane."

"**YOU'RE JOSHING ME.**"

"No sir---that's where it goes."

"Okay---Where's your aircraft?"

"On the other side of the hangar---I'll meet you over there."

"**Okay---wanna ride?**"

"No sir---I feel like I've imposed on you enough---I'll walk."

ACT VIII
"Get in the airplane and start both engines Mark."
"I'll take the cables off---then hop in and **"We're out of here."**
"Okay Captain Beck---Here---give this guy twenty bucks for his trouble."

CLEAR #1---C-CHUG-C-CHUG-C-CHUG---VROOOOOM
CLEAR #2---C-CHUG-C-CHUG-C-CHUG---VROOOOOM

"Let's go home old buddy."
"Okay Captain Beck---let's go home---You know something---Julie fell asleep when we first got here and she hasn't opened an eyelid since."

ACT IX
"Captain Beck---dial in 123.9 and see if there are any other aircraft in the area."

I keyed the mike, ---**"This is Comanche 777**---We're departing Bullhead City Airport on a Southwesterly heading. Any aircraft in this area? ---please respond."

"Guess nobodies out there. Set take-off power for me Beck."
"Take off power is set Mark---Let's go home."
"Gear up."
"Landing Gears are coming up Mark."

"WHAT THE DEVIL HAPPENED??? We lost our instrument panel lights."
"I DON'T KNOW MARK---CAN YOU SEE TO FLY?"
"I can barely see the airspeed gauge---look under the seat and see if you can find a flashlight."
"I've already looked under both seats. ---All that's under there are the jumper cables."
"Better look for traffic out there Beck---I've got my face plastered against the instrument panel so I can see the flight instruments."

"Man---its pitch black out there Mark---I'll make a radio call,"---"This is Comanche 777---we just departed Bullhead City Airport---Comanche 777 is level at---shit Mark---I can't see the altimeter---what's it read Mark?"

"The altimeter's indicating one thousand two-hundred feet Beck."

"Comanche 777 is cruising at one thousand two-hundred feet. Anybody read this transmission?"

SILENT DARKNESS

ACT X

"Hey Mark---looks like the instrument lighting is coming back."

"Yea I see what you mean---guess that at least one of the engine driven generators is operating."

"I'm gonna go back to the airport and land---put the Landing Gear down."

"OK---Gear coming down."

"SHOOT BECK---the lights went out again."

Mark, ---that's what happened when I put the gear up---remember? ---Surely the landing gear isn't electrically actuated---**IS IT???**

"I don't think so Captain Beck---Julie---are you awake? ---see if you can find a flashlight back there."

Julie---groggily---"NO I can't find one---are we having problems?"

"Yes Julie---we're having problems---go back to sleep."

"OK---G-night."

"Mark---there is no indication that the gear is down. The gear down indicating lights are not illuminated---but then again---no other panel lights are illuminated---so I'm not sure if the landing gear is down or not."

"Look out your side window Captain Beck. Can you see if the right gear is down and locked?"

"Nah---it's darker than a well digger's ass. I can barely see the outline of the wheel."

"I'm gonna head for that smoke stack on the other side of the Colorado River---it has a lot of lights around it."

"Okay Mark---are you sure that the landing gear is not electrically actuated. Sure seems funny that every time we actuate the landing gear lever that the lights go out."

"I don't know."

We made several passes around the smoke stack. The smoke stack appeared to be part of an electrical generating plant using the stack to burn off excessive energy of something or other because smoke was billowing out of it and it was making noises like a bull elephant in heat.

After many circles, both left and right, around the billowing and bellowing, we determined that the gear was down and locked.

At this point in time---I asked Mark, ---"Why don't we pull the emergency gear down cable actuated handle to make sure that the gear is down and locked?"

"I don't think that's necessary---when you pull the emergency landing gear extension handle---it rips a lot of aluminum parts off the airplane and it takes a lot of work to put it all back together again."

"I'm gonna pull it anyway Mark---I don't care about aluminum parts as much as I care about my body parts. ---Where's it at?"

"Fly the airplane Beck. I'll take care of it."

I made a couple of 360s around the horny stacks while Mark tugged at the emergency gear extension handle.

"I can't budge it Beck. I'm going to go back to the Bullhead City Airport and land. We haven't got enough fuel to proceed on to San Diego with the gear down."

"Okay"

"As we get closer to the lights of the Casinos---I'm going to have my face plastered against the instrument panel. I'm going to start my approach about seven miles out and start a shallow sink rate. At this time---I want you to watch and tell me if I'm too high or too low. Then---I will adjust my rate of sink accordingly---is that okay with you?"

"Okay Mark"

"YOU'RE TOO HIGH---YOU'RE TOO LOW---YOU'RE TOO HIGH---YOU'RE STILLTOO HIGH---CORRECTING NICELY---YOU'RE ON GLIDE SLOPE---YOU'RE GETTING A LITTLE LOW---

YOU'RE ON GLIDE SLOPE---YOU'RE STILL ON GLIDE SLOPE---OK MARK---HOLD THAT RATE OF SINK." ---
"THAT SHOULD GET YOU RIGHT ON THE NUMBERS."

At this point in time---Mark raised his head up from the instrument panel and, ---
"Greased the Comanche right on the numbers."

squeak   squeak

squeak

"Ahhh---how sweet it is---thank god that's over."

---tictictictictictictictictictictictic---
The sound the propellers make when the landing gear collapses.
SCRAAAAAAAAAAAAAAAAPE SCRUNCH
The sound the airplane makes after you hear *tictictictic*.
---WE STOPPED---A LITTLE DAZED---

Up till this time---Julie sat in the back seat---uttered not a word.
At this time---Julie was out of the back seat---came over the top of my seat and my body---was out my door just as the Comanche came to a screeching ass halt.
Mark and I sat there for a few moments---in shock.
"Mark---Let's go back over to the Riverside Casino and do some more gambling. Right now I don't feel like we have anything to lose."
"Okaaay"

*****

The one thing that I remember most as the Comanche came to a screeching ass halt---was the heat on the soles of my shoes. ---It felt like I was getting a twenty match hot-foot.

*****

We got out of the Comanche and surveyed the damage. The propellers were shaped like horseshoes and the once mighty Comanche sat sideways about 500 feet from where we first heard---

---tictictictictictictictictictictictic---

And about this time---

A Bullhead City Airport employee drove up on the runway and stopped in front of the airplane with his headlights focused on the **Crippled Comanche**.

"I'll go get a crane with a sling. I'll raise the airplane up and lock the airplane's landing gear down. You boys might just a well go back over to the **Riverside Casino** and get a room. You're not going anywhere tonight."

"I'll tow the airplane over to the hangar. I'll put it inside the hangar---sort of out of sight."

"Thank you Sir---See you tomorrow."

ACT XI

"Here's twenty bucks Beck---Julie and I are going to go back up to the Racetrack Book and bet on the Greyhounds. They're still running in Florida."

"Thanks Mark---I'm gonna play the Dollar Poker Machines, but first I've gotta call my son Mark---see if he can get me out of here. I'm still gonna try to make that zero six hundred check-in tomorrow."

ACT XII

"Ring---Ring---Ri--"
"OPERATOR"

"Yea---my name is Jack Beck---I need to call collect---619 789-6884 please."

"Ring---Ring---Ring---Ring---Ri---"
"Hello"

"I have a collect for anyone from Mister Jack Beck---Will you accept the charges?"

"Uh---oh---what---yes---I'll accept the charges."
"GO AHEAD MISTER BECK"

"Hi Markie---we had a probl---"

"Where are you at Dad? Happy Birthday. How come you're calling collect? Where are you at? How come you didn't fly over the house like I asked you to?"

"Mark---we had a proble---"

"How come you're calling collect? ---Are you still at the **RIVERSIDE CASINO**? You were supposed to be home before dark. ---Mark has poor night vision."

"**Well---if you quit your yappin'** ---I'll tell you what happened."

"Sorry Dad---Go ahead."

"The landing gear collapsed on us landing at Bullhead City Airport."

"???WHAT???"

"The gear collapsed on landing at Bullhead City Airport."

"ARE YOU OKAY DAD? ---DID ANYONE GET HURT?"

"No---we're all okay except the bottom of my feet feel scalded because of the heat that the friction caused on the bottom of the fuselage."

"How are Mark and Julie doing? ---Are they okay?"

"Yea---we're all okay. Mark and Julie are upstairs playing the Greyhound Races."

"JULIE'S GAMBLING???---Are you a back at the Riverside Casino?"

"Well---she just played "you bet your life". Guess she figures that gambling with bucks is not that big a sin anymore---and yes---we're back at the **Riverside Casino**."

"Where is the airplane? ---Is it still on the runway?"

"Nah---an airport employee picked up it with a sling---got the landing gear locked in the down position and towed it inside a hangar."

"How come you waited so long to call?"

"I didn't. ---We crashed less than an hour ago."

"Crashed???"

"Well---I call it a crash. It sure as hell felt like it when it was happening."

"How come it took you so long to get there? ---Did you stop in Palm Springs?"

"No Mark, ---we came straight to the Bullhead City Airport. We departed a couple of hours ago."

"When we retracted the landing gear---**EVERYTHING WENT DARK**---no instrument lights and the landing gears only retracted part way. It's darker than hades out here in the desert. We couldn't find a flashlight so we circled a smoke stack that had lights around it. We determined that the gear was down and came back and landed at the Bullhead City Airport---no---I worded that wrong." ---
!!!**"WE CRASHED AT THE BULLHEAD CITY AIRPORT."**!!!

"How are you feeling Dad---are you okay?"

"Yea I'm fine, except the bottom of my feet feel like I've been walking on Mayan Coals. You can't believe the heat that was coming up from the floor board. Seemed like we died and were already in hell. Anyway enough of that bullshit. ---How are you gonna get us home? ---I have an 0'dark thirty check in manana."

"Are there any flights out of there tonight?"

"I don't know Mark---I'll go check. ---Dya want to hang on?"

"No dad---I'll check on some options here about getting you back. Call me back in about thirty minutes."

"No Mark---that haint gonna work. I'll go check on the flight schedule. If there isn't any flights leaving for San Diego tonight---I'm gonna get a room. I need some rest."

"Yea that's a good idea dad. What's the phone number at the Riverside Casino?"

"Hang on Mark---here's a cocktail waitress---Miss---will you please talk to my son and give him your phone number---no, just kidding---the Riverside Casino's phone number?"

"What's his name?"

"Mark---Mark Beck---my name's Beck too. ---I'm his dad, ---he's my son."

The waitress rolled her eyes---sighed---took the phone, ---"Mark---this is Nichole Henderson---my phone number---no just kidding---the phone number at Don Laughlin's Riverside Resort Hotel and CASINO IS 298-2535."

"THAT'S AREA CODE 702-298-2535."

"Here's your phone back Mister Beck---your son wants to talk to you."

"Thank you dear. ---Mark---did you get that number."

"Yea I did dad---go get a room dad. ---I'll call you as soon as I find out something."

"Okay---bye"

ACT XIII
"RING---RING---RI---"

Groggy--- "Hello"---*groggy*

"Hi Dad---What are you doing?"

"I'M SLEEPING MARK---What time is it?"

"It's almost midnight Dad."

"What are you calling me so late for?"

"Dad---wake up---you're at the **RIVERSIDE CASINO.** ---Wake up dad."

"Oh---oh—yea---that's right---the friggin' gear collapsed. Okay---I'm awake now. What did you find out? ---I have an early morning show you know. Mark---is that landing gear on that Comanche electrically actuated? Seems like every time we moved the landing gear lever---we lost all our electrical power and the lights went out."

"I don't know about the landing gear. The landing gear should be hydraulically actuated. Yea, I know about your early morning check in dad. Here's what you're going to do."

"Okay---lay it on me. ---I'm wide awake now."

"Okay---go get Mark and Julie and get over to the Bullhead City Airport as soon as you can. Two of my students are there waiting for you."

"TWO OF YOUR STUDENTS???---shit Mark---I've already cheated death once tonight---I'm not about to try it again."

"Not to worry dad. ---both these pilots have their private pilot's license and are working on their Commercial License."

"Okaaay---what are they flying?"

"Lance---Piper Lance."

'What's a Piper Lance---single engine---twin engine---and oh yea---does it have retractable gear?"

"It's a single engine, six-place with retractable gear."

"You want me to fly over mountains---and desert---at night---in a **SINGLE ENGINE AIRPLANE?** Are you trying to collect on your inheritance twice tonight?"

"No dad---the only other choice is to rent a car and drive up to Las Vegas and try to get something out of there. Or just rent a car and drive home."

"Well---I would---but I have that zero-six-hundred check-in tomorrow, ---or is it today?"

"Do what you need to do dad. Whatever you do---at least go over to the Bullhead City Airport and tell my students of your intentions."

"Ah---I'll go find Mark and Julie and go on over to the airport. I just hope I can find them. I gave them my room number before I came up here. I'm sure the Racing Book is done for the night. That's where I last saw them. I can't believe how crowded this place is on a Monday night. I hope I can find them. I want to make my flights tomorrow."

ACT XIV

"I went up to the Racing Book to find Mark and Julie---closed---not there. I looked everywhere for Mark and Julie in---**Don and Betty Laughlin's Riverside Hotel and Casino.**

I looked for Mark and Julie in, both the **non-smoking** and smoking Black Jack, Roulette Wheel and Craps sections------not there.

I stopped a Cocktail Waitress and asked her where else Mark and Julie might be.

"You might try the Western Ballroom, they do Karaoke up there."

"Thanks, I don't think Julie sings---it's against her religion---any place else they might be?"

"There's a **Bowling Alley** And A **Movie Theater** upstairs."

"HUH? ---you mean to tell me that---Don And Betty Laughlin's Riverside Hotel and Casino has A Bowling Alley and Movie House???"

"**Yes sir---Don and Betty Laughlin have built this casino from a house to big family oriented hotel and casino. There is even a little park alongside the casino with a free boat loading and unloading ramp.**"

"**That's very impressive. It's the only casino that I have ever been in that doesn't want to take all your bucks and then kick your butt out the door.**"

"**Yes---it is nice. I enjoy working here. Don and Betty are very nice people to work for. They make their employees feel like family.**"

"That's real nice. Well---thanks for the verbal guided tour. I appreciate the information. I gotta get going to see if I can find my friends. If I knew that there was a bowling alley here---I would have gone there first. Thanks again---I appreciate it."

"Hey Mark and Julie---put the bowling balls down. We have an airplane to catch!"

ACT XV

"Hello---my name is Jack Beck. I presume that you two are Mark's students that are going to take us home to the Ramona Airport. This is Mark Landau and his friend Julie."

"Hello Captain Beck---Nice to meet cha---Mark is always bragging on you. My name is Alan Tellum---this here is my buddy Mike Madden. We're ready to roll. Nice meeting you Mark Landau and Julie."

"Where did you park your plane at Alan Tellum?"

"Up over this hill here---it's not too far. She's ready to roll. We did a walk-a-round and an exterior pre-flight while we were waiting for you."

"How long have you been here Tellum? You guys been waiting long?"

"No---not very long at all---as a matter of fact---we just landed a little bit ago and we were coming over to the Riverside Hotel and Casino when we saw you. Your son Mark gave us your room number. We figured that you were still asleep and we were coming over to the Riverside Casino to meet you."

"I appreciate that. My son called me and told me that you guys were on your way in here and for me to get my butt over to the Bullhead City Airport as soon as possible. Where did you come in from?"

"Vegas---Las Vegas. We were gonna get a hotel room and do a little fun and games. On final approach into Vegas---the approach controller told us to contact Mark Beck when we landed."

"Well---that was smart of him. I have a zero six-hundred check-in."

"This morning???"

"Yea in a few hours. What time is it?"

"Zero one-hundred hours."

"Shit---oh well---I got some ZZZs at the Riverside Hotel. I only have a five minute drive from the Ramona Airport. I should get a couple more hours of sleep before I have to get up."

"We're not landing at the Ramona Airport Captain Beck. --- We're going to land at the Gillespie Airport. The Ramona Airport closes at eighteen-hundred hours and doesn't open again till nine o'clock the next morning."

"You're kidding me. Why???"

"A man from up in the Julian area has a herd of cattle that he runs on the Ramona Airport when it's closed. He has a contract with the City of Ramona. He keeps the Ramona Airport's grass mowed and keeps his cattle fat---all at the same time."

"Yea---what's that guy's name? I think I know his son---Coal Ton Stellum. Coal Ton is a student of my son Mark Beck."

"You're right Captain Beck. Mister Stellum is his name. I can't remember his first name right now. If I remember it later---I'll tell you."

"No that's alright---Just get me home. I need to get some rest."

"Okay, ---Mark, you and Julie get in the two back seats. Captain Beck, ---get in the two seats facing them. You can lie down and maybe get some shut-eye."

ACT XVI

We boarded the single engine piper Lance Aircraft. Mark and Julie took the two aft seats leaving me two to lie down on and rest my weary bones.

!!!WRONG!!!

The twos seats were separated by a very narrow aisle that led into the cockpit. I thought about asking Mark and Julie to switch seats with me. No way Hosay.

They were ---in a word---"cuddleduptoeachother".

We took flight---across the darkened desert with some very high mountains along our course.

I waited till I heard the engine throttle back to cruise power. I got a blanket from an over head bin---laid down on the floor in the narrow aisle between the two seats just aft of the cockpit.

I was just about to go to dreamland when I heard, "Yea Mike---I know there are some mountains out here. ---We drove over this part of the country once before when I was a kid. Those mountains didn't look to be over four or five thousand feet."

"Well Allie, ---Let's stay here at six thousand five hundred feet for a while. We're pretty low on fuel and I'd rather not climb any higher. This airplane seems to guzzle the gasoline when we put climb power on the engine. We would have to climb to eight thousand five hundred feet to be at our correct cruising altitude."

"Okay Mike---I can barely make out the tops of the mountains right now. This is one dark night---no moon and the stars aren't twinkling as they usually do over this clear desert air. Let's wait till we get closer and get a better look."

"Yea Allie---Okay---good idea. I don't like being so low on fuel with no airport in sight."

"Well Mike---I was gonna top off the tanks in Vegas. We were in a hurry and I thought it would be faster to gas up in Bullhead City."

"Yea Al---that's what I thought too. Looks like they roll up the sidewalks in Bullhead City when it gets dark."

"Sure does Mike---we should be seeing something pretty soon."

"Well Al---we should be alright at this altitude. Looks good enough to me."

"Yea Mike---we're okay---no sweat."

I STOOD UP and WENT BACK and talked TO MARK.

"Mark---we're cruising at six thousand five hundred feet and I know that there are some seven thousand feet peaks out here. You had better go up front and say something to them."

Groggily---"Everything is alright Captain Beck---they know what they're doing." ---

"Besides that---it wouldn't be ethical."

"ETHICAL'S ASS---DAGONE IT---GET YOUR BUTT UP THERE AND MAKE THEM CLIMB TO EIGHT THOUSAND FIVE HUNDRED FEET."
"!!!NOW!!!"

"Okay---Okay---calm down Captain Beck. I'll go take a look see."

"I DON'T WANT A FRIGGIN' LOOK SEE."
"TELL THEM TO CLIMB TO EIGHT THOUSAND FIVE HUNRED FEET AND FRIGGIN' DO IT RIGHT NOW. I almost got killed once tonight---I don't feel like I wanna try again."

"Okay Captain Beck"

I sat down next to Julie---who was asleep---waited. I heard the engine revving up to climb power---fell asleep.

---WE LANDED---
At Gillespie Airport in Santee California.
My son Mark was there to pick me up---took me home.

EPILOGUE

"RING---RING---RI---"
"Scheduling Fred here."
"This is Beck---I'm calling in sick."
"Okay"

"ALLS WELL THAT ENDS WELL"

PRFPACPJM

--- CIRCA ---

THANKSGIVING---1-NINER-80

Our seven week strike that PSA's Minnie Mouse Union staged was finally over and everything was going great.

EXCEPT FOR ONE EGOMANYICAL JEALOUS CHIEF PILOT THAT WROTE ME UP FOR
---POOR JUDGMENT---
---RECKLESS HANDLING OF AIRCRAFT---
---CARELESS OPERATION OF AIRCRAFT---
---CHEATING PSA OUT OF MONEY ON DUTY RIG---

SCENARIO

AIRPORT of DEPARTURE---SAN FRANCISCO
                    INTERNATIONAL AIRPORT---SFO
A STOP AT---FRESNO AIR TERMINAL ---FAT
AIRPORT of DESTINATION---LOS ANGELES
                    INTERNATIONAL AIRPORT ---LAX
AIRCRAFT---BOEING 727-200
CAPTAIN---BECK
CO-PILOT---CAPTAIN JIM ROHRA
FLIGHT ENGINEER---CAPTAIN BILL WALTHERS

*****

*You people that have been reading this bullshit might have noticed by now, MAYBE, that up to this point in words that I have written in **Co-Pilots and Flight Engineers as CAPTAINS**---if later on in the course of **FLYING GIANT AIRLINERS** they achieve the---**SKY GOD STATUS AS CAPTAINS.***

*****

We were delayed at the San Francisco International Airport due to ground fog. I told the Stewardesses to go get some breakfast at the employees' cafeteria, as we had no idea when the fog would lift or how long our number for take-off would be called after the fog did lift.

We were close to being #1 as our take-off time was scheduled for 0700 hours.

The Stews left for "Ulcer Gulch".
---CO-PILOT CAPTAIN JIM ROHRA---
And
---FLIGHT ENGINEER CAPTAIN BILL WALTHERS---

Being the nice guys that they are---went back into the passenger cabin and boarded the passengers---even served coffee. Me---I studied my manuals---nah---haint nobody gonna believe that bullshit----I worked at my Sunday New York Times Crossword Puzzle.

*****

I completed a Sunday New York Times Crossword for the first time the other day---framed that puppy. If it wasn't for those crossword puzzles---I could never have written this chere book ---I haint to much in the English langwitch bullshit as you might have discovered after the foist sentence in this cher book.

*****

The fog started lifting and the San Francisco International Airport Ground Control finally gave us a departure time of 0930---**an hour and a half late.**

Co-Pilot Captain Jim Rohra ran to Ulcer Gulch, the San Francisco employee's cafeteria---brought the Stews back.

Flight Engineer Captain Bill Walthers did all the check-lists and we were ready to go when Co-Pilot Captain Jim Rohra and the Stewswae---Stewer---damn---Flight Attendants got back on the airplane.

We taxied out and made our 0930 take-off slot.

*****

*You have a ten minute plus+ or-- minus time frame on the time slot that the Tower assigns you. If you miss it ---**you go back to the end of a very, very long—sometimes a two or three hour line**---and at times—you never get to go at all and you have to cancel the trip.*

*****

Somewhere along the flight to Fresno---we found out that our scheduled deadhead home to San Diego, which by the way was Flight 182, was also delayed.

Flight Engineer Captain Bill Walthers dinged the Stews and unlocked the cockpit door.

The Head Stew came into the Cockpit. Flight Engineer Captain Bill Walthers advised her to deplane and board the passengers as fast as possible in Fresno and have the cabin ready so we could all get off the airplane in

Los Angeles as soon as possible and hopefully make our scheduled deadhead home to San Diego.
Did you say head?
   ---WE MADE THE DEADHEAD TO SAN DIEGO---
    ---THE STEWS DIDN'T---
   ---CO-PILOT CAPTAIN JIM ROHRA---
---FLIGHT ENGINEER CAPTAIN BILL WALTHERS---& SELF---
  Deplaned before the passengers even had their seat belts unbuckled---ran over to Gate 69---boarded Flight 182 for San "Diegowego" just as they were closing the "do-de-do-door".
  The Stews had to wait till the last passenger had deplaned and of course missed their deadhead on Flight 182.
*****

  Usually the Flight Crew that is taking over the airplane is there when the airplane parks at the gate. This is a courtesy to the deplaning crew.
*****

  I went to work the next day---found a note in my folder---from Chief Pilot Carbunkle.
  "CAPTAIN BECK"---"Report to the Chief Pilot Carbuncle's Office before you take your flights today."
MY THOUGHT---*"Fuck you---you egomanYical jealous asshole---I haint gonna start my day listening to your ego slobbering out of your fat fuckin' head."*
I left

  I took my flights---returned four days later.
  SCHEDULING DALE---"Beck, ---Carbunkle wants to see you before you go home."
  "Fuck him and the horse he rode in on Dale---I'm tired and I'm outta here."
  "Got a note here that reads, and I'll read it to you so you know what's happening," ---
"Captain Jack Beck
Report to the Chief Pilot's Office before you leave today
I have taken you off your flights till you come into my office."
"CHIEF PILOT CAPTAIN CARBUNCLE"

MY THOUGHT---*"I don't feel like seeing that egomanYical asshole."*
My words, ---**"I don't feel like seeing that EGOMANIACAL ASSHOLE right now."**

"Ya better go on up the iron stairs Beck---he's been in and out of here all day long---strutting around---flexing his muscles in front of the stews---looking for you."

"WHAT DJA FUCK UP THIS TIME BECK?"

"I don't know---probably talked to one of his so called girlfriends."

"His so called girlfriends"???

"Yea---if a Stew comes up in the cockpit and just says hi to him---after she leaves---he tells his crew that he's flying with, ---"I don't want you messing with her---she's my girlfriend."

"You're kidding?"

"Nope---first time I heard it---I thought that he was kidding too. I laughed and it pissed him off."

"You mean he was serious?"

"Yep---see ya---I'm going up to see the egomaniac."

"OK Beck---good luck."

"Thanks Dale---I'll probably need it."

SCENARIO

LOCATION--- up the iron stairs, ---
        ---PSA CHIEF PILOT'S OFFICE---
CHIEF PILOT---BOOBOO CARBUNKLE
ASST CHIEF PILOT---CAPTAIN RYAN
ACCUSED---BECK

Carbunkle said, ---"Here's a letter that I'm gonna put in your file Beck."

I read it---

I can't remember exactly what the letter said---but I'll always remember these words.

CAPTAIN JACK R. BECK---

YOU ARE IN VIOLATION OF FAA REGULATIONS AND COMPANY POLICY.

YOU ARE CHARGED WITH RECKLESS HANDLING OF AIRCRAFT.

YOU ARE CHARGED WITH POOR JUDGEMENT IN HANDLING OF AIRCRAFT.

YOU ARE CHARGED WITH RECKLESS TAXIING OF AIRCRAFT.

YOU ARE CHARGED WITH ENDANGERMENT TO PASSENGERS LIVES.
YOU ARE CHARGED WITH NEGLIGENCE TO YOUR DUTIES AS AN AIRLINE CAPTAIN.
AND LAST BUT NOT LEAST
YOU ARE CHARGED WITH FALSIFICATION OF YOUR PAY RECORD IN ORDER TO CHEAT PSA OUT OF MONEY.

SIGNED
CHIEF PILOT BOOBOO CARBUNKLE

"WHAT THE FUCK ARE YOU TALKING ABOUT???"

CARBUNKLE said, ---"IT APPEARS THAT YOU WERE TRYING TO CATCH AN EARLY DEADHEAD HOME THE OTHER MORNING. IT APPEARS THAT YOU CAUGHT AN EARLY DEADHEAD HOME AND THE STEWS DIDN'T. IT APPEARS THAT YOU TAXIED AT AN EXCESSIVE SPEED AT FRESNO. ---WHAT HAVE YOU GOT TO SAY ABOUT THIS?"

"BULLSHIT---THAT'S FUCKIN' BULLSHIT."---"WHERE DID YOU GET THIS BULLSHIT INFORMATION?"

"A **STEWARDESS** that didn't make the deadhead came into my office that day and told me."

"YOU WROTE THIS LETTER ON A STEWS COMPLAINT---ARE YOU FUCKIN' NUTS???"

ASSISTANT CHIEF PILOT RYAN, ---"Calm down---Beck---calm down."

"Fuck you too Ryan--this is fuckin' crazy bullshit and you know it."

About this time Carbunkle put his hands behind his head and laid back in his seat and said, ---"EVEN I TAXI TOO FAST AT TIMES."

MY THOUGHT---*"Even god taxis too fast at times."*
"Did you call in my Co-Pilot and Flight Engineer and ask them about this so called "INCIDENT"?
"NO"
"I go into every Stew class and tell them if they see anything wrong out on the line to come and tell me about so it's not necessary to talk to your crew."
MY THOUGHT---*"This is bullshit."*
YOUR THOUGHT---*"This is bullshit."*---Right?
"Did you call Fresno Tower and ask them about it, Carbunkle?"
"Not necessary."
"The taxiway at Fresno parallels the runway. There's just one small dogleg that I **slowed down for** Carbunkle."
"No excuse, Beck."
"I'M NOT MAKING FUCKIN EXCUSES."
"I'M FUCKIN TELLING YOU WHAT THE FUCK HAPPENED."
"No excuse, Beck."
"FUCK YOU---I'M OUTTA HERE."

Well---I went into see Carbuncle's boss **"The Director of Flight"** *whatever the fuck that title means* about the INCIDENT. I even put on my suit and tie.

I really can't remember the words that were said but I do remember getting up from my chair and throwing my suit coat across the room---
---THREE TIMES---
Each time the Director of Flight would kick my ass out of his office and each time I would come back apologizing ----saying, ---"Okay---okay---I'll settle down."

"Did you call my crew in and ask them about the **INCIDENT?**"
"Yes I did."
"What did they say?"
"Copilot Captain Jim Rorah and Flight Engineer Captain Bill Walthers both said the taxi speed in Fresno was faster than normal---but not unsafe."
"And you're still gonna put the **INCIDENT** letter in my file."
"Yes I am."

I LEFT.

I ran into---CAPTAIN WAYNE McCLOUD at the bottom of the "Iron Stairs". CAPTAIN WAYNE McCLOUD said, "GRIEVE IT WITH PSA'S MINNIE MOUSE UNION."

I DID---TO NO AVAIL.

There was a potty growth in the toilet.

I got the same letter from the boss of the Carbunkle egomanYicaljealous asshole.

EXCEPT HE OMITTED THE PART XXXX"YOU ARE CHARGED WITH FALSIFICATION OF YOUR PAY RECORD IN ORDER TO CHEAT PSA OUT OF MONEY." XXXX

Mainly because that was part of our new contract.

I remember saying to Flight Engineer Captain Bill Walthers when he made out our pay forms---"Bill, we can't be putting in for that much duty rig."

"Yea we can Beck, that's how it was written up in the new contract."

"You're shitting me—What the fuck did we go on strike for?"

Well---the **"INCIDENT REPORT"** went into my file.

NO BIG DEAL---YOU MIGHT SAY.

You're right---no big deal. ---No time on the beach and no pay loss.

EXCEPT---

If perchance that I got another **"INCIDENT"** pinned against me---

---WITHIN A YEAR---

I'M OUT THE DO-DE-DO-DOOR.

—The "real" F-word---Fired--- F-I-R-E-D---

See you later agitator---after while crocashit.

Adios mother fucker.

What would you do???---I'll tell you what I did. ---I called in sick---**FOUR DAYS EVERY MONTH---TWO---BACK TO BACK TWO DAY OVERNIGHTS.**

This is how I worked it. I would have four days off---call in sick for four days---have another three days off. WALLA---An eleven day vacation for the month, ---and I did it every month. I was determined to do this till Carbunkle got dethroned.

OOOPS—

I got my pay check one day---The Company didn't pay me my sick leave.

I went up to the payroll department and complained.

"CAPTAIN BECK---WE DID NOT PAY YOU SICK LEAVE BECAUSE YOU HAVE USED IT ALL UP."
"???HUH???"

MY THOUGHT---"Wow---twenty years of sick leave down the toilete.
MY SECOND THOUGHT---No more sick calls.
MY THIRD THOUGHT---"Toilette"----"Toil"---work---"Lette"---release.
I finally figured how they came up with the word "Toilette"---means
"Grunt and Groan to Dump." "The Urge to Purge."

Fortunately, a new Chief Pilot by the name of **CAPTAIN DON CONEY** was in the Chief Pilot's Office.

First thing that CHIEF PILOT CAPTAIN DON CONEY did was to call me into his office, ---"Beck, it looks like you call in sick a lot. If you are that sick---I think you might want to be under a doctor's care."

"Coney, I will not call in sick again." I neglected to tell him that I had run out of sick leave and could not afford to call in sick anymore.

"ALLS WELL THAT ENDS WELL"

PRFACPJM

--- CIRCA ---

TWO WEEKS LATER---2100 HOURS

I was in scheduling---checking out after an easy two day trip that turned into a ball-busting four day trip. *Due to fog*

Scheduling Doug came up to me, ---"Beck. I need you for a one day trip tomorrow. Check in time is zero six hundred hours."

"I can't do it Doug, ---I've already got twenty-six hours and thirty minutes in the last five days." *Maximum of 30 hours in 7 days is FAA rule.*

"That's perfect, ---This trip is a day trip and only blocked for three and one half hours."

"Doug, ---I'm bushed. These last four days have been hell. Storming in the San Francisco Bay Area---fog in the Los Angeles and San Diego areas---sweat in the armpits."

"I haven't been back to San Diego since I left. As you must be aware of, ---San Diego has been socked in (*fogged*) since I left."

"Each duty day has been fourteen hours or longer. That's almost seventy five hours of duty time in five days, ---and that's not counting the time I spent in hotels and driving or taking a bus back to San Diego from Los Angeles."

"I'm too tired to take that trip. I feel unsafe."

Unsafe *is the magic word. When you tell them that you feel un-safe, ---they usually let you off the hook. Not this time.*

Scheduling Doug, ---"I'm assigning you the trip. Be here at zero six hundred hours tomorrow morning."

"Fuck you very much Doug." ---I left. I got home---sat down---passed out.

I woke up a couple of hours later, ---
picked up the telephone---dialed.
"RING---RING---RI--"
"Scheduling Doug speaking."
"Hey scheduling Doug, ---this is Beck. Ya know that trip you gave me a few hours ago."
"Yes I do Beck."
"Well, take the trip and shove it up your ass."
"I'm gonna report you for this Beck."
"I don't give a fuck Doug. ---Goodbye."

--- CIRCA ---

---The very next day---
What time? I don't know. ---I was still a vegetable.

"RING---RING---RI--"
"Hello- *yawn* Yea ---hello –*yawn.*"
"Beck, ---this is Captain Don Coney. I want to see you in my office sometime today."
"Who is it?" ---*I was being facetious.*
"Beck, ---you know damn good and well who this is. I want you in my office before seventeen hundred hours tonight."
"I have a trip next week. Can I come in then?"
"Beck, ---I want you in my office today. Do you hear what I'm telling you?"
"Okaaaay, ---I'll be there."
I got in my '73 Chevy 464 Pickup, which I bought just before the gas crunch, and motored on down to PSA.
That '73 Chevy got 7 miles per gallon of gas. I ripped all the smog devices out of it and got 11 miles per gallon of gas.
I walked by a smirking secretary and went into Captain Don Coney's Office. Didn't even knock.
"Beck, do you know why I called you in?"
"Because I'm doing such a great job?"
"BECK, YOU KNOW DAMN GOOD AND WELL WHY I CALLED YOU IN."
"Yea, I know. Don, ---we've been getting the shit kicked out of us for the last month and a half. It's like I told Scheduling Doug, ---"Storming in the Bay Area, fog in Los Angeles, fog in San Diego and sweat in the armpits."
"The reason I didn't take the trip today, Captain Chief Pilot who at one time flew Copilot for me Don Coney, was because San Diego has been fogged in almost twenty four hours, every day, for the past month. I have had to take a bus with the passengers or rent a car several times to get home. The only airports that have been without fog or thunderstorms are Burbank and Sacramento. You can look out your window and see that the San Diego Airport is closed to landings and this is the time that I would have been landing. I

would not have been legal for any more trips and would have had to deadhead home on a bus."

"One more reason **SIR**, ---I've been doing a lot of holding and circling and I've already got a lot more flying time than I should have for the month. It's only the tenth of the month and if I don't take some time off, I'm gonna run out of time before the end of the month when you need me the most."

"Beck, I hate to do this but I'm gonna give you ten days off."
!!!YOU ARE?!!! Thanks Don, I really appreciate that."
"Beck, you're being a smart ass."
"No I'm not Don, ---I'm serious. I really need some time off."
"Beck, you're being a smart ass, ---get out of here."
"BYE DON, ---THANKS."

I went down the "Iron Stairs" to scheduling to tell them that Captain Coney "put me on the beach" for ten days.

Scheduling Doug, ---"Tough shit Beck, but we have a trip for you tomorrow. You are the only Captain available and you have to take it."

"You guys don't understand, ---Coney took me off the schedule for ten days."

Scheduling Doug, ---"We're assigning you the trip for tomorrow and you had better show up or we'll come out to your house and get you."

"Well---you better talk to the man upstairs. He's given me a reprimand and I had better honor it or he might fire me."

Scheduling Doug, ---"Stay right where you are Beck. I'll go up and talk to him."

"OK, I'll wait here, but you're wasting your time. "Cooney" was pretty mucho pissed off."

I waited.

Enter, ---Scheduling Doug and Chief Pilot Captain Don Coney.

Chief Pilot Don Coney, ---"Beck, take your flight tomorrow. I'll let it go this time."

"I figured that you would say that Coney. It's a one way street around here, I reckon."

"Beck, get out of here and you better show up for that flight."
"OK---bye."

MY THOUGHT---*"If I don't take the flights tomorrow, ---Chief Pilot Don Coney is gonna have to take it."*

MY SECOND THOUGHT---"I wonder if it would piss him off if I called in sick."
I left.
And by the way, ---I took the one day flight and got back three days later. Way, way, way over the FAA flight limitations.

Every one turned their head the other way when I wrote the time on my time sheet. Another one way street.

And by the way, way, ---I ran out of FAA legal flying time on the twentieth of the month, so I still got my ten days off.

And by the way, way, way, ---"Be kind to your Co-pilot for someday he may be your Chief Pilot."

"ALLS WELL THAT ENDS WELL"

PRFPACPJM

I got this in my E-mail---don't even know who sent it.

Subj: Fw: THE EARLY RETIREMENT PROGRAM FOR PILOTS
Date: 2/14/2005 8:54:17 PM US Mountain Standard Time
To: becksflyinghigh@aol.com
Subject: THE EARLY RETIREMENT PROGRAM FOR PILOTS
THE EARLY RETIREMENT PROGRAM FOR PILOTS

Due to the critical financial situation that our airline finds itself in after the tragic events of 9/11, the company has decided to implement a plan to offer all pilots over 50 early retirement.

This program will be known as RAPE (Retire Airline Pilots Early).

Pilots volunteering to be RAPED must apply to the personnel office before 1 March 2005.

You may be eligible for SHAFT (Special Help AFTer retirement).

Pilots who have been RAPED and SHAFTED will be reviewed under the SCREW scheme (Scheme for Retired Early Workers).

Pilots may be RAPED once, SHAFTED twice but SCREWED as many times as Chief Pilot deems appropriate.

Pilots who have been Raped may apply to get AIDS (Aircrew Income for Dependents or Spouse). Also available is HERPES (Half Earnings for Retired Pilots on Early Severance).

Obviously, pilots who have AIDS or HERPES will not be SCREWED any further.

High Intensity Training) as possible. Your company has always prided itself on the amount of SHIT it gives its aircrews. Should you feel that you do not receive enough SHIT, please bring it to the attention of the Chief Pilot. He has been trained to give you all the SHIT you can handle.

Thank You and Happy Landings Tuesday, February 15, 2005 America Online: Becksflyinghigh@aol

Here's a story worth telling---

I came home one day from a four-day trip---My **live in excunTemporty** met me at the door—super hyper---with a nose that looked like she had stuffed it in a pound of flour.

"Guess what---my cousin's husband is a drug dealer and he gave me some Cocaine."

"Wanna try some?"

"Nah---I'm gonna have a Pepsi. ---What's that Cocaine shit you say you got?"

*****

Why a Pepsi you might ask---
We both quit drinking as we were getting drunk and doing combat all the time.

*****

This went on for a few weeks---I'd come home---Snow "White" would me at the door—Acting –like a human vibrator, ---

"Wanna try some?"

"Nah"

I came home one day, ---

"I want to go to the horse races tomorrow at Caliente."

"HUH?"

"I want to go to the ponies tomorrow."

This took me aback-abit because I was the one that liked the horse and dog races and was always doing the begging to go to the races.

"Yea---Fine---I'd love to go."

"Great---let's get an early start---I wanna stop by my cousins first, ---she lives near the border."

"OK"

Next morning---

"Come on in you guys---how ya been Jack?"

"Hi---we're on the way to the horses---we can only stay a few minutes."

"Yea---sure Jack---yea---sit down." ---As he put a golden one-eighth inch spoon under my nose.

---"Sniff Jack---Sniff."---

As he held one of my nostrils closed---put the golden spoon under the other nostril.

Being an "I'll try anything once" type of a guy that I am---
I SNIFFED ---I SNEEZED
I BLEW WHITE POWDER ALL OVER
"MY COUSIN VINNY".

A dope dealer that wants to get you hooked on a drug doesn't ever give up.

"SNIFF JACK---SNIFF"---ACHOO---SNIFF JACK---ACHOO---ETCETCETC.

"My Cousin Vinny" finally got some of that white shit up my nose.
I STARTED SHAKING---VIOLENTLY.

I felt like I drank ten cups of Mexican Coffee all at once.

Mexican coffee---so strong that it could burn a hole through a ceramic cup.

I was a human 440 volt vibrator.

I left, without excunTemporary, and went through Mexican Customs with that white shit in my head. If the Federales would have busted me---I would still be in the Kingston Brothers "Tijuana Jail".

I left Mexican Customs ---went to Agua Caliente Race track.

*****

Agua Caliente Race Track---Tijuana, Mexico. A short drive across the US/MEX border. ---The Caliente Race track was leased and operated by the Alesio Brothers.

The Mexicans canceled their lease one day--- a fire accidentally broke out the next day---in five different places--- burned a Beautiful Mexican Tiled Caliente Race track to the ground.
Agua Caliente=HOT WATER
*****

I watched the Horse Races and stayed for the Greyhound Races.

It was close to midnight and I was still shaking like a dog shitting razor blades.

I stopped by Cousin Vinny's house to pick up my excunTemporary.

They were still going at the white stuff---Shooting Tequila Shooters and smoking cigarettes dipped in hish-hash.

This is a quote from the drug dealer's wife---that I never will forget, ---**"Isn't this great---we can do all this stuff and still not be hooked on anything."**
MY THOUGHT---**"WOW"**

The last I heard of them ---They were living somewhere in Arizona with their sinuses and their noses ---disintegrated. ---Dja read that kids???

As we were about to leave---my excunTemporary asked, ---"Can I buy some Cocaine to take home?"

"Sure---get a pound of it if you like---I haint using that shit no more."

Cousin dope dealer handed me a vial---three quarters full---about the size of my little finger, ---

"ONE HUNDRED TWENTY BUCKS---PLEASE."
"HUH---you're shitting me."
"THAT'S THE GOING RATE AND YOU PROBABLY BLEW ABOUT FIFTY BUCKS WORTH AWAY WITH YOUR SNEEZING."
MY THOUGHT---*"HUH---you're shitting me."*

I paid the Drug Dealer his 120 bucks which was exactly what I had won that day---so it was a break-even day except for the shakes that were now replaced by a throbbing headache.
MY THOUGHT---*"Somebody told me that Marijuana led to heavy drugs---that is a myth---especially with this kid."*

That was the first---only---last time I tried Cocaine. ---That shit sucks.

Hey---don't don't fall asleep on me now---I haint done yet.

My excunTemporary went on my overnight flights at times. ---My excunTemporary would give me that vial of white poison because she did not want to take it through the security checkpoint.

I had no idea at the time what a big deal it was to be caught with cocaine in your possession.

The most powerful drug that I had ever taken was Bayer Aspirin.

I took the cocaine vial through airport security a few times---in **UNIFORM.**

And then one day in the newspaper headlines. ---
"Hyper bowl hero gets busted with a vial of cocaine---
Has to give his hyper bowl ring back---

Also is sentenced to five years in prison."
MY THOUGHT---"WOW"

I went home that night---took the cocaine and the paraphernalia that goes with it, ---burned it in the fireplace---in front of one pissed off excunTemporary.

*****

I'm gonna turn off the Volume on Volume 1 here in a few more words. *YOUR THOUGHT---"He's a man of few words---few words he doesn't write."*

Celebrities that I have met---while flying up and down the Hollywood Coast.

---MISTER BING CROSBY---

Airport: San Diego Airplane; Boeing 727 – 200
Captain; Beck
Co-pilot---Reserve Captain Ego Esciple.

Pre-board---
---MISTER BING CROSBY---
---THECROONER---
---Der Bingo---
"Good morning, Sir."
"Mornin' Captain."
"How are you this morning, Mr. Crosby?"
"Fine Captain, sit down."
I did.
"What's your name, Captain?"
"Beck, Sir."
"Beck?"
"That's what everybody calls me, Mister Crosby."
"Well, in that case, call me Bing."
"OK, Mister Crosby."
"Call me Bing, please."
"OK, Bing."
"Where do you live?"

"Ramona, California, Mister Crosby."
"Bing."
"OK, thanx, ---Bing."
"I just bought some property at Warner Hot Springs near you. What do you think of the area?"
"I've lived in Ramona for about 15 years now and I love the area. How much land did you buy out there, Sir?"
"Bing, please, ---I bought a few acres and I think it's a nice area for the people of Los Angeles to go and relax. Don't you think Beck?"
"Yes Sir,"---"Bing."

I chatted with Mister Bing Crosby, er Bing for over 20 minutes. Actually, I, a mere mortal, talked and Bing listened.

---Quite a Man, Super Nice Man, Mister Bing Crosby---

I was about to leave and go up into the Cockpit when Co-pilot/Reserve Captain Ego Esciple entered the cabin.

Co-pilot/Reserve Captain Ego Esciple came up to us and shook hands with Mister Bing Crosby and said, ---"Nice to meet you, **MISTER HOPE**. See you when we land. I got work to do."

Embarrassed---**I LEFT.**

****

MISTER BOB HOPE

SCENARIO

Airport ---San Francisco
Location---Boarding lounge
Passenger Agent---Denise La Rocca

Denise La Rocca, ---"Mr. Hope, we're going to pre-board you now."
"Thank you, Miss La Rocca."
Location--- Jetway.
Miss Denise La Rocca, --- "Where are you going Mr. Hope?"
"Down to the ramp and talk to the mechanics and baggage handlers, Miss La Rocca."

"It's raining MISTER HOPE."
"I've got an umbrella."
Location---Underneath the wing of the airplane.
"I just came down to make sure you guys weren't smashing any bags."
"How's every thing going?"
"Except for getting wet, MISTER HOPE, everything is going fine."
"Just a little bit of San Francisco sunshine for you, guys. ---See you guys, it's almost departure time."
"Bye—MISTER HOPE."---**"SO LONG MISTER HOPE."**

MISTER HOPE
Always entertaining the troops, ---
No matter where they were doing combat.

****

JOAN RIVERS
"Is the Captain sober up here?"

Beck's words---
Co-pilot Captain Patrick Joseph McGann's words---
Flight Engineer Captain Gregory Lindamood's words---

"Of course."
"Of course."
"Of course."

****

REDD FOXX---WHAT A GUY
The PSA passenger agents would begrudgingly pre-board
REDD FOXX.
Why? You may ask
REDD FOXX was entertaining them in the boarding lounge.

Then when they did finally put the great comedian on the airplane, **REDD FOXX** would entertain us until the people started boarding

When the people started boarding, **REDD FOXX** would position himself in the Jetway and entertain the passengers as they boarded the airplane.

REDD FOXX did it very well---Funny man---Loved his "job", ---his reason for being here on this planet Earth.

REDD FOXX always had a way of making the flight fun.

Thank you **REDD FOXX**. You're quite a man.

One more thing about **REDD FOXX**.

I was in Lost Wages playing blackjack at the Flamingo Hilton. I was much into my "fun" and I hear this raspy voice.

It was **REDD FOXX** Sitting next to me.

"Are you the Captain of the flight that brought me over here?"

"Yes I am."

REDD FOXX then commenced to entertain the people at the blackjack tables---play blackjack and a shit pot full of keno tickets at the same time.

And he did it all very well.

Live entertainment.

In the long run---more expensive than the show itself, but worth the bucks.

MISTER REDD FOXX
Entertainment Personified

****

SCENARIO
Airport; Las Vegas Location; PSA Operations
Cast of characters ---Rampers, Station Agents, OPS agents, Flight Engineers, Pilots, Mechanics---
Rip Taylor.
Who?
RIP TAYLOR---
'I'm so glad that you guys let me stay in here.
I hate giving out autographs."
Congregation's thoughts, ---

"Who's gonna recognize you, anyway?"
Congregation's words, ---
"Who's gonna recognize you, anyway?"
End of story

****

—CELEBRATIES that I have NOT met—

*****

ACT I
Ding-Ding

"Guess who's on board?"
Who?"
"JERRY LEWIS, I'm so excited."

ACT II
Ding-Ding

"That guy is a flaming hassle. We're not even off the ground yet and he's demanding everything and the dipstick wants it yesterday. I haven't been able to serve another passenger since that flaming asshole slithered into the cabin."

****

California Governor Jerry Brown
Jerry Brown---the Governor of California was standing up in the aisle---messing with his bags in the overhead bins prior to taxi out
The Stewardess made the before taxi an announcement—
"LADIES AND GENTLEMAN PLEASE BE SEATED."
"WE ARE ABOUT TO TAXI."
Brown just stood there---acting like he didn't hear---messing with his bags in the overhead bin

"LADIES AND GENTLEMAN PLEASE BE SEATED. ---We are about to taxi ---FAA regulations state that we cannot taxi until everyone is seated."

Governor Brown just stood there---messing with his bags.

"LADIES AND GENTLEMAN---SIT DOWN PLEASE!!!"

"We cannot taxi until everyone is seated."

Governor Brown---closed the bin---just stood there.

A passenger finally hollered, ---

"SIT DOWN YOU STUPID ASSHOLE."

Governor Jerry Brown sat down.

The passenger? ---He got a sitting ovation.

****

president ronald reagan

Now is the time to do a little FAA talking. The Tower Operators, the Departure and Approach Controllers, the Controllers that work in the Centers across the United States of America---are worth every cent they make, ---and a lot more.

President Reagan fired these people when he was in office.

Every one thought he was a hero.

!!!WRONG!!!

He set the airline industry back ten years. The controllers that he fired grew up with the industry and knew all the safe shortcuts. His firing of these controllers cost the airlines millions of dollars in the ensuing years.

But good old Ronnie was a hero.

One day, right after Ronnie did his firing act,--I had a flight from Los Angeles to San Francisco. Normal flight time was **one hour,** ---gate to gate.

It took us five hours to do a one hour flight

---FIVE FRIGGIN' HOURS ON A CLEAR FRIGGIN' DAY---

They were manning the controller positions with supervisors that hadn't done the job in years---**and new hires.**

Very, very dangerous and very, very inefficient.

You people supported the senile old assh---oops---actor.

Well, you were the passengers that sat on airplanes much longer then you did before the firing, ---saying Ronnie's a good old boy.

Your good old senile actor took the oil out of a well oiled machine, ---and as you know, any machine without oil, ---slows down and eventually quits.

---ACTING IS FOR ACTORS---
---POLITICS IS FOR POLITITIONS---
****

And last---but not least---but the most---your good old boy has an airport named after him. Reagan National--- has the most unorthodox **NOISE ABATEMENT** *approach that I have ever done and if a pilot would do that same approach at any other airport---the FAA would ground his ass.*

One other thing that your "Good old boy" Ronnie did while he was "Acting" as President.

He stopped the "deduction of interest" on everything except your home mortgage.

---TRANSLATION---

"Hey Martha---doesn't look like we're gonna be able to take that cruise this year."

"Why not George?"

"Well, apparently that good old boy that you voted for, because you liked his looks, is taking the income tax deductions away from charge cards."

"What do you mean by that George?"

"Well, Martha, ---here's what your good old boy has done to us." ---

"I was gonna pay for the cruise with our charge cards figuring that we could deduct the interest from our income tax. I was gonna work some overtime to pay off the charge cards. My working overtime would have put us in a higher tax bracket and I was figuring that the interest deduction from the charge cards would offset any more taxes that we would have to pay."

"Oh no George---I was looking forward to our second honeymoon on that cruise."

"I was too sweetheart---and by the way Martha---forget about that fur coat that I was gonna buy you for Christmas."

*****

Explain to me why all interest is not deducible on your income tax.

It is a form of paying your employee and I know that companies sure as heck deduct what they pay an employee.

Becksflyinghigh@aol.com

Fax 928-754-5319

*****

Just happened to think of this one.

We had a two hour layover at the Hollywood "BurbOnk" Airport---so I went into the terminal to get my daily rations of hot dogs.

I came back on the Boeing 727-200 through the aft stairs.

As I walked up the aisle to get to the cockpit, ---I espied a gray haired old lady sitting in the cabin.

As it was still one and a half hours before departure, I asked Flight Attendant Muffie Burke, who was in the forward galley, --- "What the hell are you pre-boarding an old lady so early for?"

"Look around Beck."

I did.

!!!It was Marlon Brando!!!

— CIRCA —

THE END
Of Volume I
But I have to write you one more story before I start on Volume II.

SCENARIO

LOCATION—SAN DIEGO INTERNATIONAL AIRPORT
TIME—TEN MINUTES BEFORE DEPARTURE
CAPTAIN—BECK
CO-PILOT—CAPTAIN PATRICK JOSEPH MCGANN
FLIGHT ENGINEER—CAPTAIN GREGORY LINDAMOOD

ACT —FINAL

"Where are you going McGann? We are due out in ten minutes."
"I have to make a phone call."
"Make it fast—I want to push back on time."
"No problem—I'll be right back."

"Who was it you had to call? What was so important that it couldn't wait?"
"I called the Chief Pilot."
!!!HUH!!!
"I called Bryan—The Chief Pilot."
"What the fuck did you do that for? You know that they are always hawk-eyeing us when we fly together."
"I just wanted to say hi."

"GODDAMIT"

We push back. Greggy starts the engines.
P.J. McGann gets us taxi clearance.
P. J. M. got us clearance to taxi to Runway 27.

We had to taxi past the Chief Pilot's Office to get to Runway 27.
As we neared the Chief Pilot's Office—

Patrick Joseph McGann opened his sliding glass window—
Pulled down his pants—
Sat on the window sill with his bare butt out hanging out.

I looked over to the Chief Pilot's Office.
There was Chief Pilot Bryan Conn—looking out his window—in hysterics.

"ALLS WELL THAT ENDS WELL"
PRFPACPJM
er oyal laming ain in the ss aptain atrick oseph cgann

*****
From—"About the Author"
I drove the float, "The Spirit of San Francisco" from Alhambra up to Pasadena to the starting point of the "Rose Parade" at the age of 17.

I was supposed to drive the float, **"The Spirit of San Francisco." in the Rose Parade**, but they wouldn't let me because on the drive up to Pasadena, I had bounced off a couple of curbs and knocked a whole shitpot full of flowers off of the float. They had the road closed and there were no parked cars along the way.

This is why.

I had worked for two weeks *Christmas vacation* on the Rose Parade Floats and the last thirty hours *without sleep* was spent putting flowers on the Floats.

The Float---"The Spirit of San Francisco" was made up of two mountains with the Golden Gate Bridge in between them.

The engine was in the aft mountain and the steering mechanism was in the forward mountain.

My buddy, Shorty, and I flipped a coin to see who got to drive and who had to sit in the aft mountain and man the accelerator. *There was an intercom system between the two mountains.*

I won and got in the forward mountain and manned the steering wheel. I had a peephole for forward visibility. Unfortunately it was dark out and the "Spirit of San Francisco" did not have any head-lights.

I can't remember how many miles we had to drive. ---I estimate between 5&7 miles.

I steered the Float by watching the centerline of the road.

All went well for a while, but even at a snails pace, it took all my concentration to keep the Float on the center line.

We started speeding up. Now I was assholes and elbows trying to keep the float on centerline.

"Shorty ---slow down."

Shorty had fallen asleep.

Thirty hours without sleep & carbon monoxide fumes can do that to a young man.---actually---anyone.

"Shorty wake up—WAKE UP."

My plea fell on deaf ears and we kept going faster and faster.

I was still holding the center line.

When we hit an intersection —I would hold the course that I was steering till we got to the centerline on the other side of the intersection.

Unfortunately, this one intersection had a slight dogleg in it. When I finally saw the center line, which was only about a foot to my right, I turned toward it. Too little---too late.

—BUMP—BUMP—BUMP—BUMP—

Well, it woke Shorty up—he slowed down—I got the Spirit of San Francisco back on centerline.

Second verse---same as the first.

Faster and faster and faster.

"Shorty wake up—**SHORTY WAKE UP."**

This time the centerline showed up about a foot to the left.

Too little–too late

BUMP—BUMP

I was a little faster reacting this time as you can read by the number of BUMPS.

We arrived at the starting point of the Rose Parade. I believe every official at the starting gate was surrounding the Float by the time we crawled out of the mountains—shaking their heads, —"Go ahead on home boys—you've done enough damage for one day."

Shorty and I walked home.

✶✶✶✶✶

More from "About the Author"

Swam and fished in **SHIT CREEK** along Solomon Run.

The houses along Shit Creek that were too poor to have cesspools---just simply ran their sewer lines directly to Shit Creek. Every once in a while a turd would float by.

The neighborhood kids would stand on the bank and chant---"Couldn't swim---Couldn't float---A big fat turd went down his throat."

That's the bad news. The good news---The stream was fed by sulfur water that came out of the cave coal mines. All those little nicks that you get when you are a kid---gone within 24 hours.

And some more from "About the Author"
Joined the Army Airborne at the age of 18---I made twenty seven parachute jumps.

I was assigned to the 18th Airborne Corps at Fort Bragg, North Carolina---as a friggin file clerk.

I even pulled my reserve parachute once.
"STAND UP---HOOK UP---
PUCKER UP YOUR ASSHOLE AND SHUFFLE DOWN"

TRANSLATION
Stand up and hook your static line to the cable that's over your head. Turn toward the aft of the airplane and shuffle down to the "EXIT" door.

"Get ready---GO."
I JUMPED
I saw the tail of the "Flying Boxcar" fly by---then got my opening shock.

I started to raise my head to check my parachute and make sure that it had deployed right.

—I couldn't—It wasn't—
WHEN I TRIED TO RAISE MY HEAD—*normal procedure was to lower your head firmly into your reserve parachute pack to keep your head from departing your body when you got the opening shock*—**I COULDN'T.**

The shroud lines were twisted behind my head. I reached behind my head and pulled the shroud lines apart, put my head through the opening and looked up at my parachute.

"SHIT"

The shroud lines were twisted clear up to the parachute and a couple of the shroud lines had gone over the top of the parachute—giving it the form of a zillion "D CUP BRA". —*Aptly called a Mae West*

!!!IN EFFECT—I HAD TWO PARACHUTES!!!

I pulled the shroud lines apart again and saw my body passing other paratroopers on the way down. —*Either that--or they were going up*

I PULLED MY RESERVE PARACHUTE HANDLE

The reserve parachute deployed. That's the good news. The bad news—the white reserve parachute started to wrap around my body. I was going down faster than normal—but not fast enough to force the parachute to inflate.

I finally got the reserve parachute to inflate. I once again pulled the shroud lines apart on my main parachute—put my head through the opening and looked up. —!!!NOW I HAD THREE PARACHUTES!!!

I was still descending faster than normal—but not as fast as I was before I pulled my reserve parachute.

---Time to land---

I didn't know whether to put my head in back of the twisted shroud lines---or in front of the twisted shroud lines.

I opted to put my head behind the twisted shroud lines so I could watch the parachutes.

!!!WRONG!!!

As I neared the ground---the ground effect took over.

The main and reserve parachutes started to go away from each other right before I touched down.

As a result ---the main parachute pulled my head one way and the reserve parachute---pulled my body the other way.

I was practically in the prone position---with legs hanging down---feeling for the ground.

I LANDED
!!!FEET FIRST---HELMET SECOND!!!

I have one more story that I just have to tell.
CIRCA 2002

I live across the Colorado River from Harrah's Casino.

Every day I would get in my "Swifty Perception" Kayak and row across the Colorado River and eat breakfast at Harrahs.

I would leave the Kayak with the people on the beach, so they could use it to play with till I came back.

Well, this one particular day, I ate and went down to the beach to get my Kayak and come back across the Colorado River to my house.

Well the kids that were using the Kayak did not want to give it up.

I told the children that I had to get something at my house *gambling bucks* and that I would be right back.

I got my loot and started back across the Colorado River.

About halfway across---I had just rowed by a buoy and the Kayak quit Kayaking.

No matter how hard I rowed---I just couldn't go any further.

The wind was blowing upriver at 35 knots---gusting to 50.

The Colorado River looked like the Bismarck Sea.

Someone had told me that there was a giant whirlpool in front of Harrahs.

I would row upstream---I would row toward my house---I would row downstream---I would row toward Harrahs. etcetcetcetcetc

I did this for over an hour and I just could not get away from the buoy that I had passed.

Every once in a while I would look up and see the children jumping up and down---motioning for me to come over. *Must have thought that I was a real jerk.*

One time that I was drifting by the buoy---I saw some rope drifting in the water.

MY THOUGHTS---"That looks like the 25 feet of rope that I tie my canoe up to the banks with."

No shit Sherlock. ---That was my rope and I was anchored to the buoy.

???Question???

How does one dumb shit guy untie a rope from a buoy in the Colorado River?

Answer.

He crawls over the front of his Kayak and in so doing ---he overturns it and hangs on to it for dear life.

People were going by me in their boats---waving and drinking their beer while I was drinking river water.

Finally a couple of young men drove up to me in their power boat and asked, ---"Are you alright?"

I wanted to say some smart ass answer, but under the circumstances---I said, ---"No I am not. Would you guys please cut the line and tow me to the side of the river."

They did.
I thanked them and rowed back over to Harrahs.
The kids were gone.
I rowed back home.
I slept for 12 hours that night.
*****

Write you later Alligator.

THE REAL END

****

FLIGHT ATTENDANT DEBBIE MCARTHY

"Don't it make my brown eyes blue" is playing on the radio as I write this.

Debbie McCarthy was always singing this song.

Flight Attendant Debbie McCarthy was on PSA's Flight 182 when it went down in San Diego.

When I hear it---I think of her and all the finest of PSA's people that were on Flight 182 and my stomach churns---and I start to cry. Still affects me that way---26 years later.

GOD BLESS you Debbie and the beautiful people that were on that Flight 182. There's a memorial plaque at San Diego's Museum of Flying in Balboa Park to these fine people.

I'll try to get a picture of it and put it in this book.

NO---I'M NOT GOING TO DO IT THAT WAY.

As you might have noticed---this book has went from a "book"---to Volume 1 and so in Volume II, I will endeavor to put anything that you FAX or E-Mail me to put into Volume II about the people on Flight 182.

Anything that will honor the people on Flight 182 on that ill-fated day in September of 1978.

ALSO---

If you have had any experiences in the Aviation Field, in the Air or on the Ground, good or bad, that you would like to be put in Volume 11, please write me at ---

Becksflyinghigh@aol.com
or FAX me ---
FAX 928-754-5319

If I put them in Volume 11 of "Flying "High" ---

I will pay you Fifty dollars for each article, or, according to the amount of words that you have written, whichever is higher, when the book,---Volume 11 of Flying "High" is published.

For your protection---I will destroy any materials not put in the book. ---
"Flying High"---Volume II
Please include your E- Mail address or anyway that I can contact you.

I will put the above article a couple of times in this Volume, Volume I.

****

Write ya later alligator

THE FLYING BECKS

MARK RESLEY   JACK RESLEY   KEVIN SHAUN

ID#28317

ABOUT THE AUTHOR

Born in Johnstown, Pa. ---Attended Maple Park Grammar School.
Swam and fished in **SHIT CREEK** along Solomon Run.
Story---last few pages

Drove the float, **"The Spirit of San Francisco"** from Alhambra up to Pasadena to the starting point of the **"Rose Parade"** at the age of 17. *story---last few pages*

I barely graduated "out of" Alhambra High School, Alhambra, California because I couldn't understand the English "Langwich" past-participles bullshit. *So if you see anything misspelled or mis,-punctuated in this chere book---jus consider the source---poetic license--- and keep on truckin'---same as reading*

Read the Bible five times while I was growing up.
Old and New Testaments

Joined the Army Airborne at the age of 18---Made twenty seven parachute jumps. I was assigned to the 18th Airborne Corps at Fort Bragg, North Carolina---as a friggin file clerk. I even pulled my reserve parachute once. *story---last few pages*

Passed the two year college GED test while in the Army Airborne

Attended Spartan School of Aeronautics in Tulsa, Oklahoma for A&E Mechanic and Flight Engineer.

Got my Commercial Pilots Lisence---oops---er---License at Ryan School of Aeronautics in Glendale California.

---AND I HAD ONE HELLUVA CAREER---

I'm dedicating this book to---
Chief Pilot Captain Bill Butler
If, perchance, any body knows where Captain Butler's Kinfolk are, please let me know at ---
Becksflyinghigh@aol.com---FAX#928-754-5319
Thanx

About the book-
free preview page
FLYING "HIGH"
"The Fun of Fu---oops—"THE FUN OF FLYING"
CAPTAIN JACK RESLEY BECK REALLYTIRED
At this point in time---Mark raised his head up from the instrument panel and, ---
"Greased the Comanche right on the numbers."

squeak   squeak

squeak

"Ahhh---how sweet it is---thank god that's over."
---tictictictictictictictictictictictic---
The sound the propellers make when the landing gear collapses.
SCRAAAAAAAAAAAAAAAAAPE
SCRUNCH
*The sound the airplane makes after you hear **tictictictic**.*
---WE STOPPED---A LITTLE DAZED---
Up till this time---Julie sat in the back seat---uttered not a word.

At this time---Julie was out of the back seat---came over the top of my seat and my body---was out my door just as the Comanche came to a screeching ass halt.

Mark and I sat there for a few moments---in shock.

"Mark---Let's go back over to the Riverside Casino and do some more gambling. ---Right now I don't feel like we have anything to lose."

"Okaaay"
*****

The one thing that I remember most as the Comanche came to a screeching ass halt---was the heat on the soles of my shoes. ---It felt like I was getting a twenty match hot-foot.
*****

We got out of the Comanche and surveyed the damage. The propellers were shaped like horseshoes and the once mighty Comanche sat sideways about 500 feet from where we first heard---**tictictictictictictictictictictictic.**

And about this time---

A Bullhead City Airport employee drove up on the runway and stopped in front of the airplane with his headlight focused on the **Crippled Comanche**.

"I'll go get a crane with a sling. I'll raise the airplane up and lock the airplane's landing gear down. You boys might just a well go back over to the **Riverside Casino** and get a room. You're not going anywhere tonight."
"I'll tow the airplane over to the hangar. I'll put it inside the hangar---sort of out of sight."

"Thank you Sir---See you tomorrow."